S.B.S

John Parker, a journalist and former Fleet Street editor,
has undertaken many investigative projects in his writing career
with topics ranging from the Mafia to Northern Ireland.
His numerous books include several military bestsellers
including *Task Force, The Gurkhas, Commandos* and *Desert Rats*.

S.B.S.

The Inside Story of the Special Boat Service

JOHN PARKER

Bounty
Books

This updated edition first published in 2003 by
HEADLINE BOOK PUBLISHING

This edition published 2005 by Bounty Books,
a division of Octopus Publishing Group Ltd
2–4 Heron Quays, London E14 4JP

ISBN-13: 9780753712979
ISBN: 0 7537 1297 0

A CIP catalogue record for this book is available
from the British Library

Printed and bound in Great Britain by MPG Books Ltd

Contents

'Not By Strength, By Guile'

The motto of the Special Boat Service is like a clue to a cryptic crossword: there's a hidden meaning. Its operations are spectacular and dangerous, but every one of them has a twist to it, some extra element. Everyone knows that members of the Special Forces the world over are, generally speaking, portrayed as fearless hard cases who barge in, guns blazing, where others fear to tread. Even for the most overt of these groups, such as the SAS, it is never like that, of course. The 'charge' is the last act of an operation that requires meticulous planning, days, possibly weeks, of undercover surveillance, specific pre-operational training and split-second timing for the assault – otherwise the men would be falling dead in their droves when they finally went in.

This is doubly important for operatives of the Special Boat Service because they are also waterborne, and that ingredient to their operations alone requires levels of training, fitness and real-life work-outs of an extraordinary nature, which no one ever sees, nor can anyone assess, and which makes them among the most highly skilled, technically adept and versatile units anywhere in the world. The sheer diversity of their range of skills and disciplines, which will be demonstrated throughout this narrative, calls for dedicated proficiency in approaching their tasks by land, sea or air, and increasingly the SBS is in the vanguard of operations confronting military forces around the world.

They are skills that are applied to tackling the ever-threatening potential of today's world of localised wars and the growth of international terrorism but which are rooted in past endeavours. As will be evident from the text, the history of the Special Boat

Service from its foundations onwards is comprehensively explored in these pages.

Many of the SBS's major operations are recorded and recalled, often by those who were there. In undertaking this task for the first edition of this work, in 1996, the author was given unprecedented access to former SBS personnel who traditionally have kept a low profile and are exceedingly security conscious for a number of reasons. Additional material has since been researched for this new edition, bringing the SBS story up to date.

The result is an intriguing and gripping story, already praised by former SBS officers, which respects their anonymity but which allows more than a glimpse into their ultra-secret world, which embraces everything from the safety of coastal installations around the United Kingdom, national security, counter-terrorism and intelligence-gathering techniques ahead of large-scale troop movements, which involve procedures and equipment of the highest secrecy classification.

Apart from the interests of national security and their compliance with the terms of the Official Secrets Act, SBS members must also consider their own safety. In the diversity of tasks confronting them in this modern age, they are well aware that they themselves may become targets, a fact which the author acknowledged in setting out on this project.

Even so, former members of the Special Boat Service and its associated units of the Second World War assisted in the compilation of this work. Their first-hand recollections, reports and private memoirs form the basis for a running narrative from its beginnings in 1941. They have been quoted throughout the ensuing chapters, along with extracts from a vast collection of archive material, much of it previously classified but now accessible at the Public Records Office and published here with permission of the Crown Copyright Office.

The author wishes to record his sincere thanks and appreciation to all those who participated and gave their time and hospitality so freely during the numerous interviews, meetings and telephone conversations. Responsibility for accuracy of this work, however, rests solely with the author.

PART ONE

Legends and Heroes
1940 to 1945

The modern Special Boat Service emerged from a number of now-famous groups and virtual private armies formed during the darkest days of the Second World War and which were wound up at the end of it. Skills, disciplines and traditions in the particular art of clandestine amphibious raiding, invented and learned in times of great need, came forth, sometimes through careful planning but often simply from the sheer courage and determination of individuals. Many of their swashbuckling tales have been told in voluminous accounts of those wartime activities. While it is not possible to cover them all, a recap is necessary to set the scene for all that was to follow in the remaining half of the twentieth century. Part One of this book focuses on stories that, even today, remain largely untold or incomplete through official secrecy or individuals shunning publicity.

It is with the benefit of much previously unpublished material and dramatic, if reluctant, first-hand accounts that those early days and some legendary figures are remembered. A few historical vignettes are recalled from a catalogue of hundreds that abound from that era of the founders, with apologies to those involved in the many operations whose acts of bravery have, for reasons of space or repetition, been omitted. The intent here is to signpost the development of principal wartime units whose equipment and traditions (though not necessarily personnel) were merged at the end of the war to form the basis of today's SBS. The units are described on the next page.

FORMER WW2 UNITS MERGED TO FORM TODAY'S SPECIAL BOAT SERVICE

ARMY

Special Boat Sections, attached to 8 Commando, founded by Roger ('Jumbo') Courtney: 1SBS, 1940; 2SBS, 1942; 'Z' SBS, 1943; 1SBS temporarily merged with SAS in 1942 as Special Boat Squadron under Captain (the Earl) George Jellicoe in 1943

MARINES

Royal Marines Boom Patrol Detachment formed in July 1942, famous for Cockleshell Heroes led by Major H. G. Hasler; SBS today considers itself a direct descendant of the RMBPD Small Operations Group founded in 1944 by Lord Mountbatten, South-East Asia Command, with A, B, C Groups of (Army) SBS

NAVY

Combined Operations Pilotage Parties formed in great secrecy in September 1942 specifically for harbour and beach reconnaissance prior to landings of Allied forces in virtually every theatre of the war.

Sea Reconnaissance Unit, formed in 1942

CHAPTER ONE

Jumbo's army

The twenty-second of June. The date was chosen as the one on which we were to make contact, but the quiet, unassuming voice of advancing years gave me no clue that he recognised its significance. If he did, he was not the one who was going to mention it. For Lieutenant-Colonel Robert Wilson, DSO and Bar – 'Tug' to his service comrades – the day was just another, like every other 22 June that has passed during his retirement in the relative calm and total anonymity of that Regency watering-place of Royal Leamington Spa. He said he was no different from thousands of other servicemen and -women, who were just doing a job at the time. And that's right.

Their numbers are declining but, thankfully, as these words are being written there are still many silver-haired heroes of that era, able to recall, when specifically asked, what exactly they got up to, in detail so graphic that it must be imprinted on their brain cells. Any one of dozens of their escapades could have been chosen to begin this account, and we will meet more of them as these pages progress to the present day. This escapade was historic; a pinprick in the panoply of wartime activity, sure enough, but historic none the less.

Tug Wilson and his former colleagues don't make a fuss about the past because in accord with SBS tradition they dislike exaggerated accounts of their exploits, preferring to this day to remain shadowy silhouettes compared with their upfront compatriots of the SAS. Also, in the early days it was bows-and-arrows stuff compared with the operations of their successors in the Service today, who are as finely tuned fighting machines as the high-tech weaponry surrounding them. What cannot be taken away is that the original founding principles of the SBS still hold good.

Tug Wilson and others like him were the advance party. They wrote the guidebook and plotted the course. They were the forerunners of all those who followed in the derring-do traditions of Special Forces the world over and specifically in the terms of reference for this book, the SBS.

Wilson was a trailblazer in Special Operations. As novelist John Lodwick, a later volunteer to the service, wrote of him: 'As leader of the first successful raids ... he occupies a position in our hierarchy not unlike that of St Peter in Holy Mother Church.' The date of his first mission, and the first ever successful sabotage strike in wartime Mediterranean – which became the model for so many in the future – was exactly 55 years before the present author made contact for this work: 22 June 1941.

UP PERISCOPE. Lieutenant-Commander Tommo Tompkinson gave the order as His Majesty's U-class submarine *Urge* hovered under a calm sea three miles off the east coast of Sicily between Taormina and Catania. On the surface, the Mediterranean was shimmering under the late-afternoon sun of that hot summer. Mount Etna was hugely visible, a dramatic rising backdrop to this particular theatre of war as the periscope cut a wide arc through the water.

Tompkinson was on his assigned patrol for what was known by submariners as a 'billet', roaming the Straits of Messina off the coast of southern Italy along the route used extensively by enemy shipping, and lately to supply Rommel's burgeoning presence in North Africa with the Afrika Korps.

Today, Tommo had a secret weapon aboard: two founding members of 1SBS, Lieutenant Tug Wilson and his partner, Marine W. G. Hughes, a lean, small man, but tough. Wilson himself was no tough guy – he was handsome, slender and middle-class – but he and Marine Hughes shared a common bond: they were canoe fanatics, and both were desperate for action.

Their first outing together as a partnership in sabotage had been a month or so earlier, when they sailed in HMS/M *Triumph* with the object of attacking shipping in enemy harbours with limpet mines. The mission had been aborted through rough weather, and their only action on that occasion had been to sink an Italian copper-bottomed schooner, named *Tugnin F*, loaded with macaroni. *Triumph* had dropped the pair off in Alexandria but, anxious for another mission, Wilson and Hughes had hitched a ride to Malta and the HQ of the 10th Submarine Flotilla in search of action.

Captain Shrimp Simpson, boss of the 10th, was among those yet to be persuaded as to the value of such clandestine missions by free-ranging saboteurs, of sending out two men in a flimsy little canoe on demolition and attacking tasks. *More bloody trouble than they're worth!* In the end, and more by way of getting them out of his office, Simpson had signed the docket that gave them permission to go to sea with HMS/M *Urge* when she came in to refuel in the third week of June; he entered their departure in his log.

The pair stowed their collapsible canvas canoe, known as a folboat (originally spelled 'folbot') deep in the bowels of the submarine along with their cache of explosives, tommy-guns and knives, and *Urge* set off on a hunting expedition towards the southern Italian coast. They had no particular target in mind. The plan was that they would scan the shore looking for something important to blow up.

That day, as *Urge* lay submerged off the coastline just short of Catania, Tompkinson called Tug Wilson to the periscope as he swung it slowly across his horizon. Almost at the foot of Mount Etna he had spotted what looked like a tunnel serving the main railway line, which was surely a key transport link for Sicily's hefty population of Axis troops and their civilian associates. They studied their charts and confirmed the sighting.

'Will that do you?' asked Tompkinson in a challenging tone.

'Just the job,' Tug replied. 'Just the job.'

'OK. I'll drop you off a mile or so from the coast.'

Wilson and Hughes went to the wardroom to eat some ham sandwiches, study their maps for a suitable landing-site and prepare for their attack as soon as darkness fell. Then they gathered together their gear, swallowed a couple of benzedrine tablets and brought their flimsy-looking boat towards the fore-hatch, ready to launch when the submarine surfaced. They unravelled the canoe from its canvas stowing-pack. It was 4 feet 7 inches (1.4 metres) by 1 foot (30 centimetres) by 1 foot (30 centimetres) and weighed just 48 pounds (22 kilogrammes). They assembled the jointed rods that slotted together to form the frame over which the canvas was stretched.

The frame, in turn, was kept solid with six cross-members of marine plywood to make it pretty sturdy whatever the weather; or at least that was the theory. Buoyancy aids were fitted in the bow and the stern and then a canvas sheet was fixed to the top by metal clips; the sheet fitted around the two canoeists supposedly to keep them and their cargo of explosives, weapons and stores relatively dry.

The risk of capsizing, especially when the canoe was floated off the submarine casing in heavy seas, was ever present. Everything that might float away – like the paddles, the waterproof map case and the two tin tea-mugs, used as bailers – was attached to the frame by a length of fishing-line.

The summer sun had given way to moonless sky and a light mist shrouding the sea as *Urge*'s captain prepared to surface later that night. Tompkinson took his craft to within a mile of the shore, as close as he dared. Wilson and Hughes were ready, the adrenalin running high as the effects of the bennies kicked in. With the water still surging over the casing, they moved their canoe through the forehatch and completed its construction, replacing the timber cross-members that had been removed so that the canoe could be squeezed through the hatch, and loaded the 110 pounds (50 kilogrammes) of explosives.

They positioned the canoe at the bow of the casing, clambered gingerly into their positions, faces blacked up, clothes greased, paddles in hand and tommy-guns slung over their shoulders. When they were ready, Wilson gave the signal and the submarine advanced slowly forwards and then dived, allowing the canoe to float off. Wilson and Hughes paddled in unison towards the shore.

Their somewhat minimalist training, plus make-do-and-mend equipment (which included no form of communications other than a torch for signalling, covered by an old sock or some such to dim the beam) for operations that had grudging approval from the wartime hierarchy, hardly prepared them for this moment. But as Wilson recalled, nothing could prepare the human psyche for the nervous excitement that welled up as they pressed on cautiously towards the Sicilian beach and the first mission of this skilful partnership which was to do the enemy a good deal of damage.

As they struck out towards the shore, *Urge* vanished from view. She would return at a given time to an agreed position and surface when the captain spotted the pre-arranged signal by torch that the two saboteurs were heading back. As ever, the disappearance of the mother vessel left a twinge of anguish: 'Will she be there when we get back? Will we find her in the dark?' One day, as Tug Wilson would discover to his cost, she would not be, and he would be left high and not very dry. That day lay in the future. This time, the first time, everything looked to be set fair.

But on the outward journey they hit trouble.

Hughes suddenly stopped paddling. 'Voices!' he hissed.

Tiny Sicilian fishing-craft, working in darkness and not visible through the mist were dotted along the coastline. Fishing-boats were to become the bane of many SBS operations in enemy waters, not least to Tug Wilson in his future missions. On this occasion, Wilson and Hughes manoeuvred their canoe around and past them, zigzagging towards the coast without being spotted.

They had no predetermined landing-spot but discovered an inviting deserted cove with a shingle beach and a few convenient rocks where they could unload their explosives and hide their canoe before they set off inland in search of their target. The embankment from the cove was steeper than it first looked, but once at the top they could see a row of telegraph poles which Wilson knew from his maps ran by the railway line. They were less than a quarter of a mile from the tunnel, which appeared to have no guard. Even so, they had to make a couple of trips to carry their gear and explosives from the beach.

Tug Wilson selected a point 30 metres or so inside the tunnel to lay the gelignite, which they buried out of sight under the sleepers. Hughes had brought a pick with him, but they decided that using it might attract attention, the sounds echoing through the tunnel, so they moved the shale with their bare hands. The fuses were to be laid to the underside of the rail line so that the raised studs on the casing would get pressed down by a train passing along the line, igniting the detonators attached to the gelignite the moment the train passed. The exercise was, in all honesty, a bit of a hit-and-miss affair, almost a trial run – only for real – in what would become an art form of the saboteurs which the SBS men learned to perfection.

They were an hour and a half making their way to the tunnel and setting the charges. Then Hughes tapped his partner on the shoulder. The rail signals in the distance had changed to green, which meant a train was heading in their direction. Wilson tenderly pulled the safety bar from the fuse while Hughes collected the rest of their gear. They made a rapid exit and moved back down the embankment to the beach and the canoe, still behind the rocks.

At that moment there were voices again. Hughes nodded towards a couple of fishing-boats, oil-lanterns glowing on their masts, swaying back and forth on the gentle waves directly in their path 500 metres out. Wilson pointed skywards. The moon was on the rise and would be breaking through very soon. The train heading towards them would, if all went to plan, blow up at any moment, and all hell would be let loose. They had to go now.

They launched the canoe into a few inches of water and paddled silently, using single paddles, until they reached the headland and were out of the way of the fishermen. Then they stopped to refit their double paddles and moved swiftly towards the pick-up point, where, hopefully, the submarine was lingering below the surface. *Urge* came up to their starboard, and in a short time the two men were hauling themselves on to the gun platform, dragging their canoe on to the casing behind them. They stood for a moment looking back at the coastline with exhilarated satisfaction tempered by concern that there had been no explosion. Had it failed to go off? Damp, perhaps, or wrongly connected?

Quickly, they collapsed the canoe and loaded it back through the forward torpedo loading hatch and headed below themselves as *Urge* glided towards deep water. As they went, the captain summoned Wilson and Hughes to the bridge on the conning tower. Through his binoculars, he had caught sight of dim lights on the shore. The train was just entering the tunnel when Tug saw it. He was counting the seconds . . . and then – boom! – the distant sky was lit by a flash of red.

To complete his report on the attack, Tommo Tompkinson hung around the area overnight, though in the safety of deeper waters. The following morning he turned *Urge* back towards Mount Etna and, with Wilson, scanned the attack site. Activity at the tunnel entrance confirmed the hit. Scores of workers were removing debris from the scene. His log for *Urge* that day recorded the satisfaction of all concerned, especially Wilson and Hughes.

What may in hindsight be viewed as a minuscule piece of wartime history at the time was in fact important. The mission marked the first successful raid for the Special Boat Section in the Mediterranean, but for Tug Wilson and Marine Hughes the Sicilian jaunt was not quite over. With the success of the raid confirmed, *Urge* resumed her billet patrol and moved on to the south of the Messina Straits, where a new target was spotted: a pair of 10,000-ton Italian cruisers surrounded by six destroyers. Tompkinson lost no time in selecting his target, the cruiser *Gorizia*. Within minutes she was sinking, with a couple of nasty gashes in her side sustained from his salvo of torpedoes. The Italian destroyers came looking for him and dropped a hundred or more depth-charges. The submarine shuddered and shook as if it were about to break into pieces, the noise deafening and frightening.

Tug Wilson had never experienced anything like it, and the moment might have caused him to reflect: How in God's name was he, Robert Wilson, until recently quietly pursuing his rather staid career as a draughtsman in Bristol, harming no one, and with a new young wife at home with whom he should have been raising a family, now holed up in the corner of the control-room of a submarine somewhere deep under the Med, being bombed out of his mind by depth-charges, having just blown up a railway line and causing goodness knows what damage or loss of life and already thinking about his next mission?

He wanted action. He'd got it! And it was nothing like anything he had ever imagined when he volunteered for service in the Territorial Army just before the war began, or even contemplated when he was commissioned into the 5th Survey Regiment of the Royal Artillery when the balloon went up. His new wife, Marjorie, whom he had married in the early stages of the war at the local register office, honeymooning briefly in Bath, had kissed him goodbye and off he'd gone to his billet in a dirty, disused, eighteenth-century workhouse in Stroud, Gloucestershire.

Tug Wilson's story is not untypical of SBS personnel in the early years. They just appeared, as if from nowhere, to take up their duties with a strange new commando unit that die-hard military men regarded with suspicion and generally dismissed as made up of a bunch of foolhardy, undisciplined eccentrics, often scruffily attired, paddling about in canoes and carrying backpacks full of curious gadgets. It was a world away from conventional military thinking in every respect. But that was the point – it had to be.

Special units of commando-style troops had long been on the

drawing board. As early as 1924 the Madden Committee on defence, which examined some of the military disasters of the First World War – including huge losses incurred in amphibious troop landings at Gallipoli – proposed that a 3,000-strong Royal Marines brigade be set up to undertake raids on enemy coastlines and bases. But like so many other shortfalls in the British military contingency in 1939, not very much had been done about getting it formed. In fact, it took the German invasion of Norway on 9 April 1940 to spur the British military planners into action, and the first Special Forces were finally rushed into service. The move came after a British force under Major-General P. J. Mackesy landed north of Narvik on 14 April. Another force went ashore at Namsos two days later, and more troops were on their way, including contingents from the French Chasseurs Alpins, the Foreign Legion and Polish forces who had escaped during the German invasion of their own country. It quickly became apparent, however, that the vast and rugged Norwegian coastline was no place for ill-equipped British troops who had neither the clothing, boots nor transport for such conditions.

General Carton de Wiart took a scratch contingent raised from county regiments, including the Bedfordshire and Hertfordshire. He landed on 14 April with orders to attack German positions at Trondheim, supported by the guns of the Royal Navy ranged along the shore. On that day, HMS *Warspite* sank seven enemy destroyers in the Narvik fjords, while several other enemy ships were scuttled outside Oslo. On land, successes were harder to come by. Most of Wiart's men had hardly ever seen a hill, let alone climbed through treacherous, rocky terrain. Furthermore, while the Germans were kitted out in white uniforms and were equipped with skis and other made-to-measure accoutrements to suit the conditions, the 'special clothes' provided for the British troops consisted of fur coats, thick knitted jumpers, heavy-duty socks and gardening boots that leaked. As the general opined later: 'If my troops wore all of those things together, they were unable to move about and looked like paralysed bears. As far as guns, planes and transport were concerned I had no worries at all, for no such things were available.'

Wiart was forced to retreat, his force badly mauled and let down.

The early stages of this British/French expedition to help the Norwegians repel the German invaders was a fiasco from the outset. Troops were needed over a wide area between Narvik in the north and Namsos, 300 miles away, and on towards Oslo, ostensibly to prevent the Germans from setting up air and sea bases. In the wake of this unfortunate experience, there was a move to instigate the original plans for 'guerrilla companies' to be formed immediately, except that the Royal Marines were already operating at full stretch and of insufficient numbers to provide what the military planners had in mind. Thus, initially, the units were to be recruited from army personnel and formed into Independent Companies, formed from county regiments and the Territorial Army. This hurried plan was to form ten Independent Companies, each consisting of 21 officers and 268 other ranks, and because time was so short they were to be raised largely from volunteers from the second-line TA divisions still in the United Kingdom. The companies would have no specific barracks, nor even accommodation provided. They were supervised by a head-quarters company manned by officers from the Royal Engineers and the Royal Army Service Corps with an attached Intelligence Section.

Their sole object was to be deployed on raids against enemy positions and, because all of those were outside the island waters of the United Kingdom, the companies were to be organised as ship-home units: the ship carrying them to and from operations would be their base and at all other times they were billeted in private houses in the coastal towns selected by their officers as their home base. Nor were they provided with transport, all movement being by rail.

Among them was future SBS member Ernest Chappell from Newport, South Wales, who had left school a couple of years earlier at the age of 16 to work in a fish-and-chip shop and had lately been employed in a factory assembling hot-water geysers before joining the Royal Welsh Fusiliers:

I had gone through the usual initial training and [in January 1940] we were sent down to the Wiltshire area on some monotonous guard duties on Andover airport and various little Coastal Command radio stations. It was very boring, and I asked to be transferred to somewhere where I could see more active service. Eventually I was posted to No. 9 Independent Company, which was already in training at Ross-on-Wye and headquartered at the Drill Hall. This was

11

my introduction to the Independent Companies. Personally, I enjoyed every minute of it. I liked running through the countryside with scruffy clothes on and a bandolier around my neck, as opposed to the formality of the normal army regime of being smartly turned out, bolt upright and saluting anything that moved. It seemed I was a free agent. We used to wear our kit and a blanket and a mess tin and a bandolier with ammunition slung around our necks – this is the sort of scheme in a kitbag war. We were organised into troops, aimed more at raiding, landing from the sea. We had no special weaponry, nothing elaborate in those early days. We had the old Lee-Enfield rifles, mostly of First World War vintage. I liked the free style of it. Our discipline was self-imposed and brought on by respect for the people we worked with and for. We were relying on one another, and it was made clear what was expected of us. We had more scope. We operated in smaller numbers, subsections of three or four men. And if we were loose in the woods, we had to make our own minds up of how we handled a situation. We were left to our own devices. This was the style of our training, although initially there was very little time. We were supposed to land in Norway and operate behind the German lines there within a matter of days.

These early groups were clearly establishing some of the ground rules that became vital in the operation for Special Forces, but there was no real training at that stage. Their forthcoming excursions to meet the Germans head-on was ill-prepared, ill-considered and ill-equipped. The lack of preparation verged on the farcical, given the desperately difficult coastline on which they were to land and operate and the skill of the enemy troops facing them. Many of the men, perhaps the majority, could not swim. Most had never set foot in a boat, and some had never been near such an expanse of water or seen such sights as huge waves crashing ashore against the rocks and inlets of the fjords where they were to land. Every step of their journey was a new experience.

Worse still was the shortage of supplies and transport once there, and even getting to their designated locations would prove to be literally a journey into the unknown, given that the only maps available were actually taken from 'an illustrated guide to the beauty of Norway as a holiday country'. Even so, No. 1 Independent Company was on its way to Norway within ten days of its formation with orders to go ashore at the port of Mo. The only instructions to the company came by way of an Admiralty advice sheet to the Officer Commanding:

> Your mobility depends on your requisitioning or commandeering local craft to move your detachments, watching possible landing places. Keep attack from the air always in mind. Disperse and conceal but retain power to concentrate rapidly against enemy landing parties. Keep a reserve. Get to know the country intimately. Make use of locals but do not trust too far. Use wits and low cunning. Be always on guard.

Within the week, four other Independent Companies – Nos. 2, 3, 4 and 5 – were dispatched to Norway, each with a given target, and under the overall command of Lieutenant-Colonel Colin Gubbins. His orders were: 'Your Companies . . . should not attempt to offer any prolonged resistance but should endeavour to maintain themselves on the flanks of the German forces and continue harrying tactics against their lines of communications.'

A second wave of Independent Companies hung around for days at docksides with no firm instructions as to how they would actually be transported across the North Sea. In the end it was too late. On 10 May 1940 the Germans launched their Bliztkrieg across the Low Countries, and by the end of May the British Expeditionary Force was being evacuated back to England from Dunkirk, followed soon after by the British and French troops when they were pulled out of Norway, leaving that nation also in the hands of the Nazis.

Within 24 hours of succeeding Chamberlain as Prime Minister on the day Hitler began his march into the Low Countries, Winston Churchill was looking for proposals for the creation of Special Forces of a kind that still did not exist in the British military. He demanded prompt action to raise commando-style seaborne raiding-parties, saboteurs, espionage agents and airborne and parachute troops, the last having so successfully spearheaded Nazi incursions into Norway, Belgium and Holland. Thereafter, and in spite of all the other great worries surrounding him, Churchill took great personal interest in nurturing them into being, forgiving early errors and pointing the way forward to the point of insistence, as will be seen by simply tracking the dates of significant developments in his first month at No. 10.

The whole of Continental Europe was a no-go zone for any form of conventional troop landings, especially when Italy joined the war as Germany's sidekick. The only viable options for the time being were attacks from the air and clandestine, hit-and-run seaborne raids around the coastlines of Nazi- and Italian-held territory. Although the priority had turned to the defence of the British Isles, Churchill was well aware that the spirit of attack had to be maintained, if for no other reason than to boost the morale of the British nation at its darkest hour. This, he maintained, could be achieved only by raids on German-held coastlines. Churchill demanded of the military Chiefs of Staff in a minute logged on 3 June 1940:

> It is of the highest consequence to keep the largest numbers of German forces all along the coasts of the countries that have been conquered, and we should immediately set to work to organise raiding the shores on these coasts where the populations are friendly. Such forces might be composed by self-contained, thoroughly equipped units. Enterprises must be prepared with specially trained troops of the hunter class, who can develop a reign of terror first of all on the 'butcher and bolt' policy but later on or perhaps as soon as we are organised we should surprise Calais or Boulogne, kill and capture the Hun garrison and hold the place until all preparations to reduce it by siege or heavy storm have been made, and then away.
>
> The passive resistance war which we have acquitted ourselves so well in must come to an end. I look to the Chiefs of Staff to propose me measures for a vigorous, enterprising and ceaseless offensive against the whole German-occupied coastline . . . in flat-bottomed boats from which they can crawl ashore, do a deep raid inland, cutting vital communication and then back, leaving a trail of German corpses behind them.

In a single memo, Churchill had outlined the guiding principles for the formation of Special Forces – and the Special Boat Service in particular – that were just as applicable in the twenty-first century as in 1940, when the Joint Chiefs of Staff were presented with these ideas at a meeting held on 6 June. Reaction was swift. Three days later, the War Office dispatched an urgent call to all Commands requesting the names of 40 officers and 1,000 other ranks to join a 'mobile force', and it was made known that the ultimate numbers required might reach 5,000. The force was now formally to be recognised as commandos, and already in the pipeline was a plan to set up tem commando units as soon as possible, based almost entirely on army recruits because the Royal Marines were already hard-pressed. MO9 Branch was created to take responsibility for planning all commando operations, and on 12 June Sir Alan Bourne, Adjutant-General of the Royal Marines, was asked to become Commander, Offensive Operatives – forerunner of Combined Operations – with a mandate to call on the cooperation of both the Royal Navy and the RAF.

On the afternoon of 23 June, Major Ronnie Tod received his sealed orders from the War Office for what was to be known as Operation Collar, instructing him to split his force and make landings the following night at four different points on the French coast. The object of the trip was to reconnoitre the defences and capture a few Germans for interrogation and anything else that might be of use. It was also to provide much-needed morale-boosting headlines stating that in little more than three weeks after the evacuation from Dunkirk British troops had landed on French soil to harry the German invaders.

In the haste to achieve these objectives, training, planning and intelligence went awry, and the raid fell into disarray almost from the outset, as did the next, against newly established German posts in the Channel Islands. According to Lord Lovat, soon to become a leading figure in the commando movement, 'the Prime Minister was not amused by this tomfoolery and laid it on the line in no uncertain terms. Churchill ordered an immediate reorganisation.' It was a good enough signal to complete the formation of commando units as soon as possible and, as a matter of priority, to organise some realistic training in the most difficult of surroundings to equip the soldiers with strength of will for what lay ahead.

Churchill appointed his old friend Admiral Sir Roger Keyes (later Baron) as head of the newly named Combined Operations. Keyes was himself the architect and hero of one of the British military's few commando-style operations in the First World War:

in 1918, when commanding the Dover Patrol, he led raids on German naval bases at Zeebrugge and Ostend, effectively blocking the ports for use by U-boats. Keyes abided by Churchill's wishes and sent rattling memos flying from his headquarters in Richmond Terrace, London, to get the whole concept on to a permanent footing, with real training under conditions that tested the endurance of the men against all the possible hazards they were likely to meet. One training school for officers was formed, using the Scottish estate of Lord Lovat in the West Highlands. The school was formed almost as a private enterprise by a group of officers who had served together in Norway in the Scots Guards. It was originally Major Bill Stirling's idea.

He and his younger brother David – the future founder of the SAS – were cousins of Lovat and were very familiar with the countryside, having been visitors there for many years. They obtained authorisation from the War Office to set up a new training school on the Lovat property, which included six deer forests with lodges and covered a landmass for training purposes running to some 200,000 acres. Lovat himself was sent on ahead to requisition all properties astride the Fort William to Mallaig road and railway line that would be useful. Once installed, with Bill Stirling as chief instructor, they began with cadre courses for junior officers, who began arriving in the first week of June 1940. Their base was Inverailort Castle, 25 miles west of Fort William. It was a large, square building, grey and gloomy, rising like an apparition from the rolling mists in the dark dawns. Built on the shore of Loch Ailort, it provided all the opportunities for commando training, including amphibious operations, which were supervised by a naval commander. Lord Lovat himself provided men from his estate – stalkers who were great rifle shots and experts with telescopic sights – who turned up in their civilian plus-fours to give instruction.

The school was a great success. Ronald Swayne, with No. 1 Commando, remembered:

The whole commando world attracted some very strange characters to it. Some were extremely confident people who were very successful later in the war. Several were just total eccentrics, but they added a lot of imagination to training and helped and developed the eventual character of the commandos.

Those who passed through this initial training included several who were to become famous in the creation of Special Forces operations, like David Stirling himself, then a 24-year-old second lieutenant, and 'Mad Mike' Calvert, then 25, who became one of the great pioneers of guerrilla warfare. His personal exploits included assisting Major-General Orde Wingate in the famous Chindits in the Burma campaign. It was Calvert's words, spoken often enough, that were later ingrained into the psyche of many a volunteer to the Special Forces: 'The main job of the soldier is to kill people. As a guerrilla you don't achieve anything by just being present. No regular force of any nation in the world is really frightened of guerrillas unless they can see the results in blown bridges, their friends being killed or trucks being ambushed.'

Talk among returned officers was of great tests of physical endurance, a trial of strength in every respect. Roger Keyes was so impressed that he authorised the setting up of a Combined Training Centre for amphibious warfare at Inveraray. Winston Churchill himself, meanwhile, kept up the pressure, displayed in a memo dated 25 August 1940:

> If we are to have any campaign in 1941, it must be amphibious in its character, and there certainly will be many opportunities for minor operations, all of which will depend on surprise landings of lightly equipped mobile forces accustomed to work like packs of hounds instead of being moved about in the ponderous manner which is appropriate. These have become so elaborate, so complicated in their equipment, so vast in their transport that it is very difficult to use them in any operation in which time is vital. For every reason therefore we must develop the storm troop or commando idea . . . small 'bands of brothers' who will be capable of lightning action. In this way alone will those positions be secure which afterwards will give the opportunity for highly trained regular troops to operate on a larger scale.

If any further recommendation was needed, it came from his own son Randolph, who immediately volunteered to become a commando. James Sherwood, from Southport, Lancashire, who had lately been a dispatch rider with the RAMC, scuttling around Kent on a motorbike delivering messages, volunteered for 'special duties' at the same time and ended up in 8 Troop of No. 8 Commando, raised at Windsor by Captain Godfrey Nicholson. Sherwood recalled:

We were among the first batch in October 1940. We were thrown in at the deep end, and at that time each commando set about training according to its own ideas. It started out on the basic premises of weeding out those who couldn't stand the pace. Within 24 hours of arriving there, we formed up complete with our gear, full pack: rifle, respirator, tin hat and the rest of the paraphernalia. We were headed by Randolph Churchill, who looked to us to be very fat and unfit but who proved himself as capable of taking on anything that we had to do. What we could do, he could do. I remember the perspiration poured off him. He must have lost about a stone in no time at all on what turned out to be high-speed marching, which just stopped short of running. I think the aim was to do something like seven miles an hour, which, with all the gear, was some going, especially for people from units like my own who had been sitting in vehicles for most of the war.

We belted out along the road northwards by the loch with Randolph at the head going hell for leather for about an hour. Then after a brief stop we turned around and did the same thing coming back. Those who couldn't take it just fell out by the roadside and were returned to their unit the next day and never seen again. The rest of us were just doubled up with pain, and Randolph was still there, still pouring buckets of sweat, and then he shouted, 'Pick up the step,' and some rebellious spirits shouted back: 'Bugger off!' That was our first day.

However, the discipline was to be strong, and demands on strength of character heavy. Those who were judged not up to it were sent back to their units, and that included the whole of Randolph Churchill's 8 Troop. Sherwood said: 'Godfrey Nicholson, who was in charge of 8 Troop, called us together and told us, to our fury, that our standard of training wasn't considered sufficiently high by the command of 8 Commando and we were going to be disbanded – which meant only one thing: RTU [return to unit]. The men were very angry, because they considered the training to be the responsibility of the officers. There was a lot of offensive language used on parade which in other circumstances would have been acted against.'

It so happened that at Lamlash on the Isle of Arran at that time was one Lieutenant Roger 'Jumbo' Courtney, an extrovert character of some repute who had just been given permission by Lieutenant-Colonel Robert Laycock, commanding officer of No. 8 Commando, to form an experimental Folboat Section. James Sherwood and a half a dozen other disgruntled members of the disbanded 8 Troop went over to see Courtney at his headquarters in Lamlash and most were taken on to join with other recruits who were to form the basis of an important and swashbuckling crowd. Courtney, undoubtedly one of the great eccentrics, had this idea that commandos in canoes could sneak into enemy harbours and blow up shipping, or crawl ashore and sabotage railways and other vital installations.

Courtney, from his background, might well have been dismissed as a crank, and the military hierarchy believed it had its fair share of such men already. He certainly did not fit the conventional pattern of fighting men either. Naturally indifferent to authority, he was a wild, adventurous man of 40 who, between the wars, had been a professional big-game hunter and gold prospector in East Africa.

When he married at the age of 36, Courtney and his wife Dorrise spent their honeymoon paddling a collapsible German-built canoe named *Buttercup* down the Danube. Another of his own great adventures was to paddle the Nile from Lake Victoria to the delta with only a sack of potatoes and an elephant spear on board. The need to earn a living had led him to join the Palestine Police, where he reached the rank of sergeant. 'He was a big man in every way, though not very tall,' one of his wartime officers, Vere Holden-White, told me. 'He had a bashed-in kind of face and a blunt, no-nonsense manner that was intimidating on first meeting. Fortunately, that was soon dispelled by a great bellowing laugh . . . and the boast he could drink any bugger under the table. He enjoyed proving it. And a hoaxer. During the great "monster fever" of the 1930s, he discovered footprints on the muddy beach of Loch Ness, and the *Daily Express* made a great deal of his find. It wasn't until much later and many newspaper articles around the world that some bright spark discovered that the footprints were all from a left foot. Roger confessed . . . the footprint came from one of his own victims – it was from the sawn-off foot of a hippopotamus that he used as a doorstop.'

At the start of the war Courtney returned to England and joined the King's Royal Rifle Corps as a subaltern, and there he might well have remained. In the summer of 1940, however, Churchill launched his plan to 'set Europe ablaze' with Special Forces and agents to spearhead sabotage, propaganda, subversion and clandestine attack missions across Europe while the conventional forces regrouped and prepared for re-invasion.

Almost immediately, swashbucklers and the adventurers in the tradition of British privateers sallied forth, along with a motley collection of madcap scientists and inventors. Volunteer groups began to take shape under mercurial figures who answered Churchill's call.

In 1940 Courtney joined Laycock's newly formed commando units in training at Inveraray and there submitted his plan. He theorised that from his own experience he was certain that a small force of men in canoes could carry out effective sabotage by secretly landing on enemy coasts and attacking enemy shipping. The men could also be used for recce missions ahead of larger troop landings and for a multitude of other tasks.

No one was particularly impressed; in fact senior officers made no secret of their views: the plan was positively foolhardy, bloody ridiculous. So Courtney set about proving his point. He took his canoe out into the Clyde Estuary, where the commando ship HMS *Glengyle* was moored. He slid out of the canoe into the water and pulled himself up the anchor chain, over the guard rail, slipped past the sentry and grabbed a souvenir.

He went back the way he came in, paddled to the banks of the Clyde and ran to a nearby hotel, where a conference of senior officers who controlled the commando units was in session. He burst in, still dripping wet, carrying with him the equally wet canvas gun cover from *Glengyle* and dropped it on the conference table.

Well, he might do it once . . .

Some remained unconvinced; others showed a glimmer of interest. Courtney persisted and volunteered to repeat the exercise as a pre-arranged mock attack. Admiral Sir Roger Keyes, a hero of Zeebrugge from the First World War, who was now in charge of Combined Operations, agreed. Courtney was to make a second raid on the ship and place chalkmarks on the hull to show where he might have planted limpet mines.

Wearing only bathing-trunks in the ice-cold sea, he paddled undetected to the ship's mooring, once again slipped over the side of his canoe alongside *Glengyle* and placed chalkmarks along the side. At that point he could have moved away and left the navy with egg on its face once again. But a length of rope hanging over the side was too tempting. He climbed aboard, intending to make a spectacular entrance on the deck of the ship – and fell into a trap the ship's captain, aware of his impending visit, had laid. He was captured.

But the demonstration was sufficient to convince Admiral Keyes. Within a month, Courtney was promoted to the rank of captain and given the task of forming the first Folboat Troop, which was to consist of just 12 men. He began to scout for suitable recruits.

A list was already being compiled of men who had answered the call by volunteering for 'special service of a hazardous nature' – totally unaware of what that might entail. Among them was Tug Wilson, the quiet subaltern with the 3rd Survey Regiment of the Royal Artillery, then languishing at Exeter.

He described to me that day in the autumn of 1940 when he received his secret orders. His understanding wife, fortunately born into a military family, kissed him goodbye and would barely see him again for another five years. 'I was instructed to travel at once to Scotland and report to the White House, which in spite of its grand name was actually a shooting-lodge on the estate of the Duke of Montrose on the Isle of Arran. I had no idea what was on, not a clue.'

A dozen men drawn from Horse Guards, Marines, Commandos and Royal Artillery assembled on the appointed day and were ushered into an introductory talk by Courtney. In his usual colourful language and persuasive words, he outlined his plans along with his assurance that he could drink any two men under the table.

The volunteers, Courtney said, should be prepared for excitement and danger, missions with impossible survival odds and constant high-risk operations. They were to become the foundation troop of the SBS, for which Courtney had obtained his 'fleet' of eight folboats, one of which was the *Buttercup*, in which he had paddled the Danube with his new bride.

That night, after the lecture, he and Tug Wilson began a

conversation which lasted until dawn, and Wilson used a handily placed flowerpot to avoid disappearing under the table. He was mesmerised by Courtney's tales and by his plans for the small group of raiders. The whole concept captured his imagination. At the end of their conversation Courtney had appointed Wilson his second-in-command, and the next day they began mapping out their strategy. They had less than three months to train in the skills that would be required of them. Few of them knew much about demolition explosives; others had never been in a canoe; some knew little about mapreading. An eccentric Scottish professor taught them how to survive on seaweed. Courtney and Tug Wilson, so totally unalike in everything they had ever done in life and in physical and personal demeanour, came together like two pieces of a jigsaw.

Wilson was everything that Courtney sought in his recruits. He preferred the alert, almost sensitive chaps who would work out the way of attack through a side window rather than go blasting their way in through the front. (This philosophy still holds good more than half a century later, and is still an approach that can be seen as distinctly different from that of another famous group of Special Forces who brag about daring and winning.)

Courtney swore by enthusiasm, skill and coolness under pressure, and that's what he and Wilson drummed into this tiny group of men now under his command and in training at Corrie, on the east coast of the Isle of Arran, near the northern end of the island. The landscape provided its own challenge. Goat Fell towered 2,867 feet (874 metres) behind them and Sannox Bay lay before them: the best, or worst, of both worlds, depending on your view of it, for training canoeists, swimmers, divers, mountaineers, survivalists, demolition experts and killers, descriptions that could be rolled up into one and applied to any member of 1SBS, as the unit was soon to be christened.

They had no special gear to speak of; training, as Tug Wilson recalls, was done in battledress. There was no such thing as a wetsuit, no breathing apparatus, no particular work had been done on waterproofing – always a problem – and standard-issue condoms would cover a multitude of sins.

Ten days' leave at Christmas was granted amid a buzz of rumours of forthcoming embarkation to foreign parts. The rumours proved correct. General Sir Archibald Wavell, who by the end of 1940 had amassed 300,000 men in what Churchill described as Our Army on the Nile, wanted more and had heard about the commandos in training in Scotland.

In spite of his successes in the Western Desert and the capture of 35,000 Italian prisoners of war, Churchill was repeatedly critical of Wavell's supposed reticence to attack on other fronts. 'What is he going to do with these great armies?' the Prime Minister demanded. Wavell replied that he was already committed to the capture of the Italian Dodecanese Islands and planned to move on to Rhodes early in the New Year to forestall a German base being established there. He was standing in defence of Egypt and planning to move against Rommel when the 'time was right'.

Thus, his request for the immediate dispatch of the commandos was granted, and Roger Courtney – a man well experienced in the Nile regions – would take his Folboat Section to the Nile. The group was attached to 8 Commando, which joined 7 and 11 Commandos under the command of Laycock; the group would, for the time being, be known as 'Layforce'. The convoy of commando ships left Scotland under heavy escort on 31 January 1941, heading out into the North Atlantic to stay out of range of long-distance bombers. The full force of the Atlantic swell gave them all a bad time before the convoy veered south around the tedious Cape route to arrive in Alexandria on 11 March. James Sherwood, then a lance-corporal, was on one of the ships:

We were given a rousing speech by Laycock before setting off, sailing straight into a force-nine gale, and it certainly felt like it in this 10,000-ton ship carrying its landing craft slung from davits either side of what would normally be the boat decks with the commandos on board in hammocks slung in the former cargo holds, all very makeshift. There were very makeshift toilet facilities, too, merely long rows of seats with holes in them facing one another down a long alley and water running along underneath as primitive as they come and all very matey. Everybody was so sick and unhappy in this heavy sea they couldn't have cared where they sat or who they faced or anything else in their misery.

It was a fairly fast convoy, although I suppose it took us about five weeks to get out there via the Cape, landing eventually at Suez, where we were immediately struck by the discomfort of millions of flies. Our base initially was Geneifa on the shores of the Great Bitter Lake, a transit area really of ramshackle tents, very, very basic equipment, no comfort whatsoever, no showers for washing and that sort of thing. We stayed there for about a week and did a few half-hearted route-marches through sand, which wasn't very well received. Then two of us were teamed up with Roger Courtney and moved down to a naval base at Kabrit, at the other end of the lake. There we were joined by Lieutenant-Commander Nigel Willmott.

Nigel Clogstoun Willmott, a 30-year-old senior naval navigator for ships, was working on plans for a ship-borne invasion of Rhodes. As a veteran of the Narvik disaster a year earlier, when the British suffered heavy losses as they foundered on rocks and hidden shoals off the Norwegian coast, Willmott was well aware that many ships' navigators had in the not-too-distant past been civilians and at best had only amateur navigational experience. He put forward a strong case for a reconnaissance of the island. Laycock agreed and teamed him up with Courtney. The two men were to be taken under cover of darkness to two miles or so off Rhodes aboard the submarine *Triumph*.

They would then paddle away in Courtney's canoe, *Buttercup*, equipped with sub-machine-gun, tommy-gun, grenades and a thermos of coffee laced with brandy to recce possible landing-sites on Rhodes for Layforce and the mainstream troops who would follow them ashore. James Sherwood was given the task of being the backstop for the two men:

After several nights of dummy runs and training, we set off, a journey lasting a couple of days to get to our point off Rhodes. It was very exciting because I'd never been in a submarine in my life. I'd always seen them as rather romantic things. I soon came to learn that it wasn't so. My role in this was not to go ashore but to keep the two canoes in good order and maintenance and be up on the casing of the submarine for the launching and return. When it came for them to set off, it was pitch dark. The technique they developed involved sitting in the canoe on the casing of the submarine, which then slowly trimmed down, sank itself in the water, until they just floated off. It sounded simple, but it wasn't.

★ ★ ★

Courtney and Willmott slipped away under the moonless skies and paddled ashore to the beach areas that would make suitable landing-sites for Layforce, noting data such as depths and rocks in chinagraph crayon on a slate-board. Finally, Willmott went ashore, dodging enemy sentries, to make a map of the terrain and nearby roads. He penetrated to within 195 feet (60 metres) of a large Axis headquarters at the Hôtel des Roses, apparently crawling about the lawn to get an idea of its troop population. On the following night, he and Courtney made a recce of the main beach south of Rhodes town, with Willmott this time cutting through wire barricades to get on to the main highway.

A third night was spent making a beach recce through *Triumph*'s periscope, and on the fourth and final night they set off again for the shore. Courtney swam to one beach, leaving Willmott to travel a little further down the coast. Willmott was to return and pick up Courtney, who would signal his position by dimmed torchlight. Courtney, however, ran into triple trouble. He suffered severe cramp while swimming, and as he lay writhing on the beach he attracted the attention of a noisy dog, and then to cap it all his torch failed. Willmott managed to find him and brought him to safety only minutes before an enemy patrol appeared on the beach. Had Courtney been caught, he would undoubtedly have been shot.

This was the first major beach reconnaissance of its kind. Both men were decorated for the mission – Willmott was awarded the Distinguished Service Order and Courtney the Military Cross – and promoted to captain. Their meticulous charting of potential assault beaches would later become one of the prime tasks of a most secret wartime organisation called Combined Operations Pilotage Parties (see Chapter Seven), headed by Willmott himself, set up to guide major invasion forces in the latter stages of the war. COPPs, as they were called, were so secret that their very existence was not revealed until a dozen years after the war had ended. Theirs was one among the most dangerous of the clandestine wartime missions, and, as we will see, the procedure they established became one of the principal disciplines of the post-war SBS.

In this instance, however, all the dangerous work carried out by Courtney and Willmott was to no avail. The Rhodes landing was cancelled even as Layforce prepared for the assault. Rommel's

Afrika Korps had succeeded in driving Wavell behind the port of Tobruk. Meanwhile, Hitler had ordered the invasion of Greece, and the Germans were on the brink of taking Crete and Rhodes. Wavell began using Layforce in roles for which they were totally unsuited, and which bore no relation to their commando training. Frustration grew to anger, confusion and chaos reigned. Then, gradually, the force began to be cut to ribbons by misuse, bad planning and sheer bad luck.

By then, the Enigma decrypts from Bletchley Park revealed that the Germans were planning a massive invasion of the strategically important island of Crete, and the huge battle that ensued in May 1941 saw one of the most disastrous and costly reverses of the war so far: 4,000 Allied troops killed, 2,500 wounded and more than 11,000 taken prisoner. Of the 2 whole battalions of Layforce that went to Crete, only 23 officers and 156 other ranks managed to get away. James Sherwood recalled:

> The shocking outcome of all this was that Layforce was virtually disbanded and scattered around the Mediterranean in penny packets. Some went to Tobruk, some went to Crete. No. 11 Commando suffered pretty considerable losses in action against the Vichy French, in south Lebanon, just over the border from what was then Palestine. So it was really a story of disbandment of Layforce, of the three commandos, and of their reappearance in various forms, or return to unit for chaps who couldn't find employment in some other form.

Among the survivors of operations thus far was the young officer David Stirling, who was currently in hospital with a back injury after his very first parachute jump ended in drama when his canopy failed to open properly and he came down to earth with a bump. While in hospital, he mused over the plight of Layforce, in which he was still a lieutenant. He also looked at the tactics of the Long-Range Desert Group, formed a few months earlier to make long-range, self-sufficient attacks behind enemy lines, and Roger Courtney's Special Boat Section of small-group sabotage and reconnaissance missions. He thought of combining these ideas with the latest addition to the British military – parachuting – and these were the makings of a new Special Force. He used the time when he was lying on his back to set down his proposals and sent them off to the new Commander-in-Chief, Auchinleck. He liked the sound of them, and so did Winston Churchill, who needed little persuading when he visited North Africa and asked to see Stirling personally. Thus the SAS was born and given a base at Kabrit, near the Suez Canal, in July 1941. Initially it went under the grandiose title of L Detachment, Special Air Service brigade, clearly hoping to fool the Germans into believing that the Allies had a new airborne brigade.

The concept of Layforce, on the other hand, lay in ruins, but out of it emerged two vital and spectacular elements of the British military, the SAS and the SBS, whose development in the post-war years was to become a lasting tribute to their founders.

By the time the SAS came into being, Roger Courtney's section was already creating mayhem around the Mediterranean.

Chapter Two

Star of the show

Tug Wilson watched the Jolly Roger hoisted above the submarine *Urge* as she sailed into Malta under a cloudless sky after the Sicilian adventure and felt pangs of pride. On the corner of the flag, over the bar denoting the sinking of an enemy cruiser, the emblem of a dagger had been sewn in recognition of the first SBS attack. Shrimp Simpson, head of the 10th Submarine Flotilla, was waiting on the quayside to welcome them; when the full account of the raid by Wilson and Hughes was relayed, his early scepticism about the value of Tug and his colleagues vanished in an instant.

Simpson was soon requesting that Wilson and Hughes – and more like them, if possible – should join his command. He saw the opportunities for further raids, with SBS attacks on shoreline installations in addition to his submariners' general harassment of Italian and German shipping. Their base at Lazaretto Creek – known to the locals as X-base – on the sheltered side of Valletta in Marsamxett Harbour was a top priority for Axis bombers as they pounded the island daily. The strategic importance of Malta for the British fleet, lying midway between the two key Mediterranean bases of Gibraltar and Alexandria, was more vital now than at any time since the naval presence was first established in 1869. Lately, the Nazis were getting rather annoyed that the X-base subs were severely hampering the supply of men, stores and weapons to their star performer, Rommel, in his North African campaign and were in danger of stifling his spectacular advance, heading as he was towards Alexandria and Cairo. Goering ordered the Luftwaffe to blast the subs out of the island and the island out of existence. Shrimp Simpson and his 10th Flotilla, who had covered themselves with glory and won dozens of medals for sustained bravery, refused to budge – at least for the time being.

Simpson's request to hold on to Wilson and Hughes brought a swift response from Courtney in Alexandria: 'Carte blanche – and good hunting.' There was nothing Courtney would have liked better than to have had his whole team doing exactly the same. They had spent the summer training in limpet-mine attacks and other forms of sabotage and were raring to go. They were also aiding the Special Operations Executive, ferrying agents into various key Axis-held territory in the eastern Mediterranean. But the submarine fleet at Alexandria, No. 1 Flotilla operating under the general command of Combined Operations, was already hard pressed. It had fewer vessels available, and they could not be diverted from the main chance – attacking enemy shipping – to allow brief excursions ashore by SBS raiders.

In any event, Courtney's little gang had already been further diminished. One canoe team, Sergeant Allan and Marine Miles, having successfully sent an enemy ship to the bottom in Benghazi harbour with limpet mines, hit a jagged rock as they paddled their way to rendezvous with the mother sub and were captured.

Back in Malta, Simpson rapidly began to make use of his two new acquisitions, and his command was alerted to seek out suitable sites for attack. At the end of July 1941 Wilson and Hughes were assigned to the submarine *Utmost* commanded by Lieutenant-Commander Dick Cayley, a stocky man with whom Wilson struck an immediate rapport. In the following three months, the deadly duo, as they might well have been called, pulled off a series of raids that caused mayhem and disruption to the railway system of southern Italy. None of them was without incident.

The first was in the Gulf of Santa Eufemia. A main-line rail link to the north was in view, with no tunnel on the flattish terrain, and the link was obviously important enough to cause bother if disrupted. The pair made a daylight recce of the site through periscope surveillance and took to their canoe in the evening before the moon came up. They were floated off the sub casing in the usual way and paddled in to shore, carting enough explosives to blow the railway line sky-high. Everything went without a hitch. The explosives were laid under a hefty section of the track and set with instantaneous fuses, which gave them just sufficient time to take cover behind some rocks close to the beach. What they had not anticipated was that farm buildings nearby were filled with

Italian soldiers, who spewed out shouting and screaming when the explosives blew. Tug and his partner kept their heads down, wondering how they were going to get out when a curious diversion came to their rescue.

A crowd of skinny-dipping bathers enjoying the late-evening warmth of the sea were spotted further up the beach and the soldiers dashed off to arrest them, certain that they were the saboteurs. During the commotion that followed, Wilson and Hughes found a route to their hidden canoe and paddled away unnoticed.

Their next raid was planned with more care to detail, and it would be their most spectacular yet. The target was a huge railway bridge over the River Seracino in the Gulf of Taranto. The bridge was so vital that the Italians, fearing it might be a target for saboteurs, had camouflaged the seaward side, hampering reconnaissance. A clear view of it was possible only by daylight scanning from the submarine's periscope.

As darkness fell on the evening of 27 August, Dick Cayley brought *Utmost* as close as he dared to the beach, as an extra-large load of explosives was required – eight charges of 'P-for-plenty' material, packed in bulletproof and waterproof bags weighing around 30 pounds (14 kilogrammes) apiece.

Wilson and Hughes were floated off the casing, and Cayley kept the submarine on the surface to watch them go; even though the sea was calm, the heavily laden canoe was low in the water. One false move and they could have capsized; there would be no second chance. A suitable landing-spot had already been pinpointed and the two beached without problems. They were hyped up with nervous excitement as they began unloading their packages. Then Wilson looked seawards and saw that *Utmost* had not submerged, its black hull clearly visible from the beach and too close for comfort. She could be hit by any shore batteries that might be around, and also might alert the Italians to their own landing.

In spite of the precision timing, and with brilliant coolness, he climbed back into his canoe and paddled back to the sub to suggest politely to Cayley that he should draw away to a safer distance. In other words: bugger off! Back on shore he and Hughes, with Thompson sub-machine-guns loaded and at the ready, began an initial sortie of the target, first climbing a steep incline of rocks and loose shale. Over the top, they saw the bridge looming before them.

31

Wilson scratched his head as he stood looking at the thing. It was bigger than they had anticipated: reinforced concrete pillars strung with steel girders spanning a deep gorge. Wilson concluded he would have to climb into the network of steel to set his charges.

They returned to the beach, where they had hidden the explosives. It took four trips to carry the packages to the bridge, and while Hughes unpacked and kept watch Wilson began his climb into the steel, carrying the lethal packs and swinging like a monkey between the girders and occasionally hanging one-handed from them while he set the charges and detonators in place. When it was done, Wilson made one last check of the connections, rolled out a long length of slow-burn fuse to hang over the bridge, and lit it.

'Run like hell!'

Wilson didn't need to say it; he was ticking off the seconds in his mind as he and Hughes dashed away, crashing their way through the undergrowth back towards the sea.

Boom!

The whole lot went up in a cloud of shattered concrete, twisted metal and dust, showering them with debris as they scurried, stumbling and falling, down the embankment to the beach. Fortunately, the canoe was safely hidden from the flying masonry, and the two pushed it into four inches (ten centimetres) of water and clambered inside to make their escape. *Utmost* had come to about 800 metres offshore. As Wilson and Hughes came aboard they were cheered by the crew, and one more dagger went into the corner of the Jolly Roger when the sub and its bold but modest bombers received another heroes' welcome in Malta.

By now their names were taking on the proportions of local legend among the submariners and navy in Malta and Alexandria. News of their exploits brought interest and fascination from the war managers in war theatres and London. The Italians, whose own water-borne raids using frogmen and limpet mines were causing havoc in Gibraltar and elsewhere, realised that they were being hit by expert teams of saboteurs and began tightening security around rail and other coastal installations.

Wilson and Hughes were already being earmarked for further raids and were once again aboard *Utmost* when she resumed her patrol in September 1941. This time the target was another rail tunnel of the kind that could cause most disruption and chaos. It was south of Naples, and the job wasn't just an explosives one. They were to take with them propaganda leaflets to make sure the Italians knew exactly who was carrying out the wrecking missions and, secondly, to cause unrest and fear among the locals.

They made their attempt on the night of 22 September, this time using two canoes because of the weight of the leaflets and the explosives needed to blow the tunnel. They landed on a beach with a moderate incline behind it and, as usual, hid the canoes and their contents while they surveyed the scene to check for guards and likely obstacles. That done, they headed directly to the tunnel; seven trips were made to take the explosives and leaflets to the site.

Wilson and Hughes were busily laying the charges when out of the darkness came an enemy patrol. They took cover, but they were spotted. Wilson stood up, firing his Thompson sub-machine-gun, and the Italians dived for cover, back inside the tunnel. The patrol regrouped and could be heard coming back. Wilson and Hughes fired again and made tracks for the beach. Abandoning their gear and explosives, they paddled like fury back to *Utmost* and lived to fight another day – the next day, in fact. Overnight and the following day *Utmost* sped off down the west coast of Italy and on the night of 23 September was off the northern coast of Sicily, scanning the next target on Wilson's list, a three-span railway bridge over the River Oliva.

Once again they ran into trouble. The landing and locating the target went according to plan, but sentries were guarding the bridge with a group of workmen with lanterns. Out of the darkness, one of them challenged Wilson, who responded with the shout of 'Amico!' The guard was not convinced and raised his rifle. Wilson shot him. A hail of gunfire followed. Somewhere close by a Breda machine-gun crew was set up and ready. Wilson and Hughes dashed away in the dark and headed for their canoe and back to a safe return to *Utmost*.

The action was hotting up. The Italians had cottoned on and were evidently placing guards at likely sabotage targets – and that was in part the intent of the raids. The damage could always be repaired, usually within a week or so. The effect of the attacks was to divert Italian and German troops to deal with them; one more gun crew at a railway bridge meant one less on the battlefields. Even so, when Tug returned to Malta at the beginning of October, Shrimp Simpson told him that the top brass at Combined Operations were concerned that his operations were becoming too hazardous. His raids would have to stop.

Tug argued his point. Even if railway tunnels were attracting a regular protection squad, miles of track were still unprotected, and guarding it all was an impossible task for the Italians. And, anyway, he had been working on a new method of speeding up his operation, a ready-assembled device that he could leave beside the track to explode quickly when the train came by, rather than risking long periods ashore. Simpson was persuaded, and on 18 October Tug went aboard the latest T-class submarine, under Lieutenant-Commander Hugh Rider Haggard, grandson of the novelist Sir Henry Rider Haggard. *Truant* was on its way from the Barrow-in-Furness shipyard to join No. 1 Submarine Flotilla in Alexandria.

Haggard would pursue a route that would take him through the Strait of Otranto, between Italy and Albania, into the Adriatic. It was this that persuaded Simpson to allow Wilson to go along, by changing tack and hitting the east coast of Italy for the first time. In fact, it turned out to be one of the most hazardous submarine journeys Wilson had ever had. The last stage of the journey from Barrow-in-Furness provided the new vessel with a baptism of fire. *Truant* encountered a succession of high dramas and activity, including mortar attack from surface vessels and aircraft, depth-charges, torpedo action against enemy shipping and, for four hair-raising hours, being grounded on the ocean floor with only a bathtub of water over her periscope.

Even so, Tug was allowed ashore for one more attack to test his new explosives set-up. The target was the main Milan to Brindisi railway line near Ancona. The pre-prepared charges were attached to the rail in double-quick time just as a train was approaching, and his plan worked exactly as he had forecast, derailing the engine and 14 sleeping-cars, doubtless packed with Axis war executives, and causing a good deal of disruption to the line.

Wilson and Hughes spent a full three weeks on patrol with *Truant*, sailing into Alexandria on 17 November, almost seven months after leaving for Malta for what, at the time, was meant to be a brief sojourn. The date was Wilson's second wedding anniversary, though his young bride was far away in Bristol. Even correspondence between them had been at best spasmodic, although any particular news, such as Marjorie's survival of a blitz attack, had been radioed through to whichever submarines he had been aboard at the time.

Roger Courtney was in Alexandria to welcome Wilson back to the Special Boat Section based on HMS *Medway* with an anniversary present – he had been promoted to captain. Wilson noticed that the place was somewhat depleted in terms of personnel. By then the 1SBS had extended its particular repertoire of special operations, working largely from submarines. The range of tasks covered everything from beach recce for troop landings, sabotage operations on the lines of Wilson's own exploits, and rescuing Allied troops left behind after the fall of Crete in June 1941. In the month of August alone, one solitary SBS canoeist, Corporal G. C. Bremner, single-handedly rescued 125 British, Australian, New Zealand and Greek soldiers who had been hiding in the hills of Crete since it was overrun by the Germans. He brought them to safety via the submarine *Torbay* and on to Alexandria. He was eventually awarded a Distinguished Conduct Medal.

Another series of operations that became an SBS speciality during the latter half of 1941 was the insertion and evacuation of secret agents behind enemy lines across the whole of the Mediterranean theatre, and later in the Far East. These missions continued, often at great risk to canoeists, agents and the delivering submarines, throughout the remainder of the war. The situation became a familiar one: agents, often in smart civilian clothes and clutching a briefcase containing important papers and/or communications sets, would look in horror at the little canoe into which they were expected to climb to be ferried ashore; often, they ended up soaked to the skin in rough seas.

Alternatively, the SBS might be tasked to go into a particular region and bring out an agent who had been betrayed or lost. Courtney himself had to go in search of an important agent who had gone missing in Yugoslavia but failed to find him. On another occasion he sailed in HMS/M *Osiris* to evacuate a group of agents from Albania who should have been waiting for him on the beach near Scutari, but who never arrived. They were not heard from again.

Betrayal was one of the worst aspects of these operations. In September that year, for example, James Sherwood, now an SBS lieutenant, and Corporal I. Booth had the task of repatriating eight Cretans back to their island at a pre-arranged place from HMS/M *Thunderbolt*. They were floated off in a canoe each, both of them taking one agent per trip, instructing the agents to wait in hiding on the beach until all were safely ashore. By the third trip to the beach, however, the four previously delivered agents had vanished. Sherwood took a severe dressing-down from those who remained, though the fault doubtless lay with a contact in Crete who had had the agents captured and probably tortured.

Elsewhere, a major operation was in the offing that would, for the first time in history, utilise the joint skills of the SBS as well as the last remnants of Robert Laycock's much-vaunted Layforce, now operating as a special raiding-party with the 8th Army. The latter group was down to just 53 men by the end of October 1941 out of the 1,500 who had set off full of hope and ambition just 10 months earlier. Operation Crusader, a new offensive by the 8th Army to retrieve ground lost to Rommel, for which Churchill had been pressing since August, was finally to be launched on the night of 17–18 November 1941. Layforce, the SBS and the SAS were to get some ambitious side-action: a daring – some said wild, mad and plain daft – scheme to infiltrate deep behind enemy lines to cause maximum commotion on the eve of the launch of Crusader. The plan was that . . .

1. The SBS would be responsible for the delivery and recovery of virtually the entire remaining complement of Layforce, led by Laycock himself and Lieutenant-Colonel Geoffrey Keyes, son of Sir Roger Keyes, director of Combined Operations in London.
2. The raiding party would be put ashore from rubber boats launched from submarines, make their way to Rommel's villa, supposedly in the village of Bida Littoria 185 miles inside enemy territory, and assassinate him.
3. They would hit the German headquarters in the same place and blow up all telegraph and telephone installations in the area.
4. They would then blow up the Italian headquarters at Cirene and the Italian Intelligence Centre at Appollonia.
5. David Stirling's L Detachment, on the same night, was to launch a secondary diversionary raid, attacking five enemy airstrips for forward bombers and fighters between Gazala Tmimi – an historic event as the first-ever raid of the fledgling SAS.

They were to travel by submarines to a beach landing-area which had been surveyed by an SBS team consisting of Lieutenant Ingles and Corporal Severn. They were taken to the area aboard the submarine *Torbay* a couple of nights before the raid, paddled ashore by canoe and made a complete recce of the beach. They also met British intelligence officer Captain Jock Haselden, disguised as an Arab, who was to give the signal for the parties to come ashore on the night of 15 November, when the raid would get under way. The party set off after nightfall aboard the two submarines *Talisman* and *Torbay*.

The weather had just taken a turn for the worse, but the green light remained on for a landing in spite of the rough sea, with SBS men guiding the heavily laden troops off the submarine casement into their tiny craft. As forecast by the SBS men, the launching of canoes and dinghies from the submarines would take forever in those conditions. The *Torbay* carried the bulk of the raiding-party, with 36 men aboard. It took almost 7 hours to land them instead of the 90 minutes estimated. By then it was deemed impossible to land the remaining 18 men aboard *Talisman*, although Laycock, who was on *Talisman*, eventually made it ashore with 6 others. He decided to remain at the rendezvous with reserves of ammunition, leaving Keyes, the group commander, to lead the raid itself.

There was one other problem. Haselden, when told by Laycock of their intentions, was surprised: he understood Rommel's house to be at Sidi Rafa and not Bida Littoria, the designated target. Two Arabs who came with Haselden confirmed this, and Laycock was forced to switch the main attack. The depleted group set off on the 18-mile march to the inland target in driving rain, which hardly mattered because each and every one of them was already drenched from the landing débâcle, and the passage through thick mud as the march proceeded only added to their woes. At dawn, and making slow progress, Keyes ordered the men to take shelter in a cave, where they laid up for the rest of the day and began their move towards the targets at nightfall, which were reached on the night of 16–17 November.

They reached the Rommel house at around 2330. Keyes placed his men in key positions: three were detailed to put the electricity plant out of action, five were posted around the building to cover all exits, two others were placed outside a nearby hotel to prevent anyone from leaving and covered the road on either side of Rommel's house. All were in position just before midnight, when a recce was made of the house. Unable to find a way in through the rear, as planned, Geoffrey Keyes and his party walked boldly to the hefty front door and beat upon it. Captain Campbell, who spoke fluent German, demanded entry and eventually a sentry opened the door. He was set upon immediately by Colonel Keyes, but the German grasped the muzzle of his tommy-gun and backed against a wall. Keyes was unable to draw his fighting knife and neither Campbell nor Sergeant Terry could get close enough to stab the German in the throat in the manner in which they had been trained. Finding it impossible to dispose of the sentry silently, Campbell shot him with his .38 revolver.

The noise alerted others and two men came down the stairs in front of them, saw the commotion and were met by a burst of fire from Terry's tommy-gun. Off the main hall were several doors. Keyes gingerly opened the first and found the room empty. Inside the second room, from which no one had attempted to emerge, were about ten German soldiers in steel helmets. Keyes fired a few rounds and slammed the door shut. Campbell told him he would throw a grenade and pulled the pin. As Keyes opened the door, half a dozen guns blazed and Keyes fell, mortally wounded, just as Campbell hurled his grenade. It exploded, killing all inside who had not been finished off by Keyes's gunfire. Terry and Campbell carried Keyes outside, and he died within a few minutes.

Campbell went back to the house and to the side of it to round up his men and was hit by a bullet from a jumpy commando who thought he was a German, it broke his lower leg. Campbell now ordered the men to hurl all their remaining grenades through the windows of the building and to withdraw immediately and, realising the burden he would be to the men on the return journey, ordered himself to be abandoned.

Only 18 men made it back to the rendezvous where Colonel Laycock had been waiting, passing the hours away by reading a damp copy of *The Wind in the Willows* which he had taken from the submarine. They all then moved towards the beach, where they had hidden their boats, and signalled out to sea. Miraculously, the submarine *Talisman* rose up and headed closer towards the shore, but then the party discovered that their boats had gone: not a single one remained. They were stranded.

SBS Lieutenant (later Major) Tommy Langton described the moment:

We were relieved to see the arranged signal from the beach, but it was much too rough to launch a folboat. The [submarine] captain having decided to send Lieutenant Ingles and Corporal Severn on a spare rubber craft, this was attempted, but the boat was washed adrift by the swell before the crew could board it. Later, the party ashore reported they had found the boat with water and food . . . they also reported there were 22 of them. They did not know what had happened to the rubber boats which had been left on the beaches.

The submarine captain suggested in his signal to the shore that they should attempt at dawn to swim out to the submarine, which was hovering 800 metres from the beach. There were, however, a number of men who could not swim anything like that distance, and others who could not swim at all. The suggestion was declined on the basis of all or none. The submarine was in a risky position even under darkness, and, with no apparent way of rescuing them, the captain decided to put to sea and signalled he would return after dark the following day.

Langton continued:

We put to sea again . . . and closed the beach very soon after dark the next night. The sea was considerably calmer . . . but we were dismayed to see no signals from the beach this time, so after waiting some time the captain decided to send myself and Corporal Freeberry in to reconnoitre. The beach was deserted . . . [then] we spotted a light which appeared on a hillside. It was the correct colour but not giving the correct [recognition] signal, so I was suspicious of it. We walked a little further and thought we saw a movement. We both heard a shout soon afterwards but found nothing, and, since we were by then some distance from our boat and liable to be cut off, I decided to return to it and wait.

Langton and Freeberry waited for several minutes but saw nothing further and decided to launch their folboat to paddle along the shore towards the location of the light. Langton flashed his torch, heard a shout but saw no signal in return. They beached again and were upturned as they did so, losing a paddle. Then Langton spotted the glow of a lighted cigarette in the undergrowth and realised the people ashore were the enemy. They clambered back into the folboat and headed back to the submarine, a feat completed with one paddle only through the brute strength of the 16-stone Corporal Freeberry. In fact, the 22 survivors of the raid had been attacked by German troops; some were killed, others were captured and at least four escaped into the hillside. Why the enemy troops had not killed Langton and Freeberry, too, remains to this day a mystery. Those who escaped included Lieutenant-Colonel Laycock himself; with Sergeant Terry he made an incredible 36-day trek on foot through hostile countryside and desert, reaching British lines on Christmas Day.

The second diversionary raid scheduled for the night of the launch of Crusader was no more successful, although more survived. The bad weather, with high winds and sandstorms, was hardly conducive to a successful parachute landing, but after consulting his men Stirling decided they were going anyhow. The SAS detachment was divided into five groups, to drop from Bombay aircraft close to the target airstrips and blow them apart. Then they would make their escape and be picked up by Long-Range Desert Group transport.

Each group had 60 incendiary and explosive bombs for the attack. Not surprisingly, when the aircraft came in over the designated dropping zone, they had to take evasive action to avoid enemy flak and, with winds gusting at 45mph as the men leaped out, they landed miles off target out in the desert; a number of them were hurt. It was almost ten days before the survivors began wandering back, 22 of the 60 who set out making it to a patrol position, the task half done. Stirling was furious with himself and vowed such stupidity would never happen again. Next time, he promised, not a detail would be overlooked. The SAS was on the move, but for Layforce it was definitely all over.

The operation was a costly failure in its execution but was regarded as a success from two aspects: first, it had brought pressure to the very heart of the Germans' desert campaign, and, secondly, the operation of beach landings became, for the SBS, a model from which lessons were learned and corrected for the future. Decades later, the landing of raiding-groups of the Special Forces, as in the Falklands War and the Gulf, benefited from the experience, and the standard final section of reports on all future operations would include a summary under the heading: LESSONS LEARNT.

Back at base, other matters of import for the future of the SBS were developing. Roger Courtney, in failing health, went back to England in November where immediately he began gathering suitable recruits to form 2SBS. The onshore sabotage operations of the indomitable Tug Wilson and 'Wally' Hughes had been vetoed from on high because of their increasing danger, although he and other remaining SBS personnel were now regularly aboard departing submarines in the 1st Submarine Flotilla.

Wilson himself was in fact in the process of preparing even more hazardous missions, and, when *Torbay* set off on her next billet in early December, Wilson and Hughes were aboard, specifically to try out a new triple-limpet-mine device Wilson had invented. They headed towards Navarino, the busy Greek port where enemy destroyers had been spotted from aerial reconnaissance. The plan was that Wilson and Hughes would be deposited outside the harbour, paddle in with their canoe loaded with their limpets, and hopefully blow up a couple of targets. Despite paddling almost 15 miles on the first night, Wilson and Hughes found no suitable vessels for the attack. A few nights later they returned to Navarino and through the periscope found an enemy destroyer moored at the pier.

They set off in their canoe, paddling to within 150 metres of the ship. At this point Wilson, wearing only greased-up long-johns to protect him from the cold, slid into the water to swim the remaining distance, cautiously pushing six limpet mines ahead of him on a buoy. The limpets consisted of two pounds (0.9 kilogrammes) of plastic explosives in a metal case that would be clamped to the ship's hull by magnets (see Appendix I). Each mine could blast a two-metre hole in the side of the destroyer. The hefty package needed careful manoeuvring, a slow task at the best of times, and the December waters were ice-cold.

Hughes could see that his partner was in trouble within 80 metres or so. He signalled on the line attached to Wilson that he was pulling him in. Tug was hauled, protesting, back into the boat, with numb hands and chattering teeth. It was a disappointing end to their partnership. Hughes and Wilson would never work together again.

At the beginning of January Tug was summoned back to Malta to undertake a number of vital missions landing agents on the Tunisian coast complete with stores and radios, a task increasingly in the hands of SBS personnel. It was there, too, that he learned

41

that he had been awarded the Distinguished Service Order for his exploits – a fairly rare decoration for his rank. He was to be sent home on leave to England and take his decoration from the king at Buckingham Palace.

'One last task . . .' said Shrimp Simpson, after revealing the award. Two agents had to be landed near Carthage.

'Of course,' said Wilson without hesitation.

He was to travel in the submarine *Upholder*, which had the largest number of kills to her name in the Mediterranean fleet under her by-then famous captain, the tall and bearded Lieutenant-Commander David Wanklyn, VC, DSO and two bars. She had sunk 125,000 tons of enemy shipping in 16 months. Tug was to take the two agents aboard, land them in a rubber dinghy at Carthage and then rendezvous at sea with the submarine *Unbeaten* to get a ride to Gibraltar before going on to the UK.

The landing was completed without a hitch, and Tug went back aboard *Upholder* to sail for the meeting with *Unbeaten* off the island of Lampedusa. *Unbeaten*, it turned out, was limping home, damaged in enemy action. By then the sea had churned up and looked too rough for Tug even to make the transfer. Wanklyn suggested he remain aboard *Upholder*, return to Malta and get a lift to Gibraltar from there. Tug, anxious to get on his way home, decided to risk it in spite of a joking shout from *Unbeaten*: 'Piss off, Tug. We've got two feet of water in the fore-ends and aft. We'll never make it to Gib.' It was a fateful decision. Soon afterwards, *Upholder* was lost with all hands. Tug Wilson was the last person to see the crew alive.

CHAPTER THREE

Tug's last stand

Jumbo Courtney and Tug Wilson were back in Blighty, and Captain Mike Kealy took temporary command of the SBS. The original party, now topped up with additional hands, had remained remarkably intact, considering their hazardous pursuits. In the months ahead and on towards the close of 1942, that was soon to change – decimated by loss of life, loss of liberty and punctuated by some fine stuff for the glory book. There are too many examples to detail, but a few instances will give a flavour of those classic feats of human endeavour, beyond and above the call . . .

There was, for starters, the epic journey of Captain Ken Allott, who was dispatched with Lieutenant Duncan Ritchie, RN, to scout the coastline beyond the British-held position 60 miles west of Tobruk, a mission prompted by GHQ in Cairo. The planners believed they would need to get an idea of the lie of the land in double-quick time. How were they to know that Rommel would soon be rolling the British back to El Alamein, and that Allott and Ritchie were being sent off in the wrong direction?

But it seemed a good idea at the time, and the two officers were ferried 100 miles along German-held coast by motor torpedo-boat (MTB) on 22 May 1942 and dropped off with their folboat and stores (and, for the first time in any SBS operation, a radio) at Cape Ras-el-Tin, deep in enemy territory. They paddled along the coastline, noting the terrain and any troop population and eventually pulled in for a rest at a beach that provided a modicum of cover from low-growing bushes.

No sooner had they landed and shared out some chocolate than the sound of a popular Wagner tune wafted across the dunes as

43

several trucks arrived, disgorging 200 German troops. For several hours Allott and Ritchie, dug into a self-constructed hide behind a few precariously unbushy bushes, watched as the young Nazis performed various physical training exercises, then played some games, one of which appeared to be hide-and-seek. Virtually every bush other than theirs was used in the game, and the troops eventually departed unaware that they had been observed throughout by two British officers who now needed a change of underwear.

The two pushed off to sea again and began to paddle back to base, performing their recce tasks as they went. The journey ahead, often in rough seas, during which the heavy radio was tipped over the side to lighten their load, was completed in five days, often under cover of darkness. From the point they set off to arriving back at Gazala was 150 miles!

Meanwhile David Stirling, the ambitious and empire-building head of the now firmly established Special Air Service, was casting an acquisitive eye over the SBS. Their operations, he conjectured, could easily slot in to a joint command with himself at the helm. He had already established a Special Boat Squadron under Captain (the Earl) George Jellicoe, a 24-year-old, thick-set young man with a mop of curly hair, much remembered at Cambridge, where he had studied before the war, and now an officer of panache, style and wit.

Stirling's little army and the notoriety of its escapades in the desert had grown and grown. He was, said John Lodwick, the Marks & Spencer of the military. His HQ was stacked with the assorted playthings of war which were scarce everywhere else: Jeeps, weapons, stores (variously of German, Italian and British origin), a vast hoard of explosives of every kind and, in an instant, whatever air transport he required as of that moment. For months, while the SBS had been working largely from submarines around the enemy coasts or landing its chaps for highly confidential missions in enemy territory, Stirling's outfit had been rampaging through the countryside, miles inside enemy lines, raiding and pillaging, stealing and killing and causing general mayhem among the outposts of Rommel's Afrika Korps.

Attacks on airfields were a particular speciality, and they had blown up more than anyone else: six air bases in Cyrenaica were put out of action temporarily, forty planes destroyed and an unknown number of German and Italian troops killed. The aura of mystique was also being established, with the standard-issue beret badges with blue wings and a white commando dagger bearing the legend WHO DARES WINS. It was, as a motto of the day and the future, rather better than Jumbo Courtney's invention of EXCRETA TAURI ASTUTOS FRUSTRANTUR, worked out by an Oxford don and which roughly translated meant: BULLSHIT BAFFLES BRAINS.

Stirling himself could see no reason why Courtney's SBS mob should not join his own on selected joint missions, and, indeed, in June they began several back-to-back raids to attack enemy airfields around the eastern Mediterranean. The first of these joint attacks was on Crete. Mike Kealy took three sections of the SBS to the north-west of the island while George Jellicoe led a contingent of SAS canoeists to Heraklion. Kealy's own target, Maleme airfield, was too heavily guarded to attempt their raid. But Captain George Duncan's section made it through the wire at Kastelli field and blew up four bomb dumps in spectacular fashion, killing 70 or so enemy troops in the process.

Jellicoe's attack at Heraklion, with a party that included four French officers and a Greek guide, was also accompanied by a substantial display of fireworks. They were landed from HMS/M *Triton* in captured German inflatables and laid up while a recce was made of the airfield. Sixty-six aircraft were counted, and the raiders moved off on the second day to do their worst. Unfortunately, German guards discovered their wire-cutting entrance to the perimeter defences. Fortunately, before the guards could seek them out, an RAF Blenheim bomber followed three Stukas which were landing at the field and promptly dropped its payload, causing confusion and panic on the ground. This gave Jellicoe and his team the time they needed to set their explosives, timed to go off in 90 minutes.

When the first of their charges began exploding, Jellicoe's party was still inside the perimeter, but with incredible coolness he and his men tagged on behind a German patrol in the darkness and walked boldly out of the main gate, where they promptly split up and vanished into the undergrowth. Jellicoe and the Greek guide managed to reach their rendezvous by walking 120 miles across two mountain ranges before linking up with a rescue contact on the south coast, followed by a safe return to base. The four Frenchmen accepted the kind invitation of a passing Grecian to join him for a meal and were betrayed. In the shootout that followed as they resisted arrest by the Germans, one of their number was shot. The body of the traitor who led them into the trap was later discovered upside-down in a well with a bullet through his head.

To date, the SBS losses in personnel had been remarkably light. That was about to change – and how. Within the next three months more than half of the men of Courtney's 42-strong 1SBS would be in enemy hands or dead as, repeatedly, they were asked to undertake the most hazardous and exacting tasks in clandestine attacks. A change in strategy contributed to the losses. The influence of David Stirling became more forceful after Courtney himself left the Middle East in 1942 to return to England for closer liaison with Lord Mountbatten, newly appointed head of Combined Operations. Where originally SBS took light losses on their specialist tasks of hitting railways, running limpet raids on Axis shipping, ferrying agents and making diversion raids ahead of full-scale assaults, they were now being drawn into the work that was previously the domain of the SAS: they were travelling deeper inland, especially to attack enemy airfields.

In July they lost eight key members, all taken prisoner in one hit. With Malta under siege, and the 10th Submarine Flotilla having evacuated its base, SAS and SBS teams were being tasked to attack airfields in the vicinity to protect attempts by Allied convoys to reach the island with supplies and oil. They had been rehearsing with a collection of new devices specifically to be used in rapid attacks on parked aircraft.

On the night of 11–12 August 1942, Major Desmond Buchanan, a Grenadier Guards officer attached to M Detachment of the Special Boat Section, was delivered by the submarine *Una* to a drop-off point near Catania, Sicily, with seven others, including the travel writer Eric Newby. They were to go ashore in canoes laden with explosives to blow up German Junkers 88 bombers, massed at the Gela aerodrome west of Catania, for an attack on the Pedestal food convoy bound for Malta. They penetrated the airfield and split into two groups, but discovered that the Italian guards had been reinforced by a strong presence of Wehrmacht troops, so that each aircraft was guarded by an armed sentry. One group did penetrate the workshops and were planting explosives on crated engines when they were discovered. One of them made an unconvincing attempt to talk their way out, and then, in plain-as-day English, he called to the others and shouted: 'It's time we fucked off.' They made a hasty retreat, firing as they went.

One of them fell into a trench around the airfield and landed on several Italian guards who managed to grab him and his partner. The remaining six made it to the beach where they had hidden their two-man canoes, but found that one of them had been damaged beyond repair. They all piled into the remaining three canoes to paddle out for the rendezvous with *Una* five miles from shore, but in worsening conditions they failed to reach the contact point. One of the canoes, with two men aboard, set off back to the shore, but they were captured the following morning. Of the remaining two canoes, one sank, and the commander of the party, not wishing to be a burden to his comrades, swam off into the darkness. He was persuaded to return, however, and Buchanan gave him his place in the last canoe, which undoubtedly saved his life. Buchanan tried to swim back to the shore but shortly after dawn, frozen and exhausted after five hours in the water, he and the remaining three raiders were picked up and taken prisoner by an Italian fishing-vessel. Recommending Buchanan for an MC, the captain of *Una* commented that he had shown 'courage and resource of a very high order. Although the object of the raid was not achieved due to the enemy's exceptional precautions, the boldness and initiative shown are considered most deserving of recognition.'

In the same month two more members of Courtney's 1SBS, who had been in since its inception, were captured. A section led by newcomer Captain Montgomerie was tasked to attack an ammunitions dump on the North African coast near Daba, one and a half miles behind enemy lines and virtually on top of the El Alamein front line. To reach it they had to pass a tented village of German troops which included a mobile cinema and a canteen full of singing drunks.

The SBS men working in pairs, successfully laid their explosives around the dump and a few more for good measure on tents, wagons, some captured British trucks and even the cookhouse before heading back to the coast for their exit rendezvous. One pair stumbled across a German lookout post, and in the exchange of fire Corporal Gurney was wounded by a burst of machine-gun fire and Lieutenant Mike Alexander stayed behind to help him. Both were captured.

Next, Lieutenant Tommy Langton hit trouble in a raid on

Tobruk. It was a two-pronged attack that began on 22 August, when an SAS squadron was joined by detachments of Royal Engineers, Coastal Defence and, later, the Long-Range Desert Group. They filled seven three-ton lorries loaded with British soldiers dressed to look like prisoners of war, while the SAS were in German uniform, acting as guards. They were to drive through German lines, intending to reach Tobruk to coincide with the sea landing of the 11th Battalion, Royal Marines, backed up by 150 infantry and machine-gunners. They were to shoot up shore installations and German communications to hinder the advance on Egypt.

Tommy Langton, the sole SBS officer, was riding with the SAS and was tasked to guide the infantry forwards from MTBs while the marines came ashore in Palestine-built landing-craft from two destroyers. The incredible journey of the fake PoWs actually ran without a hitch, apart from one hair-raising moment when Langton and his group, under Lieutenant Roberts, encountered a nest of Germans about to point a machine-gun in their direction. Roberts shot them. On the south side of Tobruk, a building identified as a wireless station was entered; the staff inside were similarly disposed of and the building blown to bits.

On to the beach, and Langton went ahead alone to begin to call in the MTBs. Problems were evident immediately: the landing-craft were generally pretty poor; several simply packed up or were not suited to the rapid landing techniques required. Secondly, as was later discovered, a double agent had forewarned of the attack and, as the chaos of the landing began to unfold, the Germans opened fire from dug-in positions, with tracer bouncing off the MTBs and searchlights scanning the whole area. More than half the force never landed because of the conditions and the inefficient landing-craft. Most of the rest were killed or captured, although mini-battles between groups of British and German troops ran for hours.

The destroyer HMS *Sikh* was sunk by shore batteries; the cruiser HMS *Coventry* and the destroyer HMS *Zulu*, with the unlanded troops aboard, were sunk by dive-bombers on the way back. A young Royal Marines Lieutenant on board *Coventry*, Donald Peyton-Jones, survived and later became Officer Commanding SBS.

Tommy Langton and two army privates tried to make their escape in a beach MTB but couldn't get it started. Then they swam out to an abandoned landing-craft and paddled around picking up survivors, 25 in all from the beach and inshore. Langton led the bedraggled group on what seemed an impossible task of reaching Allied lines – 700 miles away – through hot Nazi territory, with little food or water and having to dive for cover virtually every few yards.

The trek was to last 78 days, and the last quarter of it in bare feet. Day by day the group became smaller, depleted by illness (mostly dysentery), starvation, German patrols and capture. After three weeks the party was down to six men. Then one more fell ill. Sergeant Evans, dehydrated and ravaged by dysentery, was too ill to go any further and was made comfortable by the roadside to be picked up by the enemy the following morning. Two others, twin brothers named Leslie from the Fusiliers, were next. One of them could not go on and his brother remained with him, to join him in captivity.

Finally, the three made it back to an Allied position – Tommy Langton and two privates, Hillman and Watler, emaciated and bedraggled and with a story of another incredible journey. Langton's only complaint was that he could not get near a radio for world news, otherwise he would have joined Monty at El Alamein. They threw a party for him later. Drink was taken, and Major Mayne accidentally drove a Jeep into the tent. Not many injured. Tommy Langton was awarded the Military Cross and was soon back in action.

While Langton was still marching, four more stalwarts of 1SBS were taken out in an otherwise very successful raid on airfields and fuel depots on Rhodes. The party was led by Captain Ken 'Tramp' Allott – so nicknamed for his total disregard of uniforms and razor blades – and Lieutenant David 'Dinky' Sutherland – the complete opposite, who would rise from a night in the depths of grottiness smartly attired and having used his last mug of water to shave himself.

Their mission to Rhodes was one of the most vital of its time and carried out to perfection. Tramp and Dinky took with them one Greek officer, two Greek guides, Sergeant Moss – a veritable superman – a corporal and three marines. They were landed on the island eight days before the raids were due to begin, bringing ashore a mound of explosives, ammunition and stores on three Carley rafts and one canoe. Each man carried a backpack of 50 pounds (23 kilogrammes) over 40 miles of rough, hostile terrain, deep valleys and steep cliffs to a cave where they would store part of the rations for the return journey. There, they split into two groups, each heading for their respective targets – two airfields from which German and Italian aircraft were harassing Allied shipping.

Each group completed its task with brilliant efficiency, and the two fields were put out of action for several weeks, giving Allied shipping an extremely unusual window of opportunity. Both groups, however, were hampered by deserting guides in their return to the rendezvous, where they would signal to the submarine that they were coming out. German search-parties scoured the countryside. One of the guides was captured and tortured, and they discovered that the rendezvous site was surrounded by 50 Germans. Dinky Sutherland's party split into two, while he himself remained with the Greek officer and Marine Duggan. He never saw the rest of his group again, and from the thud of distant gunfire he knew that they were either dead or captured.

Sutherland and Duggan reached the beach and from a hiding-place in the cliffs could see that the German intercepting force was searching the area meticulously. The Greek officer with them had gone off to try to get information on the others and never came back. Suddenly, amid a lot of commotion and gunfire, it was clear that Tramp Allott's party had been found and captured. Sutherland and Duggan were on their own.

That night Sutherland gave the pre-arranged signal out to sea with his torch in the hope that the rendezvous submarine was hovering somewhere waiting to take them off. Suddenly, Duggan spotted a faint response, flashed through the periscope; it was clearly several miles away.

They had no boats; the only course was to swim for it. They waited for an hour or more until the signal became clearer, but now they were fearful that the Italians had seen it too. They had. An enemy MTB had been launched and was patrolling up and down. Sutherland and Duggan, already weakened by lack of food and the long grind of the operation itself, had a stark choice: to give themselves up or try to swim out to the sub. They chose the latter.

They were in the water for almost an hour and a half, swimming towards the spot where they last saw the signal, with Duggan still signalling with their torch. At one point the sound of motors brought them joy until Duggan shouted 'Dive!' It was the Italian MTB. Minutes later the submarine rose from the depths beside them. Sutherland was dragged aboard, half-dead and seriously ill; Duggan was similarly in a bad way. But they had survived.

One more mishap brought gloom to the SBS and to Jumbo Courtney in particular . . .

Tug Wilson had enjoyed his home leave. He'd been reunited with his wife, had been fêted in Bristol and in his former place of work as the hero returning, and had received the royal congratulations on the presentation of his DSO. The sojourn in England, which he had reached finally in April after the eventful ride home via a limping submarine, was not entirely in the interest of his personal well-being. At one of the several top-secret experimental stations in the South of England, where all kinds of devices, gadgets, aids for agents, and other secret weapons were being tested, Major Malcolm Campbell and his group had invented a mini-torpedo for use by canoeists. (This was the same Malcolm Campbell, later Sir, who took the world land-speed record when his car *Bluebird* exceeded 300 miles an hour on the Bonneville Flats in 1935, and then achieved the world water-speed record in 1939.)

Campbell's device was ideal for the SBS. Instead of having to paddle or swim to enemy shipping and attach limpets – the current practice – they could attack from a safer distance more rapidly with these new hand-held torpedoes, which were powered by a windscreen-wiper motor. Trials had been conducted in experimental pools and home waters, but the torpedoes needed the expertise of a skilled canoeist of the SBS for a practical demonstration.

Tug Wilson was the man selected for the honour. Six of the mini-torpedoes had been produced, and he was to proceed forthwith to Alexandria in the company of a box marked 'Definitely This Side Up'. There he would join the submarine *Unbroken* and travel on to the coast of Italy to attack enemy shipping. This time he would be without his trusted aide Wally Hughes, who was ill. In his place went Bombardier Brittlebank, a solid, unflappable and courageous veteran of the disastrous Rommel raid and who, like Lieutenant-Colonel Laycock, had managed to find his way back to Egypt after enduring 40 days in the desert behind enemy lines.

51

No account of this adventure can match Tug's own placid description:

Crotone harbour was chosen by Captain G. W. G. Simpson, commanding officer of the 10th Flotilla, after a close study of aerial photographs, because it afforded maximum chances of success, and of escape after the attack. Periscope reconnaissance of harbour was carried out during afternoon from a distance of about four miles offshore. The target, a merchant vessel, was located in an anticipated position along the northern mole.

It was estimated that the operation, from leaving the submarine to the return, would take about two hours. The commanding officer of the submarine suggested that I should be launched about 2330 hours owing to the phase of the moon, which would rise about 0300 hours. He wanted the operation to be completed and under way from the vicinity of the harbour by that time. It was arranged that on return I was to flash a pre-arranged signal with a blue torch to seaward. If anything delayed my return, an alternative rendezvous was fixed at a point five miles off the harbour.

At 2340 our canoe was launched approximately 2,000 metres off the harbour, with personnel, stores and equipment. There was a slight breeze and a faint swell; otherwise it was flat calm and a clear sky above. At about 250 yards [228 metres] [from the harbour entrance] we split paddles and approached square-on to present minimum silhouette. The boom on closer approach looked rather formidable, but certainly not insurmountable.

However, we decided to investigate the bomb-damaged south mole and see if the breach gave us easier access to the harbour and found a gap that was down to sea-level. Barbed wire and rabbit wire had been erected but not very efficiently. It was possible without much difficulty to fold this upwards very conveniently over a large piece of masonry, which was luckily just awash with three or four inches of water. Having made the gap sufficiently large, it was then simple to ease the canoe through into the harbour.

Inside the harbour the stillness was intense and the sky clearly reflected on the water. The target was distinctly visible, the funnel, bridge and mast silhouetted against the sky. A large schooner was lying in the middle of the harbour in a line parallel with the target. The breach in the mole was almost directly opposite the target . . . and an ideal position for attack, since the torpedo had a range of only 400 yards.

The chances of being observed at that distance would not be great. Bombardier Brittlebank sat forward using single split paddle, myself aft with torpedoes ready for immediate action. The final approach was made at absolute minimum speed owing to the extreme stillness of the water and phosphorescence stirred up when the paddle was used with other than the smallest effort. The visibility was just too perfect and gave us need for additional caution.

Having just arrived in the attacking position, the stillness was exploded by a challenge from the schooner. This was followed immediately by a shout from the target vessel, then by the noise of people running about and shouting in an unmistakably Italian manner. I decided it would be some moments before they would recover themselves sufficiently and do something reasonable in the way of a countermeasure. I removed the nose cap of one torpedo, placed it in the water and pressed the starter button. It was necessary to make a quarter-turn of the propeller and press the button a second time. The starter functioned and the motor started, sounding extremely healthy.

With the torpedo just submerged, I took careful aim at the target (the canoe being stationary) and with a gentle push released it. Almost simultaneously I ordered Brittlebank to stand by with double-ended paddle in readiness for departure.

Having quickly found my own paddle, I stole a last glance at the torpedo. The white line painted fore and aft along her back was pointing directly at the centre of the target's length. Her depth was about five feet and appeared to be running steadily during the few brief moments I was able to follow her. There was now plenty of commotion, and lights were beginning to appear among the Italian flotilla, but as yet no shots were fired. No definite explosion was heard during retreat, and I could not guarantee a hit. The retreat was made, bearing in mind my instructions and the main point of the operation, and I rather regretted at the time having withdrawn with three torpedoes before making a further attempt in the same or another harbour later in the patrol.

But my instructions were to ensure we were not captured with the torpedoes still in our possession. I still had a formidable salvo of three of them left for use elsewhere, and I was in safe waters outside what had become something of a hornets' nest, with my parent craft in waiting at the rendezvous only some 2,000 yards away.

We made our way to the position and carried out the customary procedure of signalling. This was only used after intensive scanning of the horizon and from a few inches above the water. The swell was increasing very noticeably now, and I continued signalling at specific intervals. Then, after half an hour I located the familiar-looking blob of [what I thought to be] a submarine off my port bow and turned towards it. A moment later I saw a similar object a short distance from the first. It soon became apparent that this was no submarine but two surface craft approaching line-abreast. I turned towards them with the intention of passing between them.

Crouching low in the canoe as the craft bore down on us, I estimated the enemy's speed to be about ten knots, the bow waves now being very marked and about 60 yards apart. On the spur of the moment I quickly launched one of the torpedoes over the port side. A few moments later the knife-edge bows and low waist of the dark-and-light-grey-camouflaged ship, now very close and on my port beam, suggested a light destroyer. Between the two vessels and at such close quarters, I expected some form of challenge, so held the remaining two torpedoes in readiness to be jettisoned. Luckily, the canoe had not been seen by the enemy, and I carried on at a steady speed in a direction opposite to that of the enemy shipping.

A few unhappy moments were experienced in passing through the immediate wake of the two vessels, but the canoe withstood the test without capsizing. I realised that our submarine would most certainly have picked up HE [hydrophonic effects] and would have taken evasive action. With enemy vessels patrolling the harbour area, I gave up any hope of contacting the sub that night. It was by then approximately 0145 hours. The alternative rendezvous was to be at dawn. The weather was gradually worsening. A considerable swell with occasional white horses running diagonally across my rendezvous course created conditions most unfavourable for maintaining an accurate course in an open canoe.

To meet the submarine it would be necessary to square into the weather and patrol up and down for the next five or six hours with concentrated attention. This we managed to do, although the accuracy of my position for the rendezvous at dawn could be no other than a little doubtful. Everything in the canoe was drenched. It was impossible to wipe the compass and binoculars effectively, but Crotone could be seen, however, roughly in the right direction about six or seven miles away.

The sea had quietened considerably at dawn. Having remained in that position for about another two hours without having sighted a surface craft of any description, I decided to try to attract the attention of the submarine by creating underwater explosions. Two four-second hand-grenades were thrown astern after maximum speed had been attained by myself and Brittlebank to avoid possible damage to the canoe by fragmentation. No periscope was observed. I could only conclude that the canoe was not in an accurate position or that the captain had decided not to remain, for very good reasons unknown to myself.

Conditions now demanded that the canoe should be beached as soon as possible for maintenance, so I abandoned the area rather than run the risk of sinking. I proposed to make a bid for Malta, *some 250 miles away* [author's italics]. The condition of the canoe, however, and the equipment in our possession and the absolute necessity of frequent land-ings forced us to admit to ourselves that the odds of success of such a venture might be a little in the Italians' favour.

We proceeded south-south-east, towards Capo Calonna. Having rounded the cape, we reconnoitred that part of the coast for a suitable point of landing. A beach was selected, approachable only from the sea, being hemmed in by sheer cliffs. Before landing, the remaining two torpedoes were flooded and sunk some two miles offshore. By then, the canoe was not in a very stable condition. After some twenty minutes' work on her, we pushed off again. It was now about midday.

I set a course to cross the Golfo di Squillace. We passed

a number of fishing-craft, and occasionally we were hailed. I replied with a wave of the hand. By six in the evening we were forced to beach again. This time it was not possible to select a suitable beach. We had been observed landing. Some twenty minutes later we found ourselves surrounded by a large number of Italians. Throughout the operation, Bombardier Brittlebank's conduct and reactions to various circumstances left nothing to be desired. Also during subsequent interrogation after capture, he proved to be the model soldier.

Tug Wilson spent the rest of the war in – and escaping from – Italian and German prison camps, a classic PoW story which is a book in itself. In Germany he escaped twice, once from a moving train under heavy gunfire. He managed to get back into Italy in 1943, and became involved in the Rome escape route run by a Roman Catholic priest before finally being betrayed and captured again. He spent the remainder of the war in a German prisoner-of-war camp at Brunswick, along with other British inmates who, as a memorial to their time together, pooled part of their service pay when they returned home in 1945 to fund the formation of the New Brunswick Boys' Club in South London; the club still exists today.

The story of Malcolm Campbell's baby torpedoes was not yet over, however. The result of the trials was unknown. Had the torpedoes worked? Could they inflict serious damage on enemy shipping? They had not been successful, but with Wilson captured they had no way of knowing. Major Vere Holden-White – Harry to his service pals – was the man to find out.

Lieutenant-Colonel H. G. 'Blondie' Halser and Marine W. E. Sparks, the only two survivors of Operation Frankton, at the unveiling of a memorial to the Cockleshell Heroes at Poole. The eight who did not return were drowned or shot by the Germans.

Heroes and legends . . . creator of the wartime SBS Roger 'Jumbo' Courtney with his wife Dorrise in their canoe *Buttercup* in which they paddled the Danube for their honeymoon in 1938. *Left:* Blondie Hasler, inventor of many of the operational strategies on which today's SBS is based, in classic pose.

Nigel Clogstoun Willmott, beach reconnaissance expert and founder of Lord Mountbatten's Combined Operations Pilotage Parties which guided in invasion assault troops and equipment.

Lionel 'Buster' Crabb, Britain's first frogman and scourge of the Italian underwater raiders of the Mediterranean in the Second World War, who vanished while examining the hull of a Russian cruiser for MI6 in 1956.

Robert 'Tug' Wilson, the Bristol draughtsman who became a courageous canoeist/saboteur.

Canoe-borne raiders *Above:* early exercise of Army Commando Folbot troop in 1941. *Centre:* swimmer-canoeists in action in their Klepper during the Indonesian Confrontation in 1963. *Below:* a typical SBS beach landing, though normally under cover of darkness.

Saboteurs, reconnaissance teams and agents were often delivered to their target zone by submarine.

The *Sleeping Beauty*, codename for the wartime motorised submersible canoe developed from an idea by Blondie Hasler for sabotage attacks on enemy shipping. The pilot sat like a racing driver in the cockpit, with a hefty load of explosive charges secured inside the canoe. The *SB*, as it was known, was famously used on Operation Rimau, which originated from Australia for an attack on Japanese ships berthed in Singapore harbour. The raid went disastrously wrong and ten who survived gun battles with the Japanese forces were later beheaded by their captors. *(By permission of the Public Record Office)*

Wartime heroics of Buster Crabb, seen here at work, were subsequently overshadowed by the post-war drama of his disappearance. With primitive equipment, he made hundreds of dives to clear Italian limpets from Allied ships and towards the end of the war helped clear Venice of mines deposited by departing Nazis.

Precarious in the extreme, the *X-Craft* mini-submarine, often leaky and always cramped, in action with top secret COPPs teams guiding the Normandy D-Day troop landings, as they did with all seaborne invasion forces after 1942. On this vessel are Coppists Jim Booth (for'ard) and George Honour in the conning tower.

North African invasion for Operation Torch.

CHAPTER FOUR

Harry's game

News item, 7 November 1942:

The greatest-ever armada of ships assembled for a single operation today landed American troops in Vichy-French North Africa. It brings 140,000 men for the great Allied offensive against Axis forces following last week's decisive rout by the British of Rommel's Afrika Korps at the Battle of El Alamein. As rangers, marines and infantry landed by sea, paratroopers dropped on key airports in Morocco and Algeria. They had taken all their objectives by nightfall. The French had no desire to oppose the Allied forces. The only resistance came from naval and coastal defence guns; two small ships were lost in Oran harbour.

It was the launching of the first major invasion force of the war, famously codenamed Operation Torch. The second string to that assault – the raid on Oran harbour – was codenamed Operation Reservist. No mention was made of SBS involvement because that was a secret. The SBS were among the advance party that carried out a full reconnaissance of the landing-sites for the assault, along with the founder members of new small groups soon to be known as the Combined Operations Pilotage Parties (COPPs), formed by Jumbo Courtney's good friend Nigel Clogstoun Willmott. The SBS had also been earmarked to test a secret weapon, and behind the last dismissive sentence of the news item about the action in Oran harbour and the loss of two ships lay the dramatic sequel to Tug Wilson's trials with baby torpedoes. The man to tell the story was Major H. V.

Holden-White, MC, who led the SBS activity in the assault on Oran.

In January 1997 I met him at Huntly, the very pleasant residence for retired officers not far from the sea at Bishopsteignton, Devon. An attendant showed me to his little room, adorned with some of his own fine paintings and other memorabilia from life as an artist, living for a long while in France, after he quit the service at the end of the war. Vere Holden-White is now a frail but thoroughly charming and gentle man who also has an immediate and graphic recall of those days so many years ago.

He goes straight back to that battle off Oran, Algeria, where he was left holding the baby torpedoes that Tug Wilson had tested but had been unable to report back on. 'Bloody things,' said Vere with a mischievous chuckle. 'No bloody good at all. Damn things got ten of us captured, and I told Louis Mountbatten as much!'

Known as Harry in those days, in 1942 Holden-White was a 24-year-old second lieutenant in a battalion of the Royal Sussex Regiment, engaged on home defences since Dunkirk but about to be converted from infantry to a light anti-aircraft regiment of the Royal Artillery. Around that time, Harry's imagination had been fired at the local cinema by some newsreel of commandos; he volunteered immediately for special duties.

Before he knew what was happening, he was on his way to Scotland, where Jumbo Courtney was hastily assembling a contingent who would form 2SBS, now that 1SBS was under so much pressure at the eastern end of the Mediterranean. The new section would include some returned members of the original section, with new recruits such as Holden-White and the merging of 101 Troop, 8 Commando, the latter hand-picked by its commanding officer, Captain Gerald Montanaro. Montanaro was to be training officer of the new unit, Courtney was commanding officer and the number two was his brother, G. B. 'Gruff' Courtney. Montanaro, in particular, would bring special skills to the training of the new section. Apart from an obsession with canoes which matched Courtney's own, he also possessed remarkable technical qualifications that he could apply to key problems that daily confronted the folboatmen, including the calculation of currents, navigational aids, camouflage and improving the adhesion of limpets to the slimy hulls of barnacled ships.

Their billet was a private hotel in a suburb of Ardrossan, and soon Holden-White was being initiated into the gospel according to Jumbo. After the usual lecture, they were given a tour and shown the folboats they would use: 'a number of canoes stacked higgledy-piggledy against the side of a hut and looking at first sight unprepossessing objects in which to go to war.'

In due course, too, an old gentleman in knickerbockers turned up to face the stolid-looking audience of new recruits. 'This was,' said Harry, 'Mr Branson, the celebrated grass-eater and future great-uncle of the entrepreneur and balloonist.'

> Accompanied by an ancient bicycle to whose crossbar was attached an equally ancient umbrella, this redoubtable man had cycled all the way from London, living on mowings culled from golf courses he passed. He rightly extolled the Japanese method of gathering their food from the country-side through which they walked. Suddenly his eyes lit up as he scanned the ground outside of our hut . . . and with the air of a conjurer producing a rabbit from a hat, plucked a bunch of chickweed and announced that he was going to make lunch with it. With newly awakened interest, we watched in amazement as he doused it with vinegar and bran, which he had brought with him, and solemnly proceeded to eat it.

In the weeks that followed, Harry and his new section passed through the rigours of training as canoeists, swimmers, mountain-climbers, survivalists and the general attributes of advanced boy scouting; the real thing bore no comparison. His tales are filled with the dark humour that goes with capsizing in the rough waters of the Firth of Clyde and being rescued by the harbour-master, and with long treks across Scottish hillsides, jumping in and out of rivers and carrying the canoes on their backs, and with the emerging comradeship among his fellows.

If their training was a trifle hurried and not quite up to scratch, there was a reason: the SBS desperately needed more manpower to match the ambitions and aspirations of Lord Mountbatten and the planners of Combined Operations. And conditions in North Africa, where the Special Forces were in chaos, added some urgency. There, the remnants of 1SBS had temporarily been taken under the wing of the SAS, with George Jellicoe in control but within the sphere of David Stirling, the sole director of the vast and powerful military group he had, by now, built up.

61

Stirling ran the group largely from his head; he alone knew where everyone was. On the other hand, everyone seldom knew where *he* was – which, most of the time, was racing ahead of the 8th Army, causing mayhem miles behind enemy lines. Then . . . utter confusion. Stirling's luck ran out; he was betrayed, then captured by the Germans while laid up with his column on the night of 23 January. It was days before the enemy realised that it had caught its most wanted man. Two or three months of upheaval and uncertainty among the Special Forces set in, and matters would not settle down again until new commanders were in place. At the time there was much wringing of hands and mutters of 'What do we do now?' Later, the SAS was temporarily wound up, re-forming into two sections. Stirling's original force regrouped under the name of Special Raiding Squadron and were posted as advance troublemakers ahead of the 8th Army in Tunis and later Italy.

Jellicoe, meanwhile, became commanding officer of the SAS-controlled Special Boat Squadron formed principally from Courtney's commandos in the Middle East and from Stirling's own canoeists and raiders; the squadron retained the SAS insignia. It consisted of three detachments of 70 men each, with seven officers. The squadron came officially into being on 1 April 1943 under Jellicoe's command from a base at Athlit.

This combination of SBS personnel caused post-war confusion about the title and an argument over who was entitled to use it (as described in later chapters). 'Special Boat Section' was the title adopted for Courtney's units. 'Special Boat Squadron' was the name of the formation under Jellicoe, who owed his allegiance originally to Stirling. Jellicoe thus began a long and spectacular command with many successful missions. Meanwhile, Roger Courtney was rebuilding his Special Boat Section in Britain. It was a pressing matter with Operation Torch on the horizon. Harry Holden-White was now fired up and ready to go. His first mission in the late summer of 1942 was supposed to be a repeat of the brilliant raid by his training officer Gerald Montanaro earlier in the year.

Montanaro and Trooper F. Preece had been ferried by motor launch across the Channel to Boulogne one moonless Saturday night in spring. Two miles out, they transferred to their canoe and paddled into the harbour to attack their target, earmarked from aerial reconnaissance. It was a German tanker which had taken refuge in the port after receiving a torpedo hit in the Channel. Montanaro and Preece successfully placed delayed-action limpet mines along her side, below the water line, and were about to depart when the front end of the canoe lodged in the hole created by the torpedo and wedged between the inner and outer hulls of the tanker. Although they managed to pull it clear, the canoe was damaged and started to take on water.

In this parlous state they began their difficult two-mile paddle to the launch in heavy seas, Montanaro paddling and Preece bailing furiously. The only resistance they encountered was a German soldier slumped by the wall of the fort at the harbour entrance who did no more than throw a beer mug at them. It missed. They managed to reach the launch just as the charges exploded. An aerial photograph the next day confirmed that they had completed the job the torpedo had failed to do, and sent the tanker to the bottom.

Harry's task was intended to duplicate this exploit. However, the plane that had flown over to take aerial photographs of possible targets was shot down and the job was aborted. Not much later, however, he was thrown into action – with a baptism of fire.

In the second week of October Harry – by then with the rank of captain – was summoned to Lord Mountbatten's Combined Operations headquarters in Whitehall, where Courtney also had an office. There was something big on. Hush-hush. Destination secret for now, but the SBS had an important role to play. Holden-White gleaned enough information to guess that an attack was planned on the Vichy French and that SBS canoeists would be launched at the head of a sea-borne onslaught which, even for one quite new to the service, seemed to nullify what he assessed to be the section's greatest asset, operating clandestinely.

The big one was Operation Reservist, part of Operation Torch described in the news item at the beginning of this chapter, the massive invasion of North Africa coupled with an amphibious attack on Oran, held by the Vichy French, heavily protected by shore batteries and harbouring a number of ships. Opposition inland was judged correctly to be minimal, but the Vichy naval chiefs were still smarting over the sinking of part of the French fleet at Oran by the British in 1940 and would take drastic measures to protect their remaining vessels.

Oh, and one other thing, said Courtney. The SBS had the

honour of testing a new weapon, a mini-torpedo designed to be fired from canoes, which would hopefully cut down on the need for limpet mines whose clamping was always a hazardous business. A few days later Harry and Lieutenant E. J. A. 'Sally' Lunn went to an experimental station in Hampshire to see a demonstration of the mini-torpedoes. A stock of them was being prepared which, they were assured, would be dispatched with an officer to Gibraltar, where they would be collected by the SBS *en route* to wherever they were going (then still a secret).

The day of embarkation came. Harry took five pairs of SBS canoeists to Greenock, where they loaded their stores, weapons and canoes aboard two converted American coastguard cutters now under the Royal Navy flag and named HMS *Walney* and HMS *Hartland*. Three pairs led by Holden-White boarded *Walney* while Sally Lunn headed the other two in *Hartland*. Orders were now clear. They were to join a large convoy at Gibraltar, protected by destroyers and submarines. There, the two ships would pick up 400 American troops, who were to mount a sea-borne assault on Oran harbour and hold it until reinforcements arrived from inland.

The SBS role in all of this was to go in first, blowing up shipping in the harbour with the still-experimental mini-torpedoes. Each pair of canoeists was to be given two torpedoes, which they were to release towards suitable targets as soon as feasibly possible. The torpedoes were to be collected in Gibraltar, they were told, where an officer would explain all.

Harry takes up the story:

Well, that was the first thing to go wrong. When we got to Gib, there was no bloody officer to explain it all, no bloody instructions, and the baby torpedoes were in bits. Luckily, I had Sergeant-Major J. Embelin with us, who was a demolition expert, and he was able to assemble them. But we still had only a vague idea about range and so on, and a greater surprise was to come on that score much later.

Another problem for us was launching the canoes from ships. Normally, SBS crews are floated off submarines or lowered from MTBs. These cutters gave us a drop of eight to ten feet and our flimsy folboats could have been damaged. So on the way out we decided to practise and unpacked the canoes we had brought aboard in kitbags to assemble them, staggering about the heaving deck like some mad ballet. Fortunately, the *Walney*'s shipwright designed a sling to lower our boats into the water.

As we sailed into Oran, it was evident that the harbour was a death-trap for a sea-borne assault. Although the overall length of the harbour straddled the coast for about a mile, the opening to it was protected by a boom, which we knew about, of course. Once inside, there was no escape. *Walney* was supposed to ram the boom and, if that failed, Sergeant-Major Embelin, the demolition expert was to break open the boom with explosives. Sadly, he was subsequently killed by French machine-gun fire from the shore.

Anyhow, as soon as we sailed in, the Vichy-French shore batteries started firing. The three SBS pairs on board *Walney* were virtually thrown overboard and started paddling towards the docks. Frankly, I was so bloody glad to be away from it. Soon that feeling turned to guilt as I and my number two, Corporal Ellis, paddled off to find suitable targets for our mini-torpedoes. We had not travelled far when there was a huge explosion. We looked back. *Walney* had been hit by shore batteries and was already sinking. Then *Hartland* was hit; they were being shot to pieces and eventually we learned that around half the men on board were lost. Sally Lunn had been unable to launch his pair of canoes because they were damaged by shells. They joined escaping US troops on Carley liferafts.

Ellis and I paddled on. We had lost sight of our other chaps. We hid behind a barge to get our bearing, and as we did a ship loomed up out of the darkness coming towards us, a bloody great ship, absolutely enormous. Anyway . . . a suitable target, I thought. I fired one of my mini-torpedoes. There was no big bang, although the ship slowed down for a moment. Whether we hit it or not I do not know. She was eventually sunk outside the harbour by one of our subs. Then a submarine came out and I fired my second mini-torpedo at the sub.

Unfortunately, my arm was jolted as I put it in the water, so that one went astray. We watched it go, streaking through the water, but at least it made a bang. It hit the harbour wall just below the lighthouse, which was not, of course, lit. The lighthouse-keeper came out waving his arms; bloody furious, he was. I think he thought he'd been shelled by his own side. After that, there was nothing we could do but go on.

The original plan, in the event of failure, was to paddle back out to sea and get aboard one of the many Allied ships outside the harbour. This was now impossible. *Walney* and *Hartland*, still ablaze and listing, blocked our route. There was no alternative but to go on to the harbour and try to make our escape there and link up with troops coming inland.

Needless to say, the harbours and quays were swarming with Vichy-French troops. Holden-White and his partner Ellis managed to land but were very soon surrounded by a dozen men, who in due course carted them off to a makeshift PoW camp outside the town. The French showed particular interest in the SBS men's clothing – one-piece Tropal suits covering the body from ankle to neck and stuffed with kapok. They bore no insignias to indicate that they were soldiers and thus to be treated as prisoners of war – a fact that would cost the lives of other similar adventurers who fell into German hands later in the war.

They were marched to the camp to join the remainder of the US troops who had come ashore from the two sinking cutters and eventually all the other SBS men on the mission. French officers overseeing the remnants of this disaster were friendly enough and referred to them as 'mes amis'. One even said in English: 'Don't worry. You will be liberated soon. The Americans are coming.'

Meanwhile, Sally Lunn, who followed Holden-White to the camp, had been horrified to see one of the mini-torpedoes floating in the water near the quay where he was being marched away. Says Holden-White:

These bloody torpedoes were supposed to be top-secret. That's why the SBS had been sent to try them out, and I thought I had better get back to England as quickly as possible to report what had happened. We were freed within five days when the troops arrived from inland, but needless to say there was bloody confusion all over the place. We, the SBS, were told we would have to make our own way back to England, so I wandered around to the aerodrome to see if we could find a plane. We eventually got a lift to Gibraltar and linked up with Gruff Courtney. From there we hitched a ride on an American Fortress returning to England. We landed back in Cornwall, where we were immediately arrested. Bloody funny, really. We hadn't got any papers, of course, and wearing these odd clothes, the local police and immigration people surrounded us. We were interrogated for half an hour and eventually, after a few telephone calls, we were taken under close escort to London, where I was finally able to report on the mini-torpedo trials. It was only then, as I explained our efforts to use them, that their range for maximum effect – that is, sinking the target – was [found to be] only 50 yards. We had been firing them from 100 to 150 yards, so they were no bloody use from that standpoint.

In the meantime, Captain Peters, who was in overall command of *Walney* and *Hartland*, was killed when the plane carrying him and his report to England crashed on landing at Plymouth. Harry and Sally Lunn were summoned to the office of Lord Mountbatten, a large and sumptuously furnished room on the first floor of the Georgian mansion that housed Combined Operations. Mountbatten was anxious to hear a first-hand account of what had happened. He listened and questioned and was clearly disappointed about the baby torpedoes, for which he had high hopes. Holden-White pushed his personal concerns as far as he dare, hinting that his own bitter thoughts were directed towards 'the shameful waste of life at Oran'.

Mountbatten glared at him but let the comment pass without comment, although there was perhaps a reason for that. In Mountbatten's office at the time was Colonel Robert Henriques, who handled 'public relations'. Mountbatten now wanted Harry and Sally Lunn to agree to be interviewed by the BBC, as it was the first operation of its kind in which British and US troops had cooperated. Though the assault on Oran had ended in disaster, the overall operation had been a huge success. 'I was appalled,' says Holden-White. 'To make capital out of such a catastrophe seemed to me to be an act of betrayal to those who had lost their lives. There were and would be so many disasters. But when you think about it, the odds were very definitely stacked against the SBS and the groups like us, and I suppose when you came down to it it was a case of "If you can't stand the heat . . ." '

Holden-White scuppered Mountbatten's plans for a bit of publicity by standing his ground and refusing to be interviewed;

Lunn, seeing the vehemence of his resistance, stood by his decision. Mountbatten had no alternative but to let the matter drop. Harry Holden-White was sure, as he left the office that day, that he had placed his head on the block and it would soon be chopped off.

Not so. Mountbatten grudgingly signed the approval for Harry Holden-White's medal, the Military Cross, for his part in the Oran operation. Then, in late 1943, when Mountbatten became Supreme Commander in South-East Asia, his lordship's long-committed belief in the value of small raiding-units once again came to the fore. Almost straight away, in April 1944, he established the Small Operations Group (SOG) to bring together the skills of the several units involved largely in amphibious raiding, sabotage and recce work behind enemy lines.

Holden-White, now a major, found himself as officer commanding A Group, SBS, running operations against the Japanese on the Arakan coast of Burma. His was one of three SBS groups seconded to the SOG, along with Detachment 385 from the Royal Marines commando assault troops, four Sea Reconnaissance Units (SRUs) and four parties from Combined Operations Pilotage Parties (COPPs).

Mountbatten's commitment to these clandestine raiding-parties was demonstrated by his choice of men to command the SOG: the redoubtable Humphrey Tollemache, a Royal Marines colonel (later Major-General Sir) of vast experience in the Far East and jungle warfare and his number two Lieutenant-Colonel H. G. 'Blondie' Hasler, OBE, DSO.

The mention of that name brings us to the next set of disciplines and traditions, elevated during the war, which would ultimately be incorporated as a model in the do's and don'ts of the post-war SBS.

CHAPTER FIVE

Blondie's Cockleshell Heroes

H. G. 'Blondie' Hasler, so nicknamed by his chums in the Royal Marines for his mop of golden-red hair, which he had since all but lost, and a long moustache of the same colour, was a tall and hefty 28-year-old in 1942, an acting major and with a well-known interest in small boats that had been his passion since childhood. He had already been awarded an OBE, Croix de Guerre and Mentioned in Despatches during the Narvik operations. As a career officer, Blondie was projecting his theories about using small craft to attack enemy shipping even before Roger Courtney came on the scene. The previous year he had written a paper on the subject, but his ideas had been rejected. Now Courtney, Gerald Montanaro and others were advocating the same thing and others were following their lead.

There was something particular about Blondie's ideas, though, that distinguished him from the rest. His were perhaps more akin to the Italian way of seawolf activity, filled with ideas involving gadgetry and experimentation. His methodology was not Courtney's way, and they did not see eye to eye.

From the beginning of the war, the Italians had shown them-selves to be well ahead of everyone – British, Germans and Japanese – in their perfection of sea-borne guerrilla warfare. They also possessed an impressive array of gadgetry and some deadly missiles – among them breathing apparatus for underwater swim-mers, piloted torpedoes, miniature torpedoes and exploding motor boats.

The skill of the Italians began to worry the Allies in 1941, at a time when the British fleet was reduced to two battleships in the Mediterranean, HMS *Valiant* and HMS *Queen Elizabeth*, which lay sheltered behind torpedo nets at Alexandria. At 0330 on 19 December, two Italians were discovered clinging to the anchor buoy of *Valiant*. They surrendered immediately and were taken ashore for interrogation and then, to their dismay, back to *Valiant*, where they confessed that the battleship was about to blow up.

The crew was mustered to deck and the watertight doors were closed, but shortly after 0600 the ship rocked and shuddered as the charge set by the Italians blasted a large hole in her stern. Soon afterwards, *Queen Elizabeth* reared up from two explosions from charges attached below the water-line and both ships were temporarily out of the war. It soon emerged that the explosions had been caused by charges carried by three piloted torpedoes, driven by a team of six men from the 10th Light Flotilla of the Italian Navy, trained to remain under water for miles wearing flexible rubber-suits, breathing gear and fins. Although slow and cumbersome, the piloted torpedoes were to do a great deal of damage to Allied shipping.

In this instance, the torpedoes had been launched from Prince Julio Borghese's submarine *Scire* off Alexandria, two men astride each of the three piloted torpedoes. The men travelled to the target ship, where the time-fused warheads from each one were disconnected and attached to the ships' hulls. They then made their exit on the remaining part of the torpedo and returned whence they came. The operations even drew praise from Churchill as an example of 'extraordinary courage and ingenuity'. Escapes were always planned in advance. But on this occasion the two Italians had to adopt the course of last resort – which was to surrender to the nearest safe haven.

In fact, there was virtually no alternative to capture for the pilots of their next trick – the exploding motor boat. This was a high-powered, one-man boat with a range of up to 100 miles whose bow was packed with 500 pounds (226 kilogrammes) of explosives. The operative would aim the boat with death-defying speed at a suitable target and, at a safe distance for himself, pull a lever that ejected him and a rubber inflatable liferaft into the sea. He would then climb aboard the inflatable and paddle off to surrender to the nearest ship or shore.

The British, intrigued by these devices, captured a number of items – including the exploding motor boat and a human torpedo – which they were able to dissect.

Britain clearly had some lessons to be learned for her own

attacking force, especially for use by the small-group raiders. At the time, Lord Mountbatten had just drawn together a number of eminent military and scientific experts to look at new weapons and methods. It was at a meeting of those men at the newly formed Combined Operations Development Centre (CODC) that Blondie Hasler's paper was remembered by one of the committee members – Major Malcolm Campbell, no less.

Hasler was summoned to the CODC's base at Southsea by the head of CODC, Captain Tom Hussey, RN, and was invited to join the study-group. On the first day Hasler was shown the Italian's exploding boat, captured in an attack in Souda Bay, Crete. The following day he was introduced to Mountbatten who made clear that his top priority was to build something similar. Mountbatten seemed convinced that such boats would be ideal for use by British raiders to destroy enemy boom defences, beach obstacles and dock installations. Although the Italians had launched them from surface craft, lowered over the side by derrick, Mountbatten believed that a method could be devised to drop the boats close to the target by air.

After that meeting, Blondie Hasler was given a wide brief to 'study, coordinate and develop all forms of stealthy sea-borne attack by small parties and pay particular attention to attacking ships in harbour'. Hasler went away to draft his proposals for a new specialist detachment. And it was these original theories, dreamed up in a time of dire necessity and expanded later, that were to provide some of the key ingredients in the blueprint for the post-war development of the modern SBS.

His ideas were, of course, linked to the already well-tried and well-tested methods of sea-borne raids by stealth, engineered by the likes of Roger Courtney, Tug Wilson and Gerald Montanaro. For although the exploding boat – codenamed by Mountbatten the Boom Patrol Boat (BPB) so as not to reveal its true purpose – was his priority, Hasler still based many of his ideas around the use of canoes. Canoeists would be needed, for example, to cut their way through boom defences prior to an exploding boat entering a harbour.

During March and April of that year, Hasler sought out Courtney and Montanaro, the latter bringing his own 101 Troop to Portsmouth to give him a demonstration. Later, after Montanaro's merger with the SBS, Hasler joined them on exercises in Dover, and it was there that one of his key ideas took shape. The canoe, or folboat, used by the SBS was a Cockle Mark I, later replaced by a Cockle Mark I**.

Hasler believed they had limitations for the work he had in mind. He wanted a stronger craft, with a flat strip of timber for a rigid bottom that could take a heavy load and still be lifted over shingle or mud without breaking the canoe's back. Tom Hussey sent him to see Fred Goatley, works manager of the Saro Laminated Woodwork factory, which had recently won a War Office design award for a new river-crossing assault boat.

Blondie described his ideas to Fred, and soon had the Cockle Mark II in production – not knowing that it was to become the carrying craft for one of the most famous small-group operations of the Second World War.

The prototype delivered in July proved to be everything Hasler wanted, a strong but inconspicuous craft, very narrow and low in the water. It measured 16 feet (4.9 metres) in length, and had a 28-inch (71-centimetre) beam and a depth of just 11¼ inches (28.6 centimetres), with a collapsed depth of 6 inches (15 centimetres), and it weighed 90 pounds (41 kilogrammes). It had a flat wooden strip along the bottom made of ⅛-inch (3-millimetre) plywood with shallow bilge keels or runners underneath so that it could be launched from a beach and dragged across mud, sand or shingle. The sides were canvas or rubberised fabric, and the deck was ⅛-inch (3-millimetre) plywood on rigid wooden gunwales. The deck was held by eight hinged struts. When folded, the sides collapsed and the deck lay flat. The cockpit where the men sat was covered with waterproof fabric held by spring clips that disengaged quickly in case of capsize. Normal propulsion would be by double paddles, which could be split to singles at times of quiet operation.

It was designed to carry two men and about 150 pounds (68 kilogrammes) of equipment and stores through rough water. What was also true about the Cockle Mark II was that it would require utmost skill in its handling and in its navigation, especially on a dark night, tossed by rough waters and drawn by a tide flow running diagonally against it. The two-man crews needed utmost practice and training to be able to endure the physical effort of paddling the canoe while reading their charts, establishing their position and setting and maintaining a course by way of a mini-compass and the stars.

The exploding boat, meanwhile, was still on the drawing-board.

Not even a prototype had been planned when final details for the establishment of the Royal Marines Harbour Patrol Detachment were submitted in a paper from the CODC to Mountbatten on 12 May 1942. He approved them personally, although he did change the name to the Royal Marines Boom Patrol Detachment, and the RMBPD officially came into being on 6 July.

A memorandum to the Chiefs of Staff noted that the object of the new detachment was to evolve new methods of attacking ships in harbour. The detachment was not intended to specialise in small-scale raids on coastal positions, demolition ashore, reconnaissance of beaches or the landing of agents, which appeared to be adequately covered by the SBS.

The detachment, with headquarters in Southsea, was quite small, initially made up of two sections, each with one lieutenant, one sergeant, two corporals and ten marines, with Hasler himself as officer commanding, and with a captain as second-in-command – a total of thirty men, plus four more in an administrative section. They were all volunteers from the services for 'special duties of a hazardous nature'. (It is interesting to note that one in three of the men in due course won medals for bravery.)

Two other sections were added later, and they began training around Portsmouth and the Isle of Wight by day and night, in canoes, assault boats and fast motor boats, the latter acquired from civilian sources.

Hasler had a hand-picked cast. The men had to be young and fresh – barely out of their teens – and capable of undertaking a training routine that would bring them to the very peak of physical fitness. In the process they went through all-night marches, long swimming routines in the coldest of water, diving exercises, running barefoot across shingle to harden their feet, and paddling canoes for mile after mile. They trained in stealth manoeuvres by sea and in mock escapes from enemy territory.

The RMBPD's daily log reflects a happy, eager bunch of recruits. (On one occasion, as a reward, they were given a private screening of Noël Coward's new film *In Which We Serve*, based on Mountbatten's exploits when he and his crew went down with HMS *Kelly* with all guns blazing.) But none of them yet had the slightest idea what they were training for, and nor did their marine counterparts at Southsea to whom they became a familiar sight, and nicknamed thereabouts as Hasler's Party.

Even as these young men were beginning their training, events unfolding elsewhere were to have a dramatic and immediate effect on their future. On 9 May Lord Selborne, Minister for Economic Warfare, wrote to Winston Churchill about concerns that Axis merchant shipping was running the British blockade. He wrote again on 22 June, and in July Selborne's ministry produced a study that showed that a particularly busy port for the blockade runners was Bordeaux. In the previous 12 months, 25,000 tons of rubber had passed through that port on its way to Germany and Italy. Other cargoes important to the Axis war effort included tin, tungsten and animal and vegetable oils.

With increasing concern in those most depressing days for the British war effort, Selborne wrote again on 5 August offering definite proof that fifteen blockade runners were at that moment in French Atlantic ports and three more were on their way from the Far East. Deputy Prime Minister Clement Attlee passed Selborne's letter to the Chiefs of Staff. Lord Mountbatten, in his capacity of Chief of Combined Operations, sat on the Chiefs of Staff Committee, and it was to him that Selborne's letter was eventually passed for action.

During August and early September the war planners produced a scheme called Operation Frankton. In effect, it boiled down to a Combined Operations attack on the port of Bordeaux, reached via the Gironde 500 miles south of Plymouth on the Bay of Biscay. The proposals, however, were turned down by the Chiefs of Staff Examinations Committee because of the inaccessibility of the inland harbour, a decision that may not have been unconnected with the Dieppe disaster of 19 August. That raid, also under the auspices of Mountbatten's Combined Operations, was the biggest Allied assault on Hitler's Fortress Europe. At the end of the day, 68 per cent of the Canadian troops and 20 per cent of the commandos who landed were dead or wounded; 2,000 were taken prisoner, with nearly 1,000 dead and left behind when the battered Allied armada returned home. Though two-thirds of the overall assault force remained intact, this fact merely demonstrated how many did not get ashore. Those who did never got beyond the beach. Nothing in Mountbatten's military career earned him so much criticism as the Dieppe raid.

Even so, Operation Frankton re-emerged in mid-September at planning level, when it was conceded that the port of Bordeaux could be attacked by a small raiding-party, travelling by stealth along the River Gironde to the point where the blockade-running ships would be berthed. Blondie Hasler, by then touting for business for his new detachment, 'now ready for a small testing operation', was called to London. The idea was floated, and Operation Frankton was under way.

On 30 October Mountbatten issued an outline of the operation to the Chiefs of Staff Committee: 'Operation Frankton has been planned to meet Lord Selborne's requirements . . . that steps should be taken to attack Axis ships which are known to be running the blockade . . . [it] is the only one which offers a good chance of success.'

He summarised the intention: officers and men drawn from the RMBPD would be taken to within nine miles of the Gironde Estuary by submarine. They would then paddle the 90 miles in Cockle canoes to the anticipated location of the blockade-running ships. There they would attach limpet mines to as many ships as possible, scuttle their canoes, make contact with patriot French and escape back to England, possibly through Spain.

It all sounded so simple.

Ahead lay four weeks of meticulous planning and final training. All kinds of other hurdles had to be overcome, and scientists were enlisted to help – Professor Solly Zuckermann was asked to provide medical aids for night vision, for instance, and Major Malcolm Campbell to come up with dim-lighted torches by which the men could read charts and compasses. Then came the task of weighing and packing a vast supply of equipment and stores which would have to be stowed on board the canoes while still leaving enough room for the men to complete their journey in relative comfort.

The stores themselves were daunting enough for the anticipated four-day journey along the Gironde by six pairs of RMBPD canoeists to be led by Hasler himself (see Appendix I). The explosives package – 48 limpet mines, 12 grenades, silenced sten-guns, each with 3 magazines containing 36 rounds – weighed 400 pounds (180 kilogrammes).

The men picked for the operation were themselves not told of it – any of it – until the morning of 30 November, when they were safely aboard the submarine HMS *Tuna* and under way to the Gironde Estuary.

They learned of their task only then: to sink the 12 largest ships lying in the Bassens-Bordeaux area. (What followed was immortalised in a not very good film, *Cockleshell Heroes*, starring José Ferrer and Trevor Howard, whose London première Hasler did not attend.)

No written orders were issued. Hasler verbally briefed the men and answered their questions, not least of which was: 'How do we get home?'

The six boats and their crews were split into two divisions: A, led by Hasler himself, and B, led by Lieutenant Mac Mackinnon. Each canoe had a codename; the pairs were: *Catfish*: Major Hasler with Marine Ned Sparks, aged 22, from London; *Crayfish*: Corporal Albert Laver, aged 22, from Birkenhead, with Marine Billy Mills, 20, from Kettering; *Conger*: Corporal G. J. Sheard, from Devon, with Marine David Moffat, 24, from Halifax; *Cuttlefish*: Lieutenant Mackinnon, 21, with Marine Jimmy Conway, 20, from Stockport; *Coalfish*: Sergeant Sam Wallace, 29, from Dublin, with Marine Bobby Ewart, 21, from Glasgow; *Cachalot*: Marine W. A. Ellery, from London, with Marine Eric Fisher, 22, from West Bromwich.

The submarine *Tuna* reached the disembarkation point on the evening of 6 December and surfaced. A periscope reconnaissance revealed numerous patrolling vessels and they were forced to delay 24 hours. The next night she surfaced again and the Germans' coastal radar station picked up the signal. Searchlights flared along the French coast and all around the entrance to the Gironde Estuary, visible on what was according to the submarine commander 'a beastly clear night'. But Hasler decided to go ahead.

Up canoes. The forward hatch swung open and seamen crowded on to that narrow stretch of casing, dripping wet, from which the Cockles would be launched. The Cockle crews, faces blackened, stood nervously waiting to go up, saying their good-byes to the submariners and wishing themselves the best of luck.

Two by two they came out, and then . . . a setback. The sound of ripping canvas. *Cachalot* was damaged, fouled by a sharp corner of the hatch clamp. Ellery called to Hasler. The tear was along the side of the canoe, which he knew immediately could not be launched. Now there were five.

At 2022 they were in the water and heading for the Gironde under a cloudless sky lit by roaming searchlights giving a clear view for the marauding German patrol boats.

That night, with the Germans certain that the submarine, stationary for an hour or more, had unloaded a sabotage party,

Berlin issued a piece of disinformation along the news wires: 'Dec 8: A small British sabotage party was engaged at the mouth of the Gironde River and finished off in combat.' Southsea held its breath.

For the remainder of the narrative of this remarkable adventure, there is no better account than the report of Blondie Hasler himself, published here in full, I believe, for the first time:

The five Cockles Mark II moved off at 0822 . . . led by *Catfish*. Weather oily calm with low ground swell. No cloud. Visibility good, with slight haze over the land. Progress good. At 2350 the boats passed over Bano des Olives [sandbank] whose presence was evident from soundings and the way in which the ground swell began to build up into steep rollers over the shallows. These rollers would have been dangerous if the boats had been a little further inshore.

The force of the flood tide now began to be felt and course was altered further eastwards to follow the line of the coast, now clearly visible about one and a half miles away. Shortly afterwards, the sound of broken water ahead indicated a tidal race. This came as an unpleasant surprise, not having been apparent from the chart or the sailing directions. Owing to the strength of the stream there was no chance of avoiding the race, which proved quite severe for such small craft. The Cockle Mark II proved quite able to weather it provided it was kept head into the waves and cockpit cover securely fastened.

Immediately after passing the race, *Coalfish* (Sergeant Wallace and Marine Ewart) was found to be missing, and the force turned back to look for it without success. Since both men and the boat had buoyancy equipment, it seems possible that they had not capsized but had turned further inshore on finding themselves separated from the remainder. Nothing further was heard of this boat.

A short time later a second tidal race was heard ahead. This proved to be somewhat heavier than the first, and on emerging on the far side of it we found that *Conger* (Corporal Sheard and Marine Moffat) was capsized, with its crew in the water. As it was impossible to bail out the flooded boat, she was scuttled, and every effort was made to tow the two swimmers somewhat further inshore. During this proceeding, the tide carried the party round the Pointe de Grave, not more than three-quarters of a mile offshore and through a third but less violent tide race. The lighthouse on the point had just been switched on at full strength and lit up the scene quite brilliantly.

The two men in the water were finally left in a position one and a half miles south-east of the Pointe de Grave, since it was considered that to take them any further would prejudice the chances of the other three boats remaining unobserved. From this position the tide should have carried them very close to the mole at Le Verdon, but they were already very cold and unable to swim effectively. Both men were wearing life-jackets fully inflated.

This incident wasted so much time that it was impossible to attempt to reach the east bank of the Gironde that night. Also, the remaining three boats were now closer inshore than had been intended, and the strength of the tide compelled them to pass between the mole at Le Verdon and three or four vessels anchored lying about three-quarters of a mile east of it. These vessels appeared to be of the French Chasseur type. In order to get through unobserved, it was necessary to change to single paddles and proceed with caution, and the three boats separated to a distance of several hundred yards to lessen the chances of being seen.

On getting clear of this danger, it was found that the third boat, *Cuttlefish* (Lieutenant Mackinnon and Marine Conway) had lost the formation. Nothing further was seen of this boat, but there was no reason to suppose it met with any mishap at this stage since it was in perfectly good shape and no alarm could have been raised by the enemy without it being audible to the other two boats on such a still night.

The remaining two boats proceeded on course and picked up the west bank of the estuary near the Chenal de Talais, turning south-eastwards in order to continue up as far as possible. At 0630 the first attempt was made to land, but it was found that there was a line of half-submerged stakes on a shingle bank running along the shore, and the ground swell breaking over these obstructions made it impossible to negotiate them in safety.

The boats continued along the coast for some time without finding a possible landing-place, and it was only as daylight was breaking that they were able to get ashore at a small sandy promontory near the Pointe aux Oiseaux. The boats were concealed as well as possible with camouflage nets.

A considerable number of small fishing-boats had begun to issue from the Chenal de St-Vivien and now headed towards our beach. At the same time a number of women appeared walking towards us along the shore. We took cover as well as we could, but it became hopeless when a number of the boats landed on the beach and fishermen began to light a camp-fire and make preparations for breakfast within a few yards of us.

We were soon observed and had to explain that we were British and that our presence must not be revealed to anybody. Some of the party seemed quite unconvinced and declared that we were Germans, but we pointed out that in any case it would be better for them to keep silent on the subject, and shortly afterwards women returned to the village and the men to their boats. At about 1600 some of the women returned for a further chat, but as we were otherwise undisturbed it seemed that they had followed our instructions.

It was not possible to resume the passage until the flood stream began to run at 2330, and as this was low-water springs it was necessary to manhandle boats over nearly three-quarters of a mile of sandy mud before we could launch them. The method was to drag them fully loaded, which was only possible owing to the flat bottom and the strong construction of the Cockle Mark II.

Getting the boats clear of the shore was difficult owing to large areas of outlying sandbanks and breaking rollers which we met head-on. Eventually, we got clear and into the shipping channel. Navigation was easy as the port hand-buoys were all showing a dim flashing blue light. Weather was flat calm, no cloud; visibility good but with haze over both shores. Continuing on the same course, we picked up the east bank just north of Portes de Calonge and followed it about one mile offshore until the approach of daylight made it necessary to lie up.

At this time it became suddenly extremely cold, so much so that the splashes of salt water were freezing on the cockpit covers. We found a suitable field and put the boats in a thick hedge. During the day we discarded certain stores that were

79

no longer any value to us as we got into more inland waters.

The plan for the following night was complicated by the fact that during darkness we would only have three hours of flood tide at the beginning of the night, then six hours of ebb followed by a further three of flood before daybreak. This entailed an intermediate lying up. In order to catch as much of the tide as possible, we started somewhat earlier than was prudent and were seen silhouetted against the western sky as we launched the boats. Frenchmen from a nearby farmhouse came out to investigate and we repeated our story from the day before. They seemed quite convinced and rather upset when we declined their invitation to go to the house for a drink.

At 0630 we began looking for a place for a lying up. It was only after considerable difficulty that we got ashore near a small pier. A quick reconnaissance of the area disclosed what appeared to be a light Ack-Ack position 40 yards away, and in view of that we again embarked and proceeded further south. The situation was getting rather urgent owing to the approach of daylight, and we finally put ashore at 0730 at a point with not very good cover but placed the boats in the middle of a marshy field in long grass with the nets over them. We were not observed at all in this position, although a man and his dog came within a hundred yards of us, and at one time a herd of cattle stood around in a circle looking at us.

It had been intended to carry out the attack on the night of 10–11 December, but we had not got high enough up the river to enable this to be done with any chance of withdrawing into darkness afterwards. It was therefore decided to move to an advanced base close to the target area that night and carry out the attack early on the night of 11–12. The boats were launched at 1845 on the tenth with considerable difficulty owing to vertical and slippery banks. The weather was good from our point of view, being cloudy with occasional rain and a moderate breeze. For the first two miles we proceeded up the centre of the river, then changed to single paddles and followed close along the western passage, which was lined with thick reeds.

After an uneventful passage we passed underneath the pontoon pier opposite Bassens South and found a small gap in the reeds into which we were able to force the boats at around 2300. As soon as the tide began to ebb, the boats dried out and we made ourselves comfortable for the night. Daylight showed us that we had been fortunate in our lying-up place as we were quite inaccessible and well concealed, and at the same time by standing up we were able to observe traffic on the river. Two good-sized ships lying alongside immediately opposite us.

During the day, we rearranged the stowage of the boats so as to have all the escape equipment in two bags, and in the evening we completed the fusing of the limpets. A nine-hour setting was used on time delays. The weather was once again flat calm with clear sky and good visibility. The moon did not set until 2132, and I considered it essential to delay leaving our lying-up place until 2110, which was about 30 minutes later than we would have desired from the tide point of view. At 2100 the time fuses were started.

The plan of attack was as follows:

Catfish: To proceed along the western bank to the docks on the west side of the river at Bordeaux.

Crayfish: To proceed along the east bank of the river to the docks on the east side of Bordeaux, but if no suitable targets were found to return and attack two ships at Bassens South, which we had been studying during the day.

Both boats left the lying-up place at 2115 and separated for their respective attacks. *Catfish* got up past the entrance to the basins without difficulty, except that it was necessary to keep clear of the shore because of a good many lights, particularly around the lock gates.

Eight limpets were subsequently placed by *Catfish* as follows: three on a cargo ship of about 7,000 tons; two on the engine-room of a Sperrbrecher; two on the stern of a cargo ship of about 7,000 tons; one on the stern of a small tanker.

While *Catfish* was a little distance from the side of the Sperrbrecher, and in the process of turning downstream, we were seen by a sentry on deck who shone a torch at us. Fortunately, we were able to get back close to the ship's side and drift along with the tide without making any movement. The sentry followed us along the deck shining his torch down at us at intervals but was evidently unable to make up his mind as to what we actually were, owing to the efficiency of the camouflage scheme. We were able to get into a position under the bow of the ship where we could no longer be seen, and after waiting there for about five minutes everything seemed quiet, so we resumed our journey downstream.

The attack on the second large merchant ship was rather spoiled by the presence of a tanker alongside her and the fact that the tide was now running so strongly that I considered it unsafe to go between the bows of the two ships; this forced us to attack the stern only.

After all limpets had been placed, *Catfish* withdrew down the river without any further incident. While having a short rest in mid-stream, we were re-joined by *Crayfish*, having successfully completed their attack. This meeting was purely by chance, but it was decided to continue in company until the end of the withdrawal.

Corporal Laver reported that he had proceeded some distance along the east bank of Bordeaux without spotting any targets and, as the tide had turned against him, returned and attacked the two ships previously seen at Bassens South, placing five limpets on a large cargo ship and three on a smaller cargo liner.

In order to reach the Blaye area by low-water slack, it was necessary to abandon our previous caution. At 0600 we separated and proceeded to land independently about a quarter of a mile [0.4 kilometres] apart. Nothing further is known of *Crayfish* and her crew. Having disembarked *Catfish*, the boat was scuttled and sunk.

A full report of the escape route followed by *Catfish*'s crew has been made separately to MI9.

It is desired to draw attention to the part played by the following NCO and men: a) Corporal A. E. Laver, who handled his boat skilfully and displayed initiative and coolness in making his independent attack; b) Marine W. E. Sparks (No 2, *Catfish*) and Marine W. H. Mills (No 2, *Crayfish*), who both did their work in cool and efficient manner and showed considerable eagerness to engage the enemy.

Blondie Hasler's report was filed in April 1943 soon after he returned home – following a 1,400-mile journey which was as remarkable as the attack itself, taking him and Ned Sparks through France, over the Pyrenees, on into Spain and finally into British territory at Gibraltar on 1 April, dodging German patrols and the agents sent to look for them all the way.

Mountbatten was moved to send a memo to the Chiefs of Staff: 'This brilliant little operation carried through with great determination and courage is a good example of the successful use of limpeteers.'

The only debatable part of the exercise was its cost. The planners knew from the outset that the chances of the men returning were pretty bleak, but such considerations, at the height of desperation, are not considered in the same light as they are after the passing of years.

It was many months before news of those who vanished from the narrative, two by two, came through. The first, via Red Cross channels, confirmed the discovery of Marine Moffat. His body was washed ashore close to the point where he had been left with Corporal Sheard when their canoe capsized. Corporal Sheard was also believed drowned. As to the remainder, a fuller picture of what happened, though by no means a complete one, was in a report filed to the Office of the German High Command, Foreign Department/Security, by Major Reichel on 12 January 1944 'for possible exploitation for propaganda purposes'.

The report, headed 'Sabotage attacks on German ships off Bordeaux', read as follows:

On 12.12.42 a number of valuable German ships were badly damaged off Bordeaux by explosives below water-level. Adhesive mines were attached by five British sabotage squads working from canoes. Of the ten who took part in the attack, the following were captured a few days later:

Mackinnon, Naval Lieutenant, born 15.7.21, N. Argyllshire.

Laver, Albert Friedrich (sic), born 29.9.20, Birkenhead.

Mills, William Henri (sic), Marine, born 15.12.21, Kettering.

Wallace, Samuel, Sergeant, born 24.9.13, Dublin.

Conway, James, Marine, born 28.8.22, Stockport.

Ewart, Robert, Marine, born 4.12.21, Glasgow.

Their leader, Major Hasler, and Marine Sparks presumably escaped. Having carried out the explosions, they sank their craft and tried to make their escape to Spain in civilian clothes with the help of French civilians. There were intermediaries in two places on the Gironde, and in a bar. They were brought to the demarcation line by intermediaries with whom arrangements had been made beforehand.

All those captured were shot in accordance with orders on 23.3.43.

During Hasler's long and hazardous trek across Europe with his sidekick Sparks, the RMBPD had continued to expand and did so further on his return. New sections were formed with volunteers, principally from the Royal Marines, being trained as underwater swimmers, canoeists and limpeteers to focus specifically on small-party raiding operations against enemy shipping and German-held harbours, notably around the Greek and Turkish islands of the eastern Mediterranean and later under Mountbatten's South-East Asia command.

In the Mediterranean, they linked up with SAS and SBS units. Apart from their own sabotage operations attacking enemy installations, SAS and SBS teams were now placing men with attaché-case-style radio sets originally designed for members of the Special Operations Executive on islands and coastal sites throughout the area to report on enemy shipping and troop movements and to call in attacks by the Royal Navy or RAF bombers. Edward William Horner, a young marine who had volunteered for special duties, found himself at the eastern end of the Med with the newly formed RMBPD unit codenamed Earthworm after a long training stint in Scotland, which now included a new addition to their repertoire: parachuting into water. Borrowing from the experiences of Blondie Hasler's trip along the Gironde and Tug Wilson's sabotage raids, the Earthworm detachment had a faster – if more risky – method of reaching their targets to attach limpets to the sides of either moving or moored enemy vessels, as Horner recalls:

We now had the benefit of using a fast motor launch, a Fairmile ML 360. The scheme was that we had three canoes on board, and we were out looking for convoys or any shipping that we could attack. Orders would come through from Cairo giving movements of shipping moving down the various coasts, and the SAS and SBS teams were reporting to Cairo, and we picked up their tips.

In one of their first missions, Horner's patrol was given a small convoy of two destroyers and an escort ship, heading for Portolago Bay on the Greek island of Leros. The idea was that the fast launch would taken them as close as possible to target vessels, and then the team would disembark their canoes and paddle the remaining distance to place limpets on the sides of the ships. 'We had in our canoes our personal weapons, camouflage nets, 24-hours' rations, a Sten gun and eight magnetic limpet mines. Attacks could be made only at night and when there was a moonless sky. We were also told that there was a crack German commando unit known as the Brandenburgers patrolling the area in canoes.'

This in fact worked to the raiders' advantage on the first attack when Horner's canoe was spotted by the crew aboard a target vessel as the raiders approached. Horner had already rehearsed the cry 'Brandenburger patrol' and shouted out as the German crew began to shine torches in their direction. And they got away with it: the men on the ship thought the patrol was German. In due course, two destroyers were successfully mined and badly damaged. The irony was, however, that as they were being towed away for repair, they were bombed and sunk by the RAF, who claimed the kill! And so it was that the intrepid limpeteers went about their business, adding new disciplines to the overall expertise of these small groups, which in due course were merged to form the modern-day SBS.

CHAPTER SIX

Sleeping Beauty

By now, the intrepid canoeists were performing a broader range of tasks and were diving, with new inventions, activities that would form vital precursors to SBS operations in the post-war years. While Jumbo Courtney's SBS had concentrated largely on surface canoes for the landing of saboteurs, agents, raiding-parties and reconnaissance groups, Blondie Hasler's Boom Patrol Detachment was pioneering a number of new small craft, several for underwater work, which required new skills and a large number of swimmers. In fact, the burgeoning need for swimmers and divers led to the formation of the Sea Reconnaissance Unit, which was attached initially to Hasler's RMBPD.

Experiments were already advanced on a number of craft designs when Hasler had left for Bordeaux. On the assumption that he might not return from that expedition, his second-in-command, Lieutenant (later Captain) J. D. Stewart pressed on with the work. He had served with Hasler in landing-craft operations in Norway in 1940 and enthusiastically supported many of his ideas.

When Hasler got back to the fold after his mammoth journey across Europe four months later, he found that the programme had developed with remarkable speed. Training was in progress for specialist canoeists using a further modified version of his own Cockle design. The group had blueprints for new single-seater canoes and multi-person versions. Meanwhile, would-be pilots were getting the low-down on the exploding boat, while others were being instructed for various tasks, including the latest creation – a motorised submersible canoe which went by the name of *Sleeping Beauty*.

SB was another of Hasler's inventions. In a paper written in late 1940, he had outlined a plan for what he called an underwater glider – a single-seater submersible canoe manned by a shallow-water diver. The Admiralty rejected it as impracticable. Undaunted, he re-submitted the plan a few months later with modifications and explained how the submersible could be used for beach reconnaissance, destruction of underwater obstacles prior to beach landings and for attacking enemy shipping.

By early 1943, with Lord Mountbatten's stamp of approval, a prototype had been manufactured, and it was being trialled along with a number of small surface and submersible craft being produced at experimental stations by the Royal Navy. Mountbatten's Combined Operations headquarters was naturally interested in any craft that eased the route of the all-purpose raiders.

Up to that point, work on the exploding boat had taken priority, and by January 1943 it was undergoing trials. The boat was small – 16 feet (4.9 metres) long with a 2-foot (0.6-metre) draught – and capable of carrying a crew of one with 500 pounds (226 kilogrammes) of explosives with an instantaneous fuse in the bow. It had a maximum speed of 40 knots (74 kilometres per hour) – although it could travel silently at only 5 knots (9 kilometres per hour) – and a range of about 70 miles in calm weather.

Its key purpose was to be taken by air or sea to within range of an enemy harbour, a route through the harbour defences having been ensured by a swimmer-canoeist. The cox'n would then aim it at a suitable target and eject himself at a safe distance, to be picked up by a canoeist or to make his escape in a rubber inflatable to a waiting ship. Trials were already under way for drops by air. Six Dam Buster Lancaster bombers were converted to carry the exploding boats. Lieutenant Cox, RM was awarded the MBE for the first drop – such was its importance.

By August 1943, however, the Chiefs of Staff were still not convinced by either the boat's effectiveness or the procedures to be followed for the safe return of the pilot. Although a number of exploding boats were built, they were never used in any operation.

Sleeping Beauty, on which Hasler had worked with Sir Malcolm Campbell and others, seemed to have more versatile possibilities. The single-seater canoe was 12 feet 8 inches (3.9 metres) long, with a 27-inch (68.6-centimetre) beam, and was powered by an electric motor driven by batteries. The hull was made of mild steel and the deck of aluminium. It could travel on the surface, sailed, trimmed down, or submerged to enable the pilot to attach limpets to enemy ships. The pilot took an unusual position in the craft, lying long and low with his chin almost level with the cockpit coaming. A joystick provided control, and in theory the motor was started by the press of a button (although that did not always happen). The pilot would move the craft slowly forward until the air pressure in buoyancy tanks equalled that of the surrounding water.

Training for *SB*s proved hair-raising for some as they practised submerging in the heavy swell of waters around the Shetland Isles. Two men died in the calm of static training pools during training for the use of breathing sets. The use of such equipment, not common at the time, was very definitely a case of trial and error.

Even so, *SB* was judged ideal for beach reconnaissance ahead of major troop landings and for the more traditional role of fixing limpets to enemy ships, which could be approached submerged and remain so. The submersible had a maximum speed of just four knots (7.4 kilometres per hour) on the surface, or around two knots (3.7 kilometres per hour) trimmed down or submerged. It was designed to be carried on a MTB or other vessels, and experiments were also carried out to try dropping it and its pilot by parachute from a Lancaster bomber.

Other small craft, ingenious but of dubious value, were also being built. One of them, from designs by the British Army, was *Welman*, a midget one-man submarine, earmarked for use by the Special Operations Executive in the Far East and by the 2SBS in the Mediterranean. Twenty-nine feet (8.8 metres) long, it could be carried towards the target area in an MTB or on a submarine and was capable of carrying six 100-pound (45-kilogramme) charges or a single 560-pound (254-kilogramme) charge to attack enemy ships. It was also thought useful for beach marking ahead of invasion.

In trials, however, *Welman* was difficult to navigate, incredibly claustrophobic, and the pilot had to surface to get his bearings. Hasler could see no practical use for it, although Roger Courtney, who was totally sold on the idea, took a team of SBS for practical trials and had supported the notion of setting up a *Welman* base at

Appledore. Further trials raised additional anxieties about the usefulness of *Welman*. One report presented to the Combined Operations Executive complained: 'Eighty-five per cent of trained *Welman* operators conceive a dislike of going down in them. They say there is no way of getting out if anything goes wrong and if the fin drops off under water, no one knows which way up the *Welman* would arrive on the surface . . . the craft roll very badly . . .' Nineteen hulls were built, but *Welman* was used only once, in an aborted operation off Norway.

Then there was *Chariot*, a hefty torpedo-shaped submersible boat, driven by a battery-powered motor with a range of 24 miles. It was a copy of the two-man Maiali (sea pig) used by the Italian 10th Light Flotilla against British ships earlier in the war. Its crew, equipped with breathing sets that would allow six hours of diving, sat in the open astride *Chariot*. The boat could deliver a 1,000-pound (454-kilogramme) warhead, which would be detached and hung by magnets to the target. A delayed time fuse would allow the pilots to return to the mother ship aboard the craft without suffering the effects of underwater explosions. *Chariot*'s disadvantage was that it was difficult to manoeuvre, especially in enclosed situations such as crowded harbours. It was not considered a success, and those expected to operate it soon regarded it as jinxed. The charioteers, as they were known, were recruited from SBS and RMBPD. In the first recorded operation, Norwegian blockade runner 'Shetland Larsen' took two *Chariot*s and four charioteers aboard to attack the German battleship *Tirpitz* near Trondheim, Norway.

The submersibles could be slung, hammock-like, beneath the mother boat, and when they got close enough the divers intended to slip over the side and release the two craft for the attack. Unfortunately, about eight miles out they were hit by a major storm. The two *Chariot*s broke free and sank; Larsen had to scuttle his fishing-boat, and all aboard made for shore. The party set off on foot to cross Norway into neutral Sweden. They arrived back in England six weeks later, unharmed but angry.

Next, three *Chariot* teams were taken aboard the submarine HMS/M *P.3111* at Malta and sailed off to sink some Italian ships moored at Corsica. The submarine was hit by enemy action just short of the target area and all aboard were lost. *Chariot*s did however sink ships in an operation at La Specia.

Finally, there was the *X-Craft*, a fully equipped miniature submarine with a range of 1,500 miles, intended again to attack enemy shipping and capable of landing a small raiding-party. Lieutenant-Commander Nigel Clogstoun Willmott was looking for something similar as a recce submarine for his newly formed Combined Operations Pilotage Parties and wanted the *X-Craft*, with modifications. Willmott attended trials of the mini-sub and later described it as 'like living under a billiard-table that leaks'. Living conditions were cramped – no one could stand fully upright – and facilities primitive. Condensation was appalling, causing the labels to fall off food tins so that no one knew what they were about to eat, and body odours became overpowering after a few days. Willmott also spotted other severe flaws: 'It was found desirable for the officer of the watch on the casing to lift his head above water for breathing purposes. He is strapped to the induction pipe and has a bar to which he clings with fervour while floating on his front like a paper streamer on the bottom of the ocean. There is a vacancy for an intelligent merman to fulfil this role.' But Willmott still saw its possibilities, with some modifications, for his own unit, and the *X-Craft* came into service with COPPs during the latter stages of the war and were used for the Normandy landings.

Small-party raiders, more often than not, still had to rely on their well-tried and well-tested methods of attack and reconnaissance by canoe. Production of the new craft was slow, and some did not make it into regular service. The Special Operations Executive's Indian Mission, which was based in Ceylon, sent a requisition note for some of all the above for tasks in the Far East. Their order was for 12 *Chariot*s, 9 *Welman*s and 48 *Sleeping Beauty*s, though what exactly they planned for them all was not immediately clear.

They received only 15 *Sleeping Beauty*s, which were to be used on an operation planned and launched from Australia. Though not connected directly with either SBS or RMBPD sections, the story is recorded in the classified history of the SBS, both for its lessons and for the courage of its participants. The operation was also the only one recorded of the intended mass use of submersible canoes (although the RMBPD had trained hard for a plan to drop a party with *SB*s on to the Etang Biscarrosse lake, 50 miles west of Bordeaux, to attack four Luftwaffe Viking 222 flying-boats regularly parked there: the mission was aborted at the last minute because of the weather; the descending parachutes might have drifted off-target in the wind and landed in a nearby pine forest).

The Far East operation followed an earlier successful raid, codenamed Operation Jaywick, against Japanese ships in the crowded port of Singapore. It was led by Lieutenant-Colonel Ivan Lyon of the Gordon Highlanders, a keen yachtsman and canoeist who was attached to the Special Operations Executive 136 Force, specialising in organising resistance and sabotage. Jaywick was the India Mission's biggest success to date. Lyon's party – himself and three canoeists – approached the port aboard a captured native fishing-junk that had been converted and camouflaged to carry the raiders.

It was moored in a quiet creek among the Riau archipelago of islands, from where Lyon and his comrades took to their two canoes for the final assault on Singapore. They paddled through the filthy waters of this bustling port, unnoticed amid the conflicting smells of diesel and spices and the cacophony of noises and activity all around them. The two canoes moved silently towards their targets on single paddles so as not to kick up any phosphorescence. Unseen, they passed Japanese sentries patrolling the harbour walls.

Once in the port and under cover of darkness, they slipped in and out of the moored ships, attaching limpets to four. They made their escape back to the hidden junk, in which they then proceeded to journey on through almost 1,000 miles of Japanese-patrolled waters to reach the safe haven of the Exmouth Sound, off the north-west coast of Australia. Behind them they left more than 40,000 tons of Japanese shipping damaged or destroyed by their charges.

Buoyed up by the success of that mission, Lyon flew to England and turned up at the Combined Operations headquarters in Whitehall, where he outlined his plans for a second attack on Singapore, using the new submersible canoes he'd heard about via the India Mission. The plan was welcomed wholeheartedly, especially as Lord Mountbatten, by then leading the South-East Asia Command, had his heart and mind set on – among other things – anything that would weaken the Japanese hold on Singapore and hasten its return to British control. Sub-Lieutenant Riggs of the Royal Naval Volunteer Reserve (RNVR) trained with RMBPD in the use of *Sleeping Beauty*s and was then charged with taking them to Australia.

Lyon had gone on ahead to recruit a party of 23 swimmer-canoeists, who were to be known as Group X. After training in *SB*s, the party was taken aboard the mine-laying submarine *Porpoise*, which would deliver them to an island hideaway close to Singapore – and the beginning of what was codenamed Operation Rimau. With them went truckloads of stores: enough food for a month, clothing, weapons, ammunition and, of course, a substantial cache of charges.

Two weeks later, Lyon was taking a periscope recce in *Porpoise*, which was dived off Pulan Merepas, a small island within striking distance of Singapore. This they chose as their advance base for the operation. They unloaded their boats and their stores from the submarine, and Lyon set off with a handful of men aboard *Porpoise* in search of a native junk to capture for use as the carrier for *SB*s on approach to Singapore and in which to escape after the attack.

A long search for a suitable craft proved fruitless, and after five days they had to settle for a conspicuous white junk named *Mustika* that had no engine. The crew of nine Malays was scattered, though in what condition is unclear. Lyon and his own crew set sail for their hideout, where they were soon carting aboard their cargo for the planned assault.

Porpoise left immediately for Freemantle, scheduled to return for a rendezvous in a month to pick up the party. Lyon planned to carry out simultaneous attacks on six separate areas of Singapore harbour, approaching submerged in *SB*s. Ten *SB*s would return to the junk; the other five would travel to hideouts used by Lyon during Operation Jaywick and would be picked up later. All 15 *SB*s would be scuttled after the successful completion of the operation. That, at least, was the plan.

What happened next is, 50 or so years later, still shrouded in the mists of a Japanese cover-up. *Mustika* set sail with her raiding-party, leaving four men at the hideout to guard their stores. At some point during the operation, *Mustika* was challenged by a Malay police patrol. Lyon, certain that they would be discovered with his secret *SB*s on board, refused to heave to and a gun battle followed, killing three men on board the police launch.

Japanese troops, alerted by the incident, began a five-week cat-and-mouse chase for the raiders. Lyon scuttled *Mustika* and the 15 precious *SB*s, and his men paddled ashore in groups in canoes to hide up. They were pursued by Japanese search-parties that relentlessly scoured the islands. Several gun battles followed. In one, lasting a full two days, Lyon and another officer, along with several Japanese, were killed.

Now leaderless, the remainder of Group X continued their desperate retreat from the searchers. More battles followed; another nine men were lost. The submarine *Porpoise*, meanwhile, which should have come to collect Lyon's group, had developed engine trouble, and *Tantalus* came in its place, arriving late because its commander had to engage enemy shipping *en route*.

The remnants of Lyon's party were stranded. The Japanese refused to let go. Survivors were hunted down and eleven were captured, the last one taken 10 weeks after *Mustika* was scuttled. One died from battle wounds; the remaining ten were kept prisoner. On the orders of a Japanese general, they were beheaded on 7 July 1945, a month before the end of the war in the Far East.

Records of a court martial, produced by the Japanese after their surrender, were clearly faked to avoid war crimes accusations. They did, however, note that the men of Operation Rimau died 'in valorous spirit'. The Japanese report claimed that the men were intercepted before they reached Singapore harbour, though evidence suggests that they had, in fact, made it to the harbour and severely damaged some Japanese cruisers.

Thus ended the most ambitious and courageous project to use Blondie Hasler's submersible canoes. Once again, men were prepared to risk their lives for what were small-volume, high-risk ventures for the sake of damaging or, if they were lucky, destroying a few enemy ships or sabotaging enemy installations, which for the most part were back in operation again within a month or two. The theory was that, cumulatively, the attacks were of great value, tying up or disposing of Axis troops, guns, ammunition, support groups, transport and ships across a wide enemy arena and thus keeping them from front-line positions. And this was certainly true. By the end of 1943 and onwards, swimmer-canoeists and small raiding-parties of the various groups visited briefly in these chapters were working in ever-increasing numbers in every theatre and every department of the war, across the whole panoply of conflict.

There was, however, one more group which forms a key link in the family tree of the SBS of which we have so far only caught a passing glimpse: Combined Operations Pilotage Parties, born initially as a small section to trial a revolutionary concept in beach reconnaissance. COPPs mushroomed into one of the most vital and secret units of the war, and their techniques are still used by the SBS more than half a century later.

CHAPTER SEVEN

COPPs

Ronnie Williamson, a softly spoken Shetlander by birth and a commando in his youth, was one of the 18 known operational Coppists left when I interviewed him in 1997. Williamson looked back with utter astonishment that, as a young man of 19, he was chosen to be part of a group that was given 'Top Priority of the War' – a virtual law unto itself, and to which even senior officers found themselves giving way.

Coppists were members of the élite Combined Operations Pilotage Parties, 50 per cent of whom were officers. Two-thirds of Coppists were naval and the remainder came from the Royal Engineers and commandos. The group was officially brought into being by Mountbatten at the beginning of 1943 following the disaster of the Dieppe landings.

In a nutshell, COPPs were an SBS-style gathering of swimmer-canoeists, who were to be supremely capable of looking after themselves in any situation but who were also to be trained to perfection in the arts of navigation and hydrography. The men would be delivered by submarine, landing-craft and other carriers – including, later, the X-Craft mini-submarines – paddle inshore in their canoes and then go over the side to prepare a complete reconnaissance of assault beaches, draw their maps and charts to ensure the smooth landing of Allied armies.

The task required many hours of swimming and shore sorties for a complete survey, always in darkness, invariably in enemy territory and often on heavily guarded beaches.

At Mountbatten's insistence, and after putting his proposals direct to Winston Churchill at a private meeting, COPPs were formed on the understanding that they would have to know the secrets of Allied invasion plans ahead of their launch. Given such vital knowledge, the very existence of COPPs was strictly operated within the terms of the Official Secrets Act; their existence was never referred to in any newspaper, or in BBC broadcasts or internal services communications that did not bear the stamp MOST SECRET.

They were given a cover story of being Combined Operations Police Patrols, supposedly checking boom defences, but many senior Allied commanders below the rank of commander-in-chief did not even know of their true role. COPPs commanding officers carried orders signed personally by Mountbatten; their orders were to be produced if challenged by a higher rank, a not uncommon occurrence. COPPs men – even lower ranks – possessed knowledge of future plans in the war often before senior officers of the mainstream services were aware of them, which also put them in a most precarious position if captured. Three COPPs officers were rumoured to have swum out to sea and drowned rather than face torture by captors waiting on the shore. Coppists on missions in the Far East were provided with cyanide pills and anti-shark repellents as standard issue.

The secrecy surrounding COPPs was maintained after the war, even though they were disbanded, because of their hand-me-down connections with modern warfare. Their existence was not publicly acknowledged by the Ministry of Defence until 1959, and only then when the cover was blown by an American researcher. Public Records Office documents relating to COPPs activities did not appear for the full 30 years. Those involved remained remarkably tight-lipped among the wartime memoir-writers.

The reasons for such security dated back to midway through the war. Major troop movements lay ahead and Mountbatten, with foresight inspired by recent experience, began a campaign to ensure that beaches were properly reconnoitred rather than relying simply on aerial photographs or second-hand intelligence – which included pre-war picture postcards.

The whole assault area would be examined in detail: gradients of underwater approaches, obstacles, sand-bars, rocks, beach consistency, land surfaces, mined areas, beach defences, beach exits, natural hazards such as cliffs and hills, lookouts, sentry posts, gun emplacements and finally enemy positions . . . all to be mapped and charted ready for invasion troops. At that stage,

COPPs would be there again with canoes anchored 100 metres off the centre of the critical beach, shining a shaded torch out to sea over a predetermined arc to guide the assault forces forward. In Sicily, for example, four canoes guided in 3,250 ships.

The task was, as Mountbatten saw it, crucial, and the man he chose to form COPPs – and in effect become the inventor and pioneer of modern beach reconnaissance – was Lieutenant-Commander Nigel Clogstoun Willmott, RN. He was a close friend of and had served with Blondie Hasler in the early Norwegian operations and Willmott, it will be recalled, won a DSO when he saved Roger Courtney's life while they were on the very first reconnaissance operation on the beaches of Rhodes in 1941. Hasler and Courtney were both consulted. Willmott was selected.

They knew he had a particular bee in his bonnet about beach landings. He'd made a study of them, presented reports on Narvik and Rhodes which no one seemed especially interested in and, as a navigator on the Naval Force Commander's staff, he persisted with his theories of converting beach reconnaissance into an exact science. In this he had the intermittent encouragement of Courtney, with whom he had kept in touch. In 1942 Willmott returned from service in North Africa and found himself transferred to the Combined Training Staff in Scotland, where he started a course on beach pilotage for junior officers. In September he was summoned to Mountbatten's office and asked to put together a reconnaissance team to be dispatched immediately to North Africa ahead of the landing in Operation Torch.

Early in 1943, after Mountbatten had visited Churchill and was told to put his proposals before the Combined Chiefs of Staff, COPPs came into being, with barely enough time to train up parties to plot the course for the invasion of Sicily in the early summer.

Ronnie Williamson was little more than a boy when he volunteered for the commandos. After a rigorous selection process, only ten per cent of those who applied were selected for training and about ten per cent of those failed the course itself. Out of a shortlist of six men, a final interview by Captain Basil Eckhard, SBS, produced the three men required for COPPs teams. They then went on a further four months of specialist training.

Ronnie later rose from corporal to captain in 14 months and went on to become a close friend of the founder and his family.

(He was best man at Willmott's second wedding in 1982.) Williamson recalled:

Nigel convinced Mountbatten and Mountbatten convinced the war planners that it would be impossible to win the war unless they could land thousands of men safely on exactly the right beaches which would stand up to the heavyweight back-up of tanks, artillery, shells, transport – the whole mass of an army such as Montgomery's landing in Sicily, brought ashore in good order.

The beaches had to be thoroughly surveyed, the forces guided in and onwards, speedily and perhaps under enemy fire. To have them bogged down in shifting sands, to have vehicles or men drowned, to be unaware of underwater obstacles or mines, to be lacking in detailed intelligence of hazards unseen from aerial reconnaissance photographs . . . those were the nightmare scenarios that gripped Nigel and Mountbatten.

From my own standpoint, it shook one, as a virtual youth, to discover that you were part of something as internationally important as this; it was viewed by all of us, I know, as just a sheer honour to be part of it. You had to pinch yourself to believe it was true. Hitler would have paid millions of pounds to know what we knew. Mountbatten realised quickly that Nigel's job would be utterly impossible unless he was granted Top Priority of the War. I got this from Nigel himself. Mountbatten went directly to Churchill to explain his plans that would enable Nigel to recruit and properly equip precisely the right people he needed for this vital task. He believed that nothing and no one should stand in their way. Churchill's reply, to my surprise, was that he did not have the authority to grant Mountbatten what he asked. Mountbatten would have to put his proposals directly to the chiefs of the army, navy and RAF – but with Churchill's full approval.

They, in turn, were not at all happy about the top-priority request, in other words giving Nigel the power to overrule senior officers and even civilians to get what he needed. But what choice had they? Either they would have to promote him to an incredible height or else give him the ace of trumps. In the end, entirely due to Mountbatten, Nigel was given the ace of trumps.

That ace came in the form of a personal letter of authority from Mountbatten – golden words from him saying tactfully NOW HEAR THIS. It provided commanders throughout the war theatres with a message writ between the lines. If the officer commanding a COPPs unit experienced any difficulty at all, he was to get on the blower to the Chief of Combined Operations – Mountbatten himself. Under the heading 'Instructions to the Officer in Charge of a COPPs Unit', Mountbatten memoed:

> These instructions should be produced as your authority should such be questioned. On arrival at the station you will be under the orders of the Naval Commander-in-Chief . . . Your normal method of communication should be through the authority under whose orders you are placed. In order, however, that the general organisation, development and training of COPPs units may proceed to the best advantage . . . you should keep the Chief of Combined Operations informed on all matters of detail. This should be done by requesting the authority under whose orders you are to forward a message in the following form:
> 'Following for Chief of Combined Operations from COPPs—'
> If requirements are forwarded by letter, it should be addressed to the authority mentioned with a copy to the Chief of Combined Operations. This will enable the Chief of Combined Operations to take preliminary action.

In other words, the authorities mentioned had better watch out, and they did.

Ronnie Williamson again:

> It was quite remarkable. Nigel was given the power to do what he wanted. He was very modest about it, but the reality was that no one could stand in his way. Our COPP units also got pretty well whatever we asked. If we needed a lift on an aircraft-carrier, we got it. If we needed additional equipment, it was there. If we raided the stores of a shore-based unit, there was no comeback . . . quite incredible.

That situation was not easily reached. Some difficult hurdles and resistance had to be overcome. Early COPPs sections, such as the one Willmott took on the recce prior to Operation Torch for the North African assault, were not given the precedence that Mountbatten later ensured. Willmott mustered a force of 18 in haste, virtually all trained navigating lieutenants from the Royal Navy or RNVR and experienced SBS officers. They lacked proper equipment, especially efficient swimming-suits, and Willmott also faced some hostility among the top brass over demarcation: beach marking had always been the preserve of SBS. But these difficulties were overcome and COPPs was founded, initially under the codename of Party Inhuman, which they used for Operation Torch. The reconnaissance was a model of its kind.

It still took a major setback in terms of casualties to prod the powers that be into agreeing to put COPPs on a firm footing in the way that Willmott and Mountbatten had envisaged, with its own headquarters and establishment, training facilities and equipment. At the time, war planners were anguishing over the invasion of Sicily, anticipated for the summer of 1943. Various locations in the south of Italy and Sicily were under consideration. The Allied commanders who would lead the two-pronged assault were more or less agreed that a Sicilian landing could be achieved with the minimum loss of life.

At the beginning of January 1943 COPPs were called into action. Two COPPs sections were dispatched from England and one formed from the Middle East Beach Reconnaissance Unit and supplemented by a couple of men borrowed from the SBS. They met up in Malta and began training procedures. The party badly needed rehearsals but barely had time for them. They were due on the Sicilian recce by the end of February because their reports were required by mid-March. In fact, the assembled company was ill-prepared both in terms of expertise and equipment. That February was wintry cold, their canoes were barely adequate for the weather, and the suits used for lengthy swimming missions were ill-fitting and had a tendency to leak.

The men pressed on. They were taken aboard three carrier submarines from Malta and set off for the Sicilian coast, 75 miles away. There, after dark, they would paddle their canoes to their designated beaches to begin their recce, returning to the submarine on conclusion, the whole operation scheduled for four nights. They were dropped around 2 miles from their recce sites and would paddle inshore to a point around 200 metres from the beach. The paddler would remain in the canoe, suitably camouflaged, and attempt to maintain a stable position, unnoticed, while the reconnaissance officer would slip into the water.

He would be wearing a hefty suit of rubberised fabric, which was supposed to give him buoyancy and protect him from the cold. The suit had a built-in lifejacket that could be inflated by mouth, and pockets laden with equipment, including: a .38 pistol, a fighting knife, an oil-immersed prismatic compass, sounding lead and line, beach gradient reel, an underwater writing-tablet with chinagraph pencil, 24-hour emergency rations in case of separation and two torches to home in on the canoe for the return.

The swimmers were to record every possible detail that would be of use in pinpointing the most suitable assault site, with a profile and description of the geological nature of the beach itself to assist invasion force beachmasters to bring ashore landing-craft and to establish suitable sites for piers and breakwaters.

The Sicilian recce ran into trouble from the word go and stumbled from bad to worse nightly. All the beach sites due for reconnaissance were found to be heavily guarded, with sentries posted at around every 100 metres. The losses began immediately.

First, the leader of the COPPs expedition, Lieutenant-Commander Norman Teacher, RN, failed to return to his canoe and was presumed dead or captured. The former proved to be the case. His paddler, Lieutenant Noel Cooper, an experienced canoeist who had been on Operation Torch as a marker, returned to the submarine rendezvous completely exhausted after a long search.

In spite of that, Cooper went out again with Captain G. W. Burbridge on 2 March. They did not return and were never seen again. On 3 March two of the Middle East group, Lieutenant Bob Smith and Lieutenant D. Brand, failed to meet their submarine, although their navigation was certainly not at fault.

In rough weather, they simply paddled two and a half miles back to the same beach – i.e. seven and a half miles in all. There is no tide in the central Mediterranean, but they had to make allowances for the wind and waves for fine adjustment to their re-set course, which they had carefully memorised. They then paddled 75 miles back to Malta in just over two days and went right up to Grand Harbour in Valletta before arriving exhausted alongside a submarine in Lazaretto Creek. This was a remarkable feat of navigation and endurance without food and water. One week later, the submarine they tried to re-join returned safely from patrol.

On 6 March Lieutenant A. Hart and Sub-Lieutenant E. Folder, also from the Middle East section, did not come back.

On 7 March Lieutenant P. De Kock and Sub-Lieutenant A. Crossley failed to meet their connection, and the following night Lieutenant Davies went to look for them and did not return either. Others also went missing.

Of the sixteen who joined the mission, only four were known to be safe. Five – Teacher, Cooper, Burbridge, De Kock and Crossley – were never seen again, presumed drowned. The remainder had been captured.

The three lost officers of COPPs – Teacher, Cooper and Burbridge – were believed by some to have hit trouble and had taken the ultimate precaution against capture and torture by drowning themselves. Others disagree, and put their loss down to either accident or enemy action. The incident remains a debating point to this day.

In spite of the losses, some of the beach reconnaissances were completed successfully, and for these Lieutenant N. T. McHarg and Lieutenant George S. Sinclair, DSC, RNR, were both awarded the DSO. Smith and Brand were awarded the DSO, while one of those captured, Able Seaman James McGuire, who later escaped from an Italian PoW camp, was awarded a BEM.

In the aftermath it was concluded that the men were ill-equipped and ill-trained. In the haste to get them under way, no homing exercises had been carried out and only three, ironically Teacher, Burbridge and Cooper, had experience of the procedure.

Nigel Willmott, devastated by the losses, vowed that such a catastrophe should never happen again. He insisted that the disastrous results merely confirmed his point – that training procedures for COPPs people were paramount and could not be hurried. The men also had to be properly equipped; without adequate gear, their missions were doomed to failure.

At this point Mountbatten took the operation by the scruff of the neck and demanded full backing from the Chiefs of Staff – which he achieved. They dealt Willmott, as Ronnie Williamson described it, the ace of trumps. Nigel Willmott became the father of COPPs. He based his unit at the requisitioned Hayling Island

Sailing Club and went on to train ten COPPs sections between 1943 and the end of the war. Ronnie Williamson recalls:

> Thanks to the Top Priority, we never lost a man in COPP5. Our canoes could and did operate effectively in force eight, while our new equipment was lightweight, tailor-made and state of the art. Hardly a week passed without more high-tech items arriving. It was like the difference between coal-dust and gold-dust. The transformation took only four months and we never looked back.

COPPs took their vital place in the war effort, operating in every theatre and every major invasion of Allied forces. They were there for the Sicilian landings in July 1943, every one of the assault landings into Italy and on into the Adriatic.

Then came the greatest operation of them all, the Normandy landings, where two X-Craft mini-submarines were extensively used by COPPs, with five men aboard at times instead of four. In addition, two regiments of waterproofed tanks were guided 90 miles (145 kilometres) across the English Channel and put into the sea 2 miles offshore from Sword Bay, arriving precisely as arranged at 5.30 a.m. The margin of error allowed was just 40 yards (36 metres). They were right on target. Furthermore, there were no casualties among the COPPs men; instead, deservedly plenty of accolades, honours and medals.

COPPs sterling work continued in major river crossings, such as the Rhine, and in a huge variety of complex assignments with the Small Operations Group in the Far East, especially in preparation for the invasion of Malaya. These were led by Willmott's logical successor, the most experienced Coppist of the war, Lieutenant-Commander Peter Wild, DSC, RNVR. Although all these operations were carried out with remarkable low casualties among the Coppists, the work of such men as Wild was inadequately acknowledged, largely due to the secrecy that surrounded the group long after the hostilities had ceased.

After the war, many of the techniques and unique skills devised and practised by COPPs teams were still totally applicable to modern warfare. From tenuous beginnings, COPPs established the strategy that there should never be large-scale troop landings without prior extensive reconnaissance of the invasion beach, its underwater approaches, its surrounds and enemy positions –

techniques that hold good 50 years later and were demonstrated, for example, with the first British task force landings in the Falklands, for which the SBS opened the door.

By the beginning of 1944 the principles of small-group operations which were to provide the foundations of the SBS down the remaining half of the century had been firmly established and were being deployed across the whole spectrum of Allied action. Though many of Courtney's original SBS group had been lost in action or captured, reinforcements were trained and dispersed across the Mediterranean and the Far East.

Three new Courtney-trained SBS groups, A, B and C, were formed to join the Small Operations Group based in Ceylon under the badge of the Royal Marines in South-East Asia Command along with sections from RMBPD, Detachment 385 from the Royal Marines commando assault troops and four Sea Reconnaissance Units, the newly formed unit for the growing emphasis on underwater work. In the coming months the SOG parties mounted no fewer than 174 raiding and recce operations behind Japanese lines before its disbandment at the end of the war. RMBPD also had a section very active in the Mediterranean.

Meanwhile, George Jellicoe's Special Boat Squadron, acquisitive, well equipped and flamboyant, with a force made up of former SBS and SAS sections, bolstered and renewed after losses, had won medals by the bucketful across the whole North African arena and the Italian coastline, prior to and around the time of the Italian armistice. Jellicoe himself led some spectacular missions, by land, sea or floating in by parachute, routing Italians and giving little peace to the Nazis with his island-hopping raids off the Greek and Turkish coasts, around the Mediterranean and on into mainland adventures off the Adriatic and the Aegean.

There was, however, a clear distinction between Jellicoe's Special Boat Squadron and Courtney's Special Boat Section. The Courtney traditionalists considered Jellicoe's group to be an affiliate of the SAS from which it originated, and thus 'not one of us'. Special Forces and private armies all had their own way of doing things. There was undoubtedly dissension between the SBS and the SAS over tactics, and the glowing embers of it remain half a century later.

Gruff Courtney, 30 years after the war had ended, would recall pointedly that when the original SBS was allowed to operate in the specialised roles for which it had been chosen and trained, its casualties in major campaigns were relatively light. Losses mounted after 1942, when Roger Courtney departed the Middle East and 1SBS was employed mainly with Jellicoe on *coup de main* raiding on inland airfields, more properly the province of the SAS.

'The prime function of the SBS,' said Gruff gruffly, 'was to do maximum damage to Axis forces with the minimum of effort . . . weigh the possible loss of two men in a canoe against one or more bomber aircraft in an attack on a railway bridge and you have an example of cost-efficiency.'

He made another valid point that he seemed to equate *his* SBS and sea-borne raiders and recce parties of RMBPD and COPPs. The men whose activities we have followed in this brief sojourn in the Second World War came to the fore on the key principles of the SBS – as volunteers and as men with the physical and mental stamina to sustain them through the most difficult times. They were drawn from all walks of life – from Tug Wilson, the Bristol draughtsman, to Billy Mills, who worked in Kettering Sports and Rubber Store before he became a Cockleshell Hero.

With a few exceptions, such as Roger Courtney himself, they had no exotic past, nor were they undisciplined misfits. They were, however, individualists, loners and survivors whose sometimes latent qualities were spotted by the people who were selecting them for training. 'Their motivation,' said Gruff Courtney, 'was as mixed as one would expect: undemonstrative patriotism, youthful adventure, self-reliance, independence of mind. They were generally quiet fellows but full of spirit. A psychologist might have detected in some a masochistic urge, a hidden death-wish . . . but it never seemed to survive the actual shock of danger. Then, animal instinct for self-preservation could be expected to reassert itself with its usual force.'

It was those men and those characteristics that formed the backbone of the amphibious small-group raiders – another 'few' gathered up and trained in this particular art of warfare. Such men cut a path to the future. They possessed skills that, according to Field Marshal Lord Slim, Commander of the Forgotten Army in Burma, which he led to victory against the Japanese, and later Chief of the Imperial Staff, should not be discarded. 'There is one kind of special unit,' he wrote in 1946, 'which should be retained – that designed to be employed in small parties, usually behind the enemy on tasks beyond the normal scope of warfare in the field.'

Jumbo Courtney, Blondie Hasler and Nigel Willmott, encouraged by Mountbatten, fathered a formation that was born on a beach in Rhodes in 1941, given a cruel kicking on the banks of the Gironde in 1942, and finally came of age along the coastlines of Normandy and the Arakan in 1945. Traditions and disciplines were formed along the way.

And then, they all came home . . . but to what?

PART TWO

Peace and Wars
1945 to 1970

Hitler gone, the Japanese surrendered after the atom bombs vaporised Hiroshima and Nagasaki . . . and in the context of the war's end the specialist units seemed of little consequence. The stories of the heroes and the legends of the Special Forces were locked away in the filing cabinets marked MOST SECRET and were years away from being told. The spotlight was on the great battles and the great armies, the hundreds of thousands who never came back, the horrors of the German concentration camps and the rush to demobilise. Private armies were disbanded, which pleased many in the military hierarchy who didn't like them, didn't want them and campaigned to have them closed down. Others begged to differ. David Stirling, freed from Colditz and back with the SAS for its last knockings in the Far East, was devastated to discover that his beloved regiment was to be relegated to the Territorial Army, and for a while the amphibious raiders of SBS, RMBPD, COPPs and the swimmers of the SRU who made up SOG seemed to be heading towards the anonymity of a larger command. Barely had they begun unpacking their kit and stacking the stores and equipment being trundled in from around the world than the future reared its ugly head . . .

CHAPTER EIGHT

A troublesome rebirth

They were still a pinprick in the order of things . . . 'a speck of flyshit on a map of the world' was one description. Mountbatten was no longer there to jolly them all along. Although he'd had a war to run, there is little doubt that he viewed the canoe raiders of South-East Asia as *his* boys. Now, he and they were no more. He left Singapore on 30 April 1946: the Supreme Commander of South-East Asia was out of a job, along with the rest of them in his Small Operations Group.

The vast territory over which he had administered the British assault on the Japanese invaders was returned to civilian governments. He departed to the sound of a cliché: rumblings of discontent: Malaya, Indonesia, Burma, Borneo, Korea, Vietnam . . . 'I am afraid you are in for a rather sticky time, old chap,' he sardonically and prophetically told one of the administrators as he waved goodbye. United in their resistance to the Japanese, political factions of South-East Asia split wide apart when the Allies withdrew and mayhem took hold. Before long, SOG in the guise of the new SBS would be called back into action. But in 1946 there was little sign that anyone was really interested in what happened to the remnants of that particular party.

Mountbatten's arrival in Portsmouth for a senior officers' course not long after his return gave hope to some – and nausea to others – that he was on the verge of returning to high military office. The new Labour government of Clement Attlee had other ideas and whisked him away to India to oversee the beginning of the end of the British Empire. It would be another decade before the aura of Mountbatten returned, and, as he moved to sort out Partition, the chaps of SOG were struggling for an identity – or at least, those veterans who remained in the service were.

Many returned to civilian life and quite a few others, like Tug Wilson, who stayed on and rose to the rank of lieutenant-colonel, did not remain with the amphibians. He later returned to front-line action in Korea. Roger Courtney, ill since 1942, retired and died in 1947. Nigel Willmott returned to the navy and then went home. Things could never be the same. The impetus of war which allowed the creation of private armies and small-group raiders had gone; in its place was an anticlimactic void.

A million service personnel had been demobilised by the end of 1945. Bankrupt Britain had to tighten its belt yet again. Deep cuts in service personnel and economies across the board were being demanded by politicians. Special Forces, and their surrounding collection of experimental stations and support staff, were a small but obvious target. Who would need them in an age of A-bombs?

The War Office Tactical Investigation Committee took soundings from commanders on the future use of Special Forces. There was formidable opposition to them from commanders in all sections of the armed forces, but, equally, many remained convinced of their role in modern warfare, particularly in some of the looming troublespots, where the terrain was rough and the natives restless. Expert testimony on where those troublespots were likely to occur led the committee to conclude that 'short-term, shallow-penetration' sections should be raised and trained under the auspices of the Royal Marines.

The SAS, on the other hand, was given no quarter. Two months after the war ended, 1SAS, 2SAS and HQSAS were disbanded, while the Belgian 5SAS was handed over to the Belgian Army. As a compromise to some loud howls of protest, a new volunteer SAS regiment was to be raised as part of the Territorial Army. The mantle was passed to a distinguished old volunteer unit, the Artists' Rifles, and on 1 January 1947, the unit became the 21st Special Air Service Regiment (Artists) TA.

The sections of SOG that remained intact were placed in the charge of the Royal Marines. It would take another five years or more before any cohesive policy for their future emerged, largely because of the vacuum in terms of direction that came with post-war blues – plus the dire shortage of cash and calls for economy.

The nucleus of men who would take the organisation forwards came principally from SOG – the remains of Courtney's SBS,

RM Detachment 385, Sea Reconnaissance Unit, Combined Operations Pilotage Parties and Boom Patrol Detachment. The men had returned home from Ceylon in MV *Athlone Castle*, arriving in November 1945. In fact, only a small number from each group opted to stay on, and after their leave they reported to the Westward Ho! Hotel, which was the wartime headquarters of Combined Operations Experimental Establishment.

They amounted to fewer than 60 men, who formed up under the command of Blondie (now Lieutenant-Colonel) Hasler. He, determined to keep those wartime disciplines alive, set about producing a draft plan for their future. What remained of Hasler's former creation, the RM Boom Patrol Detachment, moved from its wartime base, HMS *Mount Stewart*, to the rather less salubrious surroundings of Harris's Boat Yard, Appledore, under the command of Lieutenant P. G. 'Pug' Davis, DSC, a future commanding officer of the SBS.

By then, his detachment consisted of just three officers, eight other ranks and two maintenance ratings – along with their stock of *Sleeping Beauty*s (now to be known as Motor Submersible Canoes), their exploding motor boats and a very useful depot ship, MFV MV *Celtic*. But Davis, too, had aspirations.

With the likes of Field Marshal Slim supporting a continued life for small-party raiders, Hasler was heavily promoting the idea of a school that would serve all sections of the armed forces to keep alive and develop their skills. Early in 1946 the Admiralty gave approval to the opening of the School of Combined Operations Beach and Boat Section (SCOBBS) at Fremington, Devon. Hasler produced a paper, his vision of the future, which turned out to be a significant blueprint, defining the role of modern amphibious Special Forces, combining all those small-party skills from the war for a single unit of saboteurs, sea-borne raiders and intelligence-gatherers.

In future warfare, Hasler wrote, there would still be a need for infiltration by small parties of troops for the key elements that had proved so successful in the war: reconnaissance of enemy-held areas, beach survey, small-scale raids, with independent objectives or in support of larger operations, ferrying agents and supplies for them. He correctly forecast that an increasing number of special operations would be entirely air-borne, but where stealth and surprise were important the approach by water would still often be the only practicable method – hence the SBS motto created ten years later: NOT BY STRENGTH, BY GUILE.

His proposal was for SCOBBS to train a substantial pool of men who would carry out water-borne operations in small boats (such as dories, canoes, inflatables and so on) and by swimming and wading. 'Such men,' Hasler wrote, 'must from the nature of their work be courageous, intelligent and resourceful. Normally the required standard can only be reached by training specially selected volunteers with a high proportion of officers and NCOs. This unit would also contain a number of specially trained RN officers with navigating or hydrographic qualifications to lead teams on beach survey operations (former COPPs role). All SCOBBS-trained ranks of the armed forces would operate in uniform . . . They may, of course, be required to work in conjunction with plain-clothes agents for certain operations.'

Hasler's vision – though perhaps not fully appreciated then – would stand the test of time. The following passages, edited here for the sake of brevity and quoted directly from his previously unpublished document, could easily have been used as the starting-point, for example, for the recapture of the Falkland Islands 35 years later:

Requirement: When the balance of power in a particular theatre of war is in favour of the enemy, so preventing large-scale operations, small-scale raiding is of the highest importance, both in keeping up morale and in forcing the enemy to deploy large forces in static defence tasks . . . [and] while the enemy is deployed in strength ensures that there are plenty of good targets.

Transport: Long-range operations must be put in by large aircraft, submarine or large surface vessel. Short-range operations can be transported by small aircraft, coastal forces, landing-craft or sometimes overland. Where there are no off-lying obstacles or risk of enemy detection, parent vessels can launch parties close to their objectives. This enables a simple means of approach, such as swimming or a manually propelled small boat.

Approach: Where parent vessels must launch parties further off, or for an operation lasting several nights, with the force remaining concealed during daylight, the approach will call for small powered craft (which may themselves carry canoes, swimmers, etc.).

Lying up: In daylight, lying up will be necessary either afloat, in a boat of low silhouette lying some way offshore and suitably camouflaged, or ashore, in thick scrub or mangrove or on some inaccessible feature. If the boats cannot be concealed ashore, they may sometimes be deliberately submerged under water. Alternatively, the use of a local type of craft may enable the force to move by day even in fairly congested areas.

Advance base: The object is to establish inside an enemy-held area a static advanced base, from which sorties are made against local objectives. The base may well operate for some time without detection.

Withdrawal: Parties usually withdraw by retracing their approach route [to rendezvous with parent vessel or transport], but should this fail there would be a delayed rendezvous at a different place, and/or an escape plan to be used after all rendezvous have failed. Alternatively, the main plan for the withdrawal may be for the party to link up with pro-allied guerrillas, or an existing escape organisation; or in the case of certain tactical operations, to stay put until overtaken by the advance of the main force.

Suicide jobs and capture: It has not been the British policy to send a member of the armed forces to do work which is certain to end in death, or even in capture. In 1943–5 both the Germans and Japanese executed many British ranks who had been captured in uniform, on infiltration operations; but these men were captured through failure of the plan, not as part of it. Some enemies have an unenvied reputation for extracting information from prisoners by torture, and men captured on infiltration work are particularly liable to suffer in this way. These facts cannot be allowed to interfere with the intention to press forward with such operations, but the following precautions should be taken:

1) Men sent out on an operation, including the OC, must never be briefed with more than the minimum information to enable them to carry it out, and 2) the whole party must be well briefed with a convincing cover story, which they can bring forward if forced to say something. 3) If a man who is otherwise sound has a dread of capture and its consequences, he should be allowed to take 'sudden death pills' with him if he wants to do so.

Difficult landing: A valuable characteristic of well-trained infiltration parties is that they can land at places which would be impracticable for a larger force; for example, through surf, or over cliffs, rocks or soft mud. This factor should be exploited to the full on a defended coast. Even on an undefended coast, most of the easy landings are usually in use by the natives and are better avoided.

Weather and climate: On an open water, wind of over force three may make it impossible for canoes and other small craft to carry out an operation. Water and air temperatures have a marked effect on the methods which can be employed. In the tropics both small-boat work and swimming becomes far simpler in that there is no need to keep the body dry; on the other hand, coral, sharks and sting-sores must be reckoned with ashore. In the Arctic swimming is only practicable in a limited way with the aid of a watertight suit, and for boat work the main problem is to keep the body dry and warm. Snow-covered country offers considerable difficulties to infiltration parties, but this is partly offset by the long hours of darkness in the winter season, and by the large proportion of uninhabited country.

Much of what Hasler identified as ideal working practices for the sea-borne raiders still holds good, and his strategy will become apparent over and over again as these pages progress in our story to the present day.

Hasler's proposals were adopted more or less as written, except in the area of control. In his vision, the school of small-party raiders should train élite squads who would be attached permanently to larger commands. The school itself would be run by Combined Operations, without specific allegiance to any one of the main service groups. In the end, SCOBBS was placed under the command of the Royal Marines. Within a year it was merged with RMBPD and renamed COBBS – Combined Operations Beach and Boats Section. At the end of August 1947 both units, consisting of 6 officers, 25 other ranks and 8 ratings, plus 17,500 cubic feet (495 cubic metres) of boxes of stores, 5 motor boats, 12 dinghies, 26 canoes and a small mobile crane, were packed ready for their move to the Royal Marines base at Eastney, Portsmouth. Their task was set out in a memo from the

Commandant General, Royal Marines, to the Chief of Staff, Combined Operations: to select and train officers and other ranks in the skills inherited from SOG and to test and trial new and experimental equipment.

An air of secrecy still surrounded this tiny group of water-borne nomads, especially concerning its inheritance of beach reconnaissance and pilotage skills. It was noted in an article by a COBBS officer in the Royal Marines magazine *The Globe and Laurel* that November. 'The days of WWII private armies are finished,' he wrote. 'In their place in the corps a unit which will retain all the flexibility and originality of its predecessors has been formed. For two years . . . it has carried out much research into small craft, frogmen, parachuting, long-range penetration, cliff-climbing and concealment . . . What we need now is a little less secrecy so that the remainder of the corps realises what we are doing and why we are doing it.'

The secrecy was not entirely across the board. In fact, in the early days the new formation was used as something of a showcase for both recruitment and public relations. From the beginning, SCOBBS and its successor, COBBS, carried out large numbers of demonstrations around the country. Frogmen were, to the British public, a completely new and exciting force, and swimming-baths all over Britain were clamouring to get a visit from these strange creatures in their black suits, masks and flippers. Several war veterans, too, were used in demonstration teams to show off other aspects of amphibious raids. Many in the service regarded these demonstrations as a rather humiliating activity. 'Frankly, we didn't like it,' one of their later additions, Captain Len Holmes BEM, told me. 'It was seen by most of us as play acting, a gimmick. No, we didn't like it at all.'

Lieutenant Pug Davis, a tough, small man so nicknamed for his pugilistic appearance and earlier life as a services boxer, won a Distinguished Service Cross for landing with six men to search for a patrol of 2 Commando on a heavily defended Dalmatian island in 1944. Now he was traipsing around supervising frogmen demos. He sent a detailed account of a visit to Sweden, and his report was found buried away in the Public Records Office at Kew. Davis reported: 'The naval attaché of the British Embassy . . . told me the purpose of our visit was threefold – to further Anglo-Swedish relations, to interest the Swedish Navy in frogmen to buy equipment from Great Britain (export drive!), and make the Swedes more reliant on the Royal Navy for training and information.'

The frogmen were fêted, photographed and cheered, and Davis gave a 15-minute interview on Swedish national radio . . . and at the conclusion . . . the defence minister presented them with a little bronze plaque which was suitably engraved.

All very nice, said some, but this ain't what we're here for. A top-level report to the Chiefs of Staff, in a later review of Special Forces, agreed, and made the point quite bluntly: 'Too much time is being taken up acting as clockwork mice for harbour defence exercises and doing parlour tricks at demonstrations.' But if there was ever a danger of the amphibious raiders slip-sliding away into the ignominy of such ventures, international tensions came to their rescue.

A few headlines: Berlin under siege from the Russians; Fierce fighting in Palestine between Arabs and Jews; Flare-up ahead of the creation of the state of Israel; Communist 'rebels' battle with British troops in Malaya; North Korea proclaims itself a republic under Kim Il Sung; Shanghai falls to Mao's army; The IRA vows to fight for a united Ireland . . .

The troubles that were to rebound down the century were stirring by the summer of 1948. By then, the designation of the COBBS team had been changed yet again, this time to become the Small-Raids Wing (SRW) of the Royal Marines Amphibious School of Eastney. Apart from training and exercises – and prompted by the international tensions – new operational tasks were approved by Combined Operations headquarters. The SRW's new brief included offensive raids and harbour attacks, deception raids, intelligence sorties, rescuing air crews and PoWs in enemy territory, and ferrying 'clandestine operatives' and stores into enemy territory.

In the summer three frogmen were dispatched to Palestine, where British forces were in action to quell continued fighting between Arab and Jewish troops and assorted guerrilla groups. They were tasked with finding and removing limpets attached to ships in Haifa harbour. They included Sergeant 'Sticks' Dodds, so called because he began his military life as a drummer universally called Sticks, who later commanded the SBS. He was awarded the Military Medal for the operation.

The success of this mission reminded the military of the usefulness of small-group raiders, and other tasks soon began to emerge. The first major European exercise since the war, Exercise Kiel/Elbe, took the whole force through the Kiel Canal and on into the Elbe, in which live limpets were used in mock attacks. In the escape and evasion phase of the exercise, more than half the SRW team evaded capture. Another major exercise took them to Northern Ireland, where they carried out mock offensive raids and escape and evasion tactics against the Royal Ulster Constabulary in the mountains of Mourne.

Even so, the SRW remained principally an instruction and demonstration unit. Demands on its limited personnel left little scope for deployment, and this was recognised. As the new decade turned, the commanding officer of the Amphibious School, Lieutenant-Colonel Houghton, was ordered to form an operational section which would henceforth be known as 1SBS, and more or less kept apart from the training routines of the SRW.

Marine Jim Earle was a new boy at the SRW at the time and recalled the activity. He had joined the service as a tearaway youth in 1947, with starry-eyed visions of becoming one of the blacked-up commandos who figured so often in the newsreels at the local cinema. He was posted to 40 Commando in the Middle East, saw action in Palestine as a sniper, and was among the last British troops to leave Haifa. He did a stint in Hong Kong, had a short stay in Cyprus, and back in Britain his sergeant-major volunteered him, as a punishment for some misdemeanour, for the notoriously tough SRW course at Eastney. 'I knew very little about the SRW,' said Earle, when I interviewed him at his home in Wiltshire. 'I knew even less about the SBS. I don't think I'd even heard of them. But I was a good swimmer and a good shot . . . got through the selection week and was accepted for the Swimmer Canoeist 3 course; they ran through grades SC3, SC2 and SC1. The course lasted about five months in three phases, intermittently progressing through the disciplines of swimming and diving, canoeing and small craft handling plus navigation and recce, then finally the tactical phase, which was escape and evasion, mapreading, survival and a parachute course.'

There were a dozen potential recruits on the course, of whom five were eventually accepted. He is the last survivor of that intake. The remaining four had been aboard HMS/M *Affray* in April 1951 to get experience of leaving and re-entering a submarine prior to an exercise. With 75 men aboard, the 1,600-ton vessel vanished mysteriously several hours after leaving port and

119

was reported missing when contact ceased off the South Coast of England.

The submarine's disappearance baffled naval experts for many days. There were numerous theories, and it was believed she had battery failure. To aid them in their search for *Affray*, the Admiralty took the unusual step of consulting a spiritualist, who apparently told them where to look. It still took weeks to locate the craft, and, with air long expired, all hands were posted as lost.

At the time the SRW was under the command of Major Donald Peyton-Jones DSC, 'a vague but lovely fellow' who stayed until 1951, later, after leaving the service, becoming a vicar. (It was a long-held ambition. He took the trouble to discover the name of the German who had bombed him during the war and wrote and told him that on that day he had decided he would take the cloth.) Under Peyton-Jones, Jim Earle moved quickly into a tactical team of the SRW which was responsible for training courses. With demands on personnel increasing, three instructors were posted elsewhere, and he was presented with immediate scope for advancement, progressing from marine to sergeant within 12 months and becoming the youngest NCO in the section.

As a member of the Tactical Training Team, he discovered for the first time some of the history of the SBS, COPPs and RMBPD; their wartime stores were at Eastney. Some of the material was still packed away in boxes at Fremington and was eventually brought to the Eastney base. Said Earle:

It was like an Aladdin's cave; the most interesting equipment we'd ever seen. Apart from the weapons, fighting knives and communications gear, there were all kinds of oddball things. There were some false rubber feet, for instance, so that the wearer could track around the beach and leave native Asian footprints instead of European ones. There were boots with thick felt soles for silent marches. There were lots of trip-switches, various booby traps, a mass of cameras and special photographic equipment, lots of literature on special operations – and all kinds of good equipment. It was a whole new world to me and, of course, a lot of the gear was used for our courses. In fact, a lot of the courses were built around the equipment we found in the stores, and during the whole time I was there, throughout the 1950s, we were developing courses and resurrecting a lot of the old skills.

Earle recalls the re-formation of 1SBS, which would include several of the originals from Courtney's SBS.

> There were still a few names from the past among them. They were sectioned off into a Nissen hut on their own. We called them the old and the bold. Those who had been in SBS during the war kept themselves pretty much to themselves. Probably thought we were all a bunch of fairies. But 1SBS came into being, for a specific reason that we didn't know about at the time. Everything in SRW and SBS was done on a need-to-know basis. If you didn't need to know, you weren't told. That was the nature of the place, and everyone respected that.

The reactivation of an SBS unit was probably inevitable in view of international tensions. Several discussion papers were drawn up on the future role of the section, allied to its possible deployment in some of the envisaged troublespots. This renewed interest in Special Forces coincided, not unexpectedly perhaps, with the troubles in Palestine and the Far East. In Malaya the CTs (Communist Terrorists) had taken a hefty toll in their guerrilla warfare against the British-installed Federation of Malay States.

By the spring of 1950 almost 2,000 civilians, police and soldiers had been killed by the CTs, who had moved back to their jungle hideouts that existed during the war. They also had an ample cache of weaponry, courtesy of the British military, which had armed their underground army to fight the Japanese. Guerrilla leader Chin Peng had been given an honorary OBE in the Victory Honours list.

Now, in what became known as the Malayan Emergency, the same arms were being turned against the British, a salutary lesson that was never heeded (as Saddam Hussein proved years later). The probability of Britain becoming involved in jungle warfare focused minds on Special Forces. The War Office also issued a new directive for the use and training of 21SAS (Artists) TA, by then a strong volunteer force of reservists and Territorials.

The directive, issued on 2 January 1950, arose partly because 21SAS was sending personnel to the Amphibious School for instruction in sea-borne techniques. Combined Operations headquarters judged this to be 'using up valuable time of instructors' and that they would merely be encroaching on the role of the SBS. Areas of operation for SAS personnel were clearly defined – deep penetration into enemy-occupied territory – and their training should therefore take account of specific tasks, which would include: harassing the enemy, impeding enemy movement, destroying stores, equipment, bridges and railways, reporting on suitable targets and operating as reconnaissance for air-borne divisions. Training would be required to a 'very high standard'.

An SBS training directive, on the other hand, showed a clear distinction. It was very much on the lines outlined originally by Hasler. It stated: 'They must reach a standard of self-reliance which will enable them to land from a submarine or carrier with necessary equipment and weapons, establish themselves ashore, live and evade capture . . .' The planners added the proviso that since detection could have serious consequences in compromising the security of future operations, SBS men must be sufficiently skilful 'to be relied upon in suitable circumstances'.

In the middle of this flurry of fresh activity, an internal row broke out when it became known on the service grapevine that the name assigned to the new operational party was Special Boat Section. The commanding officer of 21SAS (Artists) TA wrote to the Commandant General, Royal Marines, to complain. They had no right to use the title SBS, he declared, because the wartime SBS was part of the SAS and wore the same badge. Using the letters SBS would therefore be wrong! This totally inaccurate generalisation of the situation brought a firm rebuke from the Commandant General, Royal Marines. He pointed out that the Special Boat Squadron (Jellicoe's army) operated under the auspices of the SAS and was part of it. The claim for the title was not valid because it was never recognised by the War Office as a regimental title. RM, conversely, could use the title through its inheritance of its own SBS antecedents. The dispute reached the Chief of Combined Operations Staff, who promptly ordered them to settle it over a gin and tonic. The upshot was that RM continued to use SBS as a functional title. Dispute solved, and SAS (TA) retired still smarting!

Later, the SAS once again attempted to call their boat parties SBS. Combined Operations headquarters stopped them and again put down a formal distinction between the two:

SAS . . . recce at division level, deep penetration raids, harassing the enemy well behind the lines, and training partisans.

SBS . . . operations against ships and coastal installations, shallow penetration raids by water, beach reconnaissance, smoothing the path for difficult landings, and ferrying agents.

Tasks that could be done by either were harassing raids against coastal targets, landward reconnaissance, capture of prisoners and 'eliminating undesirable people'. One important difference still remained, however. SAS was a unit of the Territorial Army, while the SBS were regulars.

CHAPTER NINE

Pug takes on the Reds

Pug Davis was being sent to stop the Reds. It might have brought a few guffaws in the bar at Eastney as the 1950s dawned, but it was no joke to him or the military planners. The red shading on the map on their wall swung into a huge arc across Eastern Europe, the Soviet Union, China and down across Indo-China into Vietnam and North Korea. The Cold War was at freezing-point. There were Reds under every bed, rumours of spies in the British Secret Service, and Senator Joe McCarthy shot to fame with his Un-American Activities Committee alleging Communist infiltration of the Federal government of the United States.

Joseph Stalin, meanwhile, had made friendship pacts with the victorious Mao Zedong, given his support to Ho Chi Minh as leader of North Vietnam and likewise to Kim Il Sung, whose generals were at that moment planning the invasion of the southern half of Korea. But at the beginning of 1950, Germany once again was the focus of Europe's attention. The Soviets were pillaging their occupied eastern section and running it with an iron fist through their puppet government. Berlin became the centre of everything after the year-long blockade by the Russians ended in the summer of 1949, broken by the extraordinary airlift of Allied supplies to the city. Besieged by hundreds of thousands of East Germans fleeing to the West, the city was full of intrigue, swarming with black marketeers and flooded with agents and spies from all sides. It was the beginning of that era of Checkpoint Charlie, the Third Man and all that.

The creation of the Democratic Republic of Germany in October 1949 was worrying Britain and her NATO allies. After securing its domination of the Eastern Bloc, the Soviet Union had

125

effectively moved to the front door of the Western alliance. Would Stalin now push on into the rest of Germany? Alarm bells were ringing loudly through the corridors of Western military power. Speculation of an imminent Russian advance was sufficient for NATO commanders, with British and American agreement, to increase the number of their troops in West Germany and to form a strategic defence that included specific tasks for an SBS-style force.

In February 1950 Lieutenant Peter Davis, today 'the legendary Pug' to all his former colleagues, was ordered to form a detachment from the Small-Raids Wing in haste to join a Royal Navy Squadron on the Rhine. Davis recalled the moment for me, chatting at his home to which he had retired from the service with the rank of lieutenant-colonel. He joined the Royal Marines in 1942, was decorated, as mentioned earlier, for leading a landing-party to search for a British patrol from 2 Commando, and was one of the few 'hostilities-only' officers to become a regular after the war. 'The "w" word was being mentioned again,' he said. 'There was a real panic on.'

Having spent too much of his time in arranging frogmen demonstrations in the preceding few years, Pug was glad to be back in operational mode. He explained: 'NATO had by then drawn up an operational plan to meet a possible move forward by the Russians. The British Army of the Rhine (BAOR) would fall back to a position on the west bank of the river, which itself would then form a natural defended barrier to a Russian advance. And that's where we came in.'

With 1SBS committed elsewhere, Davis collected his new SRW detachment of 12 men to join the Royal Navy Rhine Flotilla, which became the RN Rhine Squadron, with about 250 men of all ranks, based at HMS *Royal Prince* at Krefeld on the Dutch border. The SRW detachment was known initially as the Royal Marines Demolition Unit, but Davis lost no time in preparing a paper on the possible tactical missions for his unit, from organisation to equipment. This he presented to the Staff Officer, Operations, of the Rhine Squadron, Major N. Tailyour, DSO RM, a supporter of the SBS, who submitted it to the Admiralty and won approval for the formation of 2SBS. The creation of the unit was completed in the summer of 1950, and manpower was increased later in the year and again in 1951 to create 3SBS. The SRW section based at Eastney was renamed Special Boat Wing to accommodate the revival of its operational activity.

The principal SBS role was to utilise the Rhine as the major defended obstacle to troop movements from the east. The men were tasked specifically to rehearse stay-behind parties on the eastern side as the British Army fell back. These parties would provide reconnaissance and intelligence reports on troop concentrations and carry out sabotage raids. The remainder of the SBS would, in the event of war, blow up barges that populated the river to prevent their use by the Russians and create hazards to crossings, attack bridges and generally make a nuisance of themselves. Their tasks required men with a high competence in swimming, diving and craft handling in fast-flowing waters, as well as an expert knowledge of demolitions.

The extent of the preparations, the potential involvement of the SBS and, to some degree, the seriousness with which this operation was being treated are seen in previously classified exchanges between the Rhine Squadron and the War Office in London in the latter half of 1950, viewed for this work. The squadron requested as a matter of urgency the supplies for SBS use of 10,000 limpets, hawser cutting charges to destroy enemy pontoon bridges, 31,000 pounds (14,000 kilogrammes) of plastic explosives, 11,000 detonators and 62,000 magnets to attach the charges. Unfortunately, the War Office could locate only 4,000 limpets in the British Army of the Rhine, although another 6,000 were said to be in British Army stores somewhere in England. It would attempt to retrieve them and supply them as soon as possible. Combined Operations Experimental Establishment was also alerted to begin trials on fixing limpets to wooden hulls, which were found in many of the Rhine craft.

Meanwhile, all around the SBS was the activity of the BAOR and the Rhine Flotilla itself. Preparations included full-scale exercises and training.

Captain Len Holmes BEM was an SBS corporal at the time of the West German crisis. He had been drafted to the Rhine to join the new 3SBS and found the place buzzing when he arrived. 'There was massive troop movement around the Rhine. The whole atmosphere was very tense,' Len recalled for me at his home.

Every day there seemed to be some sort of political reprisal or tit-for-tat exchanges going on, and everyone was very conscious of it. Certainly, the army manoeuvres or exercises were of sufficient strength to show the Russians we weren't there for our health. They were posturing too. We had major rehearsals in which all nations with soldiers on the Rhine took part: British, Americans, Canadians and French. Vast areas of Germany were turned into an exercise arena with literally thousands of men taking part. There were always a few casualties, quite a few people killed being run over by tanks or other accidents. It was pretty well unavoidable with the amount of weaponry and machinery about the place.

The SBS practised being left on the east bank of the Rhine and hiding up. These invariably started up travelling in a Jeep with a radio operator and two swimmer-canoeists. We would keep with the Jeep for as long as possible, until we got into an area where we would be able to see 'enemy' troops building up. It was only an exercise, but even so a very close simulation of the real thing. The Red troops were positioned and moving forward very much as the Russian Army would have done. So we moved around on country lanes until we reached an area where the Red troops were discovered and began reporting it. When the build-up of troops became so great that we could no longer use a vehicle without being discovered, we would ditch the Jeep and go off on foot into the countryside, all the time reporting the Red troop movements.

By that time most of us could speak some German, and we would hide up in local farms and villages. Some of them wondered what the hell we were doing, because we would be wearing pseudo-civilian clothes, blue trousers and old sweaters. Communications were difficult. We were still using wartime radio equipment, a massive, heavy thing in a suitcase, which hardly lent itself to clandestine work. The exercises were extremely realistic, and you knew full well that if you were captured by the Red troops you would spend a long time being interrogated and, believe me, that's a very uncomfortable experience. You got as good a grilling as you might expect from the enemy. All of us took them very seriously.

The Rhine Squadron which included 2 and 3SBS, was based at Krefeld, with a training area 25 miles away at Four Lakes Camp, near Venlo on the Dutch border, where they set up a hutted camp

128

in the woods and practised shooting and demolition training. Training in diving was performed in Moehne Dam. The camp was also to be the assembly site if war started.

Plenty of other tasks filled their time, such as diving in German rivers to locate equipment – even tanks! – lost during exercises. It was not uncommon for the tanks to be driven accidentally into the Rhine in darkness. Searching for them was a hazardous task in the fast-flowing waters because the exercise called for SBS divers to 'walk' the river to find the lost hardware. Len explained the procedure: a heavy-duty wire was strung across the river, which was around 200 metres wide, and seven or eight soldiers gripped each end. Eight SBS divers then went hand over hand and positioned themselves at intervals along the submerged line, which was walked downstream by the sappers on either bank until the tank was found. 'You could never see it,' said Holmes, 'because the water was pitch black. You made contact by running into it. Then the diver would pop up to the surface and shout: "Found One." The fast-flowing current at times reaching 7 knots (13 kilometres per hour) meant we were unable to leave marker floats. The positions were noted, and the tank would be dragged out by the army, once again using divers to attach wires. Of course, we couldn't stop the Rhine traffic while we were searching. If a barge came along, the sappers just let go of one end of the line and the divers were swept into the bank in a tangle of arms and legs.'

Still, as Len Holmes recalled, there were compensations, such as winter training, with skiing at Winterburg, Bavaria, where all SBS sections took part in the BAOR military ski patrol races. SBS sections also took part in the major BAOR exercises each year, such as Broadsword in 1950 and Counterthrust and Jupiter in 1951, with their numbers now swelled by the temporary inclusion of 4 and 5SBS formed from RM Force Volunteer Reserve. As the tension eased between the Soviet Union and the West, the German-based units found less taxing tasks in their itinerary, including two annual cruises down the Rhine to Holland to take part in sea-defence exercises and in the autumn up the Rhine to St Goar in time for the wine festival. Someone, at least, had a good nose for organisation!

Trouble was brewing on several other fronts – and running in tandem with the German expedition. First, Korea, south of Manchuria, with the Russians not far away through their port of

Vladivostok, Japan to the east and the Yellow Sea to the west. An SBS recce team would report on the mountainous peaks that ranged the full length of the Korean peninsula and on the icy winds that swept down from the Manchurian plateau.

The recce would show that the peninsula's east coast had virtually no tidal range, yet on the west it was as much as 36 feet (11 metres). A very tempting railway line wound through tunnels along the full length of the east coast between Hamhung and Ch'ongjin. This would be the first target of an SBS unit attached to a newly formed British contingent, 41 Independent Commando RM. The unit was mustered specifically for Korea and coastal raiding. It would stand for one year, perform the tasks that were needed of it, return home and disband.

History drew the battle-lines. In 1943 Western allies pledged to make Korea an independent state. When the Soviet Union joined the war against Japan, they insisted on a demarcation line along the thirty-eighth parallel, and as the Iron Curtain slammed shut Korea was split in two. On 25 June Kim Il Sung sent his troops south across the thirty-eighth parallel to pick up the other half of the country. It was an uneven match.

His armies were Soviet-trained and heavily equipped. Eight divisions led by mighty T34 tanks simply ran over the southern force, which was barely stronger than a gendarmerie. The South Koreans were backed into a corner with only light support from the United States.

The British Pacific Fleet was patrolling those waters west of Korea and was committed to the United Nations. The American 7th Fleet patrolled the east coast, which was more suited to amphibious operations. The US Marine Corps Historical Records Officer provides the following summary of the British involvement:

In August 1950, Admiral C. T. Joy, USN, Commander of the United Nations Naval Forces, suggested a small-scale raiding-force should be formed with the object of operating against the Communist lines of communication. The original intention was that this force should be composed of volunteers from the British Far Eastern Fleet [for rapid deployment]. However, it was decided to enlarge the original conception and send out a Royal Marines commando unit . . . to be placed under United States Naval Command and equipped and maintained by them.

Having accepted the invitation to provide such a force, the British found themselves in a quandary. The most suitable unit, 3 Commando Brigade RM, was already committed, fighting the terrorist campaign in Malaya. Plans to form a special unit were advanced quickly, and at the same time a small party of volunteers was sought from SBS units to run sabotage operations.

The commanding officer was given three weeks in which to recruit, train and prepare his force. Half of the men were drawn from Royal Marine establishments in the UK and the rest from a draft which was at that moment on its way to reinforce 3 Commando Brigade RM. The former were given a vast series of jabs and flown in haste to Japan in a chartered BOAC aircraft. Though hush-hush, a British newspaper got hold of the story and ran headlines: 'British Volunteer Unit for Korea'. In fact, the only volunteers were SBS and, according to archive reports, 'the reaction was swift . . . the CO received a host of letters from angry wives. They were concerned that it looked as if their husbands preferred service in faraway Korea to domestic bliss.' Several husbands also received some poignant letters of reprimand from anxious wives as the Korean situation flared up in newspaper coverage.

And so . . . 41 Independent Commando RM, joined by SBS volunteers and commanded by Lieutenant-Colonel D. B. Drysdale RM, were dispatched at once to a US naval base at Yokosuka. From there they were to be sailed to the east coast of Korea for Operation Double Eagle – operating as part of a US Army raiding-unit from the submarine USS *Perch* and assault personnel destroyers USS *Bass* and *Wontuck*.

Five SBS men were among the first in action, carried aboard *Perch* which has some historical significance, as the craft was the first troop-carrying submarine to be used in any raiding-operation of this kind. She was converted so she could carry a large number of men and a massive array of equipment that was capable of launching one motor boat, ten ten-man rubber boats and around seventy raiders with their stores.

For their first outing, the force embarked in late September 1950 and had a week to get used to life on board and carry out rehearsals. On 1 October they arrived off the target area on the east coast of Korea, where the railways and tunnels were visible. Periscope reconnaissance was carried out from the submarine submerged about seven miles offshore for a landing on the first night. However, a number of North Korean patrol boats were spotted, and they did not go away: mission aborted. The following night they were more successful and began their first operation, which set the pattern for months to come. The fear of mines and coastal radar forced *Perch* to stand off at around eight miles from the coast. There, she launched her light motor boat and ten inflatables with raiders aboard and then submerged. Using a telephone link to the surface craft, *Perch* towed the line of small inflatables to within five miles of the target area and then cast them off. The motor boat then towed the inflatables to within half a mile or so, and from there they were on their own, paddling. At 300 metres, the swimmers went in for a final recce, signalled the all-clear, and the raiding-party came ashore.

The men headed straight for their target, carrying anti-tank mines, which they laid beneath long stretches of the railway. They returned to the beach and prepared for the rendezvous with their motor boat and mother ship and had the satisfaction of hearing several huge explosions as a train came along.

Other SBS men had joined marines on *Bass* and *Wontuck*, both of which were able to sail closer to the shore during a misty, dark night. They launched their first assault party from three miles off, with landing-craft towing ten inflatables. Between them, they carried a cache of 4,410 pounds (2,000 kilogrammes) of explosives. The charges were placed in a tunnel, culverts and bridges. When they had exploded, the men went back and set anti-personnel mines in the craters of their explosions and hastily departed under enemy fire. It was during this retreat that the SBS lost one of theirs: Corporal Babbs, ironically one of the more experienced among them, and one of the few with operational parachute wings. Babbs accidentally shot himself while paddling his inflatable towards safety and did not recover from his injury.

After these initial sorties, 41 returned to Japan to be re-assigned to the US Marines at the very time the Chinese threw in its lot with North Vietnam. SBS reinforcements were waiting, including Sergeant Sticks Dodds, along with equipment and canoes. They began going ashore in two-man parties for recce and sabotage missions, which were carried out with considerable success – provided they had been given the correct intelligence, and that was not always the case.

In February Dodds and his number two, Corporal Edmonds,

were sent to ambush an enemy convoy as it passed a certain point in the coast road; they were to set charges and blow up the road as the convoy passed. They were briefed on the mission on board USS *Wontuck* by a CIA man, who claimed to know the beach well and told them to look for a large building at one end.

They paddled for miles, up and down the coast, trying to find the building but saw no sign of it. Finally, they went ashore and discovered that the building was in fact a large rock. The CIA had misread aerial reconnaissance photographs. The delay allowed the enemy convoy to pass through unhindered, but Dodds and Edmonds blew up the road anyhow.

Apart from one daylight raid in April, all the unit's tasks were clandestine missions performed at night. As the RM Corps Historical Records Officer noted: 'Most of the personnel were permanently based in islands off Wonsan on the east coast of Korea some 60 miles behind enemy lines. From here they carried out raids that varied from two-man canoes to forty men in rubber inflatables. Tasks included beach reconnaissance, capture of prisoners, blowing up railways, ambushing roads, and generally keeping the enemy occupied on his lines of communication.'

Both SBS and marines had become skilled in close approach work in rubber boats and canoes. Unlike British tactics of canoe pairs, the Americans preferred mob-handed missions, with charges carried by humping-parties, laid by assault engineers, while a covering force would form a defensive circle around them. It would take around four hours to lay the charges in 10-pound (4.5-kilogramme) packs connected in a ring with cordtex for simultaneous detonation.

Once the fuses had been pulled, and the order to withdraw given, the force would fan out again, return in a line to the beach and re-embark under the direction of a beach-master until all were clear. They would paddle out to the waiting landing-craft, which would begin the long tow back to the waiting ships. Although the US Navy was officially dry, officers would invariably break out the medicinal brandy after a successful operation.

As their stay progressed, one troop established an advance base on Yo Do Island, with motors, tents, landing-craft and canoes, and were joined later by other marines to launch clandestine missions. Another troop did the same on Modo Island, establishing a more permanent outpost – only to have it temporarily flattened by a typhoon – from which to carry out mainland recces.

Other, smaller groups established observation posts among the outer islands, where they would remain for up to two weeks at a time.

Towards the end of the year, their activity was toned down while the United Nations tried to get peace talks under way. Although it would take another two years, and a good deal more fighting, before armistice was finally achieved, 41 Independent Commando RM formally stood down in December 1951 and disbanded on its return to England on 22 February 1952. SBS men returned to Eastney, minus two: Corporal Babbs and Sergeant C. E. Barnes, the latter killed in engaging the enemy during a raid; he had been Mentioned in Dispatches. Sergeant Dodds collected another medal, the DSM, to add to his MM from Haifa.

'So ended an eventful year,' wrote an RM historian who was there, 'involving most types of operations . . . Many lessons were learned and many friendships cemented . . . A great experience and one which no one who served in 41 Independent Commando is likely to forget.'

CHAPTER TEN

To save a king

The SBS men returning from Korea brought with them stories of an experience remembered. They rabbited on about the gear, the abundance of stores, good weapons and good food. No hunting around for equipment, as they had to do in 1950s Britain, which was still in the grip of severe austerity. The armed forces were no less focused on their spending habits than the rest of the population. Politicians demanded cuts. Prudence was a regular visitor.

Major Hugh Bruce, RM, was used to making do and mending in Colditz and had to do something similar when he took over command of the SBS. As he told me:

> On the one hand we were charged with encouraging new recruits during a period of moderate expansion through demands of military activity in the Far East. On the other, our range of equipment was pretty old stuff, largely from wartime stock and quite inadequate to meet current needs. Homing devices were primitive, navigation aids almost non-existent, beach survey equipment was made up of curios and museum artefacts, and clothing and suits were poor and of the wrong material. It was all very well to say that we were keeping in touch with wartime techniques, and indeed teaching them to trainees and trainers, but it really was a burden to have to use wartime equipment too.

To top it all, the Joint Intelligence Bureau produced a study criticising the lack of beach intelligence both in the UK and areas abroad in which Britain had a specific interest, and Operation Sandstone was launched in early 1950 as a joint task between the hydrographic section of the Royal Navy and the SBS. The navy were to survey British beaches and the SBS were to do the same abroad over coming months and years. Most were done clandestinely without the knowledge of the country's government. COPPs equipment extracted from the remains of their wartime stores was largely used. More modern equipment came along eventually, but the style and report format were virtually the same as those created by Nigel Clogstoun Willmott.

Hugh Bruce, then a captain, came to the SRW/SBS in the early 1950s and brought a new impetus in terms of leading from the front. Bruce, a strong, forceful man, scared of nothing and no one, was liked by all. His own background lacked the cut and thrust of SBS field action, but he made up for it in other ways. He was taken prisoner during the defence of Calais in 1940 and took no further part in the war, at least not on any military front. Like all the British in German prison camps, he felt it his duty to escape and get back home. He worked on numerous escape schemes and got out himself three times, spending many weeks on the loose before being recaptured on each occasion, usually through betrayal.

Finally, the Germans took him to Colditz, along with other famous escapers and personalities such as David Stirling and Douglas Bader, where he spent two and a half years on the escape committee, planning the breakouts later famously re-enacted in books, film and a television series. 'In the process,' Bruce recalled, 'I learned much about disguise, deception, impersonation and some of the skills of moving through enemy countryside at night and lying up during the day. I learned about travelling incognito and how to forge papers.'

Like many in the SBS, he was a canoeing and yachting fanatic, navigated for yachts of several nations and took part in several transatlantic races. He also formed the RM Canoe Club and broke the record for a two-man canoe crossing of the English Channel and came second in the 124-mile Devizes to Westminster canoe race in 35 hours and 7 minutes. So, the SBS had a generally good egg at the helm at a particularly crucial time.

When he arrived, first to head up training and later to take over as officer commanding, Bruce discovered that the SBS – though reactivated on the back of a training school – had no current instruction manuals. He created, typed and bound three volumes as aids for instructors. Later he wrote the handbook, too, entitled

SBS: Capabilities and Techniques. It was an uphill struggle without finance and resources. Bruce recalled:

> Training and safety were paramount. Every operation, every exercise, needs a full recce, complete information; otherwise you are courting disaster – as happened so often in the past, when men went barging in without full knowledge of what might confront them. It's no good training up men who are going to get put out of action on their first operation through lack of knowledge, fitness or not being sufficiently skilled in the use of equipment, or indeed of not having the right equipment at all. SBS operators for all grades faced a pretty stiff selection procedure, and the pass-rate was incredibly low because of the standards demanded.

At the beginning of 1952 Bruce suddenly found he could use the cheque-book again. This brief and welcome respite from cash starvation had less to do with the current well-being of the SBS than an operation for which he had just received his top-secret orders. He had been instructed to prepare for a clandestine recce in advance of a possible evacuation of British nationals from Egypt. At least, that was the cover story. It was almost certainly untrue, and he was never told exactly what the operation was intended for because he never actually got to the point of 'need to know'. The jigsaw can now be pieced together.

Bruce was allowed to purchase new equipment previously requested and refused, including new drysuits for beach reconnaissance, swimmers and reels to develop distance and sounding lines, bought from Ogden's Fishing Shop in St James's Street, London. Why? The countdown to what history now terms the Suez Fiasco had begun.

King Farouk was in trouble. The dissolute and bulbous playboy monarch, last surviving member of the Mohammed Ali dynasty, which had ruled Egypt since the early 1800s, was on the verge of being ousted. Rumours of his imminent demise through assassination or some other non-accidental misfortune were rife, and he was holed up with resident harem in his magnificent Ras-el-Tin Palace in Alexandria. Gamal Abdel Nasser, head of the Society of Free Officers and courted by the Soviets, was dedicated to liberating Egypt from what he considered its three main evils: the monarchy, imperialism and feudalism.

Although the British government had withdrawn its troops from Alexandria and Cairo in the late 1940s, it could barely contemplate the risk of losing control of the Suez Canal. Two world wars had demonstrated the importance of the waterway to British security and trade. Britain retained a heavily manned base that had grown, Topsy-like, along the west bank and had become the last great monument to the country's military and economic strength in the Middle East and North Africa. Nasser wanted them out. Britain, in company with France and other foreigners, had run his country for too long.

Nasser was talking loudly about cancelling the Suez Canal Treaty, and King Farouk was shuddering in his palace. Back in Britain, Hugh Bruce was studying his secret orders. The plan, that March, was to send destroyers into King Farouk's private harbour, 10 miles east of Alexandria, ostensibly to rescue British nationals but more likely, in the first instance, to bring out Farouk himself. No one was saying. Bruce was to take a recce party to get the lie of the land; he gathered five of his best operators and flew to Malta.

More details emerged. The staff of the Commander-in-Chief, Malta, had drawn up a plan to send the SBS party into Alexandria by merchant ship. They would wear civilian clothes and, on reaching the harbour, transfer to a dory to conduct their clandestine recce. Bruce was not at all happy with the plan and put forward an alternative: they would be taken by submarine as close as possible to the harbour and travel the remaining distance by canoe. Their swimmers would then go over the side, complete their recce and return to their canoes and to the submarine. This was accepted, and the team spent the next couple of weeks rehearsing and training. But Bruce began to get a distinct feeling that the operation was becalmed. Sure enough, after six weeks in Malta it was aborted and the SBS unit returned to base in early April.

By the end of May the operation was on again. Lord Mountbatten was now in charge, having just arrived in Malta as Commander-in-Chief of the British Fleet in the Mediterranean. Captain Bruce was otherwise engaged, and so he sent Lieutenant H. B. Emslie, MC, RM, to lead the party. The men were flown to North Africa and then travelled on to Tobruk to join the submarine HMS *Teredo* under the command of Lieutenant-Commander L. D. Hamlyn.

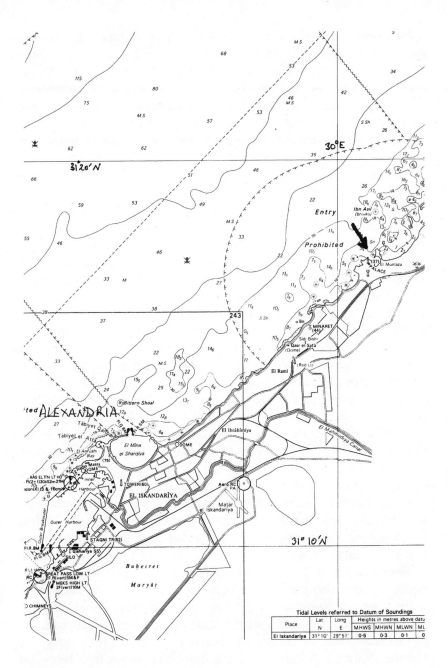

Beach recce for King Farouk's palace.

139

Hamlyn was also kept short of detail. Mountbatten told him to leave Malta and proceed westwards and await further instructions – and, by the way, 'Keep your mouth shut afterwards!' About what, Hamlyn had yet to discover. While at sea he received a signal to proceed to Tobruk. There, he learned he was to take the SBS party aboard, with the intention of floating the men off in canoes at Alexandria. They carried out a few hurried rehearsals by day on a deserted beach, and then the submarine headed off to Alexandria, intending to drop the SBS team about three miles from Farouk's harbour.

Under starlight, four of the team left the submarine in two canoes and paddled in closer. The swimmers, Lieutenant Emslie and Sergeant Moorehouse, made a final check of their suits and equipment, put their writing-tablets over their wrists, slipped into the water and swam into the harbour, splitting up when they were close enough to begin their individual tasks.

The submarine remained at a discreet distance until dawn, when Emslie and his partner returned, their recce completed. SBS Marine Geordie Vardy, keeping watch on the bridge with night binoculars, spotted the second canoe heading back but with only one man, Marine Langton, aboard. Langton reported that his swimmer, Sergeant Moorehouse, had not made the rendezvous.

Hamlyn ordered the submarine to dive and set a course for the pre-arranged alternative rendezvous, ten miles away to the south-west. As they approached it, they found an Egyptian sonar-operating frigate with an aircraft circling above, seemingly on a joint search. Hamlyn thought this was too much of a coincidence and headed back out to sea and signalled to the C-in-C, Malta, for instruction. He was told to make for Port Said, though was given no explanation.

The mystery of Sergeant Moorehouse's whereabouts began to unravel. After completing the recce of his designated zone, two sentries sitting smoking on the harbour wall delayed his exit and he missed the rendezvous with his canoeist, Marine Langton. So he had to swim for it, out of the harbour and down the coast towards his next rendezvous. After travelling about five miles, he ditched his one-piece swimming-suit so that he would not be too heavily questioned if caught, and then, wearing only his under-pants, stopped for a rest. Moorehouse was discovered – according to his own account – resting on a buoy by a coastguard patrol boat to whom he told his cover story that he had fallen overboard on a fishing trip.

He was taken ashore and asked to be put in touch with the Royal Navy or the embassy. Eventually he was taken under escort dressed in Arab clothes to Fayid, half-way along the Suez Canal, where he was handed over to Major Gordon Sillars, RM, of naval intelligence. He was given more appropriate clothes and sent to Port Said. When Lieutenant-Commander Hamlyn arrived in *Teredo*, he found him waiting on the jetty.

The navy had apparently asked the Egyptians for help in locating a man lost during an exercise, which accounted for the fact that there was an aircraft and frigate searching the second rendezvous spot. Moorehouse had not revealed the true reason why he was out alone, almost naked in the water, and the Egyptians seemed satisfied with the explanation.

To Lieutenant-Commander Hamlyn, the episode remained annoyingly unexplained. He was never told of the purpose of the mission, was not involved in its planning, nor debriefed at the end of it. Moorehouse was not entirely frank with him, either, when he was questioned aboard as to what exactly happened. Moorehouse died some years ago, and Emslie was killed on active service. Today, Major Bruce believes that the operation achieved its aim in making a full recce of Farouk's harbour.

The lack of information supplied to the operatives at the centre of this intrigue was and, to a degree, still is fairly typical. MI6 and the CIA hovered in the background of this particular mission. The CIA were clandestinely funding Nasser because it was against the British policy of attempting to make the corrupt monarchy work. The British hoped to keep Farouk alive and well, and hopefully return him to power if Nasser staged a coup. Farouk was to be rescued by a raiding-party if a coup seemed imminent.

In the end, the good work of the SBS team wasn't necessary. On 23 July 1952 Nasser seized power, and the same evening he peacefully ejected his unwanted king, who was allowed to sail comfortably away to the fleshpots of Europe, his possessions stowed in 200 trunks. But, of course, that wasn't the end of the matter . . . not by a long chalk.

Hugh Bruce was already planning another series of events that eventually became tiresome because, again, they were not what the SBS was about. 'That didn't stop us throwing everything into

141

them,' said Len Holmes, who took part, 'and especially Hugh Bruce. He was hard physically and mentally, and his big claim to fame from the SBS point of view was his meticulous planning. And what came next was not going to be any different.' The Admiralty had commissioned the SBS to test the security of all Royal Navy bases and air stations throughout Britain with saboteur or terrorist-type penetration that the SBS was itself famous for, intermittently over a period of several months. This was to be followed up with an extensive infiltration exercise against submarine defences on the Clyde, with raiding-parties using both surface and submersible canoes. Len Holmes recalls:

> On the face of it they were exercises that sounded pretty innocuous. Boring, we all thought. But Bruce had souped them up so that they were as close to the real thing as you could possibly get – even to the point of cutting wire fences, charging in with a lorry packed with SBS raiders, clearing buildings filled with 300 to 400 matelots with tear-gas, and making one helluva racket. When it became known on the grapevine that the SBS was attacking bases, it became extremely hazardous, with our small group being confronted by a large crowd of sailors carrying pickaxe handles.

Bruce's mock base attacks unknowingly laid ground rules for the future, when the SBS was charged with creating a maritime protection force for the security of Britain's coastal oil-rigs, offshore installations, and for counter-measures when the IRA began targeting mainland military bases. Bruce's time in command was also marked by the development of many new SBS training techniques. He initiated experimental work on the underwater release of SBS operatives from submarines, making it unnecessary for the vessel to surface.

He also began extensive trials dropping SBS raiders, their boats and stores by air, landing them by parachute into the sea close to the target area, saving the problem of the need for a submarine to hang around in hostile waters. It was the first time ever that the SBS dropped swimmers already dressed in full underwater kit, oxygen diving apparatus and fins. One other important development was the introduction of the first custom-designed underwater breathing sets for use by SBS teams. Colour-Sergeant Jock Swan received the Herbert Lott prize for work on this project. Piece by piece the SBS was building its stock-in-trade for the developing needs.

Curiously enough, it was also underwater work that led the SBS into a period of temporary decline, a time when, through no fault of its own, few called on its services to the point where it was almost being shunned. The troubles arose merely by association with the generic term of frogman following an MI6-sponsored mission that ended in disaster and brought unexpected implications for the SBS.

To the underwater fraternity at large, Commander Lionel 'Buster' Crabb was something of a legend. He made his name in Gibraltar in the early stages of the Second World War when, with hopelessly inadequate equipment, he led Britain's first team of frogmen to combat the attacks by Italian underwater teams on Allied shipping at Gibraltar. As we have seen in earlier chapters, the Italian 10th Flotilla, with piloted torpedoes, well-trained divers kitted out with flexible rubber suits, breathing gear and swimfins, and exploding motor boats, was causing havoc in Mediterranean harbours under Allied control, and especially at Gibraltar. The Italians' most spectacular successes came in 1941 and 1942, attaching warheads and mines to the hulls of British ships.

Buster Crabb was 32 years old and could barely swim the length of a swimming-pool on the surface when he joined the battle against the Italians in November 1942. Nor did his background recommend him for such work. After an apprenticeship in the Merchant Navy, he had lately been drifting aimlessly, with a variety of jobs ranging from petrol-pump attendant to selling advertising space.

His only pre-war contact with the water was through a friend who was trying to market the invention of a Frenchman who had designed a pair of rubber swimfins for flippers which Crabb personally had little faith in. At the outbreak of war, he volunteered for the Royal Naval Volunteer Reserve but was rejected on account of his age, and he returned to merchant shipping as a gunner on a tanker. A year later he managed to transfer to the Royal Naval Patrol Service and then volunteered for special duties, which led him eventually to join a Royal Naval Mine and Bomb Disposal Unit. He took a two-week course in explosives, and that was sufficient for him to be given a commission to lieutenant and, soon, to lead the Royal Navy's hastily prepared Underwater Working Party in Gibraltar.

There, two Royal Navy divers, equipped with the most primitive breathing gear, swam around and under Allied ships looking for mines and warheads. The original plan was to bring the charges to land, where Crabb, as bomb-disposal officer, would disarm them. That was often impracticable, and Crabb was soon dealing with the charges himself below the surface, never knowing when they might explode and take him with them. From then on, his contribution to the Allied war effort was remarkable, filled with acts of tremendous courage and endurance. Fear was not a word in his vocabulary, and he and his colleagues in the naval team pushed themselves and the boundaries of safe diving to the very limit.

After the war Crabb found himself once again in limbo. He devised many money-making schemes to utilise his skills, from discovering the size of fish shoals for herring trawlers sailing out of Great Yarmouth to underwater photography. He turned up at the SBS headquarters when Pug Davis was running the frogman demonstrations – 'and he still couldn't swim far on the surface,' Davis told me. Crabb was re-called periodically by the Royal Navy as a member of the RNVR and helped in the search for the lost submarine, *Affray*. He was employed on occasional and secret missions for British intelligence, including one still-classified 'underwater job' in the Suez Canal zone in 1953 and the examination of the Russian cruiser *Sverdlov* when she visited Portsmouth in 1955.

In April 1956 Crabb, then 46 years old, was overweight, unfit and in debt when he was approached for another intelligence mission. An agent of MI6 contacted him and outlined a proposal for a particularly sensitive task – to examine the bottom of an important Russian cruiser, the *Ordzhonikidze*, when she arrived in Portsmouth with an escort of two battleships, carrying the two Soviet leaders, Khrushchev and Bulganin, on a goodwill visit.

While MI5 were bugging the hotel rooms of the two leaders in London, MI6 hired Crabb to investigate the hull of the cruiser. Although never publicly revealed, it can now be confirmed that MI6 wanted Crabb to measure the cruiser's propeller and to discover how the ship could travel at twice the speed originally estimated by British naval intelligence. The Royal Navy urgently wanted this information. MI6 itself was also anxious to listen into the ship's cipher machine transmissions to try to break the cipher.

An attempt had been made to inspect the cruiser when she came into British waters a year earlier, using the one remaining serviceable X-Craft mini-submarine which MI6 kept at Stokes Bay, three miles from Portsmouth. On that occasion the mission had been aborted because of tight security around the ship.

On 17 April Crabb checked in at the nondescript Sallyport Hotel, Portsmouth, using his own name, accompanied by a tall, blond-haired man aged about 40, who signed himself in as 'Smith'. The following day Crabb had a reunion meeting in Portsmouth with some old friends from the Gibraltar era. That was the last anyone outside MI6 saw of him. He was not seen leaving the hotel on the nineteenth, but as dawn broke on that day he was taken by a small launch from Portsmouth harbour to a suitable distance offshore, donning his diving gear as they went.

He took an oxygen breathing set so that no bubbles could be seen on the surface. At safe range, he slipped over the side and swam towards the target ship well aware that he might have to dive below the 33-feet (10-metre) safety margin for oxygen breathing gear. What happened next remains a mystery; all that can be said is that Crabb got into some kind of difficulty – either through a heart attack, oxygen poisoning, getting caught in the propeller blades or being captured by the Russians.

When he did not return, panic hit the MI6 operatives managing the operation – and it rose all the way to Cabinet level. Feverish attempts to keep the developing fiasco from public view merely enhanced the mystery. Three days later 'Mr Smith' arrived and paid the bill for the hotel rooms for both of them, in cash, and took away Crabb's belongings. The newspapers had already got wind of Crabb's disappearance but had been put off from publishing the story by an Admiralty spokesman, who claimed that Crabb's next of kin had yet to be informed. On 29 April the Admiralty finally put out a statement claiming that Crabb had disappeared and was presumed dead after 'failing to return from a test dive in connection with trials of certain underwater appara-tus'. On the same day a detective superintendent from the Portsmouth force arrived at the Sallyport Hotel and removed four pages from the hotel register, warning the hotel owner to say nothing to anyone since the matter was covered by the Official Secrets Act.

On 4 May Prime Minister Anthony Eden, faced with mounting

pressure for an explanation of what exactly had occurred, ducked behind the barrier of national security:

> It would not be in the public interest to disclose the circumstances in which Commander Crabb is presumed to have met his death . . . It is necessary in the special circumstances of this case to make it clear that what was done was done without the authority or knowledge of Her Majesty's Ministers. Appropriate disciplinary steps are being taken.

Hugh Gaitskell, leader of the Opposition, retorted: 'The suspicion must inevitably arise that your refusal to make a statement on this subject is not so much in the interests of public security but to hide a very grave blunder.'

The Soviets promptly added their own contribution with letters of indignant protest. The Soviets' note stated that a frogman had been spotted at around 7.30 a.m. on 19 April, swimming between the Soviet ships. The British reply conceded that was a possibility, but that Commander Crabb's presence within the vicinity of the Soviet ships was totally without authorisation and was regretted.

The absence of a body and the scent of espionage brought days of newspaper speculation, discussing the possibility that Crabb had been captured, perhaps tortured, even taken to Moscow by the KGB. Finally, a Commons debate on his disappearance was granted on 14 May and lasted for more than an hour and a half. Gaitskell once again laid into the government and to the secret service, which was 'patently mixed up in this affair', although he added that he recognised that the nation would be poorer without men like Buster Crabb. Anthony Eden deplored the debate and insisted that national interests were of first importance. 'I confess,' he said, 'that all I care about is that our discussions with the Soviet leaders should in truth prove to be the beginning of a beginning . . .'

The mystery only deepened when a headless body of a frogman was washed up on the shore and was tentatively identified as Crabb's. Much later, further intrigue was added by the claim by Soviet defector Anatoli Golitsin that the Soviets had been forewarned of the impending visit to their ship by Crabb through a security leak from within MI6.

In the bloodletting that followed the débâcle in the higher regions of MI6, there was a throwback to all associated agencies, and to frogmen in particular – which in turn meant the SBS. For months afterwards the very mention of underwater activity brought a minor knee-jerk reaction among the naval and military hierarchy.

Lord Mountbatten had no such qualms. He had recently doubled his area of responsibility with his additional appointment as Allied Commander-in-Chief, Mediterranean, in which role he reported direct to the Supreme Allied Command, Europe. Now, in addition to his role as Commander-in-Chief of the British Fleet, he had the authority of NATO over the French, Italian, Greek and Turkish admirals, each commanding their national navies in the Mediterranean, and consultative powers with the American 6th Fleet.

Among his immediate NATO tasks was to prepare an immediate plan to prevent Russian submarines from leaving the Black Sea in the event of war. This, he proposed, should be achieved by the laying of a complex system of mines. These plans, and the focus on other regions around the Mediterranean where sabres were being rattled, such as Cyprus, Egypt, Libya, other parts of North Africa and the Arab oil states, brought a renewed urgency for beach reconnaissance for the Joint Intelligence Bureau. This was to be given priority treatment, overseen by AI9, a sub-section of JIB, and a major reconnaissance programme was set in motion which would go on from the mid-1950s well into the 1960s.

The JIB would require hugely detailed reports, charts and photographs which, in the main, could be obtained only by clandestine methods, inserting SBS men in civilian clothes disguised as tourists or locals. This brought fresh demands on the SBS. Mountbatten's own liking for small raiding-parties and recce teams, along with general intelligence-gathering, was the background to the hurried formation of 6SBS in Malta.

Recruiting the group fell to Pug Davis, who was about to join 42 Commando when 3 Commando Brigade, Royal Marines, returned from the Far East and took up residence in Malta. Initially, Davis recruited from the ranks of 42 Commando, which was a far from satisfactory arrangement, given the training and expertise required for beach recce and other SBS specialist tasks. A few months later the RM Commandant General formalised the establishment of the Malta party, and a new section, with one officer and ten other ranks, was formed in the UK and posted immediately to Malta, where it would for many months hence concentrate on the beach recce work required by the JIB, along with a busy schedule of other tasks. Training and development exercises were carried out around the waters of Malta, and it was an easy launch-place for other rapid missions of both recce and insertion. The exercises came as a prelude to the Suez crisis of 1956.

On 13 June the last British troops had been withdrawn from the Suez Canal garrison, where they had been for so long. The canal was to remain in the hands of the Anglo-French Suez Canal Company, which had originally constructed it. Before the month was out, President Nasser nationalised the company, beginning a series of events that some would compare to a Greek tragedy.

Eden dithered for months, and by September the Chiefs of Staff were being ordered to prepare for a full-scale invasion of Egypt, codenamed Operation Musketeer, supported by the French with some side action by the Israelis. Mountbatten was among vociferous opponents to the very last. As a serving officer, he could do no more than comply or resign, which he contemplated doing.

At Poole, 1SBS had been placed on alert, and within days half the section was given orders to proceed at once in support of Operation Musketeer to conduct a clandestine operation in Alexandria. They were given a specific task: to cut cables drawn across the harbour entrance which were being used as a boom to prevent ships from entering. Before leaving the UK, 1SBS carried out deep-dive experiments using charges. The noise was so loud, however, that a thermic cutting lance activated by oxygen was specially developed by the Admiralty Materials Laboratory at Holton Heath.

The SBS team, led by David Leigh, left by Sutherland flying boat as civilian passengers. They flew to Malta, where they were kept apart from 6SBS for security reasons. They had a further rehearsal in Malta which included practising departure and return with cutting gear from the submarine HMS *Totem*. Four canoes loaded with their equipment would be floated off. They would paddle as close as they could under darkness to Alexandria harbour, where four swimmers would go over the side and complete their task. Political uncertainty intervened. Operation Musketeer was stalled, revised and then given a new direction, and 1SBS was re-called to the UK.

Next, there was curious talk of a plan to assassinate Nasser

148

using SAS/SBS-type raiders. The hare-brained scheme was supposedly invented by MI6 and was said to have been 'favourably viewed' by Eden, though it was never activated. One of the reasons was that in the intervening period most of MI6 'assets' in Cairo had been uncovered and neutralised by Nasser, with a little help from the Soviets acting on information supplied by the British traitor Kim Philby.

The SBS was mobilised once more. Lieutenant Henry Musto, Officer Commanding, 6SBS, in Malta, was ordered to prepare his section for a submarine-borne mission off the north coast of Egypt, ahead of British landings. The men were to prepare a detailed recce of the beach landing-sites. Musto found the plan full of inherent dangers. Nasser's army was well equipped in surveillance, radar and coastal monitoring. The closest the submarine could get to deliver the SBS was 12 nautical miles (22 kilometres) offshore. The men would have to paddle to the coast in manual canoes and come ashore on a bland coastline that offered virtually no protection or cover; more than likely they would be shot to pieces.

Just before they were due to sail, the task was cancelled. Instead, 6SBS boarded HMS *Ocean* with 3 Commando Brigade bound for Port Said. The British paras dropped in to coincide with a landing of commandos on 6 November, five days after the British jet bombers taking off from Cyprus bombarded military installations around Cairo and the Suez Canal zone. The French landed in Port Fuad and the Israelis invaded from the east. Tough fighting ensued, though British casualties were light.

The attack was, as history would show, ill-timed and ill-judged. The commandos went in on the day of the US presidential elections and quickly gained control of the docks, the airports and the outskirts of the city. The American government of General Eisenhower was openly hostile to Prime Minister Eden when it learned of the attack. Thirty-six hours later, the United Nations imposed a ceasefire. Britain retreated with humiliation. Eden and his Suez masterplan were finished, and King Farouk spent the remaining nine years of his life gambling and womanising in Monaco.

Farouk wasn't the only monarch that the SBS got involved with. In 1959, a drama developed in Libya, where Britain's good friend, King Idris, seemed destined for a fate similar to King Farouk's.

Intelligence sources had uncovered an assassination plot by left-wing opponents supported by factions in the military. Idris immediately fled to his fortified palace in the desert and appealed to the British for assistance. The Foreign Office in London alerted Malta, who put 6SBS *en route* to Tripoli. A contingency plan would be worked out on the way. Somehow, they were going to reach the palace and, if necessary, get the king out. By the time they reached their point of assault, however, some gunboat diplomacy had achieved its desired effect and the SBS men were stood down. King Idris negotiated a token 'invasion' by 3 Commando Brigade, RM, as a demonstration that the British were on his side. When the forthcoming arrival of the commandos was made known, the threat to the king's well-being evaporated. He continued to live on a knife-edge and survived for another ten years before a group of revolutionary army officers, led by a young subaltern named Muammar Gaddafi, seized power while the king was visiting Turkey.

The SBS did not waste the journey to Libya. The men conducted beach recces along the whole stretch of coastline between Tobruk and Tripoli, where some of the waters were still mined from the Second World War. In fact, the SBS was still continuing with its task of beach reconnaissance on all coastlines designated by the Joint Intelligence Bureau. They landed on Cyprus, for example, at the height of the EOKA terrorist campaign and, under the guise of civilians having a beach party, surveyed numerous beaches that would be suitable for troop landings should they become necessary. By the turn of the decade, few coastlines of strategic interest around the Mediterranean had not been charted. Elsewhere more pressing matters were occurring . . .

South-East Asia.

151

Techniques learned in the Second World War were soon being called upon. *Above:* a team of divers won medals for their work clearing limpet mines from troopships in Haifa during the Israeli crisis of 1948, Sergeant 'Sticks' Dodds and Lieutenant Henry Musto (*left and centre*) were both future Officers Commanding, SBS.

Below: SBS teams joined 41 Independent Commando RM and US troops in the early stages of the Korean War to lead sabotage teams blowing up railways and vital installations, landing on a hostile coastline in their canoes and inflatables from submarines and ships stationed up to five miles offshore. *(Royal Marines Museum)*

Beach reconnaissance remained a crucial task after the Second World War and canoes remained a principal craft: here Len Holmes, a long-serving SBS member instructs new recruits.

The scene looked casual enough and their equipment in austere post-war days was described by one commanding officer as consisting of curios and museum artefacts. It fell to the SBS to make detailed charts and reports on dozens of beaches and landing areas throughout the 1960s in such sensitive zones as the Middle East, North Africa and the Federation of Malaysia (see Appendix II).

One for the album: in the Second World War, they were sabotaging each other's ships and coastal installations. In Malta, in 1959, 6SBS carried out numerous exercises with their Italian counterparts of Reparto Sabotatori Paracadutisti.

Training and exercises still account for much of SBS non-operational time. This 1960s sequence of training photographs captures the reality of launching canoe teams from submarine casing in a relatively calm sea. In a hostile situation, they get only one chance . . .

Small inflatable craft, like the one above, were developed for use in the Second World War, mainly for downed pilots, and eventually adopted by the SBS as an alternative (though not a replacement) to canoes. An outboard motor was later added – in this case an Atco lawn-mower engine.

Early multi-personnel carriers were a precarious mode of transport through choppy seas.

Faster, more powerful inflatables developed through the 1960s and 1970s brought added dimensions to SBS ability to insert both small and large raiding parties.

A four-man SBS patrol with stores and equipment required to put just two swimmer-canoeists into the water en route to a target in the Arctic during a 1972 exercise. The men had exited from a dived submarine with their gear, then skied across country and spent some time lying up, before finally swimming to the target and returning by the same route.

CHAPTER ELEVEN

Undrinkable claret

Now the SBS is in the jungle, answering the call of a Company Commander in 42 Commando RM. Out of the torrid, monsoon-drenched undergrowth, with perspiration patches under his arms and down his back, strolls Pug Davis, a little more rotund now but as pugnacious as ever. He's running Pugforce in the Borneo 'confrontation'. There standing before him is tall and lanky Sergeant Len Holmes, reporting for duty.

First it was Germany and drowning tanks. Then Malta and all that, and now the sergeant and his section are in some godforsaken sweatland of the Far East, where headhunters abound, to paddle their canoes down mosquito-infested waterways, taking care not to hit the booby traps, holed up in unprotected lookout posts in the middle of mangrove swamps, surrounded by guerrillas ready to cut them to ribbons at first chance and mingling with Gurkhas, supposedly their friends, ready to do the same if Len doesn't give the right bird-call when entering camp!

Pug's call to the wild was welcomed. The life-blood of the SBS was being 'tasked', as it still is. One of those latter-day stalwarts, Captain Neil Johnstone, an SBS officer for almost 30 years, made the same point as many of those interviewed for this book: 'Special Forces can only thrive if they are being tasked. Without tasks, we're not working . . . If we're not working, people start to question our *raison d'être*.'

The core of SBS operations moved to the Far East as Britain attempted to oversee the orderly transfer of independence to its far-flung colonial outposts. The Malayan campaign had kept British forces busy virtually since the end of the Second World War as they battled guerrilla opponents to the creation of the

Federation of Malayan States, later to become Malaysia. The SAS was reactivated into regular service with the formation of 22SAS with four squadrons. At the end of the campaign it was reduced to two again as Whitehall once more cut the defence budget.

The SBS had only a brief involvement in Malaya, when a section was formed from the ranks of 3 Commando Brigade specifically to find and capture a guerrilla leader. In 1961 a decade of political and military manoeuvres in Malaya seemed on the brink of collapsing. Military analysts were predicting a Communist 'domino' effect throughout South-East Asia. Americans would soon be pouring into Vietnam, the French having retired hurt.

Britain was committed to a heavy slice of action through its three dependencies on the island of Borneo. There, it was responsible for the defence of the Sultanate of Brunei and the colonies of North Borneo (later Sabah) and Sarawak.

Those states, it was hoped, would join the Federation of Malayan States to form a powerful and stable alliance. The 'Mad Doctor' Sukarno, president of Indonesia, was doing his damnedest to prevent it. The three British protectorates shared borders with Kalimantan, the Indonesian region of Borneo which accounted for three-quarters of its land surface. Sukarno wanted control of the remainder, to add seven and a half million inhabitants to the hundred million he already ruled. His further ambitions, inspired apparently by the Japanese plan in the Second World War, was to take over the whole of the Malayan states, with it the plum target of Singapore.

In 1961 he was poised to continue. For a year or more, Britain had been engaged in quelling riots in Brunei, largely locally inspired but fuelled by Sukarno. Guerrilla forces, backed by Indonesia, were also playing havoc in the other two dependencies by attacking strategic installations. In the same year the British government approved a hurried, if limited, military response from an initial force drawn from the Gurkhas, 42 Commando Royal Marines and the Queen's Own Highlanders.

The force resolved the Brunei crisis, freed hostages and restored order, but it was already clear that a new campaign was looming in the territory that the British hated most, jungle and swamp in a climate that ran the gamut of extremes.

Orders called for 2SBS to join 42 Commando from Malta to Singapore, and were later joined by 1SBS to create the largest single gathering of SBS personnel outside Britain since the Second World War. The men were to remain there until 1971, along with SAS squadrons, one of which was led by Major Peter de la Billière, future commander of British forces in the Gulf.

The Borneo clash was never classed as a war, just 'a confrontation'. It was confined mainly to the borders and coastal areas of the four regions of the island. The British military was tied to strict terms of engagements, codenamed Claret, which became otherwise known as 'the golden rules'. The Claret Reports of operations during this period were regarded top secret. As such, public knowledge and perception of the Borneo confrontation was unlike Korea, for example. It did not rate among the more celebrated victories of the British armed forces, even though it was precisely that. When set alongside the record of the French and the Americans fighting guerrilla warfare, the British and her allies repelled the Sukarno-backed invaders in one of the worst regions on earth for conventionally trained soldiers – the island where in 1995 a team of British soldiers on a training expedition became hopelessly lost.

The SBS succeeded, as one Special Forces commander was heard to say, with one hand tied behind its back – because of the strict rules of confrontation in a bitter struggle fought in wild, dense, watery and mountainous terrain, terrain far more hostile than the Americans faced in Vietnam. The 'golden rules' for the Claret operations were quite specific and limiting.

The rules were drawn up with two key thoughts in mind: first, the British government did not want to become drawn in to a long-running jungle war in which heavy casualties might be inflicted on British and allied forces; secondly, the terrain was so hostile that troops should not be risked on deep penetration. The overall penetration across the border into Indonesia allowed was just 5,000 metres although this could be increased to 20,000 metres for specific operations authorised by the director of operations. He in turn had to get permission from London; there could be no diversion from that chain of command, regardless of how urgent the situation on the ground and in the jungle might appear at the time.

Only experienced troops were to be sent across borders, no attacks were to be made with the sole aim of retribution or inflicting casualties on the foe, and there would be no close air support except in an extreme emergency.

The army's overall commander in Borneo was General Sir Walter Walker, who was also brigade major-general of the Gurkhas and a man of somewhat enigmatic behaviour. He was also a supporter of Special Forces. He had used the SAS and, briefly, SBS in the Malayan campaign, and he planned to use it at the forefront of intelligence-gathering over what was effectively an 800-mile front. The SBS, in particular, would be sent covertly into the toughest terrain for reconnaissance where guerrillas were most active.

Walker also knew that small parties were likely to be better received by local populations whose loyalties, in those wild regions, were never certain. The 'hearts and minds' of the locals were as important as hitting the rebels. Both SBS and SAS parties, moving into the countryside, won the support of villagers with gifts and favours such as medical attention or supplies.

They needed all the help they could get. Teams of three or four SBS men were sent into the jungle or the swamps to scout for the army patrols. There, they would build their hides and stay for three to five days at a time, radioing back to base ('when the damned radio worked!') with hourly reports. Quite often, they set up shop only to find they had pitched their hide in a position almost face to face with the enemy. They had to avoid fire fights. They were there to observe and track the movements of the guerrillas, establish their coming-from and going-to directions, their base camps and their numbers.

From this information, the assault force could take them on. It is beyond the scope of this book to record more than a summary of the events in what became a five-year campaign, but after a shaky start SBS operations came thick and fast. They reached a peak under its commanding officer, Captain David Mitchell, who had teams working throughout the theatre, often leading recce tasks himself, being landed into the most difficult regions and conditions. Mitchell himself was awarded an MBE for gallantry in 1965.

A flavour of the activity, however, can be gleaned from a ground's-eye view by Len Holmes, then an SBS sergeant who was involved in much of the campaign. His jottings, told in a matter-of-fact way that almost plays down the dramas, make it clear that the key to the SBS presence was their total invisibility:

We arrived in Singapore at a time when the furore of the

Brunei revolt was beginning to fade, and the prospects for peace in the region seemed quite good. The SBS had settled into a normal training routine, and sport was the order of the day. The section was based in HMS *Terror*.

The first indication of trouble came when we received a signal ordering us to Tawau, a major timber port on the eastern tip of North Borneo at the point where the border converges with Kalimantan [Indonesian Borneo]. Guerrillas backed by the Indonesian military had infiltrated the border area, killed pro-British headmen and terrorised the local population.

The terrorist action was centred on the island of Sebatik opposite Tawau Port. The island was divided, one half being under British control, the other Indonesian. The terrorists had attacked a kampong [village] on our side of the border, and it was anticipated that further attacks were likely to follow. The region was a mass of mangrove swamp inter-sected by rivers, and the army in Tawau requested small-boat patrols to police the waterways.

We installed ourselves with an infantry platoon of the Leicestershire Regiment, based in a saw-mill on Sebatik Island. An observation post was established by building a hide in a large tree on the border headland. We used our own inflatable craft and purchased longboats to patrol the rivers.

Small military craft of any sort were not available. The patrol channels were very shallow and unmarked; there was always the possibility that any of our craft would run aground and become an easy target. Channels had to be marked with poles, and this enabled us to keep a close watch for terrorist incursions. It also seemed to keep them at bay. Terrorist activity in the area had virtually ceased after two months.

We were summoned back to Singapore and had barely had time to unpack our stores and equipment when we received a signal from 42 Commando, located near the Sarawak area of Borneo. Intelligence reports predicted a large sea-borne incursion by IBT [Indonesian Border Terrorists] at the west end of Borneo. We loaded all our equipment back on to a Beverley aircraft and flew this time to Kuching via the RAF staging-airport on Labuan Island. From there it was a short hop by twin-rotor helicopter to Sematan, the nearest kampong to the incursion area, where a company of 42 Commando were based.

We were met by Pug Davis, the company commander, who had been my CO in Germany. As a former SBS officer, Pug had realised that this could be a worthwhile task for the section. Within 24 hours of the signal arriving in Singapore, we had two craft patrolling the headland where the border came down to the coast. This entailed carrying boats, engines and stores over a very shallow gradient beach, and with a 30-mile approach to the operating area it meant that this system of surveillance could not be maintained for long. Two three-man observation teams were inserted onto two headlands near the border.

Len's account of the first teams describes a pattern which was to be repeated many times by all members of the SBS section during the coming months:

Two teams were landed by inflatable craft, both within a few hundred yards of the border and we were effectively operating in no man's land. You never knew when you might come face to face with the IBT.

The OP [observation post] teams were put ashore on a rocky, wave-swept headland where no person in his right mind would have expected us to land at night. Having shut off the engine and paddled in the last hundred yards we searched for a large flat rock on to which to hold the craft while we unloaded our equipment. The first man ashore moved into a position where he could watch the approaches to the area and give covering fire if we were attacked. Within seconds of the touchdown, the craft was pushed off and withdrew seawards.

Two men were left in the craft to return to base when the team was landed. Two were considered necessary; in the event of engine failure – a frequent event – there was still enough manpower in the craft to enable it to be paddled to shore. But soon, the return journey was left to one man because of shortage of personnel and loss of speed in the craft through carrying one extra person on the outward voyage. The boat-handler was left to return to base alone. If the engine failed, he either fixed it, waited on a sea anchor

158

while another craft came to his aid or got swept ashore and picked up later.

The OP team moved to the jungle's edge and established a position where they could have the maximum view to seawards and then waited undercover for daybreak. At first light a quick reconnaissance was made for evidence of terrorist tracks. If we were satisfied we had a safe hide, one man was on watch to seawards while the other remained in a defensive position to protect the team. The third would brew the tea, make hourly radio contact, passing on our intelligence reports, attend to the waterproofing to keep the equipment dry and take his turn to sleep – in that order. It was monsoon season at the time; nothing stayed dry for long. We were to maintain this routine for three days, and then we would be taken off and replaced with another team.

On the third day of our first watch, sea conditions were so bad that there was no hope of us being picked up, and behind us the countryside was swarming. Communications were also a constant problem. The A41 VHF radio we were using to link OPs, boats and base had a range of 20 miles. We were 30 miles out and, even with a 40-foot aerial at our base, radio contact was a hit-and-miss affair. As always, we had an alternative RV [rendezvous point]. It was located on the other side of our headland, where there was a small island close inshore, sheltered from the storm.

We set off, carrying our gear, to reach the RV but hit jungle territory so dense and wild it was impossible to cut through and reach the other side by the RV time. The only option was to go into inhabited areas, where the IBT could be in residence. That worry had so concerned 42 Commando that they had earlier withdrawn a ten-man section from a bunker position they set up nearby to keep local residents loyal and ward off terrorists. Intelligence reports indicated an imminent large-scale incursion, and we were walking right into it.

We set off towards the village just before dark so that if we got involved in a fire fight we could track off into the gloom. We moved cautiously through the native huts and came upon a Chinese store, the only place which had any lights showing. The Chinese family, after the first shock of seeing three armed and rather trigger-twitchy men burst into their home, made us welcome and seemed quite hurt when we left one

159

man outside in the dark to keep watch.

We stayed in the store for a couple of hours, drinking tea, and then suddenly a yapping dog brought us to our feet, weapons at the ready. It turned out to be a false alarm. The dog, foraging in empty food cans under the hut, had got its tongue stuck between the lid. The Chinese thought it was hilarious. After the adrenalin surge had subsided, we laughed too.

We headed off to the RV and reached it ten minutes before pick-up time. No sign of the craft. We were in a very exposed position, sitting ducks for the IBT, and we decided to wade out to an island 100 metres offshore. We had just set off when, to our intense relief, the RV craft came into view. It was always a great feeling to see your mates in the pick-up craft.

For the next two months we maintained both OPs and offshore boat patrols in the Tanjong Datu border area, sending intelligence back. Eventually, the wear and tear on craft and operators caused by the long sea approach to the border meant we had to operate from coastal minesweepers which patrolled further out to sea. It was while I was on board one of these ships that we received a signal instructing my team to make a daylight landing in Milano Bay to establish if the IBT had moved into 42 Commando's old strongpoint.

My first reaction was that someone must be joking, but who was I to question the wisdom of such an exercise. I briefed the ship's captain on our task. He thought we were mad. The ship sailed into Milano Bay and dropped anchor 1,500 yards offshore, and we lowered our own craft. The ship's coxswain came along so that he could take it back to the ship and wait events. We were landed well to the flank of the strongpoint. One man with a light machine-gun would wait at the water's edge to give us covering fire if we hit trouble. We ran up the beach and into the cover of the coconut grove 150 yards away. Once there, we would give him cover while he joined us, and then we spread out, moving cautiously towards the strongpoint. Fortunately for us, IBT had vanished.

The journey did have its compensation because next we moved to Turtle Island, half-way between Sematan and

Tanjong Datu, the classic example of a tropical island, 400 to 500 yards long and, with the exception of the rocky shoreline, covered with dense rain forest. This cut our approach passage to the operating area by half, and we were able to keep our craft closer to the water's edge and avoided the effort of carrying our equipment over several hundred yards of beach every time we launched.

The beach, which was the only all-weather landing-place, also catered as the nesting habitat for the turtles, and it was not unusual to see dozens of them at night laboriously digging their egg-laying holes. Where the tongue of the beach joined the solid mass of the island, a beautiful wooden villa had been constructed in the edge of the trees, and it was here that we made our base for some weeks. The villa was only normally inhabited during the turtle egg-hatching period and was overseen by the curator of the Sarawak Museum, a former member of the Special Operations Executive who had stayed behind in Malaya after the Second World War.

This idyllic tropical island, which was ideal for the SBS team's clandestine mission, was also secluded enough to leave only one man guarding the stores. Now, with SBS operations groups dotted around the theatre, manpower was under pressure. It was while they were on Turtle Island that a couple of well-known SBS stalwart characters, GH and PW, arrived to throw some experienced weight before them. Both were SBS long-term tough guys and had been out tracking for 42 Commando. When they arrived on Turtle Island they had just survived a dramatic fire fight with a 40-strong party of IBT.

GH, a sergeant, was leading a DPT (Dog Patrol Team) with PW acting as signaller, and a Dyak tracker and a dog. They had been dropped into the jungle by helicopter after reports that a large band of IBT was making its way back across the border. The dog picked up the scent, and the trackers pursued at great speed. By nightfall they could still not report a confirmed sighting. GH knew that the IBT were still too far from the border to cross it before dark, so decided to take a chance and keep going, even though this meant that his team would not have time to find a lying-up area before dark.

They had moved on only a few hundred metres further when the tracker put his hand up, signalling movement ahead. GH

161

moved off the track, peered through the undergrowth and found himself face to face with an IBT sentry. The troop was in the process of preparing camp for the night. GH fired first, shot the sentry and then raked the area with his sub-machine-gun; several IBT dropped to the ground. The IBT reacted quickly. The tracker was wounded in the arm from return fire. GH was shouting orders to non-existent troops. He and PW, using rapid fire and movement, managed to dodge the IBT and escape.

As soon as they'd lost them, GH stopped to radio the position of the IBT, but the commando reaction was not fast enough to stop them crossing the border safely that night. For his leadership and bravery under enemy fire, GH received a Military Medal to add to the Distinguished Conduct Medal he had earned as a young corporal for a similar incident against the terrorists in Malaya ten years earlier. Later, he was also awarded the British Empire Medal and the Meritorious Service Medal and became the most decorated post-war NCO in the Royal Marines. Len Holmes continued his account:

By then, it was time to move on from Turtle Island. Once sea conditions improved, the IBT began to use the route again. The risk of the base being overrun was too great, and soon afterwards, the section was withdrawn again to Singapore after two more months of sheer, continuous effort. We once more had to go through the major task of moving all our equipment.

The phrase most often used about us was the 'lightly equipped fighting troops' – typical marine sarcasm. Each time we moved, we had to move house. We never knew what our role or method of operation would be when we arrived in Borneo, and had to take our whole range of boats, diving equipment, radios, weapons, ammunition and explosives with us. The total aircraft payload for it was in the region of 30 tons for a 15-man section. This meant that every one of us had to move two tons of stores from base to truck, truck to aircraft, aircraft to helicopter, helicopter to truck or ship and then finally into a new base.

So in spite of periods of high drama, the overwhelming memory of these initial operations is inevitably one of acting like coolies. Fortunately, the hierarchy had now realised that small-boat presence was needed at both Tawau and Sematan for the foreseeable future. Another 1SBS section had been flown out to Singapore from the UK and had acclimatised themselves while we were in Borneo.

Half of this section was to be based in Tawau, where they had supervised the installation of a motley squadron of small boats manned by the local army unit and Malay troops. This unit became known as the Tawau Assault Group and took over all the tasks we had performed during our first period in Borneo. A purpose-built boat-shed, office and store had been built on the waterfront for the SBS which was within the security of the local army compound. One section, complete with all its stores, could now operate on specific SBS tasks without being side-tracked on to defensive patrolling.

For the next two years both sections were based in Singapore but supplied an officer, sergeant-major and two sub-sections (sergeant, corporal and two marines) on a three-monthly rotation to carry out operations in Tawau. The whole of Malaysia was now on a war footing. Indonesian agents had been stirring up the local population, creating general unrest. There were strikes and riots, and a constant bombardment of militant Indonesian propaganda created rumours of amphibious landings and air raids.

Singapore itself was threatened with invasion by Sukarno, and from an early stage it had been realised that if the British were ever to be able to leave the area, the resistance to Indonesian aggression must begin with locally based forces. The SBS had been instructing the Malaysian Special Forces in raiding techniques, but there was insufficient time for intelligence-gathering before action was required. The periods spent by the sections in Singapore alternated between training the Malaysian and South Vietnamese forces in raiding, and carrying out the operations which would provide the Malaysians with the information on which they could act.

No British personnel, alive or dead, or their equipment, could be allowed to fall into enemy hands and become a source of embarrassment to the UK government. Permission for SBS raids had to come from the Cabinet Office in London, and these were approved only if it could be seen that the planning was so precise as to limit failure to the absolute minimum.

By this time Indonesian forces were preparing camps on

several islands within a few thousand yards of Singapore from which they could carry out military raids or launch terrorists against Malaysia. Some could easily be approached from territorial waters by launching our craft from a surface ship; others, set further back, would have to be approached by submarine. That was a complication because of the shallow approaches in some areas, and could work only if the sub surfaced several miles offshore then submerged, towing the canoes into the area by using the periscope. The new OPs were to be mounted on islands just off Singapore.

One night the SBS target was a small island, little more than a coral reef and with virtually no cover, where an IBT encampment was located. The recce OP was assigned to another of the SBS stalwarts, Sergeant CC, who had a marine as his number two. They paddled from their submarine to an offshore position, where the two operators would swim ashore and recce the defensive positions around the camp which the Indonesians had built on the island. To make sure they could locate the canoe again, one swimmer carried a thin fishing-line paid out from a reel in the canoe. The line was staked into the beach at the water-line and left while the reconnaissance was carried out.

When the work was done, enemy positions noted and landfall charted, the two returned to discover that an unexpectedly strong tide had washed away the stake, string and canoe. After a vain search swimming around the bay using compass bearings, they were approaching the time for their RV for pick-up by the parent craft. They would never make it back in time. The sergeant faced a choice: to return to the island and risk being captured, tortured and probably executed or to simply swim out to sea. Mindful of the 'golden rule' about being captured, he chose the latter. They began swimming seawards in the hope of making the rendezvous. Fighting strong currents and a hefty swell, they swam on, but found no trace of the parent.

Five hours later they were all but done in, at least 12 miles from land, with a vast open sea ahead of them. By sheer chance they were spotted by a Royal Navy Coastal Minesweeper patrolling in international waters and picked up and returned to base. Sergeant CC, the man who faced one of the most awkward decisions of his life, was awarded the British Empire Medal for his courage.

Back to Len Holmes's diary of events:

Tawau, in the north, beckoned again, but this time the emphasis was no longer on the defensive. Tasks allocated to the section were definitely offensive.

Over the preceding months, the Indonesians had established a considerable amphibious force at Nunukan. Two large landing-craft were permanently at anchor offshore, and a regiment of Alligators [Armoured Amphibious Personnel Carriers] were positioned in a large waterfront compound next to Nunukan jetty. Both landing-craft and Alligators indicated the arrival of what was probably Indonesia's élite fighting force, the KKO [Korps Kommando Operatives], Indonesia's marines. We were asked by DOBOP (Director of Borneo Operations) to carry out a sabotage raid on the Alligators and put as many as we could out of action. At first glance the operation looked feasible; the distance from the nearest border point was only 1,000 to 1,500 yards. Theoretically, it was well within the range of swimmers towing explosive charges. However, the lack of knowledge of tidal currents created the need for caution. The experience we had gained when working in the area some months previously had shown there could be strong currents during spring tides and moonless periods which we would need to operate in. For these operations, two canoes and two assault craft were used. The canoes paddled to within 200 yards of Nunukan jetty, anchored and measured the stream every 30 minutes over a period of 3 hours. Meanwhile, the two assault craft maintained a position on the border; one was fitted with outriggers so that if necessary the canoes could be picked up quickly.

The other assault boat was fitted with a crossbar so that a bren-gunner could wrap his legs around it, leaving his hands free to operate the machine-gun. The task of this craft if the canoes came under fire was to head towards the enemy, spraying them with bullets, while the other craft picked up the canoes and withdrew them. The only way to get accurate fire from a bouncing and moving craft was for the bren-gun to be fired from the hip. By using a mix of one ball to one tracer ammunition, the gunner could see the direction of his shots and spray on to the target. Even then, the results were hardly pinpoint, and we had bullets from one of our craft go through the sides of the other.

The system of measuring the tide's strength was typical SBS stick and string. While they were at anchor, the rear-seat canoeist let a partially filled plastic bottle attached to 50 feet of buoyant line into the water. The time taken for the line to go taut and the compass bearing of the direction it took was then recorded to measure the strength of currents.

We established there was a 2-knot current setting towards Nunukan along the route the swimmers would have to take. With a surface swimmer's speed of at best 1 to 1.5 knots we could reach the target but could not guarantee that they would be able to return. As a result of this information the plan to attack the Alligators was cancelled. It also became known that the KKO had a forward base on their side of the border. Two operations were mounted, involving two canoes paddling along the main Nunukan Channel and setting up a hide in the mangrove, providing confirmation that the KKO were based there and could be dealt with in due course.

Two recces of an Indonesian listening-post were also carried out, and from the info provided the post was attacked and wiped out by a troop from 42 Commando [led by an SBS officer who was awarded the Military Cross].

Next, Holmes's section was sent back to Sematan.

Our original small camp with 42 Commando had mush-roomed into a large defensive compound manned by a company from 2/7th Gurkhas, and it was from there that they once again began inserting three-man teams into OPs near the border, where they could report any incursions.

They were out on jungle patrols, up to 17 days at a time. Apart from their OPs, SBS were used to resupply them with ammunition and food. The two groups had much in common in their operational tactics. As the Gurkha history records, its operations in the jungle were governed by stealth and silence: no rifleman was allowed to eat, smoke or unscrew his water-bottle without his platoon commander's permission. At night, sentries checked any man who snored. Whenever the company was on the move, a recce section led the way, their packs carried by men from behind. Because of the long approach marches, each man could carry six days' rations . . .

Although on the face of it the sideline task of resupplying the Gurkha patrols provided the men with the security of being based within the safety of a Gurkha compound, it turned out to be one of the most hazardous they'd face, and the dangers did not always come from the enemy, as Len Holmes explained:

A few of them spoke English, and they insisted that we identify ourselves by giving a special bird-call. I can assure you it is extremely difficult to whistle anything when you're standing alone in the pitch dark trying to locate a bunch of trigger-happy Gurkhas. Life in the Gurkha compound was far from happy. They themselves are delightful, child-like warriors, but living among them produced many problems. Our food was produced separately because theirs was too highly spiced for our consumption, and we had a navy cook using two Primus stoves producing meals from food bought locally. Washing had to be done at different times as our nudity offended their modesty.

Most of us were only getting a few hours' sleep each night and were only in the camp for a rest one day in four, yet we still had to man the compound defences at stand-to each night and morning. The British officer in charge of them was also senior to our officer and clearly did not believe that the Special Boat Section were as special as his Gurkhas. That, coupled with his overbearing attitude, produced a rebellious response from our chaps which at one stage looked as though it might erupt into a mutiny. Only a great deal of common sense on the part of our team, and a visit from our brigade major, who managed to curb some of the Gurkha officer's inflexibility, prevented a most unpleasant incident.

It was a curious confrontation, particularly as the Gurkhas and the SBS, in many respects, shared a common philosophy. Their raids were by stealth, to the last moment, then all hell would break loose. Towards the end of the SBS's unhappy attachment to the Gurkhas, they received information that an IBT camp was located on the Indonesian coast just across the border from Milano.

The SBS was tasked with determining if it were still in use. If it were, the Gurkhas would mount an attack on the camp. A long-range patrol from the Gurkhas was sent to establish the jungle track the IBT used to get to and from the camp. To get SBS recce canoes within easy paddling distance of the camp, an assault boat towed them to within a mile or so of the landing-spot. The canoeists could have paddled the distance easily, but they needed a fast craft close by if they had to make a sharp exit. A coastal minesweeper was positioned a mile or so offshore, where she could sweep the area with her radar for enemy craft. The canoeists arrived at a point 200 to 300 metres away from the suspected IBT camp, and then made a landing near the camp's position. They hid their canoes at the back of the beach and waited until daylight before scouring the area to find the camp. The thick jungle and the threat of booby traps called for a daylight recce and even then only with extreme caution. If they were discovered, they were to make their way back over the border on foot, leaving the canoes behind.

After a slow search they found the camp set in a jungle clearing slightly inland from the coast. The area was deserted, but there were clear signs that the IBT had been training for a water-borne incursion. Not long afterwards, the Gurkhas stumbled on another guerrilla camp. As recorded in their historians' description of the action, the recce party discovered a riverside Indonesian army camp against whom the Gurkhas were vastly outnumbered. It was daybreak, and the Indonesians were taking a breakfast of spit-roasted pig.

The patrol edged close and prepared to launch its attack: 'A 3.5-inch (8.8-centimetre) rocket flared across the river and exploded among the breakfast party. Their hut disintegrated in a ball of flame, the men hurled in all directions. As the two assault platoons moved in . . . they were confronted by a number of totally naked, panic-stricken enemy rushing from it. These were quickly dealt with and, covered by fierce fire from the support group, we assaulted the base. Resistance had ceased but a number of dead lay scattered about the camp and blood was everywhere.'

Len Holmes looks back at his time in Borneo as a contributor to an effort which reflected great credit on the SBS as a whole. He points to the words of Colonel J. P. Cross in his book *Jungle Warfare* who in comparing the Confrontation to Vietnam said '. . . in both Malaya and Borneo their enemy were at least as formidable as the Viet Cong in the early 1960s and Indonesia just as strong militarily as North Vietnam.'

Britain could have had Vietnam on its hands if the campaign had been mismanaged, and there is little doubt as to the value of SBS intelligence-gathering tasks in avoiding an escalation of the Confrontation into a full scale war.

CHAPTER TWELVE

Paddy and the goldfish

Major Pat Troy, a 1950s old boy of the SBS, arrived in Singapore as a young career-minded captain in 1965. The Borneo Confrontation was still on, and he had been expecting to take command of L Company in 42 Commando, having just spent a chilly year or so with the RM Falklands protection force, NP 8901. He went straight into a Jungle Warfare Course in Malaya in anticipation of his new post. Many old friends and acquaintances were around, including David Mitchell, officer commanding of SBS in Singapore, who was also moving on. A new man had been earmarked to take his place but suddenly backed out.

Pat Troy was dragged reluctantly to succeed Mitchell, and the chap who turned down the job went to 42 Commando, where in due course he became a company commander and adjutant. So, he is not one of Troy's favourite officers. 'Having said that,' Troy told me from his home, 'I thoroughly enjoyed my time back with SBS. Although operations in the Borneo Confrontation were scaling down when I arrived, there was still plenty to do and we did carry out a lot of worthwhile work, particularly in experimenting with exit and re-entry of SBS teams from dived submarines on which Paddy Ashdown, who joined us in 1966, took an active part.'

Troy had been through the SBS mill at the time when its instructors included a number of old stalwarts of the section and some of them were still around. 'In those days, few officers saw the SBS as a good career move,' said Pat Troy, and continued:

We had no one at the top fighting for us in the RM. There is no doubt that there was a strong body of opinion in both

171

political and military circles that Special Forces were an expensive luxury . . . that they denuded lots of units of their best men, their leaders, and they'd have far more effect if they remained with their unit. I must admit I had that feeling, too, when I was a company commander in 42 Commando. I had an excellent company and, given the time and the tasks, I reckon I could have picked guys out of my company to train up to the job. I used to feel quite strongly about SBS demands for special equipment. They'd have a bee in their bonnet about some particular thing, and finally they'd win and it would be bought, and when that particular person left it would remain on the shelf in the stores. Demand, demand, demand, all the time.

It was also true that some RM officers still regarded SBS men as overbearing eccentrics, diffident to authority and always asking for expensive new toys. They also had a tendency to shy away from other formalities, like uniforms and hair length. It was a standing joke that when they were going on parade, it took them a month to prepare! And wasn't it one of Troy's young trainee officers, Neil Johnstone, who turned up in battledress wearing brown shoes? 'Go away and do not return until you find some suitable footwear!' And, yes, the same Neil Johnstone who became one of the longest-serving officers in the SBS is right when he says: 'For years we were never really flavour of the month, if for no other reason than the fact that we seemed to collect a bunch of guys who had a reputation for being – shall we say? – difficult. Some of them *were*, and equally a lot of those guys went on to become real stars of SBS operations and a good many of them made their name through it.'

Major Troy admits, however, to learning an early lesson or two among them:

Once, the Dutch asked us to attempt to break into their naval base to test their security. They'd been doing it for a number of years using the Dutch marines. They wanted us to take it on and bring a fresh approach, see how far we'd get. There were about a dozen of us, going in night after night. Jim 'Horse' Earle, my colour-sergeant, noticed I was trying to get a piece of the action myself. He bluntly pointed out that it wasn't my job. He took me to one side and said, 'Look, we know you can jump as high as we can and run as fast and as far and can swim and dive. But you're our OC. Your job is to tell us where to go and what to do, how to do it. And if things go wrong, get us out. If you're with us, you can't do that.' Point taken.

Now, in 1965 he somewhat reluctantly found himself OC in Singapore and incidentally confronted by the need to acquire equipment, about which he had been critical in the past. Within a few months he was joined by Paddy Ashdown, who came to the SBS after a lively spell of operational action with 42 Commando. They had both served together earlier, in the Far East. Singapore was a married posting, and Paddy had his wife with him. He spoke fluent Malay and thus had a strong rapport with the locals.

By now, apart from its operational duties, the SBS was heavily engaged in training Malay troops in the defence of their land. Selected forces from the South Vietnamese Army and, later, US Marines were also given the benefit of SBS experience in jungle and swampland warfare for their battles with the Viet Cong and the North Vietnamese Army. Initially, specially selected small groups from the South Vietnamese Army were given jungle warfare training and underwater instruction. Later, the US Marines were grateful for advice on operations in bad terrain, but their years of ineffectual confrontation with the Communists and their eventual withdrawal proved how right the British planners had been to restrict Borneo to border confrontations and not even attempt to get involved in a jungle war.

Meanwhile, Pat Troy still had some important operations, and was working well with submarine commanders. Several islands within a few thousand yards of Singapore provided good cover for Indonesian guerrillas as a base for their raids. The SBS recce teams could reach some by launching canoes or inflatables from a surface ship. Others, further afield, had to be approached by submarine, which not only put the men at risk but the submarine too. Nothing had changed in that regard: a diving submarine makes a very loud noise and draws attention not only to itself but to the men it has just floated off. It was an age-old problem, wherever the SBS men were carried by submarine.

Trials started earlier in Singapore by David Mitchell, with Len Holmes and Corporal Bob Beers during the intermission from operations, were aimed at establishing safe techniques for the exit and re-entry of SBS swimmers, their gear and boats while the submarine was still dived. They were being run under the codename of Goldfish. Similar work was being run in the UK, but Singapore had the weather and the water that made it ideal. The trials and experiments which began in these years and pursued back in Britain would provide the basis for vital improvements to the way SBS teams were delivered to an operation.

Pat Troy and Paddy Ashdown, who served together in 42 Commando, were deeply interested in the theory of underwater exit and re-entry, and they had the support of Commander John E. Moore, RN, Commander of the 7th Submarine Squadron, who was not only willing to have his boats mucked about with for experiments but also acquired much of the gear. By then all British submarines were equipped with BIBS and TABS (Built-In Breathing System and Tower Air-Breathing System).

Installed for the escape of the crew, these systems involved pipelines running throughout the boat. In an emergency, the crew could plug in a tube with a demand valve and mouthpiece. The escape tower through which the crew would have to pass to exit was in effect a small dry and wet compartment. A system of vents and floodpipes allowed escapees to enter, close the lower hatch and then flood the compartment until the water pressure was equalised with that outside, then open the upper hatch to make a free ascent to the surface.

There was a single escape tower in both Fore and Aft of the submarine in compartments which needed flooding. The built-in breathing system meant that while this was going on the men could plug in a mouthpiece and stand, rather like tube-train commuters, waiting to go. For the Goldfish experiments, the escape tower was the only access in and out of the boat. The tower, like a large tube about 4 feet (1.2 metres) in diameter and 5 feet (1.5 metres) in height, was just forward of the conning tower in the A-class submarines then in use (they were phased out in the 1970s). Other submarines had two single escape towers.

For the Goldfish trials, high-pressure air cylinders were tied inside the conning tower, with air lines and mouthpieces. Also secured inside the conning tower was a rope with a small float attached to it so that on reaching the surface the swimmers could clip the air lines and mouthpieces on to it ready for their return and re-entry into the submarine.

Paddy Ashdown was one of the key members of the team when the Goldfish trials were reaching a successful conclusion, and it was Commander Moore (a future editor of Jane's *Fighting Ships*) who provided the boats, the air tanks, and the kit to make the trials all come together. As Pat Troy recalled:

We were on an exercise when we first decided to put Goldfish to the test and do some serious exit and re-entry trials in the submerged submarine in a mock-attack situation, as near as possible to the real thing. John Moore didn't tell anyone we were going to do it. Two pairs – Paddy Ashdown and Ted Lonnegan, each with a marine – were suited up and prepared for exit while Moore weaved the submarine in and out of the ships in a deep-water bay. The two pairs swam to the ships and placed charges on the hulls successfully without being spotted. Unfortunately, as we were leaving some sharp-eyed lookout spotted our tac periscope. He didn't know what it was, so he went to the radar. He vectored a boat on to it and we hit it and holed it. We had to do an emergency surface to check for damage. At that time, Paddy and his partner were still in the tower, draining down. The boat surfaced beside Ted Lonnegan and his marine, who were just about to start re-entry procedure. It was a very good test, however, and Paddy wrote up the paper, and much more work was done both in Singapore and in the UK to perfect the procedures.

Ashdown was also working on parachuting men into submarines at sea. The problem with carrying SBS personnel in submarines was the overcrowding, as well as the men getting unfit during long journeys and, crucially, not having up-to-date intelligence. The canoes or inflatables, their engines, and their mass of gear and stores took up a large amount of space in already cramped conditions, conditions submariners had moaned about since they began carting Tug Wilson around the Mediterranean. Unlike the US, Britain had no personnel-carrying submarines, so Troy began exploring the possibility of getting the SBS to operations by air.

SBS parties in Malta, including Jim Earle and Len Holmes, had already done a good deal of work in this area, especially at the time when 'Sticks' Dodds was OC of 6SBS, although dropping men by parachute was usually for direct raids by air without involving a submarine.

Pat Troy's variation on that theme was to load up a submarine with some of the gear and then rendezvous with an aircraft somewhere close to the target zone, where the SBS men and their additional kit would be dropped into the sea, picked up and taken in by the sub for the last hop of their journey for the clandestine raid. They practised the techniques by day and by night. The RAF were very keen on the routine, too, and Troy secured great cooperation from them. The SBS also practised parachuting to the submarine while it was still submerged, with the men entering without surfacing using the techniques developed for Goldfish.

The trials were all completed very successfully, with rubber inflatable craft being brought out through the torpedo tubes and outboard motors through the conning tower. The SBS trialists managed to get motoring without the submarine surfacing. The experiments continued – and would do so for the next decade or more – and next Troy and Moore began working on a motorised underwater towing vehicle that could pull an SBS diver and his load of explosives. John Moore got hold of a Mark XXIII torpedo. Royal Navy engineers at the submarine depot-ship HMS *Medway* adapted it to Moore's specifications and added extra batteries to convert it to an underwater tug.

Paddy Ashdown was one of the test drivers, and it worked successfully enough for designs of a similar underwater towing vehicle to go into production under the codename of Archimedes, or Archie as it was affectionately known. That particular design was not ultimately successful, but the same principles were used for underwater tugs and Swimmer Delivery Vehicles that remain in service today.

Troy recalled one more rather ironic event before Ashdown left Singapore to go off to China to continue his studies of oriental languages. The Singapore contingent of the British armed forces was putting on a show for Harold Wilson's visiting Secretary of State for Defence, Denis Healey. At the time, Healey was planning to axe various prize possessions of the navy, including cherished aircraft-carriers.

He'd had a good look around, been into a carrier, talked to the troops and so on. By the time he reached the SBS and submarines, he'd got a big gash over his eye, having hit his head somewhere along the way. He complained that they kept putting him in smaller and smaller boats. He joked about it and said thank goodness it had happened in a small ship: 'You can imagine the headlines. "Healey Leaves Carrier with a Black Eye".'

His hosts then invited him to inspect the submarines. The SBS was to pick him up in a motor launch and deliver him to the submarine where Captain John Moore was waiting. There were chaps jumping out of aeroplanes and swimmers coming up all around the submarine and so on. It was Paddy Ashdown who went to pick him up in a Gemini, brought him back to Moore's boat and eventually returned him. 'Anyway,' said Pat Troy, 'we eventually got a signal from Healey saying how much he'd enjoyed his day with the navy and especially the stage-managed finale. Some time later I was up in the House of Commons, by which time Paddy was leader of the Liberal Democrats. I bumped into Healey and I asked him if he remembered the day with the navy. He did . . . remembered it very well. And no, he didn't know it was Paddy Ashdown who had driven across in the Gemini to the submarine.'

Paddy Ashdown left Singapore and the SBS after a two-and-a-half-year stint. He had been studying oriental languages at a college in Singapore and moved on to China to continue his studies. He went to an SBS reunion in 1996 – just like the old days, except that he was famous now. He was invited to do the draw, but the hubbub and noise were such that he couldn't be heard. Ashdown got on to a chair and bellowed: 'Shaaaddup!' Of course, they all jeered and yelled back: 'Shut up, Paddy, you're not in Parliament now.'

CHAPTER THIRTEEN

White arses in the moonlight

Beach recces! Dozens of them throughout the 1960s. A whole decade of scouring, plotting and charting the coastlines of the Middle East, along with a good deal of other intelligence-gathering, a fair few fire fights and a remarkable shoot-to-kill engagement fell to the lot of the SBS in a series of operations in the Middle East that ran parallel to their presence in Borneo. They were to be followed in by the SAS and other contingents of British troops, called to action once more in the deserts and desolate mountainous territory of southern Arabia.

A brief summary of events: in the aftermath of the Suez fiasco, President Nasser vowed to kick the British out of the Arab world. The southern coastal lands, from Yemen on the Red Sea around to Qatar in the Persian Gulf, were on a knife-edge. Across the Gulf, Iran and Iraq were staring at each other menacingly. Nasser stirred the pot, the Soviets threw their might behind the Marxist rebels of Yemen and anyone else willing to take their handouts, aided by the knowledge and contacts of the British traitor Kim Philby, who vanished from Beirut in 1963 and turned up later in Moscow.

British influence, political and economic, over this string of sheikhdoms, sultanates and monarchies had become the focus of bitter reaction among Arab republicans. The one remaining vestige of colonial power in the region hung tenuously in the balance in the protectorate of Aden, which Britain had ruled for 128 years. This last strategic base had been its fortress guarding the southern access to the Suez Canal at the mouth of the Red Sea and at the tip of what would soon become the People's Democratic Republic of Yemen. By 1960, it was surrounded by hostility.

British troops had faced increasingly bloody skirmishes with the Yemeni rebels since 1955, and by the early 1960s Aden was virtually under siege. The British-friendly ruler of the Yemen, the Imam Mohammed al Badr, was deposed in September 1962, and within the month Egyptian troops rolled in to support the Marxist regime. The Imam fled to the mountains and came to rest close to the border with Saudi Arabia, whose king remained a supporter. From there, and with the aid of privately contracted British mercenaries, including former serving members of the SAS, he directed a guerrilla war against the Communists for the rest of the decade.

The Conservative government of Harold Macmillan had vowed 'no surrender' to the Marxists and Nasserite factions. The Labour Party of Harold Wilson's was not so sure, and within 18 months of coming to power in 1964 it confirmed Britain's withdrawal from Aden, leaving its base to fall into the hands of the Soviet satellite.

Between the departure and arrival of new political colours at Westminster, British troops became ensnared in a sustained campaign of terrorism and guerrilla warfare around their Aden base which threatened to spread into the Trucial States (now the United Arab Emirates) fronting the Persian Gulf. If that wasn't enough, Iraq's Nasser-friendly military rulers announced they would reclaim Kuwait following Britain's ending of its protectorate of the oil-rich little state.

Britain promised to continue its military support of Kuwait and also reaffirmed its friendship with Iran, which would receive some long-term assistance in the way of training of its Special Forces from the SBS. The Israelis, meanwhile, were standing by, secretly backing the anti-Communist factions of Yemen and preparing to act when the moment was right.

Out of this turmoil, as history now records, the dominoes fell one after the other. The worst-case scenarios of the military analysts who had called for the supreme intelligence effort at the back end of the 1950s were ticked off, year by year, and onwards down the century: British withdrawal from Aden, the Six-Day War, the Palestinian crisis, Gaddafi seizing power from King Idris in Libya, Middle East terrorist outrages, plane hijackings, hostage-taking, the 1970s oil crisis, Lebanon, Iraq v. Iran . . . and so on.

The SBS was again in at the beginning and would remain well

into the crucial stages of most of the above events, carrying out top-secret recces and raiding-missions under the auspices of the Amphibious Warfare Centre and the Joint Intelligence Bureau's AI9 and MI6. SBS involvement was, as ever, a prelude to all that was to follow as the British military planners and intelligence analysts continually updated assessments of the region, identifying the troublespots, forecasting dangers to Britain, her economy or her allies, and determining best sites if and when invasion or withdrawal of troops and British nationals became necessary. All eventualities needed to be covered.

At the turn of the decade, as things were hotting up in Aden and elsewhere, 6SBS based in Malta sent a detachment to Bahrain, from where they would be deployed throughout the Arab southern regions. The SBS teams who came to Bahrain over the next ten years or so were given a fairly long leash, often working on their own initiative, usually dressed as civilians or disguised as Arabs, but all the time reconnoitring the scenery of the coast. Jim Earle gave me this account:

JIB wanted reports on beaches throughout the Middle East, assault and withdrawal sites, very detailed recces – bearing capacities, underwater obstacles, beach profiles, exits, cover . . . everything. We were doing that from Qatar in the east to beyond Aden in the west. I spent two weeks learning how to speak a bit of Arabic, and how to conduct myself with Arabs. We were being sent away on our own, as a sub-section, and we knew it might be necessary on occasions to wear Arab clothes. We were administered, supplied and looked after by JIB, which was tremendous because wherever we went they always had a secret squirrel who could fit us up with the most amazing stuff. I'd meet the squirrel, who would give me directions of where to go, what to do, and keep in contact throughout. He'd have the up-to-date aerial photographs, which he'd marked, and hand over to me for guidance. Around those areas we had to make a full beach recce. I would work under him while I remained in his area.

As an example, we were sent into Kuwait at the time of a dispute over borders with Iraq. The oil states were all in a tense mood, with Nasser and Israel, Iran and Iraq all embroiled in their historical differences. The possibility of an Iraqi invasion of Kuwait had blown up again in July 1961, and intelligence reports from Baghdad reckoned the Iraqis were about to send troops towards the Kuwaiti border. 45 Commando were mobilised to make a show of strength by turning up in Kuwait. If a full-scale shootout developed, more troops would be needed. JIB wanted precise beach recces of Kuwait, their existing ones being out of date. At the time I was down in Oman – also facing trouble with left-wing rebels – with my section when I received a signal ordering me to report to Bahrain forthwith. There, in the naval base HMS *Jufair*, we met the JIB rep. We saw him on a Thursday, and he explained the task. There were clear-cut rules about any intelligence work in Kuwait, and they were scared shitless about disturbing them. He asked me what kit I wanted, and I gave them a list. It was ready to be collected on the Monday.

They flew us up to Kuwait City and there we were met by another JIB squirrel. He directed us to recce the oil company base outside of Kuwait. We commandeered some transport – two Dodge powerpack vehicles – and drove down to Mina' al-Ahmadi, where I saw a second squirrel, a retired naval commander. He gave me precise directions as to what we were to do. There was one road straight out, two lanes, 50 miles long leading to the beach. We travelled along it until we reached a villa, which they had acquired for our use. We arrived there and just took it over for the period we were there, using it as the base while we conducted a full beach recce along the whole stretch of Kuwait coastline.

It took us about a month for that particular recce. But there were many others . . . Aden, Yemen, Muscat, Oman, a large section of the Arabian coastline and across into East Africa. Nine times out of ten we were in these places just prior to trouble, or withdrawal. In the two and a half years I was on the Bahrain posting, it was almost entirely spent on beach recces. Some of the time we were in places we shouldn't have been, and there were occasionally some tense moments with the local militia or rebels. There was a lot of anti-British activity. We were well armed and well equipped, but we were instructed to avoid trouble. We had to be invisible. We'd run rather than engage in a fire fight because that would destroy the object of the task. Once you engaged in a fire fight you'd lost. You might win the fight, but you've destroyed the object. We were forced into returning fire once or twice in the Gulf of the Yemen areas, but that was because we were being shot at – we just did enough to clear our escape.

With the continuing threat of Iraq invading Kuwait, the SBS was ordered to send a permanently based detachment to Bahrain. Lieutenant Neil Johnstone – he of brown shoes with battledress fame – was attached to 2SBS in Singapore, where during his tour with them he became a familiar figure thereabouts, driving his little MGTC. It was around this time that 2SBS was extended to cover the Middle East; the detachment later became known as 3SBD. Johnstone was tasked with taking, initially, a five-man team to HMS *Jufair*, the shore base in Bahrain, to work with the Amphibious Warfare Squadron. The detachment was destined to remain there until 1971, although the personnel changed on an annual basis.

So, a slight diversion . . . Neil Johnstone – 'one of the most decent blokes in the SBS' said everyone interviewed – came into the Royal Marines for his National Service, moved quickly into the SBS and became one of its longest-serving officers. When I arrived to talk to him at his home overlooking some spectacular countryside in January 1997, a hawk sitting comfortably on its perch on the front lawn eyed me cautiously and a beautiful white barn owl fluttered into its hide nearby.

The hunting dogs barked and the ferrets peered through their cages as Neil ushered me inside for a most entertaining five-hour briefing on his life and times in the SBS, recollections that are included at various sections of this work:

I joined for National Service and wanted to be a frogman and eventually took an SBS course and went out to join 6SBS in Malta under 'Sticks' Dodds. He was a flamboyant character and in fact created the motto that exists today. We were in his office one day and he said: 'Let's think of a motto.' I came up with one or two suggestions, and he eventually arrived at his own NOT BY STRENGTH, BUT BY GUILE. The 'but' was eventually edited out, but that became the motto and was eventually adopted when we all withdrew back to the UK.

Kuwait was being threatened and 2SBS in Singapore was extended by an officer and four men to cover the Middle East. I was sent to open up our first base for a permanent detachment in Bahrain. The building had two doors swinging in the wind. We looked inside and it was empty, so we painted our colours on it and drew a padlock and that's how we started in Bahrain.

The beaches had to be checked. We were going around all the beaches up there, updating previous intelligence. In December 1961 we were ordered to pack our kit because Kuwait was threatened again. The Iraqis had massed their troops on the border. We were embarked on HMS *Empire*, a war department LST [Landing Ships, Tanks] with 17/21 Lancers and sent up to Kuwait. We stood by off Kuwait, but nothing happened; the Iraqis withdrew and we weren't required operationally. From then on we were deployed with the AW [Amphibious Warfare] Squadron, largely on beach reconnaissance during my time there, and taking part in major training exercises along the coast and around Aden.

Exercises were also a show of strength, and the beaches of the Middle East presented a particular problem, especially for landing or withdrawal of heavy-duty vehicles. The beaches generally had very long, shallow gradients, as if the tide were permanently out, and could often be reached only by the flat-bottomed Gemini inflatables. For their crucial plotting measurements, Johnstone and his team pioneered a new kind of reel and distance line, used for their precise calculations. They also developed a new format for signalling beach recce check results, which was believed to be the precursor to a system later adopted by NATO forces.

Neil Johnstone had purchased his own wetsuit for swimming and diving while in Singapore, and as a future SBS training officer was instrumental in opening up a long-running debate and trials on the type of suit the SBS should adopt. He is credited with the description of SBS operatives coming ashore and having to discard their wetsuits, displaying the rather noticeable targets of 'white arses in the moonlight'. More about that later, when we catch up with Neil back in the UK.

The SBS also established a good working relationship with C Company of 2 Parachute Regiment, which was also based in Bahrain. They worked together on a number of exercises and projects – in and around the vital Trucial States, which abutted the Strait of Hormuz.

The Bahrain detachment continued with its recces and exercises and led by Rupert Van der Horst, went to Aden again in 1965 in support of 3 Commando Brigade on two major exercises – another show of strength at a particularly difficult time. British troops in Aden, recently reinforced after the decapitation of two soldiers captured by the Yemeni forces, were operating in a vacuum. Everyone knew that the British under a new Labour government would pull out soon. The politicians insisted that British military responses to attacks were to be defensive, almost to the point of turning the other cheek. Hence, many exercises were staged to display the British fire power and provide the basis for a hearts and minds campaign among the local population.

Into this vacuum stepped the founder of the SAS, Colonel David Stirling – by then freelance – who had realised that royal families and heads of state in the wealthy Arab world required more than just personal bodyguards. They needed force commanders with British contacts capable of organising counter-revolutionary forces, training local armies and acquiring decent equipment. The last part of the equation provided no difficulty. The British government and international arms dealers were heavily courting the Arabs. Many fortunes were made, especially among entrepreneurs like Adnan Kashoggi.

Stirling's principal involvement was in the supply of men and in tactical skills. Former SAS and SBS men, mostly of Second World War vintage, had been freelancing for years without much attention, but lately 'mercenary' had become a dirty word. That the man who founded the SAS regiment should resort to it curiously enough had the ring of British approval. Stirling, after 12 years in Rhodesia, was financially at a low ebb at the time and was trying various business schemes. He was introduced to the prospect of taking a key position in the Middle East through a Scottish Member of Parliament, former veteran Special Operations Executive Lieutenant Colonel Billy McLean, who regularly visited the region, and who in turn had the ear of the previous Tory Prime Minister, Alec Douglas-Home.

The idea appealed, and Stirling was fixed up with a contract to aid the deposed Imam run his guerrilla campaign from the mountains. Six former SAS members were flown to Yemen and onwards to the Imam's stronghold, although three of them were eventually murdered at a road-block. Soon, Stirling had persuaded the former commanding officer of 21 SAS (Artists) TA to join him, and a little later Colonel David Smiley, also recruited by his old SOE associate Billy McLean, arrived on the scene to make reports and assessments from battle areas for the Saudi royal family. He later became the Yemeni mercenaries' commanding officer before being succeeded by two former SAS commanding officers. They controlled a mercenary force of around 50 men, leading the royalist army.

Smiley himself was very impressed by their operations:

> The royalists had set an ambush in a valley between sand-dunes and rocks . . . The grim relics of the battle littered the sand on either side of the track. There was a wrecked Russian T34 tank and the burned-out shells of several armoured personnel carriers. I counted – with my handkerchief to my nose – more than 50 decomposing bodies, half-buried by sand and half-eaten by jackals. I saw, also, six decapitated corpses – executed republicans, they told me.

Some have alluded to external connections among the mercenaries, noting that they and the royalists had kept around 70,000 of Nasser's troops and many MiG fighters occupied in Yemen at the time of the Six-Day War. It is implausible that the mercenaries alone were capable of gathering such numbers of troops and obtaining such equipment. It is possible, however, that David Stirling and company, with the tacit approval of the British, formed a bridgehead while the bulk of the British force was withdrawn from Aden in 1967. By fighting on, the royalists secured and held the territory that became North Yemen. But in spite of the hired guns of the ex-SAS, the royalists were never a match for the Nasser fire power that supported the republicans, and after eight years of fighting a political and military stalemate was reached.

Around Yemen and beyond, through Oman, into the Trucial States and the Gulf, many other odd things were happening. The mercenaries were assisting in the supply of arms and weapons, often parachuted at night from aircraft by the Rhodesian Air Service and the Iranian Air Force into drop zones manned largely by ex-SAS personnel. By the mid-1960s the bodyguard and mercenary business, along with other lucrative arms sidelines, were such big business – in the Middle East, Africa and other war zones – that David Stirling had set up a Jersey-based company to exploit it.

The Arab world remained, as ever, a patchwork of delicate alliances and bitter hatreds. The British were attempting to steer a path that would ensure the best trading potential of what was emerging as one of the most valuable markets in the world, while securing its oil interests and providing a positive basis for future stability. At the same time the CIA and American government analysts, whose reading of the Middle East complexities were seldom more than naive, thought the whole problem could be solved by the recognition and acceptance of the Pan-Arabia of Nasser's dream, a view too simplistic by half, as they would learn at considerable cost.

Britain's future position relied heavily on the mass of intelligence its military and political advisers were receiving; in three years this had developed into a veritable mountain of paper, including a good deal through the activities of the SBS. The interconnections were multi-dimensional, still deeply classified and beyond the scope of this book. A few explanations and clues are available as they involved the SBS.

Oman became a particular focus as the Yemeni troubles subsided. This vast sultanate in many ways provided a cross-sectional slice of the Middle East as a whole – a place of wild extremes in its landscape, its climate and the management of its people. It was an absolute monarchy, a barbarous closed society and, until the late 1960s, its people were largely poverty-stricken, disease-ridden and uneducated. The climate is horrendous. Supper could be cooked on the volcanic rocks. Summer temperatures reached 120 degrees Fahrenheit, while in the northern mountains the winters were so cold that a water-bottle would freeze solid in minutes. In the wilds of Dhofar, there was no shelter from the vertical rain of the monsoons.

Sultan Sa'id of Oman was a small, ageing recluse with white whiskers who spoke perfect English and ran his country by fear and violence, guarded by a coterie of young men of African descent whom he openly described as slaves. With a pistol always to hand on his desk, he communicated with the outside world by radio telephone from his room and through British expatriates on his staff. He and he alone ruled, and would not permit the social improvements so desperately needed, such as in health and education, because he believed his nation was not ready for development.

British interest in this unwelcoming and forbidding country

focused on two key elements. First, oil was discovered in 1964 which made the country ripe for exploitation; but to the British, and indeed the whole Western world, that was really a side issue. Political sway in Oman and the Trucial States was linked to control of the west bank of the vital Strait of Hormuz, a slender waterway linking the Persian Gulf to the Gulf of Oman, and out into the Indian Ocean. On the east bank lay Iran.

Through that liquid Z-bend passed more than 55 per cent of the oil used by the free world. If the flow were halted, hindered or disrupted in any way, national economies could collapse, and Britain's in that pre-North Sea oil era more than most. That is why the Trucial States became a place of regular training and exercise for the SBS, and why British intelligence was so pleased when SBS Major H. B. Emslie, MC, left the service and turned up in a key role on the staff of the Sultan of Oman.

Emslie's knowledge of the Middle East and its territories was excellent. He was involved, it will be recalled, in the Alexandria mission at the time of King Farouk's departure and had kept in close touch since. Despite his departure from the British military, Emslie's position had obvious advantages, and there remained a fair degree of consultation and cooperation between the British government and the Sultan of Oman through the offices of Emslie himself.

It was he who tasked and coordinated yet another SBS recce of Kuwaiti beaches during further sabre-rattling from Iraq. Lieutenant Pentland and Sergeant Michie were dispatched to Kuwait in civilian clothes, made their way to the beach areas to make an up-to-date report of the situation, and produced brand-new charts and calculations taken entirely in a covert operation.

British expatriates in Oman were, by then, openly in collusion with a group of Omani sheikhs and aristocrats who were plotting a coup against the old sultan if he would not abdicate in favour of his son Qaboos. In July 1970 one of them walked into the sultan's office and demanded his retirement. Sa'id picked up the pistol from his desk and opened fire, wounding the rebellious sheikh, killing a palace servant and shooting himself in the stomach in the process. However, that night the sultan agreed to go and, with SAS protection, he was put on a RAF plane for England, where he died two years later.

It was around that time that military intelligence reconnaissance photographs appeared to show a group of terrorists in training in a remote region populated by primitive tribespeople bordering the Musandam Peninsula, close enough to the Strait of Hormuz to become a problem. The terrorists were thought to be Iraqi-trained guerrillas. Britain, anxious to shows its support for the new sultan, Qaboos, agreed to investigate and deal with the nest. The SBS Bahrain detachment was at the time engaged in beach recces on the east coast of the Trucial States, working from minesweepers not far from where the terrorists were thought to be encamped.

They received a signal from base commander in Bahrain instructing them to link up with an SAS squadron. The SBS, with its knowledge of the coast and inland terrain through its exercises in the region with 2 Para, were to carry out a beach recce before putting the SAS ashore and covering their backs. The rules of engagement were such that the officer commanding the SBS had orders to shoot anyone confronting his patrol.

Having completed the recces, the SBS detachment took the SAS ashore by Gemini inflatables. One suspect was shot during the landing and a member of the SAS squadron was killed soon afterwards during a night-time parachute drop into a valley surrounded by mountainous peaks. Once the SBS detachment had completed that phase it returned to Bahrain, although later Lieutenant Bagshaw and Sergeant Grant were called back to the Musandam Peninsula and spent several weeks with the SAS squadron patrolling the area, resupplying patrols by Gemini operating from Diba.

Oman was the scene of a further SBS deployment some time later during Operation Storm, which was conducted in association with the SAS at the opposite end of Oman's rambling terrain in the regions of Dhofar butting on to South Yemen at the coast and stretching up into indistinguishable borders with Saudi Arabia. The SBS detachment was deployed under the command of SAS B Squadron and, although initially brought in for beach landings, later joined fighting patrols and ambushes. In the same region the SBS joined the SAS on hearts and minds patrols, with two- and three-man teams travelling through the plains dispensing medical and other aid to villages and settlements.

But undoubtedly, throughout its time conducting operations off the coast of Oman, the most delicate tasks confronting the SBS were those concerning the Strait of Hormuz and a group of small islands at its mouth, which in the early 1970s were again under threat of disturbance. The British were playing piggy in the middle over the disputed ownership of the islands of Tunb and Musa, sited in a strategic position close to the Iran side of the strait. Iran and the Trucial States laid claim to them; Britain was courting both.

The SBS detachment was brought in for a recce, operating from a minesweeper patrolling the waters. Over several nights, SBS swimmers paddled to the islands and went ashore. Their orders restricted them to a recce; they were not to go inland, nor engage the occupants of the islands. The SBS men scrambled ashore; they collected their intelligence; they even heard voices in the close vicinity but did not investigate.

Three weeks later Iranian Special Forces occupied the two islands and, with the country still under the control of the Shah in those pre-Khomeini days, Britain had seemingly secured this vital route by proxy. Behind that manoeuvre lay another intriguing tale which would ultimately fall into the growing Middle East catalogue of lost causes.

The SBS association with Iran stemmed from a 1959 visit to Britain by the then Iranian defence minister. Britain continued to support the Shah of Iran, whose succession it had engineered, through thick and thin, in spite of mounting and widespread opposition to his regime. SBS links were destined to last for almost two decades, continuing on through the traumas of political upheaval in Iran and eventually ending in dramatic fashion. During his tour in 1959, the Iranian minister was brought to the SBS headquarters at Poole and was so impressed that he decided there and then that Iran should have a similar unit. Under British government policy of providing training packages for the military or police forces of friendly nations, SBS instructors went to Iran for five months in 1965.

From then until 1971, SBS teams were deployed to Iran twice a year for several months at a time, either to the diving school at Bandar-e Pahlavi on the Caspian Sea, or Bandar-e Abbas on the Gulf coast. The British team was tasked with selecting men from the ranks of the Imperial Iranian Navy for their Special Operations Group. They took them through a training routine similar to that established for British SBS courses, including exercises at Kharg Island for instruction on parachuting into water. In December 1969 30 Iranians were taken to Cyprus by SBS Lieutenant Richard Clifford, then the officer commanding 3SBD for additional training. That year, the Iranian government had formally approached the British government to establish an armed forces training package, because the scheme provided by the Americans was not sufficient for their needs.

A British military assessment team visited Iran during one of the SBS training missions and agreed to formalise the arrangement. Among their needs was the formation of a commando unit with a Special Boat Section attached. In 1973 the SBS sent a team to help select officers and men for SBS and commando training in the UK. At the same time the Royal Marines Advisory Team helped form its new force. Iranian personnel who were to become the nucleus of the Iranian instructors were brought to Britain for training. SBS Colour-Sergeant Jonah Jones was given a two-year assignment in Iran as part of the Royal Marines Advisory Team, working at a new Iranian training camp at Bushehr on the Gulf coast of Iran.

Come the revolution, the association ended abruptly. Ayatollah Khomeini returned to Teheran in February 1979 and exiled the Shah. The British-trained Iranian SBS was, however, credited with rescuing and evacuating one of the Iranian princes. It was probably its last act. The Iranian SBS was identified with the shah and his political associates and allies. The SBS men were all thought to have been arrested after he fled the country, their fate unknown.

Within a year, Iran was in the grip of the Islamic revolution. A hundred hostages were trapped inside the American embassy in Teheran and became pawns in a long-drawn-out cat and mouse game that saw a disastrous rescue attempt by the crack US Delta Force crash-land in the desert. In London a month later, the SAS put its name in lights for ever with its spectacular assault on the Iranian embassy in Knightsbridge, killing four of the five gunmen who had held nineteen hostages for six days.

Back in the Gulf, in 1969, Lieutenant Clifford kept the detachment up to mettle with instructional sorties to Malta for training in deep diving, to Cyprus for parachuting into the sea and trials on dropping Gemini inflatables from aircraft, and to Singapore for jungle training.

Then, activity in the Middle East was all over. In 1971 the Conservative government of Edward Heath, continuing the policy laid down by his Labour predecessors, pulled the British out of the region. The Bahrain SBS detachment was tasked to cover the withdrawal from Bahrain based on the aircraft-carrier HMS *Albion* in November 1971.

It had barely left the Gulf, however, when India and East Pakistan began shouting at each other. HMS *Albion* was detached from the fleet to assist with the evacuation of British nationals from the Pakistan regions under threat of conflict with India. A large Union Jack was painted on the flight-deck as the aircraft-carrier arrived at speed, sailing the east coast of India. A cease-fire was negotiated in the meantime and an evacuation was not necessary. The SBS flew home . . . the end of an era, for them and the nation.

And also the beginning of a new phase.

PART THREE

A New Kind of War
1970 to the Present

Black September, 1970. Special Forces are on standby to make a storming entrance, but it is too late and perhaps, anyway, an impossible task without heavy loss of civilian life. Six days of tortuous negotiations and appalling conditions for 250 very frightened men, women and children trapped in hijacked aircraft climax in spectacular fashion . . . a huge pall of smoke and flames rises into the baking atmosphere as three airliners – British, Swiss and American – forced to land on a disused RAF airstrip in the Jordanian desert, are blown to bits by Palestinian terrorists. A fourth, a Pan American jumbo, is blown up in Cairo. The planes were taken in mass hijackings over northern Europe; 200 of the passengers were released before the explosions . . . Now frantic international efforts are being made to free the remaining 56 hostages still held by the terrorists. One of the gang, Leila Khaled, who was arrested on an El Al plane when it landed at Heathrow after another failed hijack attempt, is being held in London pending talks for an exchange.

The era of the terrorist . . .

CHAPTER FOURTEEN

To save a queen

First a brief look at events leading up to it. In the early months of 1971 the SBS began to take on a new shape, chameleon-like, to meet the current trends. It was forced into doing so. SBS attachment to colonialist battles that had one foot in the past and one in the future ended with almost shocking abruptness.

At the turn of the 1970s the face of the British military map changed beyond recognition, and for ever. Suez, Aden, Bahrain, Singapore . . . the withdrawals were all virtually complete, and soon Malta, too, under its new Socialist leader, Dom Mintoff, would scrap the defence pact with its old ally and look towards Libya and Colonel Gaddafi for friendship.

Most of the great military and naval associations with territories that formed part of the old empire were at an end, swiftly and determinedly and rightly severed during the six years of Harold Wilson's Labour government. All the classic areas of maritime and commando action, the backdrop to these pages so far, were consigned to history. Only Hong Kong and a few minor and far-flung outposts of colonialism remained, along with Gibraltar, which had also been the cause of perplexing moments in White-hall in recent times: the borders with Spain were still closed; the Fascist dictator General Franco slammed the gates in June 1969 and offered all Gibraltar citizens Spanish nationality.

The locals, by and large, had no wish to give up their long and fruitful association with Britain: what would they do without Marks & Spencer? Nor could Britain contemplate losing that most strategic and handy place at the entrance to the Mediterranean, and port of call to hundreds of thousands of matelots and tommies over the years. It also held a place of special significance for the SBS as the launch-pad of so many Second World War and post-war operations.

So 6SBS was deployed in its usual soft-footed fashion to hold the fort and generally have a good look around the coast to make sure Franco wasn't planning any other surprises, such as a sea-borne invasion or, perhaps, a blockade. This niggling dispute over Gibraltar had rumbled on intermittently for years and would continue until Franco died, and still occasionally resurfaces in the Spanish Parliament. The SBS connection with Gibraltar continues to this day. A large piece of rock was brought back to England by Richard Clifford to stand as a memorial to SBS men who lost their lives in action. Today, it is positioned at the entrance to the headquarters building at Poole.

Meanwhile, the unremitting chill of the Cold War and Soviet repression of any Eastern European nation that stepped out of line ensured the continued employment of the mass of British armed forces. Cuts would still be necessary. The declared policy of the Chiefs of Defence Staff in 1961 – 'Britain must be prepared to intervene in Asia and Africa . . . Her major military role over the next decade' – was dead and buried. The review of defence in the 1970s focused on the forces' commitments to Europe and NATO, defence against the Soviets, and what was termed a policy of strategic mobility – military or naval intervention if, when and where needed – to which the politicians would add, only when absolutely necessary. Cuts and more cuts were demanded as the troops piled home after that final splurge of 1960s activity.

Everything's changing, they were saying. Air power – that's the future. The foot-soldiers will be ambulance chasers, mopping up local difficulties. Fewer men, fewer ships, and the army mustn't go looking for trouble. It's all changing fast. And do we really need Special Forces? Both SAS and SBS found themselves in a tricky situation. They had nowhere 'active' to do their stuff, no arena in which to score points or collect gongs. Not a single conflagration anywhere that might require the services of upfront raiders, saboteurs and beach recce experts. Or, at least, that's how matters appeared for a while – until terrorists and the IRA turned up the heat.

The SBS brought its sections home from the Far East and Bahrain and regrouped in Poole in new accommodation that had been designed to hold fewer sections. It found itself squeezed by a most unsatisfactory chain of command that ran through various levels of the Royal Marines and ended at a desk in the Ministry of Defence in London. If they wanted work they had to go and find it.

The SAS was promoting itself fiercely. Its last piece of action was in Dhofar in 1970, and when it ended there was nothing on the stocks, so it invented a new role for itself.

Back at its Hereford headquarters it drew up a list of important VIPs and heads of state around the world whose assassination would be against British interests. This the SAS took to London, to offer the Foreign Office, through the MoD, a unique service: it would train and equip bodyguards for these people, and Britain would be rewarded by the protected VIP with political or economic favours. In certain special or urgent cases, the SAS would itself provide the bodyguards until such time as local cover could be trained. A special house was built at headquarters for training purposes.

On a wider brief, the SAS could continue to offer training and instruction for Special Forces for the likes of the Sultan of Brunei, the Sultan of Oman or the Royal Family of Saudi Arabia, or wherever they might be needed – just as the SBS was already doing for the Shah of Iran. There were dozens of countries that would hire the SAS's services, given the opportunity, though it would become a matter of government policy as to who would be eligible for such a service.

Such training would be called Team Tasking, and it consisted of training packages devised by the Special Forces for the security forces or police forces of other friendly nations, generally to be carried out in these countries. Team Tasks were usually at the request of a foreign government and were subject to approval by the Ministry of Defence and ultimately the Cabinet. Nor were the SAS and the SBS the only forces offering this service. From the early 1970s it became a competitive business, with Special Forces of several Western countries competing for the business and more often than not managing to undercut the British charges.

Once government approval had been obtained, an advisory team would visit the host country to map out its needs. SBS training was sought by a number of countries prior to 1979, but by definition the only true team tasks were setting up the Australian commandos, creating the Malay Special Services Regiment in 1965, and training the Iranian SBS, which went on from 1965 to 1979. The SBS was not backward in looking for mainstream tasks either; it had to, or it wouldn't have survived. Successive officers commanding SBS secured operational work in the early 1970s largely through their own efforts and contacts rather than by way of orders from above.

They did, however, have a friend in a higher place or, as one who was there at the time put it, on the right hand of God. Colonel John Mottram, OBE, who had been in the SBS early in his career with Pat Troy, was by then in a senior position on the staff of the Commandant General, Royal Marines. He was in a position to influence the future of his former outfit.

This he would do by writing the SBS into a paper drumming up support for a counter-terrorist force (although that was some way into the future; at the beginning of the new decade, it was not even on the drawing-board, and no one guessed or contemplated the carnage that lay ahead). For the time being the SBS found itself taking on tasks that were different from anything it had tackled before; a wider brief took it into both civilian and military areas. The basic premise was the same, but the *modus operandi* was very different.

The first task that fell into the civilian category was a fairly small operation. The Bahamas police force had discovered evidence of a Cuban-based drugs- and arms-running ring operating from a remote part of the island of Andros. Britain was still responsible for the defence of the islands, which were just achieving independence from colonial rule. The approach to the area was such that it was beyond a safe landing for the ill-equipped policemen. An SBS detachment was sent to search the island. They discovered evidence of a shooting-range and also the skeleton of a US pilot who had crashed there. But no Cubans were found. On a second deployment to the Caribbean, in support of the Royal Barbados Police, 13 sacks of drugs, worth a considerable street value, were uncovered.

Next came an operation that would be tackled with the true panache, style and daring of an SBS pair, an SAS sergeant and a very courageous bomb-disposal expert; the story can now be told with the benefit of previously unpublished detail.

On 17 May 1972 the switchboard at the New York office of the British-owned Cunard Line received a telephone call at around 3.15 in the afternoon from an American, a mature male with a New York accent, asking to be put through to someone in charge. After explaining that he had vital information relating to the company's flagship and pride of Britain, the *QE2* – at that moment sailing across the Atlantic towards Britain – he was put through to Mr Charlie Dickson, Cunard's finance and operations director for North America.

The caller stated quickly and calmly that a series of six bombs had been placed aboard the ship, hidden in places that would never be found, on various deck levels. They would be exploded while the ship was at sea unless the sum of $350,000 in cash was paid by the following day.

He claimed to have two accomplices aboard the ship who did not care if they lived or died. One was an ex-convict and the other a terminal cancer case. They would detonate the explosives at a given time if the ransom demand were not met. He would make contact again later to make arrangements for the delivery of the money and warned Dickson not to go to the police. If the demand were not met, be assured the *QE2* would be blown out of the water. Then he rang off.

Dickson, a normally quiet and unflappable 58-year-old, was shaking slightly and his mouth was dry as he checked his watch. The *QE2* would be somewhere east of Newfoundland, heading for Cherbourg and then on to her home port of Southampton. There were 1,438 passengers aboard and around 850 crew. Immediately, he called Richard Patton, president of Cunard North America, and together they worked out a plan of action. New York City police were informed; they in turn brought in the FBI. Their advice was to treat the call seriously.

Bomb scares and security alerts in Britain were already becoming commonplace as IRA violence flared in Northern Ireland. Most were hoaxes and, at that time, the bombers had not yet struck on mainland Britain. Cunard themselves had already received a number of hoax calls concerning the *QE2*; nothing was ever found. This one was different – a New York voice that seemed to have nothing to do with politics or Ireland, and a ransom was being demanded, which was not normally the case in bomb scares. It could be a hoaxer, an almighty confidence trick, or it might be for real.

The FBI advised that the latter possibility should be taken as most probable and suggested the company arrange an immediate search of the ship without alerting passengers. Staff and crew should work on the basis that there were bombs on board which would be exploded if the money was not paid. Furthermore, the

FBI advised, the money should be drawn in cash immediately and be available for the drop, as instructed by the caller.

The search of the ship was already under way. Charlie Dickson had wired the *QE2*'s master, Captain William Law, a cool-headed, gruff 60-year-old veteran, by coded message, briefly explaining the alert and ordering a search of the ship without alarming passengers. However, the task was virtually impossible in terms of speed or thoroughness – 13 decks, over 1,000 passenger cabins, miles of corridors, hundreds of nooks and crannies.

Scotland Yard was informed and began combing the passenger list for any suspicious names. Special Branch joined the inquiry, as did the Yard's bomb investigations specialists. The list was also wired to the FBI. All shore-to-ship calls were monitored for any coded message from the New Yorker to his supposed accomplices on board. But the bands played on, the games of bridge and the chat in the bar were uninterrupted, and in the evening the gala dinners went ahead as usual. Life remained apparently undisturbed on board, the passengers unaware of the drama unfolding around them.

Throughout the night, *QE2* staff continued their search. The following morning, Victor Matthews, chairman of Cunard, called an emergency meeting of his directors in London, and they agreed to follow the FBI's advice. The ransom money would be drawn from a New York bank ready for payment. Cunard also contacted the Ministry of Defence, and the alert went all the way to the top: Prime Minister Edward Heath was informed.

The MoD put the SBS and the SAS on standby, along with the Royal Army Ordnance Corps (RAOC) bomb-disposal unit. Somehow, a team of experts had to be flown out to the *QE2*, equipped to deal with the bombs. There was no point in waiting to see if the continuing search of the ship turned up any or not. There could be an explosion at any minute. No one really knew for sure. By then, the *QE2* was around 1,500 miles from home. The only way to reach her was by air and a parachute drop of men and equipment into the sea – exactly the kind of operation the SBS had been training for in recent times.

At the Poole headquarters, SBS officer commanding, Major S. L. Syrad MC, RM, took the MoD call at around 11.35 on the morning of the eighteenth. It so happened that Lieutenant Richard Clifford, officer commanding 2SBS, was outside his door at the time. Syrad gave him brief orders: prepare to send two men by air to jump to a ship at sea. No name or location was given. Clifford decided he should go himself and collected as his number two Corporal Tom Jones. Dry diving-suits and parachuting equipment were prepared quickly by them, with a set for the explosives expert who would be joining them from the RAOC.

A Wasp helicopter was commandeered from the Royal Naval Air Service at Portland – not without some toing and froing, because operational codewords did not then exist for unscheduled covert movements in those days. In due course, however, the helicopter arrived at 1 p.m. and ferried the SBS team to RAF Lyneham. Flight Sergeant Terry Allen, AFM, the SBS parachute jump instructor, was already at the air base preparing for the flight.

Back in New York, Charlie Dickson was in his office at first light waiting for the call. Like Richard Clifford, he had decided he would go himself, personally taking the cash to the blackmailer when he was told where to drop it. He sat back for a long wait . . .

The *QE2* sailed on . . . breakfast . . . elevenses . . . lunch . . . a quiet snooze in the library . . . a walk on the deck . . . a bit of clay-pigeon shooting off the stern . . . and the officers and engineers were still searching.

At Lyneham, Richard Clifford and Tom Jones linked up with the demolitions officer, Captain Robert Williams, and Sergeant Cliff Oliver from the SAS. The four men still had no idea where they were going or which ship was involved – not an uncommon aspect of SBS tasking, as already seen. After a short delay, probably for ministerial clearance, the team boarded an RAF C130 Hercules and took off for what would be a four-hour flight to reach the ship. After 15 minutes aloft, the men were told their destination and what would be required of them. The Hercules was tracked by a Nimrod maritime reconnaissance aircraft.

One other member of the team on the sidelines was Flight Sergeant Geoff Bald, another parachute instructor. He had a particular mission: to give advice to Captain Williams, who never in his life had done any military parachuting, let alone into water – which, as any SBS man knows, is not a pleasant experience first time down, and especially into cold, rough and windswept Atlantic waters. Williams had previously completed only three static line jumps in freefall mode, which he hated.

They had around three hours of flying time to drill Captain Williams in parachuting without his actually doing it. It did not augur well for the operation when Williams announced that he did not feel too good. Geoff Bald tried to reassure him: 'Not to worry. You'll be all right by the time you reach the target.'

In New York Charlie Dickson was looking at his watch every five minutes. It was now 2.15 p.m. (local time) and he had not received a phone call. He was beginning to think the whole thing was an absurd hoax when his office door burst open and he was brought a hand-written letter that had just arrived by special delivery – 28 cents postage due! The letter instructed Mr Dickson to place the $350,000 in $10 and $20 bills in a blue canvas bag and proceed to a certain telephone booth on Route 299, two hours north of New York City, where he would receive a call giving him further directions. 'You will be watched,' the note read. 'Be alone. Any sign of police and you will have a catastrophe on your hands. Remember Hong Kong [an apparent reference to the old *QE* which had burned out in Hong Kong harbour the previous year].'

Dickson was instructed to arrive at the telephone box at 9.30 p.m. If anything went wrong, the ship would blow within the hour. The FBI wanted to send an agent to make the drop. Dickson insisted that he went himself; he dare not, he said, risk the lives of 2,300 people.

The Hercules was half an hour off the target when the four men began final preparations for their drop. They had pulled on their dry suits. Captain Williams was still feeling decidedly unwell.

The plan was that the two NCOs would carry the bulk of the equipment, and Lieutenant Clifford would carry one smaller pack attached to his body by a line with a breaking point of 1,500 pounds (680 kilogrammes). His main task would be to talk Captain Williams through the drills in the air and to make sure he did not drown when they hit the water. The parachute used was a PX, whereby the parachutist has to remove his reserve, release the main buckle and clear his leg straps when 200 feet above the sea, so that he does not get dragged in the water.

'*Attention, please . . . attention . . . this is your captain speaking . . .*'
After-lunch snoozes and the games of bridge were halted as *QE2* master Captain Law ordered 'Stop engines!' and made his announcement to the passengers at 2.20 p.m. ship's time. 'We will shortly be taking procedures to check a report that there may be a bomb on board. We have already conducted a search of the ship

and found nothing. The likelihood is fairly remote . . . However, we have to be certain. Very shortly we will be receiving the assistance of British bomb-disposal experts, who will be circling by RAF aircraft very shortly. They will be dropped into the sea and will be brought aboard. In the meantime, please try not to alarm yourselves . . .'

Crowds rushed back to their cabins to grab their cameras and line the deck railings. The games of bridge were abandoned, although one stubborn foursome at a crucial point in the game carried on with their hands. For the moment they could see nothing . . . the team had hit problems.

The cloud base was down to a variable 300 to 400 feet (90 to 120 metres) when the Hercules reached the *QE2*. The ship was not even visible from the safety of 1,000 feet (300 metres). The Nimrod, with all its radar and tracking communications, was close by, acting as the eyes and the link between the Hercules, the *QE2* and London. It was raining and the *QE2* reported a 20-knot (37-kilometre-per-hour) wind, with a long 5-foot (1.5-metre) swell running in the sea. Every one of those statistics – cloud base, wind and swell – were well outside the safety limits for jumps over water. Training manuals put cloud at a very minimum of 1,200 feet (365 metres). Their situation was not even half that safety margin; a jump from their height without clear sight below was not only unsafe but an impossibility; 1,000 feet (300 metres) was the minimum height allowed to ensure the operation of the reserve parachute in case of malfunction. This was especially important in the case of an inexperienced jumper – and their key man was one of those!

A brief conflab as the aircraft circled, flying blind through the cloud, and Flight Sergeant Terry Allen suggested a possible solution: if they first got underneath the cloud, the pilot could then open the throttle and climb rapidly, disgorging the para-drop team at the point of extra gravitational pull. Flight Sergeant Bald agreed that it could work; difficult, perhaps, and dangerous, but the only way to get them down into the water. The others agreed.

The huge plane was buffeting and banging in the turbulence. Captain Williams felt 'jolly sick', visibly green and 'scared to death'. He tried his best to look calm as the aircraft dipped below the cloud at around 350 feet (100 metres), a highly dangerous manoeuvre. Williams was barely able to look down when the expanse of water below him finally came into view.

The pilot made several dummy runs to test the plan before the first drop. The two NCOs, Tom Jones and Cliff Oliver, would go first, carrying the bulk of the bomb-disposal gear, parachuting blind in the cloud. They positioned themselves by the port door, with Flight Sergeants Allen and Bald standing by. The aircraft came around again to the drop zone, eased up to around 500 feet (150 metres), and then . . . nose up and throttle hard to climb to 800 feet (240 metres). As he did so – and only Tom Jones's words can describe the moment – 'on Sergeant Allen's command we forced ourselves through the port door against an exceptionally high gravitational force which I am positive lifted all four of us off the flight-deck. During descent we carried out the necessary drills and quickly hit the water, too damn near the bows of the ship for my liking. Although the sea was running a heavy swell, it was refreshing after so long in the plane.'

A QE2 lifeboat set off to collect them, cameras whirring and clicking among the crowds lining the deck rails. Not an inch of viewing space was spare.

Now, back again for the second drop, and as the Hercules pilot dipped low again Captain Williams threw up, every morsel of his stomach contents heaving forth. The Flight Sergeants were yelling last-minute instructions above the roar of the plane and the turbulence, and then . . . Go!

They made their jump on the next pass by the same process. Watching from the bridge of the QE2, Captain Law saw Williams land awkwardly and disappear under the water. Law was sure he had been injured. He bobbed back to the surface and appeared to be giving a signal. Lieutenant Clifford swam quickly to his side and held him afloat until the ship's lifeboat recovered them. The NCOs and their equipment were then hauled aboard, having been in the water for about ten minutes waiting for the other two to join them.

The team was taken aboard the QE2. Williams was not injured, explaining that he just felt bloody sick. They immediately reported to Captain Law on the bridge, who briefed them on what he had done so far. Captain Williams then took charge of the team and the situation. Before starting a search, Lieutenant Clifford presented Captain Law with the day's newspaper, which he had picked up on the way out of the SBS base.

The search was continued and a suspicious-looking case was blown open by Captain Williams. False alarm. Several passengers were also questioned, and two large and very heavy suitcases opened and examined. They were found to be crammed with books.

Charlie Dickson was now heading out on Route 299 to the telephone box where he was to receive further instruction on where to leave the $350,000. He reached it ten minutes before the appointed time. He waited. Disguised FBI agents were doing drive-bys. The phone rang at 9.40 p.m. and Dickson recognised the voice as the previous caller. He obviously knew that the police had been called in, and asked Dickson why he had done so – he had now put the lives of everyone on board the ship at risk.

Dickson said he had had no choice; his board of directors was involved, Cunard was a public company and he had to do it to get the money. The caller gave him further instructions. He was to drive to a small diner nearby and go straight to the washroom. There he would find a message taped underneath the washbasin. And, by the way, there would be three guns trained on him.

Dickson did as instructed. He found the message, which directed him to one more place, a deserted area further down the road. He would there discover a marker where he should leave the bag. Once the money had been received without incident, the message said, then a call would be made to the *QE2* enabling the bombs to be disarmed.

The instructions were followed to the letter. Dickson dropped the bag by the marker and drove off. The FBI remained on hand, discreetly and clandestinely.

On the *QE2*, Captain Williams and his team had found no trace of bombs, and by the early hours of the morning they were given a meal and a stiff drink, provided with cabins and began the two-day journey to Cherbourg in first-class order. *En route* they continued their checks and searches, and when that was done were entertained lavishly by grateful passengers. 'Their hospitality was embarrassing at times,' said Tom Jones, 'especially the Americans. But it was nice to see how much our efforts had been appreciated.'

The FBI was still not convinced that the call was a hoax and suggested that the ship be evacuated immediately it reached Cherbourg. In the event, that was not enacted. Twenty-four hours later the bag containing the cash was still where Charlie Dickson had left it, watched by the FBI. All shore-to-ship calls were blocked until the *QE2* docked.

She sailed on to Southampton. No bombs or any devices were ever found, and Charlie Dickson never heard from the extortionist again. The bag was picked up as soon as the *QE2* reached Cherbourg. No bombs were ever found but the caller's threat had caused a four-man team to display considerable courage in jumping into the sea to get to the ship. Each of them was awarded the Queen's Commendation for Brave Conduct. Lieutenant Clifford was also nominated the Royal Navy Man of the Year for both the *QE2* affair and his first successful crossings of the Atlantic in his own 26-foot (7.9-metre) yacht.

As for Captain Williams: 'I never want to go through anything like that ever again.' For the SBS, however, the exercise proved to be merely a prelude to another alert aboard the *QE2* – one that would require a force of 30 of its top men to handle.

CHAPTER FIFTEEN

And again . . .

Terrorists and extremists were already a reality in the United Kingdom and their activities spread across the world. Bombs and bullets soon began to shatter the lives of ordinary folk, far from any theatre of war or place of conflict, pursuing their daily lives in all innocence. And now terrorism blazes out from the television in the corner of the living-room: war on the doorstep, watched in the home.

The irony of this new twist for the military and the intelligence gurus to wrestle with was nowhere more plain than in Britain itself, and they were at last confronting it, if tenuously, by using the Special Forces. The *QE2* mission became an operational model for the future. It was dissected, and lessons were noted and redrawn into a contingency plan which would be activated for any future attacks on ships or in coastal waters by terrorists or other insurgents. It was a prophetic move. Variations on the same theme would soon be much in demand for anti-ship attacks and, more especially, for counter-terrorist activity when the oil-rigs began to mushroom in the North Sea. And if any doubts remained as to the need for Special Forces and rapid-action teams, ready to respond to any situation, anywhere in the world, the *QE2* operation and the events of the next few months would dispel them once and for all.

Urban guerrillas and bands of extremists were in their embryonic formation across Europe and the Middle East: Black September, Bader-Meinhoff, Red Brigades, IRA and PLO to name but a few. It was almost two years since the four airliners were blown up in Jordan and, in the aftermath, all Palestinians were expelled by King Hussein. Anniversary trouble was anticipated, but the Germans were not adequately prepared for the way it was to be marked – by Palestinians causing death and mayhem among the 10,000 international athletes at the 1972 Munich Olympic Games. As an exercise in how *not* to handle such a situation, this one, supervised by German security forces with politicians in close direction, was a classic.

At dawn on 5 September a group of eight Black September Arab guerrillas broke into the Israeli building in the Olympic Village. The Germans had been tipped off in advance to expect some form of attack and had 250 plain-clothes police patrolling the area. None of them saw the Arab invaders dressed in black scale the fence.

They burst into the Israeli building with sub-machine-guns blazing at 5.10 a.m. Moshe Weinberg, a wrestling coach, was killed instantly; Yosef Romano, a weightlifter, was fatally wounded as he held a door shut while two of his team-mates escaped through the window. Another 15 also escaped through the windows and side-doors. Ten were taken hostage, but one of them, Gad Tsabari, suddenly made a dash for freedom, weaving in and out and dodging bullets to escape.

The guerrillas remained holed up in the building with their nine remaining hostages. They demanded the release of 200 Palestinians held in Israeli jails and a safe passage out of Germany. Within hours the Olympic Village was surrounded by 12,000 police. The games were suspended and the remaining Israeli team members prepared to leave Munich because security measures were blatantly inadequate. With the world looking on through intense television coverage, West German Chancellor Willy Brandt arrived to take personal charge of negotiations with the terrorists. There were dramatic televised pictures of German officials talking to the guerrilla leader, who was wagging his finger at them while dictating terms.

Brandt and his advisers agreed that the terrorists would be allowed to leave Germany with their hostages and fly to an Arab country. They were taken by helicopter to the Fürstenfeld military airport 25 miles from Munich. Just before midnight the guerrillas and their nine remaining Israeli athletes began to walk across the tarmac to a waiting Boeing 727 aircraft. They had walked about half-way when suddenly all the airport lights were turned out and German police marksmen opened fire.

The rescue attempt went tragically wrong. In the ensuing gun battle all nine hostages were killed, along with four Arabs and one German policeman. Three Arabs were captured, and the other just ran away and escaped. Just over a month later the Black September group struck again, two of them armed with pistols and grenades hijacking a Lufthansa Boeing 727 over Turkey. The terrorists demanded the release of their three comrades held after the Olympic Games débâcle. Germany gave in and did as requested to avoid further bloodshed and another disaster like the one at Munich, about which they were roundly criticised.

Everyone, from governments to airlines and any organisations involving the gathering of large numbers of people, had the jitters as a world-wide terrorist campaign gained momentum, joined eventually by other groups, other extremists, and a supporting cast which included Colonel Gaddafi and assorted Arab leaders based in Beirut.

For Black September, another possible target was already moving into view – the *QE2*, with perhaps as many as 1,500 Jews on board. On 19 October 1972 it became known that the ship had been chartered by Mr Oscar Rudnick, president of Assured Travel, Worcester, Massachusetts, specifically to carry Jews from America and Europe to Israel for the celebrations of the twenty-fifth anniversary of the Jewish state the following April.

Originally billed in low-key fashion as an 'Easter and Passover' cruise, the trip provided the opportunity of joining the *QE2* at Southampton, sailing to Haifa for a ten-day stop, then returning to Southampton. Alternatively, passengers could join the ship in Haifa. The population of the ship would be almost entirely Jewish. In fact, the trip was just one of a number of international cruises being organised from various countries.

The cruise received a large number of bookings, substantially from the US, and Rudnick was anticipating that the ship would be full when she eventually sailed. However, after the Black September attack on the Olympics, a particularly active union convenor for *QE2* workers, Joe Allan, went public over a situation that Cunard had hoped to keep the lid on, at least for the time being. He made a press statement claiming that the intended Jewish cruise posed a threat to his members, who were likely to be killed in the event of a terrorist attack, and said that in view of Munich his workers would want danger money – or they would not go aboard.

Cunard made it clear that it had thought things through and

had decided to go ahead with the cruise. The fact was that since all *QE2* sailings were planned and scheduled well in advance, the company had long ago contacted the Ministry of Defence for discussions. These had reached ministerial level and were put in the hands of a committee led by the Commandant General's Chief of Staff, Royal Marines, who in turn reported to the Joint Operations Committee chaired by Prime Minister Edward Heath.

It was with the Munich disaster fresh in public focus that security arrangements for the *QE2* and her passengers was planned. Assessments of the likelihood of terrorist action presented a gloomy scenario – that Black September, specifically, was planning to infiltrate the cruise for an on-board attack or, possibly, to raid the ship by sea or air. To this threat was added a later interjection by Colonel Gaddafi, who stated bluntly that the *QE2* would be blown out of the water.

Edward Heath and his ministers laid down the policy that became the adopted stance throughout the coming decade of terrorist attacks and on into the 1980s and the IRA atrocities: that British life, institutions and commerce would not be cowed by such threats or even attacks. Cunard's chairman Victor Matthews (later Lord Matthews from a life peerage awarded during Margaret Thatcher's premiership) agreed, but obviously needed more protection than he could muster from his own security resources or private organisations.

Although Cunard had themselves introduced sophisticated security screening since the bomb threat a year earlier, only the military could mount an adequate defence or deterrent against possible terrorist attack or action by Gaddafi-backed raiders. Cunard therefore formally asked the MoD to arrange the cover, for which the shipping line would make a payment towards costs.

An operations officer from the security service and Major D. A. Pentland, the officer commanding the Special Boat Company – as it was then called – set about planning the operation. It was significant in one other major and sensitive area: it would bring the Special Forces under the media microscope for the first time and in a manner that was totally new to them. Lessons and precautions would be learned in that direction, too, leading quite quickly to what became the established code of secrecy surrounding all future SBS and SAS operations, and about the forces themselves.

In the months leading up to the cruise, a plan was devised and rehearsed. Apart from discreet naval and air cover to accompany the *QE2* when she sailed out of Southampton, there would also be a large covert contingent of SBS personnel aboard the ship. The planning and the nature of that presence was, as one might expect, governed by strict security. It would entail 30 well-armed and well-equipped SBS travelling on the ship throughout the cruise to provide continual on-board, surface and underwater surveillance. Their cover story was that they were trainee Cunard travel agents, a device which in the face of media scrutiny was later accepted as being a touch naive.

Sending any group of Special Forces into operations where they were supposed to fade unobtrusively into the civilian population was quite new. To achieve that objective, the men had to adopt the appearance of ordinary everyday citizens, with long 1970s-style hair and stylish civilian clothes. True enough, in covert beach recces in Cyprus and the Middle East SBS operatives had often disguised their military origins, but never in their home base or in this manner. The sudden appearance of SBS ranks wandering around with shoulder-length hair, coloured sweatshirts, flared trousers and sneakers caused a stir among the Royal Marines at Poole. In fact, it became the uniform of the future.

The operational plans were submitted to the Chiefs of Staff and finally approved on 30 March 1973, two weeks before the cruise began. The force commander, Major Pentland, was himself under direct command of the MoD's Director of Operations, Central. Each member of the team would carry a pistol at all times, generally a Browning 0.38 automatic. This was to be hidden in their clothing, with each carrying an underarm holster. The SBS also devised a crotch holster made of suede leather for use when the men were wearing shorts.

Their general equipment – always a feature of any SBS operation – included Sterling sub-machine carbines, rocket-launchers, explosives, their own communications radio for secure signals, and their diving gear. They would be going over the side at regular intervals to check the hull of the ship for bombs. Finally, the briefing gave Major Pentland open-ended rules of engagement – to take whatever measures were necessary in the event of an attack.

On 15 April the planes carrying American Jews who were to join the cruise began arriving at Heathrow. By then, their numbers had been dramatically reduced by cancellations. The original anticipated 1,500 passengers was now down to around 650, and the organisers stood to lose a fortune. They were ferried by coaches under strict security and police escort to Southampton to join the British passengers. The Ocean Terminal was surrounded by police and soldiers. The media focused on the new phenomenon of the security checks that would soon become a way of life in Britain, whether in airport terminals, department stores or theatres. All luggage was searched, hand baggage checked and passengers frisked with electronic scanners.

Very little had passed into public domain about the extent of the military cover involved other than the statement that the *QE2* would be shadowed by an RAF Nimrod and other long-range aircraft along with escort ships of the Royal Navy, including one capable of launching guided missiles.

John Penrose was among the small army of Fleet Street journalists who joined the cruise. He reported:

> It was a curious feeling. After all the drama of getting aboard, and passing through nine separate security checks, the ship itself was eerily silent, a virtual ghost ship. With so few passengers, corridors and bars were deserted. Bands played to almost empty rooms. Waiters stood about idly. And the ironic line in the brochure promising 'excitement and adventure' had taken on a rather sinister meaning. Apart from that, we knew that there were men of the Royal Marines on board, and that frogmen had been diving underneath to check for explosives, but their presence was especially unnoticeable.

The *QE2* sailed away with an escort of small craft seeing her off, including Prime Minister Heath in his newly launched ocean racer, *Morning Cloud*. As for the SBS, they performed their drills and recces according to plan, while up above the Nimrod appeared at critical points for overhead surveillance. The ship made one call at Lisbon, where the SBS divers once again checked for limpet mines, and then sailed into the Mediterranean, where the American 6th Fleet joined the watch. As she neared Haifa, security was tightened again. The SBS men were on permanent watch, and the Israelis provided two heavily armed escort ships at the 50-nautical-mile limit from their coast.

The journey, with its subdued and rather nervous passengers, passed without incident, and the *QE2* sailed into Haifa, where she remained berthed for ten days. This period was, perhaps, the most critical of the entire journey for the SBS team, now working in cooperation with Israeli security forces under the direction of Mossad. They were prepared for every possible eventuality, all types of attack.

One Israeli general in charge of Haifa took objection to this. His complaints, recorded in an article in the *Daily Telegraph* by R. Barry O'Brien, were that security had been too tight and over the top. Many people had been scared off what had been a wonderful project, he said, all because of the 'tremendous exaggeration' of security needs by Cunard and the British government. Within a matter of months he would be eating his words as terrorist atrocities were unleashed around the world in an unprecedented manner – including a sea-borne attack on Haifa itself. There, raiders in inflatables came ashore just south of the harbour, hijacked three buses travelling along a coast road, and killed 30 passengers and wounded 80 others.

The general's outburst, however, led London journalists who stayed for the duration, and bereft of action, to take a glance at the security cover. Some indication of Special Forces on board had been leaked by a drunken marine who spoke Arabic and had been brought along only as an interpreter. The day the return voyage began, R. Barry O'Brien ran a further story, this time in the *Sunday Telegraph*. Under the headline '*QE2* Agents Uncovered', he announced that a party of 'armed British soldiers playing James Bond roles as plain-clothes marksmen are changing their cover for the return journey'. On the way out they posed as travel agents; now they were booked in as individual tourists.

The *Sunday Telegraph* editor, was prevailed on by the MoD not to publish more of O'Brien's copy, because doing so might have endangered a particular source of intelligence in Libya. This indicated that Colonel Gaddafi had drawn up plans to launch a missile attack from two motor torpedo-boats as the ship passed the north coast of Libya. The SBS informed the *QE2* master, Captain Mortimer Hare, a veteran of Second World War Atlantic convoys. He quite coolly said he would run the ship up to maximum speed, and was quite sure that he could easily outpace the MTBs if ever they appeared. A Nimrod circled overhead to keep watch, but Gaddafi's boats didn't show up. Nor, on this occasion, did Black September, although they would not be dormant for long, and any lingering doubts about 'over-the-top'

213

security would be totally dispelled. There was no doubt that without the cover the *QE2* was a sitting duck.

The catalogue of terrorist attacks and hostage-taking beginning in the 1970s and extending into the 1990s has been written into history, including the infamous raid by a pro-Palestinian gang on OPEC oil ministers meeting in Vienna in December 1975. They seized 70 hostages, including 11 ministers and the powerful Sheikh Yamani of Saudi Arabia although they were later freed. That same month, by coincidence, the SBS was tasked to begin planning protective cover for yet another cruise on the *QE2*, again in the direction of Israel. Called The Cradle of Civilisation Cruise, it was scheduled to call at Alexandria and Haifa in March 1976, this time with many more passengers.

Taking lessons from the first cruise and, in the intervening years, intensive training on maritime counter-terrorist exercises, the SBS this time, planned a different approach. They used a two-pronged cover: an overt force, wearing Cunard uniforms, provided an obvious if discreet guard, while other SBS men went in plain clothes as tourists mingling with other passengers. All were permanently armed. There was also a careful selection of personnel, using five officers and ten NCOs. Three SBS wives even went along as part of the husbands' cover. They had with them, too, a clearance diver who made regular inspections of the hull. The operation has gone into the SBS archives as a meticulous example of planning and execution which left nothing to chance. It was, curiously enough, also regarded by some of those who took part in it as a tiring (and tiresome) engagement which required long hours of attentive surveillance which, in the end, became 'rather boring'. That could hardly be said of some of the training and operations which confronted the SBS closer to home as they prepared to meet the growing terrorist threat and IRA bomb attacks on the British mainland.

CHAPTER SIXTEEN

Counterforce

The SBS have maintained an intermittent presence in Northern Ireland since 1971 and are still there as these words are being written. Typically, they have kept a low profile and have managed to avoid the critical broadsides launched against the SAS during their time in the province. In spite of medals and commendations won, the SBS has remained out of public view and rarely mentioned in the welter of published and televised material on their counterparts of the SAS or other military and intelligence agencies in the Six Counties during the last 30 years.

Their role in Northern Ireland fell principally into two categories: first, to provide personnel for covert intelligence-gathering and for patrols on the streets, and, secondly, in their more conventional mode of sea-borne operations against gun-runners and terrorists. Admittedly, their strength there has never been high in terms of numbers, and the overwhelming media focus on the SAS was bound to follow by the very nature of the regiment's history. From its origins in desert warfare, running ahead of the charging herd, dropping in on an enemy nest, stirring up trouble behind enemy lines, and dominated by hard-man NCOs, the SAS operated in a manner once described by an American general who served with it for a time as 'soldiering turned upside-down, resembling no military organisation I had ever known'. The unit's arrival in Northern Ireland aroused both indignation and fear and was likened by one commentator as the intelligence equivalent of putting tanks on the streets.

Both SBS and SAS came to Ireland direct from their wars in faraway places. The familiar dark murderous back-streets and alleys in the Middle East and swamp battles with Communist guerrillas in Borneo were replaced with inner-city streets and ambush action in lush countryside within the United Kingdom.

SAS and SBS alike were confronted by a situation for which there was no reference section in the Special Forces handbook, i.e. confrontation from within its own civilian population. The hearts and minds of the natives of Borneo or Dhofar they could handle. Northern Ireland was a different ball game. They were unused to the disciplines of war on the streets, running side by side with the masses, going about their daily lives, surrounded by the fervour of multi-dimensional political, religious and paramilitary activists. Nor had the SAS ever faced the experience of prolonged and intense local media scrutiny that came with those disciplines. No one paid much attention to them in Oman or Sarawak!

Says one former SBS officer:

As everyone knows, the mystique and mythology that surround the Special Forces always existed. Modern controversiality, however, really emanates from the 1970s Northern Ireland experience. Until that time, the SAS – and certainly the SBS – went about their business relatively unscrutinised by the media and largely devoid of widespread public interest. The stories then were of military prowess or unconventional attitudes, and not of trigger-happy maladroits, as the SAS have lately been portrayed. Military response to Northern Ireland and modern terrorism provided the basic ingredients for controversial insight, but a particular, underlying reason for the phenomenon which opened a window upon Special Forces is often overlooked. Here, for the first time, they would be confronted by urban terrorism and anarchy among their own people, British civilians, white English-speaking faces, armed to the hilt. For both SAS and SBS it was a completely new situation. They came to Northern Ireland from the deserts and the mountains of the Middle East. I'm not sure we were either adequately prepared or briefed, at the beginning, to handle it. One school of thought reckoned that coming fresh to it was just what was needed, battered, day in and day out, as the province was, by extremist outrages. No one mentioned either, incidentally, that we would also face political shenanigans and dirty tricks from our own side in those early days which we, I know, tried to steer clear of. We were sideways on to the rivalries that existed within a very crowded intelligence arena. Very dirty stuff. We were dragged in. That's not an excuse. It's a fact. What happened after that ran in with established policy of Her Majesty's Government. There were risk-takers and even renegades among us, of course, and we have always had them. But 99 per cent of the time we moved and operated within the parameters which were set for us, no more and no less, against an enemy who showed no desire for constraint.

SAS involvement and activity in the Six Counties, not undeservedly, became the subject of acres of published material. The SAS has been blamed for many things, some of which happened but not all at the hands of the SAS. The torture of terrorists arrested at the time of the introduction of internment cast the SAS as the main perpetrators, although no SAS unit was serving in Northern Ireland at the time. Their fire power remains indisputable, however, and gave rise to the rumours of shoot-to-kill rules of engagement – between 1971 and 1990 more than two dozen extremists were shot in SAS operations.

The involvement of the SBS goes back to those early terrible, turbulent times, racked with unprecedented violence and killings. Riots flared across the province after the imposition of internment under new emergency powers. In four days that summer, 5,000 Catholics and 2,000 Protestants were made homeless when their properties were burned to the ground. Daily, the death toll mounted from bomb attacks and sniper fire.

The SBS entered this unhappy place in a year that extremist action in Northern Ireland claimed 467 lives, the peak figure for any single year during the modern troubles. Its men were to join a new reconnaissance unit, which was formed on the back of a heady atmosphere of bravado and determination to tackle sectarian violence and anarchy.

The men found themselves swimming in waters muddied by confusion, myth and lies. Law and order in the province had virtually collapsed. The battle to restore them was one in which a misty blur posed as truth. It was the time of an emerging internecine warfare between the two principal non-military

217

intelligence agencies, MI5 and MI6. Meanwhile, the Royal Ulster Constabulary's Special Branch and officers of British Military Intelligence were running their own operations and agents with little coordination between each other.

Plot and counter-plot, dirty tricks and dangerous liaisons were to become rife within a British security effort that was supposed to be fighting terrorists but spent a good deal of time setting traps for each other. Gerald Seymour wrote a novel called *Harry's Game* which was nearer the truth than any of the stories peddled and planted by MI5's media leakage department or characters on the make or with a personal axe to grind.

In the spring of 1971 the SBS was required to send a small number of men for a particular mission: to become part of the Military Reaction Force (MRF), formed as a direct response from political pressure to improve intelligence-gathering. The MRF would put soldiers on the streets of Northern Ireland in civilian clothes to carry out covert and clandestine operations against the IRA.

The MRF was not an SAS unit. It was attached to the 39th Infantry Brigade, and was created by Brigadier (later General) Frank Kitson, Commander of Land Forces, Northern Ireland, from 1970 to 1972, a veteran of the campaign against Mau Mau terrorism in Kenya in the 1950s and later one of the planners of military action involving the SAS in Oman. He attempted to apply some of the same principles used in both those operations to Northern Ireland. Principally, he was to set up a unit that would use all measures of covert activity available to track and identify the bombers and the terrorists. Kitson's most famous coup in Kenya, and copied in Oman, was to turn members of the Mau Mau and use them against their former comrades. He proposed this technique as the basis of the new unit, with soldiers in civilian clothes actively courting ex-IRA members or their supporters – known as 'freds' – to act as spotters and informers to identify active IRA personnel.

They would be photographed by the MRF using concealed camera equipment in unmarked patrol cars. Once identified, they would be entered into the picture files for future surveillance. Among the many other schemes devised to glean intelligence was their infiltration of a massage parlour. Another base for covert operations was the Four Square Laundry, on the surface an ordinary laundry but in fact fronting a forensic laboratory in which clothes brought in were tested for traces of explosives or other incriminating material.

This method of intelligence-gathering was regarded as particularly effective. Addresses from which clothing containing suspect elements was collected were noted and filed and the occupants clandestinely photographed and monitored. Some were among those raided in Operation Motorman in the summer of 1972, when 12,000 troops moved in to smash Ulster's no-go areas, principally in Belfast, Londonderry and small towns designated by Republican leaders as Free Ulster.

The existence of the MRF remained unknown to the public at large, even when two of its members compromised it after opening fire from a moving car with a Thompson sub-machine-gun on two men standing at a bus-stop in Belfast. The two MRF soldiers were arrested and charged with attempted murder. They were later acquitted, stating that they were fired on first. The date of the shooting was 22 June 1972, the very day on which Mr William Whitelaw, Secretary of State for Northern Ireland, revealed that the government would respond favourably to the offer of a ceasefire by the Provisional IRA. MI6, which had helped set up the talks, were furious that their efforts had been jeopardised.

In any event, the ceasefire, tenuous from the outset, was abandoned within the month, on 21 July, when 11 people were killed and 130 injured in IRA bomb attacks in Belfast. The MRF, with its SBS contingent, was finally betrayed by one of its informers, who had turned back to the terrorists. On 2 October 1972 the IRA ambushed the apparently innocent-looking van from Four Square Laundry, killing the driver and wounding his companion. Both were, of course, soldiers in civilian clothes and members of the MRF forensic collection unit. The MRF was disbanded soon afterwards.

Though it had been criticised for some of its more questionable operations, its demise undoubtedly dented the intelligence capability of the security forces, especially in accumulating knowledge from the no-go areas and the so-called Republican ghettos. Towards the end of 1973 a new unit, 14 Intelligence and Security Company, was formed to fill the void, and the SBS now sent ranks to that unit. Fourteen Company also operated under cover names of 4 Field Survey Troop and Northern Ireland Training and Tactical Team.

Again this was not an SAS unit, although it was placed under the command of Captain Julian 'Tony' Ball, who had come from the ranks of the Parachute Regiment and the SAS before gaining his commission in the King's Own Scottish Borderers. His experience in covert operations in Northern Ireland was considered first class, having set up the first covert observation post in the Republican areas of Belfast.

Ball's second-in-command was Lieutenant Robert Nairac, a Grenadier Guardsman and product of Sandhurst and the army's joint intelligence college at Ashford, Kent. Nairac had volunteered for special duties and, like all members of the detachment, had joined special training in which SAS and SBS instructors were used. Operationally, the men were equipped with unmarked Q-cars and had available non-standard weapons, such as Ingram sub-machine-guns with silencers, folding shotguns, small arms, cameras and an array of electronic surveillance gear.

Operations were testing even for SBS and SAS veterans. They could be lying in surveillance for hours or days at a time, or following one man for weeks. They drove around in well-used cars with hidden radios, their small arms carefully out of sight. The recollections of one, operating in 1974, sets the scene:

On my second Sunday night I went out in an old Vauxhall Viva driven by Taff, who'd been around a long time and knew the place backwards. We each had a Browning, and I put mine on my lap hidden by a copy of the *News of the World*. We stopped at traffic lights; two youths were standing in a doorway clocking traffic. They rushed forward and yanked Taff's door open. 'Get out of the car,' he screamed, 'or I'll blow your fucking head off.' His right hand was inside his bomber jacket. I thumbed the safety catch on my pistol and looked at him. Where was his shooter? Show me your shooter, you bastard. I couldn't do anything. If he was unarmed, I'd be up for murder. I glanced at the other, still standing there. To shoot or not to shoot? Taff took the decision for me. 'Fuck off, you wanker,' he said, and pulled the door towards him and smashed it back into the youth. Then Taff was off, screeching the car on the wrong side of the road . . . I radioed in . . . and realised I was shaking. This was a different type of fear than in Oman. This wasn't nervous tension, followed by the old adrenalin rush . . . This was sudden shock. I'd been close, very close, to appearing in the dock on a murder charge.

On 16 January 1975 the IRA ended its Christmas ceasefire. Six days earlier one of the commanders of the Provisional IRA, John Francis Green, had been shot in an isolated farmhouse in County Monaghan, where he was taking a Christmas break. The IRA blamed the SAS. Some years later Captain Fred Holroyd, an intelligence officer of the Royal Corps of Transport, and several investigative journalists would claim that Green was shot by Captain Ball and Lieutenant Nairac, accompanied by two unnamed NCOs from 14 Intelligence Company. They burst into the farmhouse and opened fire, then Ball took Polaroid pictures of the body before they left. According to Tim Pat Coogan, in his book *The Troubles*, 'MI6 had engineered the truce; MI5 wanted it broken down'.

Ball and Nairac were unable to answer this oft-disputed claim. They were both dead by then. Tony Ball returned to the SAS in 1975 and left the service two years later with the rank of lieutenant-colonel to command the Special Forces of the Sultan of Oman. He was killed in a car crash in Dhofar in 1978, at the age of 38, and was subsequently transferred to the place where most SAS end up – their own burial ground at Hereford.

Nairac, more famously, was a victim of the IRA. On 14 May 1977, by then a captain, he was kidnapped by the Provisionals while on a covert operation in South Armagh, lured from the bar of The Three Steps public house at Drummintree. After a massive 48-hour search by troops and police discovered only his damaged and blood-stained Triumph Dolomite, the Provisional IRA announced that Nairac had been arrested, interrogated (meaning tortured) and executed. They claimed that he was an SAS man, which was untrue, although by then a number of SAS men had joined SBS in 14 Intelligence Company.

By the time of Nairac's death, the SAS were in Northern Ireland in strength. On 7 January 1976 Prime Minister Harold Wilson announced that the 22 SAS Regiment would supply a squadron for patrol and surveillance. The statement was treated with derision within Ulster and by a number of British journalists, who claimed that the SAS had 'always been there, shooting and killing at will'. In those confused days, the MRF and 14 Intelligence Company had no lines of distinction. They were all engaged in covert operations and as such were branded as SAS regardless. The demarcation lines were further blurred when 14 Intelligence Company and its SBS contingent was brought under a new joint command with the SAS, known as Intelligence and Security Group. It was this renamed unit that Robert Nairac was attached to when he was captured by the IRA.

The arrival of the SAS was meant to be a public relations exercise on Wilson's part. It was in response to a recent spate of killings, the deaths of 49 British soldiers in the South Armagh border area with the Republic of Ireland, and mounting criticism of the government's failure to curb months of anarchy. What Wilson's announcement also meant, but did not say, was that the military was changing its method of intelligence-gathering.

From then on the SAS became the subject of intense focus and criticism, which the SBS managed to avoid, although it continued to operate within the intelligence-gathering community and later jointly on operations with the SAS.

By the time the SAS arrived in force in 1976, the main body of SBS was continuing with its more traditional business off the coast of Northern Ireland. The SBS was a natural contender to beat the gun-runners. Coastline recces for possible landing-points were carried out and have been constantly updated ever since. A number of ships suspected of carrying guns and explosives were tracked and intercepted, but by far the greater activity of the SBS from the mid-1970s was focused on the area exclusively devoted to their talents – anti-terrorism at sea, which was not especially to do with the IRA.

In 1975 the SBS was written into plans for a new and, for them, exciting Maritime Counter-Terrorist Force, which was formed specifically to guard against international terrorism raging out of control across Europe and the Middle East. The emphasis everywhere was on security, intelligence and prevention. Special government committees were formed jointly with the Home Office and the Foreign Office to coordinate a combined military and civilian strategy covering everything from day-to-day security on British streets to airports, shipping terminals and sensitive installations.

The SBS would participate in providing a prompt reaction to terrorism involving ships, harbours and coastal installations. Most of all, Britain's mushrooming and lonesome oil-rigs of the North

Sea were believed to be particularly vulnerable. The Royal Marines were tasked to provide a series of anti-terrorist reaction forces. These were divided initially into three groups: a detachment of marines who were on two hours' notice to move (NTM), an SBS section at four hours' NTM, and a rifle company at twenty-four hours' NTM.

The only dedicated force was the SBS section 1SBS; the others were to be raised on a rotation basis, although as the number of oil-rigs grew this was found to be an unsatisfactory arrangement as the task was extremely specialised and would require a dedicated force with its own command and control team, intelligence group and support team.

The SBS was involved in many training operations and experiments for the new force. They perfected greater efficiency of dropping to a target at sea from an RAF C130 or helicopter, parachuting teams with their Gemini inflatables as close as possible to the target zone without being spotted. The Geminis would be secured to platforms; inside would be packed their equipment, weapons, engine fuel and outboard motor, all in waterproof bags and all secured by a ring-main of rope. The team, parachuting separately, would, on landing, cut free the ring-main so that the platform and the engine packing would sink, then put the engine in place, load their weapons and set off for their target.

Fresh work was also carried out on the exit and re-entry of SBS men from submarines while at sea and while submerged. Many weeks of coordinated planning were needed to perfect the system because of the inherent dangers of releasing divers through a time-consuming system of breathing connections from the moment they moved into the five-man chamber in the submarine through which they would make their exit and, once outside, release their boats, equipment and weapons from housing units on the casing before finally making their way to the surface.

Delivering anti-terrorist forces by submarine was a favoured method in the Joint Theatre Plan for a clandestine approach of an occupied oil-rig, particularly if a huge rough swell were running in the North Sea. However, there were only three submarines in the British Navy fitted with five-man exit and re-entry chambers. SBS training officers were quick to point out that if such a task occurred, and there was no five-man-chamber boat available, how would they get the men near enough for a really clandestine method of entry? And if two of the five-man-chamber boats were otherwise engaged, only four men could be carried to the target rig.

What could four men do? Captain Neil Johnstone dreamed up a system of breathing apparatus and air-bottles on the casing that would allow the multi-release of up to 14 swimmers who then go to the surface and swim towards the target. This was so successful in rigged-up trials that the Royal Marines awarded Johnstone the princely bonus of £45, a Herbert Lott award, and the system was accepted into service within 14 months.

The scope of the counter-terrorist force soon began to expand. By the turn of the decade there would be 130 oil and gas installations around Britain's coastline and more being built. In April 1979 the Admiralty Board and the Chiefs of Staff approved the formation of a new, independent company of 300 ranks, called Comacchio Company after one of the Royal Marines' most famous victories on Lake Comacchio in Italy towards the end of the Second World War. They were based at RM Condor Arbroath in May 1980, and in addition were charged with providing a fast-reaction force for the protection of nuclear weapons in both static sites and in transit, and for counter-terrorist movements on offshore installations or ships at sea.

The SBS in Poole deployed one dedicated counter-terrorism team to Comacchio, which became 5SBS; 1SBS remained in Poole to provide the lead section to combat terrorist incidents on ships. Meanwhile, a series of exercises and rehearsals was planned aboard the oil-rigs with the cooperation of the United Kingdom Offshore Operators' Association. In top-level exercises, the Home Office, the Foreign Office or possibly the Cabinet Office would lead the planning.

After several studies and papers on anti-terrorist operations, the two SBS sections were amalgamated at Poole in 1987 with two rifle troops and became M Squadron of the SBS dedicated to Maritime Counter Terrorist.

By 1990, it had three troops, Black, Gold and Purple, each tasked at various levels of MCT activity and manned entirely by SBS ranks. The squadron carried out numerous operations which for reasons of security remain classified and beyond the scope of this book. Further, with a considerably greater call for underwater work in both clandestine approach to an assault target and in

Exit and re-entry of SBS raiders and their equipment from dived submarines to provide greater security for night-time clandestine operations became the subject of many trials from the early 1960s onwards. After personnel had exited in a risky manoeuvre, weapons and stores were floated to the surface in waterproof packaging, along with an inflatable craft visible in the photograph above. Although phased out by the SBS in the 1970s, it is still used by the South African Special Forces today.

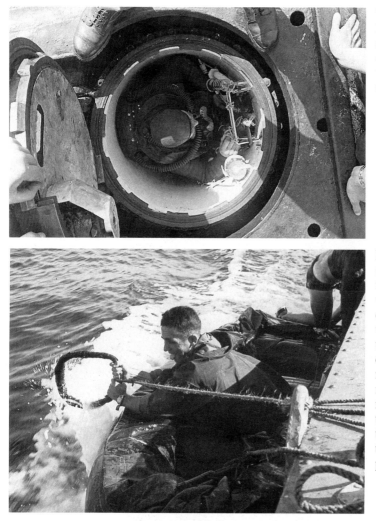

Tight squeeze: looking down upon a diver rigged for exiting a submarine with single escape chamber.

Fast pick-ups of swimmer-canoeists from the water without the parent craft having to stop, while possibly under fire from the enemy, were rehearsed with many devices. This ring connector had to be grasped by the swimmer while the craft was passing at speed.

SBS underwater activity increased dramatically through the decades as new operational tasks came into view, especially in the area of maritime counter-terrorism training. A typical suited operative in the 1970s looked a bulky soul.

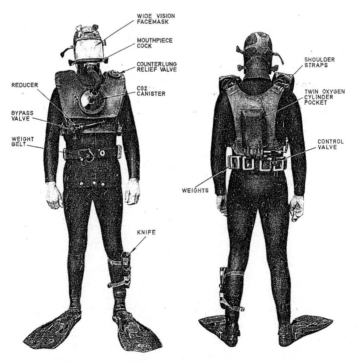

WIDE VISION FACEMASK

MOUTHPIECE COCK

COUNTERLUNG RELIEF VALVE

REDUCER

CO2 CANISTER

BYPASS VALVE

WEIGHT BELT

KNIFE

SHOULDER STRAPS

TWIN OXYGEN CYLINDER POCKET

CONTROL VALVE

WEIGHTS

SWIMMER CANOEIST DRESSED IN SCBA

Paddy Ashdown was one of the test drivers of an early underwater swimmer-delivery tug based upon a converted torpedo, designed by a submarine commander and built by Royal Navy engineers in Singapore. Various Swimmer-Delivery Vehicles were later built and trialled specifically for SBS operations from the late 1960s onwards.

An American-built Swimmer Delivery Vehicle on trial to meet the needs of the 1990s.

Another crucial SBS underwater tool for reconnaissance tasks – a beach profile recorder, first used in the 1960s.

Air drops of men, craft and stores to the target area were also the subject of many SBS trials. The stores came first followed by the men.

Similarly, air drops of SBS personnel with inflatables were also trialled. The craft is packaged and attached to the man's body to be inflated upon hitting the water. This technique was used to drop men and equipment to the threatened *QE2* in mid-Atlantic

Meanwhile, canoes were also becoming faster, although there would be no replacement for the original manually paddled type on some clandestine missions.

After aircraft drops and submarine refinements, SBS added one more delivery system to its repertoire, using helicopters with RIBs (Rigid Inflatable Boats equipped with substantial outboard power) slung below and dropped close to the target, with operatives roping into their craft.

security investigations, a dedicated Swimmer Delivery Vehicle team was founded. They were trained specifically in the use of motorised underwater tugs and towing craft for the speedy delivery of personnel to an operation.

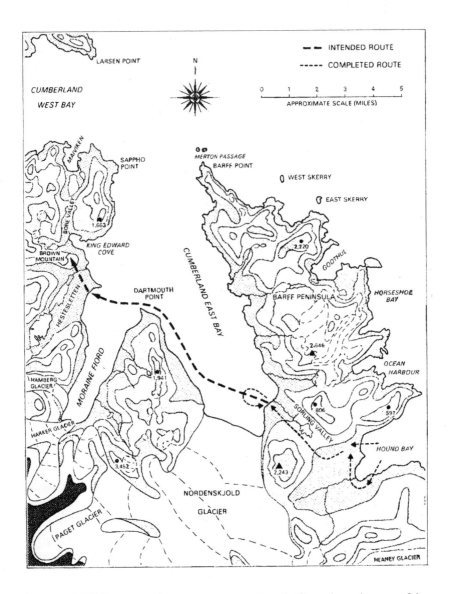

Proposed SBS reconnaissance route on South Georgia prior to taking the Argentine surrender.

CHAPTER SEVENTEEN

Bring me South Georgia!

In the voluminous accounts of the Falklands War, the controversies and the reflections, the role of the SBS has regularly been overlooked. As the largest amphibious task force Britain had mounted since the Second World War headed to the South Atlantic, SBS sections were already dashing to the scene. They were the first to deploy, playing a major part in the retaking of South Georgia, and went on to open the doors for the invasion force with surveillance operations that provided gateway intelligence ahead of the Falklands landings. SBS patrols and recce teams were operating within Argentinian positions, virtually staring the enemy in the face, up to 21 days before the assault troops arrived. They led the troops ashore and then joined the offensive and became involved in some spectacular fire fights.

There was still snow on their boots when the Falklands panic blew up. Northern Norway had once again been the setting for SBS winter exercises training for its NATO role in Scandinavia. The exercises were renowned for survival techniques in appalling conditions, leading the men to the most inaccessible mountain positions – and getting them back again.

The yelling of the NCO instructors – 'It's only bloody pain!' or 'Cold? You'll know you're cold when your balls drop off' – was ringing in their ears. The limbs of the less fit ached and toes were still numb from the wet and cold let in by boots that didn't quite match the task. 42 Commando was the only unit in the Brigade to go to Norway that year because of stringent defence cost-cutting, which was so bad that several Royal Navy frigates were lying idle in their berths because there was not enough cash to pay the oil bills. 40 Commando was left to do their training in the UK, and

227

45 Commando went mountain-climbing in Scotland after a tough six months in Belfast, although one company was jungle training in Brunei. Two SBS sections had joined the Norwegian jaunt, on Exercise Clockwork, just as it had done every year since 1970. Few in the unit had not gone through the demanding three month annual training set in the depths of a Norwegian winter; some had been through it six or seven times.

It was just as well that they had. General Leopold Fortunato Galtieri, unstable head of the Argentinian military junta, had suddenly demonstrated his impatience to reclaim the Malvinas, as he insisted on calling the Falkland Islands. The British government and its ministerial team at the Foreign Office had shown a remarkable reluctance to accept that he would even try. Due notice had been served, well in advance. A British embassy military attaché in Buenos Aires reported to Whitehall in January predicting almost to the very day when an invasion by Argentina would happen.

No one paid much heed, with London preoccupied with cost-cutting. Almost to the last, Margaret Thatcher's Defence Secretary John Nott insisted that he would proceed with the withdrawal of the Royal Navy's sole bearer of the White Ensign in the southern hemisphere, the ice-patrol vessel HMS *Endurance*, to save £3 million a year in the defence budget.

Something of a national debate opened up over the future of the ship with letters to *The Times*. The Argentinians were listening. Galtieri took the proposed withdrawal of the ship to mean that the British government didn't care about the remote sheep-farm with its 1,950 inhabitants although *Endurance*'s commanding officer, Captain Nick Barker, RN, had been warning of increasing Argentinian radio traffic since the beginning of the year.

He and others had correctly read the signs, but Lord Carrington's last-minute request to keep *Endurance* on station, was turned down by the Cabinet. Minds were only changed at the very last minute when a gang of Argentinian scrap dealers landed on South Georgia – which was not part of the Falklands – and hoisted their national flag.

The SBS, just returned from Norway, were about to go on leave, its stores still returning by sea. The men's departure was blocked even before the invasion. The SBS OC had been attending a conference in London the day before, 30 March. From what he learned, he made the correct assumption that there could be trouble at any second. The following morning he received confirmation and was alerted to keep all his units on standby.

What exactly could be done from 8,000 miles away if Galtieri did invade had yet to be decided. Some mad, mad schemes were being bandied about Whitehall. According to one who was there – and which astounded SBS people when they learned of it – a civil servant at an early planning meeting would suggest that the military 'make a loud bang in the South Atlantic by Friday 9 April' – seven days after the invasion took place. Whatever did he mean? No one seemed to know, and, anyway, short of dropping an A-bomb, there was no way of getting a loud bang of any sort to the region in seven days. Some very foolish people were around in those early days of the Falklands War, and they were not only somewhat inexperienced in handling such a crisis but they were panicking, and, as always happens when people in politics panic, they made some daft decisions and then tried to mislead the media.

When the Argentinians invaded, the SBS were among the first to learn of it and to be sent to action. Years of training and exercises for their arrival ahead of the troops, in what could only become a classic sea-borne assault, now came to the boil. The first signal at SBS headquarters at Poole ordering them to stand to came in the early hours of 1 April. Less than 24 hours later, they were on the move. Galtieri's troops had made their move on the Falklands and taken the token British force of Royal Marines prisoner. Argentinian photographers flashed around the world a photograph of them being marched away with hands over their heads. Prime Minister Margaret Thatcher was furious, and so she might be. In the words of Denis Healey, it had been 'an almighty cock-up'. Lord Carrington resigned, accepting full responsibility for 'this national humiliation', along with two other ministers. John Nott offered to stand down, too, but his resignation was rejected. He would, however, walk the plank later.

Thatcher responded on the day of the invasion by announcing she was sending a task force of 40 warships and 1,000 commandos to retake the islands. Suddenly, money was no object. As in Argentina, the forthcoming conflict deflected thoughts away from all other ills gripping the nation at the time, like unemployment and factory closures. The Poole headquarters was buzzing, although curiously enough without great conviction that a battle would result. Even so, over the next few days sections were mobilised one after the other.

First 2SBS, plus a strong command team, set off by air to Ascension Island to catch either HMS/M *Spartan* or HMS/M *Splendid* for a quick route south. That plan was aborted by operational headquarters, CINCFLEET, even as the men were *en route* and neither submarine was to stop at Ascension. 2SBS would join the Royal Fleet Auxiliary *Fort Austin* as soon as she arrived from Malta. *Fort Austin* was carrying urgently needed stores for HMS *Endurance*, now sailing around the Falklands with no port of call. At Ascension, the SBS were joined by SAS D Squadron to make a combined force of around 50 men. They would be joined by M Company of 42 Royal Marines under the command of Major Guy Sheridan, RM. The men were at sea aboard *Fort Austin* before they learned of their destination – to reclaim South Georgia as soon as possible and provide Mrs Thatcher and her politically embarrassed government with a face-saver.

Meanwhile, 6SBS travelled to Faslane, Scotland, to board the nuclear-powered submarine HMS *Conqueror* and set off for the South Atlantic. Politics ruled over military planning and instructions came from on high that *Conqueror* was to go direct to patrol the waters between the Falklands and Argentina. Later, *Conqueror* would be used to enforce the newly declared 12-mile exclusion zone around the Falklands, within which any Argentinian ships would be attacked. On the night of 6 May *Conqueror* sank Argentina's only cruiser, *General Belgrano*, with the loss of 362 men, although whether *Belgrano* was inside the zone would become a matter of some debate.

The last SB section to go out was 3SBS, deployed in Royal Fleet Auxiliary *Stromness*, with a further 12 men deployed later to Ascension, taking the SBS force up to 85 men who, by the end of the first week of the campaign, were scattered over the South Atlantic. Back in Poole, SBS Rear ran the remaining section, 1SBS, to deal with any emergencies, such as a terrorist attack in the North Sea, plus the welfare and Special Forces liaison groups.

The assault on South Georgia, codenamed Operation Paraquat, was the first objective. On the way south, both the SBS and the SAS squadron began testing their equipment and practised launching their inflatable boats over the *Fort Austin*'s high sides. SBS divers also went into the ocean and joined the drills of loading their boats with equipment, with men and kit passed down scrambling-nets in a swell that tossed the inflatables up to 15 feet (4.5 metres). Having launched in rough sea, the boat troops practised motoring around the ship. Often, they had to paddle back manually because of the failure of some of the elderly outboard motors.

This was a problem that they worked on with increasing concern. The ship's engineers joined the SBS and SAS teams in trying to get the motors to work efficiently, but even as they neared their destination the motors refused to perform well, becoming a problem that was to put the men at risk when the time came for their landings.

On 12 April *Fort Austin* sighted HMS *Endurance*, which according to one recollection was 'bouncing around on the horizon like a flaming cork'. Those soldiers who suffered seasickness in the smaller ship would find no respite in *Endurance*, which on occasions rolled in an arc across 60 degrees. For the next 24 hours the SBS and SAS teams heading for South Georgia were cross-decked from *Fort Austin* to *Endurance*, along with their stores, boats, engines, weapons and equipment, plus much-needed supplies for the crew of *Endurance*. They stood watching as the load-shifting of supplies began, cradled underneath two Wessex helicopters. The first load, a supply of food, had to be ditched when the helicopter suddenly lost power. The rest of the transfer was completed without mishap, and the Paraquat force set off for the remainder of its journey, joined now by the destroyer HMS *Antrim*, the elderly frigate HMS *Plymouth* and the large Royal Fleet Auxiliary tanker, *Tidespring*, between them carrying tons of stores and men airlifted on board while the ships were moored off Ascension.

Planning staff for the reoccupation of South Georgia had its headquarters on *Antrim*. The SBS would be put ashore from *Endurance* to reconnoitre the Grytviken and King Edward Point area. The SAS would land at Fortuna Glacier to recce Leith Harbour, Stromness and Grass Island. Their initial objective was to discover the location and strength of the Argentinian garrison, which was known to be on South Georgia, and to do so without alerting them to the imminent British assault.

Antrim and *Tidespring* sailed for a position just north of Antarctic Bay for the SAS insertion, while *Endurance* and *Plymouth* carried on towards Hound Bay carrying the SBS recce team.

231

The SAS team was to go in first. *Antrim* reached a position 15 miles from South Georgia expecting to see the island ahead of them, but the 'moderate' weather was nothing like the crew had been led to expect. A half-gale was gusting, with squalls of snow, visibility was low and the cloud base was around 400 feet (120 metres). They waited for an improvement, and a couple of hours later a helicopter took off for an inspection of the weather closer to shore. Slowly, through the murky morning, the island loomed up before them, a breathtaking vision of desolate beauty yet awesome in its implications. Sheer cliffs, the massive and threatening Fortuna Glacier which had to be crossed, the incredible backdrop of its mountains . . . all were fantastic, if you were a tourist or the film-makers from Anglia television who happened to be filming on the island at the time of the invasion.

The helicopter pilot judged that there was a sufficient break in the weather to get the team ashore. Boats were out of the question. He returned to *Antrim* and within the hour the three helicopters of the two ships were ferrying the team towards Possession Bay. But as they flew towards landfall, the weather deteriorated and they hit a wall of snow. To continue would have been foolhardy, so they returned to *Antrim* to await an improvement.

By midday, they tried again, and this time made a successful landing, buffeted horrendously by wind gusting at 80 miles an hour through poor visibility and on ground that contained hidden traps. One helicopter, landing partly on a crevasse covered with new, soft snow, almost toppled over. As the 16 men clambered out, carrying their stores and three pulks – preloaded sleds weighing up to 200 pounds (90 kilogrammes) for pulling behind them – the lead helicopter pilot radioed to all: 'I'm glad we won't have to come back to this place.'

It was the kind of remark that tempts fate.

The team roped themselves together in fours and set off towards the high rim of the glacier, hauling their sleds behind them. The terrain was toothily rough and dangerous, with deep crevasses filled with snow that collapsed when trodden upon, creating a trap to break anyone's leg. Another problem became obvious immediately: their general-purpose lightweight machine-guns froze up in spite of being heavily oiled. Worse was to come. They travelled little more than half a mile before nightfall when the troop leader, Sergeant Lofty Arthy, a climber of the Himalayas with vast mountaineering experience, decided that the journey was too dangerous for them to continue. They decided to settle in for the night as best they could.

The hard surface of the glacier made it impossible to dig any form of deep cover. They could merely hack out shallow trenches with their ice-axes into which they would bed down in their sleeping-bags. A few of the small two-man tents were pitched, but half of them just blew off into the night in the high winds.

Out at sea, *Antrim*, still anchored 15 miles offshore, had a similarly unpleasant night. A force 12 was blowing, and the ship was tossed around like a matchstick. All stores had to be lashed down, and attempts to show a movie to the off-watch officers in the wardroom proceeded only with the operator holding the projector between his knees.

On Fortuna Glacier, the weather tumbled to disaster point. The katabatic winds hurling snow at 100 miles an hour made progress virtually impossible. The men would not have survived another day of it, and finally they had to give up. At 1000 hours the team leader instructed his signaller to call *Antrim* for help. They needed to be lifted off pronto! Was it even possible? As the signaller removed his gloves to operate his set, his hands went completely numb. *Antrim* command agreed to abort the attempt.

Once more, the three helicopter pilots were forced to return to the hazardous icy slopes to pick up the team, which had switched on its search-and-rescue beacon and would release green smoke indicators as soon as the helicopters came close.

It was well past midday before a break in the weather allowed the pilots to make the attempt. In spite of still-gusting winds, the three aircraft managed to locate the men, who set off their smoke when they heard the engines. Lieutenant Mike Tidd, RN, pilot of *Yankee Foxtrot*, one of the two Wessex 5 helicopters from *Tidespring*, with an aircrewman coincidentally named Tug Wilson led the flight convoy down and settled first on the glacier amid a swirl of blown snow. The SAS men trundled forwards and threw their gear through the open doors and scrambled aboard.

Tidd, first down, was first off. He lifted safely and headed north with mountains on either side of him. Within minutes he was hit by a white-out, a snow squall that totally obliterated his vision, and he knew there was sheer rock rising all around him. The altimeter was unwinding fast as he lost sight of both ground and horizon. He shouted to Tug, who was already giving hot drinks to the six men in the back: 'We've got a problem . . .'

233

The words were hardly out when the helicopter hit the glacier surface at about 30 knots (55 kilometres per hour) and went crashing on across the craggy ice, tearing off the left side of the undercarriage, bits of metal flying all over the place. The left side of the cockpit where the second pilot would have been sitting was smashed to bits. The pilots of the other two helicopters, about to take off, watched in horror. They quickly flew to the crash site and discovered with disbelief that not one of the men on board was seriously hurt.

The men from the crashed chopper were loaded on to the other two helicopters, although much of their kit was dumped. The twin-engined Wessex 5 took the larger number of men with weapons and stores. Within ten minutes the two helicopters lifted off together to head back to *Antrim*, with the ship's own single-engined, rather ancient Wessex 3 (nicknamed *Humphrey*), piloted by Lieutenant Ian Stanley, RN, leading; Lieutenant Ian Georgeson in the larger Wessex 5 from *Tidespring* followed.

Within three minutes of take-off they hit another white-out. Ian Stanley managed to navigate through it and Georgeson followed behind using Stanley as his guide. Ahead was an obstacle neither could have foreseen, a high ridge of ice on the edge of the glacier and invisible in the white-out. Stanley went up and over without any problems. As he passed over and dipped down the other side, Georgeson lost sight of him.

He glanced at his altimeter. The ground was heading up towards him fast. The white-out had him in its grip, and he reduced speed ready for 'an involuntary landing which proceeded towards me with a certain inevitability'. He almost got away with it. The wheels touched the ground, the craft rumbled and shook and for a moment seemed to rise until it was caught in a strong gusting wind of around 50 knots (92 kilometres per hour) which swung it around and sent it crashing across the ice, ending up in a tangled mass of rotorblades and crunched metal, with the over-loaded bodycount inside on top of each other.

Ian Stanley had picked up the running commentary of Georgeson and his number two in his headphones. His own second pilot was now watching from the port cockpit side window . . . 'Steady, steady . . . Yeah, he's made it . . . No! Oh God . . . He's gone.' There was nothing Stanley could do but carry on to *Antrim*. He was fully loaded already and dare not risk the lives of the men aboard. As the last of the helicopters made its way back to *Antrim*, the signaller radioed in: 'We're on our way home. ETA 15 minutes. Regret we've lost two of our chicks.' The news was received with great disappointment in London.

Back on the ice ridge, the bodies lay on top of each other, stunned by a second crash within 15 minutes. They quickly stirred and extricated themselves from the wreckage. Incredibly, there was not one fatality, or even serious injury. Georgeson himself was trapped in the cockpit, and, in spite of the risk of fire, the SAS clambered back aboard to rescue him. The troops set off to the first wreck to recover some of their kit, including a radio and their inflatable boats, which they used to build a shelter.

On *Antrim*, Ian Stanley was watching the weather, waiting for permission to go back to see what he could find. Two attempts were aborted. Then, at 1600, there was a window in the weather for another try. There would have to be at least two rescue flights because the Wessex 3 could not carry 16 men with kit through a gusting wind. Stanley was given permission to go ahead, and by 1645 was once again heading close to the ice cliff on Fortuna Glacier, intending to bring the men home in two parties of eight.

Conditions had worsened even as he left and progressively deteriorated as he` went inshore. On the ground the crashed party's radio was now working, and Ian Georgeson made contact, ready to guide Stanley in if he ever got to see the helicopter. The weather was worsening by the minute. Stanley came down towards them through a gap in the cloud and realised instantly that he would have no chance of making two trips that night. All gear and kit would have to be abandoned and the men crammed into the back.

Stanley wasn't so much concerned about take-off; he had enough power for that. The landing might be a problem on a moving ship with slightly warmer air and less wind.

Antrim command anxiously tracked the helicopter back and watched *Humphrey* hover and come in to land. The aircraft hit the deck with a mighty thump but did no damage to itself or to those aboard. The first part of the mission to recce South Georgia was over, with two dead helicopters and a quarter of a ton of stores lost.

The SBS had reached their destination, Hound Bay on the north coast of the island, where they were to be put ashore in three recce parties by the two little Wasp helicopters from HMS *Endurance*, once again with stores and equipment making a heavy load. They were to find and estimate the number of Argentinians in that area of the island in preparation for a landing by the Royal Marines. The Wasp managed to get only a third of their numbers ashore before the weather closed in. The men on the ground waited for more than two hours, then realised that the rest of their group would not be joining them. They began to reconnoitre the area.

Moving through the now pitch-black night the SBS patrol stumbled inadvertently into a half-asleep colony of penguins remonstrating loudly for the disturbance. A little further on the patrol leader swung around, gun at the ready, when something dark reared up beside him. He had trodden on the tail of a slumbering elephant seal, which was just about to put its wide-open mouth around his ears when he made a dash for safety.

The journey became progressively worse. By midnight there had been no let-up in the weather, and the other two-thirds of the SBS patrols were still aboard *Endurance*, anchored offshore. At 0300 the Wasp pilot tried to make another attempt to land the remainder, but he was literally blown back, twice almost dropping into the sea. Heavy snow finally put paid to the attempts, layering four inches (ten centimetres) thick on the windscreen, with frozen chunks flying off and hitting the canopy and the engine.

The SBS men on board decided to attempt to land on the island by taking their inflatables through the heavy swell, a manoeuvre entirely dependent on efficient outboard motors. Manpower alone would not have been sufficient: the boats were heavily laden, six men and stores in each. They also had a longer route to follow, as landing was impossible close to where the Wasp had dropped their colleagues because of a mass accumulation of ice which would have split the rubber boats.

Captain Nick Barker took *Endurance* as close as he dare and remained while the SBS dropped over the side. Finally, they got under way, the aged 40-horsepower outboards spluttered into life, and at around 0330 they headed for shore. The swell was huge and the wind howling; by the time they reached the shore they were all very wet and cold.

The new bunch unloaded their gear while two of their number set off in search for the remainder of the section lying up around the other side of the bay, a couple of miles away. They made their way cautiously around the curve of the bay, over rocks and ice and into another area thick with angry seals and penguins. They made contact 40 minutes later and all returned to the landing-site.

The plan now was for the three patrols to make their way across the bays and inlets, through a fjord and on towards their charted position for an observation post looking down at King Edward Point, where the Argentinians were thought to be building their troop numbers on the island. To reach this observation post they would need boats to carry the three sections across Cumberland East Bay, an eight-mile stretch of water.

It was planned that they would rendezvous with the *Endurance* helicopter the following morning to accept delivery of two Geminis for the water crossing. Before first light the SBS party moved off, each carrying their 80-pound (36-kilogramme) Bergen rucksacks. They made their way over the treacherous terrain of the Soirling Valley, which normally would have presented no difficulties but now covered with ice and filled with snow-topped hazards and invisible crevasses. By mid-morning they had reached the foot of Nordenskjold Glacier, which looked on their charts a possible launching-place for the Geminis.

It turned out to be a great creaking, frozen mass disgorging icicles the size of an Exocet missile into a bay filled with growlers and icebergs. Dangerous shards filled the water. A Gemini wouldn't have lasted five minutes, and nor would they. They moved on and prepared to meet the *Endurance* Wasp at the agreed RV site. The recollections of one who was there provide an insight into the remainder of the operation:

> The helicopter arrived in mid-afternoon with the two boats and their engines slung in a net beneath the undercarriage. We saw him coming in low so as to avoid being seen by the Argentinian troops over the other side of the bay. In doing so, he probably hit the front tube of one of them on the ice. When we blew it up to full strength, it leaked badly and could not be used. We decided that we would have to split up, half remaining where they were, the others taking the second Gemini across the bay.
>
> We laid up until nightfall, making ourselves as comfortable as possible in freezing winds, with half of us still wet from the journey across. We loaded the boat and made ready for the crossing under darkness. In those couple of hours, the

weather changed dramatically. A force seven was blowing and packice was on the move – you could hear it crunching and banging. The change of wind direction was blowing it back into the bay, and it was hitting the shore-line and just stacking up. By the time we came to launch the Gemini, there was just one small channel free of ice, less than 50 yards wide and closing. Well, the others decided to make a dash for it before the ice closed up completely and headed out in pitch darkness; you couldn't see a bloody thing, and the waters were grey and impossible. Within 800 yards, they were in trouble. You could hear the motor was overworking and hitting chunks of ice; it was like a food mixer with too much to tackle. It faded and stopped several times. The ice was piling towards them – huge chunks of the bloody stuff – and they needed engine power to avoid being hit and sunk. They had to turn back and rejoin the rest of us on the shore. It was decided we would lay up for the night and make another attempt the next day.

First light showed no improvement. The ice by then had filled the bay and to attempt a crossing in a rubber boat was impossible. They radioed the Operation Paraquat planning team on board HMS *Antrim* for instructions but could not make contact. They assumed they were out of range and climbed to a higher point; still no reply. Unknown to them, there was nobody there! All British ships in coastal waters had been ordered out to sea after the Argentinian submarine *Santa Fe* was reported to be patrolling the coast, and in the dash to get out *Antrim* command had overlooked the SBS party.

They finally restored radio contact later that night, 24 April, after three very cold days ashore. The SBS asked to be taken off but there was some dissension on *Antrim*. Ought they not to make another try? Eventually, the SBS mission was aborted and the men were recovered by the two Wasps and taken back aboard HMS *Endurance*.

There was a curiously fortuitous result to the SBS's difficulties at Cumberland East Bay, which was just ten miles from the Argentinians' own base. The coded radio traffic between the SBS and *Antrim*, and then with *Endurance*, alerted the Argentinians that something was afoot. They already knew of the presence of British ships in the area, and were certain an invasion party was about to be put ashore. The submarine *Santa Fe* had been summoned to patrol that section of South Georgia and was in fact very close to where the SBS operation was aborted.

On 25 April another SBS team was mustered aboard HMS *Antrim* to be flown ashore for a further attempt. The men were landed a few miles away from the original team's insertion point, once again by Lieutenant Ian Stanley flying the *Antrim* helicopter *Humphrey*. On the way back Stanley spotted *Santa Fe* sitting temptingly on the surface on the edge of Cumberland East Bay. Stanley swooped low over the vessel, her casing gunners began firing at him, and he loosed his entire stock of depth-charges around her. They did enough damage to prevent the craft from diving and, alerted by Stanley, the Wasps from *Endurance* and a Lynx from the frigate *Brilliant* darted to the scene and blasted the submarine with a salvo of missiles and machine-gun fire.

Santa Fe limped off, oil flooding the surface, towards the British Antarctic Survey Station at Grytviken. The planners aboard *Antrim* decided the attack must be followed up immediately, but the Royal Marines in *Tidespring* were still hours away. A force was pulled together from the ships in the area, including SAS, SBS and *Antrim*'s own Royal Marines detachment of ten – in total, just 75 men, fewer than half the size of the Argentinian garrison.

They were landed at various points, now without any thought of clandestine movement, and headed for Grytviken, where *Santa Fe* had berthed. When they arrived, the whole place was decked with white sheets, and as soon as the British force turned up the Argentinians formed up beside their flag and surrendered. Later, 2SBS joined D Squadron of SAS and flew into Leith Harbour, where Captain Alfredo Astiz, the renowned torturer of Argentinian political prisoners, saluted the team leader and handed him his pistol in surrender. Not a shot was fired. In London the newspapers were already preparing their headlines: SOUTH GEORGIA RECAPTURED.

Margaret Thatcher had been given her face-saver. She came out of 10 Downing Street and made that memorable, jingoistic little speech to waiting television cameras and, waving aside questions from the assembled journalists, screeched into the microphones: 'Rejoice! Rejoice!' Whether we should rejoice for her and her government or for the troops who had performed these death-defying first efforts of the Falklands adventure was not immediately clear.

Falkland Islands.

CHAPTER EIGHTEEN

Finest hours

South Georgia secured, the SBS went off to join the advance force fleet in preparations for the main task: Operation Corporate – the recapture of the Falkland Islands. 3SBS was already aboard HMS *Hermes* sailing from Ascension, and 6SBS joined the advance force as soon as it was released from Operation Paraquat. The bulk of SBS work now would be to go ashore at crucial points around the Falklands to recce landing-sites and to report on enemy positions and on the going, terrain and beaches and possibly to clear landing-site obstacles. Three separate areas of the Falklands were to be reconnoitred and patrolled, stretching the meagre resources of the SBS to the limit. But SBS men were the first British troops to go ashore in the Falklands and were there behind enemy lines a full three weeks before Royal Marines and paratroopers stormed ashore at San Carlos Bay on 21 May.

The most crucial reconnaissance of the Falklands conflict was placed in the hands of the SBS. The task was the Trojan Horse equivalent of penetrating well behind enemy lines to provide the gateway intelligence for the major troop landings that were to follow. Without them and their intelligence reports, casualties would undoubtedly have been far higher. The British government naturally declined to confirm that any British troops had landed prior to the first major assault, and so the SBS men were once again vulnerable to the whim of the enemy if they were captured. The grey area of being treated as prisoners of war had, historically, been a bugbear ever since Hitler declared that the secret raiders should be interrogated and shot.

Their wide brief and the equally wide area to be covered meant they also had to move around the theatre of potential conflict much more than they would normally be inclined to do for recce work, so that each site could be covered. An additional discomfort for the patrols was that they could not send their reports by radio for fear of interception and had to use the slow hand-speed Morse for general communication. The more complicated beach recce reports and charts were too long and involved for transmission by any other means than personal delivery, and often the men had to go back to base or ship to report direct to their controllers and then return ashore.

The SBS patrols were flown in generally by Sea King Mark 4 helicopters, although occasionally they went ashore by more traditional method, delivered by Geminis. They were moved only at night by pilots flying on Passive Night Goggles, a brand new technique they had mastered only at Ascension on the way south with equipment borrowed at the last moment from Farnborough. The helicopters flew from up to 180 nautical miles offshore at 50 feet (15 metres) above sea-level into enemy-held territory. As soon as they were landed with weapons and stores, the SBS dug into the rolling, coverless hillsides and remained hidden for days at a time while the enemy searched for them with small aircraft, helicopters and ground troops.

As the most crucial period of the conflict approached, the SBS had observation teams scattered throughout the Falklands, watching Argentinian positions and carrying out beach recces. Patrols were deployed to Campa Menta Bay, Eagle Hill (twice), Johnson's Harbour, Ajax Bay, San Carlos and Port San Carlos for up to a week at a time before being withdrawn to report their findings and for insertion elsewhere. The stretched resources of its limited manpower also showed up the importance of the SBS in intelligence-gathering: when no patrol was available to cover Port San Carlos for a vital five days, the Argentinians moved an entire company into the area unseen.

Key Argentinian positions were under constant observation. One patrol established a post at the proposed main British invasion site, in a refrigeration plant at Ajax Bay. Another was dug in across San Carlos Water on the Inner Verde Mountains, while the recce team at Port San Carlos observed troop movements for seven days without a break.

The procedures were well established and rehearsed through years of SBS exercises and operations. The men usually worked in teams of four, although sometimes more. They would clear the landing-area quickly, one of them watching to give covering fire, then make their way under darkness across open country towards their selected observation site, often having to set up temporary bases *en route*, and lying up during daylight.

One would keep watch while the others built the hides and covered the stores. If the lookout had to stray from the lying-up site, they used the old SBS fishing-line trick: with one end attached to a Bergen rucksack in the hide, the lookout would give a pull on the line to warn of approaching danger.

Well aware that they were being hunted, the men took enormous care to ensure that the hides were virtually invisible, even if they were to be used for only a few hours. They knew that care in that direction could save their lives. The Falklands earth, when not frozen solid, was of a consistency that could be carved into small bunkers, perhaps on the side of an incline, of about six or eight feet (1.8 or 2.4 metres) square. The turves from the top were cut and saved to be used later as a roof. The men dug down to about two feet (0.6 metres), lining the sides of the bunker with waterproof sheets. The soil from the hole was placed around the hide and covered with turf. Chicken wire and netting were slung across the top, and the turves placed back with an easily removed access point and spyholes for observation.

If the job were done properly, the hides would be completely invisible from the air, and even Argentinian ground troops were known to have walked by without noticing them. Two other hides, for food and equipment, would be built nearby, where possible in a straight line for easy access during darkness and within ten feet (three metres). The stores – always a problem in their movement from place to place – were substantial, especially for a seven-day recce. Equipment included binoculars, night-sights and a tripod-mounted telescope.

The men each carried sleeping-bags and duvet trousers, a change of clothes, high-protein ration packs and tinned food that required cooking on hexamine stoves. They carried emergency rations and were well armed. Each man would be equipped with an M-16 Armalite rifle, one M-203 grenade launcher, six high-explosive grenades, one 66-millimetre (2.6-inch) anti-tank missile, 300 rounds of ammunition, smoke and phosphorous grenades, a 9-millimetre Browning pistol and a hunting knife. The hides would be used for lying up during the daytime, using the cover of darkness for recce, although that was not always possible. Food for the day had to be drawn before first light, and the men who went outside the hides for whatever reason would brush their tracks as they went back so as not to leave any footprints or flattened grass. By dawn they had to be under cover and hidden away for another long stint, taking it in turns to go on watch and often in situations where matters of personal hygiene and the call of nature had to be dealt with as best they could be.

The routine was similar, often almost identical, to the procedures described by Captain Len Holmes in the observation posts of the Borneo campaign. By day they each took a two-hour watch while the others rested, made tea or prepared their rations; cooking a meal took perhaps 40 minutes or more, each man preparing his own. The daily intake of sustenance, particularly in a cold climate, could never be ignored. At night they took one hour on watch and three hours off, and under darkness they would venture out to get a more precise view of the local situation. Making sure the hides were carefully concealed, they moved stealthily around the area, noting all that was required of them for full recce reports with charts and drawings, especially those assigned to potential landing-sites.

As usual, these all had to be checked for gradients and underwater obstacles, such as rocks and shelving. They also had to be largely free of kelp – a major problem throughout the islands and which choked motors – so that landing-craft carrying troops could make a swift, unhindered entry. The surrounding terrain had to be mapped out, and beach profiles drawn and checked for easy approaches from the landing-zones to inland positions for the massed troops. Cliffs and steep gradients were out of the question. Equally important were the inland approaches, so that the advancing troops did not become trapped by natural barriers. At Sandy Bay, for example, the SBS recce team discovered that behind the headland of one possible landing-site leading to a settlement containing Argentinian troops lay a secondary beach in which the British invasion force would have become sitting ducks.

There were many near-misses of discovery of SBS patrols, and at the most sensitive place of Ajax Bay, where they kept up a 16-day watch, it seemed that they were being specifically hunted.

Once, an Argentinian helicopter landed less than 150 metres from the hide. The pilot got out, strolled around and then stopped for a quick pee. 'A few more yards further on and he would have been pissing into our hide,' one of their number recalled. Later, another helicopter hovered virtually on top of the hide and the downdraught blew away some of the camouflage. Even then the pilot did not see the gang of four hidden just a few feet below him.

By now, the amphibious battle was hotting up. After *Belgrano* was sunk, the Argentinians began hitting the newly arrived task force with French-built Exocet missiles. The destroyer HMS *Sheffield* was sunk on 4 May with the loss of 21 lives, and the *QE2* was about to set sail with infantry reinforcements.

At the time other complications were arising from political sources in London and the United States as the US tried to intervene with a peace plan being brokered by General Alexander Haig, a plan that almost led to a ceasefire. Contingency schemes were made to withdraw the bulk of SBS and SAS, leaving stay-behind patrols. But the ceasefire proposals came to naught and the SBS was back in business.

One incident caused a good deal of concern for different reasons at SBS control: two of their corporals went missing. Apart from worries about their safety, the possibility arose that SBS operations might be compromised. The trouble hit a patrol led by Sergeant KJ as it made for a mist-shrouded hilltop to find a position for its operations. By coincidence, the same spot had been chosen by an Argentinian patrol, which was approaching from the other side of the hill at exactly the same time. The two corporals, who had gone on ahead to recce the position, crept forward in fog and heard voices. The British patrol had to make a choice: open a fire fight with the Argentinians and alert them to their position or stealthily retreat, allow the Argentinian patrol to occupy the position and be none the wiser of British presence. The British chose the latter and pulled back. The rules of engagement were clear: no fire fights unless absolutely unavoidable. This left the two corporals with the Argentinian patrol advancing on the hilltop and cutting off their route to the rest of the SBS team.

The pair made a quick retreat and went to ground, unavoidably losing contact with their comrades. They had no radio or other form of communications, and very little else. One of the corporals, TWM, was an old hand at SBS practices, although both knew the procedures. They pursued the emergency drill of moving through a list of pre-arranged rendezvous points on their map and waiting for a specified time. If the RV was not met, they would move on to the next, and follow that procedure until contact was hopefully made.

The patrol made several sorties to look for the missing pair without success. Sergeant KJ was now confronted by his own difficult decision: he had to pull the rest of the team out to meet his own RV for the helicopter pick-up, which would mean leaving the other two behind. It had to be done. The team flew back to the base ship, leaving the corporals to their own devices.

The sergeant asked to be allowed back on the ground to carry out a further search. Several days passed and no contact was made. There was a chance that the missing men had died of exposure or had been taken prisoner. Their SBS comrades were pretty certain that neither was the case. The corporals were well used to rough weather and had a good eye for self-preservation. More than likely they were following the manual to the letter, hiding up in the day and moving around at night. What they would not have done was to make contact with locals unless absolutely necessary.

It was seven days after the two were separated when the sergeant took a team back to the area and painstakingly retraced the pre-arranged rendezvous positions, a task made all the more difficult by the darkness of the night. And they would be well hidden because there were Argentinian patrols all around. But looking for an SBS hide that was built and skilfully camouflaged with the specific object of *not* being found was a needle in a haystack job. The search now concentrated on the final RV on the list, and there finally the rescuers came upon the two corporals. A barrage of expletives was exchanged by both sides, and they headed off back to base. They had a good meal, half a bottle of medicinal brandy and a good sleep before being debriefed. Within three days they were back on patrol.

Meanwhile, other issues had to be resolved. During the advance force phase, 2 and 6SBS were held in the battle group for anti-shipping tasks. In one such operation, 2SBS was dispatched aboard two Sea King Mark 4 helicopters to board and apprehend the 1,300-ton Argentinian fish factory-ship, *Narwal*, which was discovered in the British exclusion zone. Before the men reached their target, however, the ship was bombed and strafed by two Harrier jets. The vessel was already listing badly when 2SBS arrived. With the helicopters hovering above the ship, the men roped down to board her, using the procedures they had practised during their Maritime Counter-terrorist training.

The section managed to rescue the crew, some of whom were badly injured (one was dead). They also took possession of charts and operation orders before setting charges and blowing up the ship. In spite of claims by Argentina that she was an innocent vessel, the orders showed she had been shadowing the fleet and, presumably, signalling intelligence.

By now, the SBS teams were working through the most crucial stages of the reconnaissance operation. Several of the recce teams had come close to being discovered, the Argentinians were clearly attempting to root them out as the possible invasion of British troops edged closer. The main amphibious force was nearing the Falklands, carrying the major body of troops and fire power. HMS *Hermes*, the anti-submarine carrier and parent ship to the Sea Kings, headed south to accompany the task force.

With few helicopters now available, the SBS had to join the queue for use of the two Wessex 5s flying off HMS *Antrim* at the very time they needed to put recce teams back into Ajax Bay and Fanning Head to monitor Argentinian movements around Port San Carlos. The SBS had less than four days before the beginning of the biggest amphibious assault since the Second World War.

The countdown to that assault saw some frantic activity: on 16 May an SBS recce team was landed by rubber craft from the frigate HMS *Alacrity* south of Ajax Bay and set up an observation post overlooking the vital San Carlos Water. On the same day another team was reinserted to its former operations site on Ajax Bay. On the next day a third team was launched from the frigate HMS *Brilliant* to take up an observation position overlooking Port San Carlos. As this last approached the target area, however, the men saw lights and heard voices. Evidently, there was an enemy company close by, and they returned to *Brilliant* without landing.

It now became imperative to get a team into the area of Port San Carlos and in particular to that feature of it known as Fanning Head, a hill dominating the entrances to both North Falkland Sound and San Carlos Water. The exact enemy positions were not known, but if the SBS could insert its teams now, the intelligence would be covered well in advance of the troop landings.

The SBS managed to get hold of the two Wessex helicopters from *Antrim*, and 2SBS, with a half-section from 3SBS along with an SAS mortar detachment were tasked with locating and dislodging the Argentinians from its Fanning Head position in the hours running up to the landing. For this, the SBS had acquired a useful piece of equipment never previously used in any military operation. It was a thermal imager (TI), at the time in experimental use among police forces in Britain for tracking escapees from justice who were being tailed by bobbies in helicopters. The imager, now familiar to television viewers of police action programmes, could pick up the presence of bodies, live or recently dead, simply from the heat they generated.

The TI was fitted to *Antrim*'s ancient Wessex and began flying the area in square patterns. Sure enough, a company of Argentinians was picked up on the screen, from which their exact position could be calculated. This was radioed from the Wessex and for the next two hours HMS *Antrim* bombarded the target with its 4.5-inch (11.4-centimetre) guns. In the meantime the Wessex made five trips back and forth to collect the remainder of the assault team, a task fraught with danger since the landing-lights of the helicopter could be seen from some distance. Then the SBS moved in. One of their number who spoke Argentinian Spanish called for the surrender of the Argentinians. The reply was a burst of gunfire which hit the rucksack of one of the team. The SBS gave them one more chance to give up and then moved forwards. They shot and killed twelve, wounded three and took nine prisoners.

The Argentinians had been on Fanning Head manning anti-tank guns and mortars covering the straits and would have had British ships in their direct line of fire. The remainder of the company, around 60 men, were sheltering in houses in Port San Carlos area. They did not see an SBS beach reception party as it crept into position two hours before the first troop landings, by the Parachute Regiment, but the SBS did not see them either. The Argentinians moved out when the Fanning Head fire fight started. They were still in the area as the first troops went ashore and were able to shoot down two Royal Marine Gazelles which were escorting a Sea King carrying a Rapier missile battery ashore. Three of the four Gazelle crew were killed.

The landing itself was unopposed and, with the essential beach-head now in British hands, the invasion force moved ahead for the final assault and the recapture of East Falkland.

On the north coast, by Port Salvador Water, 6SBS was inserted from HMS *Fearless* to clear up ahead of the arrival of the commandos. The section faced a long journey by water at night, with three raiding craft, before establishing a forward base on the tussock-covered Green Island, four days before the Commando Brigade began its advance from San Carlos. The section carried out close recces of Port Louis and Green Patch settlements, reported them clear of enemy, and conducted one beach recce. 2SBS inserted from HMS *Intrepid* joined them, operating in the Teal area, ultimately guiding 3 Para into Teal before moving on to establish an observation post over an enemy company on Long Island Mountain.

This was followed by a small operation by the SBS to winkle out an enemy observation post. Their only casualty to date, Sergeant Hunt, was killed here on the hill forward of Teal in a blue-on-blue incident, hit by SAS fire. The SAS pointed out that the SBS team leader, an experienced commando, had strayed into their Green Patch operational zone. There were no recriminations despite the death; indeed, the incident led to closer cooperation between the two units. As we will see, they came together for one of the last, and spectacularly difficult, operations involving the Special Forces in the Falklands campaign.

By now the advance force in East Falkland was reaching its bloody but successful conclusion. The SBS continued its covert operations to the last and from 10 June began scouring the string of islands of West Falkland for enemy positions and airstrips. Teams were deployed to Port Stephens, Weddel Island, Chartres, Dunnose Head, Byron Heights, Caracass Island, Keppel Island, Saunders Island and Pebble Island, and one team went to Sea Lion Island off Laffonia.

Enemy were found on Pebble Island, estimated to number 30 to 50. The SBS planned to attack this garrison with 36 men and two Harriers, but they were overtaken by the surrender of the Argentinians at Port Stanley. An SBS major took the surrender of Pebble Island and discovered that had the SBS taken it on they would have confronted a well-armed garrison of 112 men.

Three pockets of stubborn resistance were cleared up on the west island with the SBS directing naval bombardment, one on Fox Bay and two on Port Howard. The operations were one-night stands in which the SBS teams were inserted by small boat from a supporting frigate to a point within 1,000 metres of the target.

The final deployment of the SBS in the campaign, its one remaining piece of action, was shared between a joint force of

SAS and SBS as part of the battle for Port Stanley. While the main action took the credits, this little piece of activity was barely noticed by historians, though it should have been. On 12 June 2 Para began its attack on Wireless Ridge, five miles west of Port Stanley. A six-man team from 3SBS formed a volunteer raiding-party with D and G Squadrons, SAS, with the object of creating a diversionary assault from the sea to deflect some of the hostile fire from the paratroopers. The task was unplanned, spur of the moment, dreamed up by the Special Forces, who could not possibly stand around looking on as the massed guns came blazing out.

After a day in an observation post, the SBS team was to swim across to Wireless Ridge and move forwards. In the event this was impractical, and on 12 June the team, with a troop from SAS D Squadron, were to move across the Murrell River by four fast power-boats, RRCs (rigid raider craft) brought round during the night by the trawler *Cordella* and driven by men from the Royal Marines 1st Raiding Squadron. They were hidden off Kidney Island until they were ready to launch their assault.

The next night, 13–14 June and the last day of the war, the men began their approach towards their target area. On the way they had to pass the Argentinian hospital-ship *Bahia Paraiso*, berthed in Port Stanley harbour. As they did so, the crew switched on their searchlights, drawing them in an arc across the water. The boat raiders were sitting targets. Argentinians on both sides of the water, certain they faced a full-scale sea-borne assault, turned everything they had on the SBS/SAS teams: mortars, artillery, anti-aircraft cannon, even small arms. The skies were filled with metal, hot and gleaming.

The raiders had no option but to withdraw. One of the RRCs was badly damaged and limped back on hardly any power. The coxswain steered her by the hospital-ship for a shield and the boat died on them just as they reached the water's edge. Another sank just offshore, but close enough for the team to swim to safety. Good luck and poor shooting by the enemy – plus a lot of guts on the part of the coxswains – saved the men from disaster. An SBS corporal and two SAS troopers were wounded. The RRCs were riddled with holes and had to be destroyed. This time, the combined unit of SBS and SAS admitted they had broken the first rule of raiding-parties: don't do kamikaze missions. But to be fair, they weren't anticipating the hospital ship would get involved. Even so, the exercise provided a 'terrific diversion' for 2 Para on the other end of Wireless Ridge and doubtless saved a few lives at that end.

There remains, as we come to the close of this glimpse at SBS activity in the Falklands, one other area that was a subject of controversy in the aftermath: the raiding of the Argentinian mainland. This has never been admitted by the Ministry of Defence. This book has attempted to deal only in certainties and fact and to avoid speculation, but most of the reporters of the campaign and several television documentaries would suggest that the Special Forces were involved in raids on Argentinian mainland positions before the campaign ended. The BBC's James Fox provided an account that claimed they had entered through Chile, landing in a Sea King helicopter which was then dumped.

CHAPTER NINETEEN

Footsteps to the Gulf

The Falklands experience focused military minds – as all wars do in the aftermath and the inquests – on the future. The Special Forces, whose contribution to that campaign remained oblique and guarded for many years, became the subject of numerous internal papers. An ongoing debate into their role was not fully resolved until 1987, when the present Special Forces Group command was formed. It became a brokerage for all tasks and special projects that were the speciality of Special Forces units, predominantly SBS and SAS, with support from other units from the army and the RAF.

If there were any remaining doubts as to their effectiveness, they were countermanded by the analysis of the Falklands. What Operation Corporate highlighted – and the Gulf War of 1990–91 would re-emphasise – was that where there was no contingency plan for the conflict, the specialised skills of the SAS and SBS were vital. It was perhaps significant that the SBS was chosen to join a Special Forces contingency study. Plans to counter any future attack or invasion of the Falklands by the Argentinians were drawn up. The SBS carried out a detailed recce of the islands and all the proposals were rehearsed in 1985.

To make sure that a similar problem might be averted in Belize, that other outpost of Britain's colonial past on the eastern coast of central South America, an SBS detachment was posted there in 1983. Belize, with its population of 175,000, was granted independence from Britain in 1981 and became a member of the Commonwealth. But it was also the subject of a long-running territorial dispute with Guatemala, which had periodically threatened to invade and, like Argentina, had been making rumblings in that direction around the time of independence. Britain remained responsible for defence of the country, and a contingency plan against invasion or other incursions was prepared. The SBS sent a team to join two SAS patrols, based in a military compound six miles from Belize City. They were to remain there until 1987.

At home, with a dramatic increase in the size and impact of the IRA's mainland bombing campaign, the SBS role in the Maritime Counter-Terrorist Force activity was also consolidated and extended. As we have seen, it had previously been under the control of the Comacchio Company of the Royal Marines. Soon after their return from the Falklands, the two SBS sections involved with maritime counter-terrorism were amalgamated, and command of the group switched from Scotland to Poole. After several studies and papers on anti-terrorist operations, the group was expanded further in 1987 with two rifle troops and became M Squadron of the SBS, dedicated to maritime counter-terrorism.

By 1990 it had three troops, Black, Gold and Purple, each tasked at various levels of counter-terrorist activity and manned entirely by SBS personnel. The squadron has carried out numerous operations although for reasons of security details remain scarce. By then, new areas of operations were being included in the SBS brief. These included working with anti-organised crime units within police and Customs and Excise, focusing especially on drug trafficking, and other projects that are today on-going and remain ultra-secret, including a continued presence in Northern Ireland.

Changes in the whole concept of Special Forces were under way, and not merely or in relation to their deployment and control. A lot of baggage, transported from a previous age, was being discarded. The SBS was also undergoing a significant change in its man management. In the 1950s and 1960s officers came and went after a two-or three-year stint; it was not considered a good career move to linger too long. The original theories of the likes of Nigel Willmott and Blondie Hasler of a unit with a higher proportion of officers were, in those times of crisis and austerity, diluted.

The change began falteringly when the SBS switched from its post-war role as a predominantly instructional group to an operations-led force. It remained a training ground, especially for upwardly mobile officers in the Royal Marines, and NCOs still formed the backbone of the SBS, as they do today. As the

SBS raised its profile, so too did the standards of entry and selection of men. Former SBS training officer Captain Neil Johnstone confirmed:

> People just couldn't understand the failure rate, and challenged it. We can now see that, historically, it has never been any different, except that it hardened on the side of rejection. It's got to be like it is. The summer and winter courses, which were adopted in the 1970s, for example, proved another factor that people couldn't understand. Why have two? The answer was simple. One man may not be able to withstand the extremes of the wet and the cold in winter, and conversely others might not manage the heat of summer training or operational activity. We need people who can operate in both. We always found that when you dropped one of these training situations for economy, the unit suffered later. We kept going, hardening up the selection process, and ended up with a lot of super, intelligent blokes who were very good indeed.

The point was emphasised by his story of a young marine who almost did not stay the course. 'S' was a 'ghastly corporal'. His officers constantly moaned about his attitude – 'It's S being difficult again' – and they were wondering what to do with him. He took a sergeant's course and went on to become a training colour-sergeant and was 'magic, very good indeed'. He was still reluctant to go on. His officer advised him to go for his commission: 'There's everything in the SBS now. Why don't you go for it? The alternative is to go back to the Corps and work up from there.' S stayed the course, won his commission, and later served with distinction.

Extensive training, the opportunity to learn specialist skills, from demolition to languages, and forced situations of endurance are the similarities shared between SAS and SBS. The common thread is that the men are called on to do things that they would never do voluntarily. They may look at a particular challenge, from rock-climbing to endurance swimming, and say to themselves 'I can't do that,' but they do it anyway, driven by a combination of macho bravado within the group, personal challenge or plain and simple survival. At that point, the SAS and SBS reach a fork in the road.

They differ in both philosophy and objectivity. The SBS was more likely to consider the consequences of its actions and to weigh up the alternatives to brute force and fire power. It is, perhaps, no better typified than by comparison between the two mottoes, a comparison I was repeatedly invited to consider during interviews for this work: WHO DARES WINS and NOT BY STRENGTH, BY GUILE. The end result may well be the same, once the troops under either banner have reached their target, except that with the SBS the body-count may not be as high.

The basic philosophy may not have changed, but the whole context of SBS activity has itself undergone a total overhaul in the decade or so since the post-Falklands studies began.

The Iraq v. Iran, Iran v. Salman Rushdie, Israelis v. Palestinians and others, Iraq v. Kurds, bombing them with mustard gas, Iraq massing troops on the Kuwaiti border. To veterans of the SBS, those headlines were decidedly déjà vu. On 2 August 1990 Iraq invaded Kuwait and, in the words of Senator Donald W. Reigle, who chaired a 1994 Senate Committee investigating pre-Gulf War exports to Iraq from the US, panic gripped those nations that had kept up their trade with Saddam Hussein virtually to the day of the invasion.

As Reigle recalled: 'Suddenly it dawned on people that we were going to have a real problem facing off against weapons that we had helped create . . . because [Saddam Hussein] had not been on the bad-guy list at the time.' By then, anyway, it was too late. Ill-judged assessments that Saddam would not invade, or, if he did, that it would be a temporary incursion, proved disastrously wrong. Pentagon military planners produced a stark assessment of what confronted them. William Webster, director of the CIA, said: 'The Iraqis are within eight-tenths of a mile of the Saudi border. If Saddam stays where he is, he'll own 20 per cent of the world's oil reserves, and he's within a few miles of seizing another 20 per cent. Jordan and Yemen will probably tilt towards him. We can expect Arab states to start cutting deals. Iran will be at Iraq's feet. Israel will be threatened.'

It was at this point that two of the key elements of Allied action against Iraq that could involve the Special Forces began to emerge, and for which contingency planning began by the end of the month:

1) A rescue attempt to bring out as many as possible of

hundreds of Western expatriates living and working in Iraq and Kuwait whom Saddam infamously declared he would use as a human shield against air raids from the West.

2) To stop the Scuds which, in the case of all-out war, would almost certainly be used against Israel. By the end of August the pre-war options had attracted a crowded arena of Special Forces from the US, led by the American Special Operations Central Command with 5 Special Forces Group, the US Sea Air Land (SEAL) units; US Air Force Special Force and other smaller groups. They were the initial component parts of a planning effort that would proceed under the title Operation Desert Shield.

British Special Forces were standing by at the early stages but were soon to be diverted by the plight of the hostages in which Britain had a large interest, with around 800 expatriates in Kuwait and slightly more in Iraq. Saddam was threatening to herd them into his airfields and chain them to military installations, and indeed did so at the end of October, placing 661 of them at key economic and military sites. By September SAS and SBS planners were working with US Special Forces frantically trying to produce viable plans to get them out. The options were incredibly limited and fraught with danger, both to the rescuers and to those being rescued. There was no central focus because the hostages were dispersed over a wide area. The operational planning began from the standpoint that perhaps fewer than half might be reached, and even then the prospect of heavy casualties could not be ruled out.

Historically, there were three particular experiences on which to draw: the evacuation of US expatriates from the roof of the American embassy in Saigon in 1975; the successful Israeli raid on Entebbe in 1976 in which 100 hostages were freed; and, more disconcerting, President Jimmy Carter's disastrous attempt to free the Iranian hostages in 1980 which ended in disaster when the helicopter carrying America's crack Delta Force crashed in the desert.

With political pressure mounting and civilian concerns for relatives and friends making the headlines, General Sir Peter de la Billière asked the Special Forces planners to look at a possible mass rescue. His idea was that teams would drop into Iraq by parachute or helicopter, gather up the hostages, call back the helicopters, load them aboard and ferry them to a collection point somewhere in the desert. The problem of location remained. A good deal of work was done by the Foreign Office and the Ministry of Defence, who helped to build a map of the highest concentration of Britons. The Britons trapped in Kuwait might be more easily contacted and reached, since an underground communications network was established quickly among them; some were still contactable by telephone. The BBC World Service was available for bulletins and was already broadcasting messages from friends and relatives. A sea-borne infiltration of Kuwait by the SBS was one possible option. The SBS would hopefully gather the Britons at a central point, perhaps the grounds of the British embassy, and airlift them by helicopter to safety, either to a desert rendezvous or to a ship in the Persian Gulf. The risk factor occurred in all deliberations, especially when the Americans began talking about diversionary raids to cover the evacuation. The British Special Forces were not at all happy.

By mid-November the British Special Forces command had assembled a force of around 800 men, including SBS, SAS and an RAF Special Forces section to join the Americans for the evacuation raids, although still no formal plan had been approved. At the same time, the prospect of them actually going in was diminishing daily. Amid diplomatic efforts to get the expatriates released, the Iraqi hostages were being moved around constantly, and no single human being in Iraq provided intelligence on their whereabouts. The best information came from watching CNN, and intelligence officials videoed and watched every frame of the news items. The chances of an effective round-up seemed slight. Even so, Special Forces were directed to press on and advance their plans to operational level so that, even if an all-out war did not develop, they might still be required to go in and bring out the hostages, by force if necessary.

Suddenly, that particular crisis was over. On 6 December Saddam Hussein released the hostages and said they would no longer be needed. This, in turn, gave the British Special Forces freedom to concentrate on a strategy for their own involvement in the war, if and when it came. They returned to their maps and intelligence to carve out a role for themselves, although few tasks were actually perceptible.

The US Special Forces had commandeered front-line reconnaissance as the Allied armies were arriving daily, by every means of transport available, until the Saudi Arabian desert was crammed with three-quarters of a million troops, kicking their heels and waiting for the off.

The style of the campaign was also not one that fitted the pattern of classic Special Forces operations, at least not in the beginning. It would be a high-tech, computer-controlled, satellite-directed air and missile attack, and there was no point in any Allied forces getting in the way of that. However, at the British Special Forces training base on the Arabian peninsula, planners went to work on surveying all possible objectives for an offensive role for their groups, listing attacks on military air bases to hit Saddam's supposed stock of 700 warplanes, deep infiltration to pinpoint likely targets for the Allied bombers, severing vital lines of communication and generally causing trouble.

There was, however, one other hurdle for them to overcome if they were to go to work at all. Overall commander of the Allied forces in the Gulf, General Norman Schwarzkopf, was not fond of Special Operations. He told journalists as much during one of his briefings, admitting that Vietnam border operations had left scars. He had also been let down in more recent times: the US commando tactics in the invasions of Grenada and Panama were both severely flawed, the Delta Force disaster in Iran was seared in American memories, and the aid-for-Contras scandal caused more bother than it was worth.

Then, all changed overnight. Apprehension vanished as Saddam Hussein began launching test flights of his Scud missiles from a site near Basra, day after day, test after test. US satellites tracked the missile flights and produced rapid predictions of their capability, damage and range. The last was an impossible equation because with mobile Scud launchers, Israel and Saudi Arabia were easy targets. There was also the unknown factor of his warheads. Was he bluffing or would he use them?

The CIA NonProliferation Center in Washington had a mass of data on that painful topic. The CIA had established that Saddam had been manufacturing his own Scud warheads, filled with gas and biological agents. This intelligence was to be proved entirely correct, if understated. UN teams after the war found 13,000 shells filled with mustard gas, 6,200 rockets loaded with nerve gas, 800 nerve agent aerial bombs, 28 Scud warheads loaded with nerve gas, and a stockpile of 75 tons of nerve agent – not counting that which was blown up during the war or squirrelled away for future use.

On 17 January the air war began 12 days ahead of schedule with a spectacularly televised precision blitz on Baghdad by the Coalition. The Iraqi Scuds started flying before the day was out, and with them came fear of what the warheads would contain. The chemical and biological threat is fully explored in my earlier book, *The Killing Factory*, and has since been aired fully and controversially. My opening paragraph set the scene as the Coalition prepared for Scud attacks:

'Gas! It's gas . . .! Level four, level four. Not a drill. Repeat, not a drill.' The words were shouted often as thousands of chemical detectors and alarm systems positioned across the Saudi Arabian desert among the tented cities of the Coalition forces screamed the alert and sent the troops diving for cover. Sweating buckets in their protective suits, drugged with a cocktail of 13 separate vaccines and tablets, breathing air heavily polluted by sand, dust, diesel fumes, jet fuel, pesticides, bug sprays and depleted uranium tips of armour-piercing shells, the massed armies of Desert Storm were on the very edge of their nerves . . . The tension could be sliced with a blunt bayonet.

On the second day of the war a dozen Iraqi Scuds hit the suburbs of Tel Aviv, bringing an immediate demand from Israel for air clearance to strike back. Schwarzkopf knew full well that doing so may well have compromised Arab support for the Coalition, support that was at times threatened but always vital. Apart from the sensitive political implications of allowing Israeli jets over Arab air space, an Israeli air intervention, possibly followed by a full-scale invasion, would also disturb the pre-planned and computer-programmed air attacks, with Coalition sorties running to hundreds a day. The Scud factor had to be met. The untried and hugely expensive Patriot surface-to-air missile response would not provide an absolute deterrent, and in any event they were still in short supply.

According to General Sir Peter de la Billière, he 'steamrollered' Norman Schwarzkopf into agreeing to use the British Special Forces; having done so, they now had to be adequately tasked. At the start of the air war the Special Forces were still at their training base on the Arabian peninsula. They had to move in double-quick time to get their men, vehicles and equipment to a forward holding base 1,200 miles (1,930 kilometres) away, located 650 miles (1,045 kilometres) north-west of Riyadh. With RAF Special Forces Hercules transporters making return trips, they completed the movement within 24 hours with the help of the US Tactical Aircraft Control Centre, which guided them through every mile of air space, alive with the hundreds of Allied warplanes heading north on their bombing raids.

The role of the Special Forces now crystallised into the anti-Scud effort. With no amphibious role for the SBS, a line was drawn through the map of anticipated operations across southern Iraq. The SAS was to cover the western territory, SBS to the east. Their principal tasks would be to scout Scud launch-sites, mobile Scud traffic and any other targets that eluded the air strikes. Road-watch teams were to be inserted by helicopter 140 to 180 miles (225 to 290 kilometres) behind the enemy border.

In the SBS sector of operations lay one other crucial installation that was to become the first target of the British Special Forces, and an operation exclusively planned and executed by the SBS. It consisted of a vast and complex communications network which, among other things, linked Saddam Hussein to his Iraqi forward positions. The SBS task was to locate and destroy the heavily concealed mass of fibre-optic cable buried well below ground, identified by US satellite intelligence.

The execution of the task was not a problem with SBS expertise; the dangers lay in the location – just 32 miles west of Baghdad. With barely time for their customary work-up, the SBS team of 36, led by Lieutenant 'S', prepared for their journey. Under cover of darkness on the night of 22 January, the men clambered aboard two Boeing Vertol Chinook helicopters from No. 7 Squadron's Special Forces Flight and flew north deep into Iraq to the site close to a road.

Nomadic Arabs and desert spies abounded in the area, so close to Iraq air and ground resources that a counter-attack force could have been launched rapidly. The team, heavily armed and equipped, carried 400 pounds (180 kilogrammes) of explosives. They flew direct to the site, leaped from the helicopters and sprinted to the target a short distance from the main road. The helicopter pilots kept their engines running but disengaged the rotors to cut down on the noise and to be certain of a swift exit should it become necessary. As they landed, the night sky was ablaze with Coalition bombardment of Baghdad.

The SBS team quickly located the communications cables and dug down, taking out a length to bring home for analysis, and placed explosive charges along the exposed area. Then they retreated and detonated their charges, blowing up a 40-yard (36-metre) section. The mission was described by Sir Peter as a high-risk operation carried out with great skill, determination and courage in a most hostile environment; it was a total success. The SBS party completed the task with no casualties in 90 minutes flat.

Before they left, Lieutenant 'S' grabbed one of the cable-route markers that, on his return, he presented as a souvenir to General Norman Schwarzkopf, who was so impressed by the success of the mission that he reported it immediately to General Colin Powell in Washington. Powell in turn passed the news and US congratulations back to London.

The SAS, meanwhile, was inserting three eight-man road-watch patrols to scout the Scud box and watch for traffic along three roads deep in the desert and 20 miles (32 kilometres) apart. Their exploits and the tragic compromise of one of the teams have been vividly described in various books, most notably *Bravo Two Zero*, by team member 'Andy McNab', and *The One That Got Away*, by Chris Ryan. This latter team was discovered when an enemy camp was set up almost on top of the men, three of whom died in their frantic efforts to escape – two from enemy fire and one from exposure. Four, including McNab, were captured, while Ryan made his epic journey to Syria.

Suffice to say that the mixed fortunes of the Special Forces group were perhaps most poignantly demonstrated in the command headquarters, when the success of the SBS operation was being analysed while the commander of the SAS, Colonel Andrew Massey, was in tears over the plight of his own lost patrol.

Another mission for the SBS came towards the end of the war. They were tasked with reclaiming possession of the British Embassy in Kuwait. They were personally chosen by General de la Billière, who was anxious to re-establish a British presence as soon as possible so that the nation's interests were well represented when the reconstruction of Kuwait was up for grabs.

The SBS went into action on 27 February 1991 when the men flew into Kuwait in their helicopters and set up a temporary base at the wrecked Kuwait airport. The next day, General de la Billière ordered the launch of the operation. The SBS worked on the assumption that the embassy buildings and grounds might be booby trapped, or perhaps still be harbouring a kamikaze group of Iraqi troops. Two Chinooks took off from the airport and hovered over the building. The SBS team roped down from the helicopters on to the roof of the embassy.

They had plans and a description of the building from staff who had been the last there but, when they discovered discrepancies, quickly withdrew to plan an explosive entrance, as mandated by their operational instructions. They threw stun-grenades through the windows and blasted down the huge and famous front door, designed by Edwin Lutyens. In fact, the precautions turned out to be unnecessary. The building had never been occupied by the Iraqis, and a Kuwaiti janitor who was still living nearby could have let them in with a key.

As it was, the British Ambassador, who flew in that night to take possession of his little haven among the devastation, was dismayed that the Lutyens door had been blown up.

There were other operations carried out by the Special Forces during the Gulf War, but at the time of writing they remain classified.

CHAPTER TWENTY

No licence to kill

The creation of a central command for British Special Forces had, by the early 1990s, developed a strategy of tasking that has brought new dimensions to the role of the SBS. No longer do they hang around waiting for wars or fill their time portraying the enemy in NATO exercises, although as an élite military group both remain their prime reason for being. Their commitment to maritime counter-terrorism also demands that they remain at peak readiness for any eventuality through training and exercises. But, just as MI5 began to diversify into other areas of civilian intelligence as the Cold War ended, SBS approaches the end of the century with one eye on the future – ready to work with other Government agencies.

The National Crime Intelligence Service (NCIS) may well become one of the organisations increasingly seeking SBS support. Launched in 1992, it targets the higher echelons of crime. It was one of the first services to be set up in Europe to deal with the development of criminal intelligence on a national scale, with approximately 500 staff drawn from the police, Customs and Excise and the Home Office. Its international division manages a network of European Drugs Liaison Officers and is linked up with the world-wide DLO group managed by Customs and Excise. The UK Bureau of Interpol is also based within this division, providing NCIS with direct access to Interpol's 176 member countries.

Although all projects in which the SBS is involved are security sensitive and remain well away from public view, modern tasking is leading them towards longer-term involvement in what may be regarded as ultra-secret activity. The SBS is never glimpsed by the media and especially not by cameramen, although one of its earliest 'civilian' tasks in the drugs arena did make the headlines, simply because of the size of the target: a ton of pure cocaine worth £160 million, the largest quantity ever seized in Britain.

Months of monitoring the movements of a ship, *Fox Trot Five*, and its largely British crew, culminated with a spectacular raid at Greenwich, London, with an SBS team swarming all over the vessel as she tied up on the Thames. The boat, which had been bought in America, had sailed to an island off Colombia and was tracked across the Atlantic. On 23 November 1992, she was sailing towards a mooring beside a warehouse on the edge of the Thames.

The vessel sailed on along the South Coast and back up into the Thames, where she was once again moored at Greenwich. There, in an operation that had so far included Customs and Excise, Interpol, the US Drugs Enforcement Administration and Scotland Yard and now the SBS, the trap was sprung. The members of the crew were watched as they unloaded a ton of cocaine wrapped in black polythene bags and carried it into a warehouse. At a given signal, two RIBS carrying the SBS teams, in their black gear with balaclavas over their faces, stormed across the Thames from a nearby hiding-place; the first group, armed with Heckler and Koch MP5 sub-machine-guns and stun-grenades, clambered aboard, followed by a second group in support. Meanwhile, a large contingent of armed police and customs men on the shore followed on behind a police-driven JCB as it broke down the doors to the warehouse. The job was done.

Five men were arrested at the warehouse, and later two hundred policemen raided eighteen addresses in the South-East of England. The SBS faded quietly and quickly into the background, disappearing whence it came. But for one sharp-eyed woman named Joyce Lowman, who took a picture of the SBS team as it boarded the boat, its presence would not have been revealed.

Is this the future or part future role of the SBS? It is certainly an area in which the SBS are likely to be used, but they are basically Royal Marines, in other words soldiers, commandos, complemented by a specialisation in maritime skills. They can provide skills that are unique. It is recognised now that they are able to deliver a capability that no one else has. Clearly, they have been involved in a wide diversity of operational activity. It is, however, only relatively recently that they have moved into a completely different environment. Their tasking has become substantially more positive and indeed the threatening possibilities on the international horizon have become more intense. At the same time, their reason for being is not now in accord with the popular image of the special forces, which is one of apparent personal glorification and self-satisfaction.

Survival? They are past masters of the art. And so when, in March 1994, a British army expedition from Hong Kong went missing, a joint SAS/SBS team went in to find the men and plucked them out within 48 hours of the team's arrival, a fact never publicised at the time. Lieutenant-Colonel Robert Neil of the Royal Logistics Corps led his party of ten on an army expedition from Hong Kong to the 13,455-foot (4,101-metre) Mount Kinabalu on the island of Borneo. It included himself, a fellow officer, five young soldiers and three Chinese military officers.

The region was well known to members of the Special Forces from their past involvement in this place of dense jungle and difficult terrain, which needs exceptional skills if trouble is to be avoided. Several SBS men had themselves tackled the mountain following an exercise the previous year. Its infamous attraction to adventurers, Low's Gully, is so called because colonial officer William Low toasted the British Empire in port when he became the first man to conquer the mountain in 1851. The gully is a 2,000-foot (610-metre) long, steep jungle gorge that offers virtually every possible challenge to expeditions such as theirs – sheer, vertical rock to be abseiled, a 400-foot (120-metre) waterfall to be negotiated, a rock-hopping section across deep plunge-pools, dense jungle through which it took them four days to hack through a mile, and so on. It is said that a full descent of the gully, from the top to its absolute floor, has never been achieved.

The expedition split into two for the descent from the mountain. One team managed, with difficulty, to return to the base on 12 March. The second team which included the expedition leader Lieutenant-Colonel Neil, became long overdue. Initially, an RAF mountain team was deployed to find the men, helicopters searched, and two officers put on to Low's Gully found traces of the team – empty sardine cans. Heavy rain, however, turned the gully into a fast-moving river, and the two men were flown back to base exhausted.

On 21 March the Malaysian Army provided 400 trackers and soldiers to scour the valley – without success. On 24 March the RAF went back in with a six-man team, turning back after hitting trouble on the waterfall. On the same day it was decided in London to send a Special Forces team, including five SAS men, three SBS and seven others, to conduct a search.

The team left London and two days later it was on the edge of the jungle. The first air recce used a Malaysian Army helicopter with two Malaysian airmen, and by the end of the first day the missing men were found.

Two members of the Special Forces team, a major and a sergeant, spotted flashes of light which brought them in for a closer look. It was that, and not an SOS spelled out in pebbles on the river bank – as some have suggested – that drew them to the spot. Later, they discovered that the flashes of light were made by a camera, not a mirror.

The helicopter, not entirely suited to the job at hand, went in as low as it dared and the SF team found the men, starved and in a bad psychological condition. The team signalled its discovery and returned to base to get supplies, which were winched down, along with an SBS medic. The next day the SF team acquired a Sea King helicopter for the final rescue. So ended the drama of the five missing men, hugely reported in Britain and across the world. No mention was made of the British Special Forces who got them out.

Similarly unreported and anonymously enacted was the role of the British Special Forces, including the SBS, in the finale of the bloody conflict that engulfed the former Yugoslavia in the first half of the 1990s. The SBS was placed on alert from the early stages of the war in Bosnia, virtually from the moment the first of Britain's contingent of 3,500 troops were standing by to join the United Nations Protection Force (UNProFor). The explosion of ethnic, religious and territorial violence which was to bring daily images of unimaginable horrors on to television screens for the next five years began at the turn of the decade. Serbia, the lead nation of that unfortunate combination of states forced together in the early part of this century to form Yugoslavia, tried to impress its will on the others and retain control of the disintegrating republic after the death of Tito.

First it went to war with Slovenia, then Croatia, as both states won international recognition for independence. But those conflicts were a minor forerunner to the appalling and ferocious conflict that flared in Bosnia between the Serbs and an alliance of Croats and Muslims. In the spring of that year, as the Serbs pounded Sarejevo into the dust, the international community was finally, if reluctantly, forced to act and intervene on behalf of the millions caught in the crossfire.

The British intention was announced by Prime Minister John Major on 21 August 1992 as the British contribution 'to support the United Nations High Commission for Refugees operations in the former Yugoslavia. Time is now needed to assemble and prepare such a force. There is therefore pressure for those elements of the army likely to be involved to be at a high state of readiness so that they can react should the government's offer be accepted by the United Nations.'

The 1st Battalion of the Cheshire Regiment would form the core of Britain's initial troop deployment, along with a medium reconnaissance squadron of the 9/12 Royal Lancers, and they headed for the area around Tuzla as the winter set in. There began the British involvement in what the 1st Cheshire commander, Lieutenant-Colonel Bob Stewart, described as 'one of the most vicious wars ever'.

The British Special Forces as a group began contingency planning for possible tasks as the UN gathered its force of 20,000 men in that winter of 1992. The UN role, filled with complexities, restrictions, local opposition and with one arm tied behind its back, was chaotic and for the most part impossible from the start. The UN forces were the buffer in a seemingly unfathomable civil war. As Bob Stewart said in his autobiography, 'The Cheshire group . . . were not there to "make peace"; we were not enforcers of it . . . Helping to create conditions for peaceful resolution of disputes was one thing, but forcing a cessation of hostilities was certainly outside of our charter. Peacekeepers have to react to events while enforcement troops may have to create them.'

It was the ambiguity of the UNProFor role that put the peacekeeping force in constant danger and, at the same time, imposed restrictions on assault activity of any kind, regardless of the aim – and that included the SBS. Their initial role, therefore, was a delicate one concerning the humanitarian effort but equally for precautionary measures over the deployment of British troops. As the unforgettable pictures of the starving prisoners of war, the massacres, the mass graves, the relief efforts – stalled time and again – to get food to millions of starving people, along with the desolate faces of the Vance–Owen peace negotiators, reached television screens world-wide, the SBS was already in rehearsal.

The possibility of British forces being isolated, ambushed or captured in the conflict occurred daily. In early 1993, an SBS team conducted recces of certain areas. Rehearsals were staged in Britain for possible tasks of both an operational and a humanitarian nature. The following year the then commander of UNProFor, General Mike Rose, formally requested the presence of British Special Forces, and the SBS contributed teams for patrols and reconnaissance. They were operating within the region first designated for the establishment of British troops under UN command.

In October 1995, the Dayton Peace Initiative, supported by all the major Western powers under the NATO alliance, began to set in motion the groundwork for a total cessation of hostilities. In December the SBS joined a large deployment of British Special Forces, who were to become part of NATO's Operation Joint Endeavour and the British component, Operation Resolute.

In a combined and determined effort, NATO would provide 60,000 troops, including 20,000 Americans and 10,000 British to police the ceasefire and enforce it if necessary. Optimism that this war was finally ending rose when the peace formula, eventually signed on 15 December, was accepted by all sides.

Between the beginning of December and D-Day, nominated as 18 January 1996, when the zone of separation between the various 'entities' was to be vacated, a great deal of delicate negotiation was required on the ground, particularly in the flashpoints where peace was most likely to be threatened. On that day UNProFor troops would join the incoming reinforcements under the command of NATO's Allied Command Europe Rapid Reaction Corps (ARRC).

It was in this area that the British Special Forces team of SBS and SAS was operating, linked to the complicated demarcation line, hundreds of miles of the ceasefire front, along with territory swaps and evacuations.

An SBS squadron provided important advance intelligence for the incoming US 1st Armoured Division. The American force was designated to make a tactical deployment based on a forced crossing of the River Sava. The advance was, however, significantly amended in the light of SBS contacts and reconnaissance within the region.

As a direct result of SBS recommendations, the Americans made the crossing, unforced and in relative calm, by bridge. The epic building of a new 370-metre pontoon bridge over the Sava, and another 240-metre span over its flooded surrounds – the largest undertaking of its kind since they crossed the Rhine at Remagen in the same fashion 50 years earlier – was completed by 1 January 1996. The Americans moved unhindered into position.

ARRC commanders recognised that the 'initiative, judgement and creativity of the SBS' were fundamental in allowing the US1AD to adapt to the local situation and meet deadlines set by the Dayton Peace Agreement. The SBS remained until August 1996, when the peace agreements they had helped nudge into place appeared to be holding. Then it left, as usual, without a trace of its having been there in the first place, as ever a tiny cog that helped the big wheels to keep on turning. The only clue to SBS involvement were unidentifiable mentions in the *London Gazette*, when several members of its team won commendations and medals for service in Bosnia.

The unseen and relatively unknown operations in foreign parts ran in tandem with more dramatic and headline-grabbing excursions that were increasingly becoming part of SBS workload. Experiences such as the *QE2* drop and the 1992 swoop on a drugs ship as she steamed up the Thames had provided successful precedents, and more were to follow, particularly in relation to assisting Customs and Excise officers and the National Crime Intelligence Service in the fight against large-scale smuggling of drugs into Britain by sea.

The NCIS has a specialised Drugs Team consisting of three specific units dedicated to the war on drug-runners: Heroin Intelligence, Cocaine Intelligence and Synthetic Drugs and Chemical Control Intelligence. A formal communications link was also established with the SBS by the NCIS Organised Immigration Crime Section, which coordinates the intelligence response to illegal immigration, particularly in relation to possible raids on boats used by people-smugglers. These connections, added to the established and routine involvement in the security of Britain's offshore and coastal installations, called for a constant review of training and preparation and the updating of equipment. Training for any task presented to the SBS has been a prerequisite since its creation, and civilian-linked operations such as a drugs swoop required no less preparation than full-scale military activity.

Training procedures and manuals for such raids provide all the scenarios and eventualities they are likely to encounter, and rehearsals and preparation cover the finer points of a specified task. A target vessel would, for the most part, have been located and monitored for many days prior to the point where the SBS reached the point where she could be legally challenged and boarded. New equipment specifically to meet the potential for raids out at sea was acquired. By 1998, for example, the SBS had acquired what was described as a Stealth Boat, a 40-foot (12-metre) inflatable coated with anti-radar paint to make it invisible to radar screens and capable of speeds of up to 50mph with up to ten commandos in their black divers' suits on board. The open boat was designed for versatility. She could be dropped from a C-180 Hercules transport aircraft and, powered by electric motors, the approach to a target ship could be made either on the surface or submerged with SBS men using breathing gear. The craft could even be secured to the seabed, while the SBS returned to the surface as divers to make their approach.

Surveillance and interception missions were seen as the prime use for the boat, with established routes for drug-runners by sea from West Africa, southern Europe, the Caribbean and Latin America. SBS teams worked with the crime agencies in developing the boat, although she was obviously well suited to their wider role of coastline protection. The same level of secrecy is maintained over their operations, and they leave no footprints. The potential for SBS involvement came to light when they provided their expertise to intercept a drug-running vessel in the Irish Sea, on that occasion abseiling from a Sea King helicopter to board a ship carrying three tons of cannabis.

In 1997 the SAS was involved in the arrest off the coast of Portugal of a 277-ton yacht which had sailed from Morocco, allegedly carrying 14 tons of cannabis bound for Britain. The yacht was tracked and intercepted by the Royal Navy Frigate HMS *York*, which had SBS men on board. The raid was the culmination of 18 months of surveillance by Customs and NCIS officers in which the SBS were also involved, but on that occasion their efforts were in vain. The trial of three men accused of importing an estimated £14 million-worth of cannabis ended without conviction after the Ministry of Defence refused to submit to defence requests regarding information about the role of the Special Boat Service. The Customs officers who organised the raid were also criticised over what the defence had argued involved serious breaches of international law and Britain's treaty obligations.

Exposure of the SBS to public, media and even legal scrutiny was thus once again thwarted, but not before some of the drama of such operations leaked into the headlines.

CHAPTER TWENTY-ONE

The élite

Towards the end of the 1990s and into the new millennium, the SBS profile was raised considerably. Fresh challenges were appearing across the globe in both military- and civilian-orientated actions that would test even the most highly trained units of military forces and the SBS, with their more comprehensive repertoire of key disciplines much in demand, especially where American troops were also involved. US Special Forces commanders had developed a great respect for their abilities since the Gulf War and the Bosnian conflict.

So much so that their numbers were eventually increased substantially and in due course would include recruitment from crack army units, such as the Parachute Regiment, rather than being restricted to the Royal Marines. This move was not entirely popular among the older SBS aficionados, who were keen to maintain an exclusive link with the naval heritage of the SBS – although, as some pointed out, the SBS originally emerged from army commando units rather than the Royal Marines.

However, the changing times brought greater demands, especially with the need for finely tuned personnel capable of handling the multitude of tasks confronting the British Special Forces as a whole, the modern-day version of what Winston Churchill once described as 'our own storm troops'. In the case of the SBS, this higher profile brought unwelcome media interest on a scale that had been previously reserved for their more overt colleagues in the SAS. Their fleeting but dramatic public appearances, kitted out in their sinister black garb and accoutrements on such operations as the storming of suspect ships, invariably made the front pages. But these incidents were few and far between, and for the most part public scrutiny of the SBS remained out of bounds. This is especially so in maintenance of the ongoing 24-hour-a-day 'ready-to-move' commitment to tackle any terrorist or criminal activity within the United Kingdom itself.

Long before Osama Bin Laden became a household name, the SBS had been progressively stepping up its readiness to deploy against possible terrorist activity, particularly with regard to the nation's oil, gas and nuclear installations. This permanent 'watch-tower' operation, carried out jointly with a larger general force which includes the Royal Marines, the Paras and the SAS, requires constant review and reappraisal, with a continuous programme of training and preparation in which personnel and all systems, procedures and equipment are tested in near-to-life situations. The SBS also continues to perform exceedingly realistic mock assaults against its own side, to test the protection and defences at sensitive British military, intelligence and civilian sites. It is an extension of the exercises the SBS invented to assess their own strengths and weaknesses, practised without warning, and which has now been universally adopted for counter-terrorist training routines.

In addition, their specialist assistance is in constant demand in cooperation with the police and Customs and Excise to take the lead role in raids on maritime crime gangs such as people-smugglers and drug-running ships, an area exclusive to the SBS, involving as it does sea-borne assault, either from boats or ship-launched helicopters. In recent times, the SBS has also been involved either actively or as advisers with a Royal Navy anti-drugs force, especially in the Caribbean against drug ships launched from South America.

In response to these new challenges, the SBS was reorganised into three squadrons in the late 1990s, each specialising in particular disciplines, such as swimmer and canoe operations for intelligence-gathering, covert craft and mini-sub operations for raiding-parties, and full-on assaults in counter-terrorist and ship-boarding manoeuvres launched from fast boats or helicopters. Apart from these specialisations, all SBS personnel are fully trained and available for any general assault or policing operations in the style of the SAS, with whom they occasionally join forces and often report to the same chain of command.

As the new millennium approached, these possibilities bore down heavily on the British Special Forces as a whole, and called for the movement of men and equipment to far-flung parts of the globe. In the autumn of 1998, for example, a new crisis emerged that would take them back into the Balkans, where the SBS had won much respect from the Americans for their restraint and patience in the unravelling of the Bosnian conflict. Their delicate handling of powder-keg situations on the ground became an intrinsic ingredient in the move towards the peaceful resolution in Bosnia that Yugoslav president Slobodan Milošević hated. Now, Milošević had embarked on parallel lines of conflict in the province of Kosovo, attempting to ethnically cleanse the towns and villages of the Albanian Kosovars.

As with Bosnia, the troubles dated back to the end of the Cold War, when Milošević dissolved the Kosovo assembly, and ethnic Albanian legislators in the province responded by declaring independence, which the Serbs refused to recognise. Tens of thousands of ethnic Albanians lost their jobs as Milošević ordered a clampdown in the province, and the shadowy Kosovo Liberation Army (KLA) made its presence felt by admitting responsibility for a number of bombings and attacks against Serbian police and state officials.

Fast-forwarding to March 1998, the situation had stumbled through several phases of internal crisis until the international community acknowledged, finally, that a repeat of Bosnia was already unfolding in Kosovo. Serbian police emptied village after village, and thousands of refugees from Serbian brutality were already on the move when US envoy Richard Holbrooke flew to Belgrade in June to meet Milošević to try to end the conflict. The Serbian leader gave no promises and the following day UN Secretary-General Kofi Annan cautioned NATO that it must seek a Security Council mandate for any military intervention.

All summer long, diplomatic activity swung back and forth; the Kosovars, meanwhile, were being brutalised. First reports of mass graves and many instances of the burning of houses and clearing of villages were appearing. On 24 September 1998 NATO approved two contingency plans, one for air strikes and the second for monitoring and maintaining a cease-fire agreement if one was reached. The UN High Commissioner for Refugees (UNHCR), meanwhile, announced on 29 September that 200,000 civilians had already been displaced within Kosovo since fighting began in February. International mediators continued their efforts, but months passed during which promises by

Milošević were never kept, peace talks didn't happen, NATO bombing strikes were postponed and the general air of impending doom deepened. The refugee problem had by now long ago passed crisis point and was heading for catastrophe as the winter weather set in and thousands more were moving towards Albania. Refugee camps began to appear in the most desperate and tragic displacement of whole populations since the Second World War. Observers on the ground in Kosovo reported that the speed with which the refugee crisis developed appeared to indicate that there was a plan to ethnically cleanse at least the KLA strongholds, if not the entire province, of its Albanian population. As this situation developed, the Special Forces teams would be tasked on missions that cut across all aspects of their training, including the little-publicised humanitarian aspects, as well as that of providing intelligence that would cut the loss of life collaterally and within their own military forces.

By February 1999 the humanitarian situation had significantly deteriorated, and reports of atrocities were widespread as Serbian troops advanced into the countryside. The UNHCR reported a total of 330,000 displaced Kosovars and the figure was rising. By 23 March, 23 major cities were being targeted by Serbian forces. The emptying of Kosovska Mitrovica had begun with thousands of homes and businesses looted and torched. With long lines of refugees struggling with all the possessions they could carry still heading for the borders, Western leaders proposed an airlift to take 100,000 Kosovars to NATO countries. NATO also released imagery taken by surveillance aircraft of 500 people surrounded by Serb forces in the town of Glodane. There was also evidence of many atrocities and mass graves. Serbian forces reportedly locked the members of an entire family into a house in a village in Drenica and burned them alive.

Against this background, further frantic diplomatic efforts were under way, with talks arranged in Paris, and a peace deal was hammered out that seemed to present an eleventh-hour hope of a solution. Milošević refused to sign it. Thus, on 24 March, NATO launched its air war with the assembled aircraft of 14 nations; long before they reached the start line, British Special Forces, the SBS among them, along with military intelligence units, were already surveying the landscape. As in the Falklands and the Gulf, it was inevitable that Special Forces surveillance patrols would be there, inside enemy territory, before, during and after this bitter and tragic conclusion to the Yugoslavian nightmare. They moved into the inhospitable Serbian countryside at five key points in Serbia and Montenegro. Their brief was, first and foremost, to stay out of sight and keep out of trouble, report on troop movements, ammunition dumps and other tools of war, and at the same time to offer up a range of potential targets such as important communication lines and road bridges whose importance might not be fully evident in imagery from surveillance aircraft.

Belgrade itself was rocked by bombs in the first wave of attacks. Dozens of Tomahawk cruise missiles were launched by warships and submarines – mostly American, but including one Royal Navy nuclear submarine, *Splendid*, prior to the intensive Allied bombing campaign that followed. The intelligence from inside Serbia also helped the UN human rights observers to alert the world to the continuing plight of refugees on the move in the war zone. It was estimated that 1.2 million Kosovo Albanians had by then been displaced from their homes and that 400 towns and villages had been damaged or destroyed by Serbian forces since mid-March 1999. The endgame now, as the Allies began their bombing campaign, was to degrade the Serbian military capacity for oppression to such an extent that ground forces could move in to assert a political agreement, but that possibility, vague and ill-planned from the outset, soon began to look impossible. Milošević also utilised every possible situation to discredit the NATO assault, which in the event was not difficult because there were a number of serious errors of judgement and too many collateral casualties.

With Allied aircraft making up to 650 sorties a day at the height of the campaign, the vast movement of people on the ground made the possibility of casualties among civilians and friendly forces all the more likely. Milošević knew that, and he utilised the lines of refugees as cover for the movement of troops and vehicles as the columns of human flotsam were shoved and directed along the routes to the borders. Once again, Special Forces were engaged to report as far as possible on the movement of Serbian troops in an attempt to limit the casualties, but they were apparently hampered by poor communications. The Americans had insisted on taking control of intelligence operations, but what was described to the author as 'the sheer bureaucracy' of the US intelligence network resulted in long delays – sometimes by as much as three days – in reports reaching the bombing command centre. Secure communications were also inadequate, which meant that crucial information was not being passed to attack units for fear of the Serbs hearing it. Consequently, the reports from surveillance teams inside Serbia often arrived too late to be of use, and bomber pilots found themselves directed to sites already deserted or, conversely, to points where Serbian troop movements had been replaced by refugees.

The air bombardment campaign proceeded relentlessly day after day, yet for all the damage and discomfort to his citizens Milošević refused to accept any moves towards a cessation in return for firm proposals to halt the ethnic cleansing of Kosovo and the repatriation of those he had forced out. The situation deteriorated to the point where the hawks of Europe were calling for the start of a ground offensive, which would require the assembling of well in excess of 100,000 troops. Time was running short for such an operation, which military experts concluded would have to be under way long before the start of the autumn and winter, when the troops and their transport would become bogged down in the mire of poor roads over mountainous routes. These had already been surveyed by the Special Forces, and the outlook was grim. The Americans were already reluctant to commit their troops to enter into manpower-costly ground combat, which would entail a large number of body bags being sent back to the US and a resultant political disaster to President Clinton, then in the final throes of his sex scandal, and his Democratic Party. A key meeting between US defence chiefs and their European counterparts to discuss sending in ground troops ended in stalemate.

Ministry of Defence sources acknowledged, however, that contingency plans for such a move had to remain active, especially if the bombing campaign dragged on through the summer. Time was running out, and a deadline was set for the middle of July if a successful operation was to be launched before the winter set in. British Defence Secretary George Robertson was among those lobbying strongly for a state of readiness for a full-scale invasion. Although talk of this measure was played down, contingency plans were well in hand for Britain to send a substantial contingent of troops as part of a NATO army to move into Kosovo if it became necessary. Among the plans discussed at the time was that British Special Forces and Paras would lead an airborne assault to capture one of Serbia's main airports as a precursor to a full-scale invasion. The latter prospect in turn meant a renewed alert for the Special Forces, who, as ever, would be among those preparing the way for any attack, with on-the-ground surveillance of the hazards that the incoming troops might face. The NATO commanders saw the mountainous countryside as particularly dangerous, filled with ambush places, natural anti-tank obstacles, firetraps and every other sort of terrain favourable to Serbian defence and unfavourable to NATO attack. Thus, the Americans were prepared to consider only the formation of a NATO peacekeeping Kosovo Force (KFOR). Other detractors who opposed a forced entry into Kosovo – and there were plenty – preferred to continue the NATO bombardment of key Serbian installations and troop positions until submission was achieved, although there were waverers against that too. The bombardment simply went on and on, until a diplomatic effort finally brought an agreement from the Serbian president, Milošević, on 10 June 1999 when he finally agreed to pull his troops out of Kosovo, to make way for KFOR ground forces.

By then, ground troops were already being brought to the edges of the conflict, with Britain, for example, sending 20 or so troop-carrying flights a day to deliver 5,000 troops and 20,000 tons of supplies, ammunition and army hardware. They joined contingents from other NATO partners and piled up on the Albanian side of the border as part of the UK contribution to the 11,000 troops of the KFOR peacekeeping force that would enter Kosovo under the terms of the cease-fire and so begin the West's most ambitious military deployment since the Gulf War, with contingents of British, German, French, Italian and American troops preparing to cross the border from Macedonia and Albania. Britain alone had close on 2,000 tanks, self-propelled artillery pieces, armoured troop carriers, trucks, Land Rovers and other vehicles for the move upcountry and into villages, towns and cities devastated by both the NATO bombing campaign and months of ruthless ethnic cleansing, wanton destruction and murder by the most brutal regime in that region since the Nazis.

Chinook and Puma support helicopter forces had also arrived, operating from Macedonia, with Special Forces patrols from four nations, including the SAS and SBS, moving into Serbian territory well ahead of the main forces. Their task was to ensure that there were no surprises as the peacekeeping force moved in. There were, however, plenty of potential hazards.

The route into Kosovo was banked by steep, mountainous terrain that could hide ample numbers of snipers, machine-gun nests and rocket launchers. The Special Forces also discovered two tunnels, four large bridges and about ten smaller ones which were obvious targets for boobytraps, mines and ambush hideouts for any of the remaining Serbian paramilitaries who might choose to make life difficult for the incoming troops – indeed, the welcome mat might already have been laid, and thus almost every step of the way required careful inspection before the main body of troops moved forward. Since the whole, lumbering 4th Armoured Brigade, with its vast column of men and machines, would have to negotiate the passes and bridges, speed was of the essence, and the road had to be declared safe before they even reached it.

The push forward by the British contingent signalled the start of the overall movement of the NATO troops who made up KFOR into their own designated areas of protection, with the Americans bringing up the rear. Their commanders were particularly reluctant to move their troops into Macedonia, apparently under orders from Washington that they should not advance if there was a real threat of confrontation with the Serbian army or strong paramilitary forces. And there was – all the way in, not to mention a highway and countryside strewn with mines and explosives at virtually every step and much unexploded ordnance dropped by their own side. It was the latter that subsequently killed two members of the Queen's Own Gurkha Engineers while clearing material from around a village school at Orlate, south-west of Priština airfield.

The Americans, however, kept their 2,200 marines stacked up in ships moored in the Adriatic until the all-clear was sounded, this resulting in part from assurances to be received at the border from Serbian military commanders and from the reconnaissance by the British Special Forces and the forward units of the British troops. At dawn on 13 June, the second phase of the 'invasion' was under way in southern Kosovo in spectacular style – and certainly flash enough to please the politicians in London as they viewed the movement along with the rest of the nation on their television screens. All looked good for the dash to Priština, and again the Special Forces went ahead in their Chinooks and

Pumas, followed immediately by troops from 1 Para as the huge, noisy, snaking convoys of wheeled and tracked vehicles headed for the frontier flanked by Gurkhas with heavy backpacks to take control of the ravaged state of Kosovo, and subsequently to help restore it to some semblance of normality. For humanitarian reasons alone, it was an exceedingly worthwhile effort.

The SBS would be back in the region before many months were out, but in the meantime other demands on their skills arrived thick and fast.

Barely had the dust settled in Kosovo when far-flung tensions rose in a region where the SBS originally took on board much of its heritage in covert operations – the Far East, and specifically Indonesia. This was SBS stamping ground, the heartland of literally dozens of operations in the Second World War under Mountbatten's South-East Asia Command and post-war in such long-running anti-terrorist operations in Malaya and the Borneo Confrontation. The focus now, however, was the island of Timor in the Malay archipelago, easternmost of the Lesser Sunda Islands, between the Savu and Timor Seas. The western half of the island had long been in the hands of Indonesia, while the eastern sector, 5,743 square miles in area, was a Portuguese overseas territory. In 1975 one of the major political parties gained control of much of the territory and declared its independence as the Democratic Republic of East Timor. The following year, East Timor was invaded and occupied by Indonesian forces, with the loss of some 200,000 lives, and officially became part of Indonesia.

A lively resistance movement flourished and began the struggle for the return of an independent East Timor, which the Indonesians refused to countenance, and furthermore ruled with a rod of iron in defiance of mounting international criticism. By then, Indonesia was gaining strength both as the most populous region in South-East Asia and as a powerful trading nation, especially in petroleum products, and played a critical role in the development of its part of the world. Against this background, horrific human rights abuses in East Timor went unchecked for years until, in 1999, the international community finally got around to taking action by demanding that the islanders of East Timor should be free to decide their future. After a UN-sponsored vote, East Timor was granted independence, but the Indonesians did not give way easily. Rioting and mass killings began at the hands of well-armed and out-of-control militias, some of whom were in collusion with the British-trained Kopassus, Indonesia's special armed forces.

Finally, intervention by a UN peacekeeping force was judged the only solution and, given its history, it was fitting that the SBS should take a leading role. Britain was to contribute an SBS team and a Gurkha contingent to the international force to quell the riot-torn towns and villages. The first UN peacekeepers to enter East Timor were 30 members of the SBS with a 20-strong team from the Australian Special Forces. They flew into the capital, Dili, at dawn and immediately began the familiar preparatory role of preparing the way for those who were to follow: more than 2,500 soldiers arriving within 48 hours and a further 5,500 following behind.

The SBS moved out to cover the airport perimeter as the major landings began, and they then moved off to test the water elsewhere and provide surveillance and intelligence reports for the incoming UN commanders. Their role was vital. Thousands of wild and angry militiamen opposed to independence were on the streets, along with a substantial presence of Indonesian troops whose willingness to depart peacefully was in some doubt. All around, said one of the SBS men present, the atmosphere was exceedingly tense; everyone had the feeling that the whole place could just explode into furious violence at any moment, and it would be several hours before the UN peacekeeping force arrived in any significant numbers. The prospect of heavy battles was never far away, and the Special Forces were there especially to forewarn and forestall.

As the SBS moved out, columns of black smoke from burning houses curled over the capital, apparently from fresh fires, accompanied by sporadic gunfire. The SBS made its presence felt immediately by disarming a group of Indonesian troops who rode menacingly into the port area. The SBS was soon to be joined by the Gurkhas – their partners in many similar operations over the decades – who, once again, went straight into the firing line, willingly and with their usual good humour. It was by any standards a hazardous mission. The Gurkhas came from the Brunei-based 2nd Battalion, the Royal Gurkha Rifles, and, as in Kosovo, the British Special Forces and the Gurkhas were among the first wave of troops to make their way into East Timor. They make excellent partners in such situations, the SBS with their own diverse skills followed up by the equally fearless but much feared Gurkhas, highly trained for the infantry role and urban conflict, as well as being acclimatised to the intense heat and humidity of the province. No one was in any doubt, however, that this was a potentially explosive situation, with thousands of well-equipped militiamen still on the loose on the island. At one stage rogue troops fired their weapons close to Gurkha and Australian soldiers in an attempt to intimidate them and test their reaction; the troops stood firm without firing a shot in reply. The Gurkhas were given responsibility for security at the UN compound, where many people had taken refuge, and were immediately confronted by three lorries, each carrying about 15 armed men, many with bandannas over their faces. Shots were fired and the Gurkhas chased the convoy on foot and in vehicles. The British contingent needed to demonstrate their willingness to open fire if necessary without provoking the departing Indonesian forces into hostility.

As tensions intensified, it was the Gurkhas who fired the first shots in the peace enforcement campaign, intervening in another episode where armed militiamen were terrorising thousands of refugees in a quayside shantytown. Tipped off by the SBS, a group of 20 Gurkha soldiers travelled to the eastern port of Corn to discover the incredible sight of around 3,000 refugees, who had been forcibly removed from their villages, being held captive by a dozen armed men. As the Gurkhas began to move through the area, the militiamen took flight into the hills. It was the involvement of such professionalism in the very early stages of the operation that defused a highly fraught situation and eased the grateful islanders of East Timor into independence.

It was in a similarly collaborative effort, codenamed Operation Palliser, in the summer of 2000 that the Special Forces began the first of two deployments to the war-torn African state of Sierra Leone, the former British colony, which in recent years had descended into anarchy, corruption and poverty. In conjunction with a contingent from 1 Para, whose battle group was deployed in record time, they flew in to secure an airhead for the evacuation of British and European nationals as their security became threatened. More than 1,500 civilians were trapped in the spiralling conflict between government forces and the massive rebel army. Foreign nationals and aid workers poured into one of the two main hotels in the capital, Freetown, clutching passports and a few belongings to await their escort to safety. The UN had pleaded for British help to secure the airport and assist its troops in defending the part of town that included the UN headquarters, and the incoming soldiers were tasked to provide early warning of possible rebel advances on the main airport. They themselves were fired on by a band of 40 rebels in a 10-minute fire fight in which 4 rebels were killed.

The mission, with its specific aim of providing protection for civilians, was achieved in double-quick time, and the British troops were then pulled out to leave matters in the hands of a relief force. However, in August they were back in action when 11 British soldiers, part of the UN peacekeeping force, were held to ransom by a notorious 300-strong militia known as the West Side Boys, a ramshackle pro-government army of men, women and children run by self-styled 'Brigadier' Foday Kallay. The incident caused such ructions at the Ministry of Defence and among their political masters that a full inquiry was held into the incident. The results were never fully revealed, but the author is now able to provide an accurate summary of what happened.

The missing troops, from the 1st Battalion, Royal Irish Regiment, were members of an intelligence-gathering patrol under the command of Major Alan Marshall. He had led his men into the Occra Hills of Sierra Leone in three open-topped Land Rovers. They stopped for a location check and, under the searing heat of the bush, took a drink while they pored over their maps. The patrol had two options: to carry on to check two villages some distance ahead or to return to their base at Benguema Training Camp. Marshall was the youngest major in the British army and judged to be a fine officer with a promising career ahead of him. Now, as the British infantry-covering force commander, he was tasked with gathering intelligence on both friendly and hostile forces – although it was difficult to assess which groups fell into which category – and he decided on the riskier of the two options, of pushing on towards the villages.

As one of Marshall's colleagues pointed out, officers are taught at staff college to gather intelligence at every opportunity, and he pressed on towards the villages to verify information he had received about militia movements. There was a snag in this plan, in that there was only one route in and one out, thus giving a force of rebels of any size an opportunity to surround the lightly armed British patrol. That is exactly what happened, although it was unclear whether at the time Marshall was of the view that the West Side Boys were 'friendlies'. Whatever his thoughts, the judgement was of little value. On the road to Magbeni on 25 August he encountered 25 of Kallay's irregulars and a pick-up truck armed with twin-mounted guns. It turned out that the cut-throat band, many high on dope and drink, were not at all friendly and were also exceptionally well armed. Marshall's patrol was surrounded and the young commander was viciously beaten to the ground as he tried to defend his troops. He decided that they had no choice but to go into captivity without a fight. He did manage to contact regimental commanders by radio and reported that they were being held near the town of Masiaka, about 40 miles east of the capital, Freetown.

Back in London, their capture was branded a 'national humili-ation' and a rescue operation under the codename Operation Barras was launched immediately, but no one imagined it was going to be easy. Previous encounters by Western forces against supposedly shambolic African troops in modern times provided evidence of the need for caution. Not least among those recent experiences was the disastrous American intervention in 1993, which became the subject of the film *Black Hawk Down*. In that year, the UN Security Council unanimously adopted a resolution to send in a peacekeeping force to disarm Somali warlords and to ensure that relief supplies reached the starving millions in the strife-ridden country. Although 15 Somali factions agreed to disarm and start rebuilding the country, on 5 June the forces of General Muhammad Farah Aydid, head of the Somali National Alliance, ambushed and killed 24 Pakistani UN peacekeepers.

The next day the Security Council called on states to restore a national government and arrest Aydid. When nothing was done, American troops went in on 15 June 1993, their gunships and attack helicopters pounding the National Alliance headquarters and armouries, destroying much weaponry and a radio station. In August 400 US Army Rangers were sent in to capture Aydid, but in the incredible scenes that followed they were beaten back. In further battles, 18 American soldiers were killed, and many more injured on 3 October, and, amid outrage at home, the idea of capturing Aydid was abandoned. The Rangers withdrew from Somalia on 19 October, and the following month Aydid warned that if American troops ever returned to the streets of Mogadishu he would attack again. Friction developed between the United Nations and the US over the former's acceptance of terms by Aydid, and President Clinton subsequently ordered the withdrawal of all American forces from Somalia.

In Sierra Leone in September 2000, the British military decided against UN involvement, despite the presence of peacekeepers in the country. After much discussion and a presentation of their plan to Prime Minister Tony Blair, a rescue force was immediately assembled, consisting of 150 men led by the British Special Forces. It was a risky business, and the American disaster in Somalia – backed up by the British experience in that country and other warring African states – was studied and discussed. Finally, the rescuers were given the green light. There would be one team from each of the SBS and the SAS and A Company Group of 1 Para Battle Group. They were flown to the British military's long-established training camp in Kenya, where they worked out the finer details and put the men through a mock exercise, realistically staged to rehearse the rescue before travelling to Sierra Leone to begin their attempt.

By then, five of the captured troops had been freed unharmed, but the remaining six had been spirited away to a jungle hideout fifty miles from Freetown, and the militia's commander warned that they would be shot instantly if any attempt was made to rescue them. The West Side Boys were by then holed up in two villages, also fifty miles from the capital. Special Forces teams went in ahead of the main body, moved in close to the militia camp, on foot, and buried themselves in hides from which they kept watch for several days until the day of the raid. The captives, still in limited radio contact, were alerted by coded messages that the rescue mission was on its way. In what became listed as the battle of Rokel Creek, the troops formed a pincer movement for the attack, which was launched just before dawn on 11 September 2000.

At the appointed time, the SBS team of frogmen crossed the creek, under water, and made their way towards the buildings where Marshall and his men were held and, with split-second timing, were ready to move in when, from the north, soldiers of D Squadron of 22 SAS attacked, guns blazing, while simultaneously the Paras abseiling in from their Chinook helicopters hit the village of Magabeni on the creek's opposite bank. The hostages were freed and a Lynx helicopter of the Special Forces Squadron

International terrorism of the 1970s brought new tasks for the SBS, especially around the coastline of the United Kingdom, dotted with oil and gas rigs. SBS was earmarked for maritime counter-terrorist measures, rehearsed here on an actual oil rig.

Ship protection became another area of SBS training, here boarding and taking the initiative in a counter-terrorist exercise.

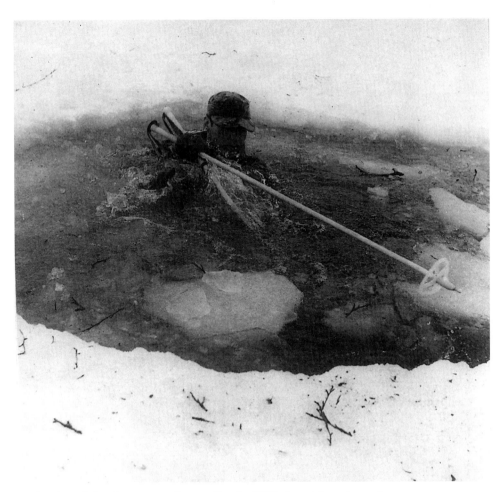

Arctic training is an annual event for the SBS. Apart from hazardous mountaineering and rock-climbing expeditions, immersion in sub-zero temperatures is one of the obligatory trials. Many a canoe has also been punctured by razor-sharp ice flows.

Arctic training stood the SBS in good stead when they were sent to the Falklands ahead of the British Task Force to gather pre-invasion intelligence. Their first port of call was this formidable glacier on South Georgia, providing a dramatic backdrop to the tiny SBS craft heading towards the shore.

In hugely unpredictable seas, the SBS inflatables were at times hopelessly out-manoeuvred by the forces of nature.

Ahead of the task force: SBS teams were first ashore in the Falkland Islands, often landing in exceedingly rough conditions under the cover of darkness and hiding up in observation posts close to Argentine positions for up to a week at a time.

The reclaiming of the British embassy during the Gulf War made headline news. The SBS team which carried out the mission were as anonymous as ever, described universally at 'British commandos'. *(Courtesy of News International)*

The raid on the ship *Fox Trot Five* at Greenwich after its alleged drug-running voyage across the Atlantic bearing a multi-million haul of Colombian cocaine. With one SBS black-garbed team on board, another can be seen in the background about to board the ship. (*Courtesy of Dr Joyce Lowman*)

An SBS team was first into riot-torn East Timor to secure the airport ahead of the arrival of a United Nations Peacekeeping force in September 1999

Versatility is the keynote of SBS operations, as here where the only silent approach in an attack may involve swimming through murky water, as they did to join an operation to rescue six British soldiers being held hostage by rebels in Sierra Leone in September 2000 (*Defence Picture Library*)

In the vanguard again, the SBS operated in the early stages of the war in Afghanistan, and a 100-man team flew in to take possession of Bagram air base north of Kabul – which was surrounded by Taliban forces – to provide security for incoming officials and troops in November 2001 (*Defence Picture Library*)

landed under fire and touched down long enough for an SAS snatch squad to get the hostages on board. The first phase of the mission had been completed successfully.

The West Side Boys' commander Kallay was woken by the sounds of gunfire and explosions as Operation Barras rocked his headquarters compound, but he and his motley gang reacted with remarkable swiftness and quickly mustered a surprisingly stiff response to the attack by some of Britain's finest. As more Paras poured into the two villages to allow the hostages to be plucked to safety, an incredible fire fight opened up.

One who was in it said:

The first part of the operation went off fine, and the rescue was achieved to perfection. But then this fire fight started. It was incredible, and very nearly a total fuck-up. There were swarms of them. Who the fuck were they? Where did they come from? Everybody thought they'd all leg it just as soon as we opened up. But they didn't, they just blazed back at us like crazy, darting and jumping about all over the fucking shop. We knocked quite a few down and then we ourselves started taking hits. You've got to ask why we took so many hits.

The gun battle lasted 40 minutes and, as with so many previous encounters by Western troops, another ragtag African army provided another lesson in their ability to threaten some of the world's most highly trained professional soldiers. 'We knew they wouldn't be a pushover,' said my informant. 'But you never can bring yourself to believe that they would be so much trouble. I mean, how can you take them seriously – kids, women and doped-up men in scruffy clothes and trainers and wearing charms to ensure they don't get hit? But these youngsters have been fighting and killing since they were strong enough to pick up a gun. It's nothing to them. They have no fear because they don't know the meaning of the word. They just keep on coming in, blasting away, laughing and shouting like it's a big game.'

One British soldier, an SAS trooper, was killed on the raid and 14 were wounded. The West Side Boys suffered 25 fatalities, with 20 or more wounded and 15 captured, including their leader. Later, the British military commander General Sir Charles Guthrie admitted that the West Side Boys were no pushover.

They fought hard and 'believe me, we were not playing some stupid arcade game'. Indeed they weren't. The SAS man surprisingly did not receive a posthumous honour of any note. He was only to be Mentioned in Dispatches. Two other members of the Special Forces team were awarded the Conspicuous Gallantry Cross, which is second only to the Victoria Cross. In addition, four Military Crosses were awarded to members of the rescue team, three to members of the Special Forces and one to a Parachute Regiment officer. Five helicopter crewmen received the Distinguished Flying Cross.

Within the month there was further action for the SBS of a rather different nature, this time back in Kosovo, where a substantial NATO force was still heavily deployed to quell civil strife between the various ethnic groups in the troubled province and later as further unrest in Macedonia threatened to result in civil war. The situation was volatile and lawless, brought about by a combination of warring political militias, Mafia-style crime gangs who were already heavily into the people-smuggling business, and Eastern European drug barons. This in turn had longer-term implications for the nations of Western Europe, and the United Kingdom in particular. These countries were the eventual target of the illegal immigrants and alleged asylum seekers being moved across country in large numbers by the gangs. A spiral of violence and crime had engulfed Kosovo since the withdrawal of Milošević's Gestapo-style police. The political factions were those who sought to continue the struggle for independence, which was not part of NATO's commitment, and over a period of several months the peacekeeping forces had performed a programme of disarming them, notably the now-disbanded Kosovo Liberation Army. More than 60 tons of weapons had been located and confiscated.

Those less committed to a more democratic process had, in the meantime, switched their interests to a more profitable form of activity, and, utilising many of the men who had been fighters in the KLA, turned to crime in a big way. Subsequently, the British discovered that they had one of the new crime bosses in their sector, an ex-KLA commander. He was arrested after lengthy surveillance by an SBS team, a key move in the attempts to enforce a significant handover of illegal weapons that had flooded into Kosovo during the crisis and which were now being used largely for criminal activity. The raid on the crime boss and his empire came after the SBS joined a force of 300 Royal Marines to track and isolate him and his henchmen. They sealed off a large section of Priština in advance of a raid on 13 bars, brothels and private homes linked to the commander's criminal clan.

The raid resulted in 28 arrests and the seizure of a large cache of weapons and £300,000 in cash, believed to be profits from drugs, prostitution and people-smuggling. The British peacekeeping forces conducted another big weapons seizure operation in the Drenica Valley, resulting directly from the SBS teams drawing on their knowledge of former KLA positions gained during their surveillance of the region and indeed liaison with the KLA themselves during the NATO bombing campaign. In this way, many caches of weapons were uncovered in the old KLA heartland of Drenica which might otherwise have been used for criminal purposes.

Once the sites were identified by the SBS, the units from 45 Commando, based at a former Yugoslav army barracks on the outskirts of Priština, raided them by helicopter. A similar hunt for weaponry was linked to the arms caches held by the Kosovo Protection Corps (KPC), a civil defence organisation that replaced the disbanded KLA. The KPC had already signified that it had ambitions to become the future army of an independent Kosovo, and its commander, Agim Ceku, boasted to the international peacekeepers that they will not be able to trace its arms dumps. The former guerrillas have maintained an underground network led by Albanian extremists whose fight for independence or international recognition was active as these words are being written. As one of the soldiers who had been there and seen it all told the author: 'This is not the end of the Kosovo story by any means. The SBS will have to go back in. You can bank on it.'

In the meantime, the implications beyond those of internal Serbian, Kosovan and Albanian politics had great implications for the rest of Europe as the movement of refugees and asylum seekers from the region showed no signs of abating. As the SBS discovered, the refugee movement was heavily promoted by the crime gangs who used it as a cover for getting people and contraband across national boundaries. The system was weighted strongly in the criminals' favour, to the extent that information from the SBS formed part of the very substantial dossier built – and constantly being updated – by both the two main British security services, MI5 and MI6, who in turn are pooling their information with their counterparts in France, Germany and Italy. In these circumstances, the prospect of further action on the part of the SBS because of their specialist knowledge of the region never seemed far away.

CHAPTER TWENTY-TWO

Afghanistan

On 7 October 2001 American ships and bombers and British submarines began their bombardment of Afghanistan after the ruling Taliban refused to hand over Osama Bin Laden in the wake of the 11 September attacks on the World Trade Center in New York. The main cities of Kabul, Kandahar and Mazar-e Sharif all felt America's wrath, and in an address to the US nation President George W. Bush said strikes by US and British forces were also taking place against training camps and military installations of the al-Qaeda network in Afghanistan and that they had been carefully targeted. The importance of that addendum to the announcement was to make clear the fact that from the outset the British and American military planners were attempting to limit civilian casualties, although it was always going to be difficult to achieve and in the event thousands of innocent people would die.

Although it was never publicly revealed, British and American Special Forces, along with CIA and Military Intelligence units, were preparing to go into Afghanistan before the bombing began. In fact, the CIA had been there for months, trying to stir up trouble for the Taliban, and now members of the British Special Forces were to be among the first on the ground to begin the vast and complex intelligence operation needed to support the massive bombing campaign launched by the Americans to oust the Afghan rulers and go in search of Bin Laden.

For the high-level bombers, finding the targets in the Afghan landscape was a massive problem. By the very nature of a nation ravaged by years of war with the Soviet Union and fighting among themselves, the wreckage of urban infrastructure where there were few paved roads made it virtually impossible to rely on aerial reconnaissance images alone. Pinpointing the caves where Bin Laden and Taliban leaders sought refuge was well nigh impossible. Thus, the logistical problems of mounting a response to the 11 September attacks were immense, and reliance on intelligence gleaned from on-the-ground surveillance was even greater than it was in the Gulf War. It was also vital to bolster the abilities of the anti-Taliban forces, controlled by diverse and dissident warlords whose murderous ways did not necessarily translate into effective military activity. President Bush and his Cabinet therefore made it clear that the Americans wished their forces to be seen as the leaders and architects of the Afghanistan campaign, if for no other reason than to salve the anger of the American people.

The British government, among a dozen or more nations who had offered to join any coalition, was equally enthusiastic, and Prime Minister Tony Blair seemed anxious to secure the No. 2 role to the American command. The British Parachute Regiment and the Royal Marines were placed on alert and began immediate exercises and training for their eventual involvement. Given that their long-established links with the SAS and SBS respectively for their particular skills in intelligence-gathering prior to any mobilisation of such magnitude meant that the Special Forces were engaged in similar work-ups for immediate action inside arenas of potential operations. Similarly, the Royal Air Force Special Forces unit, which provides most of the air transport for special operations, was, as ever, running in tandem with whatever plans were being made.

Details of the numbers and logistics of British deployments were scant, however, as indeed they were for all the nations involved. From the outset, whereas the bombing of Afghanistan was followed hourly on television, the undercurrent of secret activity on the ground was kept well away from the media. Intelligence agents and special military units from a number of the participating nations began jostling for position, and they included military rivals such as India and Pakistan. The whole scenario, over time, became engulfed in an aura of tense stand-off between military commanders and media people who faced the task of disentangling the deployment of the modern weapon of spin in order to attempt a proper assessment of British and Allied operations.

From that standpoint, the war on the Taliban developed into one of the most secretive operations in modern military history.

Even after the event, when these words were being prepared in December 2002, much of the detail remains classified. Given the devastating potential of the al-Qaeda terrorist network, such precautions were necessary, particularly in the guarding of the detail of Special Forces operations, as was proved again and again in due course by further acts of terrorism elsewhere in the world. The cautious approach was evident even before the major deployment began, largely because of the fact that British and American Special Forces were already inside Afghanistan and their safety was at risk if specific details of their deployment leaked out.

Initially, the only clues as to the likely commencement of hostilities could be drawn from what was happening among American forces, where units from US Navy Seals (sea, air and land) and US Army Delta Force commandos, equivalent to Britain's SBS and SAS, were activated. Some were sent to join the American 5th Fleet, based in Manama, Bahrain, which was dispatched to a position in the Arabian Sea in range of landlocked Afghanistan two weeks before the assault on Afghanistan began. Among them were the aircraft-carriers USS *Carl Vinson* and USS *Enterprise*, which had crews totalling almost 12,000 between them. The two could provide 170 aircraft and up to 600 cruise missiles to attack sites in Afghanistan or elsewhere. There were also 100 F-15 and F-16 jets and a dozen or so British Tornadoes in countries surrounding Iraq, previously engaged in imposing the no-fly zones in the north and south of that country. Thus, the British were able to provide RAF refuelling tankers with their protecting fighters, which were utilised to keep British and American aircraft flying around the clock.

The pounding of Taliban positions and installations had been running for more than a month before it became known that Special Forces were already on the ground. The SAS and the SBS were giving tactical and communications assistance to commanders of the Northern Alliance of Afghan warlords, whose men were fierce but ill-prepared and modestly equipped. Then, in the second week of November, the SBS was publicly revealed as forming the vanguard of British troops for deployment in Afghanistan. Speculation as to what exactly the SBS would be doing was rife in the media, and some of the reports demonstrated how little was actually known about their operations. One commentator in a British national newspaper, for example, wrote that the deployment of the SBS to the landlocked country was 'unexpected', given that there would be little scope for its famous canoe-borne operations, seemingly unaware of the SBS's own boast that it could do anything the SAS could do – and do it on, in and under water.

On 15 November 100 SBS personnel landed in an RAF Hercules transport plane at Bagram air base north of Kabul. It was a forlorn, desolate and dangerous place, a graveyard of ancient Russian MiGs, overgrown with weeds, littered with unexploded ordnance and with its buildings in a shoddy, bombed-out state. The base was within territory recently acquired by victorious anti-Taliban forces, but at that point it could not be used because the Taliban still controlled the surrounding hills. Indeed, many decaying bodies of Taliban soldiers were still around the western perimeter from recent battles with the Northern Alliance. There were also 11 Taliban tanks hidden from American planes in the deep gorges of the mountains close by, which the Alliance commandeered.

The arrival of the SBS coincided with a statement issued by the Taliban leadership, declaring that they would not give up their fight. Even as they landed, the SBS came within an ace of being fired on themselves – by supposedly 'friendly' forces of the Northern Alliance. It was later revealed that as the Afghan conflict entered the tense phase of deciding who would govern the country when the Taliban fell, leaders of the Alliance were furious about the formal arrival of the first party of foreign troops since the departure of the Russians a decade earlier. Their leaders said they had not been given the opportunity to 'coordinate' the arrival of the SBS advance party. In truth, they feared a return to the bad old days, and that the SBS would start to dictate terms just as the Russians had. The Afghan warlords remembered only too well that in 1979 the Soviets poured in men and equipment to install a puppet government to take over the country, which led to ten years of bitter conflict. Furthermore, historically when British troops have entered Afghan territory it was for making war, not ending it, although the Afghans and their tribesmen of the southern mountains invariably won, as in what became known as the First Afghan War, Britain's biggest military disaster of the nineteenth century.

The speed of the deployment of the SBS had taken everyone by surprise, and the decision, according to the *Guardian*, had come from 10 Downing Street. Dr Abdullah Abdullah, the Alliance's chief spokesman and later to become Afghan Foreign Minister, was 'very angry' about not being told of the deployment. It was left to Foreign Secretary Jack Straw to intervene personally with an urgent call to officials in Afghanistan to rescue the situation. This unfortunate turn of events led to media speculation that the decision to send in the SBS was made 'on the hoof' by Tony Blair after appeals for humanitarian aid. In fact, the appeals came from the Bush administration, requesting British troops to make the air base secure as soon as possible – as a matter or urgency, in fact – to get an access point for the intelligence community and other specialists.

That Bagram needed to be reopened to allow the commencement of flights bringing food and medical aid was true enough, but this was also the cover story for sending in the SBS. The contingent of 100 personnel flew in – albeit into the teeth of an unknown threat – and began to set their stall out, erecting radar dishes, signals equipment and air-traffic control gear, and then went to work securing the perimeters of the base, clearing unexploded ordnance and marking the minefields. They also began a detailed reconnaissance of the whole area and provided the Americans with intelligence of Taliban positions to enable the bombers to attack. They also sent detailed reports back to London to indicate the potential for resistance from Taliban forces in the area, and it was specifically as a result of these reports that any major troop deployment in Bagram was delayed for several days because of the dangers of attack. The ongoing reconnaissance by the SBS, however, subsequently paved the way for incoming flights, and they then recruited the help of Afghanistan's state security ministry – known as the local KGB – to provide security and guard against prying eyes as they set about creating communications systems with the help of an RAF Special Forces unit in conjunction with the RAF Tactical Communications Wing, all of which needed to be in place before any major movement of personnel into Bagram.

The TC Wing is a vital element in RAF overseas operations and particularly in any large-scale deployment of Special Forces, who rarely have the luxury of established landing facilities. The unit has a worldwide commitment, which may be in support of British or NATO operations. Its detachments are trained to set up, install, operate and maintain landing facilities anywhere in the world and in any kind of situation. At the time of the Afghanistan

297

emergency, the TC Wing was already operating 12 other sites overseas either for national or NATO interests. Their package comes complete with satellite communications and support facilities for air-to-air refuelling and sophisticated surveillance and photographic reconnaissance aircraft. Within a very short space of time, the atmosphere at the air base was changed totally, and the 'strictest orders' to let no one in without authority was enforced first by the SBS and later by other Allied soldiers when they took over the security role.

Within days, Western men in both casual and formal clothes began arriving on five transport flights, as did a supply of Jeeps with darkened windows. They were the American intelligence specialists who were joined by contingents of US Special Forces and military surveillance teams whose own cover story was that they were there to ensure the humanitarian aid reached its target and to enable United Nations non-governmental officers to begin the process of setting up an interim government.

Meanwhile, British Special Forces were alongside their American counterparts in northern Afghanistan, where the rout of the Taliban had moved more swiftly, so that they were now engaged in mopping up the remaining nests of opposition and concentrating more specifically on hunting down and arresting fleeing members of the al-Qaeda network. This quest took precedence over dealing with the Taliban forces, who were generally released after being disarmed and questioned. The intelligence people working with the Special Forces were much more interested in discovering and arresting those linked to Osama Bin Laden, and especially foreign nationals. The capture of an airfield close to Mazar-e Sharif, in the far north of Afghanistan, allowed the Allied troops to reach conclaves of Taliban still holding out, and in due course to take custody of the al-Qaeda suspects who were already heading towards the border in an attempt to escape.

It was this development that brought the SBS to this far-flung place and led ultimately to action in which the NCO commanding an SBS contingent of six was to be awarded America's highest honour, the Congressional medal of Honor, the equivalent to the British Victoria Cross. The recipient's name remains secret. His identity, rank and unit are officially classified information, the citation never publicly revealed and as far as the Ministry of Defence is concerned he doesn't exist. The story behind the honour, however, is this . . .

Mazar-e Sharif is 35 miles south of the border with Uzbekistan, where many of the fleeing troops, including a large number of Muslim supporters from Chechnya, were heading. The town's name, meaning 'tomb of the saint', is derived from the discovery there of the tomb of the son-in-law of the Prophet Muhammad, according to Afghan legend, in the twelfth century. A blue-tiled mosque and a shrine mark the location of the tomb, which is venerated by all Muslims, especially the Shiites. Mazar-e Sharif came under Afghan rule in 1852 and became the political hub of Afghan Turkestan in 1869. After their incursion in 1979, Soviet troops established a military command in the town and in 1980 began construction of a new road and railway bridge across the Amu Darya of Mazar-e Sharif, which was linked by air and a decent road to Kabul, 200 miles south-east. A well-known Islamic theology school was also located there.

The capture of the airfield allowed Special Forces to land in their helicopters and US Air Force F-15 Strike Eagle and F-16 Falcon aircraft to maintain a permanent presence in the air above Afghanistan, instead of relying on carrier-based aircraft which can operate only if they are refuelled in the air, flying in from the Arabian Sea. The airfield also provided a gateway to bring aid into northern and central Afghanistan. But the underlying prospect for the intelligence community on the ground was the rounding up of al-Qaeda people who were among the Taliban forces in flight, and for them at least that task and the hunt for Bin Laden stood above all else.

In the third week of November 2001, the CIA's special activities section was ready to screen more than 400 prisoners, mostly Pakistanis, Chechens, Arabs and many from Central Asian countries, brought in by local troops and British and American Special Forces. The majority had surrendered to the ruthless Uzbek warlord Rashid Dostum who, according to local legend, once tortured one of his own men to death by tying him to the tracks of a tank and having it driven around the courtyard of his headquarters. Dostum's prisoners surrendered at Kunduz, 85 miles from Mazar-e Sharif, and they were then loaded into lorries to be driven away. Most were searched and disarmed, or at least should have been.

They were taken to the airfield near Mazar-e Sharif, but there was no room for that number of men to be held for interrogation. Dostum then took them on to an old fort at

Qala-i-Jangi where he kept his horses and stores, including his weapons. The nineteenth-century fort was a huge mud-walled construction with underground caverns. It had been in the possession of the Taliban until two weeks earlier, before the Uzbek warlord took control. Dostum dumped his prisoners at the fort and went back into the fray, leaving about 80 men to guard them. What happened next was filmed by a Northern Alliance intelligence officer. (The video of events in the fort, lasting two and a half hours, was later acquired by the Americans.) The prisoners had been herded into a basement area, until the guards brought a large number into the court-yard for questioning. One official warned that so many fighters in the open might be difficult to handle. The mood was already menacing as up to 300 wild-haired prisoners were told to sit in rows, their arms tied at the elbows behind them, some with the long black silk of their Taliban-style turbans. Uzbek soldiers and police officials began searching and questioning the prison-ers. Then two men from the CIA working with them, one a tall man known only as Dave, dressed in Uzbek clothes, and the other Johnny 'Mike' Spann, appear on the film, strolling around looking at the prisoners, stopping to photograph and question them with an apparent lack of concern for security.

Spann, dressed in jeans and a black fleece jacket, an M-16 assault rifle hanging down his back, is seen astride one prisoner, then leads another prisoner away by his bound arms for interro-gation. Most of the prisoners answered the questions put to them, although many may have given false names. Another prisoner, an Iraqi, claimed to be working for American intelligence and asserted that there were up to 120 Arabs among the prisoners who were all al-Qaeda. Then he pointed to another man: he was al-Qaeda, too, and he was an American. Spann and 'Dave' came over to where the man was sitting, mop-haired, unshaven and in filthy clothes. Indeed, he was an American. They were looking at a 20-year-old Californian named John Walker Lindh, who had converted to Islam and became a Taliban fighter and who, it was discovered later, had firm links to al-Qaeda.

Spann began to question him, there and then, in front of the other prisoners and called on the video cameraman to film the interview. A short piece was recorded, and the cameraman had put on film the last minutes in the life of the interrogator Mike Spann, a married man aged 32, who was soon to become the first

American killed in the Afghan conflict, on that afternoon of 25 November 2001.

Spann wanted to know: 'What's your name?' Lindh ignored him.

'Hey,' Spann said, snapping his fingers in Lindh's face. 'Hello . . . wake up. Who brought you here? Hello.' At that Dave came close and Spann told him: 'I explained to him [Lindh] what the deal is. He needs to decide if he wants to live or die. If he wants to die, he's just going to die here.' The young American prisoner was unmoved by the threat and remained silent. What happened next is one of the most controversial episodes in the Afghanistan campaign.

There were shouts off-camera, coming from the entrance to the basement area where another 60 prisoners were being held. The videotape cuts off suddenly. This was the moment, witnesses say, when two prisoners rushed from the basement with grenades in both hands and hurled them at the nearest guards. They grabbed weapons from the guards and opened fire on the soldiers and then shot Mike Spann as well. More of the Taliban now came out of the basement and pursued the soldiers and the police, who were beating a retreat from the inner courtyard. Within minutes, scores of people were dead, and the Northern Alliance men were in danger of losing control. Between 30 and 40 prisoners sitting on the parade ground were killed where they sat, with their arms still tied, but most now escaped when the fighting broke out, freed their hands and took up arms. A full-scale riot was under way, and before long the Taliban prisoners had ransacked the weapons store and were engaged in ferocious running fire fights with their Northern Alliance guards.

Dave, the second CIA man, was trapped but managed to get to an entrance just as rescuers came in to find him: five men, wearing curious hats and with their faces shrouded by Afghan scarves, burst in and dragged him clear. They were members of a patrol from the SBS who had arrived in Land Rovers. By then, the prisoners had armed themselves with rocket launchers and rifles and moved to barricade themselves in for a tough battle with the Northern Alliance soldiers, now aided by the SBS.

A violent fire fight raged for hours, but the SBS men were able to radio for help and provide precise coordinates for aerial support flown in from the nearby airfield. Using this detail, American aircraft controversially bombed the areas where the

301

prisoners were holed up, killing many of them instantly. Even so, the battle raged on at a ferocious pace and, according to the *New York Times*, 'It took six days and the overwhelming force of American air strikes to put down the uprising.' At the end of it the huge fort was strewn with the bodies of prisoners and Northern Alliance soldiers, the latter losing 46 men killed and about 200 injured. Initially it was assumed that all the Taliban and al-Qaeda forces had been killed, especially after the Northern Alliance men had blasted tank shells into the underground areas where dozens had taken refuge. It seemed that none could have survived such an onslaught. Yet 48 hours after the battle had ended, 85 prisoners emerged from the underground tunnels, blackened and charred.

Among them was the American, John Walker Lindh, Mike Spann had been questioning just before the uprising began. He was taken into custody by the Americans, along with others, and flown out – some direct to America and others to the US base on the island of Cuba, infamously shackled and blindfolded.

Meanwhile, in the aftermath of the drama, word of the SBS involvement and their action in saving the life of Dave and their contribution to bring the situation under control reached Washington in a report on the incident to the CIA and the US Defense Department. However, no details were publicly released and the details of the SBS involvement were not at the time revealed in the UK, nor indeed were reports of Spann's death published in the American media. The significance of the SBS contribution, however, was evident from its eventual recognition when the NCO in charge of the SBS patrol was awarded the Congressional Medal of Honor, America's equivalent to the VC, the first time it has been awarded to a living foreigner. Four of his colleagues received a Presidential Citation.

The Congressional Medal of Honor, the highest award for valour in action, is generally presented by the President himself. Its history – like the British VC – forms a fascinating record of exemplary bravery. The first Medal of Honor was awarded in 1863 during the Civil War and since then just over 3,450 medals have been awarded. There are only 150 living recipients, of whom 67 served in Vietnam, and in modern times the award is something of a rarity. Two medals were issued posthumously to two US army sergeants for their actions in Somalia in 1993, but no awards were made resulting from operations during the Gulf War.

Details of the British recipient were not posted on the MoD website, and it is likely that he will remain anonymous during his lifetime. Mike Spann, who worked in a little-known paramilitary unit of the CIA's clandestine 'special activities' group, was the first of nine Americans to be killed in Afghanistan. He was buried with full military honours at Arlington National Cemetery at which George Tenet, director of the CIA, described Spann as a 'patriot who knew that information saves lives, and that its collection is a risk worth taking'. He was the seventy-ninth employee of the CIA killed in the line of duty.

One further development resulting from SBS actions was that John Walker Lindh was returned to his homeland. After an investigation by the FBI, he was charged with ten counts of conspiracy to murder Americans and providing services to the Taliban and al-Qaeda. When he was brought to trial in August 2002, prosecutors filed papers indicating the depth of his knowledge about al-Qaeda and revealing details that bore distinctly worrying possibilities for the future – and, indeed, the potential for further SBS action in the years ahead.

The FBI said that Lindh 'knew that future terrorist acts were planned, that these were likely to be even worse than the events of 11 September and that these were targeted against his fellow Americans'. They stated that Lindh knew of forthcoming terrorist acts as early as June 2001 and specifically that 20 suicide attacks involving 50 operatives were being planned by his al-Qaeda associates. No details of what was planned were given by the FBI, nor did they reveal if they had any clue what they were, but of course, in addition to 11 September, at the time of writing there have been other atrocities linked to suicide missions, including the bomb attacks on a nightclub in Bali and the Hotel Paradise in Mombasa.

The FBI conceded that it did not have evidence that Lindh was directly involved with the death of Mike Spann but that Lindh bore some responsibility for it: 'The fact that we do not have evidence that Lindh wielded the weapon that fired the bullet that killed Spann has been taken by the defence as an admission that Lindh was an innocent bystander,' the prosecution said. 'He was neither a bystander nor in any respect can he be described as innocent.'

The judge agreed, and Lindh was subsequently sentenced to 20 years in prison after sobbing through a 14-minute statement in which he repudiated terrorism, condemned Osama Bin Laden and tried to explain why he joined the Afghan movement. He stopped short of apologising for anything other than causing his family so much pain.

All elements of British Special Forces were, thereafter, engaged in various operations and actions as the main part of the campaign in Afghanistan moved towards its conclusion, at least in terms of defeating the Taliban. Over the course of the many weeks of bombing, the Americans switched from dropping so-called smart bombs used to attack Taliban installations and cluster bombs to hit their troops, often with little accuracy, and instead turned to 5,000-pound (2,265-kilogramme) 'bunker-busting' bombs to hit the networks of caves and bunkers, again generally called down by US or British Special Forces who had provided the coordinates from close surveillance. They radioed back to US air controllers at the US Special Operations Command in Tampa, Florida, who in turn sent in the US bombers with their bunker-busters.

Much of the bunker-bombing was in preparation for the arrival of ground forces before the coalition of nations began to fall apart in the face of increasing criticism of the bombing and the deaths of so many civilians. In March 2002 a second group of 60 SBS personnel flew into Bagram, paving the way for a steady build-up to 1,700 British troops. Within a month they launched Operation Snipe to clear out al-Qaeda forces along the Afghan–Pakistani border. The US Green Berets who had been training in Uzbekistan for two weeks also moved into the region through Bagram while the Northern Alliance, assisted by members of the 10th Mountain Division, took control of the high ground around the airfield to secure the airfield as a base for tactical air strikes by USAF F-15 Strike Eagles and RAF Tornado GR4 ground-attack aircraft.

The Pentagon also confirmed that elements of the SBS and SAS were in the vanguard of a bloody fight to flush out hundreds of Taliban and al-Qaeda fighters making a last stand in eastern Afghanistan. They were part of a 3,000-strong coalition force engaged in the largest land battle of the war in clearing well-defended caves at Sha-e-Kot, near the town of Gardez. Fierce fighting ensued, and the coalition troops took some of their highest casualties of the war, with many wounded being ferried away by helicopters. Some evacuated from the area told of a gruesome fight against a well-covered enemy, and of facing

Taliban fire for up to 18 hours at a time in atrocious conditions. They became dizzy from the thin air and loss of blood as they dodged from one hiding place to another to avoid mortar fire before darkness fell and they could be rescued: 'It wasn't a Mogadishu. It wasn't as though we were pinned down. We just kept the enemy fixed all day. Any time we could see a target we'd eliminate that al-Qaeda element.' The enemy had scattered, and that proved to be more of a problem than facing an organised troop movement. 'They appear to have no discernible command structure, with small groups of up to 20 fighters dispersed in bunkers or natural features suitable for defending their ground,' said one official. 'It is never clear whether they were protecting their leaders or had simply been hiding out in the hope that American troops would abandon the fight in Afghanistan and move on to other targets.'

Before, during and after the major battles, there were numerous individual fire fights involving Special Forces from Britain, Australia and America, especially among those teams operating as snatch squads. They spent many weeks searching the mountains and cave networks for Bin Laden's supposed hideout and chasing rumours that brought them to many false leads. The RAF's No. 27 flying Chinook helicopters operated with the British Special Forces in clearing Taliban stragglers from the remote regions of the country, and with the snatch squads. The Americans had laid on Pave Hawk helicopters protected by Apache helicopter gunships, and those specifically involved in the hunt for Bin Laden and his associates included teams from the SBS, SAS, Delta Force, the US Navy's Seal Team Six and the Australian SAS. Between them, they covered thousands of miles over a period extending to almost three months. Some interesting finds were made, and a relatively small number of al-Qaeda suspects were taken into custody, but Bin Laden had vanished. His influence, as events elsewhere in the world would soon demonstrate, continued to play a significant role in international affairs and the ever-mounting threat of terrorist activity.

Even as the Afghanistan deployment began to be scaled down, other possibilities of major proportions began to emerge. American military commanders were already preparing for war with Iraq, long ago threatened by President Bush if Saddam Hussein refused to accept a new strongly worded UN resolution to allow inspectors inside his country to determine his stock of weapons of mass destruction. Tony Blair had already committed the British military to a strong supporting role if war did come, and since no such operation is undertaken without considerable exercises and practices the Special Forces were immediately engaged in the initial preparations. A number of 'routine' exercises were staged in Britain and in the Middle East, and the British base on the island of Cyprus was put on high alert – both for the preparatory effort and to guard against possible terrorist attacks, after the base was identified as a possible target by al-Qaeda suicide squads.

The Americans, meanwhile, once again began to co-opt large numbers of their Special Forces personnel into CIA covert units where their counter-terrorism skills could be utilised, thus allowing the Pentagon to maintain that no uniformed combat forces were in action while the UN resolution was in force. Both Britain and America did, however, begin stepping up training for special forces. The Americans also moved thousands of troops with heavy armour into Kuwait for training purposes, but who could if necessary be ordered into action against Iraq if Bush so decided. The Pentagon had also ordered the resumption of inoculating certain troops for anthrax while the British government announced plans to make smallpox vaccines immediately available for key military and civil personnel.

In truth, the largest deployment of British Special Forces since the Second World War was underway and the sheer numbers preparing for action in the Gulf indicated the complicated and dangerous nature of their mission. As ever, their tasks would initially include the gathering of forward intelligence on the ground, to establish the exact location of Iraqi defensive and anti-aircraft installations. This would be followed by close reconnaissance of troop movements and then efforts to locate aircraft and mobile missile launchers. Every one of these operations is fraught with risks, but is necessary for the assimilation of accurate intelligence.

It will be recalled that the Special Forces were in action long before the main body of troops in both the Falklands and 1991 Gulf wars. As previously noted, SBS teams on the Falklands spent days at a time dug into hides reporting on Argentine troop movements from positions which were on occasions just yards from enemy activity. In the last Gulf War, an SBS team clambered aboard two Boeing Vertol Chinook helicopters of No. 7 Squadron Special Forces Flight, loaded with 400 pounds of explosives. They flew to a site 32 miles west of Baghdad and there, in an operation lasting just 90 minutes, blew up Saddam Hussein's vital communications cables. At the same time, the SAS was inserting three eight-man teams deep behind enemy lines to scout for Scud launchers and report traffic movement. They included the Bravo Two Zero patrol that ran into trouble and lost three men, two shot in a fire fight and one dying from exposure as he tried to escape. Lessons were learned and once again, as the prospect of a further war with Iraq loomed, the British Special Forces began lengthy training, which included tough rehearsal exercises in the deserts of Oman. The quest for reality, enacting the dangers likely to confront them, was evident from the fact that two SAS men died during training. One of the fatalities happened during a parachute practice jump, which involved leaving the aeroplane at around 30,000 feet with oxygen and opening the chute at just 1,000 feet. The second was killed during ground combat exercises in which, as ever, live ammunition was used.

One of the major improvements since the last Gulf War has been in the area of communications. The Special Forces teams are equipped with sophisticated radio apparatus with which they can relay back without fear of interception and, although British and American surveillance aircraft and satellite imagery is now capable of reading incredible detail, there is still no substitute for on-the-ground intelligence. These teams were undoubtedly in action long before the final decisions were made whether or not an American-led invasion would get the go-ahead and their surveillance was quite divorced from the UN inspection teams seeking out weapons of mass destruction. Their sole purpose was to report on active situations that related to war, and nothing else.

Both SBS and SAS teams in training for such operations do so on the basis that teams of four or eight men will live and operate covertly in potential enemy territory for up to three weeks at a time before withdrawing. In the case of Iraq, these incursions would have been made from the south through Kuwait and in the north through Turkey. The weapons they carry depend on their mode of transport – if any – once inside the target areas; whether, for example, the teams were dropped in by parachute, landed by helicopter or possessed ground transport. But the assortment of weapons likely to be carried, depending on the circumstances, might include a high-calibre rifle with a 20mm grenade launcher, a fast-fire machine gun and a 60mm mortar. They would be in permanent touch with their base, relaying information constantly, however minute. Each team would also have helicopters of the RAF Special Forces squadrons dedicated to them to arrange for a hasty exit should it become necessary. Above all, up to the point of war being officially declared, they would be under strict orders not to engage the enemy unless their own lives were in danger, nor to leave any trace of their presence. These operations were in place as the prospect of war loomed ever closer. Once the declaration is made, however, the rules of engagement change – and the teams go back behind enemy lines, this time to indicate targets, call down air strikes, and do whatever else becomes necessary in the manner in which the British Special Forces excel.

An estimated 450 men Special Forces operatives, including SBS, SAS and Australian contingents, were on the ground in Iraq preparing the way for the invasion. Although they operated independently, and in the small teams described above, they were to form part of a larger formation up to 3,000 strong known as the Combined Joint Special Operations task force predominantly led by the American equivalent to the SAS, Delta Force, and also including operatives from branches of the US and British secret service and intelligence community. Their work prior to the invasion covered all aspects of preliminary reconnaissance tasks, predominantly reporting on troop positions and movements and armoury placements, as well as probing Iraqi defences around all major cities that the Coalition forces would have to occupy.

As the possibility of the invasion drew closer, the secret war moved into higher gear, with Special Forces teams literally roaming the Iraqi desert wilderness conducting reconnaissance and sabotage missions such locating and cutting underground communications cables as well as other vital tasks which often entailed spending days in covert observation posts. They were inserted either by helicopter, or using motorcycles, four-wheel drive vehicles, gun-mounted Land Rovers and Supercat high mobility vehicles. They spent much time confirming military and command and control installations pinpointed from aerial surveillance and were equipped with laser designators, indicating priority targets to be hit by air strikes and artillery fire.

In the deep south, around the areas of potential sea-borne activity and landings, demanding work was called for that was in the mould of classic tasks for which the SBS became renowned in

World War II and beyond – that of clandestinely surveying potential troops landing areas and assessing the hidden hazard of mined areas in the sea and on land and other potential hazards to the large scale movement of troops and machines. Indeed, British forces made a key contribution towards the eventual securing of the vital Umm Qasr port. The task was made all the more hazardous because the extent of Iraqi minelaying was simply unknown, and the waterway was littered with 74 wrecks dating back to the Iran-Iraq war. Divers operating from a Mine Countermeasures Task Group under Royal Navy command and including American and Australian elements, was drawn together to encompass all the skills available, including the equipment aboard three mine-hunting vessels, underwater vehicles, mine-clearance divers and, when the invasion was successfully achieved, even the American unit of dolphins trained to sniff out mines. Later, during the clearance of the port areas of mines, the Fleet Diving Group, who describe themselves as the 'down am dirty' side of the business, covered depths where almost fingertip searches were necessary in the mud and silt, enlivened by sewage outfalls, and up to ten to 13 feet deep. In such conditions, visibility was often zero. They discovered a large number of antipersonnel mines, which they made safe.

The Special Forces teams were also watching the Iraqi oilfields, an operation which formed a major element in the covert observations. With memories of 1991, when Saddam ordered the destruction of the Kuwait oil industry by setting fire to 730 wells that took five months to put out, detailed reconnaissance was necessary to establish detailed plans to save the oilfields from destruction if the Iraqis moved to destroy them. With more than 1,000 wellheads in the southern oilfields alone, the potential for destruction was enormous. Several contingency plans were drawn up, with SAS/SBS teams linked with paratroopers and Royal Marines Commandos standing by on a ready-to-move basis. Another key issue, and one of the most controversial of the invasion, was the search for sites that might house chemical and biological weapons stocks to prevent the Iraqis from using them against the allied advance, and although no weapons of mass destruction were located, the combined task force discovered stores of the Iraqis' own NCB (nuclear, chemical and biological) protective suits and equipment, raising the fears that such weapons existed, and might be used, thus putting further pressure on the invading forces. The teams also investigated and blew up a number of sites in the desert, such as culverts and bridges that could have been used to hide missile launchers scud missile launchers, given that 39 scuds were fired by Saddam at Israel during the 1991 Gulf war.

Much of this work was carried out in the weeks prior to the invasion of Iraq and thus became the unsung, unseen war that was kept well away from the television cameras and the 'embedded' journalists travelling with the invading troop formations, for which the British contribution consisted of around 45,000 men and women, approximately a quarter of the total Coalition service personnel in the Gulf.

The onslaught began on the night of 20 March 2003 with an opening bombardment that was to be a dress rehearsal for the 'shock and awe' bombing campaign 24 hours later. A massive aerial attack on key sites was the prelude to a dramatic storming of southern Iraq, with British Special Forces in the vanguard. They called in confirmation of targets and hits as cruise missiles fired by American ships and Royal Navy submarines in the Gulf and the Red Sea slammed into Baghdad, while RAF Tornado GR4s took off from the Ali al-Salim air base in Kuwait to join the assault with US air force F15 Strike Eagle and US navy FA 18 Hornet ground-attack aircraft. As the extent and nature of the bombardment unfolded in the next 24 hours, with the world watching every move on television, the need for precise targeting and thus assistance from Special Forces on the ground, was highly evident. The second night of the bombing of Baghdad saw the release of more than 300 cruise missiles from American ships and Royal Navy submarines as well as more than 1,000 precision guided weapons launched from layer after layer of aircraft led by the giant B-52 bombers flying from RAF Fairford in Gloucestershire.

Quite apart from the precisely targeted air raids, there was a mass of overhead activity in the southern skies with helicopters and aircraft lining up for landing and takeoff from ships and ground bases. There were scores of operations of the American tank-busting aircraft and British helicopters on support missions as well as logistical duties, ferrying men, machines, transport, supplies and vast quantities of ammunition from ship to shore and then on to forward positions. That such a high volume of traffic went ahead with comparatively light casualties or friendly fire was in no small measure aided by those on the ground in highly vulnerable positions.

The SBS were especially involved in activities ahead of the herd as British troops spearheaded the invasion in the south as hundreds of Royal Marine Commandos stormed ashore in an amphibious assault on the Al-Faw peninsula, while British and American tanks roared across the frontier from Kuwait. Artillery including the 32 AS90 155-millimetre self-propelled guns of the 3rd Regiment, Royal Horse Artillery, blasted Iraqi front-line positions while Royal Navy ships *Marlborough*, *Chatham* and *Richmond* and the Australian frigate *Anzac* provided heavy bombardment cover for the Commandos, hitting targets again coordinated by Special Forces and Royal Artillery spotters. The navy began firing when an Iraqi bunker complex was pinpointed for HMS *Marlborough*, and from six miles away on the Al-Faw peninsula her shells reached the target 25 seconds later. The first rounds were fired short to give the troops the chance to surrender, and then, after ten rounds had been fired and the white-hot shrapnel burst into the bunkers, a spotter radioed back: 'Possible white flags being raised.'

Meanwhile, US navy Seals and a company of Royal Marines and SBS moved towards their first major objective, to secure the vital Kwahr al-Amaya and Mina al-Bakr oil terminals as reinforcements were airlifted in by helicopter troop carriers containing the three companies of 40 Commando, Royal Marines, from their base in Kuwait, and other units were deploying from Royal Navy ships which had steamed in to the waters of the northern Gulf.

Chief of Defence Staff, Admiral Sir Michael Boyce, confirmed in London that afternoon that the primary aim of the operation to secure the oil infrastructure in that part of the country before the Iraqis themselves can sabotage it. The enemy believes that sabotaging oil wells, that the thick black smoke such action might produce, can degrade our ability on the battlefield. The environmental repercussions of such action, especially with regard to oil being poured into the Gulf, are enormously damaging and, at the heart of our military planning in this operation as a whole, we are trying to make sure that the economic infrastructure of Iraq is left as intact as possible to benefit the Iraqi people after the campaign. As Royal Marines launched an amphibious and air-delivered assault on the Al-Faw peninsula to secure the oil infrastructure, a United States Marine Corps battalion launched its own attacks on the port of

311

Umm Qasr, and that port will be available to us as soon as our British minesweepers are able to clear the waterway up there to allow shipping to move in safety.

While the Marines dealt with that objective, combat teams began pushing forward towards the strategically important city of Basra, and their exposed flank was covered by two battle groups of Britain's 7th Armoured Brigade, including the Desert Rats, the Black Watch and the 1st Battalion of the Royal Regiment of Fusiliers. They moved quickly towards the outskirts of Basra itself, a movement supported logistically by helicopters and carried out under air cover provided by the US air force and by the Royal Air Force, whose Tornado GR4 aircraft attacked enemy artillery in the area with precision weapons, along with other military installations as far north as Al-Kut.

By 23 March the 7th Armoured Brigade (the Desert Rats) had moved to the west of Basra while the 16th Air Assault Brigade took up position at Ar Rmaylah, where they came under fire from Iraqi artillery from the 6th Division. The Coalition forces called in counter battery fire and close air support along with further and extensive bombardment from naval guns, still covering ongoing operations on the Al-Faw peninsula.

After six days of conflict, the Coalition had made steady progress towards its objectives. The Al-Faw peninsula, Umm Qasr and the southern oilfields had been secured, and Iraqi resistance in those areas overcome, with the Commandos in control allowing the US 15th Marine Expeditionary Unit to return to the 1st Marine Expeditionary Force, which was now heading towards Baghdad. It was an important development in the progress of the war in which the SBS had played its part. Indeed, the First Sea Lord, Admiral Sir Alan West, was laudatory in his assessment of the operations in which his people were concerned:

'We kicked the door open effectively. You saw the picture of a Royal Marine jeep knocking down a door; well, we rather did that in terms of letting people into the country. We were using T-LAMs from sea, and we fired a considerable number of those, and they were all very accurate and went on the sorts of regime targets I wanted to hit. In the amphibious operations in the Al-Faw peninsula, our expertise was recognised by the Americans, and we actually took an American battalion effectively under command of my Commandos so we could do that attack, and by doing that attack slightly early we actually got to all the oil infrastructure, various parts of which were wired up to be exploded. We arrived before they could be blown up, and that was a very successful outcome. We conducted operations really across the littoral; we supported our Marines from sea both in terms of logistic supply and close air support, attacking enemy tanks and the like, and the Commando Helicopter Force was there to provide mobility, which was carried out with exceptional skill, given the amount of traffic. We enabled and delivered humanitarian aid, we carried out mine clearance in the waterways, we did a lot of explosive ordnance disposal and we really were the lead people in all that, with the Americans.'

The euphoria of the completion of the invasion of Iraq and the closing down of Saddam Hussein's regime did not, of course, signal the end of the road for the Special Forces or the Coalition troops as a whole. Indeed, as things turned out, it was only a beginning and events over the ensuing months -- still in full swing as these words are being written – would demonstrate an ongoing need for the deep involvement of Special Forces, first in the hunt for Saddam and his henchmen, and then in the battle against mounting terrorist activity within the country, as well as considerable civilian unrest and disenchantment over the continuing presence of the invading forces.

This once again entailed considerable input from Joint Special Operations Task Force 20, made up of members of Delta Force, the US navy Special Forces, the SAS and the SBS. They successfully hunted down many of Saddam's former ministers and army chiefs and were involved in locating Saddam's two sons Uday and Qusay Hussein who were subsequently killed in a ferocious shootout. Much of the intelligence for Task Force 20, came from the highly secret US Intelligence Support Activity, so secret in fact that it's existence was not officially admitted in Washington. The organisation came into being after the attempt to rescue American hostages from Iran in 1980. The 'Activity', as it is known, possesses its own signals intelligence specialists and agents prepared to infiltrate agents into the most dangerous situations, and if caught would be on their own. It was while working with this Task Force that the SBS was forced to further supplement its numbers by recruiting 'unbadged' Commandos, i.e. those who had not yet become fully initiated into SBS membership. As the month went on, and the workload increased rather than subsided, it was necessary to second Royal Marines to the Special Boat Service who were still deployed with Task Force 20 on the search for Saddam, and on numerous other undercover missions aimed at hunting the burgeoning guerrilla units responsible for the succession of devastating bombings that brought considerable death and tragedy in the aftermath of the war.

One of the Royal Marines seconded for special duties, Corporal Ian Plank was sadly killed while working with American special forces in what the Ministry of Defence described as being 'outside the British area of responsibility'. As is the practice on any action in which a member of the Special Forces is killed or seriously wounded, no details were given of the operation, other than to confirm that Cpl Plank was killed when a Coalition unit came under hostile fire on 30 October. It is believed, however, that the unit was engaged on an operation targeting Iraqi terrorists loyal to Saddam Hussein in northern Iraq. The news highlighted once again the highly sensitive and top secret operations that continue to engage the SBS, and indeed all units of the British Special Forces.

Nor will there be any let up. As 2004 flicked over on the calendar, the world of international terrorism threatened, in fact promises, further outrages and in this increasingly dangerous world, the SBS will need full advantage of those two most important elements of their motto – strength *and* guile.

EPILOGUE

So you still want to join . . . ?

The SBS has always shown a remarkable cool-headedness and has seldom opened up an assault situation unless absolutely necessary. The lightness of casualties in operations filled with disastrous potential will have been evident throughout this account, even though SBS operational activity has largely been behind enemy lines and always close to fire power. Yet even accounting for those missions that have remained from public view, losses of men have been few.

Since the Second World War, casualties in action have been outnumbered by losses incurred during exercises and training. Even during the last war, after initial sorties, which saw a hefty toll in those killed or captured, the numbers were kept significantly light. This was in part due to good fortune but largely because of the insistence of commanding officers, the founders of the SBS, RMBPD, COPPs and SRU, that every member of those units should not only be willing volunteers but should be fully and expertly trained, be adequately equipped and undergo a full and realistic rehearsal of any intended operation. Additionally, the men were to be coordinated at all times by an effective command, control and administration structure fully conversant with SBS needs and demands, however eccentric they might appear at the time. This, as has been seen, was not always appreciated by conventional force commanders.

Those wartime traditions continued in the post-war formation of the SBS and remain at the very heart of its operations today. In short, training and planning have built-in survival factors – and survival is not just about armed combat or having sufficient rations to last a delayed stay behind the lines.

315

Survival is in the planning and in the training. As both Blondie Hasler in the 1940s and current CO said, the SBS and the Special Forces groups are not about sending men on suicide missions. An inadequately trained man would face certain death, and a badly planned operation spells disaster. The guidelines drawn up long ago – in 1958, in fact – have barely changed in that regard. In the manual entitled *The Organisation and Employment of Special Boat Sections* produced by the Commandant General's Office of the Royal Marines, the ground rules were specific and clear:

It is important that SBS or sub-units should avoid being engaged by superior forces. Success depends on their skill and thorough and detailed planning and rehearsals. It is essential therefore that all intelligence is made available and that adequate time is allowed for preparation before an operation is launched . . .

In accordance with the Supreme Allied Commander's policy governing Special Operations . . . directives for Special Boat Sections will be broad so far as carrying out the operations is concerned but precise in defining its object and in imposing any limitations on the operation . . .

The success of a small-scale amphibious operation depends mainly upon a carefully prepared and feasible plan in which sufficient time must be allowed for delays and taking alternative action if a turn of events or deterioration of the weather makes this necessary. The plan must be simple yet flexible, with every possible contingency thought through at planning stage. This will ensure that alternative courses of action are decided upon at planning stage . . .

The detailed plan will contain specific information and timings that are of paramount importance to each individual man taking part and which in fact must be committed to memory . . .

Planning requirements: Up-to-date Intelligence reports, large-scale maps, all available charts, detailed interpretation report; Tide tables and Atlas of Tidal Streams, the Nautical Almanac for obtaining bearing and timings of Sun, Moon, etc. Appropriate list of Lights . . .

SB operations may be considered in progressive stages of planning, preparation and rehearsal: 1) approach in parent vessel or aircraft to operational area, 2) the final approach by raiding-craft or by swimming or combination of both, 3) carrying out the task, 4) recovery and withdrawal 5) debriefing, 6) report writing.

In execution of the above and especially where a reconnaissance raid is a prelude to a larger operation, the following measures are essential: a) Time must be allowed for at least one alternative method of recovery, b) alternative swimmer recovery-positions must be laid down, c) an alternative craft homing position must be arranged, d) a suitable lying-up position ashore should be pre-located, e) recovery on a subsequent night at an emergency rendezvous, f) if all else fails, escape overland.

The above provides a brief look at the SBS operational cycle, which in practice is vastly more detailed.

To meet those demands, the selection and training of the Special Boat Service are regularly reviewed and overhauled to meet modern trends, new technology and better, faster equipment and boats. Although one of the guiding principles that have existed since the SBS and its antecedent companions were formed in the Second World War is that all candidates must be volunteers, the last standard selection procedure was laid down in January 1994. Today, candidates wishing to join the SBS will attend a Joint Special Forces selection procedure over a tough course in the Brecon Beacons, followed by wild territory in Brunei and the ultimate test at the SAS headquarters in Hereford.

Two courses, under the supervision of a joint SBS/SAS training team, are held each year. Before the start of selection, the candidate must attend a two-week aptitude test run by the SBS training team which will determine if a man is suitable to operate in the most challenging of environments.

The aptitude test consists of the following elements:

Boating Phase (1 week). Students must:
Pass a Combat Fitness Test.
Pass the SBS Swimming Test, which demands 600 metres (656 yards) in 15 minutes, plus 50 metres (55 yards) clothed with weapon and belt, and 25 metres (27 yards) under water without diving operations.
Complete all canoe trials including carrying canoe and fully

317

loaded Bergen rucksack for 3 miles (4.8 kilometres); and complete a 20-mile (32-kilometre) canoe-paddle.

Diving Phase (1 week). Complete a number of dives and then satisfactorily demonstrate all drills taught. Show confidence and a willingness to dive.

The first week is physically and mentally demanding, the second week is more relaxed, covering basic diving theory and drills in slow time, with the aim of instilling confidence and assisting those less adaptable. But that is only a beginning, a mere holiday camp compared to what follows.

The Selection Course itself consists of the following programme:

1. Brecon Beacons phase (3 weeks)
2. Pre-Jungle Training (2 weeks)
3. Jungle Training, Brunei (6 weeks)
4. Officer week/Signals Training (1 week)
5. Support Weapons Training (1 week)
6. Army Combat Survival Instructor Course (2 weeks).

The three-week Brecon Beacons phase begins with an initial passing-in programme, including a Combat Fitness Test and a hill-walking exercise of 23 kilometres (14 miles) with a 40-pound (18-kilogramme) Bergen rucksack and weapon. The second week includes a series of navigational and physical training exercises, including a swimming test. The final week includes six hill-walking exercises, covering a total of 180 kilometres (112 miles) with a Bergen and weapon.

Continuation training

1. Demolitions (2 weeks)
2. Observation Post Training (1 week)
3. CQB Course (2 weeks)
4. Individual Skills Courses (8 weeks)
5. Parachute Course (3 weeks).

During the eight-week individual training period, men are trained to become Special Forces communicators or medical specialists, while officers undergo language training and attend a Special Forces commanders' course. On completion of the para course, SBS students spend eight weeks learning the specialist skills of boating and diving, which includes aspects of submarine work, coastal navigation and tactical swimming operations. In addition, a range of well over a hundred further skills and qualifications are available, ranging from medicine to veterinary training, and from welding to law – plus tuition for virtually every language under the sun, depending on the operational requirement.

The course, says RM literature, is:

> Within the capability of most marines, particularly those with the mental commitment and determination to succeed. Training is demanding, but that's the way it has to be. The rewards are most definitely worth the effort and include: a structured career; job satisfaction; realistic and challenging exercises; extra skills training work with other SF units at home and abroad; operational employment and extra pay . . . but you earn it.

And, of course, acceptance into SBS is only the beginning. Training never ceases . . . and as reflected in these pages, the physical and psychological endurance of every man, regardless of rank, will be tested to the limit time and time again.

APPENDIX I

Equipment list

The report of Major Hasler, commander of Operation Frankton (aka Cockleshell Heroes), detailed in Chapter Five, listed the stores drawn for the operation. This list has never been previously published in full; it is printed here exactly as it appeared in the report. It formed the basis of many similar operations in the future, and even today is not unlike the requirements of a modern SBS team setting out on a mission.

The initials at the top of each column, i.e. H S L M W E, represent the team leaders.

Boats' Gear.	H	S	L	M	W	E	Remarks.
Cockles Mk. II	1	1	1	1	1	1	
Double Paddes Mk.II prs.	3	3	3	3	3	3	
Handgrips Mk.II prs.	1	1	1	1	1	1	
Bailers	1	1	1	1	1	1	
Sponges	1	1	1	1	1	1	
Buoyancy Bags	2	2	2	2	2	2	
Cargo Bags, sets.	1	1	1	1	1	1	set of 5.
Magnetic holders	1	1	1	1	1	1	
Codline fms.	20	20	20	20	20	20	
Sounding Reels, 16 fms.	1	1	1	1	1	1	
Repair Bags	1	1	1	1	1	1	Each containing Bostick cement, patching canvas, needle, waxed thread Oil bottle, Waste, Tyre Patch, Rubber Solution, spare split pins and copper tacks.
Sectional Charts sets	1	1	1	1	1	1 ∅	
Log Pads	1	1	1	1	1	1 ∅	Containing tide tables and spare paper.
P. 8 Compasses	1	1	1	1	1	1 ∅	
Correctors for	1	1	1	1	1	1 ∅	
Monoculars	1			1	1		
Pencils	2	2	2	2	2	2	Half size, sharpened.
Dim Reading Torches	1	1	1	1	1	1	
Spare Reading Torches	1			1			
Spare bulbs for	1	1	1	1	1	1 x	
Protractors, G.S.	1	1	1	1	1	1 ∅	
Camouflage Nets	1	1	1	1	1	1	Special light type.
Watches pocket, G.S.	1	1	1	1	1	1 ∅	Waterproofed.
Spare Torch batteries	2	1	1	1	1	1	
Wire Cutters		1				1	

Boats' Gear.	H	S	L	M	W	E	Remarks.
Screwdrivers		1				1	
Marline Spikes		1				1	
W.T. Matches, Tins	2	2	2	2	2	2	
Camouflage Cream, Tins	1	1	1	1	1	1	
Escape Kits							
Pieces of Chalk	2	2	2	2	2	2	
Whiting line, 4 fm. lengths	2	2	2	2	2	2	
Weapons & Explosives.							
Silent Sten 9 m.m.			1		1		
Magazines for			4		4		Each filled 32 Rds.
69 Granades	2	2	2	2	2	2	Fuzed
Limpets, Rigid, 6 Magnet	8	8	8	8	8	8	Fuzed A.C. and sympathetic.
Ampoule Boxes	2	2	2	2	2	2	Each contains 4 Red, 4 Orange Ampules. 4 Soluble Plugs. 2 Tins luting.
Limpet Spanners	1	1	1	1	1	1	
Placing Rods	2	2	2	2	2	2	
Food & Medical.							
Compact rations, days	10	10	10	10	10	10	Each day contains 3 boxes, 1 Tin Meat and 1 tin Cheese.
Water cans, ½ gallon	5	5	5	5	5	5	Filled.
Benzedrine, Boxes	1	1	1	1	1	1	Each contain 20 tablets.
Water Sterilising sets	1	1	1	1	1	1	
1st Field Dressings	2	2	2	2	2	2	
Iodine Bottles	1	1	1	1	1	1	
Toilet Paper, packets.	2	2	2	2	2	2	
Morphia Syringes	2	2	2	2	2	2	
Hexamine Cookers	5	5	5	5	5	5	Varnished.

Food & Medical.	H	S	L	M	W	E	Remarks.
Dixie, (5 pint)	1	1	1	1	1	1	With Lids.
Foot Powder (Tins)	1	1	1	1	1	1	
W.T. Ditty Boxes	1	1	1	1	1	1	
Cough Lozenges, tins	1	1	1	1	1	1	
Laxative Pills, Tins	1	1	1	1	1	1	
Cups.							

Carried in Parent Ship

Camouflage Cream, Tins	2
Mk.II Slings and Spreaders	1 set
Slip Book	1
Girder for 4" Gun	1
Purchase Tackle	1
Wire Preventer Pendant	1
Preventatives	12
Seasick Tablets, Tubes	12
Boats' Envelopes	6
Air Pumps	1
Spare P.8 Compass	1
Box of Instructional Models	1
Mineral Jelly, lbs	2
Pads for Boats	6
Needles and Twine	
Photographs	
Orders	
Intelligence Reports	

On the Men.	H		S		L		M		W		E		Remarks.
	1	2	1	2	1	2	1	2	1	2	1	2	
Cockle Suit Complete	1	1	1	1	1	1	1	1	1	1	1	1	
W.T. Trousers, Prs.	1						1		1				
Socks, Prs.	1	1	1	1	1	1	1	1	1	1	1	1	
Denim Trousers, Prs.	1	1	1	1	1	1	1	1	1	1	1	1	With knife sheath sewn on.
Braces Prs.	1	1	1	1	1	1	1	1	1	1	1	1	
Belts, Light	1	1	1	1	1	1	1	1	1	1	1	1	
Pants, Long Thick Prs.	1	1	1	1	1	1	1	1	1	1	1	1	
Vests, Woollen, long Sleeves.	1	1	1	1	1	1	1	1	1	1	1	1	
Seaboot Stockings, Prs.	1	1	1	1	1	1	1	1	1	1	1	1	
Blue Balaclavas	1	1	1	1	1	1	1	1	1	1	1	1	
V. Neck Sweaters	1	1	1	1	1	1	1	1	1	1	1	1	
Blue Scarfs	1	1	1	1	1	1	1	1	1	1	1	1	
Handkerchiefs	1	1	1	1	1	1	1	1	1	1	1	1	
Reliant Life Jacket.	1	1	1	1	1	1	1	1	1	1	1	1	
Gloves, 3 Compartment, Silk.	1	1	1	1	1	1	1	1	1	1	1	1	
Gloves, 3 Compartment Wool.	1	1	1	1	1	1	1	1	1	1	1	1	
Red and Green Identity Discs.	2	2	2	2	2	2	2	2	2	2	2	2	
P.T. Shoes, Brown Prs.	1	1	1	1	1	1	1	1	1	1	1	1	
Twine, 12" long pieces.	6	6	6	6	6	6	6	6	6	6	6	6	
Web Belts & Holsters	1	1	1	1	1	1	1	1	1	1	1	1	
.45 Colt	1	1	1	1	1	1	1	1	1	1	1	1	
Magazines for	3	3	3	3	3	3	3	3	3	3	3	3	Includes one in gun Each loaded 7 rds.
Knives Fighting	1	1	1	1	1	1	1	1	1	1	1	1	
Bird Calls	1		3		2		1		2		2		On lanyards.
Clasp Knives	1	1	1	1	1	1	1	1	1	1	1	1	
Sheet of Paper	1	1	1	1	1	1	1	1	1	1	1	1	Lining Ditty Box.

In the Bags.	H		S		L		M		W		E		Remarks.
	1	2	1	2	1	2	1	2	1	2	1	2	
Short Pants Prs.	1	1	1	1	1	1	1	1	1	1	1	1	
Toothbrush & Paste	1	1	1	1	1	1	1	1	1	1	1	1	
Towel	1	1	1	1	1	1	1	1	1	1	1	1	
Handkerchiefs	1	1	1	1	1	1	1	1	1	1	1	1	
Sea Water Soap Pieces	1	1	1	1	1	1	1	1	1	1	1	1	
Razor and Blades	1	1	1	1	1	1	1	1	1	1	1	1	
Shaving Brush	1		1		1		1		1		1		
Felt-Soled Boots prs	1	1	1	1	1	1	1	1	1	1	1	1	
Spare laces for, prs.	1	1	1	1	1	1	1	1	1	1	1	1	
Socks, prs.	1	1	1	1	1	1	1	1	1	1	1	1	
Roll Neck Sweater	1	1	1	1	1	1	1	1	1	1	1	1	
Spare Woollen Gloves prs.	1	1	1	1	1	1	1	1	1	1	1	1	
Cigarettes	20	20	20	20	20	20	20	20	20	20	20	20	If required.
Extra Matches, Bos.	1	1	1	1	1	1	1	1	1	1	1	1	If required.

326

ESCAPE GEAR.

Binoculars	1	Additional reading torch	1
Dim reading torch	1	Matches (From W.T.T.)	1
Matches (From W.T.T.)	1	Escape Kits (complete)	1
Escape Kits (complete)	1	Spare Compact Rations	
Watch	1	First Field Dressing	1
Spare Compact Rations		Iodine Bottles	1
Benzedrine Boxes	1	Morphia Syringe	1
First Field Dressing	1	Tin, Water	1
Morphia Syringe	1	Pills Boxes	1
Foot Powder (tin)	1	Pencils	1
Tin Water	1	Camouflage Cream	1
Pills Boxes	1	String, of, peices, fms.	4
Needle and Thread	1	Toilet Paper, Pkts.	1
Oil Bottle	1		
Pencils	1		
String, of, Pieces, fms.	4		
Water Sterilising Set	1		
Toilet Paper Pkts.	1		

— — — — — — —

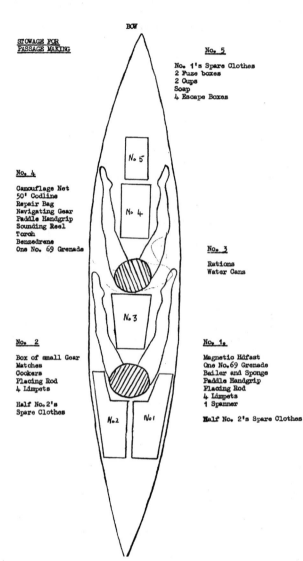

STOWAGE FOR
PASSAGE MAKING

No. 5

No. 1's Spare Clothes
2 Fuze boxes
2 Cups
Soap
4 Escape Boxes

No. 4

Camouflage Net
50' Codline
Repair Bag
Navigating Gear
Paddle Handgrip
Sounding Reel
Torch
Benzedrene
One No. 69 Grenade

No. 3

Rations
Water Cans

No. 2

Box of small Gear
Matches
Cookers
Placing Rod
4 Limpets

Half No. 2's
Spare Clothes

No. 1.

Magnetic Hdfast
One No. 69 Grenade
Bailer and Sponge
Paddle Handgrip
Placing Rod
4 Limpets
1 Spanner

Half No. 2's Spare Clothes

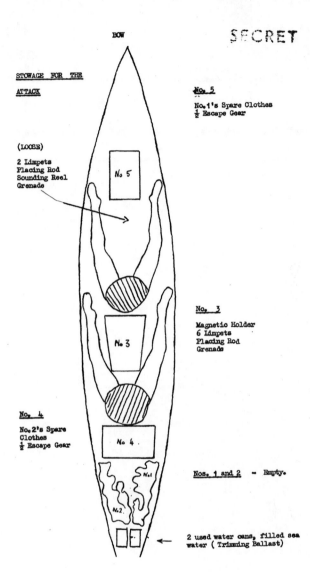

STOWAGE FOR THE
ATTACK

No. 5

No. 1's Spare Clothes
½ Escape Gear

(LOOSE)

2 Limpets
Placing Rod
Sounding Reel
Grenade

No. 3

Magnetic Holder
6 Limpets
Placing Rod
Grenade

No. 4

No. 2's Spare
Clothes
½ Escape Gear

Nos. 1 and 2   -   Empty.

2 used water cans, filled sea
water (Trimming Ballast)

APPENDIX II

Beach reconnaissance report

This is an early example of a beach reconnaissance report of the style devised by COPPs during the Second World War. It became standard procedure in the post-war activities of the SBS, and indeed employed a great deal of its manpower until the 1970s. Modern techniques and satellite imaging has lightened the task, but the basic requirements for a full and detailed reconnoitre of beach and location sites for major troop landings and deployment remains paramount.

EXAMPLE OF AMPHIBIOUS RECONNAISSANCE REPORT

Beach No. 35

PART I – COVERING PAPER

1. METHOD AND RESULTS
   (a) The required reconnaissance was carried out by No. 4 SBS working in conjunction with H. M. 'X' Craft XE 10, by periscope by day and by swimming by night in a no-moon period on 8th and 9th April, 1953. Two swimmers were used on each night.
   (b) The Pilotage Directions contained in Part III are written so as to be given as they stand (if approved) to the navigational leader, accompanied by the relevant sketches.

2. RELIABILITY OF RESULTS
   In order to show the probable reliability of the observed results the approximate route of the greatest penetration by the operators

331

is shown on the shore-line sketch. The positions of the lines of soundings are also shown.

3. Recommended Alterations to the Provisional Plan

The beach is not one which can be approached directly, and consequently it is essential that the landing craft navigational leader is brought on to the least mistakable leading line as early as possible. It is therefore recommended that a marker beacon be set up in position Cape Gremlini 027° M. 6 miles, from which position the navigational landmarks can be identified.

4. Chance of Compromise

Neither of the swimmers attracted any enemy attention and it is considered that it can be fairly presumed that the reconnaissance was carried out without leaving any trace.

5. Form of this Report

This report covers only the matters concerning Beach No. 35.

Part II contains the Beach Report and the Beach Data Form.

Part III contains the Pilotage directions and the Pilotage Approach Plan.

Appendix 'F': Surf Report.

PART II – BEACH REPORT

Beach No: 35
Classification: B
Lat.: 45° 32′ N.
Long: 6° 18′ W.

Name: BONDI BEACH
Refs:
Chart Nos.: Admty. 20002
                         40007
          Ruritan Y493
                     X755
Map No.: Series 3005
           Air Mosaic Series

Location: 3 miles North of CAPE GREMLINI on western shore of BAY.

SEA

(a) ANCHORAGE AND HOLDING GROUND

A good anchorage exists in 8 fathoms of water about 1½ miles N. of the beach. The bottom of this position is shingle and appears to provide good holding ground.

(b) NAVIGATIONAL DIFFICULTIES AND HAZARDS

Several areas of off-lying rocks, some of which are awash at low water exist to the South and East of the beach. These obstructions which are shown on the Pilotage Directions sketch, prevent a direct approach to the beach from seaward. North and inshore of these there are no obstructions.

(c) CONSPICUOUS OBJECTS AND LANDMARKS

During the approach from seaward the following landmarks are useful for the purposes of navigation. (*See* Pilotage Approach Plan.)

    (i) Capes Gremlini and Goblino.
   (ii) The Saddle: a dip in the land at the head of the bay.
  (iii) Conical Hill: conspicuous and conical shaped.
  (iv) Tower: on the rising ground between Gremlini Cape and Conical Hill.

(d) Tidal Sets

Tidal sets in Comforto Bay were found to be inconsiderable. They appear to depend on the previous night's wind. The maximum set which was encountered inside the bay was less than 1 knot.

(e) Tides

The maximum vertical effect of the tide is 13½ feet at springs. However, a wind effect is also likely which may have a varying effect on the depth of water over the bar as shown on the attached beach data form.

SHORE

(a) Extent of Beach

The extent of the beach is 600 yards.

(b) Approach and Landing Marks

On the final approach to the beach the conspicuous white tower on the rising ground behind provides a good leading mark. Even at night this can be located, since it will be clearly skylined. A bearing of 225° M. Will take a vessel clear of all obstructions. Full details of the recommended approach are given in the Pilotage Directions.

(c) Protection from Weather and Surf Conditions

Several small fishing boats were anchored close inshore off the beach, which suggests that the shelter is good from the prevailing south or S.W. winds. Little surf may be expected. A surf report is attached.

(d) Nature of the Shore below HW Mark

The beach close inshore below the HW line has a good average gradient of 1/20 up to a depth of 3½ feet where the gradient becomes less and more variable. The eastern 300 yards is not suitable for most major L/C owing to the presence of a sand-bar about 50 yards off shore. At low water the bar dries. It is considered that LST and LCT could beach on the western half one hour on either side of H.W., but the gradient sketches on the Beach Data Form should be referred to.

(e) SOUNDINGS AS OBSERVED 9TH APRIL, 1953

Yards	10	20	30	40	50	60	70	80	90	100	110	120	130	140	150	Time
Line A	3	6	5	4	4	5	6	7	7	8	8	10	12	14	14	0045
Line B	3	5	5	4	4	5	7	8	9	10	10	11	14	14	15	0130
Line C	4	6	6	5	6	8	9	11	11	11	12	13	15	15	15	0205

(f) NATURE OF THE SHORE ABOVE HW MARK

The surface of the beach from the water line consisted of sand mixed with boulders for 25x at a gradient of about 1/20. This gave way to a 50x wide stretch of shingle which was large and unlikely to jam tracked vehicles. The average total width of the beach was 75x.

SHORE LINE SKETCH

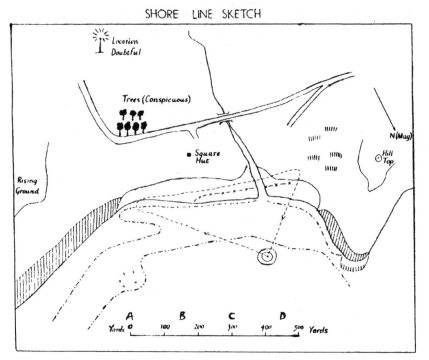

SCALE ——— OR ――― _1_ ――― INCHES TO _100 Yds_

LEGEND

⫶⫶⫶⫶	Cliffs	┄1┄	Air Beacon
⫶⫶⫶ ⫶⫶⫶	Scrub	─ · ─	1 Fathom Line
─x─x─	Wire fence	─ ·· ─	2 Fathom Line
⫶⫶⫶⫶	Rocky Shore	─────	Route of Operator
·ᐧ·ᐧ·ᐧ·	Rocks Awash	◎	Swimmer Rel & Rec Posns

	HEIGHTS	ABOVE	DATUM	
PLACE	MHW SPRINGS	MHW NEAPS	MLW SPRINGS	MLW NEAPS
Bondi Beach	14·0	10·6	2·1	0·5

MARGINAL   INFORMATION

SOURCES	_Traced From Mosaic B564 8.4.53_
DATE	_26ᵗʰ April 1953_ LAT _45°32′N._
PLACE	_Bondi Beach_ LONG _6°18′W._
MAP REFERENCE	_GSOS 1" Sheet N° 206 594327_
LOCATION	_2 Miles North Comforto Harbour._
MADE BY	_OC N° 16. SBS RM._

Shoreline sketch.

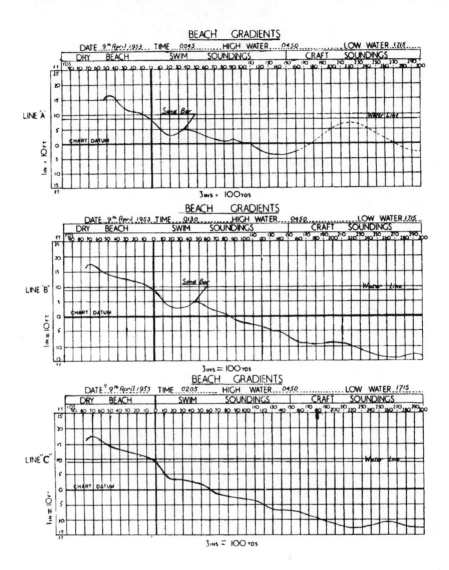

Beach gradients.

Bibliography

Billière, General Sir Peter de la, *Storm Command: A Personal Account of the Gulf War*, HarperCollins, 1992

Coogan, Tim Pat, *The Troubles*, Arrow Books, 1995

Courtney, G. B., *SBS In World War Two*, Robert Hale, 1983

Elliott, Peter, *The Cross and the Ensign: A Naval History of Malta*, PSC Books, 1980

Geraghty, Tony, *Who Dares Wins*, Little, Brown and Co, 1992 (revised edition)

Gilchrist, Donald, *The Commandos: D-Day and After*, Robert Hale, 1992

Holden-White, Vere, *Goodbye to Old Hat*, private memoirs

Holmes, Captain Len, private memoirs

Jellison Charles, *Besieged: World War II Ordeal of Malta*, UPNE, USA, 1984

Ladd, James, *SBS: The Invisible Raiders*, Arms & Armour Press, 1983

Lodwick, John, *The Filibusters*, Methuen, 1947

Macksie, Kenneth, *Commando Strike*, Leo Cooper, in association with Secker and Warburg, 1985

McNab, Andy, *Bravo Two Zero*, Bantam Press, 1993

Perkins, Roger, *Operation Paraquat*, Picton Publishing, 1985

Pringle, Major Jack, *Colditz Last Stop*, William Kimber, 1988

Ramsay, Jack, *SAS: The Soldier's Story*, Macmillan, 1996

Shortt, James, *The Special Air Service*, Osprey Publishing, 1981

Thompson, Brigadier Julian, *No Picnic*, Leo Cooper, in association with Secker and Warburg, 1985

Trenowden, Ian, *Stealthily By Night*, Crecy Books, 1995

Winton, John, *Hurrah for the Life of a Sailor*, Michael Joseph, 1977

Woodward, Admiral Sir Sandy, *One Hundred Days*, HarperCollins, 1992

Public Records Office:

Layforce WO218/89-95, plus 1, 2 and 3; SBS reports WO 218/103, 104, 112, 113, 212, 252.

RMBPD DEFE 2/988; Operation Frankton ADM 202/399, ADM 202/310, DEFE 2/216-218; Operation Rimau DEFE 2/1788, DEFE 2/650B and ADM199/1882; Sleeping Beauty DEFE 2/1144, DEFE 2/1144A and 1145; X-craft DEFE 2/1145; Welman DEFE 2/1009.

Rhine Flotilla DEFE 2/1706; Limpets DEFE 2/1719; Sea Reconnaissance Unit DEFE 2/1148 and 1145.

COPPs references, 34 separate folders viewed, on formation to operational activity, collated in ADM 234/52, DEFE 2 and WO 218, WO 203, WO 206 series.

41 Independent Royal Marines/SBS in Korea ADM 202/459; other Korean reports DEFE 2/1861; SBS post-war assessment DEFE 2/1907; Special Boat Sections, a history, DEFE 2/1621; SBS/SAS title dispute DEFE 2/1621.

SBS and amphibious warfare DEFE 2/1798. Other Second World War operations studied, all listed in ADM and WO series: Anteroom, Arenal, Bowery, Baboon, Batman, Corona, Catswhisker, Camperdown, Carpenter I, II and III, Condor 1–2, Cassoway, Chimera, Etna, Frippery, Gregory, Hawthorn, Hurry, Kelso, Kingpin, Lightning, Marigold, Postage Able, Principal, Profit, Reservist, Sandbank, Stakes, Snatch, Substract, Torch.

Other general SBS-related files and reports under DEFE 2/1373, 1545, 1546, 1720, 1453, 1454, 1447, 1736; 970, 975, 1903, 1819.

Index

Also by Robson Green

Robson Green: Just the Beginning

Robson Green
Extreme Fishing

With Charlotte Reather

**SIMON &
SCHUSTER**

London · New York · Sydney · Toronto · New Delhi

A CBS COMPANY

First published in Great Britain by Simon & Schuster UK Ltd, 2013
A CBS COMPANY

Copyright © IWC Media Limited (a Zodiak Media Company) 2013

1 3 5 7 9 10 8 6 4 2

Simon & Schuster UK Ltd
1st Floor
222 Gray's Inn Road
London WC1X 8HB

www.simonandschuster.co.uk

Simon & Schuster Australia, Sydney
Simon & Schuster India, New Delhi

A CIP catalogue record for this book
is available from the British Library

ISBN: 978-1-4711-38393-3
Ebook ISBN: 978-1-47112-750-2

Typeset by M Rules
Printed and bound by CPI Group (UK) Ltd, Croydon, CR0 4YY

I dedicate this book to my beautiful son Taylor
and to my Uncle Matheson who gave me everything
I needed to know about Fishing – *Robson*

To my darling High Tower, Mom & Pops,
Mo Granny and Robson – *Charlotte*

Fish Anatomy

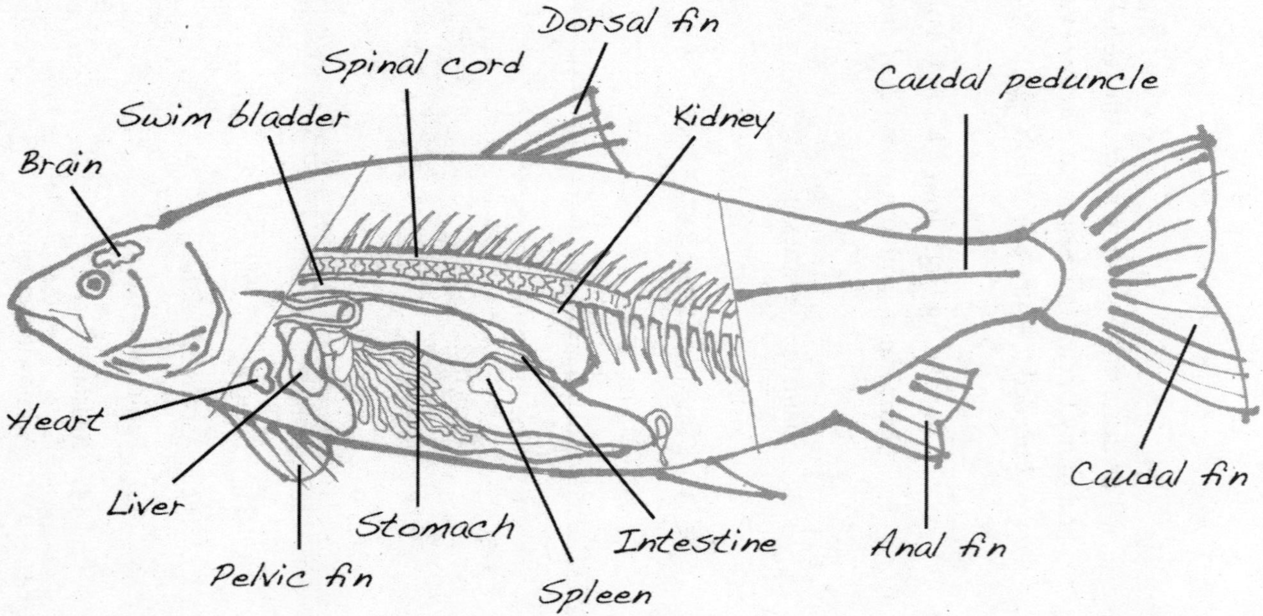

Caudal peduncle

Caudal fin

Anal fin

Kidney

Dorsal fin

Intestine

Spleen

Spinal cord

Stomach

Swim bladder

Pelvic fin

Liver

Brain

Heart

CONTENTS

Chapter One

SPAIN, THE CANARIES AND THE AZORES

'Don't Go All Scrambled Egg'

May 2008

I'm in the mid-Atlantic, off the coast of the Azores, powering through the waves on a high-tech fishing yacht. South African Captain Ian Carter and shipmate Steve Hall are taking me on a deep-sea adventure in pursuit of the Holy Grail of game fish, the Atlantic blue marlin. The sun is warm, birds are flying high in the sky above, and dolphins are leaping just metres from the boat. Conditions are perfect for catching a billfish and Ian tells me I'm here at exactly the right time, when the Gulf Stream brings the marlin within striking distance.

We've been motoring across the ocean for four and half hours and at last we're approaching our destination. Ian slows down and we put out squid lures at the back of the boat and begin to trawl. The vibrations of the boat should help attract marlin and maybe, just maybe, one will take the bait. We trawl and we trawl but nothing is going for our lures. The hours tick by. Unlike our reels, everyone is at full tension.

Suddenly, Steve tells Ian to change course. He can 'smell fish'. I sniff the air; I can't smell a bloody thing. I sniff again: nope, nothing. Ian swings the boat round and heads west. Steve points at a small slick of oil on the water; we're going to head straight through it. It's a sign that something is feeding on bait fish, possibly sardines or mackerel. We're closing in on our target. I ask Steve for some advice in case I am lucky enough to hook a blue.

He is a man of few words. He says, in his North Carolina drawl, 'I'll be watching from the corner of my eye. I'll say "Go to the chair", and you go. Just take your time and don't go all scrambled egg, do you know what I mean?'

Right, got it. No, actually I haven't. What the hell does that mean?

About twenty minutes later, and with little time left on the clock before we have to return, one of the reels starts making a loud whirring sound, like a primitive yawn. We are in! The line is taken out at high speed, 200 metres or more.

'Hold me glasses. Hold me glasses!' I say, panicking and flapping like the actor I am. My heart is pounding as I click on the harness and take the rod. The fight is immensely powerful. It *must* be a marlin but I'm not certain. I am yanked forward violently and swung round in the chair. I lean back with all my might, release and reel, ten to the dozen. And very slowly I begin to bring the fish closer to the boat. But soon it turns and runs again, stripping the line out another 150 metres.

'Please, please stay on the line. I beg you to stay on the line,' I say.

'Relax,' says Steve, but that is impossible right now.

I wind as fast as I can without letting the line go slack, otherwise I could lose the fish. *Think positive, Robson.* My muscles are burning and my arms feel as if they are going to drop off. Ian is backing up the boat to help me. *I am hard-boiled, not scrambled. Hard!* I shout at myself internally, like a fishing coxswain. *Come on, Robson. Come on!* I fight with all my might for fifty minutes, winding and pulling, when suddenly a 500-pound blue marlin bursts though the crest of a wave, piercing the sky with her spear.

She is the most amazing creature I have ever seen. Her body is midnight blue with a silvery white belly and faint cobalt stripes on her side. I am awe-struck. *Makaira nigricans*, the 'black sword' of the Atlantic (in Latin, *machaera* is a sword and *nigricans* means 'becoming black'). She is the reason we have come here and it's taken only a matter of hours to find her. It took poor old Santiago eighty-five days to catch a marlin in Hemingway's *The Old Man and the Sea.* Our budget just wouldn't stretch to that.

Jaded, I slowly reel in my beautiful fish. She is tired, too. Steve grabs the line and pulls her to the side of the boat. For this to count as a catch, he needs to get hold of the last bit of the filament, called the leader, which connects the line on the rod and reel to the hook. We can't bring the fish on board as the species is not only protected but also seriously dangerous. Steve leans out and grips the leader with his right hand and smiles at me. We have officially caught an Atlantic blue marlin.

We all stand and stare silently at the magnificent fish moving with the waves at the side of the boat. With a gloved hand, Steve carefully 'bills' the fish by firmly grasping her spear so she can't injure anyone. Marlin use their bills to slash and kill schools of fish before they feed and they have been known to spear boats and the odd fisherman, too, including one woman I read about on the Internet who was pierced through the chest when a marlin leapt onto the boat. The only thing that saved her was her breast implant. Perhaps Katie Price should be doing this show instead of me. After all, she is better equipped.

I run my hand across the marlin's back and say goodbye. Steve unhooks her and releases the bill. Capable of swimming at up to 68 m.p.h., she is gone in a matter of seconds. Everyone is pumped with emotion and adrenalin; the marlin was truly astonishing and her magic lingers. We hug and engage in male back-slapping.

'Don't forget to breathe,' says Steve.

We return to shore, the marlin flag upside down to show we've caught and released an Atlantic blue today. I am a hero and this episode is a triumph – except that this is television and our fishing adventure hasn't been quite as clear-cut as it would seem.

In reality, we have just pulled off a miracle at the eleventh hour. The show was on the verge of being cancelled and my career well and truly down the pan. *Extreme Fishing* could have been my second Vietnam, the first being my singing career with Jerome. Director Ian Lilley and I hug each other out of pure relief. He goes back to projectile vomiting off the side of the boat, which he and his assistant, Anna Hassan, have been doing for the past few days. I have done most of the filming myself, by fixing the camera to the side of the boat and talking into it. It's the eighth day of a disastrous trip and we are all exhausted. Catching the blue marlin has pulled us back from the brink and it's all thanks to one extraordinary man, Steve: The Man Who Can Smell Fish.

Rewind to eight days earlier. I've just landed my own fishing show. I am unbearable to my wife, colleagues and peers. What mortal can resist the sensuous mix of exotic travel, hard cash and fish? In every fisherman's eyes I've won the lottery. My mentor and uncle, Matheson Green, who taught me to fish as a boy, is sick as a parrot with envy; he's also very proud. I, however, am smug and heading for a fall, and it comes sooner than I think.

Some people say the anticipatory fear of doing something is far worse than actually doing it. What a load of old cobblers. From the moment I step on to the plane to Madrid I know I have made a terrible mistake. Matters aren't helped at Heathrow when an old woman comes rushing over and says, 'Eeeh, look who it is and I haven't got my teeth in.' She continues, 'I've got your album – I got it free with a chicken at the supermarket.' She thinks she is paying me a compliment, and goes on to tell me she uses the CD cover to stop her fridge from wobbling. The director, Ian, literally has to pick me off the floor, where my ego lies in tatters.

River Ebro

Our first port of call is the River Ebro in Spain. I am supposed to catch a wels catfish today but at the moment I feel I'm more likely to suffer a heart attack. I take my pulse subtly in the van – it's over 100 beats per minute. I need beta blockers. Fishing used to be my stress relief but not anymore. Not only do I have to fish on camera but I also have to present, and I'm not really used to being myself in front of, well, anyone these days. I prefer to dress up, slap on the make-up and pretend to be someone else. Anyone but me.

I swallow hard as I prepare for my first piece to camera. We enter a local drinking hole in Mequinenza, full of rowdy British cat-fishermen. It looks like the bar in *Star Wars*, where Han Solo meets Chewbacca. Talk about an owner looking like his dog; these guys all look like catfish, complete with hairy barbels.

This place is obsessed with catfish and here in Spain they grow to epic proportions. If they're not in the river, they're on the wall. A 150-pound giant protrudes out of the brown wood above the bar, like an ichthyic tumour.

'To me it looks like it's swum past a nuclear power station. It's too big; it's not right,' I say, jabbering at the camera.

Everyone is staring at me. *Just pretend you're Noel Edmonds, Robson,* I think. *He makes the camera his friend; he has a winning formula.* But I don't want to be bloody Noel Edmonds. He's a bit creepy, with too much facial hair, and I don't trust men with beards. Blind panic descends as I look around and see everyone in the bar has a beard. I don't know what the hell I'm doing and they're all staring at me thinking 'You lucky Geordie git – how did *you* get a fishing programme?' And I'm thinking exactly the same thing. I'm racing my words and I'm so tense I sound as if I've had a hit of helium. I'm somewhere between Noel Edmonds and Alan Carr, and that's not a place I'd like to be.

The first take is a disaster and we need to re-shoot the scene. It's not getting any better and my inner voices are now shouting.

Why the hell are you doing this, Robson?

Because I didn't think it through.

You're winging it and dying on your arse. You need a script. You don't even know who you are without a script. Why haven't you got an American series like Hugh Laurie or Damian Lewis?

Because I didn't go to Eton. No, it's because you're fannying around pretending to present a fishing show. Oh God, I'm a fraud. I want to go home.

'And, action!' shouts the director.

I have nothing to give so I waffle. We move outside to meet Birmingham-born contributor Colin Bunn, who is going to help me catch a catfish. Up until this point the biggest fish I have ever caught is a four-pound trout and an eighteen-pound salmon. Colin's nice but I can tell deep down he pities me.

Although I've never landed a wels catfish before, I've thankfully done loads of research. For example, I know that catfish are also known as sheatfish – and that's not a Geordie insult. ('You call this a catfish, bonny lad? I call it a sheat fish!' In fact, it sounds more French: 'Zay are really sheat fish.') I rehearse some lines in my head ready to use on camera. 'The Latin name is *Silurus glanis*, they have good hearing and can live for around thirty years. The species is not indigenous to the area and there are concerns about the ecological impact on the Ebro, including a decimation of the endemic Iberian barbel species.' Colin sets up a couple of rods and I relate the facts to camera like rapid machine-gun fire. It is another total waste of video tape.

I give up talking directly to the camera and instead get some tips from our contributor. Colin, like many other Brits, used to come here fishing on holiday and loved it so much that he moved here permanently. I want to know if these catfish really do live up to their fearsome reputation.

'I can give you an example,' says Colin. 'Put your two hands on the rod.'

I lift the heavy rod as he instructs. Colin gets on the other end of it and yanks me forward, pulling the line up and down sharply.

'That's what they're like, and they shake their heads like this so you get that banging action.'

After the demonstration we crack on with the real thing. Colin's mate, Ashley, rows the bait out into the middle of the river and drops it in. We are using halibut pellets, which are fed to farmed fish. They look a bit like pony nuts, which possibly explains why some of the catfish are the size of Welsh Cobs.

'I've heard they can take egrets off the surface,' I say.

'And swans,' says Colin.

OK, Colin, I see your swan and I raise you. 'And wild boar,' I add.

'Yeah, anything that swims in there that's big enough.'

Anglers have been known to tell a few tall tales in their time but this fish really does have an incredible reputation. In the eighteenth century, it was reported that the body of a woman had been found inside a catfish. Well, I wouldn't mind curling up in one right now, because at least I would be dying in private rather than in full view of the cameras.

One of the sensors starts to bleep. Colin hands me the rod and I pretend to know what I'm doing. The fish packs a punch and I am immediately working hard. It runs, almost pulling me into the water as Colin had demonstrated.

'Just pump and wind,' Colin says. What he means is that I need to lift the rod to pull the fish towards me, then wind it in quickly. If I just try to reel, the reel could break, or burn out the clutch. Either way, I could lose the fish and, after all this effort and anxiety, that's not something I'm prepared to do. Deep down I know I am living the dream; I'm just looking forward to the time I can start enjoying it.

The catfish hoves into view in the shallows. Colin gets hold of it by the lip and passes the large fella to me. This is my chance to share my knowledge of catfish with the viewer, but all I can say is: 'Look at the size of that! Oh, my goodness, what a beautiful creature.' I look down at it again, with its massive mouth and strange fleshy whiskers (barbels); it's certainly not a looker. Beautiful? Why did I say that? It's impressive but not pretty – a bit like Ann Widdecombe.

The fish is weighed and comes in at 33.5 pounds. I carry it back to the river and release it to swim another day. Thank God I didn't fail on the fishing side of things on my first outing: I can't present but at least I can fish. I take a breath as I look across the murky Ebro to the verdant Spanish countryside; it really is lovely here. Right, let's see if I can reel in another. Over the next few hours it's a catfish-fest. I land a dozen fish and my personal best is ninety pounds – the biggest river fish I have ever caught. All together a 400-pound haul isn't bad for a day's work.

I pick up the phone to the producer, Hamish Barbour. I want to talk about my problems in depth. He listens.

'Basically, Hamish, it's all been a big mistake. I can't present to save my life. I might have got lucky with the catfish, but I'm feeling like a total fraud – the only fishing I've done is on some streams in the northeast. Why didn't you choose Paxman? Or Chris Tarrant, an angling ninja and an actual TV *presenter*? Hamish, you've got the wrong man.'

'No, we haven't, Robson. We want you. We believe in you. You have something they don't.'

'What's that? Well, I suppose I am better looking.'

'Exactly. They'll never look as good on camera as you do.'

This is music to every shallow actor's ears – all we want to know is that we look good on camera. Hamish, the TV Svengali and puppet-master, plays me like a carp in a bucket. (No offence to carp fishermen, although they hate me already – but more on that later.) After our chat, my confidence slowly starts to return. I realise I need to embrace the opportunity and stop worrying. Everything is going to be OK.

Later that evening we travel by car to the coast just south of Barcelona. We're all tired but we have to shoot a night fishing sequence. Centuries ago, fishermen used to catch fish by putting flames on the water to attract sardines, rather like moths. Tonight we are using halogen lamps. Without sardines big fish wouldn't exist, and I enthuse about the species on camera. It's going really well.

I am on a boat with director Jeremy Cadle and two guys who don't speak a word of English. My Spanish is also poor. It's pitch black save the lanterns and a few torches, and as the fish come to the surface I say to Jeremy, 'Aren't those a bit big for sardines?'

'No,' he says.

'In fact, are you're sure they're not mackerel?'

'No, Robson, they are sardines,' he says with the utmost authority.

'Oh, OK,' I reply, assuming he must be a marine biologist. He is not.

We film for seven hours, gathering the fish in nets. I do a PTC (piece to camera) about the sardines and the fact that I have never caught so many fish in such a short time. There are thousands of them. I take one in my hands and say, 'If it weren't for sardines, big game fish like marlin wouldn't exist.' One of the Spanish guys lightly taps me on the arm but I ignore him and carry on talking. He coughs loudly. He is ruining my PTC.

'What?' I say indignantly.

'Eh, Señor, no sardine. Mackerel. Mackerel,' he smiles, revealing several missing teeth.

I can hear the blood whooshing around my brain as the pressure increases. I thank our Spanish friend and shoot Jeremy a look that could freeze concrete. *Oh, bloody hell! All the filming is wasted, utterly wasted, because I haven't said the word 'mackerel' once.* There is no way we can hide this mistake with clever voiceover and editing, and an entire night's work is now heading for the cutting-room floor. I am furious with Jeremy but inside I chide myself for being a fool. I knew they were mackerel so why did I doubt myself and trust a man who doesn't even own a fishing rod? I look up at the stars and the Milky Way as we head for shore. My Uncle Matheson appears like Obi-Wan Kenobi with a bright aura around him.

'You can do this, Robson, but first you must believe. Trust your instincts,' he booms majestically across the night sky.

Elusive Giant Grouper

Jeremy tries to make amends by telling me the size of the giant grouper I am going to catch this morning. He says, arms outstretched, 'They grow up to two thousand pounds.' *Wow*, I think, totally forgetting the fact that he's not a marine biologist. Grouper do grow to that size, but not here off the coast of Spain.

But off we go into the void, me as trusting as a child. It's like *Living in Oblivion* with Steve Buscemi.

We are fishing using glass-bottomed boxes that you put in the water and which act like large goggles. Groupers are stout ambush predators with vast mouths: their jaw pressure is around 800 pounds per square inch; a man's clenched fist is only 35–40. Their powerful mouths and gills can suck their prey in from a distance, a bit like Simon Cowell. The species are also hermaphrodites: born female, they can turn into males if there aren't enough cocks in the shoal, so to speak. (And we thought such versatility between the sexes was a modern phenomenon, when fish have in fact been gender-bending for millions of years – and a bit more realistically than RuPaul.)

We submerge the box in the water and wait ... and wait and wait. There's bugger-all down there! And after not hours but *three days* what do we catch? Diddlysquat. It has been a complete waste of time and I have come to the conclusion there's nothing in the sea. It's empty. And do you want to know my theory? It's those damned Spanish fishermen, who, by the way, we pay millions and millions of pounds every year to fish off the coast of Africa whilst our own British fishermen struggle to survive. And then they come and illegally plunder British waters as well. Not to mention the bureaucratic idiots who started the practice of discarding, whereby tonnes upon tonnes of fish are thrown back every year because of the stupid EU quota system. And these muppets get paid like footballers and only work on Wednesdays so as not to spoil both weekends. Don't get me started! But you can do your bit by supporting Hugh Fearnley-Whittingstall's incredible 'Fish Fight' campaign to bring an end to the madness and terrible waste.

Back on the boat, my patience has been tested to the max by the 'sardine' and grouper debacles. I talk to Jeremy about how the show is going and he tells me he thinks it's going swimmingly. I say, 'But we didn't catch anything today.' He replies, 'Robson, it's called fishing, not catching.' I want to strangle him.

Seeing as we have caught bugger-all so far, save the catfish, Hamish suggests we push on to the Canary Islands to see what we can find there. Everyone is winging it and it's not a comfortable feeling. Behind the scenes, Hamish is foaming at the mouth like a rabid dog. He has seen the rushes of Spain – uncut footage that will later be edited into the final programme – and says we have no more than five minutes of a show. This really is our last-chance saloon.

'Go and catch a marlin, Robson,' he says on the phone to me.

'Easier said than done,' I say. 'Haven't you read Hemingway's *The Old Man and the Sea*?'

'Make it happen. I believe in you.'

Uncle Obi-Wan Matheson echoes the sentiment in my head: 'Believe.'

But today, much like the rest of the trip, there is plenty of behind-the-scenes drama that the TV audience doesn't get to see: it transpires that our marlin fisherman in Tenerife, the one we are so heavily relying on to save the show, has had a skinful the night before and crashed his boat! So our first task is to find another contributor. Mercifully the production team manages to track down a Scottish guy called John with a big boat. Crisis averted.

I shake hands with our Scottish fisherman, who is tanned like leather. He has brought his wife and another old seadog along and boy do they all love to drink. It's like a bleeding episode of *Eldorado*.

'How's it looking today?' I ask.

'Looks great. Great weather – nice and hot,' he says.

'Fantastic. So what brought you to Tenerife?'

'The sunshine.'

'Not the fishing?'

'Nope, the sunshine.'

It quickly becomes apparent that this guy isn't remotely interested in fishing; he's just an old sailor who likes going round the islands topping up his tan.

'When did you last catch something?'

'Haven't caught anything in, er, three years.'

Oh. My. God.[1]

We end up fannying around with Scottish John for two days and – surprise, surprise – we catch nothing. I'm in mental decline.

After a day of not even catching a sea cucumber, the biggest insult to an empty-handed fisherman is to make him taste another man's fish, but the team is running out of ideas. I look at the camera and say, 'It's called escolar – because it looks like it's wearing reading glasses like an academic or "scholar". It's also called butterfish.'

The escolar is a bottom feeder and scavenger that hoovers up the dead, decomposing things that lie on the ocean floor – a bit like a vulture does on land. Part of the snake mackerel family, it is highly toxic and has to be prepared in a certain way to make it safe for humans to ingest. It's so dangerous that eating this fish

1. After the first series we always remembered to ask contributors if they had ever actually caught a fish and how long ago that was. It was a steep learning curve.

is banned in some countries – but not here. The islanders absolutely adore it; in fact, they can't get enough of it. Apparently it has a lovely buttery taste – if you get it right . . .

Joni Cejas, a restaurant-owner and chef, is going to show me how to prepare this dangerous fish. He is a silver-haired Spanish Del Boy who has his fingers in lots of pies, and now fish. A large escolar is waiting for me on a butcher's slab in the kitchen. The leathery prehistoric creature has large, frightening eyes, razor-sharp teeth and an obsidian tongue. I only have to take one look at it to know I don't want to eat it. It's as if my response has been evolutionally hardwired to my brain because an ancestor way, way back in time, some 60,000 years ago, once ate one of these fish and puked himself inside out and everyone in the Green tribe was really worried and said, 'Was it the oysters, Brian?' 'No, the escolar [puking sound effects].' And they all said, 'Gosh, well, we won't eat that again' – and that knowledge was planted in my DNA in an attempt to protect me to this very day. However, today I am going to ignore all of that good sense and eat it for the sake of entertainment on Channel 5.

Enter Joni waving two large knives at me. He shows me how to remove the toxins and cuts the meat away from the spine because this is the most hazardous part of the fish. Although any part of the skin could also send me to hospital with blue lights flashing – it's like playing a game of deep-sea Russian roulette. I wring the oily poison out of a piece of the filleted fish as if it's Russell Brand's bed sheet, and we pour loads of salt on the fillet, just as you do when you spill red wine on the carpet; in the case of this fish, the salt draws toxins out rather than wine.[2]

2. Except I've since learnt that sparkling water or white wine are much better for carpet stains, as well as being very refreshing drinks.

Joni fries the escolar without oil or seasoning for a few minutes and lunch is served. We move through to the dining area to taste our handiwork. It's like being a guest of Blofeld. I put the poison to my lips; like a fussy child attempting to eat broccoli, I open wide and nibble a small piece. It's like motor oil – but not Castrol Edge, more Mick's Garage's own brand. I turn to camera and my face starts to lie like a cheap Spanish watch.

'Mmm,' I start to say.

I chew some more and have an epiphany: 'Trust your instincts, Robson,' I hear Uncle Matheson say.

'That's horrible! That is shocking. I'm sorry, I can't eat that. What *is* that? The islanders love it? Are you mad? Mmmm, the lovely buttery taste . . . It tastes like shit. Oh dear me, I think you have left some of the toxins in it, Joni.'

But the chef decides that the reason I'm not enjoying it is because I've put too much salt on, and, oh joy of joys, he gives me another piece. It tastes a bit better but that's like saying Hitler was a bit better than Stalin. In that moment, I realise the only way this show has a chance of working is by me being brutally honest at all times.

Rock Fishing

The next day I am rock fishing with my old mate the poisonous-fish chef, Joni, and his brother. Using a twenty-one-foot bamboo pole, we're hoping to catch some delicious parrotfish, which will make a nice change from the 'I can't believe it's not butterfish' that tastes nothing like bloody butter – not even close.

I am unravelling fast today as I had little sleep during the night, convinced that I was slipping into a toxic coma brought on by my sampling of the frightening oleaginous scavenger. I clamber over volcanic rock to get into position for our first take and then stand precariously on a craggy lump of ignimbrite and attempt to explain the topography of the islands on camera.

'The Canaries sit on top of a huge underwater mountain range, causing plankton and lots of fish to well up from the depths below. Argh!'

A large crab jumps out at me from a rock pool, waving its claws angrily. I shriek like a girl and hop across to another rock. Out of nowhere a dog brushes past my leg unexpectedly, which nearly sends me over the edge. The director shouts for me to get into position – bloody easy for him to say from down there on the ground, which is *flat*. It's really dangerous on the rocks, especially as I am currently neither physically steady nor mentally sound.

I used go fishing to unwind and relax but now it's having the exact opposite effect and all I want is to hide in my wardrobe and hug my shoes. As I dangle my hook into the water below, my bottom is like a rabbit's nose on a spring day: twitchy. I've never had this symptom before; my nerves must be shot. Back at the hotel, however, I discover this twitchiness is due to something else entirely: parasites, to be precise (the word comes from the Ancient Greek for 'professional dinner guests'). That poisonous atramentous bottom feeder, the escolar, has infected me with red threadworms that are now feasting on *my* bottom and, well, I'm not happy about it. I should have trusted my instincts: I knew eating it was a very bad idea.

I rejoin Joni and his brother on a local beach to eat the parrotfish we caught earlier. It is nectar – just the most amazing-tasting fish. I share a glass of wine with them but I can't stay long – my bottom's on the move again. I head back to the hotel and take action. Standing in front of the bathroom mirror I address my behind: 'I am not food for worms, yet.' I down a litre of milky nematode-napalm.

'Hasta la vista, critters!'

Azores Marlin

The Azores aren't in the schedule. They are Hamish's last-ditch attempt to save the show, as we have maybe enough footage for about half an episode at this point. We have two days to get some usable footage or we are officially sunk. On the first day there, the heavens open up and it pisses it down. We can all tell it's not worth heading out to sea but the skipper, Ian Carter, suggests we give it a go. I suppose we have nothing to lose.

We power out of the habour into a two-metre swell. All the other boats are coming back, and fast, but we unflinchingly go against the tide. I remain cheery on camera but off it I am staring into the abyss of my own career. It is in fact the barrel of a gun with a knot in the end. That said, dwelling on my private turmoil is mildly better than staring into my breakfast, which is what Ian Lilley and Anna Hassan are both doing. This is the start of their extreme-hurling-fest that would endure for the next two days.

After what seems an eternity, Skipper Ian finally abandons the trip and we head for home. Not only are the conditions danger-ous but also the likelihood of us catching even a sprat in this weather is remote. However, the relief of heading back to land is tinged with searing anxiety: we now have less than twenty-four hours to catch a blue marlin or something – anything – or the episode will have been an expensive cock-up and the series will be panned.

There is a saying in acting circles that actors are paid for waiting around and the acting's free. This is entirely different. I feel more like one of the British soldiers waiting for his imminent demise in *Zulu*. The night is a long one and I can't sleep. I toss and turn as if still on Ian's boat on the rough seas. Tomorrow is our last chance, our only chance. We *have* to catch a fish.

The next morning I tear the curtains open. The sun is shining and the sky is blue.

Hope springs eternal in the human breast;
Man never Is, but always To be blest:
The soul, uneasy and confin'd from home,
Rests and expatiates in a life to come.[3]

We head out in Ian's boat for the very last time, on the very last day of the schedule, and, well, you know the rest of the story already. Thanks to Steve Hall's superhuman sense of smell, we are given a *deus ex machina* ending and we catch a magnificent blue marlin. Steve saves the day, and my career, and the episode is a success. You couldn't script it.

As we return to Faial Island, our marlin flag flying aloft, Ian says, 'We don't go out to catch marlin because it's easy, we do it because it's hard. And when it's hard to do something and you get it, you get so much more satisfaction out of it. You have to put in the time and you have to try.'

It's a beautiful maxim, and one I'll take with me on my unfolding adventure.

3. Alexander Pope, *An Essay on Man.*

Chapter Two

COSTA RICA

Frogs, Monkeys and Fish that Eat Fruit

June 2008

After the success of catching my beautiful marlin in the Azores, the producers now want me to recapture the magic by reeling in a sailfish, the fastest ocean predator on the planet. Sure, no sweat! I mean, seriously, where do we go after that? Waterskiing behind a Russian sub? Actually, that would have made one hell of a Bond sequence, but yet again I was overlooked for the job. I mean, what's Daniel Craig got that I haven't – apart from Rachel Weisz?

As I board the plane to Costa Rica I'm feeling calm about the journey ahead. The marlin's given me a massive boost of confidence and I've been dipping into my Stanislavski books to help me up my presenting game. The 'Stanislavski system' helps actors draw emotional truth into their performance. I'm feeling sure that Hamish is going to be very happy with the improvement on camera.

After a two-hour drive from the city of Liberia, we arrive at Playa Flamingo, the largest marina in Costa Rica. It's the rainy season so it's hot and sticky, which would be nice if I were with my wife, but I'm not; I'm with my crew of hairy Brits, who are sweating so profusely they look like human fountains. There will be no romantic beach scenes on this shoot but with the rivers swollen with water, there will be plenty of fish in the sea.

After a quick wash and brush-up at the hotel, we climb aboard Captain Jesse Baletti's boat to go in pursuit of a sailfish. The magnitude of the task ahead of me is starting to sink in and a wave of nausea hits me before we've even left port.

When I started the show I'd been a fisherman for thirty-five years, but the fish I was after were four-pound trout, not ocean predators that can get up to speeds of 70 m.p.h. and weigh as much as 500 pounds. I'm a ten-and-a-half-stone neurotic actor about to go and do something brave – the coward within is screaming. I feel like I'm in the wrong bloody play.

Before I film a piece to camera with Jesse Baletti, I go to the WC to have a firm word with myself.

OK, breathe.

I can't. My pulse is racing.

Here you are again, caught up in this madness, about to play with a monster of the deep, a veritable cheetah of the sea, and you're not prepared at all. Forget Stanislavski, you're screwed.

But what about the marlin I caught?

Luck, a simple case of luck.

'Believe,' says Uncle Obi-Wan. It's starting to get crowded in my head.

I walk purposely up the stairs to interview veteran fisherman Jesse. The American's been catching fish since he was five years old, and all his family are fishermen (the list is like the families in the Bible: it goes on a bit). Anyway, the point is it's in his DNA.

'If we're lucky enough to find a sailfish, the fight could be one or two hours,' he says. I smile and my stomach knots a bit tighter.

'And what type of tackle will we be using, Jesse?'

'What really excites me is catching big fish on light tackle,' he says.

I inspect the rods. If this is light tackle, I wouldn't like to see what he uses on a heavy day. This is so different from trout fishing it's unreal. I mean, usually I would spend my day putting a tiny fly onto a tiny hook and trying to cast as elegantly as I can. But Jesse spends his day baiting one-foot squid lures and preparing for a two-hour wrestle with no referee and no bell-ringing in between rounds. It's like comparing Creedence Clearwater Revival with AC/DC.

First Mate Steve Starbuck (genuinely his name) prepares the lines for trawling. On the lure he puts ballyhoo.

'The ballyhoo are good bait fish,' he explains, 'as they're thin and move well in the water to attract the big fish.'

He puts the lines out from two rods at the side, one in the middle and one on the top deck for Jesse. As the boat slices through the waves I suddenly become aware we are surrounded by dolphins.

'Look!' I point, 'There's about fifty!'

They are on both sides of the boat, and in fact there are

hundreds – possibly thousands. Jesse tells me it's a super-pod of Costa Rican spinner dolphins feeding on a shoal of sardines. Known for their gymnastic displays, the dolphins are leaping out of the water as if for joy. It's an awesome sight, and, for fishermen, often a good omen. The dolphins by the boat look as if they are jumping steeples in a National Hunt race. It's exhilarating to watch. As a boy I once asked Uncle Matheson, 'Why do salmon leap?' and he answered, 'If you could, wouldn't you?'

Jesse says that dolphins like to put on a show, but there's a more serious side. Under the water it's a feeding frenzy: there are dolphins, marlin, tuna, sharks and sailfish all wanting fresh sardines for lunch, washed down with a decent splash of claret. It's a ferocious battle and an orgy of food, a bit like a Mr Wu's all-you-can-eat buffet. On the surface of the water the cormorants and gannets scoop up the scraps. Gannets are not the brightest of birds and they gorge on food, trying to satiate their gargantuan appetites, until they literally can't take off. From the boat I watch them lying on the water, bellies sticking up in the air, like fat tourists on the beach in Magaluf. This is when they are most vulnerable to attacks from sharks, which, after gorging on fish, have a sudden urge for chicken. We've all been there.

'Robson!'

A reel at the side of the boat starts whizzing. Oh, my God, this is it: I'm about to join the fray. I reel like billy-o and am impressed with my strength and resolve. I keep my lines as tight as possible and I am winning. I am winning! The fish comes into sight; it's a tuna – a beautiful yellowfin tuna. Both crews (TV and boat) look disappointed, but I am wild with excitement. I leap into the air like a dolphin. I am heeding the truth within, just as Stanislavski said. I heave the fish closer to the boat. It's about twenty pounds – my biggest marine fish, save the marlin, but this time I'm landing it.

Steve Starbuck is unimpressed: 'It's a bit small.'

'Small? It's one of the biggest bloody fish I've ever caught!'

We heave her onto the boat. Her Latin name is *Thunnus albacares*, *albacares* meaning 'white meat'. This powerful torpedo-shaped creature is capable of bursts of speeds over 40 m.p.h. I think, as with many creatures we harvest, that we take tuna for granted because it comes in tins and has become a staple food in our diet. But I believe we should revere and honour this truly magnificent creature. Sadly, like her cousin the bluefin, she is increasingly becoming overfished due to the 'purse-seining' methods of many commercial vessels. They use sophisticated technology to locate entire shoals and scoop them up in one net that can hold as much as 2,000 tonnes of fish. Unfortunately they tend to scoop up turtles and dolphins, too, which is why, where possible, you should always opt for dolphin-friendly or line-caught tuna.

But today we aren't going desecrate this beautiful tuna with cheap oil, brine or vegetable broth, which they use to preserve tinned tuna in the States; we're going to sushi it! It's an amazing feeling eating tuna a couple of minutes after dispatching the fish. It gives your taste buds a unique flavour that can only be described as clean. And you don't describe fish as clean-tasting very often, do you? The tuna is healthy, fresh and bloody good for you, and today I'm eating it at the finest restaurant in the Pacific: Jesse's boat. In Costa Rica they have a saying, 'La Pura Vida', which strictly means 'pure life' but translates loosely as 'It doesn't get any better than this' – and now I know what they mean ...

Room 25, Santa Cruz

The hotel doesn't look that bad from the outside, but the ordinary exterior hides the horror that lies within. I mean, I've heard of hotels with cockroaches, I've even complained about mosquitoes in a hotel, but I've never come across a hotel that has a problem with crabs. Not one or two but thousands of the buggers.

At the beginning of the rainy season the tajalines, or land crabs, come up from their underground homes in droves and travel to the coast to lay their eggs. And they don't let *anything* get in their way – not even six-storey hotels. I try to sweep them out of my room but they are everywhere: in my bed, my bathroom, my drawers (honest!) and my shower. I banish most to the verandah and try to get some kip but all I can hear is them scratching with their tiny little claws at the door: 'Let me in. Let me in.' An army of Cathys at the French windows: 'It's me … I've come home. I'm so cold, let me in at your window …'

I put a pillow over my head to muffle Kate Bush and that's when I come cheek to cheek with cold exoskeleton. I scream and the night turns murderous as I embark upon a killing spree. I stove the crabs' heads in with my trusty priest – not a local Catholic Father, but the wooden tool I use for knocking fish on the head. And now crustacea, too. Die!!!

I return to bed, *fruits de mer* splattered across the room, put my empty wash bag over 'me night fishing tackle' and try to get some shut-eye. In the morning I close the door on room 25 and leg it from the scene of the crime. It's a room I won't forget in a hurry.

*

Director Ross Harper asks me to do a PTC about my crab hell. As I explain why there are so many of them, I pick one up for a more visual effect. Yes, it's definitely more visual: the blighter nips my little finger, and as I pull my hand away its arm comes off. Oops. There's an inhalation of breath from the crew and a squeal from me as I realise its nipper is still pinching my finger. The cameraman pulls the detached arm off. I tell viewers it will grow back, and indeed it will. I mention nothing of the crab pâté in room 25.

Upala

As you can imagine, after the night I'd experienced, I am feeling pretty rotten. Plus there was no hot water either, so morale is low. We get in the minibus around 4 a.m. and travel several hours by road to meet a man called Alex Arias, the president of El Club Nacional de Pesca de Costa Rica. The club is a big deal and I need to impress the main man. However, I am not impressed by what Alex proposes I do. He wants me to float down the hot, muddy, crocodile-infested Río Pizote – without a boat. And, what's more, while being swept down the river in only my shorts and a life-jacket, I have to fish for the toothy first cousin of the piranha, the machaca. This is madness. I need to speak to my agent – except I haven't got one.

I turn accusingly to the director and ask why he hasn't let me in on this secret before now. Ross says, 'Because otherwise you'd never have agreed to it.' Fair enough. He's right – but angry emails are going to be written later.

The thought of having a limb removed by a reptile, or my nadgers munched off by a machaca, doesn't half focus the mind. Alex, a dark and handsome smooth-talking bar steward, smiles and says, 'Don't worry, Robson, it'll be fine – but if you see a sign saying "Welcome to Nicaragua", then you've gone too far.'

'Great,' I say, grinning, beginning to draft my incandescent email to Hamish.

'But seriously,' says Alex, 'if you get to the border you need to turn around and swim upstream very fast – the guards are bored so they might "shoot you up". Understand? Apart from that, this method of fishing is perfectly safe.'

I look down at the river from the bridge. It's in full flood and swimming upstream would be impossible. A river like this in the UK would be declared unfishable – and besides, it's swimming-pool temperature, so I imagine the fish are half-cooked already. Alex says, 'Shall we jump off the bridge, Robson?'

'No, Alex, let's not. Let's leave that to Daniel Craig.'

We are using spinning rods with little lures to attract the machaca, which takes me back to when I was a lad messing about on the River Coquet in Northumberland with Matheson. When I was about twelve or thirteen, we would spin for trout using Mepps that spun through the water like shiny two-pence pieces. A fly-fishing purist like my uncle wasn't really keen on spinning but it was a guaranteed way of catching a fish or several – either that or using worms – and then you were definitely going to go home with something to cook for supper. Fish tend to swallow worms so using lures reduces the risk of damaging the fish, as the hook will usually catch the side of the mouth. This is the best method for catching and releasing a fish, whether you need to do so because of quota, size or because it's a female carrying eggs.

Alex and I put on our life jackets and wade into crocodile alley with our rods. The water soon sweeps us away. Surprisingly the machaca, considering they are members of the violent-crime piranha family who specialise in 'waste management', are vegetarian, save the occasional insect. They love to gorge on the wild figs of the *Ficus tonduzii*, known locally as the Chilamate tree, which grows along the riverbanks, its branches overhanging the water. As well as figs, the fish also eat various flowers, palm fruits and wild plums. I've never heard of a fish like it. Rumour has it they also love a cup of lemon and ginger tea after a hard day at yoga and are rather partial to tie-dyed T-shirts.

We cast our lines out as we travel downstream, trotting a piece of bait along the riverbed. It's similar to the 'drop minnow' method I use to catch trout on the Coquet, which is, as we say up north, 'deadly', basically because the bait is carried by the fast water into the mouths of the trout waiting in ambush. Thankfully, back home, we do it from the relative comfort of the riverbank, not in the drink.

Alex gets a bite but struggles to reel it in because we're in such deep water. It's a machaca but it quickly flies off the hook. We retreat to the bank and watch as fruit drops off a tree into the water and a hungry machaca snaps it up. Bam! It takes it and is gone. I'm not only really keen to win one of these fighting fish for dinner but I'm also hell-bent on joining Alex's club.

We walk up the riverbank and find a spot to wade in and see if we have better luck fishing on our feet. It's late morning and as I stare at the water I have a flashback to the tajalines crab massacre in room 25. I imagine the chambermaid's scream. My rod is yanked forward: I've got a bite. I set the rod up and let it run. Then, very slowly, I reel in the fish, which is fighting like a featherweight champion. I get it to the bank and pick it up. It's tiny, no more than a pound, but I turn to camera and proudly say, 'Look: my first ever cuchaka.'

'Machaca,' interjects Alex.

'Fuck! Machaca.'

'Machaca,' he repeats.

'Machaca,' I say, reddening with embarrassment. I pop the fish back in the water and he swims off. According to club rules any fish under a pound has to be put back in the river. The club is like the British fishing bodies, there to safeguard the health of the river and the fish, as well as to promote the sport. Alex also hooks one and it's a good size, so we're keeping it for our dinner. I carefully hold the vicious fish while delivering a piece to camera.

'Look at that: beautiful Costa Rican machaca – and what's great is, I can't believe how many fish are here. What it tells us all is that this is a very, very healthy river. This fella is for dinner. Well done, matey,' I say to Alex. 'Whoa!'

Suddenly the fish makes a bid for freedom, plops into the river and is gone. I am mortified.

'I've just lost your fish – oh, fuck! Oh, shit, I've just lost the fish!'

Alex looks at me like I'm a right member – but definitely not of his exclusive fishing club. I apologise profusely.

'It's OK, buddy,' he says.

'I'd be knocking me out if I were you.'

'Next time!' he laughs. 'You're paying for lunch anyway!'

'Because I've lost the fucking fish!'

Off camera it was even worse. I also managed to stand on Alex's best and most cherished rod just after I lost the 'cuchaka'. So stunned was I at dropping the fish that I stumbled backwards like a startled wildebeest and laid waste to his rod as if it were no more than a twig. I'll never forget the look on his face or my own toe-curling anguish. However, in spite of the mishaps, Alex still made me an honorary member of his prestigious fishing club. Dunno when I'll use it, mind!

Maleku Tribe

The next day we take a five-hour drive north, deep into rainforest. We are heading for the village of Impala to meet one of the last indigenous tribes of the region, the Maleku. The Maleku people still speak their own language and are fiercely protective of their traditions. They've been living here for over 1,200 years, so if anyone knows about jungle river fishing it's them. I greet Ulysses and two of his fellow Maleku tribesmen, 600 of whom still live on the reserve.

'Capi, capi,' they say, tapping me on the shoulder twice. I return their welcome: 'Capi, capi.'

Ulysses tells me I won't be fishing today as they are taking me on an armadillo hunt.

'OK,' I say, looking at Ross.

He shrugs and we decide to go with the flow. Well, the extreme part of it fits in with the show, at least! As we hack our way through the rainforest I am reminded of Tony Last in Evelyn Waugh's *A Handful of Dust*, who disappears in a South American rainforest and is held captive by a man who forces him to read the entire works of Charles Dickens. I wonder what would be the modern equivalent of such literary torture? Perhaps the complete works of Jilly Cooper, Jeffrey Archer or even Katie Price.

My heart misses a beat when Ulysses' machete swings dangerously close to my knee as we slowly but surely pick our way through the thick undergrowth. The rainforest is the Maleku tribe's supermarket, building supplier and pharmacy. After an hour we stop for a breather near an unremarkable-looking bush. The Maleku medicine man, a dead ringer for Frank Zappa, cuts a leaf off and motions that he wants me to try it. I look around at the director and assistant. They're both nodding, saying, 'Try it, Robson.' *Why don't they bloody try it?* I think to myself.

I put the leaf in my mouth and chew. It's vile and bitter. I spit it out. Suddenly I can't feel my tongue or throat – my whole mouth is numb! I try to speak but I sound like I've had a smack in the mouth, a root canal and then another smack in the mouth. I start choking to bring my throat back to life. Frank Zappa tells me the sensation will subside and I'll be back to normal in half an hour. Great. Meantime I'm thuppothed to prethent a thhow. He goes on to tell me the tribe uses the leaf for numbing the mouth in order to extract teeth. In fact, many of the pills and potions we have in the West are synthesised from these natural rainforest plants. It's fascinating. I chew gum manically to get some kind of feeling back, and slowly it starts to return. I realise I wouldn't last five minutes on my own in the rainforest.

After three or four hours of trudging through the unbearably humid rainforest, the Maleku locate an armadillo burrow and start digging the creature out. It takes a very long time and I come to the conclusion that they must *really* like armadillo. One of the tribesmen disappears down the hole, three others holding him by the ankles; he fumbles about and then shouts something back. He is hauled up, victorious – clutching an armadillo. I tell them they really should invest in a Jack Russell.

Instructed by the tribesmen, I knock the strange-looking creature on the head and return to camp with our supper. It's boiled up by the village ladies and served with soggy bananas. The

Maleku believe eating armadillo is good if you have asthma and it is apparently also a rich source of iron. I wonder if it helps panic attacks. My new friends all watch me take a mouthful.

'It tastes like pork,' I say.

They lean in closer wanting to know my verdict. I tell them, 'I prefer fish.' They laugh.

Man, I am looking forward to a good night's sleep. I'm dead on my feet but what an amazing day it's been. I am shown my hut in the camp ... and I immediately wish I could be back in room 25 *with* the crabs. It's a bleeding mud hut with a crappy wooden door that doesn't fit, and to top it off I'm sharing it with Ross Harper and George Hughes, the assistant producer.

As we settle down to sleep I imagine I'm in my bed at home in Surrey with Vanya. My son Taylor's tucked up in his room, safe and sound, and I have clean sheets and Siberian goose-down pillows and ... suddenly my dream is interrupted by a loud rumble. Half asleep, I come to and find both of the guys are now snoring heavily and I am stuck in between them, and the armadillo and bananas are having a very negative effect on the camp. I wake them up.

'Ross, George, you both have to go. I can't sleep with you. *You* snore like a bush pig and *you* have a bottom like Bhopal.'

They willingly rush off to nearby accommodation with running water and proper beds. I resist and I snuggle down as best I can on the hard floor. *I'm not doing a Bear Grylls and skipping off to the nearest five-star*, I think. *I want an authentic experience.*

What is it they say? Be careful what you wish for ...

Thud! Something hits the roof. Thud! What on earth? I search outside with the flashlight. The hut is under a bloody mango tree. Thud! I look closer. A monkey is throwing the mangos *on purpose*! I go back into the hut. The monkey starts pelting the roof with mangos – it's like throwing-out time on Saturday night in Newcastle. Eventually the monkey gets bored and decides to make loud calls instead. I do breathing exercises to relax my frazzled mind and slowly I start to drift off again ... *Zzz!* – a mosquito flies past my ear. *Zzz!* Then a cockerel starts cock-a-bloody-doodle-doing every twenty seconds ... and it's only 1 a.m. Dogs are barking, ants and mosquitoes are biting me, birds are tweeting – all that's missing is a bloody brass band. I am in the seventh circle of hell – get me back to room 25! I would rather read *Martin Chuzzlewit* surrounded by tajalines crabs for eternity than stand this for another night. I desperately need sleep.

Sadly, I get none. The next morning my face is creased and blotchy like a wanton hussy's bed. I tell Ross I need to phone my son, Taylor, as it's his eighth birthday. He tells me the only phone in the area is three miles up a mountain. I give him a Mel Gibson snarl and get jogging.

'Tay? It's Dad. Yes, it's really me – come on, it hasn't been that long! Happy birthday, little man. Are you all right? Me? I'm fine. Well, actually I'm not. [Cue tears] Daddy hasn't slept for three days and I look terrible and that's every actor's nightmare and they gave me this leaf to chew which made my mouth go numb and I've been attacked by monkeys, crabs and mosquitoes and ... [sniff] I killed an armadillo ...'

At this point Taylor hands the phone to his mother.

'What's wrong?' she asks.

'I'm sorry, I'm a bad father. Tell him I love him.'

This was meant to be all about my little boy and his birthday but the conversation became all about me, my utter exhaustion and obsession with my career. I drag my sorry self back down the hill. I must do better as a dad.

I pull myself together and embark on a five-kilometre hike with the Maleku through the jungle to catch the elusive machaca. After losing Alex's fish in such a humiliating fashion, I am determined I'm going to hook one of these veggie fish and keep it, maybe even frame it. On the way, tribesman Oscar shows me a poisonous frog that can kill you stone dead, bullet ants (among the largest on the planet) that will put you in A&E for a few days, and a beautiful chameleon that thankfully is benign. I look at this amazing creature and say to camera, 'Out of all the colours in its repertoire, vibrant yellows and greens – he chooses a dull shade of brown.'

The Costa Rican soundman, Alberto, pipes up: 'Stop! I can't hear anything.'

This is unsurprising as he has insisted on taking a forty-foot cable attached to the camera everywhere we have ventured, land or sea. Most other soundmen are usually connected by wireless because of the dangerous type of terrain but not Alberto, he's old-school. Earlier on today, after getting caught in the undergrowth, he fell down a steep slope taking the cameraman, Tim, with him. We stop filming to assess the extent of the problem.

'Is any of it useful or shall we film that piece again?' asks Ross.

The sound guy replies, 'Well, sometimes I hear and sometimes I don't.'

Ross: 'So did you hear any of what Robson just said?'

Sound: 'Sometimes I hear and sometimes I don't.'

Ross: 'Has this happened on any other occasion whilst we've been filming?'

Sound: 'Sometimes.'

Ross (now losing it): 'So are you telling me that sometimes you couldn't hear Robson on the boat, or with the tribe or river fishing?'

Sound: 'Sometimes I hear.'

Robson: 'Are you kidding me? Why didn't you tell anyone?'

Sound: 'You are a bad man, Robson, shouting at me! The people will hear you sometimes.'

And thus the soundman became known as 'Sometimes'. We later found out that much of the sound was poor quality but we manage to muddle through.

We trundle on through the forest. Morale is rock-bottom until, through the trees, we see the sparkling Río Venado. We hurry through to the water's edge. It's nice to get out into the open air; the forest is hot and oppressive whereas the water is clear, cool and about ten feet across. For the first time since arriving, I feel back in my comfort zone; being on the riverbank somehow restores my equilibrium.

We are using methods the tribe have relied on for 1,200 years and today our bait is the machaca's favourite food, figs. I sniff the fruit.

'Smells very nice. Can we eat it?' I ask.

Tribesman Oscar nods. 'It's nice.'

I take a bite. The fig is hard and tastes terrible, all sour and musty like grandma's tights. I spit it out. Oscar and the other lads chuckle.

I take my line with a hook baited with the horrible fruit and throw it into the middle of the river, using the minnow-drop method that Alex and I had previously tried. I suppose this could be called a fruit-drop – and anyone attempting it in the northeast would be called a reet bloody fruit-drop.

'I'm in! I'm in! Please let that be a fish! Yes. Yes! YES!'

After a decent fight I reel in a machaca and I get the name right on camera – back of the net! The fish, known as *Hiki Maleku* by the tribe, has an impressive set of razor-sharp teeth like its Amazon relative, the piranha. Its scales are silvery and tinged with green, probably from eating its five a day, unlike its crazy carnivore cousin. *Perhaps that's why one species of piranha is red-bellied, from all the blood*, I muse. I land a second fish and am thrilled. Oscar and his mate have had an unsuccessful day but are pleased that my two modest fish have made me hysterically happy. They laugh at my crazy behaviour.

'La Pura Vida!' I shout.

In spite of the arduous five-kilometre trek back to the village, I am still buoyant, and I am beginning to feel fitter and more sure-footed. Back at camp, we smoke the fish and serve it with – you've guessed it – bananas. The bananas are rank but the fish is lovely and tastes a bit like grouper, with big meaty flakes and a light texture. The machaca is such a healthy, powerful fish, mainly because it is constantly swimming against a strong current. It's no wonder the Maleku tribe are such healthy people, both physically and mentally. They enjoy a natural stress-free life and a good diet: the Omega-3-rich fish, coupled with mineral-rich bananas and a good two-hour yomp to find your food, is a winning combination. Not to mention their iron-rich armadillo – it really does tick all the boxes.

Sailfish

My journey in Costa Rica is almost over but I am returning to the Pacific to have one last outing with Jesse Baletti and Steve

Starbuck, in search of the fastest ocean predator on the planet. We meet at Playa Flamingo and head out on Jesse's boat. Hopefully this time we will manage to hook a legendary sailfish.

The midday sun beats down, making the waves shine. We've been at sea for nearly five hours now and nothing has been attracted to the lures, but all the signs are positive: the birds are scattered over the water, the dolphins are feeding, and, with the gentle sea breeze, the temperature is perfect. This is my last chance to catch this majestic billfish but I am realistic.

Suddenly the line explodes off the outrigger. *Perhaps it's another tuna*, I think. I harness up and take the rod from Steve. I've been taught all the basics of what to do but in reality, when you see the bend in the rod, all you can do is hang on for dear life. Whatever is on the end of the line is packing thirty pounds of tension on the reel. This is power – the clutch is fully on and the line is still zinging out as the fish takes off at full speed. It strips over 250 metres of line. Jesus Christ! As I play the fish, my muscles burn and I remind myself that it wasn't long ago men were fishing such creatures with hand lines. The chance of this being my ultimate prize is still remote, though. This ocean is teeming with all manner of fish. It really could be any number of species on the end of the line.

As I slowly lift and deliberately wind, the fish torpedoes out of water about 100 metres from the boat. Whoosh! It *is* a sailfish. I can't believe it! The sail is just visible and it jumps two or three times before diving back under the water, where the battle continues.

Jesse shouts over from the helm: 'All right, keep your line tight, keep it tight. It's about a hundred-and-twenty-, hundred-and-thirty-pound fish.'

I am trying to keep my cool.

'What kind of line have we got on here?'

'Ahh, you got a forty on there,' says Steve in his Carolina drawl.

'This is not salmon fishing,' I say, straining. 'He is just holding and I can't do anything. Ha, right, come on ... oooh, yes, he's starting to run again. Whoa! Gotta run, run, run, keep reeling, Robson, keep reeling. Ah, man, he's coming up, keep the line tight, keep winding – this is when it's dangerous.'

I decide to take it nice and easy with this fish, it's a once-in-a-lifetime catch and I don't want to blow it. He is near the boat, about ten feet away, and I can see his sail a metre from the surface.

Suddenly the long, slender creature flies across the crest of a wave, his navy and purple sail at full mast, iridescent like taffeta in the sunshine. The fish is dark blue on top with a bistre and silvery underside, and he has a spear like a marlin. But his sail – his sail is sublime.

After fifty minutes of playing the fish, Steve pulls the line to the side of the boat. He bills the fish and hauls the tired creature onto the side of the boat. He unhooks its mouth and unfurls its now-pitch-black sail. I hold the fish with Steve and touch the silky sail and slippery skin. Its Ancient Greek name is *Istiophorus platypterus*, which means 'to carry a sail'. The incredibly complex hydrodynamic design makes this billfish capable of extraordinary bursts of speed, the fastest in the ocean.

Steve tags the fish in order to help marine biologists understand more about these incredible creatures. He returns it to the salty waters holding it by the bill allowing oxygen back in the gills, and when it is strong enough he lets go.

What a baptism of fire. How on earth am I going to top that?

I fly back to the UK, safe in the knowledge that in Costa Rica we have made a great show.

Post-Production Meeting One Month Later.
Hamish looks me straight in the eye.

'Robson, you look good, the episode's fine, but the voiceover's shite. It sounds like your balls are up your ass. Give it some passion, some grunt.'

I am astonished. How dare he? Hamish looks at the editor.

'Well, what do you think?'

'Truthfully? It's quite boring.'

'Boring? It's fucking soporific!' adds Hamish.

I storm out of the editing studio, squeaking a few insults back at him and racking my brain for the definition of soporific. I google it and loathe Hamish even more. But you know what, he was right. The voiceover *is* terrible. I had felt I had improved so much in Costa Rica and was beginning to grasp what I was meant to be doing, but in the end I dropped the ball before the final touchdown.

Chapter Three

CANADA AND
BRITISH COLUMBIA

'The Curse of the Ocean Pearl'

November 2008, Series 2

Who'd have thought it? The four episodes of Series 1 prove to be a hit for Channel 5 and a second series is commissioned. And this time we've got eight episodes to play with.

I pack my suitcase, mentally preparing to leave my wife and son again. People who travel a lot on business, especially soldiers, will know this feeling – the wrench of leaving your nest and familiar surroundings, to face the unknown. As I lay out my three holdalls, the sense of adventure is palpable.

I spy Taylor out of the corner of my eye. Packing is a ritual I usually do on my own but this time Taylor wants to be with me. The first holdall is for thermals, fleeces and puffa jackets. The second for all types of footwear, from Arctic boots to trainers. The third is for my smalls, socks, shirts, jeans and pictures of my family – something I always take with me.

'Tay, tell me something about Canada,' I say.

'Um, there are lots of black bears and polar bears and grizzly bears,' he says, growling.

I always ask him to find out some interesting and unusual facts about the places I'm about to visit; each one I use in the show is worth a quid. It's a nice little earner for him.

'Very good. And did you know Canada is from the Native American word *kanata*, which means "village" or "settlement"? No? Well, now you do.'

He rolls his eyes at me and leaps onto the bed like a salmon.

I say my goodbyes and hug Vanya. The long absences are not easy for her. Then I turn to Taylor, who has been holding it together well.

'It's all right, Tay. I'm coming back. I will think about you every second of every day, and even though I'm away I will never ever leave you. I will kiss your picture goodnight every night until I return. Will you do the same for me?'

'Yes,' he says.

'Good lad.'

It physically hurts to get in the car and I wave and wave until I can't see them anymore. Five minutes later I phone Vanya.

'Is he OK?'

She tells me that, as soon as I turned the corner, he went to watch *SpongeBob SquarePants*. Kids these days – so shallow.

Jet lag is like being in a really crap musical you don't want to be in: you're singing the songs and dancing the dances but your mind and heart are elsewhere. It's as if you're watching yourself from the wings, wondering how you will ever reconnect with that dancing, singing twat on stage. My nightmare musical would be *Salad Days* – I bloody hated that one. After ten hours in the air, my body and mind are truly smashed, but I gaze glassy-eyed out of the window at the mountains, vast lakes, emerald-green forests of British Columbia, and they take my breath away.

Black Gold

It's 4.48 a.m. in Vancouver and my head is bouncing off the walls. In the UK it's nearly lunchtime. I witter to my diary cam about how I'm losing the plot and I really am. Unable to get back to sleep, I'm dressed, fed and ready to go by 6 a.m.

The iconic Fraser River flows through the city of Vancouver and just a few miles upstream is the largest freshwater fish in North America, the mystical sturgeon, which can grow up to five metres. To try and help me catch this prehistoric giant is Randy Beck – yep, Randy – and, seeing as there's only him and me on the water today, let's hope he doesn't live up to his name. Men can get kinda lonely fishing sometimes.

It's a cold, grey day. We jump out of the minivan at our meeting point on the Fraser River. Randy wanders over to greet us and shakes my hand firmly. He looks like Tintin's mate Captain Haddock but without the hat. I jump aboard his fishing boat and we head upriver. It really is bleak and wintry out here but the mountains in the distance lend a stark beauty to the misty monochrome scene.

We're casting from the boat today because if I hook one of these fish from the bank I'd probably end up waterskiing in its wake. Think of sturgeon fishing as a tug of war with a small car.

They grow so large because they gorge on the millions of salmon whose life cycle ends here, and in order to catch this extreme fish we are going to need some extreme tackle. Randy drops anchor unexpectedly. Clank! My heart skips a beat before going into overdrive. My nerves fray even more when Randy introduces me to what he calls a 'mangina'. I've worn one before but never heard it called that. It is basically a harness that wraps around your waist with a little codpiece at the front to accommodate the butt of the rod (it's all getting a bit Julian Clary). I tell Randy it reminds me of the heavy-metal band Saxon's lead guitarist, who wore one of these to spin his guitar mid-song. It seemed an apt story, given Randy sounds exactly like a roadie at soundcheck, but sadly the pop trivia is lost on him. I quickly move the conversation on.

'OK, Randy, let's just pretend I know nothing about sturgeon fishing.' *Er, you do know nothing about sturgeon fishing, Robson,* pipes up my internal monologue. 'Shut up!'

'What?'

'Not you, Randy. Jason, the director, was coughing.'

'No, I wasn't,' says Jason Holmes from a second boat across the way.

'So what tips would you give in order to catch a sturgeon?'

'Three things that are essential for this type of angling are courage, power and strength,' he says.

I'll get my coat.

I am lying through my teeth, telling Randy I've spent five days a week at the gym for six months preparing for this moment, when, all of a sudden, I get a nose-full of a putrid stench. If that smell is coming from Randy's bottom he needs to see a doctor *immediately*. It's like someone's just opened a coffin next to a sewage plant. I discover the culprit is Randy's bucket of 'green death' stink bait. It's shocking, a full-on dirty bomb attack on the senses. Sturgeon love putrefied salmon, it's like fishy crack and they know it's bad-quality gear, but they're addicted to it. I place the bait on the hook and am gagging. I cast out fifty yards of line and drop the lure into a natural feeding channel behind the boat. All we can do now is wait. *Please bite*, I think, *I've travelled nearly 5,000 miles and feel like I'm on a bad acid trip.*

We're using ninety-pound breaking-strain line with thirty-pound tension on the reel, as some of these creatures can weigh over 500 pounds. The odds really aren't stacked in my favour. Randy tells me that, because the price of caviar is so high, one decent fish can be worth up to $100,000 and it's not uncommon for boats to be held at gunpoint and asked to hand over their catch or else they'll be sleeping with the fishes. The thought that I could be murdered for a fish takes time to sink in. *I need to try these damn fish eggs*, I think.

Suddenly, something begins to stir in the depths and the rod gives a small but significant twitch.

'There we go!' shouts Randy.

The rod is resting in a cradle on the side of the boat; I wait for Randy's command: 'Hit it! Hit it! Hit it!' I swing the rod skywards to hook the fish – 'Reel, reel, reel!' – and I wind with all my might, but nothing's on. We've missed it. My heart is pounding in my chest.

'Bloody hell, Randy, I nearly had a heart attack when you shouted: "Hit it!"'

We don't have to wait long before we are in again.

'Now, now, now! Reel reel reel!' yells Randy.

'Yeah! I am!' I shout.

The bend in the rod is near breaking point; I feel as if I have hooked a mini submarine. The bend increases and the rod almost folds back onto itself. I wind and pull up but every time I wind in two yards, he takes me out two yards.

Finally, after what seems an eternity, the fish reveals itself close to the side of the boat and it is the most extraordinary sight to behold. It's about five feet long and forty pounds in weight. We heave her on board. I try to hold her up for the camera but she's such a strapping and awkward lass that I struggle, so Randy takes the tail and I hold her head. She is an astonishing creature whose family has survived two ice ages. She certainly looks prehistoric with the white, diamond-shaped scutes patterned down her sides, like the armoured skin of a crocodile rather than fishy scales. The Native Americans used these scutes as cutting tools, arrowheads and piercing instruments. The sturgeon was also prized for its oil content, and just a hundred years ago these beautiful fish would even be stacked at the sides of rivers or lakes, to use as firewood. ('Throw another fish on the fire, there's a good lass.' 'Throw your own bloody fish on the fire, you chauvinist pig!' Whack! Getting smacked around the chops with one of these fish could be fatal.) It was also common to see steamboats sailing along the Mississippi powered by sturgeon oil, until legislation led to the cessation of overfishing. Now they are under attack because of their eggs, which are known as 'black gold'. This particular fish is worth around £20,000, but because sturgeon are endangered, and thankfully protected in Canada, we are going to put her back.

So, I am no longer a sturgeon virgin and I'm very happy. These fish love Randy's stink bait and soon we have another strike. This one feels like the Daddy and it's moving away from me at an alarming speed. I struggle, winding and lifting, winding and lifting. Suddenly he whips round to the left – I spin with him. Now to the right – 'Where's he taking me?' I am propelled forward – he's diving down. The downward load is putting a massive strain on my back and I am not as young as I think I am. I am beginning to wish I really *had* trained for six months because I am fighting a perpendicular battle and my back is not strong enough for the struggle. There are shooting pains flying down my legs and into my boots but there's no way I'm losing what could be the biggest fish of my life. The world record is an astonishing 994 pounds, and this feels very close. I throw my hat on the floor. I am sweating profusely, the inside of my lime-green anorak smells like Randy's bucket of green death. I wrestle and struggle some more. Randy is getting a wee bit enthusiastic and decides to increase the tension on the reel to try to slow the fish down. I plead with him not to, as we are nearing the breaking tension of the leader line, but he turns the tension wheel clockwise and shouts, 'Come on, Robson. COME ON!'

'I think you need to take some tension off, Randy. He's gonna fucking take me over. Seriously, guys, get a fucking hold of me!' I yell as I lose my footing.

'I've got you,' says Randy, putting his arm around my waist, laughing wheezily like Muttley from *Wacky Races*.

I am in the hurt locker.

'Look at that – he's away. This has to be the biggest fish I've ever had on my line.'

'He's coming, buddy. Get him, get him,' Randy points.

'Come on then, son!'

I wind and lift the rod up with all my might. Snap! I fall backwards onto the deck – the sturgeon has broken off.

'Ohh, fuck!'

I swear incessantly for about three minutes. There are no other words for the feeling of loss, frustration and despair. It was 200–300-pound sturgeon – it had to be as it's just broken off a 90-pound trace.

Ever the professional, I turn to camera and say, 'But the thing is, the fish win sometimes and it's going take a better fisherman than me to bring that fish out the water. Oh, bollocks!' In reality I'm thinking, *It's all flipping Randy's fault. He put too much bloody tension on the line. I knew it and I did nothing about it. I know, Uncle Kenobi, I know I should have trusted my instincts, but it's a bit bloody hard to when I'm the novice and haven't caught one before.*

Director Jason tries to dampen the blow by offering me Champagne and caviar for dinner that evening. Pound for pound, caviar is the most expensive food in the world and it's strange to think that I'm about to put something in my mouth that is from the bottom end of a fish – but then I do like eggs from the bottom end of a chicken so why not?

'Sturgeons' eggs might be black gold, but are they worth it?' I say to camera.

I taste a small amount on a blini. The answer is, quite simply, 'no'. To my mind, caviar is a bit like some WAGs I could mention: zero calories, little taste and a total waste of money. I wash the salty eggs down with the Champagne and pour another glass. Now that stuff is worth every penny.

Kayaking, baby!

We are heading for Gabriola Island and it's blowing a hooley. I do my Kate Winslet impression at the front of the ferry but I am really not looking forward to going canoeing in this weather. I tried kayaking last year in South Africa and Costa Rica – it's always a bloody disaster and the footage is never used. Kayaking and me go together like the press and Hugh Grant, democracy and China, Scargill and Thatcher. But at least it was warm in South Africa; today it's gonna be as frosty as a miner's wife on washing day.

I meet Kim Crosby, a camp kayaking evangelist who will have to perform a miracle to convert me today. Unfortunately it appears he wants to perform something else. He peers into my canoe, his face dangerously close to my crotch. I point and bite my nails at the camera. I'm going to have to keep a weathered eye on this old sea otter. We paddle out into the Straits of Georgia, where there are sea lions, killer whales and . . . sharks. It is effing freezing and I really don't want to fall in. 'Chin-up, chest out, Robson, and stroke, stroke – no, Kim, not me, the water!'

We are heading for a reef where lingcod live – not a relative of Pacific cod but in fact a long, slender greenling. The lingcod are fierce predators with massive mouths and sharp teeth, and they can grow up to eighty pounds. Kim says the biggest fish can take the kayak with them, dragging you for hundreds of metres. I say to him, 'Stay close.' Worryingly he replies, 'Don't worry, I'm with you, baby.' I have been on some dates in my time, but this one is unique.

We arrive at the spot near some rocks where Kim suggests we throw out a line but this isn't easy and the strong wind keeps blowing us off the reef. He gets me by the paddle, trying to steady me in the waves. It's an impossible task and we are both blown and tossed further off course. I hold on tightly to his kayak, our canoes gently rubbing against each other in the bumpy waters.

I ask Kim that if by some a miracle I should catch a lingcod today and get it to the boat, how the hell do I dispatch it?

'We just grab into the gills, pull it in here, punch the shit out of the fish and down it goes.'

Right. That sounds lovely. I have a feeling that Kim might be sniffing glue or that he's two lingcods short of a picnic – and right at this moment a picnic or any kind of food seems very doubtful indeed. In two hours I have only managed ten minutes of fishing. The wind is taking the canoe in one direction and the current is taking the lure in another, meaning it's not sinking to the bottom but rather is floating on the bloody surface, which is no bloody good for attracting lingcod.

'This is fucking stupid! Ocean kayaking is meant to be breathtaking, but I think this is piss-taking,' I snap.

'But you are looking marvellous,' says Kim, trying to appeal to my vanity. Well, my vanity fucked off long ago and is currently by an open fire, sipping single-malt and puffing on a Monte Cristo cigar, and I want to join it.

We of course catch sod-all. My bottom is numb, I can't feel my toes and I've really had enough. In my eyes, Kim's credibility is at its nadir, unlike our lures. Unabashed, Kim says, 'I dropped some prawn traps earlier today. How about some lovely prawns for lunch?'

'Prawns. Perfect. Whatever. Get me out of this kayak!'

We head out on Kim's boat to pull up his prawn traps set 100 metres down. Right now I'm so hungry my stomach feels like my throat's been cut. I start to haul up a trap. It's hard work but finally it reaches the surface and ... 'Fucking hell, Kim, it's empty!'

There is not a single prawn. I feel like a right one, but Kim is a prize langoustine.

'It's OK. There are two more traps,' he says irritably.

I say, 'It's a bad omen; it's a barren wasteland out there.'

I strangle him on camera when the second one is empty as well. There is one more pot and as I yank the rope up, lunch hovers into view – a couple of handfuls of what in the northeast we call 'shrimp', of which you need to eat about fifty in order to consider it an appetiser. I wave one in the air.

'A prawn. I'm so happy.'

Kim puts his face in the camera and says, 'Extreme fishing, baby.'

No, it's not – and don't call me 'baby', punk.

Port Alberni

'I'm really looking forward to today because I've never been in a fishing competition before but I think my chances are good. There has been a question mark over my fishing ability during this show but I think a lot of questions are going to be answered today.'

I deliver the PTC by an open fire, soft-lit like a 1980s porn film.

'Today this is my type of fishing, exactly like fly-fishing on the Coquet, the Tweed or the Spey, surrounded by peace, quiet and tranquillity . . .'

Cut to loud rock music and us roaring up the Stamp River, battering into grade-five rapids in a shallow aluminium speed-boat, its engine terrifying anything within a five-mile radius. There's obviously no time for poncey scenery today.

I am here to challenge the self-proclaimed Angling King of

British Columbia, the Jedi Knight of steelhead fishing, Roly Hider, which is a totally made-up name and a really crap anagram. We decide it's the most fish that counts, not the biggest, and the loser has to swim naked in the Stamp lagoon. Roly sits cross-legged on his boat, shades down, cool as fuck, so confident in his ability, so smug and unflappable. I do hope he got bullied at school. If I lose, the water will instantly freeze my tackle off. I *have* to win or I'll become a castrato forever and be forced to duet with Aled Jones on our album, *The Very Best of Songs of Praise.* (What ever happened to that show? Mum used to love Harry 'Seagoon' Secombe singing. I always found it a bit surreal and he wasn't even very good. Don't say a word: three number ones. I was always great; it was Jerome who was tone-deaf. I carried him for years, you know. Just kidding. Love you really, Jerome.)

It's a good start: I have a fish on before Crap Anagram. I lose it but quickly coax another. It puts up a good fight and I have to concentrate hard to reel the fish to the boat, but I manage it and land my first ever steelhead. Steelheads are also known as sea-run rainbow trout or salmon trout, and the only difference between them and the plain old rainbow trout is where they spend their lives feeding and maturing. Stream-resident rainbow trout live their life entirely in freshwater, perhaps with short periods of time spent in estuaries or near-shore marine waters. Steelheads, however, leave freshwater as juveniles and migrate long distances in the ocean, where they grow to maturity before migrating back to their original streams. As they travel to the ocean as little'uns their scales turn a steel blue, hence their name.

I admire my steelhead. What a stunner! She is about five

pounds and with the most vibrant magenta hue along her side that morphs into a stunning bronze gilt around the rest of her form. After a quick 'donk' on the head it's time to get back to work. I am in the lead against the world's cockiest Canadian and I'm planning on it staying that way. Time ticks by and it's one-all, but Roly soon hooks another. It's a fabulous fish but as he reels it towards the boat it suddenly turns and is off. Oh no, he lost it! So sad. Never mind.

Three hours and fifty minutes later, it's two-all with ten minutes to go. I hook a fish and lose it. Damn. With only several minutes left on the clock, Roly shouts: 'Fish on.' He lands the steelhead during injury time and I am gutted. 'I am not going in the drink,' I mutter. 'Oh, yes, I believe you are,' he says, perking up.

Everyone is goading me from the boat. The water is a balmy seven degrees – that's only two degrees warmer than the water that killed the passengers of the flippin' *Titanic*. I'm going to die and he only beat me by one fish. But I am a man of my word. *Stiff upper lip, Robson. For Queen and Country and the Commonwealth, including Canada, which we still rule – suckers!*

I walk in *au buff*.

'I do this every day in Newcastle – not a problem!'

I dive in and burst out of the surface for air.

'Fuck! Jesus! Jesus! Oh, my God!'

My testicles retract, I sing a perfect B-flat – I have never reached that note before, or since. I run out of the water using a dead salmon to protect my modesty, which is more like a mole peeping though a set of curtains by this time.

You might think that's the worst thing that could happen, but you'd be wrong.

The Curse of the *Ocean Pearl*

From the look of the eerie trawler and its rabble crew, my instincts tell me not to board, but as usual I don't fully tune in.

'Robson, I've been looking forward to this,' shouts Captain Bob Frumani, his voice raspy from years of hard living. It's exactly what a killer would say, just before he carves you up. Bob is an unforgettable man, a man on whose face are etched the frightening things he has played witness to. His eyes are haunted – he has seen too much. His crew stand behind him like wraithy heavies from a ship long gone, except instead of wearing swashbuckling kit they are wrapped in black hoodies, which only add to the menace. Nature has played nicely with me so far but I am now about to witness her at her most despicable. I board the *Ocean Pearl* from a small fishing boat and the cameraman, Mike Carling, the director, Jason, and the sound guy, Stuart Bruce, follow me up the metal ladder. The associate producer isn't coming. Why? 'I've got loads of work to do here.' I later discover he suffers from terrible seasickness. He made the right call that day.

We've had sight of the weather forecast and it's looking untidy, to say the least. Sleet and snow are predicted, so it will be not only stormy but also freezing. We are heading out to a notorious stretch of the Pacific off the Brooks Peninsula. Explorer Captain Cook called it the 'Cape of Storms' and Bob does nothing to soften his punch: 'This is serious high seas ... It's like going to another planet. This is extreme fishing. I'm serious.'

As we head out I'm having serious doubts about this. I mean, come on, guys – it's only a bloody TV show. Isn't this too much of a gamble with all our lives? I am pacified by the director, who is between a rock and a hard place – he has to make a show or the production company could lose a lot of money. He updates me with the weather report. The storm will be heading north so we'll miss the worst of it, thank God, but we're still going to get mixed up in a gale.

I take Bob to one side to voice my concerns in private. I don't want his burly crew to know I'm scared. We go up to the wheelhouse from where he captains the trawler. As I start to relate my fears we enter the beginnings of a two-metre swell. The vessel starts to heave up and down and rolls powerfully from side to side. Bob tells me this is nothing compared with what's to come. He's really not helping.

Bob: 'When you come out here you gotta be ready to focus because it's high-end. If someone really doesn't want to come fishing with me, I don't take them. I never phone my crew guys, I never phone 'em and say "Will you come with me?" No way. They gotta wanna be here and it's the same as when you're captain: you have gotta wanna be here, so you're absolutely at your best.'

My internal monologue cranks up. *But I don't want to be here! I don't want to go fishing! I am not at my best and no one will let me get off this fucking boat! I wish you'd understand that!* I stay silent and swallow my frustrations.

Bob: 'I've been in some very serious storms where I really thought that this wheelhouse was gonna get knocked off the boat ... and you know, what I'm saying is, I've been scared before.'

'OK,' I whisper. *Robson, you pillock, listen to me – if he's been scared, you're fucked. I mean, look at the man! He's gnarly, nails, hard as fuck. He's like out of another time, where sailors wrecked four or five ships a career and that was normal.*

Bob: 'You know when you're four hundred, five hundred miles off shore and it's blowing so hard you can't even hear it . . . you think that it's peaking . . . it's just screaming, it's just woo, woo, woo, woo, woo, woo, wowowooo . . . and you think it's peaking and then it just comes: wahhhhhhhhh . . .'

I swallow.

Bob: 'And the whole boat's just shaking and you literally think your wheelhouse is gonna get knocked off . . . That's, erm . . .' – he turns and looks me straight in the eye – '. . . when you do really see God, believe me.'

I do, I see all sorts of horrible storms in those haunted grey eyes – it's like looking into one of those snow globes all shaken up, but there's a ship in there being gobbled by the waves.

'Thanks for the chat, Bob. It's really helped.'

For fuck's sake, I'm going to die. I'm seriously going to die. I feel light-headed, my teeth feel too big for my mouth, I'm delirious and I need to breathe, but the boat is all over the place and I'm on board for thirty-six hours.

As we slowly head northwest towards the Cape of Storms, the waves are already four metres high and rising, just as the temperature is plummeting. Well, at least, according to the weather report, we're going to miss the worst of it. But somehow, as time slowly ticks on, it really doesn't feel that way. The swell continues to rise and rise and the wind speed increases. Bob admits this is gale force now.

'But don't worry, Robson, this trawler is built for a hurricane.'

I do not want to test it out, I think to myself.

A conservative description of the ocean would be 'lumpy'; the reality is that its peaks and troughs are about twenty feet high. It's like driving over the tummy-lurching Northumberland Hills at breakneck speed whilst, at the same time, being thrown violently around by some prison animal who wants you to be his bitch.

'I thought we were missing the storm, Jason,' I spit.

He shakes his head: 'We're going straight into it. The weather pattern changed at the last minute.'

I am so unimpressed. To Jason, it's terrific news – this is his *Deadliest Catch* moment – but for Mike, Stuart and me it's terrifying. Especially as those guys are carrying such heavy equipment and don't have an extra pair of hands to hold on. The wind screams. I am frothing with ire.

'How dare you put us in this situation?!'

Boom! Boom! Waves hit the side of the boat and spray the deck. I am glad I'm wearing a survival suit: it'll give me three minutes of important thinking time should I fall in. That's enough time to mentally say goodbye to everyone I know and love. The crew have located their marker buoys so I need to help them get what they've come for. The sablefish are located two miles down in waters chilled by the Arctic winds. The reason why these guys risk life and limb week after week is that black cod, as it's known in high-end Asian restaurants, brings top dollar. On a good day, the *Ocean Pearl* can land £100,000 worth of sablefish. It's black gold to these men, and as we all know riches can corrupt the mind . . . and indeed it has done, because these guys are fucking mental to do this job. But not only are they addicted to the booze, the women and the lifestyle the money brings, they are also addicted to the thrill and adventure. As these men prove, the life of a sailor hasn't changed much over the last 500 years.

Deckhand Seamus is showing me the ropes. We need to bring up the pots that the crew baited and set a mile off the ocean floor a couple of weeks ago. A machine starts winching them up. We need to turn into the weather to get the catch on board, and as we do so a wave smacks me in the face like an angry wench. Her hand is bitter cold. As I recover I ask Seamus at what age he started doing this.

'Fourteen!' he shouts.

'Fourteen?' *Why on earth does he do this? There must be easier ways to make a living,* I think.

'Fucking and fishing: that's what Dad taught me.'

Wow.

Actually, Seamus and the rest of the lads are men of a certain ilk: strong, dependent on one another, courageous, fearless, and, in a strange way, really caring. Like soldiers or miners, brothers in arms in the face of adversity – in this case, Mother Nature. Their bond is essential because if there's no trust they literally could die. The number of times Seamus pushes me upright or catches me before I fall is amazing, as if he has a sixth sense for my safety. The guys work their arses off, heaving and lifting the catch onto the boat, all the while being tossed around like toys. I suddenly understand what having your sea legs means – it's not only being able to withstand the physical urge to vomit but also to move with the boat as it lurches left, right and centre.

I am put in charge of the gutting the fish. Seamus picks up a very large knife, takes a sable and bumps it on the head, then decapitates, disembowels and throws the flesh down the chute. He continues with the next fish: three bold moves with the knife and on to the next. The blow to the head of the first fish was just for TV; in reality the sablefish are decapitated before they can blink, if they could. I take the knife and wield it dangerously as I try to remain upright. I steady myself and chop the deep-sea creature's head off, gut it and throw the carcass down the chute. The smell of rancid guts is pungent and inescapable. I continue with the next. Head off, guts out, down the chute. It's a brutal, hellish scene of certain death, with potential death all around us.

Head off, insides out, down the chute. Another and another. Seamus watches over me but I can take no more. I run to the side of the boat but quickly realise I can't vomit over the edge as it will blow back in my face. I puke on deck, all over my boots, a lurid yellow goop. But, unlike with a tummy bug or after an excess of piña coladas, I get no relief; I just feel even worse. As the men heave another load onto the deck, so do I. Our work rate is in sync: every ten minutes another haul, another hurl.

It's dark now and a bit like being tossed about by a cat that's popped your eyes out and eventually will eat you whole, just not yet – there's more pawing, chasing and batting mid-air to be done – and all I want to do is die. Bob guides us through a rising swell to more marker buoys. He is a worried man tonight, not because of the weather but because he needs to balance the books. The last two locations haven't been yielding.

I have been on board for twelve hours now, working, falling and puking. I'm dog-tired. With the light gone I have no sight of the horizon and no perspective of which way is up. But although I am weakened, the anger inside me is growing and seething. As we pull up by another marker buoy, I help the lads land another pot. A wave hits me clean in the face. I can't breathe as I inhale the icy seawater. It's up my nose, in my lungs and stinging my eyes. As I try to recover another wave comes. POW! I am punched backwards and in that moment I think I'm going over into the swirling black nightmare. As everything breaks down into slow motion I yell inside: 'I don't want anyone else to be Taylor's dad. I'm his dad! I want to be there for him, no one else.'

Seamus picks me up. What I need now is a good slap but no one gives it to me so I am going to pass one on to someone else. I summon all my strength, stumble across the deck and swing for Jason: 'Bastard!' He's stood by all this time watching me puke and fall and he's the one who got us into this bleeding mess in the first place. I boom: 'Turn the fucking boat around!' The Arctic winds scream around our heads as another wave smashes port side. We fall. In the film version this is the point where I get Jason by the collar, pin him down on the butcher's block, chop his head off and gut him and throw him down the chute. As if reading my mind, Jason scrambles away.

The soundman has fetched Bob from the wheelhouse – *fuck, who's driving?* I stay on the floor. I don't want to fall anymore. Bob shouts down at me over the winds, which sound like a million banshees.

'We can't turn, Robson! The boat'll flip and then it's night-night.'

He offers me a hand up. I accept but am immediately bent double for another projectile puking fit.

Another wave smashes the side. At this point I decide to give in and accept that this is how it's going to end. I've never been a religious man but in this moment I am having more words with the Almighty than ever before. I think, nowadays, in the age of science and reason, many see religion as anachronistic and irrelevant to them, but all I can say to those without faith, including myself, is perhaps we've never been in a position where we've really needed it? Out on the high seas or on the battleground or at a refugee camp, cold reason and science are just not enough. For the first time I pray that I will be reunited with my family. I pray with all my heart and soul and I vow never to complain about being an actor again, as I don't know the meaning of hardship. All the while I'm having my spiritual epiphany, the crew of the *Ocean Pearl* graft away, landing pot after pot without a break, undeterred by the vicious storm.

Seamus takes me and the TV crew below deck. He confirms it's a force-10 storm, which is two off a hurricane (12) on the Beaufort wind force scale. The waves are over twenty feet high and the wind is reaching speeds of 65 m.p.h. He offers us some fried black cod, but we all shake our heads in unison and snaffle another couple of seasickness pills, which are bloody useless. He shows us to our digs. There are four bunks to a closet. I share with Mike and two fishermen and, like a nightmarish version of *The Waltons*, we say goodnight. The other three guys snore as if they all have serious medical issues. I diagnose sleep apnea and a very bad case of bulimia for myself, as I need to get up every ten minutes to puke.

Finally the wind drops a few knots and Bob is able, very slowly, to make a turn for home. Bob and the crew are happy to stay out fishing, but my pleading every five minutes with Jason has obviously paid off. It went something like this: I'm lying in the closet on the bottom bunk, I shut my eyes, oh God going to be sick, I run to the toilet, dry retch, dry retch, flush, wash my mouth out and knock on Jason's closet door: 'Please, Jason, I can't take anymore! For the love of God!' I go back to bed and repeat the process. It was worth the begging, though, because *we are heading home*. I get a burst of energy and rush up to the wheelhouse to see if it's really true. Bob, being the hero he truly is, has taken pity on me after thirty-six hours of hell and guides us back to safer waters. The crew are apparently pissed off – they're losing money and it's our fault. I apologise.

Bob offers me a glass of red wine and a fillet of black cod, which the crew eat for breakfast, lunch and tea.

'I couldn't, Bob, I'm sick to my toenails.'

He insists I drink with him. As I sip the claret I feel as if I've taken a quantum leap back to the seventeenth century.

'Thank you for the experience. I will never forget it, Bob.'

His face cracks into smile. We finish our drinks and shake hands.

After dropping us off, the crew head back out to endure another five punishing weeks at sea. I honestly don't know how they do it, especially in light of what I found out several days later. Just weeks before we arrived, Bob had lost an entire boat, out of his fleet of a dozen trawlers, in a force-9 gale. Sadly, eight of the crew members were also lost at sea. It's a sobering thought and one that should make us all value our fishermen all the more. So when you're next eating black cod, give a nod to Bob and his crew – and whatever happens don't you dare waste a morsel!

As soon as we reach the shore I ring Vanya. She has been trying to get me for days. She was worried and knew something was wrong. Taylor knew, too.

'I can't wait to be home with you,' I say.

Nothing on the face of God's earth is as important as my family. I've been humbled by the experience on the trawler and have discovered a new-found respect for Mother Nature, not only in her beauty but in all her might.

Chapter Four

ALASKA

'Thanksgiving'

November 2008, Series 2

Everything is alabaster, including the sky, frozen by the White Witch's own hoary hand. It's bitter, harsh, perishing, arctic, glacial, numbing, polar, penetrating, raw, COLD! But unlike in the *Narnia* books, I haven't just fallen through the wardrobe to get here; instead I have endured another commercial plane journey, over 2,000 miles this time. It's more mundane than magical – well, the flying bit is definitely magic, but the loos and the tea not so much. I mean, that's the paradox of the human spirit, isn't it? We can make a tube of metal fly through the sky with all our clobber on board but we can't improve the food or the plumbing! Well done, the Wright Brothers; buck up, Gate Gourmet.

A clinically obese passenger across the aisle from me asks, 'You been to Alaska before?' I shake my head.

'It's staggering,' he says. 'Over a hundred thousand glaciers and most places you can only get to by plane. I hope you got your warm clothes and boots or you'll be getting chilblains.'

He then goes on to tell me about the terrible problems he has with his feet. I look concerned but inside I'm thinking, *Yeah, you can't keep them out of the bloody pie shop, mate.* (Will I go to hell now?)

I walk like a zombie to a waiting transit van to begin a six-hour butt-clenchingly awful journey due south from the city of Anchorage to a place called Homer. We are driving in a blizzard in the dark, which makes *Ice Road Truckers* seem positively tame.

My *Extreme* team comprises Jonathan, the AP whose job it is to make sure all the filming runs smoothly, director Jamie Goold, Mike Carling on camera, soundman Patrick Boland and location fixer Hector MacKenzie. They have all been in Alaska for two weeks doing a recce, but it would seem in that time Jonathan still hasn't gained confidence behind the wheel. The conditions are treacherous and the van is slipping all over the place. We are all on edge. Jonathan is a luvvie like me and really shouldn't be the designated driver. I vote for Hector, who emigrated to Alaska with his wife twenty years ago. He's an old-school rough, tough, no-nonsense Scot, and, I'm betting, a superior ice-driver.

Jonathan is craning over the wheel. He can't see the road, the windscreen is frosting over and ... what's that? He hits the brakes and we go into a spectacular skid, turning round and round until we end up parked on the wrong side of the road. We have all had enough. I strongly suggest Hector drives. Jonathan is only too happy to hand over the task but starts having a tizzy because he feels the journey is just too dangerous; he doesn't want to be on board anymore. I know the feeling. He starts hyperventilating. In a bid to calm him down, Jamie suggests we change the tyres to studded ones to make it a bit safer. Unhelpfully I tell him to 'man up', hypocrite that I am: 'As my Uncle Matheson says, no place is worth going if it's easy to get to.'

Finally, after a change of driver, tyres and underpants, we arrive at our first Alaskan angling destination – Homer on the Kenai Peninsula. The Kenai, which is as big as the UK, Italy, France and Spain put together but only has a population the size of Newcastle, is a Mecca for salmon fishermen from all over the world. The fish are healthy and plentiful in this unspoiled paradise and only the very lucky, like me, have the chance to cast a line here.

It's really beginning to sink in that I am going to places most professional and amateur anglers can only dream about, and no one more so than my Uncle Matheson. For decades he has dreamt of dipping his fly rod in the Kenai River and exploring the unspoiled Alaskan wilderness. And what's more he's a trained taxidermist so he would doubly love it here, because at every turn, from the airport to the hotel, from the shopping mall to people's homes, there's always a stuffed creature, or usually several, on display. It's a fishing and taxidermy utopia. *I'll bring Matheson here one day*, I think, *but right now what I need is a stiff drink.*

Home from Homer

My first impression of Homer is, well, that I can't see a bloody thing, save a small wooden cabin otherwise known as the The Salty Dawg Saloon Bar. I enter; the smell of stale hops hits me. This is a place where men are men and moose are frightened.

Dollar bills are pinned to the walls and hanging from the ceiling, with all manner of messages written in marker pen: 'Shelly loves Buck.' 'Noah will pistol-whip Buck if he touches Shelly.' An old salty dawg sings Country and Western songs in the corner, strumming his guitar and puffing on a harmonica – except that they're more 'Cold and Northern' songs about being chilled to the bone and coming back from fishing and getting the dry-land blues. I feel slightly melancholy.

Keith Kalke introduces himself. He's an all-American hunter with a camo baseball cap, an impressive moustache and eyes that could pierce steel. Unlike the former governor of Alaska, Sarah Palin, Keith started hunting and fishing with his father aged just five. (In 2011, it was discovered that Sarah wasn't quite the outdoorsy girl she'd claimed to be.) Keith orders a beer and I order a white wine. No one including Keith bats an eyelid at this, which is disappointing as part of me (the mad part) wants a bit of a ruckus. There is none. Apparently, there are one or two Alaskan fishermen who enjoy a glass of Pinot Grigio as much as I do. Well, it goes very well with king salmon and there's certainly no shortage of *Oncorhynchus tshawytscha* (from the Ancient Greek meaning 'hook nose') up here. We'll be searching for the king in the morning, and Keith is very confident we'll catch.

I raise a toast: 'To good king salmon fishing!'

'Slammin' salmon!' says Keith, and we will be.

At this time of year, millions of Pacific salmon of all species, including the king (or chinook), pink, chum, sockeye (or red) and coho (also known as silvers), are making their epic journey back to their freshwater homes after years of feeding in the ocean. And what's more amazing is that they are returning to breed and then die. This life cycle is known as semelparity – from the Latin *semel*, 'once', and *pario*, 'to beget' – although no one knows why Pacific salmon (*Oncorhynchus*) expire after breeding while Atlantic salmon (*Salmo*) survive. It's one of life's eternal mysteries, but without their sacrifice the ecosystem in Alaska would struggle to thrive. These fish not only support human life in this winter wonderland but also the lives of birds, otters, bears – and the forests themselves. The salmon bring with them vital nutrients from the ocean, such as nitrogen, sulphur and phosphorus, which, via the wild animals that love to feast on them, fertilise the trees and plant life. Almost every organism around the river basin of Alaska has salmon in its DNA.

After a breakfast of tinned hot dogs, waffles and cream at our Travelodge-type hotel, I meet up with Keith and his son, Ross. We are going out on his boat, the *Ocean Hunter*, in pursuit of piscatorial royalty, and I'm excited. We drop anchor near Yukon Island in Kachemak Bay, part of the vast estuary where the Yukon River meets the mighty Pacific. Keith begins to explain the method of fishing we'll be using.

'We're running a twenty-five-pound test line with a flasher. This is gonna be like a school bait fish. All it's going to do is attract and get their attention and they'll come up and look at this and they'll see the bait dragging behind it,' he says in his rugged way.

'You give them a little tease and then they bite,' I say, nodding.

We're also putting on a downrigger, a weight to keep the bait at a depth of fifty feet.

Almost immediately Keith shouts, 'Fish on!'

'You are kidding me!'

The line is away. I take the rod. The odds are stacked in my favour because unlike the fly reels I use, which are basic storage facilities for the fly line with little or no tension at all, these reels provide up to fifteen to twenty pounds of tension along with a line that has a twenty-five-pound breaking strain. Nevertheless, if you don't keep yourself focused and the line tight, you will most likely lose your prize. I land the fish.

'King on deck!' says Keith.

In over thirty years of casting a line for salmon and trout, this is Keith's fastest bite ever.

'That took us, what, a minute?' says Keith.

Thirty seconds, more like. I try in vain to deliver a PTC that will enlighten, educate and inspire the viewer but what they get is, 'Hey . . . Woo, man, that's a FISH! You're the man, Keith! You're the lad!' I present my catch to the lens saying, 'This is the number-one salmon of them all. You've got your sockeye, your pink and your chum salmon but this is why we came to Alaska. Every salmon fisherman's dream is the king salmon.' I then drop the fish. I bloody drop it. Keith and his son share a look of incredulity. Their silence speaks volumes.

Some time later, I manage to mend bridges when we start talking of our shared passion for fishing. Ross says, 'Once you get addicted, you're done.' And he's right: it is an addiction, but what a healthy one – and you don't need to spend months in the Priory to get over it, which is a key point to underline to loved ones when explaining long absences and substantial financial investment in the sport. 'Yes, I know it's expensive, darling, but if I gave up fishing and took up crack . . . In the long term, fishing would be cheaper.' Google the cost of the Priory. You could come to Alaska five times over and still have cash to spare for bone fishing in the Bahamas!

*

Was that first king a fluke? Not on your nelly: within five minutes I have my three kings – a salmon hat-trick off the coast of Homer. Extreme location, extreme temperature and wonderful company – when catching salmon, it doesn't get any better than this.

Later that evening, although it's hard to tell whether it's day or night because it's dark most of the time, I cut the fish into steaks, cover them in lemon and butter and fry them on a shovel over an open fire on the beach. It's Newcastle's answer to *The Galloping Gourmet*.

There's a Moose Loose

The next day Jamie, the director, thinks it would be funny to film a PTC of me trying to attract a moose with loud calls. I think it's a stupid idea. I mean, is he trying to finish my acting career off? The only thing I'll be good for after this show is Maynard's Wine Gums – 'There's a moose loose aboot this hoose.' That's worse than Rob Brydon's Toilet Duck low. Of course I end up doing it.

Cue my moose mating calls. I stand in the middle of the woods and attempt to find one of the elusive 150,000 moose that live here. My male moose sounds like a cow and my female call to attract a male (bloody hell) sounds like I've popped my own testes with a plastic spoon. Awwwwwwahooooohhoooaaaaa! I wail into the icy tree-lined void for half an hour but to no avail. Unlike my lady fans, they don't come running, clutching their bangers and a Robson & Jerome CD, free with *Take a Break* magazine. Never mind – apparently nine out of ten men who try moose prefer women. I'm assured by Jamie that it's TV gold. I love Jamie but he is also a buffoon.

So where next for this Green fisherman? Fishing for northern pike with a nine-pronged spear through six feet of ice in the middle of bleeding nowhere, of course. After another epic journey in our uncomfortable van we arrive in Wasilla, where former Alaskan governor and prospective Veep (Vice President) Sarah Palin cut her teeth as mayor, and what a mare she is! It's 0600 hours and it's bloody cold with a high of –7°C, according to a very depressed-sounding radio weather forecaster. It must be like *Groundhog Day* at this time of year: 'What's the weather like?' 'Cold.' 'And later?' 'Colder.' *He needs to eat more salmon,* I think to myself – a portion a day will give you 90 per cent of your vitamin D intake (which is important when you're not getting enough sunlight) and it's rich in calcium, phosphorus and Omega-3.

Two people who aren't lacking fish in their wild diet are hunters Howard and Deborah Tieden. They've invited me into their home, which is a bit like a natural history museum. It seems after enjoying a good meal they like to remember it forever by having it stuffed. I imagine Howard looking up at his mounted caribou head and thinking, 'Those were the best goddamn hot dogs I have ever had.' Uncle Matheson would love this house – there's a creature at every turn: a bear, an antelope, a pheasant and a moose . . .

'Hey, I found one, Jamie!' I say, pointing.

Maybe the Tiedens have eaten all of the moose and that's why we haven't seen one yet?

In Alaska everyone with a resident's permit is entitled to shoot one moose a year during the season, which runs August through September. Howard's weapon of choice is a bow and arrow, but today we will be using a spear, because thankfully we're going in pursuit of a much smaller but nonetheless incredibly ferocious predator, the northern pike. Howard passes me the fishing spear, which looks more like Ruprecht's trident in *Dirty Rotten Scoundrels* or a really rubbish garden rake. Howard assures me it's a spear.

'We're going to use this under the ice,' he says.

I'm ready to hit the road but as I head towards the truck Howard shakes his head and opens the doors to a massive double garage, in which is parked a gleaming white plane. It's so small it looks like toy. *Oh, great,* I think. I bloody hate light aircraft.

'Where we're going is two hundred miles into the interior and only accessible by air,' says Howard.

I make Jamie check the map. Howard's right. Out of the 300 million lakes, he had to pick one miles from a bloody road.

My guide insists that the best pike are found in this lake at the bottom of Sleeping Lady Mountain, which is a mountain that – yes, you've got it – looks like a Native American lass flat on her back knocking out the zeds. Howard is an extraordinary bush pilot who fears absolutely nothing as we hurtle along at 200 m.p.h. ten feet above the treetops. His landing is perfect, and, after another change of underwear, we get down to work setting up our camp, drilling and sawing into three feet of ice and then setting a canopy over the hole we've created. It's a spin on the ancient Native American method of ice fishing that has fed families for centuries. In fact, it's pretty much the same save the tent, a better rod and the plane to get here!

We are fishing at a depth of eight feet. After laying sliced potato segments at the bottom of the hole, to reflect the light and show the outline of any predator that swims past, I dangle my simple red and white fish-shaped wooden lure down the hole and stare into the icy water below. The pike (*Esox lucius*) is an ambush predator that lies in wait before selecting its target and WHAM!, it quickly takes down its prey with its deadly jaws and teeth. Its long, slender and compressed shape is perfect for propelling it at high speeds over short distances. What I need is focus, speed and lightning reflexes – three things I lack. I open my eyes wide and raise my spear, primed for attack. I stare and wait and stare and wait. It looks almost instantaneous on camera but in reality it takes bloody ages. A long, black silhouette appears below me and smashes into the lure.

'Hit it, Robson!' Howard shouts, and in one swift movement I launch the spear into the back of its skull. It's over in a second. I have just speared my first-ever northern pike – and a fine specimen it is, too. I pull my spear out of the water and haul up an ugly and fearsome-looking creature with an impressive set of gnashers. I can see why the Latin name translates as 'wolf fish'.

Back in the UK, pike are a catch-and-release quarry, as 99 per cent of anglers believe that the fish are far too bony to eat. But it's the water quality that makes the difference. Out here it's gin-clear, whereas in Britain the lakes are earthy, which undoubtedly affects the flavour. It will be interesting to see how this pike tastes.

This lake used to hold salmon and grayling but once the pike were introduced there was only going to be one outcome: anni-hilation. As a consequence, the pike feed on pike in rampant piscatorial cannibalism.

'OK, let's do something about that and see how many I can land for our dinner before they eat each other,' I say.

Within minutes I spear my second *Esox lucius* and for the next three hours it's non-stop action. After that the only thing to do is take off from the soft, squidgy bottom of the Sleeping Lady and head back to the Tiedens' stuffed-menagerie HQ in Wasilla to poach our pike.

It's a beautiful sunset flight back to Howard's house and I am more relaxed after a good day's fishing. Howard tells me about the time he got stuck for nine days at the Sleeping Lady lake with two other pilots and nine Japanese tourists.

'It was 9/11 and the authorities closed the entire skies. We were told there was no way we could take off so we made a camp and survived on pike until the restrictions were lifted and we could go home.'

After that experience I'm surprised Howard ever wanted to eat pike again!

We land smoothly on the runway next to his house. Howard, the crew and I jump out and together we push the small plane back into the double garage. I am coming round to the idea of small planes. I mean, how cool would it be to have one in your garage? Deborah is waiting to relieve us of the pike, which she pops in the oven with butter and lemon slices. We enjoy a beer around the kitchen table before sitting down to sample Mrs Tieden's pike supper. It's absolutely exquisite. I tell them many people in the UK don't eat pike because it's supposed to be bony; Howard says it is, but only on one side, and that the flesh is easy to pull off the bone. I have to say the taste is up there with my top fish suppers. It might even have just knocked haddock off the top spot.

The Kenai

It's been a lifelong dream to come to the Kenai, a large peninsula jutting from the southern coast of Alaska, but the question is, will it live up to my expectations? The icy water is crystal-clear, tinged with an iridescent mineral green that adds a Pre-Raphaelite romanticism to the setting. Snow-dusted pine trees line the water's edge, shaken only by the occasion fish eagle jumping into flight to skim the water and take its prey. A brown bear casually tosses a half-eaten salmon aside and wanders into the forest as we arrive. It is everything I had hoped for and more, and I haven't even got out of the van!

In 1985 a ninety-seven-pound salmon was landed out of the river and it still stands as the biggest salmon ever caught anywhere in the world. But today I'm after rainbow trout, with the help of the Collette Bros. Carl and Billy are no ordinary brothers, and these are no ordinary rainbow trout – they're some of the best in the world.

Billy says, 'Let's just say they're not on the Weight Watchers programme. They're real big and they're real fat.'

Carl and Billy were, in their own words, born to fish. They also have a penchant for chewing tobacco, and as we row out into the river there is a 'phut-tink' every sixty seconds. At first I think they are unwell as I watch them perpetually hack and gob. Perhaps it's the flu or maybe bronchitis brought on by the cold? However, I soon deduce the reason they both have protruding lower lips is not owing to bundled forceps deliveries, as I had first thought, but to their sizeable pouches of tobacco. As Carl speaks I catch a glimpse of his 'gobbet' just in front of his stained yellow teeth. Within just five minutes of being in their company, I can tell that my time on the Kenai is going to be memorable.

It's as cold and quiet as a cathedral out on the river and there couldn't be a more spiritual setting for a fly-fisherman. The snow-covered mountains create one of the most dramatic backdrops I have ever seen. Otters feed greedily on the shore of the glacier-fed river and a large bald eagle watches over me from a leafless tree. Phut-tink! Carl spits another gobbet into the water. I watch it disperse like congealed blood.

As I prepare for my first cast on the Kenai, I am tingling with excitement. I am using an egg fly as my lure. Salmon eggs are the reason why these rainbow trout and steelheads, like the ones I caught with Crap Anagram in Canada, are so fat. Most are stream residents and it's difficult to tell the anadromous[4] fish apart. When the female salmon lays thousands of eggs in her riverbed redd, or nest, many are simply washed away by the current into feeding channels, where hefty rainbows are ready waiting for them, gobs open. Our plan is to replicate nature by gently floating downstream and through a series of turns, casting the egg under the noses of the rainbows that lie in wait below the surface. The water is so clear that I can see the fish moving about fifteen feet down and I can tell by their darting moves they are hungry.

Fly-fishing has a rhythm to it. I relax into my casts and remember a few tips Uncle Matheson taught me. I gently take the rod back, whisking the line over my shoulder until it's nearly straight; I pause and then, bringing my arm gently forward, watch the loops of the line unfurl and straighten on the water about twenty metres in front of my rod. I am happy with my cast. I feel a nibble and set the rod by quickly bringing the tip up from the water to

4. Meaning they spend most of their life in the sea but return to freshwater to breed.

the sky. This action hooks the lip of the fish and, as we say on the show, 'I am in.' I can see the trout: it's about seven pounds in weight but is fighting like a twenty-pound salmon! She runs, taking twenty-five metres of line with her. These rainbow trout are true Olympians of the river – think Jessica Ennis (well, any excuse!). Her run is continuous, powerful and downwards. That's the difference between rainbows and brown trout: rainbows fight deep, whereas browns flap on the surface.

There is no way this fish is going to come in quickly. I just need to keep her away from the fast-moving current, the boat and the hungry eagles lurking in the treetops, ready to launch at an unsuspecting angler's quarry. I let her run again and she takes the line upriver like a champion. Then, very slowly, I begin the retrieve and reel her towards me, keeping the line tight. She runs again but after about fifteen minutes the angling stalemate is over. She is spent, and I am able to gently guide the fish into the landing net and celebrate her beauty with the world. Her scales are pinks, greens and yellow hues, all the colours of the rainbow.

A hundred years ago prospectors came looking for gold in the Kenai but today I struck something else that is far more precious – and, more importantly, edible: *Oncorhynchus mykiss*. I give her one, mwah, and, holding her under the water for a slow release, allow the oxygen to gently circulate in her gills. I let go and she darts away. Closed-season rules dictate we must release our trout today – these rules protect the species and allow them to thrive and prosper.

Nanwalek

The last part of my journey in Alaska is to travel further south along the Kenai Peninsula to the incredibly remote village of

Nanwalek, home to the Sugpiaq tribe who will be taking me fishing for an Alaskan legend, the silver salmon. Although it's not far,
the only way to get to Nanwalek is by plane – another very small
plane. I turn up at Terminal 1 – it's a shed. What's more worrying is that the pilots are children, who toss a coin to determine
which of the spotty adolescents will take us. The thirteen-year-
old loses the toss to the eleven-year-old.

'Isn't it past your bedtime?' I ask, begging the director not to
make me board.

He reminds me that boats can only occasionally make the
crossing, and it's impossible to reach by road.

So my eleven-year-old pilot turns out to be Alaska's answer to
the Red Baron (I was going to say Douglas Bader but then had
images of an eleven-year-old being known as 'Stumpy' and it all
got a bit messy in my head). It's a twenty-minute flight through
freezing fog and a white sky. It's a bleak landscape and I get a
good view of it as the ground comes up to meet us fast, but the
child lands the plane perfectly.

'Well done,' I say, tapping him on the shoulder. God, not only
do I feel inadequate as an adventurer, but I feel bloody old!

Over the years, the Sugpiaq tribe have seen Russian and then
American rulers, after Alaska was sold to the US by Russia in
1867 for $7.2 million, which is under 2 cents an acre! Just
think what you pay for a 400-square-foot flat in London nowadays – it was a steal. The tribe now govern themselves
and village chief Wally Kvashnikoff is at the airport (another
shed) to greet me.

Although Wally's name sounds like a heavy-assault weapon,
he is a modest man of few words with kind eyes. He is also an

excellent hunter and fisherman. Owing to the remote location, everything has to be brought in and out by plane, so the villagers are almost completely self-sufficient. In fact, 95 per cent of Wally and his family's diet comes from the land, the sea and the rivers, so angling isn't a sport for him – it's survival.

Today Wally and I are going in pursuit of the silver salmon (or coho), which we'll eat at a village feast tonight. It's 27 November and Thanksgiving here in the remote American state of Alaska. Everyone is looking forward to the party, so Wally and I cannot return empty-handed. At this time of year, as the silvers arrive home from the Pacific to the quiet backwaters where they were raised as parrs, they quickly turn from silver to red and green, showing that they are sexually mature. It really is extraordinary to think that the final act of these beautiful salmon before they die will be uninhibited lovemaking with their partners ... so at least they'll pass away with a smile on their faces! I comfort myself with this thought but I can't help feeling choked by the sheer magnitude of this species' journey, followed by such a tragic yet passionate end. It's their beautiful and poignant sacrifice that touches my luvvie soul. That said, I still want to catch one for our supper – especially seeing as it's going to die anyway. They can't all be for the bears.

The snow flutters down as we cast our lines. I am freezing to the bone and need to stamp my feet and clap my hands every few minutes to keep my circulation going. Wally quietly casts, seemingly unaffected by the cold. After two hours of non-stop casting the fishing, like the conversation, is going nowhere.

'Are there fish in here?' I ask Wally.

'Yes, we just have to find them,' he replies.

Honestly, if my family lived and relied on my fishing prowess to provide food, sadly they would starve and eventually leave me, standing alone with my rod like an impotent angler. But November is a difficult time to catch a fish in this part of the world; these guys are weakened, waiting to die, and therefore not really in the mood for feeding.

Time after time salmon between ten and twenty pounds swim into view, but even when I cast right in front of their noses they're not interested. As salmon are technically unable to feed once they hit freshwater, because their stomachs can't digest food, I need to provide an irritant to the fish. The males become incredibly territorial and very possessive over their area and their partner, so any intruder, no matter how small, would wish they'd never ventured anywhere near the horny salmon. I cast a spoon lure, which has worked for me before on the River Coquet, and – yes, you guessed it – absolutely nothing. Time after time the fish just don't want to know.

I deliver my final PTC informing the viewers that on tonight's menu is fish surprise . . . the surprise being that there is no fish. It's a sad angling end to a beautiful backdrop but just as I'm reeling my line to the bank to perform my last cast of the day, WHAM! I get a take! My spoon is no more than ten feet from the bank but astonishingly a female silver has decided to attack my lure. Everyone is astounded and no one more than me. Even though this girl's travelled thousands of miles, has spawned and is on hunger strike, about to die, she fights like a woman possessed.

She runs, and just when I think I have her she leaps five feet out of the water and runs again, taking another thirty metres of line with her. All I can do is keep the line tight. One of us has to tire and this time it's not going to be me. Wally and his large family are expecting food on the table and they are relying on me to get it there. I reel her in and get her to the snow-covered bank. She is a fifteen-pound silver, a dark burgundy colour, similar to a sockeye salmon. I pick her up to inspect her and she is covered in snow like icing sugar. Her tail is worn from creating her redd (nest) on the gravel riverbed, in which she will have laid her eggs. This tail is so powerful that it has not only migrated 4,000 miles but then also dug a hole while fighting the current – and all on an empty stomach.

'Happy Thanksgiving, Wally. Last cast! Get in!' I say.

I am so chuffed not to be going back empty-handed and also proud that I have landed a silver on the famous Kenai. Wally says he never doubted me for a second ... Millions would, Wally, millions would.

Wally's wife prepares all the ingredients for our Thanksgiving feast, including locally grown vegetables as well as herbs and spices. She uses every part of the fish save the entrails. The fish head is used to create a delicious soup. All I'm thinking is that I hope it tastes as good as it smells, because the aroma is unbearably beautiful. We all agree fish tastes wonderful when you have caught it yourself – though these people have probably never tasted the supermarket stuff.

That said, many of the tribe do not eat as healthily as Wally and his family. Unfortunately the Sugpiaq suffered terribly in 1989, along with their fellow Alaskans, when the oil tanker *Exxon Valdez* spilled over 10 million gallons of crude oil. The spill, at that time the largest in US history, affected 1,100 miles of Alaskan coastline and killed or poisoned almost all the fish. As a result the tribe was sent an abundance of processed food by

American charities and well-wishers. Concerned about contamination during the years after the spill, native people abandoned about half the wild foods they would normally have eaten. Their bodies were unable to assimilate the imported food and sadly there is now an obesity crisis within the tribe, just as there is across most of the West. Hopefully, with Wally at the helm of the tribe, the Sugpiaq people will return to their healthy lifestyle and the eating patterns of their forefathers.

Down at the village hall, the party is underway. Thanksgiving is the celebration of the first time native people shared their food with British settlers. Four hundred years later they are just as generous. We arrive with our stewed salmon and soup and I sit down and join Wally and his family at the table and tuck in – it's delicious. I try other food on offer, too. With a little Nanwalek ketchup, which is seal blubber boiled down into a waxy paste. It tastes like, well, erm, seal fat. It kind of has the Marmite effect: you love it or hate it, and let me tell you I hate it! I later discovered that it has been known to cause botulism. This strangely didn't concern me. Well, I work with actors with faces full of botox – a deadly strain of the bacteria. A couple of air kisses could be as lethal as a bad portion of seal fat – it's a good reason to avoid kissing Simon Cowell, ladies! Anyway, before you think of freezing your faces in permanent surprise, digest this: botulism is a lethal toxin that blocks nerve function and causes paralysis. I mean, what muppet wants to inject that into their face? All I can say is it's bonkers.

After a bellyful of delicious local food there is only one way to end this Thanksgiving evening, and that's with a song. I get hold of a guitar and perform an old northeastern folk song entitled

'They Don't Write Them Like That Anymore'. I can see one of Wally's teenage daughters thinking, 'Thank the Lord for that.' I hit the final chord.

'Goodnight, Nanwalek, it's good to be back! Happy Thanks-giving, everyone.'

Chapter Five

BOSTON AND CAPE COD

Follow that Fish

November 2008, Series 2
As I walk through Boston Arrivals I spot the director, Jamie
Goold, among the throng. Immediately I can see something's
wrong. He walks purposely over to me, stony-faced.

'What's happened? [pause] Is it my dad?'

'Yes.'

'Is he dead?'

'No, he's had a heart attack.'

It's a surreal and emotional introduction to Boston.

I phone the Freeman Hospital in Newcastle. Dad is in intensive
care but able to talk.

'Are you OK? Jesus, Dad.'

'I'm all right, son.'

'I'm organising a flight home first thing tomorrow.'

'Don't you dare get on the plane. All the family are here, and we love you and I am fine.'

'But I want to be there.'

'There's nothing you can do. I know you were in *Casualty* but an actor in a hospital is about as useful as a chocolate teapot,' he laughs, short of breath.

I really didn't want to stay. The truth is that I was scared to death and I wanted to be with my family. I had never faced the possibility of life without Dad before and it shook me to the core.

'Dad, did it hurt?' I ask, like one of Job's Comforters, part of me wanting to know how serious it was, the other what it will be like when I go through it later on!

He says, 'I have never felt pain like it.'

This is a man who has worked down the mines all his life and has suffered slipped discs and a crooked back, like his father, a miner before him, all of this resulting in a perpetual stoop when he walks. He's endured severe nerve damage in his fingers (vibration white finger) from working at the coalface but never complains. He's always managed the pain by swimming for miles in the North Sea, irrespective of what time of year it is. Now that's hardcore.

'Imagine you are in a room and the walls are closing in,' he says. 'And they start to squeeze your ribs from right to left and the crushing is not stopping and the pain is getting worse. It takes a lot to drop me to my knees.'

I imagine him bent double in searing agony. I've never seen my father vulnerable before. Growing up, Robson Senior, or Big Rob, as he is known to his mates, was the hardest man in the village. He's only five-foot-nine but stocky with huge shoulders, built like a juggernaut. When people ask me to describe my father, the best word is 'huge'. He is huge both in character and stature, not an ounce of fat on him, and boy, could he handle himself in a fight – of which there were many. Like the time when a young guy knocked all my teeth out and Dad went round to his house, pushed him aside and chinned his father! Or if ever he was woken up by people on the street outside, he would thunder down the stairs, give someone a smack in the mouth and ask questions later. No one dared to interrupt his sleep. If David, Joanna, Dawn or I did, we knew not to be in the same postcode.

My younger brother, David, inherited Dad's build and toughness, but that gene wasn't passed on to me. I always say, 'A runner is better than a fighter and an ego heals faster than a broken jaw.'

'Make a good programme, Robson.'

'I will, and I'll be over to see you in six days.'

The phone clicks off. I exhale deeply, feeling as though there is a tight band around my head. I am poleaxed by anxiety and want to blub like a child.

Tonight we are meant to be going out on a trawler for three days in pursuit of Atlantic bluefin tuna, a fish that can grow to record sizes of over 1,400 pounds. Men risk life and limb to hunt these creatures because one that size could be worth around half a million dollars on the Japanese market. Our timing is perfect: the bluefin are running. But after the news of my father, and indeed the ordeal of the *Ocean Pearl* a few weeks ago, I just can't face it. Mercifully Jamie has asked the trawlermen if we can postpone our trip until the morning, explaining the situation, but my dad being poorly means nothing to them – they have to make a living – so they go without us.

Jamie calls a production meeting with Jonathan, the AP from the Alaska episode, cameraman Mike Carling and the soundman Patrick Boland, and we decide to go out on the trawler at the back end of the week. We'll just have to pray we haven't missed the bluefin run. We re-jig the schedule as best we can. Luckily Jamie is an expert at thinking on his feet.

After the meeting Mike takes me to one side.

'What you're going through with your dad – I've been there. If you need to talk I know exactly how you're feeling.'

Mike is ex-army and built like a brick shithouse. He's also got a massive heart. We'd bonded on the *Ocean Pearl* trawler, during thirty-six hours of hell, which was a hundred times worse for him with a heavy camera on his shoulder, but, unlike me, Mike never complained once. Over the next few nights I talk about my dad and how to face the inevitable. I regale Mike with stories of my childhood, such as the one and only time Dad took us out fishing in Devon, when I was seven and David was five. David and I were really seasick so the captain suggested he turn the boat around but my father said, 'No way, I've paid five pound. We are staying out 'til we get a fish.' We came back with one mackerel, which Mum cooked and made a right mess of. Dad doesn't get fishing – to him it's inactive and boring. His favourite hobby is drinking; he loves it and could have won many medals had dipsomania been an Olympic discipline. I once witnessed him devour eighteen pints and still manage to walk home – I have never been so proud. He fell over the hedge in the front garden but it was a grand effort all the same.

Cape Cod, Massachusetts

Seeing as we aren't going out on the trawler to catch tuna, we have to find something else to film. So we decide to do a PTC on Cape Cod and the history of the name. In 1602, a chap called Bartholomew Gosnold, an eminent English lawyer, explorer and privateer, went fishing and caught a few cod with a collective weight of 1,000 pounds, as you do. (Sadly we're not going to catch any today as the cod are too small due to overfishing and therefore not extreme enough.) Having rather a lot of sway and also having discovered the area first, he decreed it should henceforth be known as Cape Cod. He also named Martha's Vineyard after his daughter. I wonder if they'll name a place after me one day? Perhaps a cricket field in Northumberland – Robson's Green – or a bridge I once fished off. I can dream.

(I actually wasn't named Robson when I was a baby. Believe it or not for two days my name was Gary Green, but then Dad turned up, took the band off my arm and gave me his own name. Thank God he did. I can't think of many hip Garys off the top of my head. Well, there's Gary Oldman: extremely cool. Gary Lineker: quite cool. Gary Glitter: hmm, death penalty springs to mind. I'm very glad I'm Robson. It's a name that belongs to the mining communities of the northeast and it's common for the eldest son to have a surname as a first name. In fact, in my class at middle school there was me, Robson Green, and my mate Robson Brown. I kid you not.)

Anyway, the history of this part of New England is also pivotal in the founding of modern America. In September 1620 the *Mayflower* set sail from England and that November she landed on the shores of Cape Cod, most probably near Provincetown, aka 'P-Town', nowadays the gay capital and party town of Massachusetts.

Probably not what the highly religious Pilgrim Fathers had in mind, but I've heard Burger Queen is worth a visit. In December 1620 the Plymouth Colony was founded and the rest, as they say, is American history. But there is also another important historical fact associated with the Cape and this one I actually know a lot about. Here's a clue: the famous score is just two notes played on a cello, over and over again. Dur-nur, dur-nur, dur-nur-dur-nur ... faster and faster ... That's right, it was the setting for *Jaws*. Over the summer of 1974, when Steven Spielberg was just twenty-seven, they filmed all around here and Martha's Vineyard. Usually movies were shot in a studio, but the young maverick Spielberg wanted to prove himself and took the gamble to shoot in the ocean. There were many near-drownings and the film was fraught with setbacks, not least when the $250,000 mechanical shark was finally ready for his close-up and turned out to be cross-eyed and a bit, well, rubbish-looking. He also sank to the bottom of Nantucket Sound and all his electricals had to be overhauled. Not to mention that Jaws was worse than me in the high-maintenance stakes: every night he had to be hosed down and freshly painted. Spielberg knew he was facing a flop so he went back to the drawing board. He later said, 'I had no choice but to figure out how to tell the story without the shark. So I just went back to Alfred Hitchcock: "What would Hitchcock do in a situation like this?"' He realised 'it's what we don't see that is truly frightening', and thus made a classic by featuring the shark as little as possible.

Great whites are in fact rare off Cape Cod but there are plenty of other sharks, such as the vicious mako, which is what I'm off to catch this morning. Known round these parts as 'the taxman', mako can take 70 per cent or even 90 per cent chunks out of your quarry when fishing, which is known as being taxed.

A giant wels catfish that, I have to say, bears no resemblance whatsoever to a cat

'OK Robson, be interesting, insightful and entertaining.' And . . . action!

Let's just say this carp is no stranger to the dessert trolley (or isn't on the Weight Watchers diet!)

A super-pod of dolphins. A rare and extraordinary sight that just makes your heart sing

Show-off! If I could leap like that I could be my own stunt double

The sailfish. The marine equivalent of a Ferrari!

'Sometimes I hear, and sometimes I don't!'

Dinner is served, Costa Rican style

A survivor of the terrible massacre in Room 25

The setting for the iconic 1970s movie *Jaws*. I don't think my tackle is big enough . . .

A bluefin tuna that really put the *Extreme* into Extreme Fishing

Two crayfish and a prawn

Has anyone seen my drum kit?

Even in the Amazon jungle there's always a pap lurking in the undergrowth. Thankfully I'm not topless

How on earth are we going to top this? I came in search of the ultimate angling experience, and I think I've found it!

Check out the mahi-mahi (and the Mangina!)

It's the only way to travel, especially if I'm at the controls

The last picture ever taken of the bloody cockerel that kept me awake in Costa Rica

An actor with a harpoon, what could possibly go wrong

Mine's bigger than yours, Tarzan

If I run the caiman gets me, if I swim the piranha get me, it's a Catch-23 (which is like a Catch-22 but worse!)

Cuba. A 1950s paradise, and one of my favourite places on the planet

A rose between two thorns. Or should I say barracudas?

What more does an angler need? Well, a bathroom would be nice!

And then a storm removed our humble abode from the earth

As I walk down to the aptly named Green Harbour (hopefully not named after a forebear who lost his life to a shark), the only question is: are we going to need a bigger boat? I meet Tom de Persia and his son, Jeff, who run several sports fishing charters off the Cape. Today we're heading two hours east into the Atlantic to go in search of this ultimate predator. It's beautiful out at sea, the sun is rising, the dolphins are swimming, but bloody hell, Tom is driving the boat like an utter madman. It's obvious he hasn't skippered in a while by the way he is battering the boat at speed into the waves. Jeff is more of an able seaman and is losing patience with his father's incompetence. As we are all thrown around the boat, Jeff shouts, 'What the hell are you doing, Dad?' Let's just say they seem to have a somewhat strained relationship. I think Tom is just desperate to be on camera.

The mako shark is the fastest shark in the ocean and the third-fastest creature on the planet. They are capable of jumping twenty feet out of the water and are responsible for taking many a chunk out of fishermen who land them on their boats. We will not be landing our mako, as shark fishing is part of a catch-and-release programme, which means any taxmen we catch will be electronically tagged so that marine biologists can study feeding, breeding and extreme fiscal pillaging, and other habits of this fearsome creature.

To attract these predators we have got to get the smell of blood in their nostrils, so out goes the chum crate full of ground-up smelly fish. We drag the crate behind the boat, to encourage sharks to head straight for us – it's definitely counter-intuitive. I am looking for dorsal fins in the water, trying to act casual. When the sharks do get near the boat we are going to try to hook one using balloons.

'Are we throwing the mako a party?' I ask.

Jeff explains that the balloon acts as a bobber, so when the shark bites the balloons pop. Because of the waves and the swell it's sometimes difficult to see where the bait has dropped; in this instance we're using bonito, which is a medium-sized mackerel-type fish. The bright-coloured balloon is an extreme version of a fish float, and if we accidentally fall asleep (which is quite possible when out fishing) the loud bang will hopefully wake us up. Well, that's the theory.

Jeff has been fishing since he was born. In fact, when he came out of the womb, the first thing his parents gave him was a rod – well, almost the first thing. They probably gave him a kiss and then a good glug of milk and *then* the rod. Jeff is fascinated by sharks and saw *Jaws* before he went on his first shark-fishing trip with his dad. He has seen the film twenty-six times at the cinema. I myself saw *Jaws* six times at the Newcastle Odeon (now a car park) with my best mate Keith Jobson; we watched *Star Wars* sixteen times.

As I wait for a bite, I jabber at the crew and camera. The sun gleams on the water and I check every bump and ripple for signs of movement. I really don't want to spot a grey dorsal fin cutting through the waves like a scalpel, but then again I really do. What is it about humans and the need to scare the shit out of ourselves? Spielberg is right, it's the things we can't see that scare us the most, so I suppose shark fishing is a way of facing your fears, literally. It's also borne out of pure curiosity to see and know more about what lurks beneath. To my mind it's bloody bonkers, but I am contractually obliged!

I imagine I'm in the barrel scene of the movie. The shark is circling Quint's boat. Quint loads a harpoon and attaches it to a plastic barrel. He shoots Jaws. The predator is now very pissed off and takes the barrel on a very fast journey. He disappears and so does the barrel. Where's the shark gone? John Williams's cello music is playing in my head: dur-nur, dur-nur, dur-nur. Every glimmer looks like movement and my eyes are in overdrive. I'm seeing shapes everywhere. I stare at the balloon waiting for it to pop. I wait. But a watched balloon never bursts.

Two hours later and we've got bugger-all, I am still in one piece and I'm bored. I'm also absolutely freezing my nuts off out here. Quint never looked cold but then, compared to Orkney Islander Robert Shaw, who played the grizzly fisherman, I am a soft Southerner. He was probably warmed up by rum, as he wasn't shy of a drink. Shaw was an incredibly talented man and actually wrote the USS *Indianapolis* monologue scene in which Quint explains his violent hatred of sharks. Watch it again, it's brilliant. He died in 1978 of a heart attack but is on my imaginary list of top five people of all time to go on the lash with, the others being: Oliver Reed, Peter Sellers, Errol Flynn and, weirdly, Michael Bublé.

Suddenly I swear I see something break the surface of the water. Jeff isn't sure. The balloon starts moving towards us very slowly. I don't think we are going to need a bigger boat. It's about the pace of a Chihuahua paddling under the surface. We pull up the line – 'It's a shark!' Just the wrong bloody kind. It's a small spiny dogfish. I grab him by the tail and hold him up to camera. He's got two small dorsal fins and really rough skin, and reminds me of an ex-girlfriend.

As we pop him back, Tom suggests we perhaps try to catch a bluefin tuna instead. Jamie says no, because we are now going to do that on a trawler at the end of the week and our catch is likely to be much bigger than it would be here. We all agree to stick with the shark fishing. But right at the time of the discussion, Jamie's phone starts beeping. It's a text from the captain of the trawler 100 miles out at sea. It simply says 'They've gone', meaning the tuna.

'Thank fuck we didn't go out with them. It would have been a complete waste of time,' I say.

I have never been so happy in my whole life to miss three days on a blinking trawler without the prospect of catching a single fish. And it's all down to my dad.

Jamie looks at his phone for a while.

'OK, let's catch a bluefin,' he says.

Thank God for that. I'm always happier catching a fish we can actually eat, rather than one that wants to eat me. We head further out into the Atlantic, now in pursuit of *Thunnus thynnus*, which can grow to the size of a small car and put up one hell of a fight. The birds are feeding, which means only one thing: big fish are gorging on bait fish.

We set out our lines, baited with plastic jelly skip bait that replicates sardines or mackerel in the water, and begin to trawl. Jeff can see bluefin tuna leaping 100 yards away. We head towards them. The suspense is killing me but after half an hour there are still no bites. Surely I'm not going to miss out again. All of a sudden, one of the reels starts to scream. I take the rod, with the help of Jeff, and plug it into my special 'mangina'. The pull on the line is incredible. It feels like a massive bluefin tuna but that could be wishful thinking. The muscles in my back are stretched to their limit but still the fish keeps running.

'This is a big fish! Such a strong, powerful, ocean-going Ferrari!'

I slowly wind in but the fish takes out more and more line.

'You hear that? That is the sound of power. He's turning me round, he's turning me round. Oh, stop, please! This is some beast, I'm telling you now we're in for some shock if we get this on board,' I yell out to anyone who's listening.

After twenty minutes he seems to tire and I can wind him in again ... As the fish gets nearer, the pull gets stronger. I am in real trouble; my back is knackered and I'm in serious pain.

'Oh, it's going under the boat!' I shout.

Shooting pains are making me feel sick but I can't lose this fish. I ask Jeff if I am doing something wrong or standing incorrectly.

'No, this is what they do to you,' he says, as I heave the rod up and reel with all my might. 'You're gonna want to stay right in this corner and swing him out. There you go, get a crank.'

'I can't!'

'There you go, you're doing good,' says Jeff. 'We got colour!'

I look at the side of the boat. It's a monster. How on earth are we going to get it on board? I am dizzy with pain.

'Ready, 3, 2, 1 ...'

Jeff and Tom heave the tuna on board and I go mental, like a schoolboy with ADHD, shouting, 'That's why we came here! Look at that fish! Oh, yes, man, get in! Whoah! This is why we came to Boston, this is why we came to Cape Cod. We did it, Jeff, you're the man. Tom de Persia's the man. What have we got, a hundred and twenty, hundred and fifty-pound?!'

Jeff confirms it's a 150-pound bluefin. It's astonishing. I suddenly experience a release of tension; all the anxieties I have been storing up about my father are exorcised in that moment. This bluefin symbolises that everything is going to be OK. I sit on deck holding the fish in my arms, completely overwhelmed. I can't stop looking at every inch in admiration. The Latin name *Thunnus* means 'to dart away quickly', which is spot-on because this shinning metallic and silvery creature is made of pure muscle and is one of the fastest animals on the planet. Its design is incredible: the dorsal fin fits into a slot and comes up like a small jib when needed and then goes down again into a groove to make it streamlined, like a jet. It is beautiful, quite beautiful, but its striking eyes seem doleful and part of me is sad to have taken this creature from its home in the ocean. It's a paradox of emotions: I'm overwhelmed at the hunt but it's tinged with melancholy at the fish's sacrifice. However, nothing will go to waste and that is how we show respect for the creatures whose lives we take, by not wasting a morsel and, like the Native Americans, giving thanks in our hearts. This fish will now become a part of me, and much bigger parts of my hungry crew.

Bluefin tuna is around $40 per pound, so ours is worth over $6,000. We take a slab of the vibrant pink meat to a sushi restaurant near the harbour, where Kong the chef prepares it. He explains that the best part of the tuna for sashimi is the o-toro cut, which is the fattiest part of the belly, up near the head. It's a very pale pink meat that melts on the tongue. Other cuts are the akami, pure red meat from the back of the fish (my favourite), and chu-toro, marbled pink belly meat that is rich and buttery in taste. We eat with Tom, Jeff and the rest of crew. The sushi is delicious, among the best I have ever tasted; just like the tuna I tried off the coast of Costa Rica, it tastes clean.

Back at the hotel I have a shower and phone Dad. He is feeling better and tells me he is going to be fine. He's hoping to get 'released' tomorrow. I tell him he inadvertently saved me from another trawler journey from hell.

'Saved you from a bit of hard work, eh?' he chuckles.

I lie on the bed reflecting on how different our lives have been. Compared to his life down the pit, it is amazing how lucky I've been and I know he is very proud of me. Dad started out as a putter (pushing the coal carts), then a face worker, and worked his way up to deputy leader of a team – a role that demanded the respect of the lads underground, which he had in abundance. Whatever he asked, they delivered. However, his favourite job was looking after the pit ponies. Dad adored horses, just like his brother, Matheson. It was their shared passion.

As I lie there I swear I hear a whinny followed by a long neigh. I sit up on the bed. My mind is playing tricks. I must be exhausted. I lie back down. No, there it is again. I sit up and listen intently. Now more like a short groan, the kind of sound I make when I put my socks on in the morning. Another whinny accompanies the groan – someone's in pain. I suddenly twig: it's the elderly couple in the next room going 'at it', pensioner-style. Oh, my God! Whatever they're doing sounds sore. I head downstairs for a pint of American lager, trying to rid my head of the sepia imagery. I take a sip of my Sam Adams. I am lobster fishing tomorrow. I smile as Peter Cook and Dudley Moore's Jayne Mansfield/lobster sketch pops into my head. Now, that would be sore.

Lobster Fishing

Lobster boats go out in all weathers to get their catch, and thinking about how cold it is at the moment I opt to wear a survival suit, a special type of waterproof dry suit that will protect me from hypothermia should I end up in the drink. Unfortunately I am roasting like the proverbial trussed up like this, and when I meet Jim Ryan, he is dressed in only a pullover and waterproof dungarees, *not* a full-on survival suit. Now, unlike women, men freak out when they aren't dressed the same and at this party I have turned up wearing the wrong kit – it's embarrassing and Jim takes the piss immediately. I warm to him instantly. He is a jovial soul with a laugh like The Joker from *Batman*. For eight hours he doesn't stop laughing.

Jim and his first mate Matt harvest and bait up to 400 lobster pots a day. The forecast is for rough seas but we head out anyway. These are normal conditions for lobstermen and there is no turning back. After the curse of the *Ocean Pearl* in Canada, I laugh in the face of a mere choppy sea.

We bring up the first pot, which has two lobsters in it. Anything that has a body measuring between three and five inches is a keeper, anything smaller or larger must go back. It's only a three-man boat but there is still a pecking order. One of them catches the pots; the second job is to remove the lobsters, size them and put elastic bands around the claws to prevent the amputation of fishermen's fingers or other lobsters' pincers when they get a bit feisty, and the third job is to re-bait the pots before putting them back out to sea. Rather like Peter Mandelson or Camilla Parker Bowles, I am the third man. You'd have thought an extra pair of hands would have been helpful to a two-man crew, but in reality I am a bloody hindrance. Re-baiting is the job you give to the genetically challenged bloke – it's pretty straightforward: you fill the traps with cod skins, which are honking, and throw them back out to sea – but I *still* can't master it and am slowing the whole process down. The closed season is limited to only three months a year (January–April), which means these guys need to catch as many lobsters as possible five days a week. I fear I am beginning to have a negative effect on their bank balances.

'Jim, I'm covered in fish guts, you can't go home to your girl-friend smelling like this ... or maybe she likes the aroma of rotting herring ... cod skin and rotting herring, guaranteed a girlfriend or your money back,' I say, still baiting the pots.

Jim beams at me and cackles like The Joker. These guys absolutely reek of fish and now so do I; cod skin is in every pore. They fish all day, go to bed and then fish all the next day. I don't think they've seen a bar of soap for months. It's like when Napoleon sent the apocryphal message to Josephine: 'Home in three days. Don't wash!' So typically French. Whether it's true or not is unimportant; let's just say we all know why the French invented perfume.

Matt gets me to start bringing up the pots, and nineteen later I'm exhausted – it's tough work. Jim says: 'It's not for everyone.' He works ten hours a day, doing 400 pots five times a week, and why? Because he absolutely loves it. For some, like Peter Cook, it would be possibly 'the worst job they've ever had'.

Jim gives me a *Homarus gammarus* anatomy lesson. Each lob-ster has a crusher claw and a pincer claw, and can be left- or right-handed depending upon which side the crusher claw is on.

'The female tails are fatter and the crusher claw is smaller,' he says. He turns one over: 'See that he's got two pricks? They're hard.' He picks up a female: 'See her, she got soft ones, kind of like real life, right?'

I tell him it's a family show.

To explain more fully, lobsters have feathery appendages called swimmerets under their tail, which help them swim and also helps the female carry her eggs. The first pair of swimmerets closest to the head are soft on a female and hard on the male. These are what Jim was referring to as 'pricks'. Lobsters nest in rocky areas where they can hide, but they also burrow like rabbits in the sand and live in depths of up to 400 metres or shallower waters. Their main diet is a daily platter of *fruits de mer*: crab, mussels, clams, starfish (not the chocolate ones), marine worms, small fish and shrimp. Another bit of trivia is that the creature's anus is at tip of its tail, so bear that in mind next time you order lobster arsehole salad.

Back on dry land we cook the lobsters for a feast on the beach. The correct way to kill a lobster isn't by tossing it in a pot of boiling water, but in fact by placing it in a pan of cold water and gently heating it up. The warm water sends the lobsters to sleep before the water begins to boil, and it is a much more humane method of killing these creatures. The major pigment in lobster shell is called astaxanthin, which in live lobsters is bound to proteins that change colour, to green, greenish brown or blue. As we cook the lobster the bond between the proteins and the astaxanthin is broken down to release it to its free state and true colour: red. So now you know why their shells turn scarlet!

We settle down and eat our bounty. Jim and Matt cover theirs in loads of butter ('Butter makes everything better,' Jim smiles.) I have mine steamed with a hint of lemon, just like I do at J. Sheekey's in London. I'm such a ponce. They slurp the butter like gravy, dipping their bread in it. The lobster tastes remarkable, not that they'd know it as they may as well have had Krispy Kreme doughnuts with theirs. I suppose eating lobster gets boring after a while. I'm glad there's such a good perk to a very tough job.

Wild Bass Chase

Cape Cod isn't all about heading out into the wild Atlantic; some great fish lurk in the creeks and rivers that feed the Cape. However, winter's on the way and finding fish that haven't migrated south yet is going to be a real challenge. I meet Mike Rice, who will be showing me where to catch striped bass. The thing I love about the striper is that it's covered in black and white stripes just like my beloved football team, Newcastle. To catch a Geordie of the ocean is my destiny.

I shake hands with Mike, a good-looking, charismatic, lean guy who reminds me of Jon Bon Jovi. At this time of year, the local fishermen here have to cooperate on an almost military level to maximise their chances of catching, so we join Mike's fishing buddies, Brian, Pete and Scotty, to discuss strategy.

'So, what's the plan, Mike?' I ask.

Mike's all over it: 'What we'll do is split up. Pete's going to one area, Scotty's going to another, we're going to go to a small creek. They're all pretty close, within twenty minutes of each other, so if one spot starts to get active we can jump in the truck and be there pretty quick.'

These fishermen tell us the striped bass are in their thousands in this area and it's just a matter of finding them. I'm excited – the chase is on! Mike and I head for Scorton Creek, which is flat and marshy but conditions are perfect for catching bass on the fly. The light is constant and not too bright, and I'm starting to feel pretty confident.

After three or so hours of relentless casting I am tired and very bored. 'I don't think there's anything here,' I say to Mike. 'But you know it's not just about catching fish, is it?'

'No. It's about being out here,' he replies.

'And the companionship,' I add.

'Some of my best days on the water have been when I haven't caught a thing,' he says nonchalantly. Alarm bells ring in my head. I remind him I've travelled 4,000 miles.

'I've got a wife and kids, Mike. A personal reputation. There's a career at stake here,' I say.

Mike knows I'm not going to be dicked around on some kind of wild bass chase. He is under pressure so he checks to see how the others are doing. Brian's caught and released a fourteen-inch shad. If shad are feeding, the bass could be, too. Time to head to Brian's spot to see if we have better luck there. We arrive at Sandwich Harbour and the first thing I see is a seal. This is not a good sign as they like to eat all the fish, but the other lads caught here earlier so we decide to stay in spite of the competition.

We cast our lines out again and again in the hope that maybe, just maybe, we'll bang into some striped bass. Twenty minutes later it looks as if Mike's hooked something. The seal is interested, too.

'That seal's just gone for Mike's fish,' I say to camera. 'It's just gone for Mike's fish! Oh, he's right here, he's right in front of me. Look at him. Lovely to look at, but at the moment that seal's a right bastard.'

Jamie wants me to deliver more lines about the seal to camera while the pinniped (from the Latin *pinna*, 'fin', and *ped*, 'foot') is still in shot. I continue: 'People may look at the image of a seal and think, "What a wonderful, inspiring sight" – but to an angler they are a menace as they scare off all the fish and, surprise, surprise, today our fate is sealed. There's no bloody fish here!'

In the middle of the take a car pulls up in between me and the camera on the road behind. A guy jumps out.

'Hey, guys, you makin' a movie?' he asks in a distinctive Brooklyn drawl. 'The name's Mike, from Mike's Automobile Collectibles. How yoo dooin'? What's the movie called?'

'Well, Mike, thanks for destroying our take. It's called *Extreme Fishing with Robson Green*,' I say, grinning at Jamie, who is looking distinctly pissed off.

'That's awesome. Who's Robson?'

'Take a wild guess, Mike.'

'You're Robson? That's awesome! Here, I got some caps for you all with my logo on it! Google me. I buy and sell old cars . . . I'm *on* the Internet. I've had four hundred thousand hits!'

'I think you're *on* drugs, Mike . . . Could you please get out of my shot?'

'Have a keyring and my card. You guys are awesome . . . Robson, we definitely got something going here,' he says, shaking my hand.

'Yes, Mike, it's called mild irritation,' I say, putting on one of his hats.

He gives us a wave, jumps in the car and drives off. Basically he wanted me to plug his company on the programme – and actually, you know what, you have to applaud the guy's chutzpah. Mike is going all the way! However, had my dad been here he would definitely have chinned him! I chuckle at the scene in my head of Big Rob throwing Mike across the bonnet of his own car. I look round at fisherman Mike and imagine doing the same to him. I'm beginning to get tired of being Yanked around.

After another fruitless hour we are heading back to Scorton

Creek, again. Morale is low and everyone is frustrated. In the truck, I try to lighten the mood by regaling Mike with tales from my glittering music career.

'The act was called Robson and Jerome. We knew we had to stop when a woman brought her two guinea pigs, Robson and Jerome, on a show called *Animal Hospital*. Rolf Harris says, "What's wrong?" She says, "It's Robson, he's not right." And then, in front of millions, Robson wobbles about on his back, fitting. Rolf says, "There's only one thing to do about this poor little fella." The vet gets a large needle out and live on TV they put him down. Robson died! My mum rang up, "Have you seen you're on the other side? You're a guinea pig." "*Was* a guinea pig, Mum." And in that moment I realised that's exactly what I had been – Simon Cowell's bloody guinea pig. Thankfully I've moved on (considerably richer) and he's now practising vivisection on One Direction.'

Mike is completely uninterested in my stories and I miss Jim the Joker. He was my type of guy – laughed at anything.

It's three o'clock when we arrive back at the creek. The tide is in and everyone thinks this is now *the* place to hook a striped bass. I'm determined to be the first to get one. But as the light starts to fade, none of us has caught a single fish. I've been thrashing the water for six hours, my hand is blistered and it looks like the bass have buggered off.

'Where's the bass, Mike?' I yell.

Mike and his mates conclude that we have missed them and they will already have travelled south. Defeated, we head back to the hotel. On the way we pass a psychic's 'salon'. Jamie and I look at one another. It's time for drastic measures. We are now willing to try *anything*.

The Clairvoyant

The next morning I find out that Dad is being released from hospital. He's got to have a stent fitted and possibly undergo a bypass but at the moment, owing to flu-like symptoms and a kidney infection, he's not well enough for surgery but he is well enough to go home. I can't wait to see him. Perhaps the lady I am seeing next will tell me exactly when that will be.

We walk into the psychic salon and meet Tammy the psychic. I shake hands with the buxom blonde, who is a cross between Doris Day and Kirstie Alley at the height of her drink and junk-food problem. She looks into my eyes, still holding my hand, and no word of a lie says, 'How's your father?' I gasp. Now, on reflection of her subsequent bonkers behaviour, I've taken this to possibly be less a comment about Dad's heart attack and more a how's-yer-father, nudge-nudge, wink-wink, fancy-a-bit scenario. Either way, this whole psychic thing is playing tricks on my mind. We sit down at a table and Tammy reads my palms, her tarot cards and my mind. She looks into my eyes seductively.

'Robson, I honestly believe, on this journey, you are in a location where you are destined to be, but you're not in the right spot. There is a spot and you will find what you are searching for. You're going to become a winner – you always have been, and you always will be. You're a lover, not a fighter. You will succeed in what you're looking for.'

I only hear the words 'winner' and 'lover'.

Robson: 'Tammy, can I ask you a question?'

Tammy: 'Sure, sugar.'

Robson: 'Will you be my agent? No one has ever said those things to me. And if not my agent, will you marry me?'

Quick as a flash she gives me her ring.

Tammy: 'Yes, here's a ring. Just put it on me.'

I suddenly realise I'm in unchartered and dangerous waters here. She wants my number . . . so I give her Jonathan's. Thinking it's mine, she clutches it to her enormous bosoms. What on earth have I done? *You haven't bloody thought it through again, that's what,* cranks up my inner monologue. *You have just asked a lonely woman of a certain age to marry you and she doesn't see it as a joke; she thinks you are her white knight finally come to free her from the shackles of perpetual loneliness and suffering, like Prometheus bound to the mountain every day, an eagle pecking at her liver. And then you ride into town and offer her a glimpse of hope to break the bonds and stop the pain. You bloody fool, you've really gone and done it now.*

Tammy ends her reading by saying: 'You are not catching fish because the fish have moved. You need to follow the fish.'

Jamie: 'That's brilliant – she's a genius.'

'*I* could have told you that!'

But Jamie is already out the door shouting, 'Follow the fish!'

Back at the hotel it's all hands on deck as we plot where the fish have gone and how we're going to locate them. Mike and his gang think they have moved to Manhattan, and that's exactly where Jamie wants to go. I'm not so sure it's a good idea but he wants to shoot the unfolding story of us trying to track down these elusive stripers. Jamie calls Hamish in Glasgow, who thinks it's a brilliant idea, so it's settled: we're going to New York.

'Are we going to fly there?' I ask.

Jamie: 'No. We are going by van.'

Robson: 'What? But it's miles!'

Jamie: 'No, it's less than an inch on the map.'

Robson: 'Jamie, this is America!'

I am reminded that there is no money left in the budget because of me. I shut up.

Jonathan's phone rings. He answers. It's Tammy-the-psychic trying to get hold of me! I signal that I am not here, shaking my head vigorously. He tells her I'm unavailable. She calls back a few more times but by late afternoon the calls have stopped, and we think she has got the message that I don't really want to marry her.

Later that evening we wander down to the hotel bar to get a few drinks and something to eat. Standing in the lobby is Tammy. Before she sees me, I turn and leg it up the stairs, leaving Jonathan to deal with her, again. She tells him she really needs to talk to me. Jonathan tells her I'm not here. She says that's not true because she's been waiting out in her car and she knows I haven't left the building. She's been staking me out! Jonathan finally persuades her to go and we hit the bar. It has slightly freaked me out but then I think, if she'd been any good at clairvoyance, she should always have been ahead of me. Now that would be scary.

The next day we embark on a nine-hour road trip to New York in a van. I'm dreading it but it actually turns out to be one of the nicest journeys I have had. We really bond as a team, stopping to eat burgers and nachos and all kinds of other really bad junk food, and singing songs. We are all squished in – well, they are. I am at the front, of course. It's the *Extreme* boy band on tour.

The next morning, our new striped bass expert finds us in the restaurant of the hotel having breakfast.

'They're here,' says Tooch in a sharp Bronx accent.

He looks like a character out of *The Sopranos*. We head over with him to Sandy Hook Bay and meet his friend Brian. It's very early but these guys are wide awake and bang up for action. As we head out across the sparkling water on a small speedboat, the hazy silhouette of New York's skyline unfolds in front of us like a giant poster ... Wow. It's awesome to be here, especially as Brian tells me we are definitely going to catch striped bass today. Brian receives a text from another local fisherman: the bite is on and we're heading at full-throttle to the spot. We have found the fishing G-Spot, as foretold by the Boston stalker, and I'm excited about going in for a tackle against the Alan Shearer of the ocean.

The birds are feeding and the bass are here in their thousands. Unlike trying to catch the bass on the fly, as I did with Mike (even though they were here all the bleeding time), today we're not taking any chances. We are sinking lines and using toby lures to try to tempt the fish. Brian says that if we want to eat tonight this is the most practical method – there's no time for purist sentiment on this boat, I want me a striped bass! If dynamite were another option I'd have gone for that as well.

Ten minutes later Tooch has a striper on the end of his line. The camera crew and I are ecstatic. Brian and Tooch are taken aback by our reaction. Tooch's fish has to go back, as the legal size is twenty-eight inches, but it's a stunner, a piscatorial zebra.

At last I get a bass on the end of my line as well. It fights like a rainbow trout, as it's strong, fast and likes to run. It's crucial I keep my line tight and don't put too much drag on it or the fish will come off. After a couple of runs, including one under the boat, the fish tires and I reel him in. He shoots! He scores! He lands a bass! Sadly it's too small to keep so I have to release it, but what a stunner. It's like a skipjack tuna but stretched. Under the water they appear dark green but in the light you can see the black and white curved stripes. I pop it back. I don't mind; I'm one very happy fisherman.

With the Empire State Building in the background, it's a fantastic end to a fantastic trip. Don't go to New York for the shopping – go for the fishing.

A week later, back in the UK, Dad is as right as rain. I visit him at his huge eight-berth caravan near Bamborough Castle, where he lives with his girlfriend of seven years, Yvonne. He loves the outdoors and would have had us all growing up in a caravan if he'd had his way.

'Are you taking it easy, Dad?'

'Yes, Robo. I'm drinking less, which is a bloody shame but I did have a swift pint at the Black Bull last night with Plum. First time out since the attack, mind. Plum says to me: "Big Rob, your lad's never off the TV." I said: "I know, we call it interference."'

Chapter Six

THE PHILIPPINES

Robson Crusoe

February 2009, Series 2

Hamish Barbour and I are enjoying a good lunch at the Two Fat Ladies in Glasgow, talking about the possibilities of Series 2. We gulp more wine and come up with a few ideas, Hamish as excitable as ever. I regard him across the table – he looks like a Swan Vestas match, with his tight red hair and pale lean body from all those triathlons he does at the weekends. The comparison suits his personality, too. He ignites all the programme ideas by slowly getting the wet logs (the TV suits) to light up about something, anything. It's an unenviable task and he almost burns himself out trying to get them to finally spark. I suppose Hamish is a creative firestarter; if he had crazier hair and Keith from The Prodigy had an eating disorder, they could be twins.

'What about *Robson Crusoe?*' says Hamish, combusting, 'You

are cast away for twenty-four hours and have to survive on your own, using all the skills you've learnt to feed yourself from the ocean?'

'Fantastic! But maybe I should do it for seventy-two hours because I have learnt a lot, Hamish. I think I really would be fine for that amount of time. A bit loopy, granted, but fine. I've been watching a lot of Ray Mears, which should come in handy.'

'Great. Great. Twenty-four hours will be fine, Robson. I'll get Helen Nightingale [the series producer] to set it up. [To the waiter] Can we have the bill, please?'

The NeverEnding Journey

The *Extreme* team and I are travelling 7,000 miles to the 7,107-island archipelago of the Philippines, on the western edge of the Pacific Ocean. It's a three-day journey and Jamie Goold wants to film the first few minutes of the show on my diary cam. He says I'm not to shave because I need to film the intensity of the journey and its effect on me. Well, thanks, Jamie. It's the first time I've thought 'Fuck me, I'm middle-aged' and it's depressing. I'm entering the autumn of my years but today it looks like bleak midwinter. Jamie, Craig Herd (a Kiwi cameraman), and Peter Prada, the soundman who from this point on becomes part of the *Extreme Fishing* furniture, are with me on this odyssey. We travel via three different planes, each getting progressively smaller, until the smallest finally takes us to Manila. It's a terrifying flight and I'm glad it's over.

As we drive through the capital in a brightly painted minibus I realise that we couldn't be any more conspicuous. The city is a chaotic mixture of traffic, noise and humidity. Thousands of tuk-tuks, all beeping, zoom down the streets, there are minibuses crammed full of people, high-rise flats line either side of the road, and there is a hot, damp smell of fuel, drains and people. Every time we stop in traffic, the locals stare at us. It's a place where you need to look like you know where you are going, because if you don't, urban predators will smell your fear. This is a Third World country with Third World problems, including great poverty, corruption and violent crime, and because of that we have a team of security guys to look after us and they are tooled up to the max. I later find out that the kidnapping of Westerners for ransom is fairly common.

As we approach the edge of the city, Jamie reveals that he wants to film the rest of the journey with me travelling in a tuk-tuk behind the van. So while the rest of the crew are sitting in relative luxury, I am forced to endure a three-hour noisy and very bumpy journey to the coast southeast of Manila. It's like taking a motorised chair from Newcastle to Liverpool. When we finally arrive, my bottom is numb and I'm feeling cranky but it's straight onto a boat for another three hours, heading to our final destination: the teardrop island of Siargao in Surigao del Norte province in the Philippines Sea.

It's an open-topped boat and we've barely left port when it starts to pee it down. We are not prepared – no one is. Even though we are filming a TV show, the fixer has overlooked the fact that we would have all of our camera equipment with us. In order to save the thousands of pounds' worth of recording equipment, we are forced to surrender our waterproofs and get soaked through. It's like a hairy wet T-shirt competition on board. I feel sick. Apparently it rains a lot here. *Maybe staying on a desert island for twenty-four hours is not such a good idea*, I think. *Rubbish, it'll be fine, you big Jessie*, replies the other voice within.

*

Siargao is a tropical paradise, white sand and a clear blue sea, as well as dense mangrove forest and wetlands that help protect costal areas from erosion and storm surge. We are staying at one of the Philippines' best-kept secrets, the Pansukian Tropical Resort. This place is so amazing and opulent that even the president stays here. I'm staying in his room, aptly named the Presidential Suite, where there's enough space to swing a cat, a dog and a bleeding horse, and all the crew's 'quarters' are the same: absolutely massive. It's been well worth the ball-breaking effort to get here. I clean my teeth and look in the mirror. I am dishevelled and look so much like my dad, who has thankfully now made a full recovery and is back up to flying speed. *Why do we have to perish and decay?* I wonder. Still, at least with age some other things have improved, like my monobrow now being consigned to the past. I didn't even know I had one until I started dating Vanya. Pretty much after our first date she attacked me with tweezers. I used to look like Frida Khalo and didn't even know it.

Before Tweezers   *After Tweezers*

With that thought in mind, I crawl into bed and black out.

*

I wake up at 6 a.m. and walk outside onto the verandah. The ocean is twenty metres from my door, iron flat and turquoise, with only beach between us. Men, women and kids are fishing in bancas, traditional dugout canoes with crude bamboo outriggers to keep them stable. They are all using basic hand line methods, about a dozen of them floating in the shallows pulling up fish. It's wonderful to see, but these families are not fishing as a hobby – it's a way of life and they need to put food on the table. Jobs are hard to come by in the area and people live off the land as well as the ocean, growing rice and breeding animals. To most people here, every day is about survival.

Junior

I meet Junior Gonzalez, one of the finest fishermen on the island, I'm told. There are loads of fish here and they are varied but, as I discover, they are very small. The locals either eat them or sell them at the market. Junior has no technology to help him catch fish, no GPS, no sounder, no mobile phone, no two-way radio and not even a compass. He does what families have done for generations in Siargao: he relies on his knowledge of the stars, landmarks, tides, the weather and the moon. He also uses bird life to guide the boat, knowing certain species never fly far from the shore, and high birds or feeding birds mean fish. Low-flying birds, skimming the waves, tend to be just passing through, using the air from the waves to save energy on their journey.

Junior has fished like this since he was a little boy. He appears to be around sixty years of age but could be younger; he has a face that is well lived-in. We head out on Junior's banca, which looks more like a tourist river boat that he's hurriedly converted into a fishing vessel by putting a couple of pipes on it to hold rods and the odd plank to rest your feet against. Junior's six-teen-year-old son, Grieshan, is in another banca and to be honest I've got ship envy. His is way better.

Junior starts the engines. It sounds like a cross-channel ferry – the fish will hear us coming from about twenty-two miles away – and I stick my fingers in my ears. We get a gentle speed up but the boat is all over the place, rocking and lurching. Thankfully it doesn't matter too much today as we're staying 500 metres from the shore, but tomorrow we'll be travelling to the Philippine Trench. I hope he's got a bigger boat. At a maximum known depth of 6.54 miles, the trench is the third-deepest body of water in the world, the deepest being the Mariana Trench, near Guam, which is 6.86 miles deep. It's mind-blowing stuff, like considering the size of the universe and what it all means when you're really, really tired. It's so much to ponder that it makes me feel queasy. But then again, that's probably just Junior's crappy boat.

We try to fish from the diesel-glugging beast but to no avail. I look over the way – young Grieshan is hauling them in. I suggest, very strongly, that we change boats, and my request is granted. As we head back to shore, Junior tells me a story of the time he went out with Grieshan, aged four, to catch a swordfish. Swordfish are nocturnal deepwater fish so are caught at night when they come up to feed on squid. He was forty miles out over the Philippine Trench in an oversized canoe with a toddler and no GPS, radio or phone, in the middle of the night, when the mother of all storms hits. Storms in this area tend to come very fast and out of nowhere. Junior and Grieshan are tossed about in their banca until it's eventually smashed to smithereens and sinks. Never letting go of his son's hand for one second, he flings Grieshan on his back and, clinging to a piece of wood, begins to slowly swim and float to shore. Since that day they have been inseparable. It's an amazing tale that completely blows *Life of Pi* out of the water.

I switch boats.

'This one's much better, Junior!' I say.

He smiles. It's quieter, too, which is what we need to catch coral reef species and pelagic fish that live near the surface of the ocean, not the bottom. We're hoping for wahoo or maya maya (red snapper) to come our way. The red snapper is a beautiful red fish, which strangely makes it an excellent predator, because in the underwater spectrum of light, red isn't seen, so the fish is almost invisible.

Nine hours later, I finally get a bite. It's a dog tooth tuna and it's not coming in easily. It's fighting the current and the speed of the boat, and even though it's small it's still quite strong. It's a hard fish to land and I don't want to get my fingers anywhere near its ferocious canines. A member of the *Scombridae* family – not a mad Highland clan but a subclassification of fish that includes bonitos, mackerels and tuna – the dog tooth tuna, in spite of its name, has more in common with its bonito cousins than with pure tunas. It's fast in the water but it's the impact and bite that kills the prey. *One down,* I think to myself

My next fish comes five minutes later. It's a good fighting fish and we have a decent tussle. I reel it in but am unfamiliar with the species. Junior calls it an 'oyung-oyung'. It's definitely my first one of those. I manage to land it. It's a strong, compact fish with a powerful jaw lined with triangular razor teeth and a blue-green skin. Junior tells me that in English it's called a bluefish. Bluefish are found all around the world in coastal areas favouring continental shelves, surf beaches or rocky headland. (I've got a continental shelf problem: everything's on the way down.)

My mood has soared and we all head en masse to the market to see what we can get for this brace of fish. I tell Junior about my desert island experience in two days' time and he says, 'Robson you are a natural, you could survive on any one of these islands.' Then he gives me double thumbs-up. I am optimistic. *I am actually really good*, I think.

At the small open-air market I get 200 pesos, about three quid, for our catch. I give the cash to the children of the locals who have gathered around to watch us film and everyone's happy. The people here are incredibly charming and friendly in spite of their abject poverty. It's paradise here but surviving in paradise is far from easy. I'm sure I'll be OK for a day and night, however.

Port Pilar Harbour

Today we're heading out to the mighty Philippine Trench forty miles from the shore, and our target is dorado. I have the idea that we will only eat what we catch for breakfast, lunch and dinner. We have cooking facilities on board our fishing boat and I intend to show off my culinary skills like a Northern Rick Stein. The four deckhands, wearing classic lampshade hats, ask me if they can bring some food on just in case. I say, 'No way. We'll catch loads of fish. I caught two in five minutes yesterday.'

'Yeah, after nine hours.'

'Shut up, Craig. Right, everyone turn out their pockets for contraband. If this show's going to be a success we have to play by the rules. I don't have anything on me. Does anyone else?'

They shake their heads.

'Are you sure?'

They nod.

'Good.'

We set out to the trench. I am experiencing a great high today. The sun is shining; life is good. Deep down, I wonder if I am experiencing one of my manic episodes but I don't think so. I breathe in the air. *I am a fishing god*, I tell myself, and I am buzzing with energy and chat. As we are trawling, Junior explains he is looking for bird life, floating debris, which makes false reefs, or any other natural indicators that put us in the right place for a magnificent dorado. We are fishing as nature intended and I can't wait for our first strike.

Junior says, 'One year I went fishing every day of the year to work out the best days.'

'Three hundred and sixty-five days? Wow. And what did you discover?'

'The fourth day before a new moon is the best.'

'Is that today?'

'No,' he laughs.

I suss out the tiny kitchen area, which is basic and no more than two feet wide. As I leave a deckhand enters and places something quickly in a cupboard. I open the door and find a tin of corned beef inside. I look at him.

'Oh, ye of little faith. I'm very disappointed. That's really bad.'

He looks at me sheepishly. The four of them go into a huddle talking in Filipino, probably calling me a name used by British carp fishermen.

*

Six hours later I am feeling like a prize James Blunt, as we have got nothing. The sea is getting lumpy and the sun is due to set in seven hours' time, which seems a long way away but we need to get back to shore in that time.

Jamie says firmly, 'We have to catch a fish and we'll stay here all night if necessary.'

We are starving, I'm feeling faint and I am getting some filthy looks from the crew. I sidle up to the one with the corned beef – I can't remember his name so let's call him David.

'Psst, David. How much for the tin of beef?'

'What?'

'How much?'

We are very subtle; it's like scoring shabú – methamphetamine pills – the drug of choice in South East Asia. I give him a large amount of pesos and wander casually down to the toilet to gorge my contraband. After seven hours of nothing to eat it doesn't touch the sides. As I wander out, Craig catches me.

'You bastard. You fucking sneaky bastard.'

I start to giggle nervously. Craig is furious.

'Jamie! Peter! Robson's just snaffled a whole tin of corned beef.'

I walk upstairs. Peter looks grey with hunger and Jamie regards me like a bitterly disappointed teacher. But I feel much better. I have a new lease of life.

Another seven hours later the effects of the corned beef have worn off and we still haven't had even a sniff of a fish. If I thought I looked bad when I arrived, I now look like I'm decomposing. I hear a rustle and see Craig open a bag of crisps.

'Where d'you get those?'

'Wouldn't you like to know?'

He shares them with everyone apart from me in retaliation for the bully beef. Craig produces another bag of crisps, again none for me. He eyeballs me, munching mouthful after mouthful. I ignore him and talk to Junior.

'Well, the fishing's been great but the catching's been appalling.'

Junior says, 'In all my years of fishing, this has been one of my worst days.'

I believe him. I am a jinx and a corn beef criminal. Suddenly, two terns appear above us out of nowhere. Junior points; they are flying high – they have seen something. We see it too: it's driftwood, no more than eight feet long and six inches in diameter. Junior turns the boat around; we trawl the lines past it, and bang! I'm into a mahi-mahi. Also known as a dorado or dolphinfish, this creature's brain size in proportion to its body is large. Some say this is one of the most intelligent species of fish as it can follow simple instructions, but I say, 'Did they invent the internal combustion engine? Was Pythagoras a dorado? Let's put it in perspective.' They're about as bright as a Sunderland Supporter after a heavy weekend on the piss.

As I wind in the dorado, he comes to the surface and leaps. He's magnificent, his vibrant green, gold and blue skin glistening in the setting sun. Dorados fight hard and they fight aerially. He jumps again like a Lycra-clad acrobat doing somersaults. Morale has soared, the crew is going to eat and it's going to be delicious.

I shout, 'I have caught us supper. You all doubted me but I did it!'

The aerial fight cranks up a notch; I must bring this fish in. I give it one last leap and he jumps off the hook and is gone. The crew is catatonic with shock and I am in the seventh circle of hell, but Jamie is going mental, shouting, 'That was fucking brilliant!

One of the best sequences I have ever filmed. The under-fish triumphed – adversity works so well on telly.'

We all want to deck him.

'Fuck the programme! We want something to eat.'

I am so pissed off with myself. The deckhands won't look at me, especially the one who sold me the corned beef. He's visibly stiffened with internal rage. To make matters worse, Jamie declares he wants us to fish into the night and catch a swordfish. We beg him to let us go home but the footage has given him a second wind. He gives me a piece of bread.

'Thank you, master,' I snivel.

But Junior has a cunning plan. We are going to drop a line for swordfish very deep, and with six miles below us we're never going to touch the bottom. We bait the rod, which is huge and a bit like a marlin rod. The swordfish is a billfish and is known as one of the 'big five', along with blue marlin, black marlin, striped marlin and sailfish. This striking, dark grey fish has huge black eyes, which help it to see in the deep water over half a mile below the surface, where it resides in the daytime. Its bill is massive in proportion to its body, which it uses like a sword to cut down its prey. It is thus known as the gladiator of the sea, from its name *Xiphias gladius* (from the Latin *gladius*, meaning 'sword').

To help us catch, Junior lets the boat drift using the wind. In order to slow a conventional boat down, skippers use something called a drogue – an underwater parachute that impedes forward motion. Junior doesn't have a drogue because he can't afford one, so ingeniously he uses palm leaves, tied in such a way that they have the same effect. He says nature always solves the problem of a lack of technology. The second part of Junior's plan is to use two kerosene lamps to try to attract squid. We use a lure like a plastic shrimp with upturned barbs on the end. I drop it ten metres and slowly pull it up towards me. I do this about a hundred times before I finally catch a cephalopod (Ancient Greek for 'head-feet', as these creatures have no body). The squid I pull up is seven inches in length and basically a meal for one. By this time I am so tired and hungry I am starting to hallucinate. Junior suggests we use my one and only squid as bait.

I say, 'But I don't want to use it as bait, I want to eat it.'

He says, 'We will catch many with that one.'

I do as I am told and I slowly pull up the hand line.

'Oh, my God, I have got another one!' I cry.

'It's the same bloody one!' everyone replies in unison.

All in all, I catch two. Fishing for swordfish has been a complete disaster. It's the wrong conditions and by 3 a.m. we've all had enough. We've been twenty-two hours without a proper meal and Craig is beginning to gnaw the edge of the boat, like a pony on its stable door. He's started to kick the side of the boat as well; he is not a happy pony. He is even unhappier when, after finally reaching land, he hops out of the boat and promptly breaks his ankle. Cameramen with broken ankles are not good news, but luckily, unlike ponies, he can be mended and not shot.

The doctor back at the hotel bandages it up and tells Craig not to walk on it. We could have saved him a job and the production company a call-out fee. The fixer, Enrico, steps in: 'It's OK, guys. I know how to operate a camera.'

Thank God for that – we can sleep easy now.

'Ooh, looks sore. You OK, mate?' I say sympathetically to Craig.

'Yeah, it's just bloody annoying.'

'Get some rest. [pause] Oh, and Craig, by the way, your broken ankle – it's all about karma. That was for the second bag of crisps. The first bag of crisps was fine. We were even. Level playing field. But not sharing the second, you Kiwi bum pirate? The universe knows, Craig. The universe knows.'

And the universe does indeed know because, back in my room, as I deliver my final piece to camera about how exhausted I am, a bug starts flying around my head, dive-bombing me like a kamikaze pilot. Argh! It's a beetle the size of a blackbird.

'Go away!'

I get a wet hand towel and start to flick at the air, incandescent with fury. Neeeoooooowwww! It goes into flat spin like a World War II bomber at my head, pulling out just before crashing into my ear. I fight back for another ten minutes, waving what I later realised was basically a white flag around my head, before passing out fully clothed and face down on my bed. God knows what it did to me that night. I don't want to think about it.

I'm feeling like shit the next day but if I'm slightly off colour it's nothing to the pain poor old Craig is in. However, he carries on like a true champion cameraman. We're going out by boat to a small island called Kasulian with a guy called Charlito. This area has been declared fishing-free, to encourage fish stocks to recover, and the initiative is going so well we've been given special clearance to fish here – just enough for our supper.

I'm on a banca again and this time we're using hermit crabs as bait. The crabs live in beautiful shells that are shaped like the ice-cream part of a Mr Whippy. Cruelly we have to tease them out and then use them as live bait on our hand lines, but this is what the locals do and I'm not here to judge, I'm here to learn.

'Charlito, I've seen some hermit crabs in my time but these are enormous.'

I look into the turquoise waters at the reef below where I can see there is an abundance of coral reef fish but none is more than three inches in size. We throw out the hand lines while Craig films everything from a special chair. If you watch the sequence you'll see everything is shot from chest height!

Looking into the sea below, it's like a tropical aquarium. We can't be eating these, surely?

'Charlito, they're a bit small, don't you think?'

'Then we need many,' he says.

The hand lining is not going according to plan, mainly because the crabs are four inches bigger than the fish and our bait is actually scaring the fish away! Charlito is becoming restless. Suddenly he produces an enormous spear gun out of nowhere.

'Let's go snorkelling!' he commands.

What is so impressive is that he's made his entire diving kit himself, including his goggles from discarded rubber and plastic for the lenses, and his flippers, which are wooden panels attached to his feet. I decide to be a spectator today. What I'm about to witness is akin to blasting a sparrow with a twelve-bore shotgun. The head of the spear gun is bigger than some of the fish! It doesn't feel right to me but it's completely normal to Charlito, and, more importantly, it works. It's a crude method but it gets results – and the fish he needs to feed his sizeable family.

We eat five of these pretty fish-tank fish each with casaba, a type of muskmelon that is grown on the island and looks like a honeydew but tastes more like a potato. The fish taste nice enough but it truly is like eating Nemo.

*

Back at the hotel, I decide to do some research on why the fish are so small in this area and stocks so depleted. I find my answer swiftly: it's all down to dynamite fishing, a method whereby desperate people can kill whole shoals in one go with a lump of dynamite and an accurate throw. But it's disastrous long-term as whole reefs are disappearing and thus ecosystems are wiped out. And reefs take a very long time to recover. Dynamite fishing is illegal but sadly it's going on all over the Philippines.

This afternoon the production team has arranged for me to meet an ex-dynamite fisherman who is now helping to educate other fishermen about the importance of protecting the reefs. We travel to a very different part of the island from where our hotel is located. It's a poor, dusty village with a collection of sparse shanty huts. We are greeted by Tootya Alvarez, who did six months inside for dynamite fishing, and his judge, Bimbi, who translates for me. As we walk towards a lagoon that Tootya and others destroyed, he tells me, 'I did it because it's very easy to catch fish. We can catch a large amount and it will be big money for us.' And do you know what? If I were in the same position as Tootya I'd probably do it, too. It's a means of escape from poverty.

'How much of the reef has disappeared because of dynamite fishing?' I ask.

'Outside the lagoon, the reefs are not good anymore because they are already annihilated, but inside the corals are starting to grow already,' says Tootya.

Thankfully, with the help of local investment and efforts to conserve the reefs by former dynamite fishermen like Tootya, attempts are now being made to help the damaged reefs to recover. It is now illegal to fish in certain areas, such as the one I went to with Charlito after permissions were granted. This work needs to continue or a bad situation could, further down the line, turn into an environmental and humanitarian crisis, where the local people literally have *no* fish to live on.

Desert Island

Late next morning we leave Siargao. It's castaway time and I will be living on a desert island completely on my own for twenty-four hours. I'm apprehensive but also really looking forward to getting away from this smelly crisp-munching rabble. Craig's ankle is still buggered so we've left him behind and brought our back-up cameraman, fixer Enrico, with us.

We are heading south to the uninhabited island of Tabili. Two hours into the boat trip and I'm beginning to think this is a really stupid idea.

'How far away is it?' I ask.

'About another half an hour,' says Jamie.

'What? You mean I'm two and half hours away from civilisation and, more importantly, help? I thought I'd be just across the way like Lindisfarne to Seahouses and if, for whatever reason, I needed to swim back I could! I'm going to be miles out, in the middle of the Pacific all on my own. What the hell have I signed up to? This isn't funny.'

We arrive at Tabili. It's basically a mound of sand with a few palm trees. I beat my chest in an attempt try to knock down my growing anxiety. *Don't worry*, I tell myself, *you're the Ray Mears of the North.* You *are Ray Mears!*

Are you out of your fucking mind? comes the reply. *That's like saying Dame Judi's bloody Bruce Parry.*

We start shooting some footage of me preparing for the next

twenty-four hours and it quickly becomes apparent that, although Enrico is a lovely guy, he's perhaps not a natural behind the camera. Jamie is getting increasingly agitated but we muddle on as best we can. In the end, Jamie decides that the best solution is to shoot the whole of the island sequence on my diary camera, and with that said everyone buggers off on the boat, heading straight to the hotel bar, where it's trebles all round. I watch the boat become a speck in the distance. I am alone with only my camera and my thoughts. It's a weird feeling but the sun is setting so I need to be practical and make a fire. I gather together firewood that I collected earlier and, using coconut husks as kindling, create a small fire. Well, it's easy when you know how and you have a Bic lighter.

My next task is to make some kind of shelter. Ray Mears made a bivouac on his show so I'm going to do the same, but the light is fading. I um and ah before deciding it might be better to catch some food first. So what's on tonight's menu at the Castaway Café? I could catch a few crabs, or I could cast a line for some small reef fish similar to the ones I caught with Charlito. I walk along the water's edge, half-heartedly looking for crabs. What am I doing here? This is crackers. I think about casting a line out and then I have a much better idea. Hidden among the few supplies I've been allowed to bring is a bottle of white wine and a corkscrew.

I find a coconut and draw a face on it in homage to Tom Hanks in *Castaway*, set up the camera and open the bottle of Chablis. As the last of the light fades, I raise a toast to my new date, Julia (after Julia Roberts, because of her massive mouth). I take a sip of the wine and then drain the contents of the glass. I pour another and another.

'That's better,' I say to Julia. 'It's all a bit more fun now I'm getting pissed.'

As I finish the bottle, and open the Sauvignon Blanc, I start talking nonsense to the coconut and the camera.

'Have you heard of the notion that many dog-owners look like their pets, Julia? Well, they tried an experiment to see how true it was. They took an architect and his dog, an engineer and his dog and an actor and his dog, and under laboratory conditions tested to see how each reacted to a pile of bones in the middle of the room. The engineer's dog goes first and makes a complex cog system with gears, reflecting the behaviour of the owner. The architect's dog constructs a bridge. Next up is the actor's dog. He eats all the bones, fucks the other two dogs and asks for the rest of the day off.'

I roll around laughing but Julia is po-faced.

'You need to lighten up, Jules, have some fun.'

I reel off my CV, and she tells me hers. I feel inadequate but quite horny. I think I'm in with a chance with Jules when suddenly there is a loud clatter of thunder. Boom! As if someone's lifted a grand piano and dropped it. Immediately the heavens open. It's not a light shower but rain of biblical proportions, like someone has a hose over my head and I haven't made a fucking shelter and – shit! The cameras! I manage to get the Z-camera, batteries and the diary cam wrapped up in my waterproof coat. The fire is well and truly out, one torch has died and the other is on life support. I take a swig from the bottle of wine, grab Julia and stumble over to shelter under one of the coconut palms. What the fuck am I doing here?

It pours and it pours and it pours down for over four long and lonely hours and then that's when the REALLY BIG storm hits, and with it there is thunder, sheet lightning and, of course, more rain. The water takes out all the batteries and the Z-camera so all I have is my diary cam. I am soaked to the skin and sozzled and I want to go home – this isn't funny anymore. The only connection I have with the outside world is a satellite phone so I ring Jamie. No reply. I ring again. No reply. I can't get hold of him because he's at the bar with Craig and Peter and they are all off their tits. Bastards. They're lording it up in opulence and I'm sitting here on my own on an island in the middle of the Pacific, under a fucking waterfall, talking shit to a coconut I quite fancy.

I scramble around in the undergrowth, trying to make a last-minute bivouac with palm leaves. The rain has washed away a pile of coconuts under a tree and I can see a polythene bag. I shine my torch on it. It's a plastic carrier bag. *That's odd*, I think. I look inside and my heart stops beating. It's full of money. Oh. My. God. I'm going to be kidnapped by terrorists or drug runners and murdered in a scene out of *Scarface* with a chainsaw. I don't fucking want to be on Treasure Island anymore. I'm in grave danger and I need to get off this fucking island.

I calm down and decide to count the money. It's torrential rain but at least counting gives me something to do. My heart beats rapidly against my chest. There's 68,000 pesos! Jesus Christ, 68,000! It's a big stash. (Which I later discover is only £1,000, but it is still a great deal of money in these parts.) As I put the notes back in the bag I suddenly see lights coming towards me across the water. I shut my eyes and open them; I must be mistaken . . . but I am not. Lights are coming this way and I stop breathing. Very slowly I hide the money back under the pile of coconuts and move back under the tree. This is now not only inconvenient, it's fucking terrifying.

I dial Jamie. There's no reply so I phone the series producer, Helen Nightingale, in Glasgow, and wake her up.

'Hello?' she says sleepily.

'Helen? Get me off this fucking island!'

'Robson, are you OK? Have you spoken to Jamie?'

'I've tried; he's not answering, none of them are. They're all pissing it up.'

She says, 'OK, I'll phone him now. Don't worry, I'll sort it.'

'Send a boat, a fucking pigeon, do whatever. I am going to die!'

I get on the satellite phone again and ring my business partner, Sandra, who has got me out of many scrapes in my life.

'Sandra, whatever you're doing, wherever you are, get me off this fucking island.'

Between them, Sandra and Helen finally manage to get hold of Jamie and the team, now in their beds. The whole team is woken up and ordered to come and get me, immediately.

There isn't an inch of me that isn't wet and I'm starting to get cold. The lights are very close to the island now and I can hear men talking. The rain continues to pour down and they are talking loudly over the sound of the waves as two men drag their boat ashore. I don't move one single muscle and barely dare to breathe. They are just yards away from me and the images of what they are going to do to me flood my brain like a virus-infected computer on its way out. In fact, later on I realise they were actually fishermen coming to shelter from the storm but after discovering that stash of money all I could think of was cold-blooded killers.

Jamie and the team finally arrive around 3 a.m., half asleep. I'm cold, reeking of bevy and exhausted from being terrified.

Jamie thinks the whole thing is hilarious and wants to do some filming but I'm not in the mood.

'Come on, Robson, it'll be great material.'

I tell him where to go. He examines the cameras.

'Are you sure you can't just stay here until the morning, filming on your diary cam?'

'Fuck you!' I roar, throwing the bag of money at him and taking a swing for him. Jamie's six-foot-two, I'm five-foot-nine, and punching high isn't a good way to box. I of course miss. AP Finlay McCray holds me back. Jamie is now furious, too, and also has to be restrained by Finlay. This adventure is now less *Robson Crusoe* and more *Lord of the Flies*. I feel like Piggy, the kid with glasses that they bullied and ultimately killed.

On the boat I change into some dry clothes. I'm so wet my fingers are all wrinkled. I'm not Bear Grylls or Ray Mears, I'm Robson Green. I'll leave those guys to fight the wilds. As we bounce across the gentle waves, I can see there are hundreds of lights out at sea, like street lamps. They twinkle across the water. Each light is a fisherman who, night after night, provides food for his village and family. They are proper fishermen, unlike me.

I have never been so pleased to see a bed in all my life. I luxuriate in it, hugging a soft pillow, and sleep soundly. In the morning, in spite of everything and all the hell I've been put through, I wake up full of warm feelings of love towards my *Extreme* team. After all, they did come and rescue me in the end. Jamie has taken the money I found to the local police and all order has been restored.

Before we head to Manila I decide to pop to the shop to load up with supplies for the long journey ahead, buying fruit, juice, sweets and loads of delicious things for the whole team to gorge on. I walk outside, laden with food, and notice both of the production cars have gone. *That's weird*, I think, looking this way and that. I wait around for a few minutes, imagining they've gone for a quick toilet stop. Ten minutes later no one has returned, and this is when it dawns on me that they have fucked off without me and are on their way to Manila. I am really upset, and what's more I've got no signal on my phone. Fuck! It is twenty minutes before anyone notices I'm not in the car. Each group thinks I've gone with the other but thankfully Peter Prada decides to double-check. He phones Jamie.

'Is Robson with you?'

'No, we thought he was with you,' says Jamie.

Fuck!! Loud screech of brakes.

I'll tell you what, I am devastated. I thought I was part of this great team and they didn't even notice I wasn't there – or maybe they did and left me on purpose? They eventually turn up to get me and I peevishly give all the food I've bought to some random locals. Well, at least they appreciate the gesture and there's no way these bastards are getting a thing from me now. I sulk all the way to Manila. During the trip I turn to Jamie and say, 'I thought we were like a rock band on tour.'

'We are. But sometimes it gets crazy on the road and shit happens.'

He's right, it certainly does.

Chapter Seven

THAILAND

Accentuate the Positive

February 2009, Series 2

It's a twelve-hour flight to Thailand and, knowing that jet psychosis is waiting for me at Arrivals, I decide to follow a close friend's advice and take two sleeping tablets called Stay Knocked. They contain melatonin, the hormone in the brain believed to maintain a regular sleeping pattern – my friend assures me that I will sleep like a baby, awake feeling refreshed and as if I've had a hot shower completely synced to Bangkok time.

I fall asleep all right; I stayed KO'd for the entire flight and am only able to shoot one piece on my diary camera as I'm coming into land. I feel like some deranged squatter has laid waste to the delicate furniture of my mind; the sofa's on fire, the coffee table's broken and he's nicked the telly. When we touch down, Jamie takes one look at me and decides it's best to shoot me in wide because a close-up and the effects of Stay Knocked may scare the children. Bangkok Airport is insane, hectic, nuts, crazy, bonkers, and I'm watching it happen through bevelled glass.

We head out to film in the busy streets, avoiding tuk-tuks, elephants, women whose chest hair goes all the way down to their testicles, spider sellers, scorpion sellers and ladies who have turned ping-pong into a whole new art form. It's all here in this hot, sweaty and vibrant city of sin and serenity. This is the land of contrasts. No sooner am I shown to my room in the hotel than my face hits the pillow and I dream I am swimming with a giant stingray, one of the chief quarries of this particular adventure. It flaps its wings like a rubbery raptor, so graceful in the water. I am feeling relaxed and I touch the creature. It winks at me. I become aware that I'm not swimming alone – there is another man, an Australian. It's Steve Irwin.

'Hello, Steve,' my voice echoes strangely underwater.

He smiles and waves at me. The stingray lifts its tail. Nooo! I sit bolt upright, gasping for air.

Market

Today I am feeling more human but my nightmare has left a residue of acrid fear. Why the hell do I want to hunt a giant freshwater stingray after one harpooned one of the greatest wildlife presenters in the chest? What does the experience add to the show? Oh, yes, I forgot: it's called _Extreme Fishing_. Why on earth didn't I sign up for some gentle fly-fishing?

We hop in a tuk-tuk and go to the Bang Kapi market to meet contributor Eddy Mounce. Originally from Ipswich, he came to Thailand on a fishing trip six years ago and never caught the flight home. He now works as a fishing guide for tourists from all over the world. Here we stock up on bait for our first fishing adventure. My deli counter at Tesco looks nothing like this: everything is fresh, i.e. ALIVE! Fish flap, eels squirm, cockerels cock-a-doodle-doo, crabs scuttle, frogs jump – and one desperately tries to break out of a net bag, attempting to part a hole with its strong green arms. It's brutal; there are about twenty all piled together in the bag. I want to help them but it's how things are done here.

I must admit the market is a full frontal assault on my Western sensibilities, however it also seems more real and truthful. Back home we are shielded from the suffering and visceral, bloody destruction of the animals whose lives we take. Everything is stewed and neatly packaged in ready-meals or cling-wrapped with pretty pictures to mask the violent slaughter and butchery that befalls the creatures. But I am very proud of the animal welfare standards we have in the UK. In my opinion, limiting suffering should be top of the list when harvesting fish or dispatching any animal.

Eddy interrupts my contemplation by shoving a bag of chopped-up mackerel in my arms, which we are going to use as bait. I then have to ask, in my best Thai, for several bags of cow's blood. The woman bends down and reaches under the counter, passing me one gallon at a time. I bung the two transparent bags of burgundy under each arm, pay the woman at the stall and wander off to go fishing with Eddy. This place is as mad as a bag of frogs.

Lake IT

The city of Bangkok and all its madness is a world away from the simple life of many people who inhabit this beautiful country, where once again fishing is a lot more than a hobby – it's a way of

life. The humidity smacks you in the face, you are battered by the
relentless sun and you're leaking from orifices you didn't think
you had.

Sixty miles south we head for a lake known as IT Lake
Monsters, and it's a world away from the madness of Bangkok.
I'm pleased to be out of the oppressive city and in the countryside, with open plains and tropical vegetation. We arrive at a
man-made lake a bit like the ones we have back in the UK, only
the weather's nicer and this lake is stocked with some of the most
amazing predators from all over the world. Unlike Loch Ness,
there are real monsters of the deep lurking under the surface.

Eddy introduces me to Alley Lungtong, the singing fisherman.

'Sawadee-krup, Robson.'

'Sawadee-krup, Alley.'

Alley tells me the lake is stocked with barramundi, tigerfish,
alligator gar, redtail catfish and arapaima, and even though some
are endangered species, parks like this help protect them, so I can
fish with a clear conscience. The arapaima is incredibly rare in
the wild. In fact, you have more likelihood of catching an arapaima here than in South America, where it is from originally. I
am desperate to catch this great predator today. It hunts by scent
so we are hoping it likes the cow's blood. I chuck jam jars of
blood across the lake, 'chumming' the water. Much like fishing for
shark, the blood will get into the arapaima's nostrils and hopefully bring them towards our bait. I have only chummed for
sharks before and never anything else.

It's midday and the heat is overpowering, plus it's 95 per cent
humidity, but I don't have time to complain because within
thirty seconds I am in. Alley thinks it's a redtail catfish, but whatever it is it's big, and the pull on the line and the heat are wearing

me out. Just when I think I can't reel anymore, the redtail catfish comes to the surface. It is about thirty to forty pounds. Its red tail mixes into orange on its underbelly; a stunning creature. We put it back – the policy is catch-and-release here and the lake wouldn't stay stocked for long if it weren't.

I ask Alley what he does while he waits for a bite.

'I like sing-song.'

Perhaps he could be a replacement for Jerome, I wonder to myself, although I'm still hoping to hear back from PSY. Imagine it: Geordie Gangnam Style.

Suddenly I feel a yank on the line.

'We're in.'

Straight away it's off.

'Oh, bugger.'

I teach Alley the correct British fishing phrases. 'Oh, bugger,' he says over and over.

But the wait isn't long before we have another bite. It's an alligator gar! I reel him in and hold him up to the camera. The alligator gar is an extraordinary-looking ray-finned fish that has existed for 100 million years. He's known as an alligator gar because of his crocodilian head and rows of sharp teeth. They can grow up to ten feet in length and are found in the brackish waters of the southern United States, although this fella can survive for up to two hours out of water. No one needs to be in this heat for long so I pop him straight back. This mean-assed predator's got business to attend to in his lake. He's the Godfather fish because he will eat anything and anyone, even turtles and wildfowl.

As we continue to wait for the arapaima to make an appearance, Alley bursts into a rendition of a Thai favourite. I join in: 'I love Thailand, I like Patpong. I like Thailand, I love Patpong,' we croon.

'What's Patpong, Alley?'

I quickly work out it's the Bangkok ladies he loves. Patpong is the 'entertainments' district of the city.

'OK, let's end it there. It's a family show and I'm not Wayne Rooney.'

With no hat on I'm beginning to feel the symptoms of sunstroke. In this kind of heat your blood thickens and takes longer to circulate round the body. I try not to think about a syrupy chum trying to force its way around my veins. I really should take an aspirin but there's no time because I'm 'in' again and whatever's on the end of my line feels very different. As I begin to reel the fish in I can see it's an arapaima (or pirarucu, as the species is known by the Amazonians), one of the largest freshwater fish in the world. I bring in this dinosaur of the deep. Her tail is like an eel's and she has distinctive red speckles on her body. I put her back into the lake, mission accomplished. I shake Alley's hand and thank him for a great day. It's time to head back to the mayhem of Bangkok and not before time. I think my brain's boiled.

After a quick shower and change of clothes at our very kitsch hotel, which looks as if it is made of sequins, and with all the female staff bowing every five seconds, saying 'Sawadee-ka', the crew and I head out to dinner. Assistant Producer Finlay has booked a table at one of Bangkok's top restaurants and I'm looking forward to indulging in some delicious Thai cuisine. But the restaurant's not quite what I expected and the name is truly terrible: it's called 'Cabbages and Condoms'. I reluctantly enter.

The place is packed and there is a long queue for tables. We breeze past the line and a waiter with a johnny on his head (no lie) takes us to our table. He's got it all the way over his eyes and nose, only his mouth is uncovered, and it is inflated at the top. *It must be a femidom*, I find myself thinking. Oh, God – I really don't want to consider this when I'm about to eat. There is a tree made of condoms next to our table, and there are lights, chairs, tables and flower arrangements all made from brightly coloured willy sheaths. Apparently the proprietors are concerned with raising awareness for sexual health and family planning. I'm really not sure if the message is getting through, or whether it's even relevant to the affluent middle-class patrons here, but the food is amazing. I'm not a fan of the doggy bags, though ...

Mekong Catfish

The next day I'm back with Eddy again. We're heading forty minutes outside of Bangkok to Bungsamran Lake, which in Thai mean 'Luxury Lake'. It's a twenty-acre stock lake containing over fifty species. We're after the Mekong catfish, another enormous freshwater fish, so it should be a good rehearsal for the giant stingray. My heart races and I go weak at the knees when I consider this quarry. Thankfully it's still a few days away.

We put big balls of hard-packed rice husks above a hook and throw them out a good thirty-five yards. It's a bit like casting a tennis ball. The Mekong catfish is sadly facing extinction in its eponymous river, so fishing is tightly controlled. They are threatened partly through overfishing, but partly owing to decreased water levels because of upstream damming in the People's Republic of China.

'There're restrictions now on the Mekong River,' says Eddy, 'so fishing parks like this one offer anybody the chance to hook fish they wouldn't be able to catch elsewhere.'

A 100-kilo catfish was pulled out of this very lake so it's possible I could become a record-holder today – it would be nice to put a different kind of record to my name. In the wild they can grow to between 150 and 200 kilos in just six years. I yank the rod up and we're in. I reel and reel – giant Mekongs love to run. This one takes me up and down the pontoon and round the houses. It has an amazing amount of sustained power. I run up the pontoon again. Where's he taking me now? He tries to go down to the bottom when something in my back tweaks slightly. It feels very sore, like red-hot needles. Pulling him in is a test of stamina. He won't give up but nor will I. Wow! He peers through the surface.

'Look at the girth on the fella.'

He's a good fifty pounds – OK, by no means the biggest, but handsome all the same. Eddy and I pick him up and he looks at us with his big eyes. These Mekong catfish have seriously dangerous spikes on their pectoral fins, which can do some serious damage, so Eddy carefully puts him back into the lake and I head straight to the physiotherapist.

River Kwai

After a quick Thai massage with a happy ending – not a Patpong happy ending, but my back's much better now, thank you – I head west with Eddy and the crew to the Burmese border. We stop off at the iconic Bridge over the River Kwai, which is actually pronounced 'Kway'. Kwai ('kwhy') are in fact buffalo, and many drink from the River Kwai ('Kway'). Two hundred and sixty thousand men laboured on the Death Railway that stretched 258 miles from Bangkok to Rangoon in Burma and was built by

Japan to support its forces during World War II. More than 90,000 Asian labourers and 16,000 Allied prisoners of war died of accidents, starvation and disease during its construction; 6,318 British personnel lost their lives. Others were luckier, including Ronald Searle, the British cartoonist and creator of St Trinian's, who managed to survive the war.

On the bridge a young man in a plaid shirt and jeans is playing the violin. *How lovely*, I think, until I tune into what he's playing and start howling with laughter. I join in: 'Hitler has only got one ball, the other is in the Albert Hall. Himmler had something similar but poor old Goebbels had none at all.'

The busker takes me aside: 'Do you know Hitler has only got one ball?' He puts his finger to his lips. 'Nobody knows – only one ball.' Well, they do now.

Despite the heat I can't resist getting my rod out to try to catch a few perch. Eddy tries all manner of bait, including bananas. I instinctively know we are not going to catch one today, especially with the gathering crowd behind us, so it's time to go. The cows and buffaloes have come to drink, pee and poo in the river.

Indian Carp

In the late afternoon we arrive at Khao Laem Dam, 180 miles west of Bangkok, where I'm meeting Air Lekkham, who's lived on the reservoir all his life. It's like the Lake District with jungle attached to it. This freshwater fishing heaven exists because of the Khao Laem Dam, built in the 1980s to supply water and electricity to the area. It's a world away from the comforts of the city. I spot our hotel – it's a raft with a roof, in the middle of the lake. It's primitive but I'm sure it's as comfortable as the Hilton, and I certainly won't feel fiscally plundered in the morning. Our accommodation is open-plan and we are all sleeping in one room, but it's the only way to get an early start tomorrow.

At 10.30 p.m. we are still sorting out fishing gear for the morning and as we finally settle down for the night the insects come alive and start attacking us. We are covered in them: mayflies like pterodactyls, the high-pitch whine of mosquitoes, moths that are all over me like a busy jumper. I film a piece on my diary camera recording my suffering by moonlight. My therapist said it's good to share, and that's why I got into TV! I am exhausted and I desperately try to settle down to sleep again. I put my headphones on in an attempt to drown out the noise of mosquitoes and Jamie's snoring, which is getting on my man-tits. After what seems an eternity, I finally drift off.

Eddy wakes me up with a start, singing 'In the jungle, the mighty jungle . . .' at the top of his voice. I want to kill him and so does the rest of the crew. I've had only four and a half hours of fitful sleep and this guy has the brass neck to sing. I drag my sorry behind out of bed.

This morning we are fishing for Indian carp (rohu), which isn't native to Thailand but actually originally from India and Pakistan. It's the staple diet for families here, and what they don't eat they sell at the market. However, whatever we catch we are going to eat and I'm excited. No one eats carp back home because it's a bottom feeder and hovers up silt, weed and other gunk, apparently making it taste muddy, so I can't wait to give my verdict on rohu. Carp only feed at certain times, so we wait for sunrise. Eddy asks me to cast out three metres past a float and to the right. I'm so tired I can't hit a barn door but finally I make a good cast. Eddy is impressed but the fish couldn't give a toss; two hours later there is still no sign of life.

'Up at three forty-five, no sleep on a raft, to catch carp. This better be worth it, Eddy,' I say grumpily. 'You've got six rods out there and there hasn't been a bend in one of them.'

I'm hot and tired and I feel like a seven-year-old. Minutes later I moan from the hut.

'When are we going to get one, Eddy?'

'In terms of carp fishing we've been here a very short time,' says Eddy.

He's right, and that's why I don't like carp fishing: it's inactive and boring. The carp fishing posse can 'troll' about me as much as they like on the Internet, I care not. Some people don't like curling or tai chi – I don't like carp fishing.

I take shelter from the burning rays on a 'day bed' in the hut. I just need an opium pipe to deal with this interminable ennui and I'm set for the day. Eddy is the watchman and our six rods are primed. We wait restlessly and another three hours pass before a rod springs into action.

'Keep it pumping, Robson.'

I've got to keep him off the bottom, otherwise he'll be in snags, vegetation or dead trees that hold the fish or catch the line and I'll lose him. I don't lose him and we land the fish. I am very pleased to have caught such a fine-looking rohu and, after a very long morning, I'm really looking forward to devouring it.

We cook the carp five ways: steamed, shallow-fried, deep-fried, grilled and baked. It's a lovely white fish – not in my top three but very nice. We enjoy five courses, including tom yum carp soup. It tastes beautiful and nothing is wasted. Here they even eat the swim bladder that helps the carp float in the water, but this doesn't stay in my mouth long. Rather like prairie oysters, it's an acquired taste.

Buddhist Temple

So the day of reckoning is here: we are going after a giant stingray today and I am wetting myself. We travel to a place called Chachoengsao, fifty miles from Bangkok, and Jamie wants me to visit a beautiful Buddhist temple to bless the day. It's something I've never done on a trip before but I'll take all the positive vibes I can get. Buddhism is an amazing philosophy and one of its key tenets is to accentuate the positive and eliminate the negative.

I deliver a piece to camera: 'Yes, I'm after the world's largest freshwater fish. A fish that can weigh up to one thousand pounds. A fish with a barb so deadly that it can kill in seconds. We're going after a giant stingray!'

One of the crew's phones rings. Oh, for goodness' sake: not in the middle of a take – and in a Buddhist temple, of all places . . . I try not to get uptight. Buddhism is about achieving calmness and training one's willpower to overcome emotional responses and act rationally, so I have a go. But actors are the most unstable creatures on the planet – far worse than francium, the most unstable element in the Periodic Table. Maybe that's why they call it a periodic table . . . *Accentuate the positive, eliminate the negative, Robson.* I breathe in the incense and stare at Buddha. Finlay walks over to me, the phone outstretched.

'Robson, you need to ring Sandra urgently.'

Sandra, my business partner, is my rock. She is Paul Burrell to my Diana. She answers after a single ring.

'Robson. I'm so sorry.'

'Has Dad passed away?' I ask, sensing what has happened.

'Yes, he has. [pause] Joanna, Dawn, David and Yvonne were all with him. He had an aneurysm in his stomach.'

She goes on to tell me Big Rob was with his girlfriend Yvonne watching TV, when all of a sudden he gasped with pain and experienced the fatal burst.

'Did he suffer?'

'No, it was so quick.'

I stagger outside the temple. I'm feeling light-headed and the picture distorts. I desperately search for a corner to break down in but I can't find one. *Keep it together, Robson.* I walk towards a tree, the mobile drops from my hand and I collapse on my knees, sobbing alone in the heat. Two guys are staring at me. Maybe they think it's part of the show. Maybe they are thinking, 'Wow, this guy is really good.' I want to tell them Big Rob's dead but I don't.

Jamie comes and hugs me.

'I'm sorry, Robson, I'm so sorry'. He turns to everyone: 'OK, we are all going home now.'

A Buddhist monk silently makes his way over. He looks at me and holds my hand. His presence is so calming. He strokes my face and looks at me in the eye.

'Was he not well?' he asks.

'No,' I say, still choked.

'He has moved on to a good place, but he is still here with you. He is within you. You look like him. You are him.'

It's an extraordinary moment. I will never forget the way he looked at me.

Later on I realise I have learnt one of the four truths of Buddhism: life is challenging. For everyone. Our physical bodies, our relationships – all of our life circumstances – are fragile and subject to change. We are always accommodating.

I guess grieving is part of accommodating.

Big Rob

I visit my mum first. She's OK, I think because she and Dad parted years ago. She sips her tea and says, 'I was at the Spanish Ballroom in Whitley Bay when I first clapped eyes on your dad. The first thing he said was, "I've been watching you dancing all night. You're the most beautiful woman here." 'Course I knew straight away he was after something and I was right. He said, "Are you here next week, because I'd love to dance with you?" I said, "I'll be here." He said, "Oh, good. Can you lend us ten pence to get the bus home? I'll pay you back." The cheeky so-and-so had spent all his money on drink. Your dad was a wonderful dancer: he glided across the floor – and he paid me back, just as he said.'

I see my two sisters, who live just yards from Mum. They are taking it very badly but my brother David is reserved as ever. As we remember Dad our sadness turns to laughter, especially when we recall his preference for going everywhere bare-chested, including restaurants!

'What about the time in Devon, we were going for dinner and Dad had his top off. The guy at the door said, "You can't come in", and Dad says, "You try and fucking stop me."'

He was as hard as nails. He thought it was completely normal but as kids we knew something was wrong. No one else's dad was half-naked all the time. Come rain, shine or Arctic winter, he never had a shirt on and was always as brown as a berry. I remember him digging the garden on a cold winter's day with only his trousers and boots on. He was a great horticulturist and grew prize-winning vegetables. He also had a beautiful flower garden where he grew roses, carnations and exquisite blue corn-flowers, which he gave to family, friends and local people.

The funeral service is at Whitley Bay Crematorium, with 200 people crammed into a very small space. Dawn and Joanna both say a few words and then it's my turn. David stands by my side as I speak; he is catatonic with grief.

'Dad loved his football and he followed his beloved Newcastle United around the world. I remember a time in Nice when Monaco slaughtered Newcastle. Before the game I took Dad to the Colombe d'Or – a famous restaurant patronised by Matisse and Picasso, who paid their bills with paintings, which are still on the walls today. Dad thought the paintings were shite. "I don't get it. It's not my cup of tea." He ordered the soup; it was gazpacho. He took a sip and in broad Geordie summoned the waiter over. "How! Bonnie lad, this soup has never touched the flame." Antwerp made me smile, too. Dad was very anti-German. At lunch they had all the different flags of Europe on the table. He walks over, seizes the German one and says, "You can take that one off for a bloody start." Next to go is the Italian ensign, which he plonks down on the table. I say, "Dad, you weren't even in the war!" "So what! I still hate those bastard Krauts and I'll never trust the Eyeties." He makes a sudden grab for the Tricolour: "Almost forgot this one," he says. "Bloody collaborators."'

I take a breath and end my speech by plagiarising Jimmy Dean's 'Big Bad John':

Ev'ry mornin' at the mine you could see him arrive
He stood five-foot-nine and weighed two thirty-five
Kinda broad at the shoulder and narrow at the hip
And everybody knew ya didn't give no lip to Big Rob.
That was my Dad.

Stingray

One week later and I'm back at the Bang Pakong River in Chachoengsao Province, ready to catch a giant freshwater stingray. I meet stingray expert Que at his wooden house on stilts at the river's edge. The river is deep, fast-flowing and the colour of British Rail coffee with a hint of long-life milk. I try on the tackle and kit needed to fish for one of these prehistoric giants and Que trusses me up like a Christmas turkey.

We set up the rods on the bank outside his house while Que's mate rows the bait out and drops it in the middle of a brackish river. We use a sardine as live bait. The hook is fastened under the spine of the fish, which is brutal but it's the local Thai method. When a fish is hurt it sends out a distress signal that attracts other fish, and today we're hoping this little sardine appeals to a stingray.

By 11 a.m. the lines are set. There is only a loose tension on them because giant stingrays don't eat immediately and will take the bait somewhere to feed later, so we must wait for the moment they swallow the bait. Come midday there's 100 per cent humidity and the heat is unbearable. I am on the corner of a makeshift bed, trying to rest, and all the team is asleep except for Que, who is our watchman. The jungle behind is alive with the buzz of insects, the squawks of monkeys.

'Fish! Fish! Fish!' yells Que.

We scramble to our feet. I take the rod and it is quickly apparent that the fish is not going to come to us. We are going to have to go to the fish. We set the rod, put it on full tension and jump on a boat to float down the river. I put on the harness and take the rod, keeping it on full tension as I try to pull up. It really hurts my bollocks and my back. This fish is 300–400 pounds or even larger, and it's desperately trying to go to the bottom and bury itself in the mud. I soon realise that, because of the tension on the rod, reel and body, I can't do it alone, so Que takes over. The boat is very unstable and we almost capsize. We need a bigger boat! Considering this cartilaginous fish is a relative of the shark family, this seems appropriate. We jump in a larger model and the fight continues. The rod is bending in Que's hands, almost back on itself. He sits on the rod and it continues to bend over the edge of the boat. I've never seen anything like it.

Giant freshwater stingrays are bottom feeders and hunt for crabs, snails and clams by detecting their electrical impulses through the mud. They have sophisticated electro receptors called ampullae of Lorenzini, named after the seventeenth-century Italian scientist who discovered them, which are also found in other rays, sharks and chimaeras (ghost fish). Giant stingrays are such complex creatures that little is known about them, nor do we know how many still exist, but they are thought to be endangered in Asia and critically endangered here in Thailand. Unfortunately the Bang Pakong River is known to be polluted, with prawns and other fish stocks dwindling, possibly from industrial pollutants upstream. Many other species are endangered here, including the Irrawaddy dolphin, owing not only to pollution but also to overfishing, soil erosion, and getting caught in nets. It's a sad state of affairs, and, with the human population set to rise to 8 billion by 2030, one we need to address before it's too late.

I'm back in the hot seat and inch by inch I'm gaining some ground. It's been fifty minutes; landing this fish is like hauling John Prescott out of the water. Que pulls up the line as I reel in. But even working together the two of us still can't bring it in.

Que's friend takes over – it's become a three-man fight in the searing heat. After an hour and a half the ray nearly takes the boat over and I am screaming in agony – the load is too much. Que helps me. It's piercing agony. The way a stingray moves in the water it's like pulling up a huge plate with water on top: it's the ultimate amount of drag. Suddenly we see the fishing weight appear out of the coffee, and then a wing, flapping like an elephant's ear, breaks the surface. We see her and she truly is like something out of a sci-fi movie. Her wingspan is ten or eleven feet, and her length from head to tail is thirteen or fourteen feet. We guess she's around a quarter of a ton but these rays can grow to over a thousand pounds!

On the edge of her tail is a spike. If it comes near us we are in trouble. The spike can measure up to fifteen inches, is shaped like a bayonet and covered in a sheath of toxic mucus that is capable of piercing bone. A stingray has just killed Steve Irwin, and now Que is telling me to get in the water and hold the fish.

'Are you insane?' I yelp.

All the stingray has to do is quickly flick her tail to the side or over her back like a scorpion, the spike deploys and it's game over. They can kill sharks; they can kill anything. It's like a trigger and it's lightning-quick. I stay back while Que and his friend cover the tail with a blanket, wrapping it round and tying it down tightly. The fish is no longer a threat.

There's no way we can get this creature on the boat so I really do have to go in, according to Jamie, whom I now loathe once more. He was lovely after my father's passing but now he's reverted to his old sadistic ways. I get in the water and wade slowly towards this alien life-form. I am petrified. I hold her with Que and his friend, quickly spout a few facts about this giant to camera, and it's time to let the awesome creature off the hook. We take the metal out of her mouth and she glides gently away back to her home on the bottom of the Bang Pakong.

I wish I could tell my Dad about the experience. I phone Uncle Matheson instead.

Chapter Eight

KENYA

Addiction

September 2009, World Tour, Series 3

As I look out over Kilimanjaro for the first time, I think this programme is actually going to work. It might even be a success. As a team we have started to know what we are doing and it turns out *Extreme Fishing* isn't really a fishing programme at all; it's a travelogue that explores different cultures and places, with the common link of fishing. Fishing is quite literally my passport to the world. (Sir Winston Churchill once said, 'Polo is a passport to the world.' Mine is fishing and I don't need six horses to do it.) I have turned down several acting jobs to do this series but the locations of Manchester, Rochdale and Cowgate in Newcastle didn't really come close to the savannahs and exotic wildlife of Africa, not to mention the record-breaking angling to be had off the east coast. This is the place to catch the big five: blue marlin, black marlin, swordfish, sailfish and striped marlin.

It's the stuff of dreams and it blows *Waterloo Road* firmly out of the water!

As we come into land at Nairobi Airport, it also dawns on me that I am addicted to the show. It's like a fix and when I don't get my hit I feel sad or that something is missing, and that's just the days in between episodes. Time passes slowly when I'm back in the UK – tick, tick, tick – like the hand of a faulty clock stuck on the same minute, unable to budge. But when I'm filming the show I feel so upbeat and occupied in a positive way. If I'm honest I'm a lot healthier because of this gig – fishing has replaced drinking, which is par for the course in this business. I knew I had a drink problem when I found an olive in my urine sample – thank you, Keith Richards.

From Nairobi we take another plane to Watamu National Maritime Park in the Indian Ocean. The light aircraft is falling apart and I spot a gaping hole in the wing mid-flight! It reminds me of the good old days of Dan-Air (aka Dan Dare). We survive the rickety African flight and carry on to our hotel. We are staying at Hemingway's, named after the author, traveller and hunter who spent many years in Kenya. I didn't realise that he'd shot and fished for anything that moved. In 1933, inspired by the legendary hunts of President Theodore Roosevelt, Ernest borrowed money from his wife's uncle and set off on a three-month safari.

I look at the gigantic stuffed fish adorning the walls of the hotel: there's a giant black marlin and a beautiful golden dorado. I'm determined to catch both on this trip. The dorado won't outsmart me this time, as it did in the Philippines. I still carry the sinking feeling of that loss. Totally my fault, but it won't happen again. I've come here to set the record straight.

But first things first: I need a haircut, because right now I look like Richard Clayderman. I ask at reception if they have a salon and they tell me they have an expert stylist who comes in. I make an appointment and continue filming. A few hours later, enter Fatima.

'Come this way,' she says, leading me to a room with bright lights and a mirror. I sit down in front of it. Fatima crosses the room with a pair of electric shears, dragging the lead noisily across the hardwood floor. She plugs the shears in and sets them at grade 3.

'Hang on! Do you have any scissors?' I venture.

'No, I have a comb and shears – it will be fine.'

'But I just want you to tidy it up,' I say, putting my hand up to prevent the shears taking me a step closer to Yul Brynner. 'Just a trim would be great,' I say firmly.

'I am very sad,' she says, sighing.

'What?'

'I just buried my sister. I miss her so much. We put her in the earth at the top of a mountain.'

Inside I am thinking, *OK, that is very sad* – but I still don't want an emotionally vulnerable woman to come anywhere near my head with a pair of electric shears.

'You shouldn't be here, you must be traumatised,' I say, looking at her in the mirror.

'No, I'm fine.'

The tears are streaming down her face as she brings the shears down on my head. She gets to work like a champion sheep-shearer and it's over in a matter of seconds.

I walk outside and find the crew. They take one look at me and their faces fall. I have gone from Clayderman to Charles Bronson within fifteen minutes and now everything we have shot before the 'attack' is unusable because of continuity.

'What the hell happened?' asks Alistair.

'Let's just say she wasn't in the mood for a trim. I think I got off lightly.'

Alistair shakes his head sadly: 'How can you manage to fuck up a haircut, Robson?'

Thankfully I'd brought my trusty Nanogen in my Mary Poppins make-up bag. It's a scalp filler that makes you look like you have twice as much hair. Think David Guest but more subtle. And yes, I carry a make-up bag. Actors and presenters have all manner of tricks to avoid looking shiny, sallow or dog-rough on camera.

If you are an Alpha male, feel free to skip this paragraph but for the gays and ladies here're my top beauty tips: I apply a Clinique green cream, which covers up any redness or sunburn, and it's great if you suffer from rosacea or are a raging alcoholic. Then I apply a primer, which evens the skin tone. Next I lighten under the eyelids and use concealer as necessary. I then apply powder. I add a little eyeliner on the lower lashes because when you are filming in hot, bright countries there is high contrast, so features need to be accentuated. I also use MAC mascara for the top lashes, and on my lips I use Zam-Buk, a green ointment that protects and highlights them. I only wear make-up when I am filming, not every day – honest. And just so you know, even butch men like Matt Dawson, Bruce Parry and Ray Mears all wear make-up on TV.

Anyway, we crack on with filming. It's a hot day but we are all relishing being outside after the shocking weather back home in the UK. However, none of us has applied enough sunscreen so our faces, heads, necks, arms and ears are all scorched by the midday sun. A few hours later we look like *Viz* magazine's 'Brits Abroad'. Peter is singed the worst and that evening I suggest he try my Green Cream to cover his badly burned face.

'I am not putting any of your poofy muck on my face!'

'It's not poofy muck, it's Clinique!'

He suffers like a man; I suffer like an actor.

El Dorado

The next morning I tear the curtains open. I am red-hot with sunburn but the prospect of catching a golden dorado this morning is like lidocaine.

We walk down to the harbour to meet Callum, a strapping Kenyan fisherman and my guide for today. We board his gleaming white sports fishing boat and set off a mile out to sea, to a place known locally as Sailfish Alley. The sun is hot and it's a beautiful day to go fishing. On the way we come across a sperm whale carcass floating on the surface, about forty feet in length. As we get closer the aroma is abhorrent. It is an oily, sweet, rotten stench of death. Callum thinks the whale has either died of natural causes or been hit by a boat, which sadly happens all too often. Every year thousands of whales lose their lives to container ships, like flies on a car windscreen. It's a tragedy that will hopefully one day be preventable through technology. We slowly pass the carcass. It moves strangely in the water, its tail swishing from side to side. At first I think it's gas escaping but then I see a dorsal fin, in fact several of them – 800-pound tiger sharks are taking bites out of the whale like Brie. They are incredible-looking fish, with stripes like the eponymous big cat and just as vicious. I shudder. There are only two types of people who are not scared of sharks: psychopaths and dead people.

After just twenty minutes' motoring across the waves we reach our destination, Sailfish Alley. It's a huge drop-off and natural feeding channel for pelagic, billfish and other species that have a penchant for bait fish. We rig our skip bait, large bonitos, relations of the mackerel family, and trawl the live bait behind the boat. It's not something I'm used to fly-fishing in Northumberland, but it's the way they do it here in Kenya. Almost immediately I get a take. I set the rod and pull the line in tight. It's not a dorado, as the fish doesn't become airborne within twenty seconds, but whatever it is nimbly jumps off the hook. I reel in the bait; half of it is missing. Something has cut through the fish like a serrated knife through butter.

Ten minutes later this happens again: our bait is taken and the predator misses the hook by millimetres. Callum thinks it's a wahoo nicking our bait but on the sixth attempt I catch the culprit. I am convinced it's the same one that's been eating all the pies and now, overfed, has got sloppy and made a fatal mistake. I bring the twenty-pound fish onto the boat. It is a wahoo – the Usain Bolt of the ocean (cue lightning pose). We knock it on the head and keep it for our supper. Wahoo tastes absolutely delicious, as its Hawaiian name suggests. It's a bit like mackerel but with a softer, more delicate flavour.

I don't have to wait long for my next strike and it's gold, as the shining dorado bursts out of the water. I know how tough this pulchritudinous fish is to catch and I'm not going to lose her – she is my greatest prize. She leaps athletically out of the ocean again. If I don't keep her under control she'll turn off the hook and be free. She is so powerful she can exceed 50 m.p.h. in short bursts, and she's smart – I've underestimated the golden maverick once before but this time I play it safe and use all the skills I have learnt to land her.

I've done it! I am ecstatic. A quick bump on the head and we've got a fifteen-pound mahi-mahi (the Hawaiian name for dorado, meaning very strong) for our supper to complement our wahoo – I am a very happy man. As we head back to shore I take in the stunning coastline. Callum points to the starboard side of the boat and as I cross the deck I see a female humpback whale and her calf. We are all rendered speechless. She ejects seawater out of her spout like a geyser while her calf expels a faint mist more like a lawn sprinkler – he'll get there in the end. They swim by the boat for a while, dive down and are gone.

Back at Hemingway's, I eat the wahoo and dorado with the crew and Callum. I look around at the other clientele in the bistro. There are a conspicuous number of rotund German women in their sixties having candlelit dinners with young African men. Around the world, I've seen my fair share of saggy ageing men with fresh-faced nubile girls, which is repugnant, but I didn't know there was sex tourism the other way round. These boys have been groomed by these grey-haired pornograannies, seduced with cars, money and treats. They say many a good tune is played on an old fiddle, but looking at some of these women, I would definitely take up a new instrument.

Dhow Fishing
I wake up with images of haggard German women on heat and feel sick. At breakfast there are old Italian boilers in on the act and we all decide to get some air. Today we are heading to Malindi, a former port and tourist resort on the east coast. I am

dhow fishing with Hassan, Mohammed and Mohammed (Mo for short), three guys who fish together day in, day out and who are like the Kenyan angling equivalent of the Rolling Stones, all with faces that could tell a thousand stories. They are all wearing the traditional dhow dress of plain coloured kilts. We greet one another and I hop aboard their boat.

Dhow boats are Indian in origin and design and have been used in the area for centuries; today we are going out in a vessel Hassan says he has designed and built himself. The craftsmanship is truly outstanding. Coming from a shipbuilding background I appreciate the design and execution. As a lad out of school I was accepted for an apprenticeship as a draughtsman at Swan Hunter, where I worked in hull design and shell expansion, but I quickly realised that, if shipbuilding and I were both to survive, we would have to go our separate ways. I know the industry has been struggling since the 1980s, when I coincidentally worked at Swan Hunter, but I would like to take this opportunity to underline that the decline in shipbuilding in the northeast was down to Margaret Thatcher and not my ineptitude as a draughtsman. Honest!

The men unfurl the sail and we tack across the water. It's amazing how the boat glides through the waves; I feel this is how we are meant to fish. It's so natural and more like the poetry of fly-fishing that I love so much. It is also in complete contrast to the big white petrol-guzzling craft we went out in yesterday. I stare at Hassan, in awe of him for building this boat. As we sail across the sea I turn to him on camera and say, 'This really is an amazing dhow boat, so beautiful and perfect for catching reef fish. I understand you built it yourself?'

'No, I didn't,' he says.

My pupils dilate. WTF? 'Oh? A little bird told me that you had built it.'

'No, a local businessman built and paid for it.'

'Did you have any hand in it at all?'

'No.'

Basically he'd spun me a right old yarn until he realised he was going to be on camera and it might tie him in knots later.

But whatever the genesis of the dhow boat, one thing is irrefutable: Hassan and his friends know how to fish. I've never seen anything like it. They work the lines not only with their hands but also with their feet, playing the fish like puppets on strings. Their feet and hands all bear the scars of their work but over time the skin has hardened and they feel no pain. Each of them pulls up four fish, sometimes two at a time, without ever tangling the lines; it's an incredible feat. They are the masters, with extraordinary coordination and great strength to fight not only the fish but also gusts of wind and lumpy water. They make it look easy but I assure you it is not.

I'm hoping to catch a grouper or red snapper but first I have to don the traditional dhow fishermen dress. Well, it's more of a skirt or sarong that fits from the midriff to the ankles. I feel like David Beckham. In this part of the country it is shameful for men to show their legs, which is unfortunate because I have been told I have lovely legs. Peter Prada needs to cover his; in fact, I don't think they have ever seen the light of day. Alistair's are like pipe cleaners and Craig has Kiwi cankles. But my legs are shapely, like Richard O'Brien's, only younger.

I put on my welding gloves to protect my actor's hands. Hassan explains that fishing without gloves allows him to feel every movement of the fish so he knows exactly when to pull the line up. (I guess it's a bit like a rider keeping a gentle contact with the horse's mouth to make small adjustments in speed and direction.) He confiscates the gloves – if I'm going to be a dhow fisherman I need to feel the fish and understand the technique.

We drop anchor at the edge of a reef, lowering bait to the bottom. A grouper fish tends to come out of its cave, take the bait and then try to swim back into the reef. You have to take a grouper quickly otherwise you'll lose it.

Mo gets a bite and heaves up a chakashangu, or a green job fish. I'm up next – at first I think it's a snapper but I've actually hooked a coral fish. I heave it up. Its colours are a stunning palate of purples, reds and yellows. It's part of the grouper family and it's the best-looking fish we catch all day, not that looks count.

Hand lining looks easy but it's a technique that takes time to master. The boys are pulling them up like they are going out of fashion and I am losing them at the same pace. They catch job fish, snapper and emperor fish. Hassan gives me a quick tutorial: 'If you lift [the line] quickly then [the fish] will know it's a trap, so you have to lift it slowly.' His words of wisdom work. I casually pull up the bait and bam! I get a second bite. As I wind in the line with my hands, the fish fights and the nylon tears into my skin. I think Hassan wants me to have 'dhow lines' on my hands as marks of honour so that I can look at the scars in years to come and remember this incredible day. I ignore the burning and con-centrate on winning the battle.

'It's a grouper! I have always wanted to catch one of these!'

It's the biggest fish of the day and in my opinion the second-finest-tasting fish on the planet, after haddock. Its Ancient Greek name is *Epinephelus lanceolatus* (*epinephelos* meaning 'clouds') and its striking brown and grey markings do make it look as though it's reflecting the altocumulus clouds in the sky above. This fish with clouds on will bring a good price at the market, and in all we have eighteen of them. We later sell them on the beach to the locals for the going rate: 400 shillings a fish (under £3). It's a good day's work – my dad would be proud that I'd done at least one decent day's graft with scars to prove it.

Tana River Delta

I cannot believe the pilot of our plane, Gary Cullen, is best mates with the headmaster of my son's school! The clichés gush out of my mouth: 'It's such a small world, Gary. I mean, here we are on the way to the Tana Delta talking about people in Surrey! Unbelievable.'

The crew groan and stick their earplugs in. They think I'm such a twat today. Sod them. I natter away and Gary asks if I would like to have a go at flying. Would I? Would I? I smile from ear to ear: 'I have always wanted to be a pilot but I didn't have the aptitude skills or leadership qualities to join the Royal Air Force.' I once had to take five guys to a river with three planks and rope to build a bridge to cross it. The way I constructed the bridge ensured all five lads were swept away, with me standing on the bank wondering what to do next. We also had to lay a minefield, but first of all I didn't ask if any of the guys had done it before, which is a glaringly obvious mistake as one was an expert. Secondly, I didn't work out that it would be best to place all the mines on top of the ground before we dug them in and risked detonating them while trying to plant the others.

After a quick lesson, I take us to 11,000 feet. The Tana Delta is stunning from above: this is where the sea comes inland and forms an estuary and hundreds of little tributaries that bleed off it. I am reluctant to give the controls back to Gary but he insists on landing the plane, apparently because it's windy, we're landing on a sandy beach and, er, I've never done it before.

The crew still think I'm a twat: 'Oh, my God, I can't believe you know John Whatshisface. Such a small world,' they mimic.

We have dinner and go to bed. My room, a very smart colonial jungle tent, has no walls and 360 degrees of views and fresh air. There are only mosquito nets to protect me, which won't help against lions, hippos and other big beasts. I don't sleep a wink with all the wildlife noises, particularly the hippopotami feeding nearby. One of the most dangerous animals in the world, and the most dangerous mammal in Africa, it's not a beast you want to piss off – but in only a matter of hours I will be casting a small bait fish over a pod of hippos' heads and landing it into their dung in the hope of catching a larger fish. No, I haven't been drinking: that's my brief and I can hardly digest it myself and nor, from the sound of it, can the hippos. It's like a cacophony of dishwashers on drainage cycle.

As the sun rises we head off in a 4x4 with my guide, Keke, to a tiny village on Tana River. Here we're meeting the fishermen who risk their lives every day because of how and where they fish. It's the first time I've been on a fishing trip with a chap carrying a .303 rifle. Sporting an army green shirt, trousers and a kufi cap, this geezer looks the business. We walk in single file along the bank of one of the thousands of tributaries in the Delta and scramble down the sides to the water's edge. Five metres in front of me is a pod of hippos trying to wallow, snooze and defecate in peace. Bait fish like nothing more than chomping on hippo poo and where there are bait fish, there are predators. I cast a line as near to the pod as possible. This is extreme hippo-poo fishing. Only in Africa; only on this show.

I have to admit I am more than a little cynical, but as I bring the line in by hand I have a take. It's a small red snapper but I am happy. I ask Keke what 'beautiful fish' is in Swahili.

'Samaki Mazuri,' he says, grinning at the size of it.

Well, he can laugh but four hours later it's the only fish we have and I am more likely to be bored to death than gored to death. I spy a man in a dugout canoe catching loads, so I decide to ditch my two losers and hang out with him. Call me fickle.

Swab and his son take us upriver in their battered canoe to a secret location supposed to be full of fish, and most importantly away from hippos – the temperature is rising and they're becoming agitated. As we pass by, two of them scramble to their feet looking menacing, while the others scatter and dive under the water. I conclude that I'd prefer to watch them from the bank, not a canoe. The sun is baking and the chance of catching a fish remote. My gut instinct is to call it a day but Swab sets out crab lines – in my experience shrimp and crabs are always a last resort of a contributor. Well, after all the faffing about with poo and hippos we end up with one tiny crab, which looks like something I pulled out of a rock pool in Seahouses aged seven, a small bream and a red snapper. I cook them on the fire and eat them with all the other poo fishermen. It's a poo-tiful scene.

Lake Victoria

Gary's back and he's taking us inland to Lake Victoria, the second-largest freshwater lake in the world and bigger than Wales. However, this time I'm allowed nowhere near the controls of the plane. When the production company, IWC Media, found out I'd flown, they went ballistic.

'You are not insured. We are not amused,' said Hamish.

All the crew got into trouble so I am straightjacketed onto the plane and seated at the back, where I can't touch anything. The fact that I had always wanted to be a pilot isn't a good enough excuse to bend the health and safety rules in IWC's eyes, the killjoys.

After one aborted landing owing to a cow on the 'runway', we touchdown on a bumpy field where kids are playing football. When we've all coughed our tongues up, we head by boat to Mfangano Island in the middle of Lake Victoria.

Local fisherman Gilbert is waiting to meet us. He is a charming man with a kind manner. He welcomes us to his fishing village, which comprises square mud-and-wood huts with crude corrugated roofs. Children run around naked at the water's edge as mothers wash their clothes and cooking pots. Men busy themselves with carpentry and repairing boats ready for tonight's fishing. The lifeblood of the island is omena fish (think whitebait), which the locals catch and sell on the mainland.

As we set foot onto land, the little children rush over to greet us. Scores of them appear from nowhere and I high-five to greet them. It quickly becomes apparent that there are many more kids on the island than grown-ups, as many of these youngsters' parents have been casualties of the AIDS epidemic. According to Kenya's National AIDS Control Council, there are around 1.5–1.7 million people living with HIV out of a population of 43 million. It's eye-opening to see the effects of the disease so clearly here; in some cases grandparents are looking after twenty children.

I have a few hours to kill so I teach the kids the *Extreme Fishing* mime, where you cross your arms in an X, cast out a line and reel in the fish. It's become shorthand for the show and we are beginning to use it in the opening title sequences more and more.

Gilbert asks if I'm hungry and the crew nod their heads eagerly. He takes us to meet a lady called Paulina in the woods behind the village. She is dressed in a black and white patterned dress and a headscarf tied at the back to keep the sun off. She is waving a big cake bowl around her head, humming a tune, surrounded by a cloud of flies attracted by the resonance. Inside the bowl is a gloopy mixture that the flies stick to. These flies are the other main source of food on the island; they contain seven times more protein than steak. They might not taste as good as Aberdeen Angus but they will keep you alive. I have a go at catching some. Paulina giggles as I hum and do something akin to the 'Agadoo' dance – I could do a song from my own album but that might put them off. I have millions of flies in my face but none in the yellow bowl I'm waving around. I waft it about my head a bit more and look inside: 'I've got three!' But I need a plateful and it could take all night.

Luckily this is a TV show so, in the best tradition of TV chefs, Paulina produces a few thousand she's caught earlier. Who the hell discovered this technique and then decided to make fly burgers out of the paste? It's ingenious but all I can say is that they must have been really sick of fish. Paulina poaches the paste in milk – it looks like two mud balls and smells like acrid green meat. However, the kids love it. It's their version of M&Ms and they queue up excitedly for some.

It tastes like it smells but certain situations call for a swallow, especially in the presence of such a kind lady. Her love for the children is humbling. I discover that she is in her late fifties and is looking after sixteen kids on her own. Her selflessness, warmth and goodness make her a privilege to meet. We all fall in love with Paulina.

As we start to prepare to film the next sequence, night fishing for omena, a massive storm comes out of nowhere.

Gilbert says, 'We need to take cover – it's a bad storm.'

There is a bit of wind, the clouds turn black and within sixty seconds a hurricane hits. I've never experienced anything like it. It's quick, violent and like being mugged by Mother Nature. We run to a hut; the rain is pouring down, the wind thrashing us. We cover our heads and leg it. One by one we enter the hut. There is a thud, like a melon being split open with an axe. Alistair has smacked his head into the edge of the corrugated roof and is on the ground. We get him inside where we see the blood is pumping down his face like a waterfall. Everyone is panicking trying to keep the claret in the bottle. It's a deep diagonal gash across his skull – three inches long and an inch across. Alistair is in a blind panic; the more worked up he gets, the more blood he's losing. I want to slap him.

'Alistair, calm down. You're going to be fine.'

His eyes are haunted by an accident he had in 1991, when he was dragged under a car as it screeched to a stop over about fifty metres, subsequently trapping him under it. His bald head still bears the physical scars from that terrifying incident and now he's suffering the mental fallout. His heart rate is in overdrive. I use my shirt to stop the bleeding and pinch the wound together with my fingers. Craig finds a small first-aid kit in his camera bag and I grab the iodine.

'Right, Alistair, I need you to bring your breathing down. This is going to hurt but you need to breathe through it.'

Donning the latex gloves, I pour iodine into the wound. He whimpers and hums. I tell him to stop humming or he'll attract the flies and he raises a smile. We clean the wound with water and sterile dressings, then I cut a dozen thin strips of gaffer tape and begin to pull the wound together with the tape. It's a crude method of butterfly stitching but all I can say is thank God I played Jimmy the Porter in *Casualty*.

Alessandra gets on the satellite phone to Helen. She is amazing, and a flying doctor arrives within the hour. The doctor stitches Alistair up properly and he tells us that whoever taped the wound up was a genius who saved Alistair's life. I push past Craig and Peter and tell him it was me. He shakes my hand. Peter and Craig groan. The doctor tells Alistair he must rest and there is no way he can film the night sequence. Alistair is really upset and frustrated, and reluctantly we take him back to the hotel. On the way back, the Machiavelli in me rears his head – if Alistair's out of action this could be my directorial debut, my chance to be an actor/director like Tim Robbins, Kenneth Branagh or Mel Gibson. As Mel would say: 'If any of you have a bleeping problem with that I'll put you in a bleeping rose garden. But you have to bleep me first. I deserve to be bleeped first!'

All this megalomania is clouding my mind. I check on Alistair, like Macbeth on Duncan. He's in bed. He feels OK now and he wants to get up. I push him back down and put another pillow behind his head. He doesn't want to be mothered, he wants to direct.

'Alistair, you're badly injured. We'll be fine without you. Besides, I've been asked to direct before.'

'What?'

'*Doctors*.'

'*Doctors*? That shitty BBC excuse for a drama?'

Alistair sits up energetically. I push him down again firmly and walk over to the bathroom, returning with a hand mirror.

'Look at the size of your head!' I say dramatically. I show him the close-up.

'Oh, my God,' he whimpers.

'You look like one of the waiters in Cabbages and Condoms – you can't direct a night-fishing sequence looking like that, can you?'

'No,' he says, sinking under the duvet.

I tuck him in extra tightly so he can barely move. In my room I don a red cravat, select a Montecristo No. 2 from the thermidor, and I am ready for my directorial debut. I summon the crew together for a pep talk.

'OK, guys, this is how I see it.' I give them the vision. Four guys from the village are standing in front of me looking bewildered, while Gilbert translates. Peter thinks I've been chewing khat.

'The opening shot is of Gilbert, the fishermen and me heading off into the night. It's a beautiful balmy night and the stars are shining. Everything is perfect.'

Craig sets the camera up on the shore and I jump in the boat and we head out into the lake. We quickly lose sight of Craig and the crew. It's pitch-black on the lake and the only way the fisher-men know where they are is by looking at where they've come from. It's Irish GPS. We wait for the crew to catch up and I call out their names, impatiently. Nothing. I get out my mobile.

'Craig? Where are you?'

'Waiting on the bank, watching you fuck off into the night.'

'You're meant to be following in the other boat.'

'You didn't say that.'

I apologise to Gilbert and the fishermen as we row back to shore. I'm well aware they have livings to make and, although we do pay all contributors, we like them to still carry on with their livelihoods where possible. I call a meeting but there is immediate dissent in the ranks.

'Let's talk to one another, work as a team and direct this sequence together,' says Craig.

I want to throw a boot at his head, like Ferguson did to Beckham, but I stay quiet. We row out again and crack on with the fishing. We're floating lamps on the water to attract flies that are snapped up as tasty snacks by the omena fish.

'Craig, I want you to film this sequence in a serendipitous way.'

'What the fuck does that mean?'

'Don't force it, just let it happen.'

'Where do you want me to point the camera, Robson?'

'At the fish, Craig.'

As we wait for the lamps to be surrounded by fish, the Kenyans sing a song, 'Naru naru'. I join in.

'Film it, Craig.'

'What does it mean?'

'I don't know, my Swahili's a bit rusty. How's your Maori?'

I sing the Northumberland folk song 'When the Boat Comes In'. It seems to go down well.

Fish begin to surround the first lamp. The throwers lower the nets off the side of the boat and the rowers, like me, paddle like crazy to encircle the fish. If our rowing is too slow the fish will escape. When we've rounded them up, we haul them in. It's back-breaking work and we won't know until the last moment if it's been worth it. We have a football-sized haul of omena, known as silver treasure by the islanders. They usually get thirty or forty times that in a ten-hour period and it's taken us five hours to film one cast. Not a big haul and worth about a quid.

We send the fishermen on their way so they can claw back some of the lost time. They will go from lamp to lamp for hours to catch enough to feed the village and make some money. Alistair is on the shore waiting for us. He is very irritable and feeling sorry for himself. We all tell him it went really well.

'One of the best sequences of the series,' adds Peter Prada.

Black Marlin

Alistair is much better the next day and there is no way on God's earth he is going to miss the black marlin sequence. We fly back to Watamu and are back on a big white flashy sports boat, with our new Kenyan fishing guide Jackson at the helm.

'Are you confident we'll catch today?'

'Why not?' he says in his rich-treacle voice.

'Exactly, why not?'

'Why not?'

The exchange continues thus for some time.

We're heading for Sailfish Alley, where I caught my dorado. Jackson and I set three rods, cast the lines and trawl them behind the boat. We're looking for bonitos with small squid lures, and within forty-five seconds a reel starts screaming like a small child: Waha! Waha! The line keeps going out and out and out. A bonito wouldn't take a line like that. Jackson and I look at each other. We've got a black marlin on forty-pound test line. No one's ready and the tackle's way too light: the density of a marlin leader line is 150 to 200 pounds breaking strain. I have to make a decision. Do I hard-play the fish and snap the line? (The problem being that the type of hook for bait fish isn't dissolvable – although the theory is that nature will take care of it and it will eventually come out like a splinter.) Or do I try to land this fish on tackle meant for a fish a third of the size? As I'm mulling it over the marlin blows out of the water like a missile. Craig misses the shot. We've all been caught on the back foot.

For the next two hours I play the fish and let the marlin run and run until he tires. I get the fish close to the boat for over an hour, but then it turns tail and I have to start all over again. It's a titanic battle that, slowly, I'm beginning to win. I bring the marlin back towards the boat while Craig puts the underwater camera beneath the waves to film the vast fish. It's a large male. Females are up to three times bigger.

To count as a catch I need to get as much tension on the line as possible so that Jackson is able to get hold of the leader (the last bit of line). I reel with all my might until the black marlin rises like a submarine. I can see the leader. Jackson puts a glove on and 'bills the fish', grabbing its lethal bill to make it safe. Just as he's about to get hold of the last bit of line to confirm a catch, the fish turns and bolts. The bill flicks Jackson into the air and he bombs into the water behind the boat.

'Jackson! Jackson!' We all shout helpful advice from the side: 'Don't thrash!' 'Get back on!' It is very telling that no one contemplates jumping in. He leaps back on board. I am freaking out but Jackson is calm.

'Let's carry on,' he says.

After nearly two hours he gets his hand on the leader again and I have caught a *Makaira indica*. Jackson tags the marlin to monitor migration patterns, removes the hook and then releases the giant, as heavy as a racehorse, back into the blue. He sends up the black flag so that everyone can see I caught a black marlin today.

My knees are buggered, my back's broken, but what a hit of pure adrenalin. I am in a state of manic elation. My pulse is racing, my breathing is short. I don't want it to end. I don't want to go back. But I have to.

'Hakuna Matata, Jackson.' I say, slapping him on the back. It loosely means 'Don't worry, be happy' in Swahili.

'Why not!' exclaims Jackson.

Chapter Nine

BRAZIL

The Big, the Bad and Arianna

November 2009, World Tour, Series 3

The Amazon River is so vast I can see it from 38,000 feet in the air. This freshwater system is home to over 5,600 known species of fish, possibly even accounting for 60 per cent of the fish reported to exist on the planet. Many species remain undiscovered, such is the complex network of tributaries that branch off the world's second-longest river, after the Nile. And I am going deep into the dense jungle in search of three legendary denizens – the piranha, the arowana and the arapaima. Coming with me are three other monsters of the deep: Craig, Peter and sadistic director Jamie.

We board a flight to Manaus and head deep into the planet's lungs, the Amazon rainforest. Amazonia comprises 40 per cent of the world's remaining rainforest, which filters carbon dioxide and pollutants out of the atmosphere. It's our medicine cabinet, and one of the most bio-diverse places on Earth, home to extraordinary creatures and plant life that we are only just beginning to discover. Scientists believe that less than 1 per cent of plant species have been identified. I am rattling with facts and swept up by the ecology, so it seems strange to be setting foot into a huge city slap-bang in the middle of the rainforest.

Manaus, which means 'Mother of Gods', is home to 1.5 million inhabitants and was created in the late 1800s by wealthy businessmen in the rubber boom. Latex was discovered in the sap of the rubber tree and you don't need me to tell you how revolutionary the natural material has been to all our lives: fewer babies and nicer cars. It's an ornate city and I only need to look at the opera house, Teatro Amazonas, to comprehend the opulence of the rubber magnates. It's quite beautiful in an over-the-top neo-Classical fashion. We walk into the main auditorium, where the Manaus Philharmonic Orchestra happens to be rehearsing the *Bolero* (think Torvill and Dean). It's hard to get my head round the fact I am in the middle of a theatre, in the middle of Manaus, in the middle of the Amazon rainforest.

Outside it's seriously hot and the humidity is 100 per cent. After looking round the opera house we drive to our hotel, which is again very ornate in its décor – even the tea-making kit in the room is very proper, with fine bone china cups and saucers and hand-painted tea caddies. It's a reminder of how things were during the boom times before the inevitable bust, when the British Flashman type Sir Henry Wickham smuggled rubber seeds out of the country and used them to cultivate plantations in Malaysia and Sri Lanka. Thus the British Empire took control of the rubber market and the barons in Manaus faced financial ruin.

I'm feeling rather Flashy today. Full of the yearning for adventure, full of bluster, and trying to keep the inner coward under lockdown until it's strictly necessary to run. The china teacup rattles in the saucer as I take it over to the window. I look out over the city and at the green canopy beyond but it's no good: I really don't feel in the mood for piranha fishing. Jamie bangs on my door. It's time.

Piranha 3D

Waiting for me at Lake Balbina, as well as the legendary shredding machines, is a man with a round face, grey hair, a handlebar moustache, not to mention moobs and a tummy to rival the average darts player. I choke when he says his name: 'Tarzan? Like the bronzed hunk who swung through the jungle?'

'Yes, Tarzan,' he beams.

He looks more like Bernie Winters to me.

I set out with Tarzan in his boat, and, no, he doesn't have a wife called Jane nor a chimpanzee – I did check. Balbina is an artificial lake created by flooding part of the forest in order to provide hydroelectric power to the city of Manaus. It's an eerie place. We quietly meander through lifeless trees sticking out of the water, haunting and rigid, as if marking the spot of a horrendous atrocity or meteoric event. The water is jet-black, and there is silence. The lack of wildlife or any life whatsoever makes what is below all the more menacing. We continue to gently motor in between the ghostly pale trees. It is a vast lake and I ask Tarzan how he finds his way back. He says he orientates by the trees – he knows and recognises them. Some look like pillars of salt.

We sail for forty-five minutes, more than enough time to let my imagination run away with me. We are after red-bellied piranha (*Pygocentrus nattereri*), the one species (out of approximately twenty in the region) that has a particularly vicious streak and has attacked humans on several well-documented occasions.

'If I swim naked, will they strip me to the bone, Tarzan?' I ask with wild eyes.

He tells me it's doubtful. Apparently, in order to attract the fish, you have to be bleeding profusely or have a chunk of flesh hanging off.

'Blood in the water excites them to madness,' wrote President Theodore Roosevelt in *Through the Brazilian Wilderness*, the account of his epic trip to Amazonia in 1913 with his son Kermit (I kid you not, he shared a name with the world's most famous frog). To test the theory, some local fisherman blocked off part of the river for several days to starve a school of piranha. They then pushed a cow into the river (quite possibly with an injury they inflicted beforehand) and observed as the ravenous piranhas tore the poor beast apart in a state of frenzy. I wonder what Roosevelt's holiday snaps looked like.

I certainly wasn't going to put my feet in to test the blood-excitement theory on the bunch of marauding meatheads below. I'd already tried a fish pedicure in the Philippines and I'm not up for trying the piranha version, particularly as I have athlete's foot. According to some experts, if the fish are hungry enough a fungal foot infection or a pimple on your leg is all it takes to become skeletal in seconds.

Tarzan places a big chunk of raw meat on a ruddy great hook, considering the size of the fish. The leader is wire. I've never used one before and it's bringing home how deadly their teeth are. These fish can grow to up to eight pounds with gnashers to match. They can cut through wood and leave bite marks in metal, so it's no wonder their teeth and jaws were used by Amazon tribesmen for hunting tools. I cast the bait by the side of the boat and lower the meat to twenty feet. Tarzan splashes the water to mimic the sound of a struggling fish ... or actor. Bam! Thirty seconds and I think there's a take. It's a split-second sensation. I bring the hook up – all the meat is gone.

'That was like a hit and run!'

No fish comes close to the pace of the piranha so all I can do is hope that when the fish strikes the bait, it will take the hook with it. This is a matter of luck, not skill. Over the next ten minutes I experience some violent takes, the line twitches, the rod is yanked frequently up and down, up and down, in a matter of milliseconds, and each time there is neither meat nor a fish on the end of the line. After another strike I reel in half the bait; it looks as if it has been carefully sliced by a surgeon's hand. It must be terrifying to be a bait fish down there – like a permanent *Saw* movie. You pop out in morning to get the papers and wham! You're a toothpick in a matter of seconds.

Tarzan tells me I will catch a piranha after fifteen minutes. He's dead right: I carefully reel in the piscatorial pitbull and take a look. I let Mike hold the piranha first. The red-bellied fella is short, stubby and compressed with a jaw area packed with razor-wire teeth, the type that would keep trespassers out of a military camp or a top secret nuclear facility, all tightly packed and interlocking to puncture and shred their prey. I put a knife between the fish's teeth and it clamps down hard. I remove it and show the scratches to camera. It's my turn to hold this fish and it's a bit like trying to pet a rabid dog. I take hold of it by the caudal peduncle, the narrow part of the posterior end towards the tail fin, where there are fewer spines and more importantly fewer teeth. Its armoury is all at the anterior end (front).

We catch a total of four piranhas and grill them back on land. It's definitely a fish you don't associate with eating, more with *being* eaten, but they taste very good, with a surprisingly delicate white meat. I'm not sure if the taste measures up to the risk, however.

Fish Market

The next morning, at 4 a.m., we go to the bustling local fish market in Manaus to introduce ourselves to the other ferocious predators we are hoping to meet on this adventure. The market is on banks of the Rio Negro (Black River) and is alive with fish, fish sellers and the ugliest transvestites in the business, still plying their trade. It is a case of fish and very foul. Honestly, these two blokes are so hideous they look like Harry Redknapp and Avram Grant in wigs and thongs. Think about that for a moment, then add the smell of fish! It is wrong on so many levels. The gathering crowds jeer and shout as they pass through.

As well as the trannies on display, there are catfish, piranha, peacock bass, arowana and arapaima (like the one I caught at IT Lake in Thailand, known locally as pirarucu), one of the largest freshwater fish in the world and the largest in the Amazon basin. I examine the serpent-like fish. She is nightmarish in her looks and proportions but perversely I still want to pull one ... out of the river. She is an air-breather and has a lung-like labyrinth organ that allows her to survive in oxygen-deficient oxbow lakes or even in mud, in times of drought. A fearsome predator, she uses her bony tongue to crush her quarry against the roof of her mouth, be it fish or foul, she's not fussy.

And, by the looks of it, neither are some of the men from Manaus, as the trannies trot past again. They want to be on camera and start peering over my shoulder. Another bloke wants to sell me an armour-plated catfish. I don't want an armour-plated catfish but he's desperate to be on TV. We turn away from him and move off. Undeterred, he runs after us, sticks a live fish in his mouth and does a dance, the tail still swishing. He makes the cut in the final edit; it's too weird to miss. Perhaps he could be a contender for *Brazil's Got Talent*? It beats the dancing dog act.

Rainforest Digs

As if the market wasn't strange enough, we are booked into a Fawlty Towers, Amazon-style. To get there we head up the Rio Negro for two hours by boat. The Rio Negro is one of the biggest of the Amazonian tributaries and the largest blackwater river in the world. Blackwater rivers are coloured like strong Yorkshire tea by all the tannins leaching into the water from decaying vegetation. I look across to the horizon and cannot see the other side of the river. It looks like a dark, foreboding sea.

As we arrive at the rainforest hotel, we see pink river dolphins leaping alongside of the boat. It's a heart-warming sight and I wish Taylor could be here to see them. Maybe I'll take him swimming with them one day. I catch Jamie staring at me. His eyes flicker with the flame of a cunning plan. I shake my head – me and them in the drink together, no way. He nods with a sadistic smile. Thankfully we don't have time in the schedule.

We jump off the boat and hike our bags and equipment up to our mad eco-hotel on stilts. At the moment the river is really low but during the rainy season it can rise up to sixty feet. We march across the treetop platform to reception and there to greet us is a woman who could have been out of Papa Lazarou's circus. Except I don't want her to be 'my wife now', with her coconut-encased boobs, headdress made of green and purple crêpe paper, feathers and all sorts of nonsense going on around her lady parts. She howls 'Welcome!', puts a necklace on me and wants a photo. Bewildered, I am shown to my room. It's as I suspected: the accommodation is exactly like our coconut-clad hostess, a bit strange and definitely past its best.

Peacock Bass

The man who is taking me peacock bass fishing this afternoon is Mike Cartwright, who looks a bit like Tarzan, heavy-set with a grey moustache, except Mike's wearing specs on a cord and a crazy camo T-shirt with a metal chain around his neck. He could be the ageing MC Hammer in a *Never Mind the Buzzcocks* line-up.

We hop into a fifteen-foot fishing boat with a basic prop engine and head a couple of miles upriver to some deserted islands. My tummy begins to gurgle and churn. I inwardly hope it's not the prelude of some dire Amazonian tummy bug.

I ask Mike about his name: 'Mike Cartwright doesn't sound South American.'

'I'm from British Guiana,' he explains, referring to his country (now Guyana) by its old colonial name, as if to help me place it.

'What brought you to Brazil?'

'A messy divorce.'

My tummy growls again, but thankfully Mike can't hear it over the noise of the boat.

'Ah, divorce,' I say, knowing one or two things about the topic.

'The Latin word meaning "to rip out a man's genitals through his wallet".'

He chuckles, but his doleful eyes do not share the same merriment.

Mike tells me that, pound for pound, peacock bass is one the most powerful fighting fish in the world. The impact on the lure or bait is superlative.

'I heard that the greatest fighting fish is the Papua New Guinean black bass,' I say, my stomach making a loud noise like an industrial drain.

'No, the peacock bass is incredible,' Mike assures me.

Because the water level is low we are going to trawl for tucanaré, as peacock bass are known here in Brazil. Lower water levels mean the fish tend to congregate together in a much smaller area. We are using man-made lures (rapala) that replicate a distressed bait fish. Mike sets four rods. We trawl and cast for hours in the blistering heat and catch ... nothing. We've brought no umbrellas to shade us and my tummy is now spasming. I let a silent one go and realise that I'm about to follow through. Help!

'Jamie, I desperately need to go to the toilet!'

We head to the riverbank but nature doesn't wait and I am humiliatingly forced to let the hydrant gush over the side of the boat. The more I go, the more dehydrated I am becoming and I'm starting to get in a bad way. Jamie announces, in his typical tyrannical fashion, that we have to catch a peacock bass today because not only is it an iconic fish but also they have spent a great deal of money on the steamboat accommodation, which we are travelling on to Jaraua for our next assignment.

Hours later and I finally catch a very small peacock bass, but I return him to the water as he is too small. Jamie announces a new plan: 'We will stay another night at the crazy rainforest hotel and will fish again tomorrow morning, starting at four a.m.'

We are all pretty miserable about this but Mike's face looks like he's back in touch with his ex. Obviously not an early riser, then. On the positive side, at least we're going to call it a day: I need to get to my bathroom and fast. I am about to step out of the boat when Jamie puts his hand out to stop me: 'Wait. I know you're ill, stressed and in need of a little relaxation. I have a surprise for you.'

I immediately know it's not a spa treatment.

'It's the bloody dolphins, isn't it?'

'Yep.'

As luck would have it Mike knows just the place for me to swim with dolphins at sunset. And, what's more, his friend Igor Andradis is an expert who specialises in pink river dolphins and their behaviour. Igor tells me he has such an amazing way with these creatures that if he calls them they come to him. Well, most animals would if you wave a big bucket of sardines in their face. Unfortunately, I am blissfully unaware that Igor a) isn't a marine biologist and b) has been feeding the dolphins swimming in front of us. I hang off his every word.

'Are you sure it's safe to swim here? What about piranha, caiman or other predators?'

'Trust me, it's fine. No one has ever come to any harm,' he says.

'In you get,' says Jamie. My tummy groans, mimicking my emotions. I could really do with giving this experience a miss. I dive in wearing my pants and shirt. I wish I had worn trousers.

Everyone says swimming with dolphins is a once-in-a-lifetime experience and it probably is if you don't have Igor throwing sardines and sending them into a feeding frenzy with me in the middle. They thrash the water, violently butting me out of the way. One nuts me square on in the chest; it's like being at a Newcastle game with my dad. Another takes a bite at my leg. Referee! He nips my thigh and his friend leaps at me again, so I take a swing and bash him on the pecker. This is supposed to be a life-affirming experience with gentle creatures that heal your soul, but they're more like a bunch of Sunderland supporters. But then again, I can't entirely blame them for wanting to take a pop at me – it's like someone crashing your Sunday lunch and jumping up and down on your Yorkshires. If someone did that to me I'd butt them in the chest, too.

I am furious with Igor and Jamie. I want to kill both of them. What fucking expert puts someone in the water with a bunch of dolphins at feeding time? Haven't I learnt anything from making this show? Never trust a contributor who says they're 'an expert' when they blatantly are not. It's like a bloke who feeds ducks in the park sometimes calling himself an ornithologist. Jamie loves the commotion – 'It's TV gold, Robson. TV gold!' – and my vanity perks up. I waterboard her into submission and refocus on being angry. However, my ire doesn't last long – my bottom is in charge once more. I leg it back to the hotel.

Countless explosions later I drown my sorrows in a bottle of wine. It's going down so well that I have another few glasses. The crew joins me, then I remember I have to be up at 3 a.m. to film at 4 a.m. and it's now 11 p.m. I sink another glass and stagger to bed.

*

After three and half hours' sleep I feel like hell but the sunrise a few hours later is so spectacular that the lack of rest and the raging hangover evaporate. It's far better than the nitrous oxide I used to inhale on the set of *Casualty* most mornings before work. Everyone looks like a bag of shit. Mike is monosyllabic and stooped with morning grumpiness, like the troll under the bridge. We head out. We are going to find a peacock bass and we're not coming back until we have.

Three hours later we have nihil, nada, nichts. My patience is worn through, like my bottom, and the red mist starts to rise ... and wham! I get a bite, but I lose the fish. This happens several times. Finally, another flipping three hours later, I get a bite and this time I bring home the bass – it's a two-and-a-half-pound speckled peacock bass. Other subspecies include the three-bar, popoca and butterfly, which have different markings but they all share one detail in common: on their tail fin is the eye found on a peacock's feather. The theory is that predators think that's the front end and attack, and the bass is able to escape, perhaps with a damaged tail, but with his life. This speckled fish is eating size so we're going to keep him. Mike and I tuck in back at the hotel. The bass is seasoned and grilled and it tastes delicious. We're behind with the schedule, though, so after shovelling up lunch the crew and I need to get a move on to our next RV point.

Fitzcarraldo

I take one look at the steamboat and want to run. It's exactly like the one in Werner Herzog's epic movie *Fitzcarraldo*, where this mad Caruso-loving wannabe rubber baron with delusions of grandeur tries to get a steamboat over a mountain and everyone suffers or dies.

Goodspeed to all who sail in her

Jamie is morphing into Fitzcarraldo with the scale of his extreme ambition. He's not going to take me with him. This boat is meant to be our floating hotel for the next four days. I look around and it is immediately clear we have a major problem.

'Jamie, can I have a word?'

He comes over.

'I just want you to know that there is no way I am sleeping in this rat-infested, drug-smuggling, sailor-spunked-up gambling brothel on water. I wouldn't have a dog in it. It's disgusting. Even Craig agrees it's terrible and he's from New Zealand.'

Once again I get on the phone to the production manager and Helen Nightingale.

'I'm not travelling on this vessel. It's not river-worthy, for a start, and whatever's happened on this boat – let's just say I don't think they missed out a sin. The marks of all seven are here and some have been done to death.'

'But it's the only boat available in the area,' says Helen on the phone and Jamie in unison in my ear.

The captain comes to see what the commotion is about. He

couldn't look dodgier if he'd spent six hours in make-up, fraternising with Abu Hamza. And then there is Arianna. Dear, sweet Arianna, the cook who comes with the vessel – a podgy twenty-eight-year-old with a pretty face and an eagle eye for the fellas. She winks and smiles at me saucily and when that is ignored I find her staring at me, communicating with her twinkling eyes that she wants to ride me like Seabiscuit. I am not alone in this strange compliment – she wants Craig, Peter and Jamie as well. She wants us all.

Having no other choice, we set off on HMS *Shitpit*. I take the diary camera around the rooms of this floating hovel with its sweat-ridden beds, stained sheets and toilets to rival the one in *Trainspotting*. The engine is like an MRI scanner and we've got to sail five hours into the night to Jaraua. The sun is setting and I film a piece to camera: 'Well, this is as bad as it gets ...'

Suddenly there is a klaxon. It sounds again. We all look panicked. What's happening? People are boarding the boat. Suddenly we are eyeballing half a dozen soldiers pointing large guns at us. We put our hands up and they want to know who we are, what we're doing. They want our paperwork. They arrest the captain of the boat, who is led away in handcuffs. The vessel is not seaworthy and they are not happy with his documents. We are ordered to leave the boat immediately so we grab our stuff as quickly as possible and start to pile it up on the bank. When the last of our bags are unloaded one of the soldiers pulls up the anchor and sails the boat away. Another smiles, waving.

'Welcome to Brazil!' he shouts.

We are left stranded on the riverbank, the sun setting, wondering what the hell we are going to do now.

A little way up the bank is Arianna, surrounded by all her pots, pans and utensils, which, by the way she's looking at us, she doesn't just like to use for cooking.

'I'm not going to leave you,' she says reassuringly.

She grabs my hand roughly and looks at it: 'Are you married?'

'Yes, happily.'

'Cabrão. Cabrão!'

'What?'

'I believe it's Portuguese for bastard,' says Peter coolly.

I can't confirm this as our translator, Alessandra, is tucked up in a hotel in Manaus because Helen Nightingale doesn't think a boat, with all us boys, is the right place for a young lady. Looking at Arianna we all strongly disagree – we need her here to protect us.

Jamie is straight on the satellite phone to Alessandra to work out a way of getting to our destination. But Craig, Peter and I have other ideas of getting the fuck back to Manaus and hitting the bar. Eventually we get the fixer to rustle up a tiny speedboat with a local from Manaus who can navigate us up the Amazon at night to our destination. So the whole team, along with psycho Arianna, who keeps asking me to take my wedding ring off, head into the night, embarking on a seven-hour journey to Jaraua.

São Raimundo do Jaraua, Mamirauá

We arrive at the Jaraua Reserve in the pitch-black. Our first concern is where are we going to sleep? A kind lady vacates her hut on stilts and the whole team piles in, proceeding to install hammocks so we can swing ourselves to sleep. This will be our abode for the next four nights. Five blokes snoring, farting, gurgling, dreaming, fidgeting, and all acutely aware that Arianna could jump us at any moment.

Arianna is really pissed off she can't share the same hut as us and she's not going to bed without a protest: 'She is cold and lonely in her hut.' We ignore her and slowly all drift off to sleep when suddenly I become aware of a warm sensation by my ear.

'I can't sleep. Can you?' Arianna whispers seductively.

'I could until you woke me up. Go back to your hut, Arianna.'

'Come with me, Robson.'

'No,' I say, turning my back on her as best I can in a swinging hammock. Silence descends once more.

'Jamie?' she mummers.

'Mmmn?'

'I can't sleep.'

The whole hut is now awake.

'Go away, Arianna – bugger off!' we grumble collectively.

The next morning, after little rest because of Arianna going bump in the night, we try to film our first sequence: my counterfeit arrival in the village. I step off a small boat looking like a sexually molested hobo in desperate need of lager and therapy.

'There's no one here. I wonder where everyone is?' I say.

Well, I know bloody well where all the men are: they've gone out fishing and we've missed them because we overslept. Unable to have the meet-and-greet he planned for, Jamie decides to see what the local Jaraua women are up to, and that's when we discover a scene given by God. They are playing football, of course, and Jamie asks me to join in their game. They are happy for me to do so and I need no encouragement. The girls are lovely and fit, with a kick like a frigging mule. I run round trying to play like a professional: I fall dramatically at tackles, call for the referee and run around with my shirt over my head – well, that's what the paid ones do. I pass the ball to a very cute Amazonian lass and she fucking belts it into the back of the net.

'GOAL!' I jump around hysterically inviting us all to hug and kiss but there are no takers and with the way I'm behaving there is no way I'm going to score! Arianna watches from a distant hut, arms folded like a jealous wife. She stomps inside and continues to poison our lunch.

Eventually a few guys return from their morning's fishing, including father-and-son team Fernando and Juma. Fernando, I'm told, is sixty-five but has the body of a ripped thirty-year-old gymnast. Juma is charismatic and good-looking and, I've heard, the best fisherman in the village. I hate him. Our objective is to catch tea for Fernando's wife Alija so she can cook and feed her family. Thank God Juma is with us, then, because by the way I look and feel there is no way I could catch supper on my own.

We set off in search of a Jaraua favourite: the silver arowana. The Japurà River channel is bustling with activity. The waters are alive with small fish feeding – I've never seen so many – and we all know that small fish signify predators. As we hum up the waterway, I see black caiman, alligators that can grow up to fifteen feet long. In front of us, a 500-strong congregation of white egrets takes flight, cormorants dive for fish, a barrel of squirrel monkeys call in the trees, and a wake of black vultures on the banks inter the remains of a dead animal into their lead-lined stomachs.

I am busy observing one snapshot of nature and missing the next – there is so much to see. In front of the boat there are thousands of small fish jumping out of the river, splashing back down like an ornate fountain. They are only a couple of inches long but can leap about five to ten feet and some land in the boat. I pick one up; it's iridescent silver and gold. Fernando suggests they are escaping predators but he doesn't know what they are called and neither do I. (Possibly marbled hatchetfish – answers on a postcard, please.) I go to put the little chap and the other fliers back in the water.

'No! For the soup!' says Fernando, preventing me.

However, these small acrobats pale into insignificance when compared to the mighty flying fish of the Amazon, the arowana. This fish loves to leap out of the water to devour insects. It is a long, silvery compressed fish with a strange oblique mouth and a large gape to swallow its prey. Fernando drops anchor and we start to roll out a gillnet, vertical walls of netting set across the Japurà. We are working in tandem with men in smaller boats a quarter of a mile upstream, who act as beaters, driving the fish down towards the nets like driven pheasant across the line of guns. When our net's in place they slam their paddles on the water to flush the fish towards our trap. Within minutes the gill-net starts twitching and I haul up half a dozen silver arowana. I pick one up; it's an extraordinary-looking fish with the power to fling itself two feet out of the water. And what a mouth! It's like the top of a pedal bin. It reminds me of Janet Street-Porter – only this must be her cute little sister!

The arowana is classified as *Osteoglossum bicirrhosum*. In Ancient Greek *osteoglossum* means 'bone-tongued' and *bicirrhosum* means 'two barbels', which are found under its lower lip like a couple of Rasta dreadlocks. These are thought to house the taste buds of the fish to help them search for food in the murky water. The arowana, like the arapaima, crushes its quarry with its bony tongue to eat it . . . I'm thinking Janet S-P again.

Fernando and Juma are working together in unspoken shorthand, gathering in the fish and re-laying the net. I help where I can but am conscious not to interrupt their synergy.

After a long and fruitful day out fishing, we return to the village. Aliga cooks the arowana over an open fire and Fernando, Juma and his younger brothers and sisters, the crew and I sit down to eat. The fish is placed in front of us, accompanied by manioc (cassava), which has been cultivated here since around 7,000 BC. The starch of this tuberous root produces tapioca. The manioc we are eating this evening is a dried powder that you stuff in your mouth, followed by a piece of fish. It has the consistency of small ball bearings in self-raising flour. I gave it a miss and delight my palate with Aliga's beautifully cooked arowana.

As the sun is setting I do a PTC explaining that the Amazon River system is not only where the villagers source their food but is also where they bathe and wash their clothes, as well as being their transport network. The river is a lifeline to these families and without it they would perish.

We finish for the evening and face another night in the hut-from-hell with an undeterred Arianna on the prowl. We take turns as lookout but we are useless: one by one we fall asleep on duty and the hut is left unguarded. Arianna makes a grab for Peter. There are swinging noises, creaking ropes, a frantic scrambling sound, followed by a primal scream.

'Get the fuck off me, you crazy woman!' yells Peter, falling out of his hammock.

He is in pain as well as shock. Arianna has squeezed both his testicles. She is frogmarched back to her shack and I am concerned: 'With all the cooking equipment she's got we could be murdered in our beds.'

'Shut up, Robson. Or I'll get the mad mare to cut yours off,' says a still-shaken Peter.

After a fitful night's sleep, disturbed mainly by a bloody cockerel that crowed from 2 a.m. onwards, we wait for breakfast. It doesn't come so we make our own. Arianna is on strike and is refusing to cook any more meals for us. What's more, she's copped off with a local Jaraua fisherman, the poor bloke. He'll need as much manioc and fish as he can physically digest to survive her wanton lust.

Pirarucu

I am determined to catch a pirarucu today to feed the village, and more importantly Arianna's poor sexually ravaged fisherman, so I set off with Jorge. One look at him and I know he's the business. He's dressed in pink trousers, a yellow cardie and a straw hat – only a tough guy could get away with that outfit. He has a kindly way about him and he finds me amusing. But I know he's thinking 'Who the hell is this guy? Bruce Parry was way better.'

This morning the village has received some good news. There is a sustainable fishing policy enforced across the reserve and a government official is here to tell the village their quota for pirarucu hasn't been caught; as a result, over the next ten days, they are allowed to catch 500. Although the government has banned commercial fishing of pirarucu, catch-and-release is permitted in certain areas of the Amazon basin and native tribes, like the Jaraua villagers, are allowed to harvest this giant on a strict quota system. Thanks to these restrictions the pirarucu's numbers are beginning to recover.

I ask Jorge, using my best mimes, where he stores the nets and fishing tackle? To my dismay I discover we are using a harpoon.

(Nets, rods and reels are just too expensive.) It's brutal but that's not why I am anxious – I was useless at javelin at school. I have never had any upper body strength. I was crap at shot put, rubbish at throwing the cricket ball but was very good as Captain Hook in the school production of *Peter Pan*. Armed with a couple of spears, Jorge and I head upriver looking for signs of the large serpent-like creature to surface and show itself. The pirarucu is an air breather and comes to the surface in a swishing motion every ten to fifteen minutes to take a gulp of air. The fish is only visible for a split second but it's enough to pinpoint and launch our harpoons. Well, that's the theory.

The temperature is nearing fifty degrees and there is no shelter. Remember, the heat is reflected off the water so it's a double whammy, and the sunscreen is applied and re-applied as it trickles off. We slowly glide along looking for signs of disturbances in the water.

SWOOSH! SWOOSH! Jorge raises his hand, indicating I need to and keep quiet as we are now in stealth mode: we have spotted our target. And there is more than one, so all we can do now is wait. Wait and stand, arm raised with the spear like a coiled spring. Waiting and standing and waiting. After three minutes my arm begins to ache.

(Loud whisper) 'Jorge, my arm is about to drop off.'

He looks at me, smiling. I see something move in the weeds so I raise my harpoon.

'Jorge, what's that?' I say dramatically, ready at any moment to deploy my weapon.

'Alligator,' he says.

'Oh.'

I'm sure poor Jorge has been told I'm an expert from Europe

and now he's discovered that I am in fact a puny, whingeing, mediocre harpoon-throwing lad from Newcastle upon Tyne. Actually he doesn't know I'm a crap harpoon thrower yet – but he will. Now I wish ex-Royal Marine Bruce Parry were here as well.

I need to lower my harpoon but Jorge signals for me to keep it raised – I only have a second to fire and if I'm not primed it'll be too late. Whoosh! To our right, about thirty yards from the boat, the fish takes a big breath like a drunk lass preparing to go into a stinky public lav, and Jorge fires his harpoon – he just misses. Seconds later after the fish has disappeared without trace, I fire. I miss, just. In fact, I'm short by about twenty-five yards. Jorge laughs. He's never seen anything so funny in his life.

'The thing is,' I try to explain in an elaborate system of arm gestures, 'I had no rehearsal for this and Jamie, that "cabrão" of a director, thought it would be a good idea not to tell me the method of fishing.'

In this moment I know for a fact that if I aimed the harpoon at Jamie I would get a flipping bullseye.

The scene of Jorge just missing and me throwing like Bridget Jones continues for hours and hours. The unrelenting heat is getting to me and so is Jorge's chuckling.

'You might be laughing at me, Jorge, and you may think my technique leaves a lot to be desired, but quite frankly, bonny lad, you've caught fuck-all as well!'

He smiles and ups the ante, starting to throw like Fatima Whitbread.

Seven hours go by and I am delirious. Jorge spots a disturbance in the water twenty yards directly in front of the boat. He fires. It's a hit, and the rope attached to the spearhead tightens. We are in.

'You are amazing, Jorge. Simply amazing!'

Then the rope slackens and the fish is off.

'No! Jorge, no!'

The spearhead is retrieved and all that is on the end is a single scale of a giant pirarucu, equal in size to the palm of my hand. It would appear to belong to a 200-pound-plus fish. Morale is rock-bottom.

'Don't worry, Jorge. All we have to do is get the other part of the fish.' I suggest helpfully.

We spot the creature time and time again but I keep missing and finally, near to a swoon, my deltoids shot, I collapse and lie prostrate in the bottom of the boat. A passing fisherman takes pity on me and lends me his umbrella. So there I am, fanning myself like Helena Bonham Carter with a white parasol, while Hercules is primed and ready to take out the serpent. Splosh! Jorge strikes again and it's a hit! And this time the rope is running, the spearhead is secure and Jorge has a victorious expression. I can only stare in awe at the man's endurance, strength and skill.

'We did it, Jorge! We did it!'

Jorge throws me a look.

'*You* did it! *You* did it!'

The creature shows itself in the distance to be a 100-pound pirarucu. Jorge takes the rope and starts to fight the fish, trying to bring it to the side of boat. Unsure of what to do, I find a wooden club.

'Do you need this?' I enquire.

It's a veritable cardinal rather than the modest fishing priest I use to dispatch brown trout on the Coquet. He asks me to do the honours, so, raising the club, I bring it down on the fish's head with all my might. It's brutal but swift and efficient, and it's how these guys survive.

As I sail back to camp I have time to reflect on what an astonishing journey along the world's most iconic river this has been. It's been a great privileged. To top it off, the fixer has ferried in 140 cans of Skol and an electric piano out of nowhere – this river really is the giver of life. Our classically trained sound engineer, Prada, starts banging out the tunes. I sing 'Proud Mary' as Arianna gyrates in front of us, trying to show us what we've all been missing. And thank the Lord we missed it! Her fisherman beau takes her away by boat – now that truly *is* a great river.

Chapter Ten

CUBA

'The Land of the Lotus Eaters'

December 2009, World Tour, Series 3
As I lean out of the cab window taking in the sights, I am hit by the distinctive smell. It reminds me of when I was on holiday as a kid in Binibeca, Spain – the smell of baked terracotta in the warm air, only this time mixed with the savoury smoke of cigars. I inhale deeply. Havana is alive with colour: the faded colonial architecture, the fabulous 1950s cars, the women, the street musicians, and the vibrant blue ocean. I feel heady with excitement. Jamie, Peter and Craig are caught up, too. Cuba has an intoxicating flavour and I want to lap it up, bathe in it and lick the bowl.

We pull up at the iconic Hotel Nacional, where Sinatra, Marilyn, the Rat Pack, Rita Hayworth and Ant & Dec have stayed before me. We dump our kit and take a wander round Havana. Americans haven't been able to legitimately visit this Caribbean island since the Cuban Missile Crisis in 1962, and the embargo is still in place today. As a result of these tough sanctions, Cuba is a place that has remained unhomogenised by the outside world. Florida is only sixty miles away but the cultures couldn't be further apart. And even though the islanders have been held in an iron grip by Communist dictator Fidel Castro since he seized power in 1959, and are now ruled by Fidel's younger brother, Raúl, their sense of identity feels so defined, their self-worth defiant.

We walk past a cigar factory and pop in for a quick look around. I want to stay longer but there's no time to film – our schedule is so tight. Contrary to popular myth, Cuban cigars are not rolled on the thighs of virgins, but the factory girls do stretch the tobacco leaves on their laps as they sort and grade them. A professional storyteller reads to them as they work. Cuban women are like no other – beautiful, with classical features, healthy skin, no make-up and plenty of life in their eyes. I listen for a while before asking the name of the book. It's Harry Potter. The reader tells me she also reads Dickens and Hemingway. Cuba might have a terrible human rights record but it has one of the highest literacy levels in the world and most people speak English fluently.

Jamie has decided he wants to celebrate the Cuban clichés. Across the road is parked a blue open-top Cadillac in immaculate condition. The Cubans not only take great care of their vehicles, polishing and buffing like the average classic-car geek in Britain, they also engineer the parts themselves. I jump in the back of the Cadillac Eldorado and Jamie hands me a mojito. I'm liking this new non-sadistic style of directing. I sip my drink. Only a Cuban mojito tastes this fresh. My taste buds give the minty rum syrup a full-on snog while Jamie cuts a cigar and lights it. He hands over my Montecristo No.2 and I am taken for an elegant tour of the town. I feel like Sinatra.

Malecón Promenade

Before sunset we film a fishing sequence on the Malecón Promenade in Havana. Fidel Castro, worried his citizens would attempt to flee his regime, strictly controlled access to all boats. As a result of this, all fishing boats are owned by the state and use is only for the privileged few. This is bad news for Cubans, but good news for fish stocks, and better news for me. One of the only ways for people to catch fish is off the promenade. Hundreds of men and women line the sea wall, day and night, using rods and hand lines to catch bait fish, snapper and sardines, which they eat or sell to the government-owned restaurants, some of which are house-based. Basically you can go to people's houses and they will cook for you but the money earned has to go to the state, otherwise they will go to prison. This is enforced by the secret police, who, dressed in plain clothes, are indiscernible from regular citizens. We have been followed from the moment we arrived and I know that two men in a black Ford are watching us right now. It's a strange feeling.

There is a knack to fishing off the promenade but if you don't know what you're doing, like me, it's like casting a line into a washing machine! A wave smacks the sea wall and we all get drenched. *Ah, that's why everyone's wearing anoraks*, I think to myself. I had thought maybe it was going to rain. The trick is to put your line out in water, jump behind the wall and then jump back up. The waves bring the fish in. Lots of people are catching fish, except me, so I ask some guys across the way what bait they are using. Shrimp. We buy their whole supply. But it's not the bait that's getting fish, it's the spot they are fishing in. There are lots of sardines and small jacks and we're in the wrong place. But there's no room. I cast again in the same barren spot and vainly hope something might swim by. A wave slaps me in the face.

The sun is beginning to go down and the light starts to change. Out of the corner of my eye I see a pelican stealing one of the fishermen's bait. I chuckle. Then I realise the pelican is actually on the end of his line. *It must be an accident,* I think – it's not. This dude is purposely catching pelicans for a local restaurant to roast. Alessandra, our AP, gets deeply upset. The man yanks the pelican in, grabs it, closes its wings and binds its beak and feet. Alessandra is now beyond distressed.

I tackle him: 'That's not a fish!'

He looks at me as if to say 'So what? Mind your own business', and I begin to get upset myself. But then I start thinking *What's the difference between catching a fish or a bird? Am I being hypocritical?* I look at the pelican – his distress somehow seems more poignant, more dramatic. To ease Alessandra's inflamed sensibilities I offer to buy the pelican from the guy. He's over the moon. He'll just go and catch another one but I'm pleased with myself, thinking I've done a good turn. Alessandra hugs me and dries her eyes. And then the pelican attacks me. I untie the bird's beak first and it goes berserk. Now, I want to carefully explain my rationale here; I know what you're thinking 'Why didn't you unbind the feet and *then* the beak?' Well, I didn't want to untie the feet first in case it escaped with a taped beak destined for a slow death by starvation. I couldn't think of anything worse, so now I have to deal with this furious-feathered-fucker viciously pecking me on the arm. I'm bleeding. Bleeding! I hurriedly untie the pelican's feet, deciding that all pelicans are inherently racist. I yell at him in my head.

'I'm the good guy who rescued you from the bad guy, you idiot! But you think we all look the same, don't you? You racist.'

He looks at me with his blue eyes as if to say, 'Yeah, like you can really tell us pelicans apart, you asshole? I bet you probably thought I was a fucking heron or a swan first of all, didn't you?'

'No, how dare you? Never in my life have I met such a rude ... pelican! I want you to know I only saved you because she,' I point at Alessandra who is now crying again, '*she* wanted me to. I should have let you roast.'

He pecks me on the arm again.

'Ow!'

I let him go and he flies off without so much as a kind look behind. I wait for him to circle above or do a fly-past like animals do in the movies but I get nada.

'Bloody pelicans.'

'Did you get that on camera?' Jamie asks Craig.

'No, it was too ridiculous,' he says.

Jamie is disappointed. As you know, he loves a good sequence where I experience pain, especially at the hands of nature.

After more than enough excitement for one day we walk back to the hotel. The Cuban Film Festival is on and there is a bustle of activity with press and filmmakers. I try to do a bit of schmoozing with a couple of directors but I soon tire of their company and want to be back with my team. We decide to have 'welcome to Cuba' mojitos and an early night ... by 1 a.m. we are all shit-faced, our speech slurring, like we're electing a new pope. We all have a taste for the Cuban elixir.

Freshwater Tarpon

At breakfast we are all feeling like poo. Why do we do it to ourselves? We travel an hour and half by van southeast of Havana to the River Hatiguanico National Park. I am freshwater tarpon fishing with Lazuro Vinola, who, according to our fixer, is the best tarpon fisherman in Cuba, if not the world. Philippe Rodriguez, who is supposedly the best guide in Cuba, if not the world, accompanies him. No pressure on them then.

We motor up the sparkling river on a state-owned boat, driven by Lazuro, who is also the park's head ranger. I ask the guys to give me one piece of advice for tarpon fishing.

'Patience,' they say in unison. 'You will need a lot of patience. It's very difficult to catch tarpon. You will lose many fish today. Take, take, take, off, off, off,' adds Philippe.

'Oh, ye of little faith,' I say, fronting it.

I mean, that's not to say I haven't had my bad days, I think to myself. We all have. There was the time I lost the monster sturgeon in Canada but that was totally Randy's fault. Or what about the dorado in the Philippines, which was gutting. The worst was probably dropping another man's machaca in Costa Rica. That was a real low moment. Lazuro and Philippe trade glances and smile, knowing that, because of my fly-fishing background, I will automatically set the rod incorrectly and the fish will come off. They keep schtum.

Philippe slows the boat down and we come to a stop, and he cuts the engine.

'Tarpon spook easily,' he tells me.

As we gently drift down the middle of the river I try a few practice casts. The tarpon tend to hide in the root systems of overhanging trees and Lazuro tells me I need to cast two feet from the edge of the root. We travel downriver all day, perhaps twenty miles, and never see a single soul.

Lazuro practises his cast. Wham! A tarpon takes the lure and leaps three feet out of the water. It's a twenty-pound fish but it comes off and he's gutted. I commiserate with him: 'It's an awful feeling,' I say.

He speaks to Jamie in the boat across the way: 'Please don't show that.'

'No, of course not,' says Jamie, with his fingers crossed behind his back.

We drift to the spot where Lazuro says I'll catch my first tarpon. I'm using a popper – a weighted plastic lure in the shape of a sprat. I cast and I'm in range. I pop the floating line across the water a foot at a time to mimic a bait fish. Pop, rest, pop, rest. Wallop! A tarpon is on. I immediately set the rod up like a fly line. The fish comes off. Little do I know that it is impossible to set the hook in the upper part of the mouth because it's solid bone; the trick is to set the hook in the lower part of mouth. I lose seven tarpon before the guys let me in on this secret.

'You need to set the rod away from you, parallel to the water,' says Lazuro.

Set down, away and down again, tip to the surface of the water. Got it. On the eighth take I forget everything I have just been told and set the rod up. Of course I lose the fish and have the biggest hissy fit ever.

'I cannot lose EIGHT fish!'

One of them whispers in Spanish (picked up by Alessandra): 'What a drama queen.' It's true – today I am channelling Ava Gardner.

Nine, ten, eleven and twelve all stay on but come off during the fight. I set the hook correctly in the mouth, but the fish leaps and it's over. After fish number twelve Lazuro lets me in on the second crucial secret: 'Tarpon are known as the Silver King, and when a fish leaps you must bow to the king and drop the rod to the water.'

The fish are bigger than the leader on the line in terms of weight, so when they jump the dead weight will snap the line, hence needing to angle the rod downwards.

'Thanks for the top tip, guys,' I say, wishing they'd bloody told me this earlier.

Tarpon number thirteen is on. I set the rod away, bow to the king when he leaps and catch my first ever tarpon! I bring him aboard with the help of Lazuro. He is a bright, clean-looking fish with scales of sterling silver. His distinctive upturned mouth reminds me of the arowana's pedal-bin trap and, just like the Amazonian fish, the tarpon is an air-breather, extracting oxygen with the help of a modified swim bladder. These fellas are very adaptable fish and can reside in a variety of habitats, from low-oxygenated stagnant ditches or ponds as newly spawned tiddlers to freshwater rivers or brackish creeks as juveniles, to the saltwa-ter of the ocean as adults. As long as the water's warm they don't care. They're a bit like me sister Joanne when it comes to the cold – they just can't stand it. Her house is like a sauna, I tell you.

When tarpon reach sexual maturity between the ages of seven and thirteen, they return to the ocean to join the other adults migrating. And at the end of this trip we are going after a Big Daddy tarpon that could be ten times the size of this youngster today and measure up to eight feet. I pop tarpon junior back into the river – apparently these guys aren't for eating, as they are too bony.

Strangely we feel similarly about the hookers who chat to us in a bar later that evening. Naïvely we think they are friendly locals who want to trade a bit of banter – that's before we meet their pimp, Scarface. We tell them firmly we're not interested and they scarper. Some things are not meant to be caught and taken home – they should be released very quickly or never fished for in the first place!

Bonefish

The anglers who have done it say it's the most exhilarating feeling in the world, and those anglers who haven't done it dream of the day they will try it. I'm talking about bone-fishing. It's the exotic aspiration of the fly-fishing fraternity and I just hope it lives up to the hype.

From our hotel we head 200 miles northeast to the island of Cayo Romano, via El Pedraplén, a thirty-mile-long causeway, which in places is treacherous. I had wondered what the planks in the back of the van were for and I soon discover they are for making ad hoc bridges where the road ceases to be. We make several of these temporary crossings where the waves from the ocean have taken great chunks out of the tarmac, like marzipan. At one point I get out of the 4x4, as there is a ruddy great drop to the sea below. I'm not staying on board taking bets as to whether the car is going to make it across or not. The driver negotiates across a crude wooden bridge that the locals have built. Castro might well have taught everyone to read but his roads are crap.

The island is empty, as is the sea. There's no one around because no one is allowed a boat. I meet Eddie who, my fixer says, is the best fisherman in Cuba, if not the world. He has a handsome face with a big moustache but unfortunately he doesn't speak a word of English. We muddle on with sign language.

Bonefish are notoriously difficult to catch because they are very skittish, reacting to every sound and vibration. One slip-up and the fish is gone. Known as the 'grey ghost', its silver design reflects everything around it, making it invisible, like a moving mirror. The best way to spot this pelagic phantom is by its shadow on the sea floor. I am using my own seven-weight fly rod I've brought with me. It's a Hardy Zenith with a Hardy Angel fly reel given to me by Val McDermid, the writer of *Wire in the Blood*. I show my rod to Eddie and he shakes his head and laughs.

I say, 'Hardy's is the best in the world!' but he shakes his head again. 'Listen, I have caught some big trout with this rod.'

It's our only conversation; from now on I have to be totally silent. This is the hardest part of fishing for me.

Eddie cuts the engine and begins to punt across the gentle lapping sea. The water is shallow and gin-clear as we head out to the salt flats, where the bonefish reside. They are powerful fish that take off at incredible speeds, which is extraordinary given that shallow saltwater contains little oxygen. These fish extract oxygen from the water in a hyper-efficient way in order to move like forks of lightning. Eddie stops punting and lets the boat float with the current. We are fishing from a platform boat, specifically designed for bone fishing, with a high umpire's chair for spotting fish. Eddie is sitting high in the chair and I am at the front of the boat, ready to cast. I need to be accurate – two feet off its mouth will spook it, but four feet away is too far. It's a windy day so it's not going to be easy.

*

Eddie puts his finger to his mouth, signalling to be quiet. He sees something and points.

'Cast,' he says softly.

'Cast at what?' I whisper back.

'Fish,' he hisses.

'I can't see it.'

I pull the line out from the reel, ready to load the rod, but the whir of the reel spooks the fish. Eddie puts his hands on his head in despair.

'It's gone,' he says.

'I never saw it anyway,' I say, grinning.

Using a mixture of English, Spanish and sign language he tells me, 'Pull the line out beforehand. You need to be prepared.'

After the first unsuccessful attempt I suggest Eddie uses the clock system to tell me where to cast. He understands and we are set. Five minutes pass.

'One o'clock,' whispers Eddie.

I see a shadow. I do two false casts that don't touch the water. Over, over, out, my first cast is on the money. He gives me the OK sign. A fish comes towards the lure. I have to keep a three-foot distance to replicate an insect moving jerkily along the water's surface. I do this using a figure of eight retrieve, winding the line gently around my fingers. It's a very effective method of pulling the line in. The fly I am using is like a bug-eyed nymph or caddisfly with large eyes, and it's weighted. Bonefish also like small fish, but they are particularly partial to their insects.

A six-pound bonefish gobbles my fly and WHOOSH! It shoots off like an underwater bullet, creating a bow wave in its wake. Faster and faster it turbocharges off in a straight line, zipping off right, straight again, and back to the right. It's taking the leader, fly line and backing line out to sea and I only have fifty metres of backing because I use this rod for trout and the odd salmon in Northumberland, and no fish has ever taken this much line this far out before! As it gets to the backing I start to panic. I am going to run out of line and – oh, holy mother of Jesus, son of God, no – I haven't tied the backing onto the reel with a fucking arbor knot! The fish is going to fuck off to the Bahamas with my entire line. I grab the line with my hand and put the brakes on. The line snaps and the fish is away.

Arbor Knot

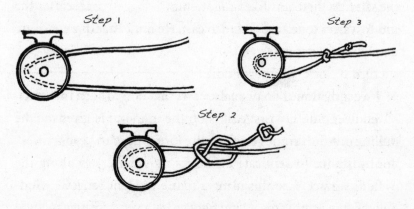

Step 1

Step 2

Step 3

Eddie is agog. He cannot believe what I have done. I didn't think I needed the extra backing or to tie it on with a knot. It's one of the most stupid mistakes of my career. Eddie continues staring at me with absolute incredulity, but on the plus side I realise now that bone-fishing really *is* as incredible as everyone said it was! This is no consolation for Eddie and he is still poleaxed.

'What an extraordinary fish! And the run – while it lasted – was out of this world. Unbelievable.'

I can't meet Eddie's eyes. He steps down from the umpire's chair, shaking his head. He silently takes my rod and winds in the line, then passes me his own. It's a 10-weight, built for the job with 150 metres of backing, fixed with an arbor knot . . .

I feel so ashamed of myself and wring my hands anxiously. Jamie, however, is all smiles. He fucking loves it. My catastrophes are his triumphs and I hate him like a Frenchman. Eddie punts over to a new spot but the water is so shallow that the draught of the boat is touching the bottom. We get off and wade in the turquoise water, like real hunter-gatherers in pursuit of our bony quarry. No one is about and the distressed trees of the salt flats look beautiful. Eddie is focused. He genuinely wants me to catch a phantom today. He also knows I hate myself enough for two people and gives me a kind look, willing me to succeed.

We gently wade out when I see a shadow. It's a huge bonefish.

'Eddie. Eddie!' I stage-whisper, wading towards the fish and pulling out the line.

The fish fucks off.

Eddie says, 'You have got to shush.' I upbraid myself internally. *Eddie is the spotter, yer numpty. You need to concentrate on being prepared for when he calls a fish.* But after the adrenalin rush of the first run I am way too excited. Seconds later he says, 'Two o'clock.' My first cast is short; my second cast is in the window. The fish takes it and flies. It penetrates the water like a Lockheed SR-71 Blackbird. I don't know what the equivalent of Mach 3 is in water but this baby's packing some Gs. Whoosh, it continues to run and I have enough line and now the experience to know how to slow it down – it's been a quick learning curve.

I start pulling the fish back in but it changes direction and bolts towards me. I strip the line to keep it tight and he keeps on coming. I wonder if he'll break my legs on impact. He darts away again taking out 150 metres of line at top speed. It's incredible. But this fish is built for short bursts of speed and not endurance. He's Usain Bolt, not Mo Farah, and his race is run. After a fifteen-minute battle I reel in the grey ghost. I look at him and can't believe he's not panting after that incredible run. What makes bonefish so spectacular is that they are so unassuming in appearance. His shallow slope at the head is more elliptical in design than other powerful fish and he has a proportionally larger forked tail to his body, which helps him move through the water, but he isn't solid muscle like a barracuda or jack. His power comes from within, somehow. A bonefish is, I guess, a bit like Bradley Wiggins: not much to look at, being so lean and almost gangly, but the power within him to win a Tour de France and then Olympic gold makes him magnificent.

I raise my silver medal – he is only four pounds in weight, relatively tiny for the race he has run, and as I pop him back I imagine what it must be like to catch a bonefish three or four times his size.

Supper and Salsa

We head back with Eddie across the causeway to the hillside town of Trinidad. It's a beautiful old place with cobbled streets, where old men and girls are dancing and laughing and there's not a single tourist. A band is performing in the square: twelve guys playing double bass, trumpet, maracas and guitars. People have just come from work – they stop by to dance salsa and enjoy a drink. There is a raw beauty to the Cubans that does not require make-up or costumes.

A stunning woman dances with her friend, and when she sees us she asks me to dance. *My father was a champion ballroom dancer so I must have his genes*, I think. *I pray*. She grabs me and says, 'Uno, dos, tres, cuatro, cinco, seis.' She is doing salsa; I am doing Dad-dancing. Yet again I have brought shame on the family name. She counts again: 'Uno, dos, tres, cuatro, cinco, seis.' I am trying to keep up but it's a terrible situation. I'm the guy who doesn't know the dance, surrounded by people who do. I have an idea. I show her 'the lawnmower'. I pull the cord three times left to right, then dance forward pushing the lawnmower. She kisses me on the cheek and goes to dance with another man. I am stranded. Jamie is pissing himself laughing and decides that we need to film a sequence where I am taught how to salsa properly. He says, 'If you catch lots of fish tomorrow, I'll hire a seriously hot instructor.'

Barracuda

I spring out of my bed extra early the next morning.

'I need to catch me some fish,' I say, stretching.

I do my morning exercises, limbering up in preparation for another evening of salsa. But first the fishing . . .

Guillermo Perez and Jorge are going to show me how plentiful the ocean is around here. They are government fishermen and have one of three boats in Trinidad Port, which are used as game-fishing charters for tourists. After shooting some meet-and-greet footage, we are marched off the boat by the police. They want to check our passports and documents, which we have to carry with us at all times. We are taken to an office nearby and after about an hour they are satisfied we aren't CIA spies and we head out to sea.

'Ha-ha! Fooled them again,' I chuckle.

Apparently fishing trips, birdwatching and charity work are classic forms of deep cover.

Barely out of the harbour, we start to trawl our Rapala lures, which are shaped like small bait fish and mimic them in the water. I film a piece to camera saying, 'Today we could catch grouper, jacks, barracuda . . .' – but as I'm speaking both lines go off simultaneously. Moments later we have two barracuda around four and a half pounds apiece. I pick up one of the ambushed predators and put it in front of the camera. I open its mouth for a close-up.

'It's equipped to kill,' I say. 'Remember, this is the guy who killed Nemo's mum.'

On board is a metal priest with a wooden handle. I haven't used one like this before – they are usually all wood. I hold up the fish and go to strike it but it twitches and I miss and smash the glass of a little gate at the back of the boat. Jamie can't breathe from laughing; tears are streaming down his face. Peter and Craig are bent double. Thankfully Guillermo and Jorge are up top and didn't hear the crack. I panic, trying to hide the cracked glass with my body. Peter finds a towel and I casually drape it over. IWC never broadcast the footage, afraid the Cubans would kick up a fuss and bill us for thousands of pounds, and I just want to say here and now I am truly sorry.

I dispatch both barracudas and dinner is on me. I am going to cook them back in Trinidad.

'How good-looking is this dance instructor going to be, Jamie?'

'If you catch some more fish, Eva Longoria level.'

This time I want to see if we can catch another type of fish for our supper. I set the lines again. Wham! Wham! It's barracuda again and they are everywhere. I pull them in.

In order to get another species, we anchor the boat and go in pursuit of bottom feeders. I am after grouper, with some squid on the hook, and before long I catch a beauty. The trick is to pull the bait in such a way that you do it very slowly. But when there is a take you need to yank up the line very fast. I'm not as quick off the mark as I should be and the grouper takes the bait back to its cave. Internally I start to panic, thinking the line will snap, but Jorge tells me to let it go slack and wait for the grouper to come out of his cave. I take the tension off the line and wait. The grouper swims out of his lair, the line goes tight and I pull him up. He's a brown-spotted grouper, covered in red and tan speckles. His dorsal and tailfins are jet-black with white edges and the first seven spines are iced with tartrazine, warning of their toxic nature.

I take the smorgasbord of barracuda and grouper to a restaurant in Trinidad and, in my best sign language, say we would like them cooked with chips. The chef tells me in Spanish how he will prepare them. I nod, not understanding a word. We sit out on the cobbled street, enjoying the warm evening. It's mojitos all round again. I've certainly got a taste for them and am beginning to get a little mojito belly.

Half an hour later the waiter returns with fried, poached and grilled grouper and barracuda, accompanied by a mountain of patatas fritas. I try the grouper first.

'It's sensational – a salsa on the senses,' I declare.

The crew groans. Surprisingly the barracuda is just as good. The poached fish is more succulent but I am a fan of all of it. A

Cuban band starts playing and everyone gets up to dance. Jamie has set the whole thing up and – surprise, surprise – no one wants to dance with me. Cue ravishing salsa instructor (Jamie's done well) who takes me by the hand and encourages me to go with her, and I really want to on so many levels. It's an intoxicating mixture – mojitos, salsa and Latin women. We glide to the music. Midway I say, 'Do you know the lawnmower?' I do the dance and she loves it. We do the lawnmower together.

'You are so funny,' she says. I completely charm her. She looks over my shoulder at Jamie as if to say, 'When am I getting paid?'

I drink another six mojitos and we dance the night away. This truly is the Land of the Lotus Eaters and I don't want to leave, ever.

Giant Tarpon

One man who came to Cuba fifteen years ago and never left is Fabrizio Barbassa. The charismatic Italian married a seriously red-hot smoking Cuban lady and is living the dream, taking tourists tarpon fishing in Cayo Las Brujas. Fabrizio wasn't always a fisherman; he used to be a Formula 1 driver until he suffered a terrible collision in 1995 in which he broke his legs and an arm and sustained severe chest and head injuries. After that he decided to get out of the fast lane for good, and I don't blame him.

Today we are in pursuit of giant grown-up tarpon, which can grow up to eight feet and leap their own height. That's like Lawrence Dallaglio doing the high jump. We are on a similar platform to the bonefish boat except this one has an F1 400 b.h.p. engine. We motor across the iron-flat ocean. Samuel Yeras

On its day, Ascension Island is the greatest fishing destination on the planet

The one that *didn't* get away

Honestly, it was THIS BIG!

On this adventure I have caught the weird, the wonderful . . . and the downright dangerous

During this extreme journey it was only a matter of time before I caught king crabs

Wouldn't a worm
be better?

WE.ARE.IN!

A bigger version of
something you might
see in a bowl at home

Some of the scenery on this trip can only be described as simply breathtaking

'Team Extreme' living the Dream in Patagonia

Not for the first (or indeed the last) time, we play the waiting game

Rarely a case of 'one man and his boat' and barely enough room to swing a minnow, you could cut the atmosphere with a cricket stump

There are so many lovely folk in the world, and my philosophy is you should try to meet as many of them as you can

Table for two, please

Travelling the globe and catching fish most anglers only dream of, where do I sign up?

Err... Erm... I think this is its head

One lean, mean, killing machine

The crew in
Costa Rica

Pound for pound the
Papuan black bass has to
be the greatest fighting
fish on the planet. Think
of it as Muhammad Ali
in fish form

Spot the guy who
thinks the plan for
today *isn't* a good one

My Uncle Matheson, the Obi-Wan Kenobi of fly-fishing and the man who taught me everything I needed to know about angling. Can you tell he's genuinely gutted I got the gig and he didn't?

My dad, Robson Senior, or Big Rob as he is known to his mates. My Rock, well, more a mountain

Pompa, Fabrizio's assistant, tells me what I can expect from today's trip.

'There are thousands of tarpon here. You will catch many,' he says.

I take it with a pinch of salt. I'm just happy to see what happens. However, after the bone-fishing and my earlier tarpon experience with Lazuro and Philippe, I am beginning to realise the Cubans don't bullshit.

We arrive at the spot where Fabrizio thinks the tarpon are. He cuts the engine. As we wait I wonder whether he can smell fish, like Steve Hall in the Azores.

'The fish will come to us,' he says presciently. 'There are giant shoals in the area that move around. They will come.'

If they are nearby and something spooks them they will leap out of the water. They also show themselves by rolling to the surface in order to breathe. This is when they are most vulnerable to predators and piscivorous fishermen.

We wait two hours for them to show.

'Any size will do, Samuel,' I say.

Jamie is starting to get irritable, but Fabrizio is super-cool with not a care in the world. All of a sudden the vast shoal of tarpon show themselves to us. They are running by the side of the boat, like the superpod of dolphins in Costa Rica. We start casting out fly lines forty yards from the boat. I use a 12-weight rod – not like a Spey rod; much shorter. I get a take. I set the rod parallel to my hip bone, keep it down and set the line as if pulling back a bow. I reel as quickly as I can. It leaps. Wow! It comes off. Bugger. What did I do wrong? I realise that I forgot to bow to the king when it leapt, that's what. I raised my rod up like a revolutionary and put two fingers up to the king. I'm a big fan of royalty – well, Elvis, Freddie Mercury's Queen and now the Silver King – and next time he leaps I'm going to kowtow, nay grovel like Uriah Heep at his feet.

Fabrizio senses my inner turmoil.

'Don't worry, it happens, Robson. In the moment you forget what to do,' he says generously. 'They're here. They're here. We will catch.'

I cast again, a tarpon takes the lure, the king leaps, I bow my rod and for the next hour Fabrizio and I take it in turns to bring this giant fish to the boat. The fish is running, leaping, and diving down to the bottom, which causes real stress on the body but my back is fine because I'm using a fly-line and not a harness. I slow down the barrel of the reel with the palm of my hand. Only a wuss would ask for a glove – real men do it with skin. I now have real calluses to prove my machismo. I used to be a hand model before this show.

I love fly-fishing and somehow this method seems a fairer fight than all the heavy-duty tackle used for game fishing. I feel closer to Santiago – after all he caught a marlin on a hand line in Hemingway's novel *The Old Man and the Sea*, which the author wrote and set here in Cuba. With the help of Samuel, we get the fish on board. It's breathtaking. Its silver scales are like elaborate chain mail. This is *Megalops atlanticus*, which loosely mean 'big eyes of the Atlantic'.

Nothing can top this extreme fish. Nothing can top Cuba. I found love here, not in a person, but in a culture and a place that I haven't experienced before, other than with Newcastle. Fabrizio fell in love, too, and he is now at peace with himself, he is serene. I look at him and think it must be a great feeling to be at peace with yourself. In the material world we have such high expectations of our lives and ourselves and sometimes our goals are impossible. Dissatisfaction and depression creep into the void between our expectations of how things should pan out and how they actually are. If we don't expect too much and we remember to get pleasure from the natural world and simple pleasures, we too can feel at peace. Especially in Cuba!

None of the team wants to leave the next morning; we all want to stay here forever. Maybe we could miss the plane and go another day? Where are we going next, anyway? I don't really care. In the distant recesses of my mind, Taylor and Vanya call to me. I snap out of my reverie; the spell is broken. I have to manhandle Jamie, Craig and Peter into the cab to the airport. Peter is worst of all.

'Go on without me. I'll only slow you down. There are others who have the gift of sound.'

'Well, none like you, Prada. You are a fucking one-off, my friend,' I say, booting him into the passenger seat.

Had I not had a beautiful wife and child to return to I would still be there to this day. Cuba is one of the most enchanting places I have visited on this fishing odyssey.

Chapter Eleven

PATAGONIA

Hostage of Fortune

January 2011, At the Ends of the Earth, Series 4

After what was a bit of a bumpy start, *Extreme Fishing* is becoming a veritable 'beast', a term we use in telly to denote a successful show. It's a case of 'be careful what you wish for', though, as there's little time for anything else work-wise and I can forget about a social life.

But everyone is talking about *Extreme Fishing*, and now in the street I am harangued thirty or forty times with, 'Caught any fish yet?' or: 'Off fishing?' I was even on the loo minding my own business when some guy popped his head over the stall wall and asked, 'Caught any extreme fish lately?' I bombarded him with toilet rolls until he left me alone. When I was Jimmy Porter in *Casualty*, I used to get 'Oi, Robson, I hurt my finger.' When I was Tucker – 'Where's Paddy?' And when I was the surgeon in *Reckless* I would have grannies winking at me, asking if I could do reconstructive bowel surgery. I definitely prefer the fishing questions.

In this latest series, our objective is to go to the ends of the earth, and there's no place further south than Patagonia. Patagonia is the tail region of South America, with territories shared between Chile and Argentina. The British Falklands Islands (Islas Malvinas) are just off the east coast of Patagonia on the Atlantic side, but it's best not to mention the war! It's even more important they don't know I was in *Soldier, Soldier,* for obvious reasons. Personally I don't know what all the fuss was about – some small rocks in the middle of the ocean. I mean, it's not like they found oil, minerals or gas there. Oh, they did, did they? Now, fancy that.

Torres del Paine

After a fourteen-hour flight to Buenos Aires and another internal flight, we are travelling eight hours by bus to Torres del Paine National Park in Chile. Our plan is to fly-fish for the king salmon, or chinook as it is also known, and then continue to Tierra del Fuego in Argentina, where I hope to land the biggest brown trout of my career.

The hitchhikers we have picked up along the way, one German and two American girls, think we have a great plan. They are all travelling alone in search of adventure and I am envious of their pluck. I don't think I could have done that at their age. They are impressive kids who can all speak three languages. They seem to hit it off with each other, crammed in like sardines in the small minivan, and they start to hatch a plan to travel together for a while.

We arrive in Torres del Paine around 3 a.m. It's pitch-black so

I can't get much of an idea of my surroundings. I'm too tired, anyway. My head hits the pillow and zzzz . . .

I pull back the curtains of my cosy log cabin and stare open-mouthed out of the window. The panorama is incredible, mountainous and dramatic. The name Torres del Paine (pronounced 'pie-nee') is from the Tehuelche Indian word for 'blue', and *torres* is Spanish for 'towers'. It refers to three jagged granite peaks that violently pierce the sky; they are magnificent and defiant. The largest horn, the Grande Paine, is over one and a half miles high. In front of the mountains is a lake, Lake Pehoe, perhaps five miles across; its bright azure colour indicates its icy temperature and mini icebergs float around in it. The frozen breeze ripples the water. In Patagonia the wind can be cruel and unrelenting. Locals call it 'the broom of God', as it can literally sweep everything away. As I walk outside to take some photographs I feel like I have been superimposed here by special effects.

Chinook Salmon

Patrick Marcos looks like a revolutionary. A young Fidel Castro, without the cigar and beret. We are standing next to the Serrano River, only minutes from the hotel. I am hoping to catch a hefty chinook (or king) today, the biggest of the species.

The chinook is thought to have made its home here some time in the twentieth century, after hundreds of non-endemic salmon were released by fishermen in the 1930s and again in the late 1970s, in the hope of establishing the species here. Only DNA tests can reveal their true mitochondrial heritage, but many are thought to have come from North America. But one thing is for sure: they have set up home here and are thriving, making the 600-mile runs from the Pacific back to their new-found rivers and tributaries. It's spring and we have arrived during this epic journey, when thousands of them return from the sea to spawn and then, as we discovered in Alaska, die.

Today Patrick is my ghillie, which is a combination of best friend and fishing mentor in one. He will be there to give me assistance on casting techniques, where the best pools are, where the fish congregate and rest, and the best lures or flies to use. Patrick knows this river like the back of his hand and he says he knows the back of his hand really well. I'm not sure I could spot mine in a line-up but he says he could. ('It was *that* hand that stole the handbag, officer. I never forget a hand.')

I tell him the biggest salmon I ever caught weighed eighteen pounds.

'You could triple that in this river,' he says. The biggest fish Patrick caught here weighed sixty-four pounds!

'That would be a record in Britain, Patrick.' In fact, it would match the enormous salmon caught by Georgina Ballantine in 1922, a UK record that remains unbeaten to this day.

We start casting at his favourite spot – the weather is slightly overcast and it is about four degrees. We are using spoon lures, which look nothing like spoons but instead like small silver fish that replicate a distressed minnow. The salmon don't attack the lures because they want to eat, and I ask Patrick why they go after them – his theory is that you're trespassing on the fish's property. My theory is that we are trespassing on their love-making.

I say, 'Imagine if I cast a spoon over you while you are making love to your wife, Patrick.'

'I would kill you,' he says.

We wade out into the river. I am dressed up to the nines in technical fishing gear that keeps me cosy and, more importantly, dry. I dangle the spoons in the water and cast. As I am casting, a stranger appears to my right. He walks into the water and sidles up to me, within about five yards. He then starts to cast. I am incensed. Angling etiquette dictates you don't walk into another fisherman's beat. This guy is trying to nick my spot. Patrick very politely asks him to leave and suggests he find his own spot. If that had happened on the Coquet, I would have decked him. I know how the salmon feel about our lures. I want him to bugger off.

I carry on casting. Patrick's reel starts screaming.

'Robson, I have a present for you,' he says, and passes over his rod.

This is the first time this has ever happened on the show, as I always have to catch my own fish.

Patrick says, 'I want you to feel this fish. You think you have caught a big salmon – you have seen nothing yet!'

I take the rod off him and immediately the chinook becomes airborne, like the helicopter of the same name. Cameraman Keith Schofield keeps his lens on the fish as it leaps – it's the biggest 'springer' I have ever clapped eyes on. Bosch! It leaps again and flies across the river, jumping five or six times, left to right, showing itself.

'Oh, my God!'

Salmon: derived from the Latin *salmo*, and possibly the verb *salire*, meaning 'to leap'. And boy, can this fish leap. I can tell it's a male because of his large gib. When males become sexually mature, the bottom part of their lip passes over the upper lip –

it's like putting your bottom lip over your nose – and it looks extraordinarily phallic.

He's still fighting hard. I play him, and it's one of the most beautiful plays I have ever experienced. Finally I start to slowly reel him into the shallows. I am excited. Patrick is hysterical – he forgets he is the ghillie. He thinks it's one of the biggest fish he has ever seen. It's certainly the biggest I have ever seen. I bring it ten feet from the bank, and to my disbelief, Patrick goes over and tries to pick the fish up. It's a forty-five-pound-plus salmon. He kneels down in two feet of water and puts both arms underneath it. I'm not sure this fish is ready to bring in – it could run again – but I rush over to help Patrick. He drops it but manages to corral it with his legs and get hold of it again.

'Don't lose it. Don't lose it,' I say, trying to hold it by the caudal peduncle. (This is known as wristing a fish and it's the correct way to take hold of them.) But Patrick can't keep hold; the fish struggles one last time and is away, motoring with its powerful tail.

The silence is deafening. I stare at him. He stares into the water. The greatest salmon I have ever seen and he's let it slip away. He stands chest-high in the water and wipes his eyes as if hoping he might awake from a bad dream. He rubs his whole face with his hands, trying to take in what has just happened. He silently walks off and stands and stares into space. Alistair, however, is elated.

'That was brilliant! So many corridors of drama: elation, conflict and despair.'

We look over at the sad figure of Patrick.

'Go and console him, Robson,' says Alistair, never one to miss an opportunity. I go over.

'Robson, you cannot broadcast that. It will be the end of my career,' he says.

'No, it won't. Everyone in the area thinks you are the best. We are all fallible. Fishing is a battle: we lost and the fish won.'

There has been a paradigm shift. I am now the comforter rather than the comforted and it's a nice position to be in. Thank God it wasn't me that fucked up this time! Patrick is still glum. We sit on the bank together.

'To paraphrase Gene Wilder in *Young Frankenstein*, "If fishing teaches us anything, it teaches us to accept our failures, as well as our successes, with quiet dignity and grace."' I pretend to sob uncontrollably, then turn to him and say, 'But if we catch another fish like that and you lose it, I will wring your fucking neck!'

He smiles for the first time.

Back at the hotel I take Patrick for a beer. The bar is packed, news is breaking that the government has raised gas prices in the south by 50 per cent as an austerity measure. The people are very angry and there is going to be a general strike.

'Life is hard enough here, why are they doing this to us?' one lady says on the news.

With very few trees and little coal, gas is the only source for cooking and heating in the area. The unions announce that, unless the government backs down, they will go on strike and they call on all Chileans to support the cause. All roads will be blockaded – there will be no way in and no way out. Supply lines will be cut, tourism will cease and there will be a general stand-still.

Patrick says, 'This will never happen. They can't implement these measures. They will sort it out.'

We call Helen to update her on the situation.

Daniel, our fixer, says, 'It should be OK. Governments do some stupid things but this would be suicide.'

He says, however, that it is up to the office whether we stay or leave. Alistair liaises with Helen and they agree we should stay put. Unbeknownst to us, this is a bad plan because the government goes ahead and implements the austerity measures overnight.

Inflatables and Escape

We have an early start with Patrick at Lago Sofia, about half an hour away. We do not get a chance to catch the news, and besides I'm trout fishing, which is far more important than politics. Today we are fly-fishing with a difference: it includes flippers, a pump and an inflatable. It looks like I'm getting ready for a Conservative Party Conference.

Rainbow and brown trout were introduced here more than a hundred years ago and they grow to sizes never seen back home. The biggest trout I ever caught was on the Coquet and weighed four and a half pounds, which is a decent fish for that particular stream. Here many grow closer to the size of the British record, which currently stands at thirty-one pounds. For many years the record was thought to be thirty-six pounds but it turned out the guy who took the title had actually found dead brown trout in a lake at Dever Springs. He held the record for seven years until he could no longer live with the guilt. His behaviour became erratic, his marriage broke up, and he never fished again. He was to fishing what Lance Armstrong is to cycling: a big fat cheat.

Patrick has blown up his inflatable and it's now my turn to

pump. I say to him, 'I know it gets lonely out here but this is ridiculous.' From a distance it would look very wrong!

Inflatables are used in the UK for trout fishing, but they tend to be a bit rustic – mainly the inner tubes of tractor tyres. It's never really appealed to me but it's time to give it a go. I finish pumping and behold my comfy chair, complete with a drinks holder – it can even recline! It's far more appealing than an old tractor tyre. An inflatable allows for a stealth approach and is powered by your flippers. I have my waders on and several layers of thermals, but I am already freezing my cojones off.

I stand on the edge of the natural lake, with my webbed feet, fly rod and inflatable, looking ridiculous. I feel like Ade Edmondson in *Bottom*. Patrick is alongside; he always looks cool. We paddle out together. It's quite breezy today – and inflatables and wind don't tend to mix. The broom of Patagonia starts to gently brush me across the lake, and I attempt to steer myself back on course, my flippers going ten to the dozen. It's not easy but trying to cast into the wind is nigh on impossible. I cast again and the fly drops a few metres away, nowhere near the point I was aiming for. I look over at Patrick. Where is he? What? He's now back on shore, chatting on the phone. Great, I am the butt of a Chilean practical joke.

I shout, 'Help, Patrick, help!' but he doesn't look round. Unbeknownst to me, he is on the phone to his wife, who is frantically telling him to 'get out now': they are closing all the roads and two protesters have been killed. (Two people have been knocked down by a car, which many think to have been an accident. However, others think it was done intentionally and it's causing a lot of friction.)

We stop filming immediately and Alistair yells over to me:

'You need to get back here. We have got to get over to Argentina.'

I paddle with all my might, but keep being swept away by the ubiquitous broom. It is pushing me further and further from the shore. I paddle as fast as I can, trying to use my hands to row, but it's no good. I am stranded. Eventually a boat is sent over and I am rescued. We jump in the van and scream off to the hotel. It's deserted. Everyone has left. The receptionist says, 'All the roads are blocked; you will never get out. You should have left earlier.'

My stomach lurches, not because of the unfolding crisis but because I am having a bout of badly timed bottom explosions. All the gear is packed up and everyone is ready to leave, but I have to use the toilet, urgently. I feel dreadful and I look ashen. I hang on tightly to the toilet seat, ready for the diarrhoea roller-coaster ride, humming the hymn 'Dear Lord and Father of Mankind', which seems to help relieve the burning pain in my tired bottom.

Each time I get to the van, I have to rush back to the hotel again and my bowels ultimately cost us forty-five minutes; a critical amount of time when trying to escape a country. We head to the border, where 200 protesters and three coaches block the road. It's the only way out. Several men stop the van. I jump out, run for the nearest private area, drop my trousers and make my own dirty protest. I peep at the protesters from behind a rock, thinking no one can see me. One looks back at me straight in the eye. He is full of aggression but I am too dehydrating and poorly to be alarmed. Daniel, our fixer, is trying to negotiate for us to be allowed across but it is no use: the protesters say the van has to stay here and we have to walk over. The border is twenty kilometres away and our gear weighs half a ton. It's impossible for us to continue on foot. We have to keep trying to get our vehicle through.

I do my paperwork and reappear from behind my rock. My bottom is so sore it takes my breath away. I mince over to speak to Daniel.

'Tell them what you are working on, Daniel. Tell them who you are with, but don't mention the singing – it could sway it.'

Daniel, Patrick and our driver, Nelson, go to talk to the protesters again. Keith continues filming covertly on GoPros, tiny hidden cameras, as we watch from the safety of the van. There is no way they will let us through the line. They shout at Nelson and tell him he has to join the protest. It is clear there will be consequences if he doesn't. Patrick is debriefed as well. He explains he is a fisherman and needs to take us back to the hotel. He says he is not working for us. They are furious that, as Chileans, they are not supporting the strike. Thankfully Daniel is Argentinian, and therefore not betraying the cause, so he tries to pacify the ringleaders. We watch as Nelson is taken away to help man the blockade. He waves at us, smiling but slightly shell-shocked. I'm not sure this is how he expected his day to turn out. Patrick jumps in the driver's side and Daniel climbs into the back.

'It's no good, they won't let our vehicle across and are keeping Nelson here as well. We've got no choice but to go back.'

'Have they taken Nelson hostage?' I ask.

'Yes, it's serious. Basically we had to swap drivers because they were angry with them as Chileans for not supporting the strike so they asked one of them to stay as a guarantee and only that way are we allowed to get back to the hotel.'

'So we could have been taken hostage,' I venture, as I take on the scale of the situation.

'Yes.' Patrick turns the minivan around and we skedaddle.

Daniel says, 'We really should have left earlier.'

I blanch. My diarrhoea has scuppered our *Extreme Fishing* adventure and we are stuck here indefinitely. This could go on for weeks. I berate my bottom.

'Well, at least we'll be safe at the hotel,' I say, noticing the petrol gauge. 'Patrick, I don't want to worry you but have we got enough fuel?'

'I hope so,' he says.

'And what if we haven't?'

He looks at me and shrugs. The hotel is about an hour and a half away and all the petrol stations are being picketed.

'Great, so I was nearly held hostage and now we're going to run out of fuel and we'll be stranded in the middle of nowhere, surrounded by llamas.'

Daniel chimes in: 'Gonachas.'

'Gonachas? Gonachas to you as well!'

The llamas, or gonachas, are everywhere. I start to make a mental plan of how we might kill and eat one if we do become stuck in the wilderness. *We'll be OK*, I think. *Patrick and I can fish; I can make a fire and I can make a bivouac, although if it's anything like the one in the Philippines we may perish, quickly. We could use the fat and skin of the llama to keep warm, like the natives used to. It'll be fine.* But after the Philippines experience I really don't want to try it. The winds are punishingly cold. I glance at the gauge again: 'It's on fucking empty!'

'We'll have to use the reserve tank,' says Daniel.

'Oh, good. Have we got a reserve tank?' I say, turning round.

'No,' says Daniel, pissing himself.

Oh, cojones.

The van makes it to the hotel but we glide in on no more than fumes. The hotel is empty – it's like *The Shining*. Alistair and Alessandra get on the phone to Helen and Hamish, who are looking at every option to get us out, including rescuing us by helicopter, Navy SEAL-style! Calls are made to the British Embassy. They send an email with the latest advice and as I read I become increasingly nervous. What started off as a mild inconvenience has turned into quite a serious situation: 'The mood is getting progressively ugly and there is a tendency to violence. The best advice is to stay where you are.'

This is not good news. I need to be back for Taylor's parent-teacher meeting and to film *Joe Maddison's War* with Kevin Whately and Derek Jacobi, but I can't think of that right now. I am so poorly and now it's gushing out of both ends. I take to my bed. Besides, I can think of worse places to be trapped. It suddenly hits me that we are stuck in the world's biggest open prison. For some reason I start thinking about Jeffrey Archer. He went to an open prison and could go home from time to time and work in a theatre, and he got to keep his title. That doesn't sound like punishment to me, but then I can't remember what he actually did. Was he charged with crimes against literature? OMG, I might be charged with crimes against music. But if I go down I'm taking Simon Cowell and Louis Walsh with me.

'Robson. Robson!'

'Yes?'

Alistair is staring at me. I realise I am delirious with dehydration.

Patrick fetches a doctor from the village. He checks me over and gives me a potion to get rid of a parasitic infection, most probably amoebic dysentery. Lord knows how I got it but somehow I did. That night I sleep soundly and so does my bottom.

Salmon Fishing Part Deux

We still can't leave Patagonia so it looks as if we're going to have to make the best of the situation. One thing the protesters can't stop us doing is fishing, especially with the Serrano River located right by the hotel. We have another chance of catching a giant chinook with Patrick. But before we start fishing, we start off by setting the mood. Patrick plays the guitar, I sing, and Alistair has written us a song to perform. We sit next to the Serrano on chairs, wearing shades, while Patrick strums his guitar and we perform the Chilean Blues.

> I woke up this morning
> I couldn't get out
> I couldn't get about
> Need to catch me a trout
> It may be fate
> It may be a fluke
> But I need to catch me a chinook.

Patrick says, 'You have a lovely voice, Robson.'

I start to tell him about my time in the music industry: 'I had three number ones and kept Michael Jackson and Oasis off the top spot…'

Patrick gets up and leaves midway.

I turn to the camera: 'He'll be back – there's no fuel in the van!'

*

I spy a little boy fishing on the bank. I wander over.

'Please don't tell me you caught something.'

The little boy replies, 'Yes, I catch a trout.'

He takes me to his dad's car to inspect it. I'm about to be upstaged by a twelve-year-old. He opens up a plastic carrier bag. It's a decent size but thank God it's not the size of the chinook we – I mean Patrick – lost. I take it out to inspect it.

'That is a beautiful wild brown trout . . .' The fish twitches and I drop it! I try to pick it up. 'I'm sorry. Sorry. So sorry.'

It's all going to hell in a handcart. I have never felt so harassed as an angler – trapped and held captive in Chile. But if I'm feeling the extreme pressure, Patrick looks one seriously worried man. As we prepare our lines he confides in me, 'I have never felt so much pressure in my life; it's like my whole life depends on catching the salmon. That cannot be right – I'm not enjoying this.'

But this is Patrick's chance to redeem himself and he needs to show the world what an excellent angler and ghillie he truly is. We wade out and start casting. After five minutes, one of Patrick's beautiful casts gets a fish. He knows how to play the lure better than me, and lets it drop much deeper. I think my retrieve is too quick but it's sometimes hard to judge. Salmon will take at any depth and it's your job as an angler to find the right level; Patrick instinctively knows in these waters. It's important to take into consideration the weather, for example; with low pressure they stay down, while high pressure brings them up. When it's sunny they take lures below, when it's windy it keeps them down as well. If you can judge by sight, all the better – but this depends on the water clarity.

Patrick hands me the rod and, as I start to gently play the fish, it leaps. It's a glorious platinum chinook. She's not as big as the last one but her bright silver scales mean she has just come up from the sea. After a few days she will start to take on the colours of the terrain. As I begin to reel her in she turns towards the bank – I am the wrong side of her! I try to bring her round but at the moment she's in charge. She swims towards me.

'I am too close!'

The closer the angler is to the fish, the more likely the line will go slack and we'll lose her.

'Walk back slowly,' says Patrick. 'Slowly.'

I keep walking backwards. I'm on the bank, still pacing back. I fall down a rabbit hole and into the gorse. I get up, still bringing the line towards the bank.

'You did it! You're there. Perfecto!' Patrick lands the fish and we both go wild. I start to breathe; I didn't realise I had been holding my breath.

'You did it!' Patrick is jumping for joy and I am so happy. We hug.

'I have never been so scared in my life. Oh, my goodness!'

It's a thirty-pound king salmon, so healthy, so vibrant; it's a credit to the species, *Oncorhynchus tshawytscha*. And that's easy for me to say! She has come up to spawn and who am I to stop her? Well, I kind of did, temporarily. I release her into the icy waters saying, 'Go forth and create other king salmon of good health and size.'

I run around the hotel grounds naked to celebrate my victory. I feel liberated. They can keep me here against my will but my spirit will not be broken. During my victory lap, Alistair gets a call.

'Put your clothes on, Robson, we need to get across the border NOW! The British Embassy has negotiated us a two-hour window.'

The van is still packed up and we leap in, me dressed in full fishing gear, unable to locate my clothes at the bottom of the baggage mountain. We bid a fond farewell to Patrick and Torres del Paine. The British Embassy has played a blinder and we are waved on through the barricades. It is only thanks to the negotiations and tireless efforts of the British diplomats and Helen Nightingale that we got through, as the strike continues for many more days.

We cross the border into Argentina. Just like the salmon, we are free once more.

Chapter Twelve

ASCENSION ISLAND

Shark Back Mountain

October 2010, At the Ends of the Earth, Series 4

It's 2 a.m., I'm in a cab on my way to RAF Brize Norton, Oxfordshire. As we enter the military compound I see floodlit razor wire and men with attack dogs. My stomach lurches. I'm definitely outside my comfort zone.

After rigorous security checks by military personnel, including an iris scan, fingerprints and tabs in my passport, I enter the strange airport lounge. Three hundred servicemen are asleep on chairs, trying to get some last-minute shut-eye before journeying to far-flung places such as the Falklands Islands, Iraq, Afghanistan and Ascension Island, which is where I'm heading. The passport-control man looks at me steadily; he wants to know why I'm going to Ascension.

'I'm off to fish there,' I reply.

His face breaks into a smile: 'You'll enjoy yourself. On its day it's the greatest fishing destination in the world.'

Billed as the Jurassic Park of fishing, Ascension Island is a tiny dot seven miles wide and nine miles long in the middle of the vast Atlantic Ocean, about halfway between West Africa and South America, and because of the island's remote location I'm told it's home to some of the best game fish in the world, as well as many unique and strange species. The only way to get there is to catch a lift with the armed forces, who fly there once a week.

As I creep past the sleeping soldiers I'm keenly aware I'm out-numbered by people who get shot at or shoot at others for a living; they have been in some extreme situations in the real sense, not like Ross Kemp or me with a back-up team and a nice hotel to sleep in. These are the men in the arena who live life on the edge and have seen some frightening things, and they are paid a pittance to risk their necks. As my dad used to say, I just ponce around wearing make-up for a living.

Suddenly a soldier, who's spark out across a row of chairs, sits bolt upright and does a quadruple take: 'Fuck me, it's Tucker!' I automatically put my hands up in surrender. 'Is this heaven?'

'No, welcome to hell, my friend.'

The incident wakes up many of the lads; just what I didn't want to happen. Spot the odd one out. I can tell what they're all thinking: 'Here's a reet pansy who thinks he's a hard man.'

Come on, Robson, man the fuck up. You're a well-respected actor, singer and presenter – a pillar of the community.

Pillock of the community, more like.

I hate my internal monologue. Of course, I have nothing to worry about: all the guys and girls are brilliant and a lot of them turn out to be fans of *Extreme Fishing* – well, they're only human.

*

Things are getting weird. It's time to depart but not by military plane, as I'd assumed – no, by Air Seychelles. As I board the aircraft I discover it really is a completely normal plane with seats, overhead lockers and no leg room. Unthinkingly I ask the air hostess where business class is located and all the soldiers look at me like I've just burnt down their houses and peed on their children. I'm escorted to the front of the plane by the base commander and offered the best seat in the house – next to the pilot. I'm living the dream. Take-off is my favourite part. It's exciting, especially when you're near all the knobs. If I were eight I'd now be swinging my legs in my chair, humming in contentment.

I'm looking forward to the adventure ahead. The first time I ever heard of Ascension Island was during the Falklands War, when Britain used it as a military base to fight the Argentinians. I don't think many people knew it even existed until then. Well, apart from the Portuguese, who discovered it on Ascension Day back in 1501. They owned it until 1815, when the Brits stole it off them, and Ascension has remained a British territory ever since. Today the island is still used by the RAF and US Air Force as a strategic outpost and communications base.

As we land I swallow hard: the runway is only a mile long and is cut into a mountain that we're approaching very fast. World War II pilots named the airfield Wideawake because they had to be wide awake to find Ascension in the first place, and then seriously alert to land there safely. There's no second chance. Mercifully our pilot's a pro and I'm right behind him if he needs me. It's three o'clock in the afternoon by the time we land. It's been a thirteen-hour flight but there's no time difference from the UK, so at least I won't be hit between the eyes with jet lag. As we disembark, the base commander asks if I would like to sing for the people of Ascension. I pretend not to hear him.

My first thought as I step off the plane is *Shit, I'm tired*. My second is *I'm not fucking singing*. I'm scooped up by the welcoming committee, who think the Beatles have finally arrived, but instead it's some dog-tired Geordie they've never heard of. I follow them into the airport, if you can call it that – it's more a shed. The whole population of the island is out to greet me – all seven of them. Although the island has no indigenous population, it is home to 900 residents, who are a mixture of UK and US military personnel and St Helenians, known locally as the Saints. As I make my way through the 'crowd', I am honoured that the governor of the Falklands Islands and the garrison commander have come out to greet me.

On the way to the hotel, I survey the scene. Ascension is a cross between Thunderbird Island and Los Cristianos in Tenerife, albeit without drunken Brits doing 'The Birdie Song' or 'Agadoo' by that really annoying band. The strange volcanic landscape is littered with cutting-edge *Star Wars* technology: giant golf balls protrude like cysts out of mountain tops and spider webs of wires form listening devices to communicate with anything from space stations to nuclear submarines. NASA even tested their moon buggy here – I can see why: I think I've landed on a different planet.

I loved *Thunderbirds* as a kid. Those were the days before political correctness when puppets could drink and smoke as much as they goddamn liked. And they smoked ALL the time. Lady Penelope was a forty-a-day girl – she must have stunk like a bad kipper. Apparently when *Thunderbirds* was rebroadcast on the BBC ten years ago, Lady P was criticised for smoking, wearing furs and shagging in the back of her car without a seatbelt on. How times have changed.

I drop my luggage off at my accommodation, and I use the word 'accommodation' loosely. It's a horrid pre-fab building that reminds me of a place called Killingworth in Newcastle, now condemned. There is nothing starry about the aptly named Obsidian Hotel. *Bear Grylls would definitely complain,* I think to myself – it would be too much like camping for him. Not that complaining would do him any good; it's the only hotel on the island.

Spear Fishing

There are only two sports boats on Ascension; one is owned by a German called Olaf Grimkowski, the other by South African Colin Chester, who I'm spear-fishing with today. I'm going deeper than I've ever gone to get a fish. We head out in his boat, the *Wide Awake II*, to Boatswain Island, which is a bird sanctuary. It's also a major fish attractor. There's a funny smell in the air and I discover from Colin it's bird guano – that's bird poo to you and me. It smells bad up top but looks beautiful down below, as the water is gin-clear. According to Colin it's the most spectacular spear-fishing on earth, and he should know as he's a spear-fishing champion. I'll be starting with fish such as black trevally or black jack.

I'm actually very nervous about diving down so deep – we'll be going down a full fifty feet – and we have to prepare our bodies properly to be able to free dive in one breath. I start holding my breath for ten seconds, fifteen seconds and then twenty seconds. Then I repeat the exercise holding the spear gun. After an hour I manage thirty-three seconds, which doesn't sound a lot but when you're holding a spear gun, diving down and moving around you get through a lot of oxygen. If I were going down under any other circumstances I could hold my breath for two minutes.

We clean out our masks and get ready to dive down. I watch Colin, who makes it look effortless, but it's deeper than I've ever dived before and with the adrenalin pumping it feels like your lungs could burst. The waters are choppy, which doesn't make it any easier. I'm bricking it.

Colin explains what I should do when I spot my target: 'Take a few deep breaths, go down and approach the fish. Your natural instinct will kick in. You point the spear where you want to shoot it and your finger will do the rest.' Simples.

No sooner have I put my head under the water than I spot a black jack – my heart is thundering in my ears. I hesitate. I'm so glad Colin's with me as he's such a relaxing influence.

'Take it easy, Robson, just dive down and fire,' he says.

The spear gun is heavy and the recoil great. The trick is to aim at a fish ten metres away or nearer. I take three big breaths and follow Colin's advice. He's right: my hunting instincts kick in and I quickly pursue the grey pocket torpedo. A black jack's turn of speed is phenomenal, so the secret is to get close and hover, like a kestrel over a vole. The knack is to let the fish come to you, and to my astonishment it glides towards me, then turns profile on and I fire. To my utter amazement it's a direct hit.

Even though I train hard every day, running and resistance training to keep fit for this job, I can't believe how truly exhausting this is. However, I feel very comfortable in Colin's company. Psychologically he is a safety net and somehow any sense of fear melts away. The breathing definitely helps, too – when you breathe in and out properly or concentrate on your breathing for an extended time you achieve a Zen-like state. Omm . . .

Colin spots a fish – three breaths and he's down. His lungs are champion-sized, he is a natural hunter and is totally in tune with the ocean environment and his prey. He brings a healthy-sized black jack to the surface. Colin is doing something he was born to do. When I watch Rooney play football, I never worry what he's going to do with the ball; I'm always excited. Many other players are scared and unsure in the arena whereas Rooney belongs there; he was born to play football. I feel the same about Colin and fishing. I really envy his inner contentment with who he is and what he is doing. Too many people leave this life with a bewildered look on their face, unfulfilled and having done something they hate for too long. Colin's one of the lucky ones.

Colin's down again. I watch through my goggles as he strikes a medium-sized blue fish. Suddenly, his catch attracts a Galapagos shark. It propels itself towards Colin and from where I'm positioned it looks as if the shark is trying to remove his hands.

I start yelling: 'There's a shark eating Colin, there's a shark eating Colin!'

I splash around like a lunatic and, like the true coward that I am, hurl myself into the boat, leaving Colin for dead. I gingerly peer over the edge before Colin emerges without his blue fish but with both hands. Hooray! He thought it was wise to give that particular fish away.

After twenty minutes the sharks have vanished and I'm back in the water. I'm ready for my next fish and this time I've got something bigger in my sights – much bigger. One, two, three, I suck as much air into my lungs as possible and propel myself down after the fish like an ancient hunter. I shoot, I strike, I score. The speared fish bolts for the rocks, followed by dozens of hungry trigger fish after a meal. Colin dives deep to bring up my prize. I'm exhausted and gasping for air but I can barely believe what I've caught. It's a dog snapper – named because of its extraordinary canine gnashers. These fish are ambush predators that lie in wait for their prey to glide by and BAM! Their iridescent blood-orange colouring is surprisingly perfect camouflage, as the colour red is taken out of the white light spectrum as it hits water, so they appear almost invisible to unsuspecting bait fish. Rather like Jean Reno in the movie *Leon*, dog snappers are silent assassins.

At twenty-two pounds, my beautiful fish is easily the biggest I've hunted with a spear. Colin is thrilled and convinced I've smashed a spear-fishing record.

'Now, that's a fantastic fish. A winning catch, Robson!' he says.

It's all down to my tutor. Colin has the experience and knowledge of a true expert; he is a special person who cares deeply about what he's doing and wants to do it as well as he can. Some people have a notion that we don't belong down there in the world below, but I think as a species we are naturally drawn to water. It's not so much the need to escape or get away from it all, but perhaps more a need to get back to how it was. My father swam in the North Sea most of his life. Maybe he was subconsciously freeing himself from chains of oppression. But one thing I know is that when you enter water you cross a border, one that is mysterious, sometimes dangerous, but in the end always magical. Whatever it was he was always happy and now I'm ecstatic.

*

As we head back we are in agreement that there's no harm in casting a line. Immediately we're in – it's a yellowfin tuna *and* it's a ninety-pound monster. It's the biggest yellowfin I've ever seen, let alone caught. The lack of pollution and water temperature, which is about 17 degrees, makes conditions perfect for pelagic species, such as tuna, dorado and marlin, to thrive. I give the yellowfin to Colin's deckhand – at that size it should last him and his family a couple of years!

What better way to end the day than by eating what we caught? Our piscatorial smorgasbord comprises blue fish, black jack and dog snapper – it's an anglers' version of a Renaissance feast.

Kenny G

Today I'm taking part in a 'fish fry', which is basically a local knees-up disguised as a fishing competition. We meet at the Saints Club in town – the Saints (St Helenians) love to fish. My team-mates are Justin Wade and Adrian Henry, known as Kenny G. Not the cheesy 1980s sax player, but hopefully a great fisherman. They are both sullen-faced and kicking their heels; as it turns out they have been reluctantly shoved into something they really don't want to do. To them, fishing with me is worse than national serv-ice, being made to dress up as women or being sent to Rochdale.

I say, 'You guys really don't want to be here, do you?'

They shake their heads miserably. OK, so I've got my work cut out today to jolly along two kids who don't want to play with me. I tell them that losing is NOT an option. We are Team Extreme, living the dream – yes, I am as cheesy as my pop career and Kenny G suggest. Cue 1980s sax music as we walk down towards the ocean as Team Extreme.

As the ice starts to thaw between us – and believe me, I expelled a lot of hot air to achieve the melt – I realise their initial reluctance was actually a case of shyness. They were both completely star-struck ... No, not really, but incidentally I am well known on the island of Saint Helena. Many women approached me (yes, they were older; they're always older) and showed me their VHS recordings of *Soldier, Soldier* and Catherine Cookson's *The Gambling Man*. DVD players haven't quite made it to these parts, but I have.

We head down to the coast. We've got three hours to fish for our target: grouper. There is a prize for the biggest, smallest and largest number of fish caught.

'I see we're using snapper as bait, Justin.'

'No,' he says. 'They're squirrel fish.'

'What have you been smoking? They're snapper, matey.'

These boys may have highly qualified jobs as marine engineers but they just make things up as they go along. As we arrive at Justin's favourite fishing spot there's a problem as we discover another team has nabbed it. One of them is Justin's girlfriend, and seeing as she's no stranger to the sweet trolley there's no arguing. We are left with a small pier to fish off. The boys handline and I have a rod. I've never won a competition before. I'm not the competitive type, but today I'll make an exception.

Our neighbours appear to be catching but Justin's mind doesn't seem entirely on the game. In fact he's far more interested in his girlfriend than he is in grouper. Luckily Kenny G's all over it – fishing like a man possessed. He pulls up a medium-sized grouper and it's beautiful, with its speckled patterning and sharp fins. I handle it up carefully as the dorsal spines can do some serious damage. It's well equipped to defend itself but it's also equipped to attack, with its cavernous mouth, powerful jaws and razor-sharp teeth. Kenny pulls out another beauty – a three-pound rock hind grouper. This guy may be a moody bastard in the morning but he can certainly fish.

Justin and I have so far caught bog-all. But just when I think all hope has disappeared, something explodes onto my bait. Sadly it's a jack trevally – I've never been so sad to see a fish. I put it back and start again. Soon Kenny G has another fish on the end of his line – a seven-pound grouper. He may not have the other Kenny G's blonde highlights but this man has a magic all of his own. I feel sure Team Extreme is going to romp to victory. It's all about teamwork. Kenny G's not so sure.

As we gather at the Saints Club for the weigh-in it becomes crystal-clear we're up against some stiff competition, so I try to find out from organiser Suzie how Team Extreme is doing. I hypnotise her with my signature blue eyes – she wobbles for a moment, before giving me a look that could freeze my chestnuts and hides the figures. I'm asked to hand out the prizes and guess what? We didn't catch the most fish. We didn't get the smallest or the biggest. But the runner-up for largest grouper goes to Mr Robson Green, and being the narcissist that I am I go completely wild. I take the award and accept it but then I see Kenny G backlit and hazy and I have to confess to everyone that I didn't catch any of the fish – it was all down to him.

The Old Geordie and the Sea

I'm slightly apprehensive this morning. I'm back with my mate Colin Chester and we're going marlin fishing. A *Makaira nigricans* would be a huge catch and we've got an unnervingly small boat; the giants out there could do a lot of damage to it and, more importantly, me. I'll be hiding behind burly Colin if a marlin jumps on the boat. I've left him for dead with a Galapagos shark once before, and I'll gladly do it again.

The topography of the island is also the reason fishing is unbelievably good here. Ascension Island is situated on the Mid-Atlantic Range, a divergent tectonic plate boundary located along the floor of the Atlantic Ocean. Part of the longest mountain range in the world, Ascension is essentially a mountain peak that rises 10,000 feet up from the sea bed. Because of this you don't have to go too far out to find deep-sea fish.

Here in the rich Atlantic waters, blue marlin grow to record-breaking sizes and are among the fastest and most powerful fish in the ocean. If anyone can catch one, my new buddy and I can, as we are the angling equivalent of Starsky and Hutch, Butch and Sundance – or is it Laurel and Hardy? To my amusement, Colin decides to remove the fighting chair: 'It's a wonderful way to fish for marlin as you're in direct contact with the fish. It brings us back to our roots, fishing like the old boys did in the frontier days,' he says.

Colin shows me what the pressure will be like on my body when we hook a marlin; as he pulls the rod down, my back groans. It's a lot of pressure. So we are going back to the days when men were men and fish were frightened. Colin tells me I need to 'man up' and I say, 'That's going to be difficult – I wear make-up for a living.' Our banter continues and the morning disappears. Soon we've been trawling for three hours but haven't caught a thing. Once again I feel like Santiago in *The Old Man and the Sea*, waiting and waiting. OK, he did it for eighty-four days, but we live in a far more impatient age nowadays. Maybe the waters off Ascension Island are fallible?

After what feels like an eternity there's a sign: dolphins. These beautiful mammals always bring luck, and suddenly something attacks the lure. Colin and the deckhand signal the driver to speed up the boat. I know I'm into something big by the sound of the reel – it's an angling symphony – and on the end of the line is the Holy Grail of game fish.

'It's a marlin!'

Colin holds on to me to stop me disappearing overboard. I'm hooked on to one of the largest and fastest ocean-going predators – if you want to know what it feels like, cast your line of 150 pounds and test it at full tension on a high-speed train. I have never done this and neither should you, but you get the idea.

As I tighten the line, the marlin explodes out of the water 200 yards ahead of me. It's ten feet long and 450 pounds of dynamic power. His bill alone, which he uses to slash through dense schools of fish like a carnivorous gladiator, is at least three feet in length. No superlative can accurately describe the sight of this creature other than 'awesome'. He takes off sideways at about 50 m.p.h. – I can't even travel at 5 m.p.h. in water and I'm a bloody good swimmer! I'm reeling in with everything I've got – I shout for Justin to turn the boat to the left.

'Quickly!'

It's enormously powerful so I dig deep and turn the reel with all my might. I am instantly reminded of Santiago again – it wasn't so long ago that guys would fight a marlin on a hand line. If I did that I think this beast would dislocate both my arms from their sockets. The one thing you can do when hooked into such a predator is: nothing. It becomes a test of strength and endurance between hunter and quarry. We both try to exhaust each other. He starts to tire and the retrieve begins. If I let this line go slack for even a split second the fish is off.

After thirty-five minutes there's colour. In the next thirty seconds I will be up close and personal with the greatest fighting fish on the planet, but at this precise second my rod whiplashes and I'm sent reeling back. He's off. Gone. And I am totally and utterly empty. The feeling is an overpowering sense of loss and failure, an emotion that I am sure is rooted in the hunter not being able to provide food for his family and the pending disappointment it will bring. I can't believe it: twenty metres away and we lost him. It's hard to take but this marlin has got the better of us today.

Colin says sagely, 'There's always another marlin out there to catch, Robson.'

And he's right: there are plenty more fish in the sea, especially around here. I go to bed early and dream of the mystical creature that got away.

Green Mountain

Ascension Island is mostly dry and volcanic but rising up in its centre is something very different: a green mountain called, er … Green Mountain. It's where I'm heading today.

The mountain is a man-made forest in the clouds that generates rain. When the early explorers first found the island they discovered they couldn't live here because there is no natural source of water. It's is thought that, in the nineteenth century, some bright sparks, possibly Charles Darwin himself, conjured up the idea of the forest, with vegetation from around the globe, in a grand experiment to see if they could create an environment conducive to habitation. It truly is a miraculous place.

I'm meeting the conservationist who looks after Green Mountain, Stedson Stroud. Stroud, as well as having an extensive knowledge of botanical life, also knows a thing or two about fish, particularly moray eels. So off we trot to a weird landscape of volcanic rocks by the sea.

Our bait is rotting tuna heads, which eels have a penchant for. As I dangle my stinky bait in the water – waiving it around a bit to get maximum blood in the water – I'm thinking this is hardly the poetry of fly-fishing. Robert Redford would definitely have turned down directing the moray eel version of *A River Runs Through It*. I'd do it. I'd do anything. But it's not long before we get some interest in the form of a spotted moray eel. Quickly I bring the gaff down and try to hook it, but he gets away. They're slippery sods. I see another one and pull it out the water; Stedson hooks it up onto a rock and then rather surprisingly lands some thundering blows to stop it going back in. Yep, that's stopped it right in its tracks – Stedson isn't the hippy I thought he was. But blows to the head are the only way to dispatch a moray eel. It isn't pretty but if their teeth get hold of you they will sink right in and they won't come out. They use the same principle as a fishing hook: they hook around the prey and have barbs that you can't pull out. These eels are vicious, but in spite of that I still think they are beautiful. And apparently very tasty.

Later, as Stedson cooks the eel over a fire on the beach, he explains that moray eel tastes like Dover sole and the skin is the equivalent of pork scratchings. He uses the berries, wild rocket and other salad leaves we picked earlier on the mountain as delicious accompaniment. Eels are common fish around the world but not usually served for dinner. I think we'll have to change that. I try the eel. It's sensational and, you know what, it tastes just like chicken. No, Stedson's spot on: it has the delicate succulence of Dover sole. He's way off the mark with the pork scratchings, though.

German Shark Fishing

Tonight I'm going shark fishing and I'm apprehensive. In fact, I feel sick. A fucking cello plays over and over in my head as it did when I went mako fishing off Cape Cod. Dur-nur, dur-nur, dur-nur . . . I feel worried because I have a sixth sense that we're going to hook one tonight.

I really don't want to see a shark, let alone catch one, but paradoxically I'm compelled to find out more about what lies beneath these waters, however frightening. I need to discover if Ascension Island really *is* the Jurassic Park of fishing. And the only way to find out is to catch one of its most fearsome prehistoric creatures. Luckily the man who is going to help me catch a monster is no lightweight. He's big, he's German and his name is Olaf. He's quite frankly built like a brick scheisshaus. Olaf owns *Harmattan,* the only other sports boat on Ascension. He fires up the engine. Oh, God – this is really happening.

As we head to a shark feeding ground about a mile out, I try to appear casual, nonchalant even.

'The biggest fish I ever caught was a 500-pound blue marlin off the Azores,' I say, and Olaf nods, seemingly with angling approval – we're bonding.

'On a good night,' he replies, 'I would catch a fish four times that size.'

I nod with angling approval, disguising the fact in my mind I've plucked a pistol out of thin air and just shot myself.

'The largest shark I've seen up close was an eleven-foot, four-hundred-pound reef shark in the Gulf of Mexico,' I say, beginning to hate the sound of my own voice. *For pity's sake, Robson, put the spade down and step away from the hole.*

'Really? Wow!' says Olaf. 'Well, tonight, my friend, you are going to see something three or four times the size of that.'

Shit. The. Bed.

According to Olaf there are some very ancient species in this part of the ocean: mako sharks, thresher sharks, and Galapagos sharks – like the one who tried to eat Colin's hands the other day. But also under these inky waters lurks a true dinosaur whose design hasn't changed for nearly 200 million years. The particular monster we're looking for is a sixgill shark, or cow shark.

Like many deep-sea creatures, the rarely-seen sixgill is known to take daily vertical migrations, moving up to the epipelagic zone (the surface) at night and returning to the mesopelagic zone (the middle) of the ocean before dawn. The sixgill, which has six gill slits instead of the usual five, is one of the few surviving members of the Hexanchidae family. All its other relatives, apart from the dog tooth and Greenland shark, are only found in fossils. Sixgill sharks get up to around twenty feet here, which is too big to land (can you imagine?), but if we get it to the side of the boat and set it free it counts as a catch. That said, getting it to the side is down to me, and the impending sense of dread is suffocating. At this moment in time all I can think about is the bloke on the Discovery Channel who had his calf bitten off in an attack. This really isn't a safe situation.

Olaf hands me some of the most extreme gear I've ever seen. There are buckles, ropes and a codpiece to rest the rod. So, just to recap, I'm on a boat in the pitch-dark in the middle of the

Atlantic Ocean, wearing some seriously kinky fishing gear with a hulk of a German – we all know what they're like – and to make things worse I'm about to invite Jaws to the party. Olaf manhandles me again: 'I'm testing the pressure, ready for you to reel in a sixgill,' he says. But it feels more like he's giving me a heart attack and a hernia all at the same time.

'Please be gentle with me, Olaf,' I whimper.

I'm only a five-foot-nine actor weighing ten and a half stone (I know, I know, there are girls heavier than me). He's a bear of a man, six-foot-four and probably nineteen stone of pure muscle. There's no way I'm messing with this SOB; he could break me in two with his little finger. Forget Popeye and spinach, I think it's all the prehistoric fish he's been eating – he's pumped up with Omega-3.

Olaf places a massive piece of yellowfin tuna on the hook. I throw it in. There is total silence as the bait descends into the dark depths. The tension is set. Olaf ties an extra knot at the small of my back just in case. I wait. I wait. I wait. The only sound is of the water lapping gently against the boat's hull – click, click, click. I look into the night beneath. How many sea-monsters are lurking down there? I'm reminded of scary stories from my childhood in the north of England, like the Loch Ness Monster or Jenny Greenteeth, who stole people's children and drowned them. I think that's partly why we're so fascinated by this other world, all the myths and legends that surround lakes, rivers and oceans are as important as what we scientifically know. Fishermen are very superstitious people, you know. In fact, fishermen and sailors both believe that bananas on boats bring bad luck. It's true, because bananas give off spores that spoil other fruit, which would have been a disaster on board ship back in the 1700s: your whole fruit and veggie supply would perish. That's why you should never put bananas with other fruit but instead place them in a separate bowl. I'm dead useful, aren't I?

Bananas to one side for a minute, I feel a very distinct and sharp yank on the line.

'We have an enquiry,' says Olaf. He continues ominously: 'It's time.'

I put on the instruments of torture: an S&M harness from Herr Flick and Helga's fun cupboard, and immediately the pressure is absolute hell. The reel is on full tension. The rod starts to bend and keeps bending until I think it will snap. I am straining, gurning, sweating, but Olaf calmly holds me steady from behind.

Suddenly I get the full force of this gigantic fish going through my body like a pickaxe in my spine, tearing my spinal cord. I knew it would be tough but nothing prepared me for this. I'm jerked forward. Shit. I head for the inky water but manage to wedge my feet on the side of the boat. One more yank from the creature and I'll topple over. I'm attached – if the reel goes in, so do I – but Olaf keeps me upright and holds on to the reel. Whatever it is down there I've now really pissed it off. Another deckhand joins in the group hug. I've never been so pleased to have two men hugging me from behind before in my life. They're so close I can feel their conkers brushing against the backs of my thighs, but there's no time to be squeamish. I've got a shark to wrestle. I'm yanked violently forward again. This seems impossible – I'm suppose to get this fish to the surface but it seems more likely to pull me down to the depths. My harness and reel are re-connected again. I've got to bring this beast up more than 300 feet and I'm already losing my nerve.

The shark yanks again and I feel something explode in my back. I scream. I have a terrible sinking feeling – I know I've injured myself badly but I have to continue fighting the monster. The pain in my back starts shooting down the backs of my legs. Why didn't I do that TV drama instead? At this point I'd present *Daybreak*. I'd even go on *Strictly*, it's that bad.

I whine to Olaf, 'It's just too heavy – I can't do anything.'

Olaf says, 'Try and use a bit of fishing technique. Lift it slowly.'

His advice gets right on my wick: what does he think I'm bloody doing?

'I'm *trying* to lift it slowly,' I snarl.

As I finally get into a rhythm I start to get somewhere.

'Ja, Robson, I like the way you do it.'

I say, 'Liking your accent at the moment, Olaf; it's very Germanic.'

My muscles and head feel like they are going to pop, my face burns and I have a big hairy German standing behind me, watching my every move.

Olaf shouts, 'Faster!'

I dig deep. *Come on!* I get angry with whatever that thing is out there that's sapping my strength and has prolapsed a disc in my back (as I later find out). One–nil to the big guy – it's my turn. Robson's coming back for more.

Unfortunately my success pisses off the creature more and he swims down, yanking the heart out of my chest. Olaf tells me it's all OK and puts a big arm around me again – I'm so not happy now. *Dad, I know you didn't want me to be an actor, I should have listened to you – this is punishment. Or maybe it's poetic justice for* Unchained Melody. *Don't punish me; it was all Simon Cowell's idea. We didn't even make that much money out of it. He took the lot! Feed* him *to the sharks. Actually, he's quite a strong guy,* I think to myself, *he could do this. I'm not sure who would be the bigger shark though, the sixgill or him? It would be an interesting fight. Perhaps it could be a new programme format:* The Fishing Factor? *Maybe not.*

I mute my inner monologue and try to stop thinking of Cowell in a harness.

'Are we nearly there yet, Dad?' I ask Olaf.

'You have another eighty metres to go,' he replies. 'Lift slowly, go fast forward and wind at the same time.'

But just as I'm making progress the pressure on my body starts to tell in a completely unexpected way. I let out a ripper. Well, something had to blow – I'm just pleased it was my bottom. I apologise to Olaf, who is still holding me from behind – he must have felt the rumble: 'It appears my belly retired and my bum backfired.' I need the costume department and fast. Well, that's what happens when you've been wrestling with a shark for thirty minutes. But the change of cacks will have to wait. Slowly but surely I'm starting to win.

Suddenly the shark breaks the surface right by the side of the boat. Whoosh! Only swear words can describe my reaction. I instinctively move to the other side of the boat – it's an enormous sixgill, just what we were after. Its head is almost a metre wide, its mouth gaping open exposing a set of ragged brutal teeth almost two inches in length. And the eyes, oh, the eyes – in them is only death. They are two green fluorescent holes that flash menacingly in the torchlight; it really is a true dinosaur of the deep. The creature is about fourteen feet long and a massive 1,100 pounds. I tell Olaf I want to let it go now. I know it's an amazing fish and incredible to think he and his relatives have been lurking on the ocean floors for 200 million years, but it really is time to say goodbye.

When I get back to the hotel I take some painkillers and sleep like the dead.

Noddy

I wake up in searing pain and feel mortified. Not only have I done my back in, I also farted on camera. Oh, the shame of it. As I try to get out of bed, I find I can't, and when I move the shooting pains in my legs are now like red-hot pokers.

A month later I have an MRI scan back in the UK, which shows the shark has prolapsed discs in five of my vertebrae. Some of the extreme fishing I have done over the course of the show has put such an incredible load on my lower back, and my consultant says that if I haven't engaged my core correctly, even for one moment, damage will have occurred. He says I will need an operation in the future but for now all I have are painkillers and a vague idea that something's wrong with my body. Suddenly I'm reminded of Chelsea Charms, the woman with the biggest boobs in world. She was on *This Morning* with Fern and Philip and I shared a green room with her. Imagine what her back must be like, having to hold up double-Xs every day. She must be in permanent agony, poor thing.

The man I'm meeting today would like Chelsea Charms a lot, in fact he's got tattoos of big busty ladies all over his arms. His name is Noddy and not only does Noddy have proper seafaring tattoos, but he also actually looks like a proper sea fisherman, suitably weathered. Completely desiccated, to be honest. I'm told this fishing Saint can turn a short boat trip into a fishing extravaganza, so I jump at the chance of spending the day with him.

Noddy has been fishing these waters for twenty-six years and is *the* Ascension Island fisherman. He is the only one who provides a daily catch for the locals to eat. His boat might not be the biggest (it's not much bigger than a dinghy) but Noddy is the real deal. Today we're looking for fish with a market value. With the rods we're going for tuna and wahoo, and with the hand lines we'll be fishing for deepwater fish like snapper, jack and our main target: deepwater bullseye.

But we've also got to keep a keen eye on the local boobies. These naughty seabirds are well practised at stealing a fisherman's catch. Boobies hunt fish by diving into the sea and chasing their prey underwater – they have facial air sacs under the skin that cushion the impact as they dive-bomb the water from a significant height. 'Booby' is possibly derived from the Spanish slang *bubie*, meaning 'dunce', as they are not the cleverest of birds and indeed were often captured and eaten when they landed on the decks of sailing ships, Captain Bligh and his companions most notably living off them after being set adrift by Fletcher Christian following the mutiny on the *Bounty*.

Only moments after putting out our hand lines there is a tug on the other end of one and I start to pull it up through the water. I pull and pull and pull.

'How far is this line down?' I ask.

Noddy tells me 400 feet – I'm going to be here for a while. You could make a cuppa, run a bath and probably have a good night's kip in the time I'm still yanking this line up from the depths. I didn't know I was going to get a full-body workout. It's taking an eternity but at last it's exactly what we hoped for: a bullseye. It is the most amazing fish I've seen and it's the first time I've ever seen one in the flesh. Its orange colour is so vibrant it's like a

giant prehistoric goldfish. The bullseye has massive eyes, which is
how we can tell it's a deepwater fish, as it needs large pupils to let
as much light in as possible in order to see anything at all down
below.

'What a great start, Noddy!' I yell.

He smiles and nods, calmly reeling in another fish at the back
of the boat. He hands the rod to me and I take over. Thanks to
him I just have to bring it in the last few metres. It's a beautiful
yellowfin tuna and Noddy tells me it's twenty-five pounds. The
unspoiled ocean is teeming with tuna. Shockingly Noddy will
only get £15 for such a beautiful fish. I tell him that in a British
supermarket it would be worth over £150. It seems crazy. The
Latin name for yellowfin tuna is *Thunnus albacares*. And if you
remember, *Thunnus* derives from the word meaning 'to dart
away quickly' and these fellas can accelerate from 0 to 50 m.p.h.
in the blink of an eye.

Suddenly fish start coming from all directions, throwing
themselves at the boat. I'm back on the hand line trying to bring
another fish up from 400 feet – I'm certainly earning my boat
ride. Noddy is at the back of the boat playing his rod like Jimi
Hendrix – he is a fishing virtuoso. Noddy's tuna comes in and
there's a black jack, too. My line is feeling strangely heavy so I
keep hauling it up. At last the reason I'm done in becomes clear:
it's a double whammy of amberjacks.

I'm back on the rod again, tackling another Ascension predator, and it's pulling like a train. It could be the biggest tuna of the
day but it's going to be a long fight to get this one up and I'm
feeling every bit of it. However, this time I remember to keep my
sphincter under control. Paddy and Noddy laugh as I have to put
a harness on to keep hold and help me pull up the large fish.

Well, little do they know that I'm actually suffering from serious spinal injuries. It hasn't gone away and still bloody hurts. I'm here carrying on like a brave soldier but all the while I'm in terrible pain, you know, especially with a giant tuna yanking me about. I know I'm a weakling compared to those guys but eventually I land the tuna. It's a whopper and in just an hour and a quarter we have caught a ridiculous amount of fish. Back on land, they use a crane to bring in the haul. We've never needed one of those before. It's some catch, including seven beautiful tuna, which would make about £1,000 back home. After every trip Noddy fillets the fish with the help of his friend Paddy. I have a go but it's not easy. They are like surgeons and I'm more like a butcher – a bad butcher. The job is to remove the fillets as neatly as possible. Mine are rubbish so I give up. Sometimes it's better to let the masters do their work.

I throw the discarded tuna heads down from the pier head to the triggerfish fifty feet below. They turn the water into a frenzied whirlpool as they drag the carcass down and devour it. It's such a fantastically healthy ecosystem. Everything is in perfect harmony.

So it's time to leave. I really hope I can bring my son, Taylor, to Ascension one day and meet up with Colin and his kids. I want to take Taylor free diving and let him experience Ascension life before it changes. I hope it doesn't. I'll keep in touch with Colin on email and Skype. It's amazing that in such a short space of time I have found a new friend.

Sadly Noddy passed away in the summer of 2011. He was a very special man and I feel privileged to have met him. I hope he's catching marlin and massive tuna up there in the sky. I'll keep in touch with Noddy in my thoughts and perhaps through a medium, but not the Boston stalker!

As the plane lands at Wideawake Airport, suddenly there's an almighty bang. Seeing as this is the aircraft we are due to fly back on I take quite an interest. It turns out the undercarriage has collapsed in on itself! Now I'm not an aeronautical engineering expert or anything, but I believe the undercarriage of a plane is rather important. It turns out I'm correct. We are delayed for several hours as they try to stick the plane back together again. Oh well. I don't want to leave anyway.

When I was first asked to join *Extreme Fishing* they said, 'Robson, would you like to venture the world in search of the ultimate fishing experience?', and on Ascension I think I discovered it.

Chapter Thirteen

PAPUA NEW GUINEA

The Lost World

December 2010, At the Ends of the Earth, Series 4

Papua New Guinea (PNG) is exactly like the land described in Sir Arthur Conan Doyle's *The Lost World*: lush rainforests, virgin waters and smouldering volcanoes. It's not hard to imagine a passing stegosaurus tearing the tender leaves off a tree or a leathery pterodactyl gliding over the cerulean bay. It's home to 800 tribes with legendary tales of witchdoctors and other folklore. I am excited – this is the start of a strange and thrilling adventure.

The journey has been epic and we are all done in. We have travelled 13,000 miles, on five planes, over three days, and now, finally, we are heading by boat to Kimbe, the capital of West New Britain. The island was 'discovered' in 1699 by William Dampier, a celebrated British explorer, and it's incredible to think that it probably hasn't changed much since he came here all those years ago. Even though PNG is situated ninety miles from the northeastern coast of Australia, there was little contact with the West until after World War II. In 1942 New Britain was invaded by the Japanese, who established it as a key military base, and the territory was crucial to their proposed invasion of Australia. The plan never came to fruition and the Japanese forces surrendered in 1945, but they left a lot of their kit behind. Strewn across the rainforests are Japanese fighter planes and other military hardware, abandoned and decaying. It makes the prehistoric landscape seem all the more curious – like a deserted movie set. Underneath the ocean lie unexploded bombs and torpedoes, above it smoking volcanoes and steaming seas. It is a place full of obscure dangers, ancient secrets and hopefully many exotic species of fish.

I have followed Jamie's instructions not to shave whilst travelling and I have the beginnings of a beard. I can see my reflection in Peter's sunglasses: it's grey and ginger and I am devastated. What throwback gene is this? There are no gingers in my family. I think about phoning my mum. Hang on a minute, the man from the Providence loan company – he was a ginger! I start to dial but there's no mobile phone signal out here.

We head to the hotel and drop our bags off. As always we're on a tight schedule and need to crack on with filming shots of the landscape, culture and people to establish our setting. The streets are lined with poverty and the banks guarded by ten armed guards with attack dogs. But what is most strange about this place is that everyone has red mouths and red teeth.

I discover that the red in the people's mouths isn't blood but dye from chewing 'betel nut', areca nuts wrapped in betel leaves with a sprinkle of crushed seashells, which act as a lime alkaline to release the stimulant properties of the leaves. They produce a feeling of mild euphoria and alertness but the downside is everyone knows you're 'off your nut' because your mouth turns a vibrant shade of scarlet. I look at the men, women and children all chewing it – it's like a national drug. I suppose it's a bit like alcohol in Britain – after all, red wine stains your lips and teeth.

Our hotel is a beautiful paradise retreat with a wooden reception area and thatched huts overlooking the ocean. The chambermaid is still preparing my room as we arrive and she flashes me a crimson smile. She is blatantly 'on the nut' and is rather friendly, to say the least. I am not sure if she wants an extra tip but let's just say I think she's suffering from desert disease – a bad case of wandering palms. Still, she's only human. I'd want to paw me all over, too.

That evening we head to the bar. There is nothing quite like a cold beer after days of travelling. We are all in good spirits and clink our glasses, toasting to this 'ends of the earth' experience. We dine on steamed Papuan black bass, perfectly cooked by the hotel chef. It's the taste of things to come.

Papuan Black Bass

'Pound for pound the black bass is the world's toughest fish,' says Riccard Reimann, my fishing guide and black bass guru.

He's intelligent, at ease with himself and good-looking – we instantly have a lot in common. It's early morning and we are at the Kulu River in search of this legendary game fish. Indigenous to only this part of the world, the Papuan black bass is a prize fighter, explosive on the line, and has been known to snap many fishermen's lines by the way it takes the bait. I am coiled with anticipation. We stand on the edge of the crocodile-infested river and Riccard tells me that so far this year three guys have been taken from the banks while baiting their hooks. They were never seen again. Well, bits of them were. The crocs here are exactly like the ones found in Australia and they look for routines before they attack. If patterns of behaviour are the same, they remember them, then like serial killers they will watch and wait in the shadows before they strike. If there is a group, they will attack the smallest. I am a lot smaller than Riccard! I look around me in panic but Peter is smaller than me and with his shiny swede has a lot more skin on display. I think I am safe.

We set off in a small boat with Riccard's assistant, Chris, and I keep one eye on the vicious archosaurs as we drift along the slow-moving brackish water. We are using torpedo lures with propellers to make disturbance on top of the water – creating a wake with small pops of the line. Riccard points to some tree roots in the river.

'This is where the bass are hiding. They will be sitting deep in the snags or at the top. You have to get your lure as close as possible,' he says in hushed tones.

'So accuracy is an important factor today?' I ask, casting straight into the trees.

'Yes,' he smiles.

I am snagged and I can't get the hook off – it's a terrible cast with no sense of distance or height. I am yanking and yanking, desperately trying to untangle the line. Craig is filming, grinning.

'Will you just pan off while I get my five-a-day?'

Jamie is loving my failure. As a director, he brings out the worst in me.

I am jet-lagged, freaked out about crocodiles and for some

reason I can't get 'She Drives Me Crazy' by the Fine Young Cannibals out of my head. I hum it over and over, still trying to untangle my line, but it snaps and the lure is left dangling in the tree. There's no way I can get it. It's a twenty-pound leader attached to a forty-pound braid line – an expensive mistake. Riccard is so patient: 'Don't worry. It happens all the time.'

He casts his line out and places the lure perfectly by a floating log. Wham! Riccard lifts his rod up and starts wrestling the fish.

'As soon as he hits the lure he's turning and it's just like a steam train. If it's a big one you just have to hold on,' he says, reeling.

It's only a four-pound black bass but it's a massive fight for such a small fish. Many black bass come in at around fifteen to twenty pounds here, but several have been seen over thirty pounds in size. I imagine it would be like hooking a charging herd of mammoths.

The black bass is a fine-looking fish with shimmering silver, pink and gold scales the size of shirt buttons, and a spiky dorsal fin. The Latin name is *Lutjanus goldiei* and it's actually part of the snapper family, which inhabits fresh and brackish water. The two canines on its upper jaw and smaller teeth below allow this fish to feed on whatever comes his way: small fish, mammals, crabs, baby crocs … he's not fussy. He is the biggest predator in this river, save the reptilian rippers.

After setting up again, I cast out my line. I need to be between three and six inches from the edge of the structure, in this case a fallen tree trunk. *Come on, Robson, don't mess this up.* I get vegetation again.

'Can you please stop filming me doing stupid casts?'

Or maybe I could just stop doing stupid casts in the first place.

I am annoying myself intensely. I want to become a troll on my own Twitter page. Jamie grins: 'Just take a deep breath and relax. Calm down,' he says, knowing this will wind me up even more. Thankfully, I get the lure back this time and save Riccard £12. I cast again, this time three inches off my target. It's a cast that deserves a fish and I get one.

'Hold on, Robson,' says Riccard.

Just as he predicted the bass is fighting like a commuter train in full motion. And I lose it.

'I did everything right, Riccard! I did everything you told me!'

God, I hate myself today. I want to swap bodies and be Riccard – or even Prada – but not me. I exhale loudly. There is a way to fight a black bass and I put too much bloody tension on the reel – when the fish runs, you need to let the line go a little slacker and put just enough tension on, but not too much. This comes with experience and, as usual, I'm learning the hard way.

Riccard casts effortlessly with one hand. It's beautiful to watch and he is so precise. I need two hands and two minutes to get myself sorted; I'm all fingers and thumbs. Riccard's in. The one thing you must do with a black bass is move it away from the structure as quickly as possible because the fish wants to go back into his hiding place. In fact, as he attacks the lure, he is already turning for home.

'They bolt so quickly,' says Riccard. 'He's taken me into the snags.'

'What do you do when he's returned to his lair?'

'Give a bit of slack but not a loose line, and watch him.'

He swims out but the line is caught about ten feet down. The fish can't get off the hook and Riccard can't bring him in. It's stalemate – someone has to go in and retrieve the fish.

'In you go, Robson,' says Jamie.

'What about the crocodiles, Jamie?'

'I can't see any. It's fine,' he snorts.

'They are stealth hunters – they are not saying "Here I am, over here!"'

'Well, you've got a head start.'

Jamie would secretly love me to be attacked by crocodiles – to him it would be TV gold. I can imagine him shouting, 'No! Don't rescue him yet, don't rescue him yet! Let him have a little bite of your leg, Robson, just a nibble. You'll get a BAFTA! Maybe an MBE! It'll be worth it.' I fold my arms. I'm not going anywhere. So Chris puts his goggles on and dives in, holding his breath for nearly two minutes. He comes up and says the line is well and truly snagged and then suddenly he is yanked down. A nine-pound fish has just pulled a 170-pound man back into the water. He emerges victorious with the bass on a lip grip and passes it to Riccard. It's an amazing fish: solid, healthy and powerful.

That evening we eat the two black bass Riccard caught, garnished with my vegetation. I need to up my game.

Good Head

The next day we are in Rabaul in East New Britain – well, what's left of it after a twenty-foot blanket of ash buried the town in 1994. As with the World War II military hardware in the forest, they haven't quite got round to tidying up yet. The volcano erupted, the ash fell and everyone fled, and that's how parts of the area have remained. It's a tropical Pompeii. Mount Tavurvur smoulders ominously in the background, a sinister reminder of the red-hot bubbling danger beneath. Tavurvur is part of a horse-shoe of volcanoes – active and potentially deadly – surrounding an aquamarine bay. The water is beautiful and serene, like a lagoon, but it is in fact Rabaul Caldera – the eye of a supervolcano – and if this baby blows, the town won't be the only place in trouble. They will feel the effects in Newcastle. No wonder people are 'on the nut' here. It's a case of 'live for today, because tomorrow you could be covered in boiling hot lava'.

The topography is terrible news for Rabaul, bad news for the planet, but great news for fishermen. The area is alive with billfish and I am hoping to catch a Pacific blue marlin. It's been over two years since I caught my first marlin, an Atlantic blue, off the Azores. Today game fishing enthusiast and pervy lure maker John Lau is going to help me.

I meet him at his workshop, where he is busy working on a lathe. John's lures are known in game fishing circles throughout the world. We shake hands and he presents me with a lure he's made especially. 'It's called a "good head",' he says with a twinkle. His other lures are the Linda Lovelace and his personal favourite, the Monica Lure-insky. We walk down the private jetty to his gleaming white yacht, the *Stephanie*. After the saucy lures I can't help wondering how Stephanie, whoever she is, got a whole boat named after her. The mind boggles.

Soon we are powering through the waves and immediately we can see there are billfish feeding at every turn. There are sailfish circling a bait ball of rainbow runners, lashing into them just 100 yards from the boat. On the starboard side a marlin is tucking in to another shoal of bait fish. There is activity all around.

I tell John that I am changing the name of my lure to Marlon Brando.

'Why?' he asks.

'Marlin Brando – geddit?'

'No,' he says, looking blank.

'I'm gonna make that fish an offer it can't refuse.'

He looks at me, bewildered. It wasn't funny to start with and by the time I've explained it five times I want to stick an orange in my mouth, wind my head in electrical tape and jump off the side. Maybe that's the sort of stuff Stephanie was into? I want a boat named after me. I'm game.

We trawl through the feeding area with our lures but after thirty minutes we have no takers. There are tuna feeding as well, but none of them are bothered about Marlin Brando when they have the real thing, and the heat is starting to become unbearable.

'Let's give them fresh bait,' I say.

We send out Rapala lures for rainbow runners. The deckhand pulls them up with ease. After half an hour I finally catch one. We slowly trawl the live bait but after three hours we get nothing. A tuna goes by, looks at our bait and turns away at the last minute. These billfish are well fed and ready for an afternoon nap. I tempt them like Mr Creosote: 'Surely, Mr Marlin, you have room for one more wafer-thin rainbow runner?' Nope. They are positive.

I have never seen so many billfish in my life. We must have spotted about twenty-five in total, as well as porpoises, whales and dolphins all wading into the fray to enjoy a good old buffet. John Lau points at the leaping dolphins: 'Such beautiful creatures.'

'Yes,' I say, looking at Jamie. 'But have you ever swum with them? There is a dark side to dolphins.'

'Oh, you're not still going on about the pink river dolphins?' says Jamie. 'So what, one nipped your leg and butted you in the chest.'

'I have been doing some research, Jamie. Dolphins are rapists and are even into gang attacks – you look it up.'

'Really?'

'Yes, really. And it's the same with moles.'

'Moles? What the fuck have moles got to do with anything?'

'There's a dark side to them, too. Moles are misogynists. Ask David Attenborough.'

'Ah, it's funny you should mention him. Do you like bird-watching? Because I've just signed you up for some this evening.'

We jump off the boat and thank John for an enjoyable day at sea. After a quick wash and brush-up it's time for me to fall on the grenade and judge the annual Miss Billfish Competition, a beauty pageant for game-fishing enthusiasts.

I loathe and despise Jamie as I'm really not feeling this event. I stand next to John, the event's compère, curl my toes and fix a grin. There are about fifty people crammed into a makeshift marquee with plastic chairs, a dodgy red carpet and a table where judges sit. I'm one of four. It's thundering and lightning outside and the rain is cascading down. Kids and dogs are running around, screaming and pissing on the carpet. It's a shambles. John taps the microphone loudly and everyone has a mini heart attack.

'Good evening' – the feedback is excruciating – 'tonight we have a movie star all the way from England. I would like to extend a huge welcome to Robson Green.'

One person claps.

'Thank you. I'm still available for panto.'

My job is to interview the contestants, who are wearing a variety of costumes this evening. I come up with a great Miss Billfish question: 'If you were a fish, what kind of fish would you be?'

'I'd be a marlin so I could travel the world, as I've heard they migrate a lot,' says one shy young woman.

One lass says: 'I don't want to be a fish. Why are you asking me that question?'

Question two: 'Do you like working with children?'

'Yes, because I've got a lot to offer and I am a kind and giving person.'

'Do *you* like working with children?' I ask another hopeful.

'No,' she says flatly. Come on, that's beauty queen basics – you have to love kids and want world peace.

Question three: 'Who's your favourite actor? By the way, I'm an actor.'

'Tom Cruise. Never heard of you.'

I ask a girl in blue. 'Heath Ledger,' she says.

'Oh boy, do I have some bad news for you.' She hasn't got a clue he's just died.

'He's so talented and handsome.'

'Not any more, he's not.'

'What?'

I tell her. She puts her hands to her face. I have turned into Larry David from *Curb Your Enthusiasm*; my humour is becoming as dark as the atmosphere. I really don't want to be here.

The fashion parade begins, to the soundtrack of the dodgiest 1970s soft-porno music. It's all a bit surreal. The women are judged on their interviews, personality and their outfits, and the other judges are taking it very seriously. There is a female Aussie tourist guide, a young guy who fancies all of them, and some pervy old guy. I give them all maximum points for each category.

One model has a Naomi Campbell-style fall as she hits the cat-walk. She gets back up and bravely continues. A dog jumps up at her and barks and kids run round in deranged circles. The next two models walk down the runway wearing only very small bikinis. Suddenly the generator fuses and the lights go out. About ten minutes later the problem is fixed and the parade continues. How much longer can this go on?

Finally the girls line up and the announcement is made: 'And the winner is . . .' – cue drum roll – 'Miss Billfish, winning by a nose, the girl in blue.' I put a ribbon over her and a tiara on her head. She is very chuffed.

We escape back to the hotel, sharpish. It's after midnight. I'm about to put my light out when there's a knock at my door. It's Jamie. He's had his bag stolen.

'With all my money, cards and my bloody passport, Robson.'

We call the police.

The day before, Jamie had gone to do a quick recce in Kimbe. He'd heard there was something called 'condom fishing' so he had driven to a pharmacy to see if they stocked prophylactics (it's an unlikely story but absolutely true!). He jumped out of the van, leaving his bag on the front seat. The pharmacy did indeed stock an array of condoms and the owners were happy for us to film in their shop. Having organised this set-up, he jumped back in the van and joined us at breakfast. Only now has it dawned on him that his bag had been nicked out of the van, which he admits he didn't lock. I shake my head disappointedly.

'Basics, my sadistic friend, basics.'

The police arrive at the hotel. They are the picture definition of 'dodgy' but couldn't be more helpful. They think they know exactly who has his bag.

'Leave it with us and we'll get your bag back,' they say.

Jamie calls IWC in Glasgow. He is very concerned about the next shoot in New Caledonia. Without his passport he won't be allowed in. Helen says if he goes back to the UK within the next two days they can issue him a new passport straight away and he can be back in time for the New Caledonia shoot, but it's a logistical nightmare. Jamie is stressed. It's nice to watch. Usually I'm the one sweating.

Eggs and Fish

Meanwhile we have a show to make, and this morning I am going hunting for eggs and hand lining with the Tolai tribe. We head by boat across the Rabaul Caldera, straight for the ACTIVE volcano, Mount Tavurvur. The lava has turned into metallic grey rocks of pumice. Every tree is a scorched post and the volcanic heat turns the waves to steam as they lap against the black shore. We navigate through a channel in thirty- to forty-degree heat. Local man Robot and three friends are waiting to greet me. They are dressed in sarongs and bare-chested like my dad, which, given what we're about to do today, feels particularly apt. I'm going to be mining. But not for minerals under the earth: for megapode eggs buried deep in the ash.

The native bird, which looks like a rooster-sized moorhen with massive feet, uses the heat of the volcanic ash to incubate its eggs, and apparently they're very tasty. Robot and his guys are going to help me find them. It's really not that hard – you just start digging where the footprints stop! I start burrowing and soon am grey with ash. Dad would be proud of my newly discovered mining capabilities. *It's in the genes*, I think, as I dig like a champion. He used to say: 'You graft? Your skin wouldn't bloody graft!'

Bloody hell, these birds certainly bury their eggs deep. I've been slogging away for two hours and I have ash in my eyes, ears, mouth and nose, but about four feet down I'm getting close. The air is hot and dry and so is the ash. I start to shovel and part the grey slag with my hands. I reach down into the hole and find an egg. It's like a large duck egg. I find another. I am triumphant but Jamie and Craig now want more footage on a different side of the ACTIVE volcano and I want to go before it starts to spew molten lava at us. Robot takes me to another spot and we start digging. The ash is acrid in my eyes and Jamie, all clean and Lynx-fresh, is sadistically enjoying my transformation into an ashen spectre of my former self. I dig for another *four hours*, finding half a dozen more eggs. Finally Jamie's happy he's got the footage he needs.

I pass the eggs to Robot and his team who will sell them for the equivalent of about 40p each; with all the eggs I've helped them find, they should make about four quid. They give me five to take for dinner. I thank them, hurriedly leaving the dry, dusty, ACTIVE volcano, and head by boat to a beautiful island paradise, home to the Tolai tribe. As I arrive, kids are diving off a tree into the turquoise-blue waters and playing tag on the sand. On the shore I am greeted by tribal leader Kevung, who reminds me of Nelson Mandela. He beams a wide smile. I shake hands with two other guys wearing very random T-shirts.

'Are there some big fish out there? What kind of big ones?' I ask.

'Breams,' replies one of them.

'Big bream? They're very tasty fish. Do they go well with eggs?'

'No,' he says bluntly.

'Oh, right.'

He gazes out to sea. I read his thoughts: 'Who is this guy? Who the hell eats fish and eggs?' *Note to self, Robson, next time just bring a nice Chardonnay.*

We go out in canoes with an outrigger on one side, a bit like the bancas in the Philippines. I'm sharing with Kevung. Out here the water gets very deep, very quickly. Even in these tiny hand-made canoes, we'll be fishing depths of more than 500 feet and using a hand line will be a test of endurance. Luckily I've brought my trusty chamois gloves. I'm not stupid. Besides, Kevung wears a glove too so I'm just copying the locals.

We send down weighted hooks with squid as bait. Anything more than ten pounds in size at this depth will take hours. And bingo! I've got a fish. I start pulling up the line, which I predict will take about fifteen minutes. The line winds against a carved-out tree branch.

'Pull,' says Kevung. 'Pull. Pull. Pull. Pull,' he says, getting me into a rhythm like a fishing coxswain.

The fish is fighting and my arms are aching. I start dreaming about electric reels. I'm usually not a fan of them. What's the point? Hard work is all part of it but now I'm beginning to think they are one of the best inventions of the modern age, along with penicillin and the Pill.

'Pull it faster,' says Kevung.

'I am pulling it fast. I can't pull it any faster, Kevung.'

My arms are a blur with motion.

Kevung gets a fish, and across the way so has George, but mine's nearly at the surface. It's a four-pound mandara, or perch, but the line gets caught around the side rigger of the boat and becomes taut. The fish flicks its tail and is off.

'Shit!'

I am so upset. That fish has just taken me fifteen minutes to pull up and now I've lost it.

All the guys pull up lovely fish. They wind in the line with ease. Kevung is about twenty years older than me but he is so strong he pulls the line up like a man taking it easy on a Sunday afternoon. These guys don't have any fancy boats or equipment; they are using what nature gave them. The only expense is the nylon line and a hook. And I've just lost one. Later, when we arrive back on shore, I give them one of mine and they are so grateful. Out here, it makes a difference. I think about Riccard's lure, still in the tree. Maybe I could tell them about that one, too. Poor Riccard – I need to give him one of my lures. Luckily I'm seeing him tomorrow and I might be directing myself, because it looks like Jamie will have to fly back to London after all.

George pulls up a six-pound mandara and he paddles over for me to inspect it. It will make a great meal for the villagers. I congratulate him and pass it back but I didn't travel 13,000 miles to hold another man's fish; I need to catch one of my own and I'm staying out here all night if necessary – and Jamie says it is necessary. Me eating eggs on camera with the Tolai tribe won't really cut it with the producers back in the UK. *Extreme Egg Hunting With Robson Green* might not get another series.

I drop the line and hope the fish are hungry. I wait. Nothing. I am impatient. I want a fish. I can't face the villagers without catching anything. I'm in. *Please, please stay on, otherwise it's boiled eggs and soldiers for me and I don't want that. Come on. Use your core, Robson. Straight back . . .*

'Oh . . . I'm fucked.'

Kevung laughs. He tries to improve my technique but I am in a rhythm. *Nearly there, come on. Oh, for fuck's sake, where's the bloody fish?* I keep pulling and pulling. It's never-ending. And finally I pull up the smallest fish ever. It must be no more that a pound and I haven't got a clue what it is. It's definitely not the bream I was dreaming of. I've lost more weight pulling in this blinking fish than I'll gain from eating it. Kevung informs me that it's a loueer – it's a sweet little thing with bright yellow markings. I knock it on the head. He's my contribution to the feast tonight, as well as the megapode eggs, of course.

Between us we have caught three large mandara, two decent-sized bream and my loueer, which, placed next to the other fish, looks like a rotten banana. That night we eat with the tribe, cooking the fish and megapode eggs over an open fire. I tell the children how I found the eggs, digging in the ash. They don't understand a word I'm saying but are transfixed by my mimes. The megapode eggs are delicious, all yolk and no white but do you know what, George was right: eggs and fish really don't go well together.

Giant Goldfish

Early the next morning Jamie calls the police to see if they have made any progress, and they have. They turn up at the hotel holding his bag. They've got the culprits. Jamie is so relieved – we all are. Everything is there save the cash. He kisses his burgundy passport and shakes the hands of the policemen. He has just narrowly avoided six days of the most arduous travelling imaginable.

The police tell us the story of how they got his bag back. They battered down the door of the suspects, who made a run for it, so they shot them in the legs and went after another guy with a machete. Jamie and I look at one another out of the corner of our eyes. What? Did we just hear right? The senior officer invites Jamie to go with them to the hospital to see that justice has been done. In

fact, we can all go. Strangely we unanimously decide to give that
particular treat a miss. Jamie shakes their hands again and they are
on their way. All I can say is don't nick anything in PNG because
they don't mess around like they do in Britain, where you'd get
three meals a day, a telly and an endless supply of narcotics.

After a spot of snorkelling we drive back to Kimbe in West New
Britain. Riccard's taking me out on his big boat. We are reef fishing about 600 feet down, and in answer to my prayers we are
using electric reels! Riccard takes us to spot where he has caught
unknown monsters.

'There are some big things down there that we haven't managed to pull up. I've had this reel here smoking sometimes,' he
says in a light Aussie drawl. 'There's actual smoke coming out of
it because it's going backwards and you know they straighten
these big hooks.'

We send the squid hooks down and no sooner have they hit
the bottom than both reels go off. They whine like distant sirens.
Suddenly mine stops: the fish is off. I take the other rod port side:
600, 590, 580, 570 . . . kick gears click on. With forty feet to go the
alarm sounds to alert you to the fact that the fish is near to the
surface and it's time to reel in by hand. As I start winding, the rod
bends acutely. I wind with all my might and what comes into
view is astonishing. It's a giant goldfish! Like something Gulliver
would have won at the fair. I am so astonished that all I can
manage on camera is a load of 'wows' and platitudes.

It's called a ruby snapper and the Latin name is *Etelis
carbunculus*, which means 'ancient stone' – hence ruby. It is a
vibrant orange with a shimmer of gold and massive black eyes,
because it's dark down there in the benthic zone where it resides.

Wow! It's a forty-five-pound goldfish! All I can say is we're going to need a bigger bowl. I mean, imagine flushing this one down the loo when it's dead. But we're not going to do that today, we're going to eat it.

The goldfish has whetted my appetite. What else is down there? What about one of the monsters Riccard was speaking about? One of the lines beeps. The electric reels perform their magic.

'We've got something very, very large on the end here,' I say. 'OK, we're at forty feet. We're at thirty feet, Riccard. We're at twenty feet, we're at ten, nine, eight, seven . . .' I start winding with all my might. 'Oh, that's a weird-looking fish – look at that. What *is* that?'

Neither Riccard nor I know. In fact, we don't find out for a couple of days and begin to think we've discovered a new species. I am hell-bent on calling it a Robson – even though it's as ugly as sin, I want a fish named after me. But, God, it's a minger – a cross between a barracuda, an oilfish and a gar with a black sail, like a ghostly pirate ship. I think of names that actually suit it, like the Cowell. Yes, that works. Or maybe the Mandelson, or even better the Janet Street-Porter, although the mouth's not big enough.

Three days later we find out from a marine biologist that it is a barracouta, or black snoek. Identifying fish can at times be very difficult, particularly as they're known by different names around the world, which is why the Latin term in the universal language of classification is so helpful. This is a *Thyrsites atun* – it's a versatile, oily, bony fish that can be grilled, fried and tinned. It was hated in Britain during World War II because canned snoek was associated with deprivation and rationing. Ask your Great Aunt Margaret, or anyone of that generation, if they remember tinned snoek. Just from the look of it Riccard and I don't fancy a bite, so we pop it back to go and frighten the other fish.

We decide to try our luck one more time and immediately something enormous fights with the reels. We pull it up and it takes the line back down. This happens again and again, until the reels are screaming under the pressure. The motors whir. Is it a shark? Riccard says it's not fighting like one but whatever it is it's enormous. The reels pull the fish to forty feet, thirty feet, ten feet, and then the creature takes the line back down to fifty.

'It's going to burn the engine out,' says Riccard.

'What the hell is it?' I say, imagining the undiscovered and mysterious creatures down there, like the one Riccard's never been able to land. Perhaps it's a world-record-breaking giant goldfish over 100 pounds? But, then again, it's more likely to be a bull or tiger shark holding on to the fish I've just caught, desperately trying to steal my prize for himself. The motor continues to struggle, until crack! The line snaps – it's over and the fish is gone without a glimpse or even a clue. But whatever it was has just broken a line built to take 250 pounds! I look at the rod.

'It's busted the whole rig. I'm kind of glad that we didn't bring it up,' I say. 'As I have come to realise on this journey, some fish aren't meant to be caught.'

We put the ruby snapper I caught on the barbecue and cook it until the flesh is succulent. I scoop up the meaty white flakes with my fingers and, as I chew, wonder if I'll ever discover 'the Robson'.

'You will have to come back and fish for longer with me next time,' says Riccard. Then maybe, just maybe, we will land one of the undiscovered monsters of this strange but incredible lost world.

Chapter Fourteen

RUSSIA

Crime and Punishment

November 2010, At the Ends of the Earth, Series 4

Arriving in Moscow sets the tone for the rest of the trip. It's cold, grey and not one person is smiling. At our hotel, the reception has no reference of our booking. The middle-aged shot-putter behind the desk is a thoroughly unpleasant individual who grudgingly finds us a few rooms for the night. It's a dour place and it's so bloody cold as we carry our stuff up the rickety stairs to our rooms. I open the door to reveal my threadbare bed with a minimum of battered 1950s furniture. This hotel is so bad, even Lenny Henry wouldn't advertise it.

I look out of the window onto the streets below. It's snowing. Everyone is wearing Cossack hats and furs and walking with their heads down. It's like a Norman Cornish painting. Norman, who is still going strong at the time of writing this book, is a pitman painter from the northeast who captured the factory workers and miners, their heads lowered as they trudged to work.

They probably had stoops a bit like my dad from being cramped in unnaturally small spaces underground. But there's no mining here: people have their heads bowed because of the biting cold and probably a good old dose of Russian melancholy. Have you ever read a cheery Russian novel? I haven't, but then again I'm not sure I've managed to finish one.

The rest of the crew go to bed but Peter, our indefatigable soundman, and I stay up and drink vodka for medicinal purposes. I take a sip and immediately choke – it's like rocket fuel. An old boiler, wearing the dress she was buried in, bangs some cold sliced beef in gravy on the table. This is accompanied by cold peas and potatoes (all tinned), pickled fish and boiled eggs. Everything is cold – it reminds me of a trip to East Germany before the Wall came down. The vodka dulls our senses and anaesthetises our taste buds, and we are slowly able to ingest the food. We take another shot of the firewater and retire to bed. It is so cold I get under the covers fully clothed and watch my breath make steam. As I drift to sleep I decide *not* drinking vodka is more of a risk than drinking too much here. I vow to top up for the rest of the trip in order to keep out the chill.

In the morning the same woman, wearing that same sage-green dress, slams our breakfast down. It's not much of an improvement on dinner. Today we're heading for Eastern Siberia. The new director, Matt Richards, is an energetic, affable guy, full of ideas. Sadly Jamie is booked up with other work so can't join the gang back on tour this time. I miss Jamie but am warming to Matt's ideas on how he wants to expand on the humour side of the show. I smile at Peter and Craig Herd, back behind the camera, and say, 'Yeah, Siberia's going to be rich territory for gags. The land of hundreds of Soviet forced-labour camps, where millions perished under Stalin's rule. There was a reason why he sent people to Siberia, you know?'

'Why?'

'Because there was no chance of them coming back. It'll be a laugh a minute, this episode.'

Matt smiles. He remains upbeat and ever the optimist.

Khabarovsk Krai

On the plane to Khabarovsk, I have never seen such a bunch of glum people in my life. The pilot makes an announcement that sounds almost cheery: 'There is a technical problem with the plane. I will keep you informed.' Twenty minutes later he comes on the intercom again. This time he sounds like his dog has just been intentionally run over by the men who burgled his house and killed his wife: 'The technical problem is now fixed so we can take off.' The passengers' faces fall further and as the engines start they go from glum to looking like members of a funeral cortège. We must be heading to a really bad place.

The atmosphere gets worse as we come in to land. The mood goes from funereal – the dipped heads of Norman Cornish paintings – to Edvard Munch's *The Scream*. If I thought people in Moscow were miserable, the Khabarovskians are suffering from chronic depression. I am now seven time zones away from Moscow and 3,000 miles away from home. Even the gulags didn't make it this far. Right now I would give my left testicle to be back in Britain, drinking a pint (of Sauv Blanc) in my local, standing by a warm fire and hearing laughter again.

On the way to meet the fixer, Isabella, the Khabarovsk landscape is barren, lonely and grey. The winter is brutal in the far east of Russia, and the temperature drops below −30 degrees. I look across the Amur River and it's like the face of the moon: a rocky field of ice. Only the middle is still flowing. People pick their way across looking for a spot to dig a hole and perhaps, if they are lucky, find a fish.

We get out of the van. It is so cold that it almost burns. In spite of this, however, Isabella is dressed in a blue skirt, thin tights, flat summer shoes, a pink headscarf and a cardie, complete with a white handbag. She stands there shivering. I am not sure she's built for the job. We introduce ourselves and quickly discover she also doesn't speak a great deal of English. As a fixer you have to be a translator – it is part of the job spec. Matt looks panicked. It's as if the real fixer has double-booked and his mum's agreed to stand in. ('Your fixing job is easy. I shall make you proud. Go to your other job, Josef.' 'But you don't speak good English, Mother.' 'No, but I will learn. Nothing is as hard as Russian.')

As I prepare to film a PTC dressed in full Arctic gear, five layers of thermals and Arctic boots, I glance over at Isabella, still shivering, looking like she's just popped down to Tesco on a mild spring day. I smile. Maybe Matt is right about finding the humour on this trip.

. . . And action!

'Khabarovsk sits at the edge of Russia, less than twenty miles from the Chinese border. It's on one of the world's longest rivers, the Amur – and apparently because of its spectacular beach and similar latitude to the French city – it's known as the Nice of the Far East.'

Yes, it's guinea-a-minute here. I look at the moon rocks. It's not a beach, it's more like a coastline, because it's –20 and everything is frozen over. And it's on the same latitude as Nice?

So what! I've been to Nice and it's nowt like this bloody place. I've spent many a day on the Beau Rivage Plage, in my Speedos, doing my Daniel Craig impression. If I did that here, my testicles would retract to my ears and you'd have to call me Susan. I don't think the French Riviera is in trouble yet.

Nanai, Sikachi-Alyan

Isabella comes with us in the van to meet the Nanai tribe in our first filming sequence. The roads are treacherous with ice but that doesn't seem to bother our driver, who is motoring along at an enthusiastic pace, talking all the while on his mobile phone. In fact he's never off the damn thing. We begin to slow and turn off onto a beaten track leading into the forest. As we climb, the trees become denser and denser, and the snow gets deeper. At 1,000 metres up we hit a three-foot bank of snow. The fixer's job, during the recce before the shoot, is to let the director know that they can get from A to B safely. But it is now obvious that Isabella has never fixed anything in her life. She encourages the driver to keep pushing through. He tries, revving the engine and putting the tyres in a spin, but we slip backwards. We are stuck deep in the forest, halfway up a hill, trying to explain to Isabella that there is no way we can make it through. She finally agrees and says, 'Yes, it's terrible, isn't it?'

Not quite the response we are after.

'What shall we do?' says Matt.

'I don't know,' says Isabella.

Matt takes charge. The driver is still glued to his bloody phone. We get his attention. In my mind, I imagine slapping the back of his head and throwing his phone out the window but instead Matt puts a firm hand on his shoulder and suggests he hangs up.

The driver turns his head to look into Matt's black, angry eyes. He cuts the call and starts to turn the van around. But we have no snow chains, no snow tyres, and we're in a little minivan like a Bedford Cruiser, full to the gunnels; like the fixer, it just isn't built for the job. The driver is ignoring our protestations. He will do things his way. He tries to go forward again, then back. It's like *Austin Powers* in the snow. The engine whirs as he tries to get traction; he puts the steering wheel in full lock; he tries the same in reverse until smoke billows from the back. Finally he puts his hands in the air.

'We are stuck,' he declares in Russian.

Yeah, well done, mate, we told you that half an hour ago. We all look at Isabella for a solution. She looks back at us and starts to cry.

'I worried we are in the middle of woods with much snow. My cat? How will she eat?'

She meows and mimes eating, to get the importance of her message across. We are all agog. From that moment on, it's not about the show any more, it's about her hungry ginger tom.

After an animated discussion it is decided that Isabella and the driver should remain with the van. We leave her to organise a 4×4 to pull the van out of the snow and solve her pussy problem. The debacle reminds me of a time when I had just set up Coastal Productions and we were filming *Come Snow, Come Blow* with Tim Healy and Rodney Bewes from *The Likely Lads*. The crew and I were on our way to a recce when I said to the driver, 'Hang on, we're going in the wrong direction.' He said, 'No, I am late for my trumpet lesson.'

'What? But we need to be in Ashington.'

'Well, I need to be in Newcastle – my band's in the National Brass Band Championships.'

'Well, why the hell did you agree to drive us?' I said, infuriated.

'I thought it would work out but it didn't.'

It was of course his first, and last, driving job, and the band didn't even make the finals.

The crew and I unpack the van. We now have to lug our stuff half a mile up the hill, through three foot of snow, to a wooden shack where the Nanai are waiting to do a dance – well, they do! Peter and I bemoan the fact that we have no vodka with us. Everything is slowly coming apart at the seams. Matt's blood pressure is rising but veteran Craig tells him to keep on filming the story and it will be OK. I am carrying the least, as usual, so I bound on ahead to act as crevice spotter.

'If I disappear, then it's deep!' I shout.

I start throwing snowballs at the crew. None of them thinks it is funny. I get Peter slap-bang on his baldy head.

'Stop it, Robson!'

'I am just trying to boost morale,' I say, throwing more.

At the top I am pelted in a revenge attack. Snowball fights always improve spirits.

At the top of the hill we find the Nanai people. There are two women wearing traditional purple embroidered tunics and holding long sticks, and a larger lady in a red outfit with a woolly hat, who's on drums. They couldn't be less pleased to see us. We are an hour late, and because of that the men have buggered off. A dog bounds out of the woods and runs at Prada. It looks like a Rottweiler. Prada, carrying his heavy sound pack and boom, legs it through the snow like John Cleese. This dog is obsessed with him; it snarls and barks as Peter runs in the opposite direction, knees high. It's comedy genius but Peter is genuinely scared. We look to the women to stop the dog. They look over vacantly and do nothing.

Without anyone to translate, Matt is using sign language to communicate to the tribeswomen. There is a ten-foot square of space next to the hut. The large lady hits a Mike Oldfield-style drum with a stick: boom, boom, boom, boom. She is bored and looks as if she is waiting for a bus. The other two girls move their sticks side to side, up and down, and stomp the ground. There is no moving, no singing – that's it.

Matt wants me to react. I say, 'That has to be the worst dance I have ever seen, and if this is a blessing, we are not going to catch anything.'

It's like bad Morris dancing without beards and bells.

The drumming and stick twizzling stops. 'Thank goodness for that,' I say.

It starts again, only this time with one of the girls wafting cotton wool around. Craig is shaking with laughter, Matt is despairing and Peter is still dealing with a growling dog. We can't find the two Nanai guys, Alexei and Andrei, who are meant to be taking us fishing. After the stunning musical and dance performance that could rival the Bolshoi, we finally find them out on the frozen Amur River. There is no meet-and-greet, no hole to be dug – they are on stools, already fishing. I walk over and they don't even flick me a look.

The Amur River is half a mile across and not totally frozen. The middle is still flowing, but where we are is solid ice. There are huge blocks of ice floating down the centre. The theory is that pike, frightened by the ice blocks rubbing together, flee from the vibrations and take shelter under the ice. Well, now I am going to drill a couple of holes into that shelter with my corkscrew drill. To maximise their chances, the experienced fishermen here use two rods and two holes. I set up my fishing camp midway between Alexei and Andrei. I am piggy in the middle. They sit stock-still and expressionless, and they stay like this for hours.

It's painfully clear I'm not going to learn anything from these two today so I get on with the task in hand. I've got my two twelve-inch rods, which are two sticks with line tied to them, and my lure. I am using a brass circle an inch across with legs like a little crab. These brass crabs bounce off the bottom six to seven feet down. Pike have a voracious appetite and will eat almost anything, so hopefully one will come along, take a look, and wallop. Pike are vicious and strike fast so there won't be any doubt about a nibble.

I look over hopefully at Alexei. I've been proactive and am all set up for fishing; maybe now he'll acknowledge me. Nope. After an hour in the sub-zero temperatures the blokes still haven't said a word to me; talk about being sent to social Siberia. I jabber away to camera: 'I am so glad I am with these guys. I am having so much fun. Since the moment we got here we haven't stopped chatting. Alexei just doesn't shut up. Such fun. Such a bond.'

Even though I am mentioning their names loudly, neither of them moves. Finally Andrei moves his arm. I say, 'Thank God for that. I thought you had frozen to death.'

He looks at me like I am a Chechen separatist. Still, it's significant progress. Andrei suddenly gets up and silently walks across the ice to drill a hole somewhere else. The crew are wetting themselves.

'I don't think he likes you,' says Prada.

'I'll set the dog on you again,' I warn him.

I look over at Alexei and say in Russian, 'Where are the fish?'

He grunts an inaudible 'dunno', but I am happy. At last I have got him to speak. My objective this week is not landing an extreme fish, it is getting two fishermen to say anything at all. But of course I know why these guys are not up for talking: the secret to this method of fishing is total silence. It's the vibrations of my voice that are quite possibly frightening the fish. I shut up and it does the trick – Alexei and Andrei both catch an Arctic pike. I am thrilled and run over to Alexei, lauding praise on him. I want to go in for a hug and pick him up but I know that might end in violence so instead I hold his fish forth and say, '*Esox lucius*, from the Ancient Greek *lucus*, meaning "wolf", which refers to the fish's predatory skills.'

It's been five hours, it's dark and I haven't got a fish because I have been talking all the time. Alexei and Andrei are either side of me holding their pike up for the camera and I say, 'There you have it: Alexei caught a fish, Andrei caught a fish, and as you can see, they are over the moon, not only to have caught two lovely pike but also to have met me.'

They look stony-faced, not even a flicker of a smile or even a glower, just total and absolute indifference.

Deflated and tired, we trudge through the snow back to the van. Isabella has had the van pulled out of the snow by a 4×4. However, instead of transferring us into the 4×4, she has sent it away again. The shitty van makes its way down the hill, through the snow and ice, slipping sideways. Isabella is not speaking to us either; she is still obsessing about her cat. Louise Allen, our assistant producer, has been trying to organise another fixer with the office in Glasgow. When we arrive in Khabarovsk Matt and Louise take Isabella off for a word. She is paid and free to get back to feed her hungry ginger Tom.

Peter, Craig and I all trudge off to bed while Matt and Louise head to a bar. Matt needs a stiff drink. As luck would have it they bump into some students who are studying media studies in Russia. One girl called Anna has particularly good English and agrees to help us. She turns out to be a wonderful breath of fresh air.

Khabarovsk City

'Are you Red Fox?' I ask a random man. 'The seagull flies high tonight,' I say to another. I have on a large Russian hat and am hamming it up. I whisper to an old lady, 'Are you Red Fox?' She hits me with her handbag.

Matt wants to set up a thread of espionage and my mission is to find the agent who will help me succeed on my latest fishing assignment. I sit by the Amur River waiting for a signal, any signal. I get a tap on the shoulder. It's Anna; she is Red Fox and she has come to rescue me from this fishing debacle. She takes me to a tackle shop in town. We're fishing on the Amur in the centre of the city today, so I need to buy a rod and variety of lures. We are going for lennock, char, grayling and catfish. In the shop there is a wide variety of lures, many of which I have never seen before. There is a mouse lure the size of a field mouse, a hamster lure, and a squirrel lure the size of an actual bloody squirrel with a hook hanging out of its bum.

'What kind of a fish would go for these?' I say.

I ask the shopkeeper if it is a joke but he assures me it isn't. Apparently Amur catfish love squirrels. I nod but know he's talking out of his bottom. I get loaded up with a variety of lures, including a squirrel lure for fun (honest).

Anna takes me to the river, where supposedly a contributor is waiting for me. We scan the lunar landscape and indeed there is a fat Russian sitting on a seat. He raises his hand and then immediately lets us know that he doesn't want to be filmed. Anna translates, 'He thought he was just here for advice.'

He has the same depressive demeanour as many others I have met on this journey. Matt is overwhelmed with frustration but just when I think this episode has hit rock-bottom, enter a larger-than-life old guy called Victor, who saves the day. He has a bag of swag on his back full of fish. And he is *smiling*. He talks to us in front of camera and says, 'You have got the wrong equipment, it's the wrong time of day . . .' He inspects my luminous green rod.

'Ohhh. I have no words,' he says.

He picks up the rod and mimes throwing it away. He looks at my corkscrew drill with contempt and starts digging a hole with his spear. It's a wooden branch with a metal end, which gouges out the ice. I have just paid the equivalent of £75 for the drill and it's no use. He tells me the hole will be too small to get the fish out. With a spear he can make a hole four times the size.

I show him the squirrel lure. He chuckles, his whole body shaking visibly, and he agrees it must be some kind of joke. He tells me to use the crab lures. The temperature is plummeting to −20 but Victor has warmed our hearts. He shows us his haul, around twenty small Amur catfish, then bids me good luck and walks off across the frozen river. I am now on my own. I say to camera, 'It's hard to make friends in this part of the world. Victor has gone and I miss him.'

Off camera we tried to keep him. We offered him money, fame, friendship, but he said, 'No, no', and went about his business. In this place people wander on and off the stage when they want to – it's like being in a perpetual Beckett play.

The temperature has now plummeted to −25 and my line is frozen. There are no fish here – Victor must have taken them all.

The guy who sold me the squirrel lure saw me coming and the drill is as much use as a chocolate fireguard. I throw it down in disgust and walk off. I need a drink and a strong one. *No wonder there are so many alcoholics here*, I think.

That night all the crew, save Craig, who's the sensible one, go to the pub with the one sole mission of getting mullered with the locals. An AC/DC tribute band is singing 'Highway to Hell' in heavy Russian accents. The band are all overweight and drinking beer as they play. It's a brilliant atmosphere. We go long and we go wrong. It's a 'Whole Lotta Rosie' and a whole lot of Vodka. My face hits the pillow at 4 a.m.

Petropavlovsk, Kamchatka Peninsula

I wake up an hour and a half later at 5.30 a.m., fully clothed – but then that's normal in Siberia. We are meant to be flying to the Kamchatka Peninsula. I am so hung-over and the flight is at seven. Craig pops his head around the door.

'Don't ask. You have no idea what these eyes have seen,' I groan.

He shakes his head. Louise helps me pack by shoving everything into bin bags. She's in the hurt locker, too, but as the AP it's her job to grip the situation. At the airport, I hold Peter's hand.

He says, 'Shall we go upstairs to the café?'

I say, 'Please don't leave me.'

I am so vague and frightened. Peter is florid and I am concerned about his blood pressure. I squeeze his hand. I am on the verge of a theatrical breakdown and think I am going to die. I keep telling myself that it's just a hangover, but it is the mother and father of them all.

*

We fly to Petropavlovsk, the capital of Kamchatka, situated between the Bering Sea and the Sea of Okhotsk. The salmon-shaped peninsula is twice the size of Britain but with a population the size of Cardiff. The facts rattle around in my head as I throw litres of water down my neck; it feels like sand. My raging thirst is unquenchable. As I wave to the air hostess to bring me more, she huffs like Kevin the Teenager and flounces back with another cup. I drink. The prospect of going out to sea today is increasing my mania. Matt has arranged for us to go out on a trawler. My stomach knots a bit tighter.

We pile into a van and head to the coast. By the side of the road, someone has fashioned several snowmen and -women. They are really good with sculpted noses and detailed boobs, and all of them are smiling and waving. They are some of the most cheerful people I have come across on this journey, save Anna, Victor and the people at the bar last night. Louise's phone rings. It's the office. There are no trawlers going out today because the sea is too rough, too cold and parts of it have iced over. My colour returns but Matt goes grey. It's day four and we still haven't caught a single fish.

We go to various landmarks and film some GVs (General View shots), which help the viewer establish where the hell in the world we are. However, the weather's closed in overnight and what is meant be a spectacular view, a view to end all views on a clear day, is obscured by monochrome cloud and mizzle.

Matt says, 'Just say something about the view, Robson. Anything.'

'But we can't see a bloody thing!'

The facts spin in my head and I feel sick again. The Red Bull is beginning to repeat.

'Err ... Kamchatka is in the Ring of Fire and the bay that you can't see behind me is surrounded by a chain of volcanoes. There are more than a hundred and sixty volcanoes here, twenty-eight of which are active, but if one erupted today you'd only hear it; you wouldn't see it. Lava could be spewing out but nature's fireworks would be completely wasted. I've travelled five thousand miles for this stunning, breathtaking view. I could be at Whitley Bay, Northumberland.'

Poor Matt is now looking terrified. We need to get out of Petropavlovsk and fish in the Siberian wilderness, fast. We meet up with Sergei and Tatiana, who are descended from the Itelman tribe, Kamchadal natives who have lived here for hundreds, if not thousands, of years. We are hoping – no, praying – that they might help us catch a fish. Any fish will do, we're not fussy!

Tatiana comes up with a brilliant idea – she suggests we visit the fish market (!) to buy the ingredients for a traditional Itelman soup called Uuka. The main ingredients are crab, Arctic char and whole salmon, including its eyes and head. I'm not sure about the eyes, I don't like my food staring back at me, but some of the best meat is found in the cheeks and under the gill plate of a fish. It's always worth using in a soup or adding to a meal. At the market we look at the various fish. I spot Stalin crab, introduced to the area as a source of cheap crabmeat. Like king crab, they can grow to huge sizes and are very deadly predators. Everything is frozen and nothing is fresh, as it has been caught in the warmer months. I buy the salmon, and know to my core that we are not going to catch anything today – that's why Tatiana is getting us to buy all the ingredients. In spite of my deep-down reservations I say to Tatiana, 'Leave the final ingredient to me.' I am determined to catch an Arctic char – or at least try my damnedest.

We head straight to the fishing location on the Kamchatka River at a place called Pinchoseheeva (*pinch* means 'fire' in Russian). Here the river is the same size as the Coquet, but it's −20 by midday and will plummet to −42 at night. Despite this, the river has not frozen over and that's because of the hot springs heated by the molten lava of the volcano, which keeps the water flowing. We don't need to ice fish here, I can cast a spinner. First of all I build a fire for Tatiana at the edge of the river, and get it going.

I tell her, 'Stay here, it's going to take a real man to catch a fish today ... [pause] ... and here he is, Sergei Lukiv.'

Sergei crumbles in front of the lens, staring at Craig as if he is pointing a Kalashnikov. We try to warm him up but he is not one for small talk. Sergei would also rather stand by the fire and watch me fish than have a conversation.

The river is freezing and I need to wade in to get a decent cast. Almost immediately I can't feel my toes. In order to cast I use bare hands, which I need to warm up every few minutes. I'm using Tatiana's old tights filled with salmon eggs as bait, which I trot along the river and let the current take downstream. It's an unusual method and an unusual use of tights. I like to keep my wife's hosiery to buff up my brogues or polish the car. It comes up lovely.

The cold is perishing, my fingers are painful and the whole experience is far from enjoyable. Everyone is by the fire, including the crew. Craig is using a long lens and Peter has good signal – they are nice and toasty. There are no fish in this bloody river. Off in the distance to my right is a half-formed oxbow lake. Water is still flowing in and there are fish in there. We go and inspect. I can see dozens of char, but it's difficult to cast into and impossible to wade.

Luckily Sergei has a plan. I dangle my line into the lake while he runs upriver to scare the fish towards my balls of eggs. Slightly surprisingly he starts throwing snowballs at the fish, pounding lumps of snow into the water. Splosh! Sure enough the fish head in my direction, but the last thing anyone being pelted with snowballs wants to do is *eat*. When I smacked Prada on the bonce with one on the hill up to the Nanai, he didn't react by saying, 'Do you know what, I really fancy a steak sandwich now.' God help us! However, we are so up a frozen Shit Creek that all ideas, however bonkers, are being considered. Suddenly I feel a faint nibble on my line. I reel in a small parr (baby salmon) about three inches long. Sergei smiles; he's delighted for me.

'Wow, I feel so butch now.'

I pop it back in the water quickly and feel seriously depressed. This is getting ridiculous but then if the producers had wanted to make it easy they would have sent us here in the summer. That bastard Hamish Barbour has a lot to answer for.

Desperate times mean desperate measures but it turns out that Tatiana has an amazing plan. She announces she knows an old Itelman method, used for centuries to feed the tribe over difficult winter months. She makes two little fish lures out of reeds. I look at them.

'Are they meant to be fish-shaped?'

'Yes,' she smiles.

I smile back. They are truly rubbish. I am utterly sceptical but willing to give anything a go. She wades into the river and, on very short lines, she bends over and drags them backwards through about six inches of water. As she 'trawls' the lures she says, 'Here, fishy-fishy. Here, fishy-fishy.'

I've seen it all now, but she is determined this method is going to work. But it doesn't take an Oxford don to work out – it does not. I tell her if she catches a fish I will eat my own head. Only the most academically challenged salmon would go for this method. I can't stop laughing and she is genuinely offended.

'Here you fish for subsistence, not just for fun,' she explains.

'Well, the philosophy of what we do, you know, on this journey is that we eat what we catch, which I think will be pretty difficult today. But I tell you what, I'm really glad you're here. Do you know why? Because you brought a bit of glamour to the show. You smile, you're a lovely person, and you've cheered me up,' I say, gushing.

She blushes. 'You're very enthusiastic, too.'

'Very enthusiastic and handsome, right?'

'Of course,' she giggles coyly.

'Thank you, Tatiana.'

And that's how we end the sequence – me lamely fishing for compliments. It's the best we can do.

Having caught nothing, we return to Tatiana's village, where her mother and family are sitting down ready to eat the Uuka soup, without the Arctic char. They are not happy about it and neither am I. I feel like a failure. Imagine all those years ago, that sinking feeling of the hunter-gather returning from days of hunting, the expectant look on his wife and children's faces.

'What you got, Dad?'

'Nowt.'

I'd have gone AWOL for days rather than face that.

'Could you apologise to the chefs that I haven't brought any arctic char?' I ask Tatiana.

'Of course,' she says.

An exchange starts in Russian. The mother says, sarcastically, 'How did our butch friend get on?'

Tatiana says, 'Our butch friend took the piss out of our straw lures and caught bog-all.' (to paraphrase)

'Stupid Geordie pillock!' says Mum, or words to that effect. I don't care – it's the butch comment that cut deep. I'm not *that* scrawny.

The Uuka soup is delightful and really tasty. We eat in their wooden log cabin, which is basic but rather like a Swiss chalet. The family is very close and unified. In order to survive out here you all need to work together and be made of stern stuff. It strikes me as quite a matriarchal society. I have always said there would be no more war if women were in charge; just twenty-eight days of serious negotiations.

That night I am staying with the family in the Village of the Damned. The house is a kind of granny flat with a definite granny smell, depressing pictures of Tsars and religious icons all over the walls and some very worn and basic furniture. I am staying here without the rest of the team, who are all in different houses. I've lucked out with a vodka-juggling trio. I think the old fella's Sergei's grandfather but I can't be sure. He offers me vodka but I politely decline. He takes umbrage. The younger man passes me a plate of cubed horsemeat – *he obviously shops at Tesco*, I think. I politely decline again. He too takes umbrage. He clunks the plate down on a side table and we sit in silence, in the dark, with only the glow and crackle of the fire to warm the atmos-phere. The old lady in the corner gurgles and dribbles in her chair. I think she's had a stroke, poor dear. The old man kindly wipes away her drool with his hand and takes another cube of horsemeat, *with the same hand*! He offers me the plate again. I smile, swallowing a gag reflex and, once again, politely refuse. I wasn't keen on the horsemeat to start with but now I'm defiant.

I am already sitting on my bed, a worn leather settee with a crocheted blanket and a cushion as a pillow, by the fire. The family soon melts away into the dark and I am left to a fitful night's sleep. The young man wakes to stoke the fire throughout the night – three o'clock, four o'clock, five o'clock, he puts logs on to keep it burning. Obviously word has got round that Butch would probably freeze to death without the fire. I thank him for his kindness.

Dolinovka

'To misquote a US president: "We don't do this extreme fishing because it is easy – we do it because it is hard." And one of the most insidious crimes an angler commits is when his ambition falters and he accepts his fishing limitations. I will triumph over adversity. I will catch a fish and put an end to this fishing deba- cle.'

'Hoorah!' Sergei and my band of brothers cheer, and we get in the truck and travel 300 miles north to Dolinovka. Matt said it was only four hours away – more like nine in our piece-of-shit army truck.

Oh my God, it has to be the most uncomfortable journey of my life and a bit like travelling in a freezer, only a freezer would have been warmer as it's only −18 degrees. The condensation on the windows has turned to ice. I am shivering and I am wearing an Arctic coat and trousers, two layers of thermals and another five layers under the coat. But the views are astonishing. The vast wilderness of Siberia is like nothing I have seen before. It is the most untouched, unspoiled and unpopulated place on the planet. We stop and take pictures at every turn. And in the villages there are massive murals of Yuri Gagarin on the sides of buildings, as well as other national heroes of the space race. Time, too, is on ice here.

We jump out of our *Apocalypse Now* truck at a place on the Kamchatka River, near Dolinovka. It's frozen over, and the ice is about four feet thick in places. Matt decides to have an ice-fishing competition to catch steelhead, Arctic char or grayling.

It's me versus Sergei, who is wearing some curious-looking camo ski gear that looks like it is from World War II – and it probably is. We have four hours and the winner is the one who catches the greatest number of fish. Sergei has already beaten me at poker on the bus, and we are pretending that I need to win back my watch. But this is a serious competition, not a TV set-up, and we are both VERY competitive. He is the Russian Bear, I am the British Lion and this is our very own Cold War. He stares at me with a steely gaze but I am strangely confident. I have learnt enough to ice-fish alone from Victor, the old man at the Amur River who taught me how to present the lure to the fish, how to dig a hole with a spear and what size, and from Alexei and Andrei, who taught me to shut up.

I keep my distance from Sergei, who is making a racket using his drill. I dig my hole with a spear made from a branch with a knife tied to the end of it. I have gone for thinner ice, and I feel there might be a feeding channel below. It's just a hunch but I'm going with it. I don't say a word, I just slowly bring up the bait, just as the dhow fisherman taught me in Kenya and Howard showed me when fishing for pike in Alaska.

After five minutes I get my first bite and I pull up a one-and-a-half-pound stone char. It's a pure char, indigenous to the area. The signature of char compared to a trout is they have a light background and dark spots, whereas trout have a dark background with light spots. Char also have brilliant white leading edges on their pectoral, pelvic and anal fins. The char is part of the salmonid family and it is its adipose fin that distinguishes it as game fish. No one's totally sure what this mysterious fatty fin is for but it is thought to help with swimming function. This turns out to be the first of many, and very quickly it's 7–0 to me.

I say, 'It's like Man-U playing Accrington Stanley. It's a battering, Sergei.'

Sergei has a fit.

'Why are you doing this to me? Why are you making fun of me? I don't understand. I have done everything you have asked.'

With ten minutes to spare, Sergei catches a grayling. I have never seen one before and am genuinely excited – it's an extraordinary fish with a dorsal fin like an angel's wing. Sergei is a good fisherman and has helped us a lot – I hug him and concede that he has caught the best fish of the day. I recite an anonymous quotation: 'She is sometimes called the silver lady of the stream and in the pure water, essential for her existence, she is as graceful and as clever as any of her rivals.'

As we enjoy the tender, delicate meat of the grayling and Arctic char by a makeshift fire, Matt turns to me and says, 'There is something in this competition lark.'

I agree. It's like the missing element of the show – the Higgs boson. Men behave in an entertaining way when they compete – the rivalry, history, preparation, winning and failing, and the struggle. As it turns out, when Hamish sees the cut he agrees, and picks up the phone to Channel 5 to pitch the new idea. They commission a fifth series almost immediately.

In spite of all the trials and tribulations of this final journey, the *Extreme Fishing* show is really beginning to work, and what a privilege it has been to work alongside and meet some of the most talented and amazing people on the planet. My dad always said, 'There are lots of wonderful folk in the world and you have to meet as many of them as you can.' I've done that against the backdrop of truly astonishing locations and connected with people of all nations through the universal passion for fishing. Except with Andrei and Alexei here in Russia – they were difficult nuts to crack – but everywhere else I've experienced nothing but kindness and enthusiasm, like from my old friend Sergei here. Long may the show continue.

And now it's time to drink vodka! Sergei and I clink glasses and the firewater blows my head off again.

Fade to black.

ACKNOWLEDGEMENTS

Thank you to Team Extreme (you know who you are) for allowing me to not look like a jerk at one end of the line waiting for a jerk at the other. Special thanks to Directors Jamie Goold and Alistair Smith who 'got it', along with the irrepressible Sound Supremo Peter Prada ... thank you for staying with me guys ... millions wouldn't! I can't leave out Hamish Barbour, Helen Nightingale and Gerry Costello, not only for giving me the dream gig but for throwing me a life line every time I was drowning in front of the lens, which was quite often. Sandra Jobling and her Husband Ken for being there when it mattered most, especially the phone call which went along the lines of 'Get me off this F****** Island!' The unending support of my mother Anne, two sisters Dawn and Joanna, along with my kid brother David. My Uncle Matheson for teaching me everything I know about fishing (yes it was his fault everyone). Briony Gowlett and the gang at Simon & Schuster, and my co-author Charlotte Reather for turning my notes, diaries and this extraordinary, extreme and sometimes absurd adventure into a beautiful and entertaining story. I miss our daily six-hour Skype calls. Thank you to Vanya for being a wonderful mother to our beautiful son Taylor. If I have forgotten anyone it's because I'm heading towards fifty and even though the wheel is still turning in my memory the hamster is well and truly dead.

Charlotte would like to thank High Tower for his unwavering support, love and belief, Mom and Pops for being there through-out my rakish journey for backing, supporting me and loving me without limits (even when the rozzers were involved). Maurice Gran for being the best confidante and chief cheerleader a girl could have, and Robson for his belief, integrity and friendship. You are amazing people and so are all my wonderful friends who have always known I am a star in waiting. Is this Kate Winslet enough?

ABOUT THE AUTHORS

Born in Northumberland on 18 December 1964, **Robson Green** is one of the best known faces on British Television. He has been associated with a number of the most celebrated television dramas of recent times including *Soldier Soldier, Reckless, Touching Evil* and *Wire in the Blood*. Robson still lives in Northumberland and spends whatever spare time he has seeing his son Taylor, reading, walking, going to the gym and fishing.

Charlotte Reather first spied Robson Green across a sea of meatheads and spray-tanned strippers at a cage-fight at the Radisson Edwardian, Heathrow, and asked if she could interview the actor for a magazine.

Robson says, 'It was fate and when I read the article I instantly knew Charlotte was the only person who could write this book. She is a serious talent, hilarious, gifted and inspired.'

Charlotte writes comedy scripts for TV and film. She is a columnist and contributor to several magazines and newspapers including *NFU Countryside, The Field, Country Life* and the *Telegraph*. Originally from the Cotswolds, she lives with her husband in Washington DC. This is her first book.

www.charlottereather.com

'Charlotte is incredibly funny, fearless and terrifyingly ambitious. Look out world!' Maurice Gran, co-creator of *Birds of a Feather*.